International Symposium on Molecular Spectroscopy (ISMS 2021)

Online
21 – 25 June 2021

ISBN: 978-1-7138-3523-3

Printed from e-media with permission by:

Curran Associates, Inc.
57 Morehouse Lane
Red Hook, NY 12571

Some format issues inherent in the e-media version may also appear in this print version.

International Symposium on Molecular Sprectroscopy-University of Illinois
170 Roger Adams Laboratory
600 South Mathews Avenue
Urbana, IL 61801

Phone: (217) 244-0984

www.isms.illinois.edu

Additional copies of this publication are available from:

Curran Associates, Inc.
57 Morehouse Lane
Red Hook, NY 12571 USA
Phone: 845-758-0400
Fax: 845-758-2633
Email: curran@proceedings.com
Web: www.proceedings.com

Welcome to the 2021 Virtual International Symposium on Molecular Spectroscopy

On behalf of the Executive Committee, I extend a heartfelt welcome to all the attendees of the 2021 Virtual Symposium.

The Symposium presents research in fundamental molecular spectroscopy and a wide variety of related fields and applications. The continued vitality and significance of spectroscopy is annually re-affirmed by the number of talks, their variety, and the fact that many are given by students. These presentations are the heart of the meeting and are documented by this Abstract Book. Equally important is the information flowing from informal exchanges and discussions. As organizers, we strive to provide an environment that facilitates both kinds of interactions.

The essence of the meeting lies in the scientific discussions and your personal experiences this week independent of the number of times that you have attended this meeting. It is our sincere hope that you will find this meeting informative and enjoyable both scientifically and personally, whether it is your first or 50th meeting. If we can help to enhance your experience, please do not hesitate to ask the Symposium staff or the Executive Committee.

Ben McCall and Josh Vura-Weis
Symposium Co-Chairs

SCHEDULE OF TALKS

ABSTRACTS

2021 INTERNATIONAL SYMPOSIUM ON MOLECULAR SPECTROSCOPY

Please send correspondence to
Ben McCall
International Symposium on Molecular Spectroscopy
Department of Chemistry
600 S. Mathews Avenue
Urbana IL 61801 USA
e-mail: chair@isms.illinois.edu
http://isms.illinois.edu

Mini-Symposia

LARGE AMPLITUDE MOTIONS

Organized by **Isabelle Kleiner** (CNRS, Université Paris-Est Créteil et Université de Paris) and **Vadim Ilyushin** (Institute of Radio Astronomy of NASU). Deals with progress and unsolved issues in treating spectra of molecules or complexes with LAM's, and with analyses, theory and quantum chemical calculations on rotation-vibration-torsion or intervibrational interactions in molecules with one or several LAM's. Invited Speakers: **Jens-Uwe Grabow** (Gottfried-Wilhelm-Leibniz-Universität), **Ronald Lees** (University of New Brunswick), **Maria-Luisa Senent** (Instituto de Estructura de la Materia, CSIC).

PRECISION SPECTROSCOPY FOR FUNDAMENTAL PHYSICS

Organized by **Shui-Ming Hu** (University of Science and Technology of China) and **Nick Hutzler** (Caltech). Focuses on the study of fundamental physics by performing precision spectroscopic measurements in molecules. Invited Speakers: **Ronald Garcia-Ruiz** (MIT/CERN), **Nick Hutzler** (Caltech), **Fréric Merkt** (ETH Zurich).

SPECTROSCOPY WITH UNDERGRADUATES

Organized by **Jacob Stewart** (Connecticut College) and **AnGayle (AJ) Vasiliou** (Middlebury College). An exploration of the ways spectroscopy can be used to engage undergraduate students in research labs, teaching labs, and the classroom. Invited Speakers: **Garry "Smitty" Grubbs II** (Missouri University of Science and Technology), **Laura R. McCunn** (Marshall University).

Rao Prize

The three Rao Prizes for the most outstanding student talks at the 2019 meeting will be presented. The winners are **Mark Babin**, The University of California, Berkeley, **Lidor Foguel,** Yale University, and **Sommer L. Johansen,** The University of California, Davis. The Rao Prize was created by a group of spectroscopists who, as graduate students, benefited from the emphasis on graduate student participation, which has been a unique characteristic of the Symposium. This year three more Rao Prize winners will be selected.

Miller Prize

The Miller Prize was created in honor of Professor Terry A. Miller, who served as chair of the International Symposium on Molecular Spectroscopy from 1992 to 2013. The Miller Prize for the best presentation given by a recent PhD at the 2018 meeting will be presented. The winner is **Fang Liu**, Columbia University.

Sponsorship

We are pleased to acknowledge the many organizations that support the 2021 Symposium. Principal funding comes from the **National Radio Astronomy Observatory** (NRAO). We also acknowledge the many efforts and contributions of **The University of Illinois** in hosting the meeting, including financial contributions from the Departments of Chemistry, Electrical and Computer Engineering, and Astronomy.

Our Corporate Sponsors are **BrightSpec**, **Bristol Instruments, Elsevier/JMS, Ideal Vacuum Products, Journal of Physical Chemistry/ACS, Lumibird, MONSTR Sense, Teledyne Princeton Instruments,** and **Toptica Photonics**.

We are also pleased to acknowledge **Amplitude, Light Conversion USA,** and **The Coblentz Society** as Contributing Sponsors.

MA. Plenary

Monday, June 21, 2021 – 8:0 AM
Room: 2021 Online Everywhere

Chair: Cathy Murphy, University of Illinois at Urbana-Champaign, Urbana, IL, USA

Welcome **8:00**
Susan Martinis, Vice Chancellor for Research and Innovation
University of Illinois at Urbana-Champaign

MA01 **8:10 – 8:50**
PREBIOTIC ASTROCHEMISTRY IN THE "THz-GAP", Susanna L. Widicus Weaver

RAO AWARDS **8:55**
Presentation of Awards by Jennifer van Wijngaarden, University of Manitoba

2019 Rao Award Winners
Mark Babin, University of California Berkeley
Lidor Foguel, Yale University
Sommer Johansen, University of California Davis

MILLER PRIZE **9:05**
Introduction by Michael Heaven, Emory University

MA02 ***Miller Prize Lecture*** **9:50 – 10:05**
ENHANCING NONLINEAR OPTICAL RESPONSE IN ARTIFICIAL STACKED 2D MATERIALS, Fang Liu

COBLENTZ AWARD **10:10**
Presentation of Award by Ellen Miseo, Coblentz Society

MA03 **10:15 – 10:55**
PARA-ORTHO HYDROGEN CONVERSION; SOLVING A 90-YEAR OLD MYSTERY, Ad van der Avoird

TA. Mini-symposium: Large Amplitude Motions

Tuesday, June 22, 2021 – 8:0 AM
Room: 2021 Online Everywhere

Chair: Sonia Melandri, University of Bologna, Bologna, Italy

TA01 *INVITED TALK* **8:00 – 8:02**
MOLECULES' ROTATION SIGNALS (AND THEIR OBSERVATION): TORSION, INVERSION, FLEXIBILITY, CHIRALITY, PHASE, Jens-Uwe Grabow

TA02 **8:08 – 8:09**
BROADBAND MICROWAVE AND COMPUTATIONAL STUDY OF HEXAFLUORO-O-XYLENE: HIGHLY COUPLED CF3 ROTORS, Sven Herbers, Sean Fritz, Piyush Mishra, Yongbin Kim, Lyudmila V Slipchenko, Timothy S. Zwier

TA03 **8:12 – 8:13**
2-PROPIONYLTHIOPHENE: PLANAR, OR NOT PLANAR, THAT IS THE QUESTION, Christina Dindić, Wolfgang Stahl, Ha Vinh Lam Nguyen

TA04 **8:16 – 8:17**
Ka BAND MICROWAVE SPECTRUM OF METHYL TERT-BUTYL ETHER, J. H. Westerfield, Kelly S. Meyer, Sommer L. Johansen, Kyle N. Crabtree

TA05 **8:20 – 8:21**
MENTHYL ACETATE. A NEW LINK IN THE CHAIN OF ACETATES STUDIED WITH ROTATIONAL SPECTROSCOPY, Anna Krin, Pablo Pinacho, Cristobal Perez, Melanie Schnell

TA06 **8:24 – 8:25**
MICROWAVE SPECTRA OF A POTENTIAL FOUR-FOLD INTERNAL ROTOR, PHENYLSULFUR PENTAFLUORIDE, Joshua A. Signore, Christopher Falls, Susanna L. Stephens, Daniel A. Obenchain, Carlos A Jimenez-Hoyos, S. A. Cooke, Stewart E. Novick

TA07 **8:28 – 8:29**
LOWERING THE TORSIONAL BARRIERS BY STERICAL HINDRANCE: MICROWAVE SPECTRUM OF THE THREE-TOP MOLECULE 2,6-DIMETHYLANISOLE, Lynn Ferres, Joshua Spautz, Wolfgang Stahl, Ha Vinh Lam Nguyen

TA08 **8:32 – 8:33**
LOCAL AND GLOBAL APPROACHES TO TREAT THE TORSIONAL BARRIERS OF 4-METHYL-ACETOPHENONE USING MICROWAVE SPECTROSCOPY, Sven Herbers, Sean Fritz, Piyush Mishra, Ha Vinh Lam Nguyen, Timothy S. Zwier

TA09 **8:36 – 8:37**
STERIC EFFECTS ON TWO METHYL INTERNAL ROTATIONS OF 2,6- AND 3,4-DIMETHYLFLUOROBENZENE, Safa Khemissi, Julie Melan, Ha Vinh Lam Nguyen

TA10 **8:40 – 8:41**
INTERNAL ROTATIONS OF METHYL PIVALATE BY ROTATIONAL SPECTROSCOPY, Nobuhiko Kuze, Yoshiyuki Kawashima

TA11 **8:44 – 8:45**
CHARACTERIZATION OF *SEC*-BUTOXYTRIMETHYLSILANE BY CHIRPED-PULSE FOURIER TRANSFORM MICROWAVE SPECTROSCOPY, Freya E. L. Berggötz, Himanshi Singh, Melanie Schnell

TB. Instrument/Technique Demonstration

Tuesday, June 22, 2021 – 8:0 AM

Room: 2021 Online Everywhere

Chair: Anna C. Wannenmacher, University of California, Davis, Davis, CA, USA

TB01 **8:00 – 8:01**
MIXING SYNCHROTRON RADIATION AND LASER SOURCES: DUAL-COMB SPECTROSCOPY IN THE SUBMILLIMETER-WAVE REGION, Francis Hindle, Gaël Mouret, Thomas Sandow Hearne, Olivier Pirali, Marie-Aline Martin-Drumel, Zachary Buchanan, Sophie Eliet, Jean-François Lampin

TB02 **8:04 – 8:05**
HIGH-RESOLUTION MICROSECOND-TIME-RESOLVED DUAL-COMB SPECTROSCOPY OF TRANSIENT INTERMEDIATES, Pei-Ling Luo

TB03 **8:08 – 8:09**
DIRECT FREQUENCY COMB CAVITY ENHANCED SPECTROSCOPY FOR TRACE GAS DETECTION USING MID-INFRARED INTERBAND CASCADE LASERS, Charles R. Markus, TzuLing Chen, Douglas Ober, Lukasz A. Sterczewski, Mahmood Bagheri, Mitchio Okumura

TB04 **8:12 – 8:13**
HIGH-RESOLUTION SPECTROSCOPY OF COLD SAMPLES IN SUPERSONIC BEAMS USING A QCL DUAL-COMB SPECTROMETER, Josef A. Agner, Pitt Allmendinger, Urs Hollenstein, Andreas Hugi, Karen Keppler, Markus Mangold, Frédéric Merkt, Martin Quack

TB05 **8:16 – 8:17**
HIGH-RESOLUTION COMB-BASED FOURIER TRANSFORM SPECTROSCOPY IN THE 3.3 μm AND 7.8 μm RANGE, Adrian Hjältén, Matthias Germann, Chuang Lu, Francisco Senna Vieira, Aleksandra Foltynowicz, Ibrahim Sadiek, Michael Stuhr, Karol Krzempek, Arkadiusz Hudzikowski, Aleksander Gluszek, Dorota Tomaszewska, Grzegorz Soboń

TB06 **8:20 – 8:21**
HIGH-PRECISION MID-INFRARED SPECTROSCOPY WITH A WIDELY TUNEABLE SI-TRACEABLE FREQUENCY-COMB-STABILISED QCL , Nicolas Cahuzac, Mathieu Manceau, Dang Bao An Tran, Rosa Santagata, Etienne Cantin, Olivier Lopez, Dan Xu, Michel Abgrall, Yann Le Coq, Paul-Eric Pottie, Rodolphe Le Targat, Anne Amy-Klein, Benoit Darquie

TB07 **8:24 – 8:25**
TOWARDS REAL-TIME PROCESSING OF DUAL-COMB SPECTROSCOPY DATA WITH QUANTUM CASCADE LASERS, Michele Gianella, Simon Vogel, Béla Tuzson, Akshay Nataraj, Kenichi Komagata, Stéphane Schilt, Thomas Südmeyer, Andreas Hugi, Markus Mangold, Pierre Jouy, Filippos Kapsalidis, Johannes Hillbrand, Mattias Beck, Jérôme Faist, Lukas Emmenegger

TB08 **8:28 – 8:29**
TWO-COLOR, INTRACAVITY PUMP-PROBE, CAVITY RINGDOWN SPECTROSCOPY, Jun Jiang, A. Daniel McCartt

TB09 **8:32 – 8:33**
MEASURING ROTATIONAL SPECTRA IN EXCITED VIBRATIONAL MODES: A NEW TECHNIQUE BASED ON A QUANTUM CASCADE LASER-PUMPED MOLECULAR LASER, Paul Chevalier, Arman Amirzhan, Marco Piccardo, Federico Capasso, Henry O. Everitt

TB10 **8:36 – 8:37**
DEVELOPMENT OF A CBGB SOURCE AND A QCL LASER SYSTEM FOR STUDYING THE IR SPECTROSCOPY OF CLUSTERS, Gregory T. Pullen, Gary E. Douberly, Heather Lewandowski

TB11 **8:40 – 8:41**
HIGH-TEMPERATURE HYPERSONIC LAVAL NOZZLE FOR NON-LTE CAVITY RINGDOWN SPECTROSCOPY, Eszter DUDÁS, Robert Georges, Abdessamad Benidar, Shuvayan Brahmachary, Vinayak Kulkarni, Samir Kassi, Christine Charles, Nicolas Suas-David

TB12 **8:44 – 8:45**
INTRACAVITY LASER SPECTROSCOPY INTEGRATED WITH FOURIER TRANSFORM DETECTION, Jack C Harms, James J O'Brien, Leah C O'Brien

TB13 **8:48 – 8:49**
CHARACTERISATION OF A 17 μm QUANTUM CASCADE LASER AND SPECTROSCOPY OF THE ν_2 FUNDAMENTAL MODE OF N_2O, Mathieu Manceau, Thomas Wall, Hadrien Philippe, Alexei Baranov, Michael Tarbutt, Roland Teissier, Benoit Darquie

TC. Dynamics and kinetics

Tuesday, June 22, 2021 – 8:0 AM

Room: 2021 Online Everywhere

Chair: Elsa Yan, Yale University, New Haven, CT, USA

TC01 *Coblentz Society Award Lecture* **8:00 – 8:02**
NONCOVALENT INTERACTIONS OF HYDRATED DNA AND RNA MAPPED BY 2D-IR SPECTROSCOPY, Benjamin P Fingerhut

TC02 **8:08 – 8:09**
UREA-WATER DYNAMICS IN PROTEINS: AN ULTRAFAST SPECTROSCOPIC STUDY, Sneha Banerjee, Rapti Goswami, Pankaj Mandal

TC03 **8:12 – 8:13**
STRUCTURAL FLUCTUATIONS IN AN AZEOTROPE: UNDERSTANDING THE BENZENE-METHANOL AZEOTROPE, Sneha Banerjee, Sohini Sarkar, Pankaj Mandal

TC04 **8:16 – 8:17**
ACOUSTIC STUDIES OF RELAXATION PROCESSES DUE TO CONFORMATIONAL TRANSITIONS OF FURFURAL MOLECULES, Farkhad Akhmedzhanov, Sirojiddin Zainievich Mirzaev, Kamoliddin Egamberdiev

TC05 **8:20 – 8:21**
DYNAMICS OF COPPER PHTHALOCYANINE MOLECULES INSIDE AN OPTICAL CAVITY REVEALED BY TWO-DIMENSIONAL ELECTRONIC SPECTROSCOPY (2DES), Tuphan Devkota, Kenneth L. Knappenberger, Jr.

TC06 **8:24 – 8:25**
ULTRAFAST PUMP-PROBE PHOTODISSOCIATION DYNAMICS OF CO_2 FOR THE PRODUCTION OF MOLECULAR OXYGEN, Jacob M Garcia, Scott G Sayres

TC07 **8:28 – 8:29**
USING COMPUTATIONAL CHEMISTRY TO DESIGN A PUMP-PROBE SCHEME FOR MEASURING NITROBENZENE RADICAL CATION DYNAMICS, Hugo A. López Peña, Derrick Ampadu Boateng, Shane L. McPherson, Katharine Moore Tibbetts

TC08 **8:32 – 8:33**
ULTRAFAST COULOMB EXPLOSION OF FORMIC ACID CLUSTERS AND PRODUCTION OF TRIPLY CHARGED CARBON MONOXIDE, Shaun Sutton, Scott G Sayres, tarakeshwar pilarisetty, Dane Miller

TC09 **8:36 – 8:37**
SITE-SPECIFIC CHARACTERIZATION OF P450CAM SUBSTRATE RECOGNITION *VIA* 2D IR SPECTROSCOPY, Sashary Ramos, Claire C Mammoser, Megan Thielges

TC10 **8:40 – 8:41**
THE RISE OF THE EXCITON IN SOLID AMMONIA, Andrew Cassidy, Rachel James, Anita Dawes, David Field

TC11 **8:44 – 8:45**
REIMAGINING OF OPTICAL KERR EFFECT SPECTROSCOPY: DEVELOPMENT OF A NEW SPECTROSCOPIC TECHNIQUE, Matthew M Brister, Richard Thurston, Liang Z. Tan, Thorsten Weber, Niranjan Shivaram, Daniel S. Slaughter

TC12 **8:48 – 8:49**
HIGH SENSITIVITY BROADBAND TRANSIENT ABSORPTION SPECTROSCOPY OF MOLECULAR BEAMS, Myles C Silfies, Grzegorz Kowzan, Neomi Lewis, Thomas K Allison

TD. Fundamental interest

Tuesday, June 22, 2021 – 8:0 AM

Room: 2021 Online Everywhere

Chair: Trevor Sears, Stony Brook University, Stony Brook, NY, USA

TD01 **8:00 – 8:01**
PERTURBATIONS OF THE A'$^1\Pi$ AND $C^1\Sigma^+$ STATES OF CaO, Sean Michael Bresler, Joel R Schmitz, Robert W Field, Michael Heaven

TD02 **8:04 – 8:05**
THE MOLECULAR CONSTANTS OF THE X2Σ+, A2Π, B2Σ+, AND C2Π ELECTRONIC STATES OF THE CALCIUM MONOHALIDE RADICALS, Robert W Field, Guy Taieb, Chiheb Bahrini

TD03 **8:08 – 8:09**
A LIGAND FIELD THEORY VIEW OF THE ELECTRONIC STRUCTURE OF CaX (X=F, Cl, Br, I, AND O), Robert W Field, Christopher Cummins, Michael Heaven, Guy Taieb

TD04 **8:12 – 8:13**
THE MOLECULAR CONSTANTS OF THE $X^2\Sigma^+$, $A^2\Pi$, $B^2\Sigma^+$, AND $C^2\Pi$ ELECTRONIC STATES OF THE CALCIUM MONOHALIDE RADICALS, Chiheb Bahrini, Robert W Field, Guy Taieb

TD05 **8:16 – 8:17**
THE DIATOMIC MOLECULAR SPECTROSCOPY DATABASE: DATA-SCIENCE DRIVEN APPLICATIONS, Xiangyue Liu, Stefan Truppe, Gerard Meijer, Jesús Pérez-Ríos

TD07 **8:24 – 8:25**
NONLINEAR FOURIER-TRANSFORM SPECTROSCOPY OF SINGLE GOLD NANOPARTICLES, Megan A. Steves, Kenneth L. Knappenberger, Jr.

TD08 **8:28 – 8:29**
A GENERALIZED BADGER'S RULE QUANTIFYING THE STRUCTURE-SPECTRA RELATIONSHIP FOR HYDROGEN-BONDED SYSTEMS, Mark A. Boyer, Ondrej Marsalek, Joseph P Heindel, Thomas E Markland, Anne B McCoy, Sotiris Xantheas

TD09 **8:32 – 8:33**
HIGH-SENSITIVITY FRANCK-CONDON FACTOR MEASUREMENTS ENABLED BY OPTICAL CYCLING, Benjamin Augenbraun, Zack Lasner, Nathaniel Vilas, Timothy Steimle, John M. Doyle

TD10 **8:36 – 8:37**
HIGH-RESOLUTION AND HIGH-PRECISION LASER SPECTROSCOPY OF A-BENZANTHRACENE, Masaaki Baba, Sho Yamasaki, Akiko Nishiyama, Masatoshi Misono

TD11 **8:40 – 8:41**
HIGH-RESOLUTION LASER SPECTROSCOPY OF TRANS-STILBENE : NONPLANAR STRUCTURE IN THE GROUND STATE , Akira Shimizu, Kosuke Nakajima, Shunji Kasahara, Masatoshi Misono, Masaaki Baba

TE. Comparing theory and experiment
Tuesday, June 22, 2021 – 8:0 AM
Room: 2021 Online Everywhere

Chair: Edwin Sibert, University of Wisconsin–Madison, Madison, WI, USA

TE01 **8:00 – 8:01**
ANALYSIS OF THE CORIOLIS- AND FERMI-COUPLED TRIAD NEAR 315 cm^{-1} OF BENZONITRILE (C_6H_5CN), Maria Zdanovskaia, Brian J. Esselman, R. Claude Woods, Robert J. McMahon, Zbigniew Kisiel

TE02 **8:04 – 8:05**
BRIEF SUMMARY OF THE MILLIMETER-WAVE ROTATIONAL SPECTRA OF 2-, 3-, AND 4-CYANOPYRIDINE: THEIR VIBRATIONAL GROUND STATES AND THE CORIOLIS-COUPLED DYADS OF THEIR LOWEST-ENERGY VIBRATIONALLY EXCITED STATES , P. Matisha Dorman, Brian J. Esselman, R. Claude Woods, Robert J. McMahon

TE03 **8:08 – 8:09**
HIGH-RESOLUTION FTIR SPECTROSCOPY OF BENZALDEHYDE IN THE FAR-INFRARED REGION: PROBING THE ROTATIONAL BARRIER , Yue Liang, Yichi Zhang, Csaba Fábri, Jiarui Ma, Jianbao Zhao, Brant E. Billinghurst, Ziqiu Chen

TE04 **8:12 – 8:13**
IMPROVED SEMI-EXPERIMENTAL EQUILIBRIUM STRUCTURE DETERMINATION AND THEORETICAL PREDICTION OF HYDRAZOIC ACID (HN_3), Andrew N. Owen, Nitai P Sahoo, Brian J. Esselman, John F. Stanton, R. Claude Woods, Robert J. McMahon

TE05 **8:16 – 8:17**
UPDATES TO AUTOFIT: PROGRESS AND PROSPECTS, Arianna T Rodriguez, Steven Shipman

TE06 **8:20 – 8:21**
MOLECULES PROBED WITH A SLOW CHIRPED-PULSE EXCITATION: ANALYTICAL MODEL OF THE FREE-INDUCTION-DECAY SIGNAL, Guillaume Dhont, Daniele Fontanari, Cédric Bray, Gaël Mouret, Arnaud Cuisset, Francis Hindle, Robin Bocquet, Kevin Hickson

TE07 **8:24 – 8:25**
FREQUENCY COMB ASSISTED, CAVITY RING-DOWN, LAMB-DIP SPECTROSCOPY OF ACETYLENE AT 1.39 μm., Antonio Castrillo, Eugenio Fasci, Stefania Gravina, Giuseppe Porzio, Livio Gianfrani

TE08 **8:28 – 8:29**
THEORY OF INTRACAVITY NEAR-RESONANT TWO-PHOTON ABSORPTION, Kevin Lehmann

TE09 **8:32 – 8:33**
CAVITY RING-DOWN SPECTROSCOPY MEASUREMENTS OF RESONANCE-ENHANCED TWO-PHOTON ABSORPTION BY N_2O, Gang Zhao, Adam J. Fleisher, D. Michelle Bailey, Joseph T. Hodges, Kevin Lehmann

TE10 **8:36 – 8:37**
AN EDGE-SPECIFIC SCHEME FOR EQUATION-OF-MOTION COUPLED-CLUSTER CALCULATIONS OF X-RAY ABSORPTION SPECTRA, Xuechen Zheng, Chaoqun Zhang, Lan Cheng

TE11 **8:40 – 8:41**
DENSITY DEPENDENCE OF SPECTRAL DETAIL IN PRESSURIZED AND SUPERCRITICAL CARBON DIOXIDE ELECTRONIC ABSORPTION SPECTRA, Timothy W Marin, Ireneusz Janik

TE12 **8:44 – 8:45**
DYNAMICS OF NITRO-NITRITE REARRANGMENT IN NITROMETHANE RADICAL CATION, Mi'Kayla D Word, Hugo A. López Peña, Derrick Ampadu Boateng, Katharine Moore Tibbetts

TE13 **8:48 – 8:49**
TRAJECTORY-BASED SIMULATION OF FAR-INFRARED CIA PROFILES OF CH_4-N_2 FOR MODELING TITAN'S ATMOSPHERE, Artem Finenko, Iouli E Gordon, Eamon K Conway, Bruno Bézard, Yulia N Kalugina, Daniil Chistikov, Sergei E Lokshtanov, Sergey V Petrov, Andrei Vigasin

TF. Linelists

Tuesday, June 22, 2021 – 8:0 AM

Room: 2021 Online Everywhere

Chair: Frances M Skinner, Harvard-Smithsonian Center for Astrophysics, Malden, MA, USA

TF01 **8:00 – 8:01**
HITRAN2020: ACT (ACCURACY, COMPLETENESS, TRACEABILITY), Iouli E Gordon, Laurence S. Rothman, Robert J. Hargreaves, Robab Hashemi, Ekaterina Karlovets, Frances M Skinner, Artem Finenko, Eamon K Conway, Kyle Nelson, Tijs Karman, Yan Tan, Roman Kochanov, Christian Hill

TF02 **8:04 – 8:05**
A URANIUM ATLAS IN ASCII FORMAT, 20000 – 27000 cm^{-1} , Amanda J. Ross, Patrick Crozet, Dennis W. Tokaryk, Allan G. Adam

TF03 **8:08 – 8:09**
THE ELECTRIC QUADRUPOLE SPECTRA OF DIATOMIC MOLECULES, Wilfrid Somogyi, Sergei N. Yurchenko

TF04 **8:12 – 8:13**
EXOMOL ROVIBRATIONAL LINELIST FOR NaO, Georgi B Mitev, Jonathan Tennyson, Sergei N. Yurchenko, Alexei Buchachenko, Andrey Stolyarov, Steven Taylor

TF05 **8:16 – 8:17**
AN *AB INITIO* STUDY OF ELECTRONICALLY EXCITED STATES OF SiN AND SO, Gap-Sue Kim, Ryan Brady, Nicholas Clark, Wilfrid Somogyi, Mikhail Semenov, Sergei N. Yurchenko

TF06 **8:20 – 8:21**
AB INITIO AND EMPIRICAL STUDIES OF ELECTRONICALLY EXCITED STATES OF PHOSPHOROUS MONONITRIDE (PN) AND ITS ROVIBRONIC SPECTROSCOPY , Mikhail Semenov, Nayla El-Kork, Sergei N. Yurchenko, Jonathan Tennyson

TF07 **8:24 – 8:25**
SPEED-DEPENDENT VOIGT LINESHAPE PARAMETER DATABASE USING DUAL FREQUENCY COMB LASER ABSORPTION MEASUREMENTS OF PURE AND AIR-BROADENED H_2O FROM 6656-7540 CM^{-1} UP TO 1100 K, Scott C Egbert, Nathan A Malarich, David Yun, Keeyoon Sung, Sean Coburn, Brian Drouin, Gregory B Rieker

TF08 **8:28 – 8:29**
A THEORETICAL RO-VIBRATIONAL LINE LIST OF H2CS USING A NEW APPROACH TO CONSTRUCT THE EXACT KINETIC ENERGY OPERATOR, Thomas Mellor, Sergei N. Yurchenko

TF10 **8:36 – 8:37**
MEASUREMENTS OF NEW LINE POSITIONS AND EFFECTIVE LINE INTENSITIES OF CIS-HONO OF THE ν_2 BAND AROUND 1660 cm^{-1}USING QUANTUM CASCADE LASER ABSORPTION SPECTROSCOPY , Nhut Minh Ngo, Qian Gou, Nicolas Houzel, Tong Nguyen-Ba, Cécile Coeur, Weidong Chen

TF11 **8:40 – 8:41**
SHOCKGAS-IR: A HIGH-TEMPERATURE AND HIGH-PRESSURE ABSORPTION CROSS-SECTION DATABASE, Christopher L Strand, Yiming Ding, Sarah E Johnson, Wey-Wey Su, Ronald K Hanson

TF12 **8:44 – 8:45**
A NEW STRATEGY FOR COLLECTION OF HIGH-TEMPERATURE BROAD-BAND ABSORPTION SPECTRA FOR GAS-PHASE MOLECULES IN THE MID-INFRARED, Yiming Ding, Sarah E Johnson, Christopher L Strand, Ronald K Hanson

TG. Plenary

Tuesday, June 22, 2021 – 9:0 AM

Room: 2021 Online Everywhere

Chair: Robert W Field, MIT, Cambridge, MA, USA

TG02 **9:03 – 9:43**

IMAGING ROTATIONAL WAVE PACKETS IN MOLECULES AND CLUSTERS, Yasuhiro Ohshima

TH. Mini-symposium: Large Amplitude Motions
Tuesday, June 22, 2021 – 10:0 AM
Room: 2021 Online Everywhere

Chair: Kaori Kobayashi, University of Toyama, Toyama, Japan

TH01 *INVITED TALK* **10:00 – 10:02**
THE EXCEL-ERATION OF METHANOL SPECTROSCOPY: ISOTOPIC TUNING OF TORSION-VIBRATION INTERACTIONS, Ronald M. Lees

TH03 **10:12 – 10:13**
A NEW PROGRAM FOR RADICALS WITH INTERNAL ROTATION, J. H. Westerfield, Kyle N. Crabtree

TH04 **10:16 – 10:17**
1- AND 2-DIMENSIONAL POTENTAL FUNCTIONS WHEN V_3 IS NOT THE BARRIER , Peter Groner

TH05 **10:20 – 10:21**
GLOBAL ANALYSIS OF THE CD_2HOH MOLECULE ROTATION-TORSION SPECTRUM, L. Margulès, R. A. Motiyenko, F. Kwabia Tchana, L. H. Coudert

TH06 **10:24 – 10:25**
NEW MEASUREMENTS AND ASSIGNMENTS IN THE $v_t = 0, 1, 2$ TORSIONAL STATES OF CD_3OH AND CH_3OD: FROM MILLIMETER-WAVE TO FIR SPECTRA, V. Ilyushin, Yan Bakhmat, E. A. Alekseev, Olga Dorovskaya, Holger S. P. Müller, Frank Lewen, Stephan Schlemmer, Sigurd Bauerecker, Christof Maul, K. Berezkin, Ronald M. Lees, Li-Hong Xu

TH07 **10:28 – 10:29**
A SIMULTANEOUS FIT OF THE TORSION-WAGGING-ROTATIONAL LEVELS FROM THE EXCITED (V_t = 0, 1 and 2) STATES OF METHYLAMINE USING A HYBRID (TUNNELING AND NON-TUNNELING) HAMILTONIAN FORMALISM, Isabelle Kleiner, Iwona Gulaczyk, Marek Kreglewski, R. A. Motiyenko, Prakash Gyawali, V. Ilyushin

TH08 **10:32 – 10:33**
ULTRAHIGH-RESOLUTION LASER SPECTROSCOPY OF ACETALDEHYDE : TORSION-INVERSION-ROTATION INTERACTION IN THE EXCITED STATE, Kosuke Nakajima, Akira Shimizu, Shunji Kasahara, Masatoshi Misono, Masaaki Baba

TH09 **10:36 – 10:37**
MULTI-DIMENSIONAL PROTON TUNNELING IN 2-METHYLMALONALDEHYDE, Iwona Gulaczyk, Marek Kreglewski

TH10 **10:40 – 10:41**
A UBIQUITOUS KINETIC COUPLING BETWEEN TORSION AND IN- AND OUT-OF-PLANE XH_3 WAGGING VIBRATIONS FOR AN -XH_3 GROUP ATTACHED TO A PLANAR FRAME, Jason R. Gascooke, Warren D. Lawrance

TH11 **10:44 – 10:45**
ROTATIONALLY RESOLVED $S_1 \leftarrow S_0$ ORIGIN BANDS OF DIFFERENT METHYLINDOLES AND THEIR INTERNAL ROTATION EFFECTS , Marie-Luise Hebestreit, Hilda Lartian , Hajo Böschen, W. Leo Meerts, Michael Schmitt

TH12 **10:48 – 10:49**
STUDY OF LARGE AMPLITUDE MOTIONS OF METHYL GROUP IN 9-METHYLANTHRACENE BY HIGH-RESOLUTION SPECTROSCOPY, Masatoshi Misono, Sho Yamasaki, Shunji Kasahara, Akiko Nishiyama, Masaaki Baba

TI. Instrument/Technique Demonstration

Tuesday, June 22, 2021 – 10:0 AM

Room: 2021 Online Everywhere

Chair: Brant E. Billinghurst, Canadian Light Source Inc., Saskatoon, SK, Canada

TI01 **10:00 – 10:01**
THE HEROES OF TERAHERTZ SYNCHROTRON SPECTROSCOPY, Thomas Sandow Hearne, Olivier Pirali, Marie-Aline Martin-Drumel, P. Roy, Jean-François Lampin, Marie-Hélène Mammez, Dominique Mammez, Francis Hindle, Gaël Mouret

TI02 **10:04 – 10:05**
CHARACTERIZATION OF A THZ ELECTRIC FIELD BY MOLECULAR ION SPECTROSCOPY, Florin Lucian Constantin

TI03 **10:08 – 10:09**
AN HETERODYNE SPECTROMETER FOR TERAHERTZ SPECTROSCOPY, Dominique Mammez, Marie-Hélène Mammez, Francis Hindle, Gaël Mouret, Thomas Sandow Hearne, Marie-Aline Martin-Drumel, Olivier Pirali, Sophie Eliet, Jean-François Lampin

TI04 **10:12 – 10:13**
THZ FABRY-PEROT SPECTROMETER, Francis Hindle, Coralie Elmaleh, Fabien Simon, A. Pienkina, Robin Bocquet, Arnaud Cuisset, Gaël Mouret

TI05 **10:16 – 10:17**
TECHNICAL ENHANCEMENTS OF A SUBMILLIMETER-WAVE SPECTROMETER: LABORATORY DETECTION OF NEW LINES OF METHANOL RADICAL DERIVATIVES, Jean-Thibaut Spaniol, Olivia Chitarra, Thomas Sandow Hearne, Marie-Aline Martin-Drumel, Olivier Pirali

TI06 **10:20 – 10:21**
OPTICALLY-PUMPED AMMONIA TERAHERTZ LASER UP TO 5.5 THz, Marie-Hélène Mammez, Francis Hindle, Gaël Mouret, Jean-François Lampin, Sophie Eliet, Stefano Barbieri, Marie-Aline Martin-Drumel, Olivier Pirali, P. Roy

TI07 **10:24 – 10:25**
CONSTRUCTION AND DEMONSTRATION OF A MICROWAVE THREE-WAVE MIXING SPECTROMETER AT THE MISSOURI UNIVERSITY OF SCIENCE AND TECHNOLOGY, Nicole Moon, Amanda Duerden, Joshua E. Isert, G. S. Grubbs II

TI08 **10:28 – 10:29**
TWO INSTRUMENTS IN ONE: A NEW CP-FTMW EXPERIMENTAL SETUP TO MEASURE MULTIPLE FREQUENCY BANDS SIMULTANEOUSLY , Cristobal Perez, Amanda Steber, Melanie Schnell

TI09 **10:32 – 10:33**
IMPROVING THE SENSITIVITY OF CHIRPED-PULSE FOURIER TRANSFORM MM-WAVE DETECTION IN UNIFORM SUPERSONIC FLOWS, Omar Abdelkader Khedaoui, Brian M Hays, Ilsa Rose Cooke, Thomas Sandow Hearne, Theo Guillaume, Divita Gupta, Myriam Drissi, Ian R. Sims

TI10 **10:36 – 10:37**
A CHIRP PULSE FOURIER TRANSFORM MICROWAVE SPECTROMETER WITH MULTI-ANTENNA DETECTION (MAD-CP-FTMW), Amanda Duerden, Nicole Moon, Christian Swanson, Frank E Marshall, Joshua E. Isert, Kristen Donnell, G. S. Grubbs II

TI11 **10:40 – 10:41**
A HEIGHT ADJUSTABLE LASER ABLATION SOURCE FOR A CP-FTMW SPECTROMETER AT THE MISSOURI UNIVERSITY OF SCIENCE AND TECHNOLOGY, Joshua E. Isert, Josie Glenn, Amanda Duerden, Nicole Moon, Frank E Marshall, G. S. Grubbs II

TI12 **10:44 – 10:45**
MICROWAVE SPECTROSCOPY: LINESHAPE APPROXIMATION FOR SQUARE-WAVE FREQUENCY MODULATION, E. A. Alekseev, V. Ilyushin

TI13 **10:48 – 10:49**
MILLIMETER-MILLIMETER-WAVE DOUBLE-MODULATION DOUBLE-RESONANCE SPECTROSCOPY, Oliver Zingsheim, Luis Bonah, Holger S. P. Müller, Frank Lewen, Sven Thorwirth, Stephan Schlemmer

TI14 **10:52 – 10:53**
MILLIMETER-WAVE DETECTIONS OF LASER-ABLATED SALTS WITH A MINIATURE SPECTROMETER, Alexander W Raymond, Kelvin Lee, Michael C McCarthy, Eric Mazur, Brian Drouin

TJ. Astronomy
Tuesday, June 22, 2021 – 10:0 AM
Room: 2021 Online Everywhere

Chair: Brett A. McGuire, Massachusetts Institute of Technology, Cambridge, MA, USA

TJ01 **10:00 – 10:01**
METHYL-CARBON CHAIN CHEMISTRY IN TMC-1: THE FIRST INTERSTELLAR DETECTION OF METHYLCYANOTRIACETYLENE (CH_3C_7N), Mark A. Siebert, Anthony Remijan, Kelvin Lee, Andrew M Burkhardt, Michael C McCarthy, Brett A. McGuire

TJ02 **10:04 – 10:05**
DETECTION OF CH_3NCO IN THE GALACTIC CENTER STAR-FORMING REGION SAGITTARIUS B2(M) BY RADIO ASTRONOMICAL OBSERVATIONS, Yuki Ohno, Mitsunori Araki, Yoshiaki Minami, Takahiro Oyama, Shuro Takano, Nobuhiko Kuze, Yoshihiro Sumiyoshi, Koichi Tsukiyama

TJ03 **10:08 – 10:09**
FIRST INTERSTELLAR DETECTION OF ISOCYANODIACETYLENE (HC_4NC), THE LARGEST ISOCYANIDE MOLECULE IN THE ISM, Ci Xue, Eric R. Willis, Eric Herbst, Anthony Remijan, Ryan A Loomis, Andrew M Burkhardt, Kelvin Lee, Brett A. McGuire

TJ04 **10:12 – 10:13**
INDIVIDUAL DETECTIONS OF POLYCYCLIC AROMATIC HYDROCARBONS IN TMC-1, Andrew M Burkhardt, Kelvin Lee, Bryan Changala, Christopher N Shingledecker, Ilsa Rose Cooke, Ryan A Loomis, Hongji Wei, Steven B Charnley, Eric Herbst, Michael C McCarthy, Brett A. McGuire

TJ05 **10:16 – 10:17**
A SENSITIVE LINE SURVEY OF TMC-1: THE CHEMICAL COMPLEXITY OF A COLD DARK CLOUD, Jose Cernicharo, Carlos Cabezas, Marcelino Agúndez, Belén Tercero, Pablo de Vicente, Nuria Marcelino, Juan R. Pardo

TJ06 **10:20 – 10:21**
IDENTIFICATION OF PHOSPHORUS MONOXIDE ($X^2\Pi_r$) IN THE ORION MOLECULAR CLOUD: FURTHER EVIDENCE FOR THE UBIQUITOUS P-O BOND, Jacob Bernal, Lucy M. Ziurys, Lilia Koelemay

TJ08 **10:28 – 10:29**
RADIAL LOCATION OF SGR B2 MEASURED FROM H_3^+ AND H_2O^+ ABSORPTION SPECTRA, Takeshi Oka, Thomas R. Geballe

TJ09 **10:32 – 10:33**
METHANOL AT THE EDGE OF THE GALAXY: NEW OBSERVATIONS TO CONSTRAIN THE GALACTIC HABITABLE ZONE, Jacob Bernal, Lucy M. Ziurys, Cathryn Sephus

TJ10 **10:36 – 10:37**
PUSHING THE LIMITS OF MOLECULAR COMPLEXITY IN THE OUTER GALAXY - THE SEARCH FOR FORMAMIDE (NH_2CHO) AT VARIOUS GALACTOCENTRIC DISTANCES, Maryam Hami, Anthony Remijan

TJ11 **10:40 – 10:41**
COMPLEX ENVELOPE CHEMISTRY AND DYNAMICS OF NML CYGNUS, Ambesh Pratik Singh, Jessica L Edwards, Lucy M. Ziurys

TJ12 **10:44 – 10:45**
RESOLVING THE NEW CHEMICALLY-ACTIVE OUTFLOW HH114, Aditya Pothanaboyina, Andrew M Burkhardt, Qizhou Zhang

TJ13 **10:48 – 10:49**
MOLECULES IN OUTFLOW OF HIGH-MASS PROTOSTAR IRAS 20126-4104, Bore Gao, Andrew M Burkhardt, Qizhou Zhang

TJ14 **10:52 – 10:53**
ALMA CN ZEEMAN OBSERVATIONS OF AS 209: LIMITS ON MAGNETIC FIELD STRENGTH AND MAGNETICALLY DRIVEN ACCRETION RATE, Rachel E. Harrison, Leslie Looney, Ian Stephens, Zhi-Yun Li, Richard Teague, Richard Crutcher, Haifeng Yang, Erin Guilfoil Cox, Manuel Fernandez-Lopez, Hiroko Shinnaga

TJ15 **10:56 – 10:57**
A SEARCH FOR LIGHT HYDRIDES IN THE ENVELOPES OF EVOLVED STARS, Mark A. Siebert, Anthony Remijan, Brett A. McGuire, Christopher N Shingledecker, Andrew M Burkhardt

TK. Comparing theory and experiment

Tuesday, June 22, 2021 – 10:0 AM

Room: 2021 Online Everywhere

Chair: Karl K. Irikura, National Institute of Standards and Technology, Gaithersburg, MD, USA

TK01 **10:00 – 10:01**
VAPOR-PHASE INFRARED AND RAMAN SPECTRA AND THEORETICAL INVESTIGATIONS OF π-TYPE INTRAMOLECULAR HYDROGEN BONDING IN 3-CYCLOPENTEN-1-OL AND 3-CYCLOPENTEN-1-AMINE, Esther Juliana Ocola, Jaan Laane

TK02 **10:04 – 10:05**
VIBRATIONAL SPECIFICITY OF PROTON-TRANSFER DYNAMICS IN ELECTRONICALLY EXCITED 6-HYDROXY-2-FORMYLFULVENE, Lidor Foguel, Zachary Vealey, Patrick Vaccaro

TK03 **10:08 – 10:09**
THE MYSTERIOUS CASE OF THE MISSING NH STRETCH TRANSITION, Karl N. Blodgett, Timothy S. Zwier, Edwin Sibert

TK04 **10:12 – 10:13**
ABNORMAL RAMAN BANDS OF AROMATICAL AMINES AND BENZYL RADICALS ADSORBED ON METAL SURFACES, De-Yin Wu, Zhong-Qun Tian

TK06 **10:20 – 10:21**
CONFORMATIONAL ISOMERS OF NICOTINE, NORNICOTINE AND THEIR HYDRATED CLUSTERS , Garrett D Santis, Naoya Takeda, Shun-ichi Ishiuchi, Kazuya Tsuruta, Masaaki Fujii, Sotiris Xantheas

TK07 **10:24 – 10:25**
TOWARD 0.1% UNCERTAINTY FOR CO_2 THEORETICAL IR INTENSTIES, Xinchuan Huang, David Schwenke, Timothy J. Lee

TK08 **10:28 – 10:29**
ACCURATE PREDICTION OF VIBRONIC LEVELS AND BRANCHING RATIOS FOR LASER-COOLABLE LINEAR POLYATOMIC MOLECULES: APPLICATIONS TO CAOH, SROH, AND YBOH, Chaoqun Zhang, Lan Cheng

TK09 **10:32 – 10:33**
SPECTROSCOPIC-NETWORK-ASSISTED PRECISION SPECTROSCOPY AND ITS APPLICATION TO WATER: THE EXPERIMENT, Roland Tóbiás, Tibor Furtenbacher, Attila Császár, Irén Simkó, Meissa Diouf, Frank M.J. Cozijn, Edcel John Salumbides, Wim Ubachs

TK10 **10:36 – 10:37**
SPECTROSCOPIC-NETWORK-ASSISTED PRECISION SPECTROSCOPY AND ITS APPLICATION TO WATER: THEORETICAL FRAMEWORK, Roland Tóbiás, Tibor Furtenbacher, Attila Császár, Irén Simkó, Meissa Diouf, Frank M.J. Cozijn, Edcel John Salumbides, Wim Ubachs

TK11 **10:40 – 10:41**
VIBRATIONAL LAMB-DIP SPECTROSCOPY OF WATER ISOTOPOLOGUES: HYPERFINE STRUCTURE IN $H_2{}^{17}O$ AND PERTURBATIONS IN $HD^{16}O$, Meissa Diouf, Frank M.J. Cozijn, Edcel John Salumbides, Wim Ubachs, Mattia Melosso, Cristina Puzzarini, Roland Tóbiás, Attila Császár

TK12 **10:44 – 10:45**
COUPLED-CLUSTER APPROACHES TO ELECTRIC POLARIZABILITIES FOR LONG-RANGE FORCE FIELDS, Stephen L Coy, Timothy J Barnum, Robert W Field, John F. Stanton

TK13 **10:48 – 10:49**
LONG-RANGE POLARIZATION MODEL OF VIBRATIONAL AUTOIONIZATION IN RYDBERG STATES OF NITRIC OXIDE, Timothy J Barnum, Gloria Clausen, Stephen L Coy, Robert W Field

TL. Ions

Tuesday, June 22, 2021 – 10:0 AM
Room: 2021 Online Everywhere

Chair: Stephan Schlemmer, I. Physikalisches Institut, Köln, Germany

TL01 **10:00 – 10:01**
VIBRATIONAL SPECTROSCOPY OF H_2He^+ and D_2He^+, Oskar Asvany, Stephan Schlemmer, Ad van der Avoird, Tamás Szidarovszky, Attila Császár

TL02 **10:04 – 10:05**
KINETIC AND SPECTROSCOPIC STUDIES OF C_2^- IN A CRYOGENIC WIRE TRAP, Markus Nötzold, Robert Wild, Christine Lochmann, Roland Wester

TL03 **10:08 – 10:09**
THE SPECTRUM OF ν_3 BAND OF CH_3^+ IN HELIUM NANODROPLETS, Swetha Erukala, Deepak Verma, Andrey Vilesov

TL04 **10:12 – 10:13**
HIGH-RESOLUTION DOUBLE RESONANCE ACTION SPECTROSCOPY IN ION TRAPS: VIBRATIONAL AND ROTATIONAL FINGERPRINTS OF $CH_2NH_2^+$, Charles R. Markus, Sven Thorwirth, Oskar Asvany, Stephan Schlemmer

TL05 **10:16 – 10:17**
THE ν_1 VIBRATIONAL MODE OF HC_3O^+ OBSERVED AT HIGH SPECTRAL RESOLUTION, Oskar Asvany, Michael E. Harding, Stephan Schlemmer, Sven Thorwirth

TL06 **10:20 – 10:21**
NITROUS OXIDE IS NOTHING TO LAUGH ABOUT: $Au_2N_2O^+$, Kai Pollow, Marko Förstel, Taarna Studemund, Robert G. Radloff, Otto Dopfer

TL07 **10:24 – 10:25**
INFRARED SPECTROSCOPY OF SINGLE-TURN AND DOUBLE-TURN TETHERED ALPHA-HELICES IN THE GAS PHASE: DON'T LET YOUR LEFT HAND KNOW WHAT YOUR RIGHT HAND IS DOING., John T Lawler, Timothy S. Zwier

TL08 **10:28 – 10:29**
PROBING THE CONFORMATIONAL LANDSCAPE AND THERMOCHEMISTRY OF DINUCLEOTIDE ANIONS VIA HELIUM NANODROPLET INFRARED ACTION SPECTROSCOPY, Daniel A Thomas, Rayoon Chang, Eike Mucha, Maike Lettow, Kim Greis, Gerard Meijer, Gert von Helden

TL09 **10:32 – 10:33**
DOUBLE-RESONANCE SPECTROSCOPY WITH A CONTINUUM: APPLICATION TO THE $Mg(3d_\delta)Ar^+$ $^2\Delta$ STATE OF $MgAr^+$, Matthieu Génévriez, Dominik Wehrli, Thomas Berglitsch, Frédéric Merkt

TL10 **10:36 – 10:37**
VIBRONIC SPECTRA OF GROUP 13 METAL-PIPERIDINE COMPLEXES, Micheal Okeke, Dong-Sheng Yang

TL11 ***Post-Deadline Abstract*** **10:40 – 10:41**
INFRARED SPECTROSCOPIC OBSERVATION OF THE MCLAFFERTY REARRANGEMENT IN IONIZED 2-PENTANONE, Yoshiyuki Matsuda, RYO YASUMOTO, Asuka Fujii

TM. Lineshapes, collisional effects
Tuesday, June 22, 2021 – 10:0 AM
Room: 2021 Online Everywhere

Chair: Keeyoon Sung, Jet Propulsion Laboratory/Caltech, Pasadena, CA, USA

TM01 **10:00 – 10:01**
INVESTIGATION OF ZEEMAN STATE-TO-STATE COLLISION-INDUCED TRANSITIONS IN NITRIC OXIDE USING TWO-COLOR POLARIZATION SPECTROSCOPY, Ziqiao Chang, Aman Satija, Robert P. Lucht

TM02 **10:04 – 10:05**
LINE MIXING STUDY ON THE NITRIC OXIDE FUNDAMENTAL BAND NEAR 5.3 MICRONS, Wey-Wey Su, Christopher Almodovar, Yiming Ding, Christopher L Strand, Ronald K Hanson

TM03 **10:08 – 10:09**
AIR-BROADENING IN NEAR-INFRARED CARBON DIOXIDE LINE SHAPES: QUANTIFYING CONTRIBUTIONS FROM O_2, N_2, AND Ar, Erin M. Adkins, David A. Long, Joseph T. Hodges

TM04 **10:12 – 10:13**
REVISING THE LINESHAPE PARAMETERS FOR AIR- AND SELF- BROADENED CO_2 LINES AT A SUB-PERCENT LEVEL, Robab Hashemi, Iouli E Gordon, Thi Ngoc Ha Tran, Roman V Kochanov, Julien Lamouroux, Yan Tan, Laurence S. Rothman

TM05 **10:16 – 10:17**
DUAL FREQUENCY COMB ABSORPTION SPECTROSCOPY OF CO_2 AT HIGH PRESSURE AND TEMPERATURE, Ryan K. Cole, Nazanin Hoghooghi, Gregory B Rieker

TM06 **10:20 – 10:21**
ADAPTATION TO HIGH RESOLUTION OF AN ALGORITHM TO RETRIEVE THE INSTRUMENT LINE SHAPE OF A FOURIER TRANSFORM SPECTROMETER, Thibault Bertin, Jean Vander Auwera

TM07 **10:24 – 10:25**
A POTASSIUM LINE SHAPE STUDY AT STELLAR ATMOSPHERIC TEMPERATURES OF BROWN DWARFS, Yiming Ding, Joshua A Vandervort, Christopher L Strand, Ronald K Hanson

TM08 **10:28 – 10:29**
CONTINUING INVESTIGATIONS OF ORTHO-PARA-DEPENDENT PRESSURE BROADENING IN THE $\nu_1 + \nu_3$ BAND OF ACETYLENE , Eisen C. Gross, Kimberly A Tsang, Trevor Sears

TM09 **10:32 – 10:33**
CO_2 COLLISION-INDUCED LINE PARAMETERS IN THE ν_3 BAND OF CH_4, Thibault Bertin, Jean Vander Auwera

TM11 **10:40 – 10:41**
COMB-ANCHORED, CAVITY RING-DOWN SPECTROSCOPY OF THE 1.27 μm BAND OF O_2, Helene Fleurbaey, Zachary Reed, Erin M. Adkins, David A. Long, Joseph T. Hodges

TM12 **10:44 – 10:45**
AB INITIO CALCULATIONS OF QUANTUM SCATTERING AND LINE-SHAPE PARAMETERS
IN O_2 PERTURBED BY N_2, Maciej Grzegorz Gancewski, Hubert Jóźwiak, Franck Thibault, Ernesto Quintas Sánchez, Richard Dawes, Piotr Wcislo

TM13 **10:48 – 10:49**
SUBPERCENT AGREEMENT BETWEEN AB INITIO AND EXPERIMENTAL COLLISION-INDUCED LINE SHAPES OF CARBON MONOXIDE PERTURBED BY ARGON, Grzegorz Kowzan, Hubert Cybulski, Piotr Wcislo, Michał Słowiński, Piotr Maslowski, Alexandra Viel, Franck Thibault

TM14 ***Post-Deadline Abstract*** **10:52 – 10:53**
PREDICTION OF LINE-SHAPE PARAMETERS AND THEIR TEMPERATURE DEPENDENCES BY REQUANTIZED CLASSICAL MOLECULAR DYNAMICS SIMULATIONS, Ha Tran, Ngoc Hoa NGO, Huyen Trang NGUYEN

WA. Mini-symposium: Large Amplitude Motions

Wednesday, June 23, 2021 – 8:0 AM

Room: 2021 Online Everywhere

Chair: R. A. Motiyenko, Université de Lille, Villeneuve d'Ascq, France

WA01 *INVITED TALK* **8:00 – 8:02**
AB INITIO CALCULATION APPLIED TO THE STUDY OF ORGANIC NON-RIGID MOLECULES WITH (AT LEAST) THREE TORSIONAL MODES, Maria Luisa S Senent

WA02 **8:08 – 8:09**
CHALLENGES IN CONFORMATIONAL ANALYSIS OF FLEXIBLE MOLECULES, Malgorzata Biczysko

WA03 **8:12 – 8:13**
INTERNAL ROTATION AND CHLORINE NUCLEAR QUADRUPOLE COUPLING IN 2-CHLORO-4-FLUOROTOLUENE EXPLORED BY MICROWAVE SPECTROSCOPY AND QUANTUM CHEMISTRY, K.P. Rajappan Nair, Sven Herbers, Daniel A. Obenchain, Jens-Uwe Grabow, William C. Bailey, Alberto Lesarri, Ha Vinh Lam Nguyen

WA04 **8:16 – 8:17**
GUIDED DIFFUSION MONTE CARLO APPROACHES FOR STUDIES OF WATER CLUSTERS: APPLICATIONS TO WATER HEXAMER, Victor G M Lee, Mark A. Boyer, Anne B McCoy

WA05 **8:20 – 8:21**
GUIDED DIFFUSION MONTE CARLO BASED ON BONDING ENVIRONMENT: AN EFFICIENT APPROACH FOR STUDYING MOLECULAR VIBRATIONS IN PATHOLOGICAL SYSTEMS, Jacob M Finney, Anne B McCoy

WA06 **8:24 – 8:25**
LARGE AMPLITUDE MOTIONS AND π-HYDROGEN BONDING IN THE THIOPHENE–WATER COMPLEX CHARACTERIZED BY ROTATIONAL SPECTROSCOPY AND QUANTUM CHEMICAL CALCULATIONS, Weslley G. D. P. Silva, Jennifer van Wijngaarden

WA07 **8:28 – 8:29**
VIBRATIONALLY AVERAGED STRUCTURE AND FREQUENCIES OF $(XeHXe)^+$: COMPUTATIONAL MOLECULAR SPECTROSCOPY STUDY, Tsuneo Hirano, Umpei Nagashima, Masaaki Baba

WA08 **8:32 – 8:33**
LARGE AMPLITUDE MOTIONS IN THE 1,1,1,3,3,3-HEXAFLUORO-2-PROPANOL BINARY WATER COMPLEX, Bowei Wu, Nathan A. Seifert, Soenke Oswald, Yunjie Xu

WA09 **8:36 – 8:37**
LARGE AMPLITUDE MOTIONS IN 2,2,3,3,3-PENTAFLUOROPROPANOL AND ITS BINARY WATER COMPLEX, Bowei Wu, Nathan A. Seifert, Soenke Oswald, Wolfgang Jäger, Yunjie Xu

WA10 **8:40 – 8:41**
COUPLING OF TORSION AND OH-STRETCHING IN *TERT*-BUTYL HYDROPEROXIDE AND ITS RADICAL ANALOG, QOOH, Rachel M. Huchmala, Mark A. Boyer, Anne B McCoy

WB. Instrument/Technique Demonstration

Wednesday, June 23, 2021 – 8:0 AM

Room: 2021 Online Everywhere

Chair: Marie-Aline Martin-Drumel, Université Paris Saclay, CNRS , Orsay Cedex, France

WB01 **8:00 – 8:01**
ENTANGLED PHOTON SPECTROSCOPY OF MOLECULES, Scott Kevin Cushing

WB02 **8:04 – 8:05**
A NANOSECOND-RESOLVED ULTRAHIGH-DENSITY SPIN-POLARIZED HYDROGEN MAGNETOMETER, Alexandros Spiliotis, Michalis Xygkis, Konstantinos Tazes, George E. Katsoprinakis, Giorgos Vasilakis, T. Peter Rakitzis

WB03 **8:08 – 8:09**
POLARIZATION CONTROL OF ROTATIONALLY RESOLVED 2DIR SPECTROSCOPY, Grzegorz Kowzan, Myles C Silfies, Neomi Lewis, Thomas K Allison

WB04 **8:12 – 8:13**
HIGH RESOLUTION COHERENT MULTIDIMENSIONAL SPECTROSCOPY FOR OVERCOMING SEVERE SPECTRAL CONGESTION, Peter Chen

WB05 **8:16 – 8:17**
NOISE IMMUNE CAVITY ENHANCED OPTICAL HETERODYNE ZEEMAN MODULATION SPECTROSCOPY, Anna C. Wannenmacher, Charles R. Markus, Kyle N. Crabtree

WB06 ***Post-Deadline Abstract*** **8:20 – 8:21**
QUANTITY DETERMINTATION AND TRACEABILITY FOR SUPER-RESOLUTION MID-INFRARED LASER ABSORPTION SPECTROSCOPY, Zhenhui Du

WB07 **8:24 – 8:25**
THE FAR-INFRARED BEAMLINE AT THE CANADIAN LIGHT SOURCE, Brant E. Billinghurst

WB08 **8:28 – 8:29**
NEAR-FOURIER-TRANSFORM-LIMITED LONG-PULSE YAG-PUMPED DYE LASER SYSTEM, Holger Herburger, Urs Hollenstein, Frédéric Merkt

WB09 **8:32 – 8:33**
DEVELOPING PROBABLISTIC MACHINE LEARNING MODELS FOR ION IMAGING ANALYSIS, G. Stephen Kocheril, Kelvin Lee

WB10 **8:36 – 8:37**
SPECTROSCOPICALLY IDENTIFYING FROM GAS-PHASE REACTIONS OF DISTONIC BENZONITRILEH$^+$ RADICAL IONS IN AN ION-TRAP MASS SPECTROMETER, Oisin J. Shiels, Samuel Marlton, P. D. Kelly, Gabriel da Silva, Stephen J. Blanksby, Adam J. Trevitt

WB11 **8:40 – 8:41**
A MODULAR DESIGN FOR REACTION TRAPS IN CRYOGENIC ION TRAP MASS SPECTROMETERS, Gina Roesch, Etienne Garand

WB12 **8:44 – 8:45**
SOFTWARE IMPLEMENTATION OF A MULTI-CHANNEL, MULTI-FREQUENCY LOCK-IN AMPLIFIER , Amrut Nadgir, Daniel S. Slaughter, Richard Thurston, Matthew M Brister, Niranjan Shivaram

WB13 **8:48 – 8:49**
LLWP - A NEW LOOMIS-WOOD SOFTWARE AT THE EXAMPLE OF PROPANONE-$^{13}C_1$, Luis Bonah, Oliver Zingsheim, Sven Thorwirth, Holger S. P. Müller, Frank Lewen, J.-C. Guillemin, Stephan Schlemmer

WB14 **8:52 – 8:53**
SPATIALLY ENHANCED ELECTRIC FIELD INDUCED SECOND HARMONIC (SEEFISH) GENERATION FOR MEASUREMENTS OF ELECTRIC FIELD DISTRIBUTIONS IN GASES AND PLASMAS , Sai Raskar, Keegan Orr, Igor V. Adamovich

WC. Dynamics and kinetics

Wednesday, June 23, 2021 – 8:0 AM

Room: 2021 Online Everywhere

Chair: Scott G Sayres, Arizona State University, Tempe, AZ, USA

WC01 **8:00 – 8:01**
TIME-RESOLVED CAVITY RINGDOWN MEASUREMENTS OF HO_2 RADICAL IN A HEATED PLASMA FLOW REACTOR , Elijah R Jans, Ian Jones, Xin Yang, Anam C. Paul, Terry A. Miller, Igor V. Adamovich

WC02 **8:04 – 8:05**
MEASURING TIME-RESOLVED CONCENTRATIONS OF FREE RADICALS IN CHEMICAL REACTIONS WITH CAVITY RINGDOWN SPECTROSCOPY, Ian Jones, Elijah R Jans, Terry A. Miller, Igor V. Adamovich, John F. Stanton

WC03 **8:08 – 8:09**
SINGLE SUBSTITUTION KINETIC ISOTOPE EFFECT MEASUREMENTS FOR CH_4 + $O(^1D)$ USING CAVITY RINGDOWN SPECTROSCOPY, Douglas Ober, TzuLing Chen, LINHAN SHEN, THINH Bui, Mitchio Okumura

WC04 **8:12 – 8:13**
PREDICTING FLUORESCENCE QUANTUMN YIELD of NO $A^2\Sigma^+$ VIA STATE-TO-STATE COLLISIONAL ENERGY TRANSFER MODEL, Zeyu Yan, Shengkai Wang

WC05 **8:16 – 8:17**
OBSERVING CHEMICAL REACTIONS IN LOW-TEMPERATURE SUPERSONIC FLOWS USING CHIRPED PULSE FOURIER TRANSFORM MILLIMETER WAVE SPECTROSCOPY, Theo Guillaume, Divita Gupta, Brian M Hays, Ilsa Rose Cooke, Omar Abdelkader Khedaoui, Thomas Sandow Hearne, Myriam Drissi, Ian R. Sims

WC06 **8:20 – 8:21**
SIGNATURES OF HYDROGEN ATOM QUANTUM DIFFUSION: H + N_2O REACTION IN SOLID PARAHYDROGEN, Kelly M. Olenyik, Fredrick M. Mutunga, Aaron I. Strom, David T. Anderson

WC07 **8:24 – 8:25**
N AND H TALIF MEASUREMENTS, $N_2(A^3\Sigma_u^+)$ TDLAS MEASUREMENTS, AND KINETIC MODELING OF NANOSECOND PULSE DISCHARGE PLASMAS IN N_2-H_2 MIXTURES , Xin Yang, caleb richards, Elijah R Jans, Sai Raskar, Dirk van den Bekerom, Igor V. Adamovich

WC08 **8:28 – 8:29**
CHARACTERIZATION OF HYBRID NS PULSE/RF PLASMAS AND ATMOSPHERIC PRESSURE PLASMA JETS, caleb richards, Elijah R Jans, Dirk van den Bekerom, David Kyle Mignogna, Igor V. Adamovich

WC09 **8:32 – 8:33**
KINETICS OF $N_2(A^3\Sigma_u^+,v)$ GENERATION AND DECAY IN REACTING GAS MIXTURES EXCITED BY NANOSECOND PULSE DISCHARGE PLASMAS , David Kyle Mignogna, Elijah R Jans, Igor V. Adamovich

WC10 **8:36 – 8:37**
THERMAL DECOMPOSITION OF CYCLOHEXANE BY FLASH PYROLYSIS VACUUM ULTRAVIOLET PHOTOIONIZATION TIME-OF-FLIGHT MASS SPECTROMETRY: A STUDY ON THE INITIAL UNIMOLECULAR DECOMPOSITION MECHANISM, Kuanliang Shao, Xinghua Liu, Paul Jones, Ge Sun, Mariah Gomez, Blake Riser, Jingsong Zhang

WC11 **8:40 – 8:41**
THE STUDY OF DIRECT D ATOM INCORPORATION IN RADICALS AT LOW TEMPERATURE PROBED BY CHIRPED PULSE mm-WAVE SPECTROSCOPY , Nureshan Dias, Ranil Gurusinghe, Bernadette M. Broderick, Arthur Suits

WC12 **8:44 – 8:45**
REACTION DYNAMICS OF PROPARGYL + NH_2 PROBED USING CHIRPED PULSE ROTATIONAL SPECTROSCOPY IN A PULSED QUASI-UNIFORM FLOW (CPUF), Ranil Gurusinghe, Nureshan Dias, Alexander M Mebel, Arthur Suits

WC13 **8:48 – 8:49**
LASER INDUCED FLUORESCENCE MEASUREMENTS OF VIBRATIONALLY EXCITED OXYGEN PRODUCED BY RECOMBINATION OF O ATOMS, Dirk van den Bekerom, Keegan Orr, Elijah R Jans, Xin Yang, Anam C. Paul, Igor V. Adamovich

WD. Non-covalent interactions

Wednesday, June 23, 2021 – 8:0 AM

Room: 2021 Online Everywhere

Chair: Gang Feng, Chongqing University, Chongqing, China

WD01 **8:00 – 8:01**
MICROWAVE SPECTRUM OF TRIFLIC ACID DIHYDRATE AND TRIHYDRATE: EVIDENCE FOR COMPLETE PROTON TRANSFER IN A MICROSOLVATED SUPERACID , Anna Huff, Nathan Love, Kenneth R. Leopold

WD02 **8:04 – 8:05**
EVIDENCE FOR SPONTANEOUS PROTON TRANSFER IN THE COMPLEX FORMED FROM TRIFLIC ACID AND TRIMETHYLAMINE: MICROWAVE SPECTRUM AND COMPUTATIONAL ANALYSIS OF THE TRIMETHYLAMMONIUM TRIFLATE ION PAIR, Nathan Love, Anna Huff, Kenneth R. Leopold

WD03 **8:08 – 8:09**
HOW INTERMOLECULAR INTERACTIONS EFFECT ESTERIFICATION REACTIONS? A MICROWAVE STUDY OF THE GAS-PHASE COMPLEXES OF FORMIC ACID WITH TWO METHANOL DERIVATIVES AND THEIR ESTERIFICATION PRODUCTS., Wenhao Sun, Melanie Schnell

WD04 **8:12 – 8:13**
CONFORMATIONAL EQUILIBRIA BETWEEN ALDEHYDES AND ALCOHOLS: ROTATIONAL SPECTRA OF ACROLEIN-METHANOL AND ACROLEIN-ETHANOL COMPLEXES, Dingding Lv, Wentao Song, Luca Evangelisti, Assimo Maris, Sonia Melandri

WD05 **8:16 – 8:17**
ROTATIONAL SPECTROSCOPY AND CONFORMATIONAL SPACE OF GLYCEROL DIMERS, Jiarui Ma, FAN XIE, Nathan A. Seifert, Yunjie Xu

WD06 **8:20 – 8:21**
INVESTIGATING INTERMOLECULAR INTERACTIONS WITHIN NAPHTHOL DIMERS USING BROADBAND ROTATIONAL SPECTROSCOPY, Arsh Singh Hazrah, Nathan A. Seifert, Wolfgang Jäger

WD07 **8:24 – 8:25**
OBSERVATION OF 2-NAPHTHALENETHIOL HOMODIMER USING ROTATIONAL SPECTROSCOPY, Rizalina Tama Saragi, Marcos Juanes, Alberto Lesarri, Lourdes Enriquez, Martin Jaraiz

WD08 **8:28 – 8:29**
INVESTIGATING SUBSTITUENT EFFECTS IN DISPERSION-CONTROLLED ACETOPHENONE-PHENOL BALANCES, C. Zimmermann, Martin A. Suhm

WD09 **8:32 – 8:33**
BINDING SITES SWITECHED BY ALKYL SUBSTITUENTS: ROTATIONAL SIGNATURES OF $C_6H_5(CH_2)_nOH$-CO_2 (n = 0-2), Hao Wang, Junha Chen, Qian Gou

WD10 **8:36 – 8:37**
P...N PNICOGEN BONDING INTERACTION IN PHOSPHORYL CHLORIDE...NITROGEN BASES: EVIDENCE FROM MATRIX ISOLATION INFRARED SPCTROSCOPY AND QUANTUM CHEMICAL CALCULATIONS, P K Sruthi, Nagarajan Ramanathan, K Sundararajan

WE. Theory and Computation

Wednesday, June 23, 2021 – 8:0 AM

Room: 2021 Online Everywhere

Chair: Inga Ulusoy, Heidelberg University, Heidelberg, Germany

WE01 **8:00 – 8:01**
STACKED ENSEMBLE LEARNING FOR RANGE-SEPARATION PARAMETERS, Cheng-Wei Ju, Ethan French, Nadav Geva, Alexander W. Kohn, Zhou Lin

WE02 **8:04 – 8:05**
TOO MANY UNKNOWN MOLECULES IN THE LABORATORY ITSELF , Krishnan Thirumoorthy, Amir Karton, Nisha Job, Inga Ulusoy, Andrew L. Cooksy, Venkatesan S. Thimmakondu

WE03 **8:08 – 8:09**
IMPROVING SPECTRAL SYNTHESIS PERFORMANCE BY UP TO 5 ORDERS OF MAGNITUDE WITH THE DISCRETE INTEGRAL TRANSFORM APPROACH, Dirk van den Bekerom, Pankaj Mishra, Erwan Pannier

WE04 **8:12 – 8:13**
PARTICIPATION RATIO AND QUANTUM FIDELITY SUSCEPTIBILITY AS TOOLS TO CHARACTERIZE BENT-TO-LINEAR SHAPE TRANSITIONS, Jamil Khalouf-Rivera, Miguel Carvajal, Francisco Curro Pérez-Bernal

WE05 **8:16 – 8:17**
ASSIGNING THE COMPLICATED DISPERSED FLUORESCENCE SPECTRUM OF PhCCCN, James H. Thorpe, Khadija M. Jawad, Timothy S. Zwier, John F. Stanton

WE06 **8:20 – 8:21**
SUB-EV ACCURACY DELTA-COUPLED-CLUSTER CALCULATIONS FOR HETERO-SITE DOUBLE CORE-IONIZED STATES, Xuechen Zheng, Junzi Liu, Lan Cheng, Gilles Doumy, Linda Young

WE07 **8:24 – 8:25**
MODELLING THE DIPOLE MOMENT FUNCTION OF CARBON MONOXIDE CAPABLE OF PREDICTING THE ROTATIONAL DISTRIBUTION IN THE 7-0 BAND, Emile S. Medvedev, Vladimir G. Ushakov

WE08 **8:28 – 8:29**
GLOBAL ROVIBRATIONAL ANALYSIS FOR THE 20 LOWEST VIBRATIONAL BANDS OF HYDROGEN SULFIDE ($H_2^{32}S$), Miguel Carvajal, Jamil Khalouf-Rivera, Francisco Curro Pérez-Bernal, Renato Lemus

WE09 **8:32 – 8:33**
COMPUTATIONAL NMR STUDY OF ION PAIRING OF 1-DECYL-3-METHYL-IMIDAZOLIUM CHLORIDE IN MOLECULAR SOLVENTS, Dovile Lengvinaite, Vytautas Klimavicius, Vytautas Balevicius , Kestutis Aidas

WE10 **8:36 – 8:37**
XANES SPECTRA OF VANADIUM COMPLEXES CALCULATED BY TWO TDDFT METHODS, Jun Yi, Zhou Lin

WE11 **8:40 – 8:41**
COMPUTATIONAL INFRARED SPECTROSCOPY OF PHOSPHORUS-CONTAINING POTENTIAL BIOSIGNATURES, Juan C. Zapata Trujillo, Anna-Maree Syme, Keiran N. Rowell, Clara Sousa-Silva, Laura K McKemmish

WE12 **8:44 – 8:45**
MOLECULAR FRAGMENT MACHINE LEARNING TRAINING TECHNIQUES TO PREDICT CLUSTER ENERGETICS AND FREQUENCIES IN BROWN CARBON AEROSOL CLUSTERS, Emily E. Chappie, Daniel P. Tabor, Nathanael M. Kidwell

WE13 **8:48 – 8:49**
IMPROVING THE ROTATION VIBRATIONAL LINE LISTS FOR OZONE, Apoorva Upadhyay, Oleg L. Polyansky, Jonathan Tennyson, Alec Owens, Nikolay F. Zobov, Eamon K Conway

WE14 **8:52 – 8:53**
NON-ADIABATIC CALCULATIONS OF SPECTRA OF OPEN-SHELL DIATOMIC MOLECULES, Sergei N. Yurchenko

WF. Linelists

Wednesday, June 23, 2021 – 8:0 AM

Room: 2021 Online Everywhere

Chair: Amanda J. Ross, Universite de Lyon, Villeurbanne, France

WF01 **8:00 – 8:01**
LINE LISTS FOR HIGH RESOLUTION STUDIES OF EXOPLANETS, Jonathan Tennyson, Sergei N. Yurchenko

WF02 **8:04 – 8:05**
EXPANSION OF THE HITEMP DATABASE, Robert J. Hargreaves, Eamon K Conway, Iouli E Gordon, Laurence S. Rothman

WF03 **8:08 – 8:09**
THE NON-LTE SPECTROSCOPY OF MOLECULAR REACTIONS USING THE EXOMOL DATABASE, Victoria H.J. Clark, Sergei N. Yurchenko, Jonathan Tennyson

WF04 **8:12 – 8:13**
EXOPLINES: MOLECULAR ABSORPTION CROSS-SECTION DATABASE FOR BROWN DWARF AND GIANT EXOPLANET ATMOSPHERES, Ehsan Gharib-Nezhad, Aishwarya Iyer, Michael R Line, Richard S Freedman, Mark S Marley, Natasha E Batalha

WF05 **8:16 – 8:17**
MODELING PLANETARY OPACITIES WITH HITRAN AND HAPI: TEST CASE OF AMMONIA MICROWAVE ABSORPTION SPECTRA UNDER JOVIAN CONDITION, Frances M Skinner, Robert J. Hargreaves, Iouli E Gordon

WF06 **8:20 – 8:21**
MOLECULAR LINE LISTS FOR HOT ROCKY SUPER-EARTHS, Alec Owens, Sergei N. Yurchenko, Jonathan Tennyson

WF07 **8:24 – 8:25**
BUILDING A HIGH RESOLUTION LINE LIST FOR ALUMINIUM MONOXIDE, Charles A Bowesman

WF08 **8:28 – 8:29**
LINE LIST FOR THE LOWEST FOUR STATES OF NO, Qianwei Qu, Sergei N. Yurchenko, Jonathan Tennyson

WF09 **8:32 – 8:33**
UPDATING CH_4 SPECTROSCOPIC MODELS FROM 6770-7630 CM^{-1} WITH DUAL FREQUENCY COMB ABSORPTION SPECTROSCOPY UP TO 1000 K, Nathan A Malarich, David Yun, Keeyoon Sung, Scott C Egbert, Sean Coburn, Brian Drouin, Gregory B Rieker

WF10 **8:36 – 8:37**
THE SECOND RESONANCE SYSTEM OF HC_3N. NEW RO-VIBRATIONAL GLOBAL ANALYSIS FOR ALL THE EXCITED STATES BELOW 1300 cm^{-1}., Luca Bizzocchi, Mattia Melosso, Cristina Puzzarini, Filippo Tamassia, Andrea Pietropolli Charmet, Marie-Aline Martin-Drumel, Olivier Pirali, Barbara Michela Giuliano, Paola Caselli, J.-C. Guillemin

WF11 **8:40 – 8:41**
A RE-EXAMINATION OF THE QUANTITATIVE INFRARED ABSORPTION CROSS-SECTIONS OF ISOBUTANE, Kendall D. Hughey, Steven W. Sharpe, Robert L. Sams, Timothy J. Johnson, Tanya L. Myers, Thomas A. Blake

WF12 **8:44 – 8:45**
INFRARED ABSORPTION CROSS SECTIONS OF NEOPENTANE AND ETHANE, Randika Dodangodage, Peter F. Bernath, Andy Wong, Brant E. Billinghurst, Jianbao Zhao

WF13 **8:48 – 8:49**
MEASUREMENT OF CROSS-SECTIONS AND PSEUDOLINE GENERATION FOR TOLUENE(C_7H_8) IN THE 7-15 μM REGION AT 240 – 298 K, Keeyoon Sung, Deacon J Nemchick, Geoffrey C. Toon, Conor A Nixon

WG. Plenary

Wednesday, June 23, 2021 – 9:0 AM

Room: 2021 Online Everywhere

Chair: Melanie Schnell, Deutsches Elektronen-Synchrotron (DESY), Hamburg, Germany

WG02 **9:03 – 9:43**

MOLECULAR COMPLEXES ON THE BRINK OF CHEMICAL CHANGE, Kenneth R. Leopold

WH. Mini-symposium: Large Amplitude Motions

Wednesday, June 23, 2021 – 10:0 AM

Room: 2021 Online Everywhere

Chair: Miguel Carvajal, Universidad de Huelva, Huelva, Spain

WH01 **10:00 – 10:01**
EXCITED TORSIONAL STATES OF DIMETHYLETHER $(CH_3)_2O$, V. Ilyushin, Yan Bakhmat, E. A. Alekseev, Olga Dorovskaya, Brian Drouin, Stephan Schlemmer, Christian Endres

WH02 **10:04 – 10:05**
FAR-INFRARED AND MICROWAVE SPECTROSCOPY OF $HCOOCH_3$ II., Kaori Kobayashi, AKIO ITOH, Masaharu Fujitake, Nobukimi Ohashi, Dennis W. Tokaryk, Brant E. Billinghurst

WH03 **10:08 – 10:09**
MICROWAVE SPECTRUM OF ACETIC ACID: THE THIRD AND FOURTH EXCITED TORSIONAL STATES, V. Ilyushin, Yan Bakhmat, Olga Dorovskaya, E. A. Alekseev

WH04 **10:12 – 10:13**
EXTENDING THE MILLIMETER/SUBMILLIMETER ROTATIONAL SPECTRUM OF GROUND STATE PYRUVIC ACID, Connor J. Wright, Jay A Kroll, Susanna L. Widicus Weaver

WH05 **10:16 – 10:17**
LARGE AMPLITUDE TORSIONS IN NITROTOLUENE ISOMERS STUDIED BY ROTATIONAL SPECTROSCOPY AND QUANTUM CHEMISTRY CALCULATIONS, Anthony Roucou, Manuel Goubet, Sabath Bteich, Isabelle Kleiner, Arnaud Cuisset

WH06 **10:20 – 10:21**
NEXT LEVEL ACHIEVEMENT OF THE *XIAM* CODE IN MODELING MICROWAVE SPECTRA OF MOLECULES WITH VERY LOW TORSIONAL BARRIERS, Ha Vinh Lam Nguyen, Sven Herbers, K.P. Rajappan Nair, Jens-Uwe Grabow

WH07 **10:24 – 10:25**
INTERNAL ROTATION OF THE ACETYL METHYL GROUP IN METHYL ALKYL KETONES: THE MICROWAVE SPECTRUM OF OCTAN-2-ONE, Maike Andresen, Damian Schoengen, Isabelle Kleiner, Martin SCHWELL, Wolfgang Stahl, Ha Vinh Lam Nguyen

WH08 **10:28 – 10:29**
COMBINATION OF IODINE QUADRUPOLE COUPLING AND ESSENTIALLY FREE METHYL INTERNAL ROTATION IN 3-IODOTOLUENE, Joshua A. Signore, Ha Vinh Lam Nguyen, Wallace C. Pringle, S. A. Cooke, Stewart E. Novick

WH09 **10:32 – 10:33**
STRUCTURE AND DYNAMICS OF METHACRYLAMIDE, Assimo Maris, Sonia Melandri, Luca Evangelisti, Camilla Calabrese

WH10 **10:36 – 10:37**
THE EFFECTS OF PROTON TUNNELLING, ^{14}N QUADRUPOLE COUPLING, AND METHYL INTERNAL ROTATIONS OF PLANAR SECONDARY AMINES, Kenneth J Koziol, Wolfgang Stahl, Ha Vinh Lam Nguyen

WH11 **10:40 – 10:41**
ACCURATE TORSIONAL BARRIER HEIGHT OF TRIFLUROACETIC ACID, Luyao Zou, R. A. Motiyenko, L. Margulès

WI. Mini-symposium: Precision Spectroscopy for Fundamental Physics

Wednesday, June 23, 2021 – 10:0 AM

Room: 2021 Online Everywhere

Chair: Benoit Darquie, Laboratoire de Physique des Lasers, Villetaneuse, France

WI01 *INVITED TALK* **10:00 – 10:02**
PRECISION MEASUREMENTS IN FEW-ELECTRON ATOMS AND MOLECULES, Frederic Merkt

WI02 **10:08 – 10:09**
MEASUREMENTS OF np–2s TRANSITIONS IN THE HYDROGEN ATOM, Simon Scheidegger, Josef A. Agner, Hansjürg Schmutz, Frédéric Merkt

WI03 **10:12 – 10:13**
DETERMINATION OF THE IONIZATION ENERGY OF THE METASTABLE 2 $^1S_0$ STATE OF ^{4}He THROUGH RYDBERG-SERIES EXTRAPOLATION, Gloria Clausen, Paul Jansen, Josef A. Agner, Hansjürg Schmutz, Frédéric Merkt

WI04 **10:16 – 10:17**
PHOTOLYSIS PRODUCTION AND PRECISION MEASUREMENT OF THE HIGHEST VIBRATIONAL STATES (v = 14) AND QUASI-BOUND RESONANCES IN $X^1\Sigma_g^+$ H_2, Kin Fung Lai, Maximilian Beyer, Edcel John Salumbides, Wim Ubachs

WI05 **10:20 – 10:21**
IONIZATION ENERGIES OF PARA-H_2 FROM ZERO-QUANTUM-DEFECT POSITIONS, Nicolas Hölsch, Frédéric Merkt

WI06 **10:24 – 10:25**
PRECISION MEASUREMENT OF THE IONIZATION AND DISSOCIATION ENERGIES OF THE DEUTERIUM MOLECULE, Joël Hussels, Nicolas Hölsch, Maximilian Beyer, Edcel John Salumbides, Christian Jungen, Frédéric Merkt, Wim Ubachs

WI07 **10:28 – 10:29**
PRECISE MEASUREMENT OF A FUNDAMENTAL VIBRATIONAL TRANSITION FREQUENCY IN HD, Arthur Fast, Samuel Meek

WI08 **10:32 – 10:33**
SUB-DOPPLER FREQUENCY METROLOGY IN HD FOR TESTS OF FUNDAMENTAL PHYSICS, Frank M.J. Cozijn, Meissa Diouf, Edcel John Salumbides, Wim Ubachs

WI09 **10:36 – 10:37**
COMB-CALIBRATED NONLINEAR SPECTROSCOPY OF THE Q(1) 1-0 LINE OF MOLECULAR HYDROGEN , Marco Lamperti, Lucile Rutkowski, Daniele Ronchetti, Davide Gatti, Riccardo Gotti, Giulio Cerullo, Franck Thibault, Hubert Jóźwiak, Szymon Wojtewicz, Piotr Maslowski, Piotr Wcislo, Dario Polli, Marco Marangoni

WI10 **10:40 – 10:41**
A WIDELY TUNABLE HIGH-POWER CONTINUOUS-WAVE OPTICAL PARAMETRIC OSCILLATOR (CW-OPO) SYSTEM FOR MID-INFRARED SPECTROSCOPY AND FREQUENCY METROLOGY, Hamzeh Telfah, S M Shah Riyadh, Jinjun Liu, David B. Foote, Walter Hurlbut, Matthew J. Cich, Ulrich Eismann, Adam Heiniger, Chris Haimberger

WI11 **10:44 – 10:45**
NARROW LINEWIDTH OPO LIGHT SOURCE FOR PRECISION SPECTROSCOPY, Zitan Zhang, Cunfeng Cheng, Yu Robert Sun, Shui-Ming Hu

WI12 **10:48 – 10:49**
PRECISE FREQUENCY MEASUREMENTS OF THE $2\nu_3$ A_1 - ν_3 BAND TRANSITIONS OF METHANE WITH COMB-REFERENCED INFRARED-INFRARED DOUBLE-RESONANCE , Hiroyuki Sasada, Sho Okubo, Hajime Inaba, Shoko Okuda

WI13 **10:52 – 10:53**
COMB-LOCKED CAVITY RING-DOWN SPECTROSCOPY FOR MOLECULAR TRANSITION FREQUENCY MEASUREMENTS BELOW 10^{-12} RELATIVE UNCERTAINTY, Zachary Reed, David A. Long, Helene Fleurbaey, Joseph T. Hodges

WI14 **10:56 – 10:57**
COMB-LOCKED CAVITY-ASSISTED DOUBLE RESONANCE (COCA-DR) SPECTROSCOPY OF MOLECULES WITH kHz ACCURACY, Changle Hu, Valery Perevalov, Cunfeng Cheng, Tian-Peng Hua, An-Wen Liu, Yu Robert Sun, Jin Wang, Yan Tan, Shui-Ming Hu

WJ. Astronomy

Wednesday, June 23, 2021 – 10:0 AM

Room: 2021 Online Everywhere

Chair: Harshal Gupta, National Science Foundation, Alexandria, VA, USA

WJ01 **10:00 – 10:01**
HIGH-RESOLUTION GIGAHERTZ AND TERAHERTZ SPECTROSCOPY OF THE ISOTOPICALLY CHIRAL MOLECULE TRANS-2,3-DIDEUTERO-OXIRANE(c-CHD-CHDO) , Ziqiu Chen, Sieghard Albert, Karen Keppler, Martin Quack, Volker Schurig, Oliver Trapp

WJ02 **10:04 – 10:05**
MICROWAVE AND MILLIMETER WAVE SPECTRUM OF STYRENE OXIDE $C_6H_5C_2H_3O$, Pascal Stahl, Benjamin E Arenas, Sergio R Domingos, Guido W Fuchs, Melanie Schnell, Thomas Giesen

WJ03 **10:08 – 10:09**
THE PURE ROTATIONAL SPECTRUM OF THE HYDROXYMETHYL RADICAL REINVESTIGATED TO ENABLE ITS INTERSTELLAR DETECTION, Olivia Chitarra, Marie-Aline Martin-Drumel, Bérenger Gans, Olivier Pirali, Silvia Spezzano, Valerio Lattanzi, Holger S. P. Müller, J.-C. Loison

WJ04 **10:12 – 10:13**
SUBMILLIMETER WAVE INVESTIGATION OF TWO FORMAMIDE ISOMERS: FORMALDOXIME (CH_2NOH) AND NITROSOMETHANE (CH_3NO), Luyao Zou, L. Margulès, R. A. Motiyenko, J.-C. Guillemin

WJ05 **10:16 – 10:17**
A ROTATIONAL STUDY OF INTERSTELLAR ACETOHYDROXAMIC ACID, A GLYCINE ISOMER , Miguel Sanz Novo, Iker León, Santiago Mata, José L. Alonso

WJ06 **10:20 – 10:21**
MICROWAVE AND MILLIMETER WAVE SPECTRUM OF FIVE CONFORMERS OF CYSTEAMINE AND SEARCH IN SAGITTARIUS B2(N), Wentao Song, Assimo Maris, Luca Evangelisti, Dingding Lv, Sonia Melandri

WJ07 **10:24 – 10:25**
MILLIMETER-WAVE SPECTRA OF 5-METHYL HYDANTOIN IN ITS VIBRATIONALLY EXCITED STATES, Minami Awadu, Hiroyuki Ozeki, Kaori Kobayashi, Soichiro Watanabe

WJ08 **10:28 – 10:29**
LABORATORY SPECTROSCOPY OF ALLYLIMINE AND ITS TENTATIVE DETECTION IN THE INTERSTELLAR MEDIUM, Mattia Melosso, Luca Bizzocchi, Ningjing Jiang, Davide Alberton, Paola Caselli, Victor Manuel Rivilla, Andrea Pietropolli Charmet, Luca Dore, Cristina Puzzarini

WJ09 **10:32 – 10:33**
HIGH TEMPERATURE FOURIER TRANSFORM SPECTROSCOPY OF THE B $^1\Pi$ - X $^1\Sigma^+$ TRANSITION OF ZrO, Jason J Sorensen, Peter F. Bernath

WJ10 **10:36 – 10:37**
THE PURE ROTATIONAL SPECTRUM OF THE SiP RADICAL ($X^2\Pi_i$), Mark Burton, Phillip M. Sheridan, Lucy M. Ziurys

WJ11 **10:40 – 10:41**
HIGH RESOLUTION INFRARED SPECTROSCOPY OF CYANO-OXIRANE (c-C_2H_3OCN) , Sieghard Albert, Ziqiu Chen, Karen Keppler, Philippe Lerch, Carine Manca Tanner, Martin Quack, Jürgen Stohner

WJ12 **10:44 – 10:45**
HIGH-RESOLUTION INFRARED SPECTROSCOPY OF DC_3N IN THE STRETCHING REGION, Ningjing Jiang, Mattia Melosso, Filippo Tamassia, Luca Bizzocchi, Luca Dore, Elisabetta Canè, Davide Fedele, J.-C. Guillemin, Cristina Puzzarini

WJ13 **10:48 – 10:49**
STUDIES OF IRON MONODEUTERIDE, FeD, VIA LASER EXCITATION SPECTROSCOPY AND DISPERSED FLUORESCENCE SPECTROSCOPY, Dennis W. Tokaryk, Allan G. Adam, Ryan A. R. Harvey

WJ14 **10:52 – 10:53**
IMPROVED CENTRIFUGAL AND HYPERFINE ANALYSIS OF ND_2H AND NH_2D AND ITSAPPLICATION TO THE SPECTRAL LINE SURVEY OF L1544, Mattia Melosso, Luca Bizzocchi, Luca Dore, Zbigniew Kisiel, Ningjing Jiang, Jürgen Gauss, Cristina Puzzarini

WK. Theory and Computation

Wednesday, June 23, 2021 – 10:0 AM

Room: 2021 Online Everywhere

Chair: John F. Stanton, University of Florida, Gainesville, FL, USA

WK01 **10:00 – 10:01**
UTILIZATION OF NEURAL NETWORKS FOR GPU-ACCELERATED DIFFUSION MONTE CARLO FOR VIBRATIONAL PROBLEMS, Fenris Lu, Ryan J. DiRisio, Anne B McCoy

WK02 **10:04 – 10:05**
DIFFUSION MONTE CARLO USING MACHINE LEARNING POTENTIAL ENERGY SURFACES, Ryan J. DiRisio, Mark A. Boyer, Jacob M Finney, Fenris Lu, Anne B McCoy

WK03 **10:08 – 10:09**
PHYSICS-GUIDED CURVE FITTING FOR POTENTIAL-ENERGY FUNCTIONS OF DIATOMIC MOLECULES, Karl K. Irikura

WK04 **10:12 – 10:13**
JIM WATSON AND THE THEORY OF VIBRATION-ROTATION INTERACTION, Takeshi Oka

WK05 **10:16 – 10:17**
A SPARSE LINEAR ALGEBRAIC APPROACH TO ARBITRARY-ORDER VIBRATIONAL PERTURBATION THEORY, Mark A. Boyer, Anne B McCoy

WK06 ***Post-Deadline Abstract*** **10:20 – 10:21**
RECONSTRUCTION OF TERM DIAGRAMS WITHOUT USING A MODEL HAMILTONIAN, Stefan Brackertz, Sven Kristkeitz, Oskar Asvany, Stephan Schlemmer

WK07 **10:24 – 10:25**
A DISCRETE VARIABLE APPROACH FOR INVESTIGATING TUNNELING SPLITTINGS AND VIBRATIONAL WAVE FUNCTIONS IN RARE GAS-ASYMMETRIC TOP HETERODIMERS, Ezra Arumi Alexander, Mark D. Marshall, Helen O. Leung

WK08 **10:28 – 10:29**
VARIATIONAL ROVIBRATIONAL CALCULATION FOR LINEAR TETRAATOMIC MOLECULES: I. THE C8V4 APPROACH, Benjamin Schröder

WK09 **10:32 – 10:33**
VARIATIONAL ROVIBRATIONAL CALCULATION FOR LINEAR TETRAATOMIC MOLECULES: II. THE B11244 STORY RETOLD, Benjamin Schröder, Peter Sebald

WK11 ***Post-Deadline Abstract*** **10:40 – 10:41**
SIMULATION OF THE ABSORPTION SPECTRUM OF CHLORINE PEROXIDE (ClOOCl), Megan R Bentley, John F. Stanton

WK12 **10:44 – 10:45**
VIBRONICALLY COUPLED STATES: COMPUTATION AND CHARACTERIZATION OF VIBRONIC AND ROVIBRONIC SPECTROSCOPIC PARAMETERS, Ketan Sharma, Terry A. Miller, John F. Stanton

WK13 **10:48 – 10:49**
VIBRONIC AND SPIN ANGULAR MOMENTUM IN ROTATIONALLY RESOLVED SPECTRA OF JAHN-TELLER ACTIVE MOLECULES, Ketan Sharma, Terry A. Miller, John F. Stanton

WK14 **10:52 – 10:53**
ACCURATE PREDICTION OF VIBRONIC LEVELS AND BRANCHING RATIOS FOR LASER-COOLABLE LINEAR POLYATOMIC MOLECULES: THE CONSTRUCTION OF THE QUASIDIABATIC HAMILTONIAN, Chaoqun Zhang, Lan Cheng

WL. Large molecules

Wednesday, June 23, 2021 – 10:0 AM

Room: 2021 Online Everywhere

Chair: Etienne Garand, University of Wisconsin-Madison, Madison, WI, USA

WL01 **10:00 – 10:01**
ELECTRONIC AND INFRARED PHOTODISSOCIATION SPECTROSCOPY OF THE GREEN FLUORESCENT PROTEIN CHROMOPHORE IN VACUO, Wyatt Zagorec-Marks, Madison M. Foreman, J. Mathias Weber

WL02 **10:04 – 10:05**
MICROSOLVATION OF THE GREEN FLUORESCENT PROTEIN CHROMOPHORE ONE WATER MOLECULE AT A TIME, Wyatt Zagorec-Marks, Madison M. Foreman, J. Mathias Weber

WL03 **10:08 – 10:09**
LOST AND BOUND: UNDERSTANDING THE ELECTRON DETACHMENT PATHWAYS OF THE TETRACENYL ANION ISOMERS, Cole R Sagan, Etienne Garand

WL04 **10:12 – 10:13**
LABORATORY IR SPECTRA OF PROTONATED FULLERENES, Julianna Palotás, Jonathan K Martens, Giel Berden, Jos Oomens

WL05 **10:16 – 10:17**
ELECTRONIC AND INFRARED PHOTODISSOCIATION SPECTROSCOPY OF PROTOPORPHYRIN IN VACUO, Wyatt Zagorec-Marks, Madison M. Foreman, J. Mathias Weber

WL06 **10:20 – 10:21**
STRUCTURAL CHARACTERIZATION OF METAL BIPYRIDINE COMPLEXES VIA CRYOGENIC ION SPECTROSCOPY, Madison M. Foreman, Wyatt Zagorec-Marks, J. Mathias Weber

WL07 **10:24 – 10:25**
THE ROTATIONAL SPECTRA OF FLAVONE AND FLAVANONE: LASER ABLATION AND HEATING METHODS FOR VAPORIZATION., Susana Blanco, Alberto Macario, Juan Carlos Lopez

WL09 **10:32 – 10:33**
A ROTATIONAL STUDY OF 1-SUBSTITUTED BARBARALONES, Mauro Mato, Miguel Sanz Novo, Iker León, Elena R. Alonso, Antonio M Echavarren, José L. Alonso

WL10 **10:36 – 10:37**
DAPPERS: A NEW PROGRAM FOR THE RAPID ASSIGNMENT AND FITTING OF DENSE ROTATIONAL SPECTRA BASED ON SPECTRAL PROGRESSIONS , Nathan Love, Anna Huff, Kenneth R. Leopold

WL11 **10:40 – 10:41**
A MICROWAVE AND COMPUTATIONAL STUDY OF CARBOXYLIC ACID ANHYDRIDES, Nathan Love, Anna Huff, Kenneth R. Leopold

WL12 **10:44 – 10:45**
MICROWAVE AND COMPUTATIONAL STUDIES OF HYDRATED ACID ANHYDRIDES: CAPTURING A LOCAL POTENTIAL ENERGY MINIMUM AND EXPLORING THE EFFECT OF $C(CH_3)_3$ AND CF_3 SUBSTITUENTS, Nathan Love, Anna Huff, Kenneth R. Leopold

WL13 ***Post-Deadline Abstract*** **10:48 – 10:49**
CHEMO-DYNAMICAL MODELING OF CHA-MMS1 TO PREDICT NEW SOLID-PHASE SPECIES FOR DETECTION WITH JWST , Miwha Jin, Kaho Lam, Jeroen Terwisscha van Scheltinga, Robin T. Garrod, Zhi-Yun Li, Melissa K McClure, Adwin Boogert, Eric Herbst

WM. Radicals

Wednesday, June 23, 2021 – 10:0 AM
Room: 2021 Online Everywhere

Chair: Mitchio Okumura, California Institute of Technology, Pasadena, CA, USA

WM01 **10:00 – 10:01**
MEASUREMENT OF THE $\tilde{A}\leftarrow\tilde{X}$ BAND OF 1- AND 2-METHYLALLYL RADICALS USING CAVITY RINGDOWN SPECTROSCOPY, Charles R. Markus, Wen Chao, Gregory H Jones, Mitchio Okumura

WM02 **10:04 – 10:05**
HIGH-RESOLUTION INFRARED SPECTROSCOPY OF JET COOLED HCBr SINGLET BROMOCARBENE DIRADICAL, Ya-Chu Chan, Andrew Kortyna, David Nesbitt

WM03 **10:08 – 10:09**
INFRARED SPECTRUM OF THE 1-IODOPROPYL RADICAL PRODUCED FROM REACTION OF I + PROPENE IN SOLID PARA-HYDROGEN , Wei Lin, Huei-Ru Tsai, Yu-Hsuan Chen, Yuan-Pern Lee

WM04 **10:12 – 10:13**
INFRARED SPECTRA OF GASEOUS (Z)-3-IODO-BUT-2-EN-1-YL [$C_2H_3C(CH_3)I$] RADICAL, METHYL VINYL KETONE OXIDE [$C_2H_3C(CH_3)OO$] CRIEGEE INTERMEDIATE, AND $C_2H_3CI(CH_3)OO$ PEROXY RADICAL PRODUCED UPON PHOTODISSOCIATION OF (Z)-1,3-DIIODO-BUT-2-ENE [$(CH_2I)HC{=}C(CH_3)I$] IN OXYGEN , Yuan-Pern Lee, Chen-An Chung

WM05 **10:16 – 10:17**
PRODUCTION OF $HOCH_2CO$, HOCHCHO, AND HOCHCO IN THE REACTION H + GLYCOLALDEHYDE ($HOCH_2CHO$) IN SOLID p-H_2 AND ITS IMPLICATION IN ASTROCHEMISTRY , Prasad Ramesh Joshi, Yuan-Pern Lee

WM06 **10:20 – 10:21**
AB INITIO SPECTROSCOPIC PARAMETERS OF PYRIDYL RADICALS, Kelly S. Meyer, Sommer L. Johansen, J. H. Westerfield, Anahut Sandhu, Jasmine Keane, Kyle N. Crabtree

WM07 **10:24 – 10:25**
COUPLED CLUSTER CHARACTERIZATION OF 1-, 2-, AND 3-PYRROLYL FOR VIBRATIONAL AND ROTATIONAL SPECTROSCOPY, Sommer L. Johansen, Zhongxing Xu, J. H. Westerfield, Anna C. Wannenmacher, Kyle N. Crabtree

WM08 **10:28 – 10:29**
ELECTRONIC SPECTROSCOPY OF *CIS*- AND *TRANS-META*-VINYLBENZYL RADICALS , Sederra D. Ross, Jonathan Flores, Daniel M. Hewett, Neil J. Reilly

WM09 **10:32 – 10:33**
THE GROUND AND EXCITED STATES OF AROMATIC OXIDE RADICALS VIA ANION PHOTOELECTRON SPECTROSCOPY, Steven J. Kregel, Etienne Garand

WM10 **10:36 – 10:37**
VIBRATIONAL ANALYSIS OF DF SPECTRUM OF THE NO_3 $\tilde{B}\ {}^2E' - {}^2A_2'$ SYSTEM (II): COMBINED ANALYSIS WITH CRYO-SEVI PE SPECTRUM OF NO_3^- , Masaru Fukushima

WM11 **10:40 – 10:41**
GATEWAY STATES OF THE $1^2\Delta$ STATE OF CaH., Shota Yaguramaki, Jin Furuta, Kaori Kobayashi, Yoshiki Moriwaki, Stephen Cary Ross

WM12 **10:44 – 10:45**
ELECTRONIC STRUCTURE AND VIBRATIONAL SIGNATURES OF THE DELOCALIZED RADICAL IN HYDRATED CLUSTERS OF COPPER ("II") HYDROXIDE, CUOH+(H2O)0-2, Elizabeth G. Christensen, Kevin T Lutz, Ryan P Steele

WM13 **10:48 – 10:49**
CHIRPED-PULSE MILLIMETER-WAVE SPECTROSCOPY OF ASTROPHYSICAL RADICALS IN A PULSE JET DISCHARGE EXPERIMENT, Olivia Chitarra, Bérenger Gans, Olivier Pirali, Marie-Aline Martin-Drumel

WM14 ***Post-Deadline Abstract*** **10:52 – 10:53**
HIGH RESOLUTION ANION PHOTOELECTRON SPECTRA OF CRYOGENICALLY COOLED SILICON CARBIDES, Mark C Babin, Martin DeWitt, Marissa L. Weichman, Jessalyn A. DeVine, Daniel Neumark

RA. Rotational structure/frequencies

Thursday, June 24, 2021 – 8:0 AM

Room: 2021 Online Everywhere

Chair: G. S. Grubbs II, Missouri University of Science and Technology, Rolla, MO, USA

RA01 **8:00 – 8:01**
THE 130-360 GHZ ROTATIONAL SPECTRUM OF THE CHLORINE ISOTOPOLOGUES OF CHLOROBENZENE AND ITS EXCITED VIBRATIONAL STATES, P. Matisha Dorman, Brian J. Esselman, R. Claude Woods, Robert J. McMahon

RA02 **8:04 – 8:05**
MILLIMETER-WAVE SPECTROSCOPY OF THE EXCITED VIBRATIONAL STATES OF THIOPHENE (C_4H_4S) , Vanessa L. Orr, Brian J. Esselman, Yotaro Ichikawa, Kaori Kobayashi, R. Claude Woods, Robert J. McMahon

RA03 **8:08 – 8:09**
THE ROTATIONAL ANALYSES OF 2-CYANOPYRIMIDINE ($C_5H_3N_3$) AND 2-CYANOPYRAZINE ($C_5H_3N_3$): VIBRATIONAL GROUND STATES AND DYAD OF LOWEST-ENERGY VIBRATIONALLY EXCITED STATES, Houston H. Smith, Brian J. Esselman, R. Claude Woods, Robert J. McMahon

RA04 **8:12 – 8:13**
ANALYTICAL QUARTIC CENTRIFUGAL DISTORTION CONSTANTS BY FOURTH-ORDER RAYLEIGH SCHRÖDINGER PERTURBATION THEORY, Peter R. Franke, John F. Stanton

RA05 **8:16 – 8:17**
PHASE DETERMINATION IN MULTI-ANTENNA DETECTION CHIRPED-PULSE MICROWAVE SPECTROSCOPY, Christian Swanson, Nicole Moon, Amanda Duerden, Joshua E. Isert, G. S. Grubbs II

RA06 **8:20 – 8:21**
MICROWAVE STUDY COMPLEMENTED WITH COMPUTATIONAL DATA OF MONO-CHLOROBENZALDEHYDES, Maria Dohmen, Sean Arnold, Pablo Pinacho, Gordon G Brown, Melanie Schnell, Daniel A. Obenchain

RA07 **8:24 – 8:25**
CYCLOHEXANE VIBRATIONS: HIGH RESOLUTION SPECTRA AND ANHARMONIC LOCAL MODE CALCULATIONS, Peter F. Bernath, Edwin Sibert

RA08 **8:28 – 8:29**
SPECTROSCOPIC CHARACTERIZATION OF *E*- AND *Z*-PHENYLMETHANIMINE, Alessio Melli, Lorenzo Spada, Vincenzo Barone, Sven Herbers, Kevin G. Lengsfeld, Jens-Uwe Grabow, Mattia Melosso, Luca Dore, Cristina Puzzarini

RA09 **8:32 – 8:33**
THE MILLIMETER/SUBMILLIMETER SPECTRUM OF 2-CHLOROETHANOL, Hayley Bunn, Susanna L. Widicus Weaver

RA10 **8:36 – 8:37**
ROTATIONAL SPECTRUM OF 2-CYCLOPROPYLIDENEACETONITRILE - A NEW ISOMER OF PYRIDINE, Brian J. Esselman, Samuel M. Kougias, R. Claude Woods, Robert J. McMahon

RA11 ***Post-Deadline Abstract*** **8:40 – 8:41**
CHEMICAL DISTRIBUTION OF ACETALDEHYDE IN ORION KL , Miwha Jin, Anthony Remijan, Robin T. Garrod

RA12 **8:44 – 8:45**
THE MILLIMETER- AND SUBMILLIMETER-WAVE SPECTROSCOPY OF ISOPRENE., Daniel J Tyree, Ivan Medvedev

RA13 **8:48 – 8:49**
THE MILLIMETER/SUBMILLIMETER SPECTRUM OF DIACETYL, Jonathan Rebelsky, Chase P Schultz, Susanna L. Widicus Weaver

RA14 **8:52 – 8:53**
INVESTIGATION OF PURE ROTATIONAL SPECTROSCOPY OF ETHYNYLBENZONITRILE ISOMERS USING CHIRPED-PULSE W-BAND SPECTROSCOPY, Jean-Thibaut Spaniol, Kelvin Lee, Olivier Pirali, Marie-Aline Martin-Drumel

RB. Mini-symposium: Precision Spectroscopy for Fundamental Physics

Thursday, June 24, 2021 – 8:0 AM

Room: 2021 Online Everywhere

Chair: Andrew Jayich, University of California, Santa Barbara, , USA

RB01 *INVITED TALK* **8:00 – 8:02**
SPECTROSCOPY OF SHORT-LIVED RADIOACTIVE MOLECULES, Ronald Fernando Garcia Ruiz

RB02 **8:08 – 8:09**
THEORETICAL STUDY OF PROPERTIES OF RADIUM MONOFLUORIDE , Aleksandra A. Kyuberis, Anastasia Borschevsky, Lukáš Félix Pašteka

RB03 **8:12 – 8:13**
INFLUENCE OF VIBRATIONS ON THE SENSITIVITY OF RAOH AND YBOH MOLECULES TO THE P, T-VIOLATION, Anna Zakharova, Alexander Petrov

RB04 ***Post-Deadline Abstract*** **8:16 – 8:17**
CALCULATION OF THE CORRECTION ON THE MAGNETIZATION DISTRIBUTION IN THE NUCLEUS TO THE HYPERFINE STRUCTURE OF HEAVY ATOMS, Sergey Prosnyak, Leonid V. Skripnikov, Daniel E. Maison

RB05 **8:20 – 8:21**
SEARCH FOR PARITY VIOLATION USING ^{177,179}HFF^{+} CATIONS, Igor Kurchavov, Alexander Petrov

RB06 **8:24 – 8:25**
TANTALUM OXIDE SPECTROSCOPY TO FACILITATE EXPLORING NEW PHYSICS BEYOND THE STANDARD MODEL, Timothy Chung, Matthew Charles Cooper, Yan Zhou

RB07 **8:28 – 8:29**
TAO^{+} CATION FOR THE STUDY OF QUADRUPLE NEUTRON DISTRIBUTION IN NUCLEI, Gleb Olegovich Penyazkov, Leonid V. Skripnikov

RB08 **8:32 – 8:33**
ACCURATE PREDICTION OF CLOCK TRANSITIONS IN A HIGHLY CHARGED ION WITH COMPLEX ELECTRONIC STRUCTURE, Charles Cheung, Marianna Safronova, Sergey Porsev, Mikhail Kozlov, Ilya Tupitsyn, Andrey Bondarev

RB09 **8:36 – 8:37**
QUANTUM LOGIC CONTROL AND SPECTROSCOPY OF A SINGLE MOLECULAR ION, Alejandra Collopy, David Leibrandt, Dietrich Leibfried, Chin-wen Chou

RB10 **8:40 – 8:41**
SPECTROSCOPIC CHARACTERIZATION OF A THERMODYNAMICALLY STABLE DOUBLY CHARGED DIATOMIC MOLECULE: MgAr^{2+}, Dominik Wehrli, Matthieu Génévriez, Frédéric Merkt

RB11 **8:44 – 8:45**
HYBRID LINE LIST AND SPECTROSCOPIC MODEL FOR CN, Anna-Maree Syme, Laura K McKemmish

RB12 **8:48 – 8:49**
VIBRATIONAL BENDING MODES METROLOGY IN THE 670-720 cm^{-1}RANGE, Marco Lamperti, Riccardo Gotti, Davide Gatti, Mohammad Khaled Shakfa, Elisabetta Canè, Filippo Tamassia, Paolo Laporta, P. G. Schunemann, Aamir Farooq, Marco Marangoni

RB13 **8:52 – 8:53**
MULTISPECTRUM ROTATIONAL STATES DISTRIBUTION THERMOMETRY, Riccardo Gotti, Marco Lamperti, Davide Gatti, Szymon Wojtewicz, Thomas Puppe, Yuriy Mayzlin, Bidoor Alsaif, Julian Robinson-Tait, Felix Rohde, Rafal Wilk, Patrick Leisching, Wilhelm Kaenders, Paolo Laporta, Marco Marangoni

RC. Astronomy

Thursday, June 24, 2021 – 8:0 AM

Room: 2021 Online Everywhere

Chair: Mitsunori Araki, Tokyo University of Science, Shinjuku-ku, Tokyo, Japan

RC01 **8:00 – 8:01**
A STATUS REPORT ON THE COLOGNE DATABASE FOR MOLECULAR SPECTROSCOPY, CDMS, Holger S. P. Müller, P. Schilke, Stephan Schlemmer

RC03 **8:08 – 8:09**
ASTROCHEMICAL FORECASTING WITH MACHINE LEARNING, Kelvin Lee, Andrew M Burkhardt, Michael C McCarthy, Brett A. McGuire

RC04 **8:12 – 8:13**
LABORATORY ICE ASTROCHEMISTRY AT LARGE FACILITIES, SERGIO IOPPOLO

RC05 **8:16 – 8:17**
SPECTROMETER USING SUPERCONDUCTOR MIXER RECEIVER (SUMIRE) FOR MICROWAVE SPECTROSCOPY OF MOLECULES IN ASTRONOMICAL INTERESTS , Yoshimasa Watanabe, Akemi Tamanai, Nami Sakai

RC06 **8:20 – 8:21**
THE 2021 CENSUS OF INTERSTELLAR, CIRCUMSTELLAR, EXTRAGALACTIC, PROTOPLANETARY DISK, AND EXOPLANETARY MOLECULES: WHAT ARE THE PRESSING SPECTROSCOPIC NEEDS FROM THE LABORATORY?, Brett A. McGuire

RC07 **8:24 – 8:25**
A RIGOROUS K/KA-BAND HUNT FOR AROMATIC MOLECULES (ARKHAM): UBIQUITOUS AROMATIC CARBON CHEMISTRY AT THE EARLIEST STAGES OF STAR FORMATION, Andrew M Burkhardt, Ryan A Loomis, Christopher N Shingledecker, Kelvin Lee, Anthony Remijan, Michael C McCarthy, Brett A. McGuire

RC08 **8:28 – 8:29**
SPECTRAL STACKING AND MATCHED FILTERING AS A RIGOROUS DETECTION TECHNIQUE FOR INTERSTELLAR MOLECULES, Ryan A Loomis, Kelvin Lee, Ci Xue, Andrew M Burkhardt, Christopher N Shingledecker, Steven B Charnley, Martin Cordiner, Eric Herbst, Sergei Kalenskii, Brett A. McGuire, Michael C McCarthy, Anthony Remijan

RC09 **8:32 – 8:33**
LABORATORY SPECTROSCOPY FOR ASTROCHEMISTRY: A ROTATIONAL INVESTIGATION OF 3-AMINO-2-PROPENENITRILE, Davide Alberton, Valerio Lattanzi, Christian Endres, Paola Caselli, Luca Bizzocchi

RC10 **8:36 – 8:37**
HIGH-RESOLUTION, ROTATIONALLY-RESOLVED FTIR SPECTRUM OF THE 3300 cm^{-1} TRANSITION OF ASTROPHYSICALLY-RELEVANT HCN, Jessica Palko, Thomas Howard, Leah G Dodson

RC11 **8:40 – 8:41**
COMPREHENSIVE ROTATIONAL SPECTROSCOPY OF METHYL CYANOACETATE FOR ASTRONOMICAL SEARCHES, Gayatri Batra, Pablo Pinacho, Amanda Steber, Melanie Schnell

RC12 **8:44 – 8:45**
LINE LISTS FOR THE $b^1\Sigma^+ - X^3\Sigma^-$ AND $a^1\Delta - X^3\Sigma^-$ TRANSITIONS OF SO , Peter F. Bernath, Ryan Johnson, Jacques Liévin

RC13 **8:48 – 8:49**
HIGH-TEMPERATURE SPECTROSCOPIC DATA FOR EXO-PLANETARY STUDIES: THE e-PYTHEAS PROJECT, Vincent Boudon, Athena Coustenis, Alain Campargue, Robert Georges, Vladimir Tyuterev

RD. Non-covalent interactions
Thursday, June 24, 2021 – 8:0 AM
Room: 2021 Online Everywhere

Chair: Malgorzata Biczysko, Shanghai University, Shanghai, China

RD01 **8:00 – 8:01**
IMAGING THE NONREACTIVE COLLISIONAL QUENCHING DYNAMICS OF NO ($A^2\Sigma^+$) RADICALS WITH O_2 ($X^3\Sigma_g{}^-$), K. Jacob Blackshaw, Naa-Kwarley Quartey, David J. Hood, Christian D. Hettwer, Nathanael M. Kidwell

RD02 **8:04 – 8:05**
N_2O-AR AND N_2O-KR: SYMMETRY BREAKING OF INTRAMOLECULAR BENDING MODE OF N_2O IN THE PRESENCE OF A RARE GAS , Chris Gergess, M. Dehghany, A. J. Barclay, A.R.W. McKellar, Nasser Moazzen-Ahmadi

RD03 **8:08 – 8:09**
THE 4.2 MICRON SPECTRA OF CO_2-CO DIMER FOR BOTH THE C- AND O-BONDED ISOMERS, INCLUDING SPLITTING OF THE DEGENERATE ν_2 BEND IN THE PRESENCE OF CO, Praveen Wakwella, A. J. Barclay, Bob McKellar, Nasser Moazzen-Ahmadi

RD04 **8:12 – 8:13**
INFRARED SPECTROSCOPY OF TITANIUM CATION ACETYLENE COMPLEXES: CATION-π COMPLEXES VS REACTED STRUCTURES, Anna G Batchelor, Joshua H Marks, Michael A Duncan

RD05 **8:16 – 8:17**
SPECTROSCOPIC CHARACTERIZATION OF PSEUDOCARBYNES: INTERACTION BETWEEN –C≡C– CHAINS AND METAL CLUSTERS, Hyunsub Kim, Scott G Sayres

RD06 **8:20 – 8:21**
INFRARED SPECTRA OF THE METHYLAMINE DIMER AND METHYLAMINE-WATER COMPLEXES IN SOLID NEON BETWEEN 80 AND 5500 cm^{-1}, Pascale Soulard, Benoît Tremblay

RD07 **8:24 – 8:25**
WETTING TRIACETONE TRIPEROXIDE ALLOWS ITS DETECTION BY MICROWAVE SPECTROSCOPY, Susana Blanco, Alberto Macario, José García-Calvo, Andrea Revilla-Cuesta, Tomás Torroba , Juan Carlos Lopez

RD08 **8:28 – 8:29**
A BROADBAND MICROWAVE STUDY OF ISOLATED α-METHOXY PHENYLACETIC ACID: STRUCTURE, INTERNAL ROTATION, AND MICRO-SOLVATION, Himanshi Singh, Pablo Pinacho, Daniel A. Obenchain, María Mar Quesada-Moreno, Melanie Schnell

RD09 **8:32 – 8:33**
EXPLOITING F LONE PAIR$\cdots\pi_{AROMATIC}$-HOLE INTERACTION BETWEEN BENZALDEHYDE AND TETRAFLUOROMETHANE, Hao Wang, Junha Chen, Qian Gou

RD10 ***Post-Deadline Abstract*** **8:36 – 8:37**
STRUCTURE AND NON-COVALENT INTERACTIONS OF THE BENZOFURAN-FORMALDEHYDE COMPLEX EXPLORED BY MICROWAVE SPECTROSCOPY AND QUANTUM-CHEMICAL CALCULATIONS, Xiaolong Li, Silvia Alessandrini, Yang Zheng, Lorenzo Spada, Kevin G. Lengsfeld, Jens-Uwe Grabow, Cristina Puzzarini, Gang Feng, Vincenzo Barone

RD11 **8:40 – 8:41**
COLD ION SPECTROSCOPY OF B_{12} DERIVATIVES: STRETCHING THE LIMITS OF THEORETICAL INTERPRETATION, Alexandra Tsybizova, Larisa Miloglyadova, Peter Chen

RE. Atmospheric science

Thursday, June 24, 2021 – 8:0 AM

Room: 2021 Online Everywhere

Chair: Christopher J. Johnson, Stony Brook University, Stony Brook, NY, USA

RE01 **8:00 – 8:01**
WATER VAPOR NEAR-UV ABSORPTION: LABORATORY SPECTRUM, FIELD EVIDENCE, AND ATMOSPHERIC IMPACTS, Lei Zhu, Linsen Pei, Qilong Min, Yuyi Du, Zhe-Chen Wang, Bangsheng Yin, Kai Yang, Patrick Disterhoft, Thomas J Pongetti

RE02 **8:04 – 8:05**
TRENDS IN ATMOSPHERIC COMPOSITION FROM THE ATMOSPHERIC CHEMISTRY EXPERIMENT (ACE) SATELLITE, Peter F. Bernath, Chris Boone, Jeff Crouse

RE03 **8:08 – 8:09**
SULFUR DIOXIDE FROM THE ATMOSPHERIC CHEMISTRY EXPERIMENT (ACE) SATELLITE, William D Cameron, Peter F. Bernath, Chris Boone

RE04 **8:12 – 8:13**
ABSORPTION COEFFICIENT (ABSCO) TABLES FOR THE ORBITING CARBON OBSERVATORIES, Vivienne H Payne, Brian Drouin, Fabiano Oyafuso, Le Kuai, Brendan M Fisher, Keeyoon Sung, Deacon J Nemchick, Timothy J. Crawford, Mike Smyth, David Crisp, Erin M. Adkins, Joseph T. Hodges, David A. Long, Eli J Mlawer, Aronne Merrelli, Elizabeth M Lunny

RE05 **8:16 – 8:17**
THE MICROWAVE SPECTRUM OF 2-CHLOROETHYL RADICAL, CH_2ClCH_2, Michael J. Carrillo, Wei Lin, Yasuki Endo

RE06 **8:20 – 8:21**
DETAILED ANALYSIS OF THE INFRARED SPECTRUM OF SiF_4: AN UPDATE, Vincent Boudon, Laurent Manceron

RE07 **8:24 – 8:25**
MICROWAVE SPECTROSCOPY STUDY SUPPORTED BY QUANTUM CHEMISTRY CALCULATIONS OF LIMONA KETONE, A KEY OXIDATION PRODUCT OF LIMONENE, Noureddin OSSEIRAN, Annunziata Savoia, Pascal Dréan, Manuel Goubet, Therese R. Huet

RE08 **8:28 – 8:29**
REVEALING LONG-RANGE SUBSTITUENT EFFECTS IN THE LASER-INDUCED FLUORESCENCE AND DISPERSED FLUORESCENCE SPECTRA OF JET-COOLED $CH_XF_{3-X}CH_2O$ (X = 1, 2, 3) RADICALS, Benedek Koncz, Gabor Bazso, Md Asmaul Reza, Hamzeh Telfah, Kristof Hegedus, Jinjun Liu, Gyorgy Tarczay

RE09 **8:32 – 8:33**
SENSITIVE INFRARED SPECTROSCOPY OF ISOPRENE AT THE PART PER BILLION LEVEL, Jacob Stewart, Jacob Beloin, Melanie Jean Fournier, Grace Kovic

RE10 **8:36 – 8:37**
A COLLISIONAL TRANSFER MECHANISM FOR SULFUR MASS INDEPENDENT FRACTIONATION IN WEAKLY INTERACTING EXCITED ELECTRONIC STATES OF S_2, Alexander W Hull, Shuhei Ono, Robert W Field

RF. Spectroscopy as an analytical tool
Thursday, June 24, 2021 – 8:0 AM
Room: 2021 Online Everywhere

Chair: David A. Long, National Institute of Standards and Technology, Gaithersburg, MD, USA

RF01 *Post-Deadline Abstract* **8:00 – 8:01**
MICRO-PARTICLES IMMUNOASSAYS FOR EARLY DETECTION OF OVARIAN CANCER USING LASER INDUCED BREAKDOWN SPECTROSCOPY., Robinson Karunanithy, P Sivakumar, Torrey E. Holland

RF02 *Post-Deadline Abstract* **8:04 – 8:05**
LASER INDUCED BREAKDOWN SPECTROSCOPY FOR DETECTION OF HEAVY METALS IN CANCEROUS AND HEALTHY COLON TISSUES , Mohammed A Gondal

RF03 **8:08 – 8:09**
STUDY OF MOLECULAR BAND PRESENT IN THE LASER-INDUCED PLASMA OF CHOLESTEROL GALLSTONE, Zainab Gazali, PRADEEP KUMAR RAI, Surya Narayan Thakur, A. K. Rai

RF04 **8:12 – 8:13**
COMPOSITIONAL ANALYSIS OF GREEN TEA LEAVES USING LASER INDUCED BREAKDOWN SPECTROSCOPY (LIBS) , Tejmani Kumar, Abhishek Dwivedi, Zainab Gazali, Abhishek Rai, A. K. Rai

RF05 **8:16 – 8:17**
COMPOSITIONAL ANALYSIS OF AYURVEDIC MEDICINE USING LIBS ALONG WITH PAS TECHNIQUES, Reshu Kumari, Zainab Gazali, Abhishek Dwivedi, A. K. Rai

RF06 **8:20 – 8:21**
LOOKING FOR CACAO IN ALL THE WRONG PLACES: AN ANALYSIS OF MAYA POTTERY WITH 2-PHOTON RESONANCE SPECTROSCOPY, Ann Williams , Mattanjah DE VRIES

RF07 **8:24 – 8:25**
DEVELOPMENT OF A SUPERSONIC WIND TUNNEL FOR A CAVITY RINGDOWN SPECTROMETER, Elijah R Jans, Terry A. Miller, Igor V. Adamovich

RF08 **8:28 – 8:29**
OPTICALLY-SWITCHED DUAL-WAVELENGTH CAVITY RING-DOWN SPECTROMETER FOR HIGH-PRECISION ISOTOPIC RATIO MEASUREMENTS OF METHANE δD and ^{13}C IN THE NEAR-INFRARED, TzuLing Chen, Douglas Ober, ROBIN MIRI, THINH Bui, LINHAN SHEN, Mitchio Okumura

RF09 **8:32 – 8:33**
HIGH RESOLUTION INFRARED CAVITY ENHANCED ABSORPTION AT LOW TEMPERATURES , Carlos Manzanares, Suresh Sunuwar

RF10 **8:36 – 8:37**
SPECTROSCOPIC DETECTION OF METHANE AT A PPT SENSITIVITY LEVEL IN MID-IR WITH A LONG-PATH MULTIPASS CELL, Hans A Schuessler, Jinbao Xia, carlos Rodriguez, James R Bounds, Alexandre Kolomenskii

RF11 **8:40 – 8:41**
A PHOTONIC GAS SENSOR FOR THE MID-INFRARED, Travis A Gartner, Paul Barclay, Nasser Moazzen-Ahmadi

RF12 **8:44 – 8:45**
MEASURING ACCURATE STIMULATED RAMAN SCATTERING CROSS-SECTIONS OF LIQUIDS, Prasenjit Srivastava, Kristen H. Burns, Christopher G. Elles

RG. Plenary

Thursday, June 24, 2021 – 9:0 AM

Room: 2021 Online Everywhere

Chair: Martin Gruebele, University of Illinois at Urbana-Champaign, Urbana, IL, USA

RG02 **9:03 – 9:43**

INFLUENCE OF NATURALLY-OCCURRING AND SYNTHETIC MODIFICATIONS ON THE STRUCTURES AND GLYCOSIDIC BOND STABILITIES OF DNA AND RNA NUCLEOSIDES, M T Rodgers, Ranran Wu, Yanlong Zhu, Lucas Hamlow, Chenchen He, Zachary J Devereaux, Harrison Roy, Erik O Soley, Chase Leslie, Giel Berden, Jos Oomens

RH. Mini-symposium: Large Amplitude Motions

Thursday, June 24, 2021 – 10:0 AM

Room: 2021 Online Everywhere

Chair: Arnaud Cuisset, Université du Littoral Côte d'Opale, Dunkerque, France

RH01 **10:00 – 10:01**
MOLECULAR ROTATION IN FLOPPY MOLECULES: HE-H_3^+, Thomas Salomon, Oskar Asvany, Dieter Gerlich, Igor Savic, Ad van der Avoird, Michael E. Harding, Filippo Lipparini, Jürgen Gauss, Stephan Schlemmer

RH02 ***Post-Deadline Abstract*** **10:04 – 10:05**
SYMMETRIES of CH_5^+, Stefan Brackertz, Benjamin Nukic, Per Jensen, Stephan Schlemmer

RH03 **10:08 – 10:09**
$^{14}NH_3$ ROVIBRATIONAL IR ANALYSIS AT 6000 CM^{-1}, Xinchuan Huang, Keeyoon Sung, Timothy J. Lee, David Schwenke, Geoffrey C. Toon

RH04 **10:12 – 10:13**
THE BENDING-ROTATION APPROACH APPLIED TO THE METHYLENE RADICAL CH_2, L. H. Coudert

RH05 **10:16 – 10:17**
TUNNELING AND RING OPENING IN THE CYCLOPROPYL RADICAL AND CATION , Nadav Genossar, Bryan Changala, Marie-Aline Martin-Drumel, Bérenger Gans, J.-C. Loison, Joshua H Baraban

RH06 **10:20 – 10:21**
STATE-DISTRIBUTION CONTROL OF LARGE AMPLITUDE VIBRATION IN SUBSTITUTED BIPHENYLS WITH INTENSE LASER PULSES, Makoto Nikaido, Kenta Mizuse, Yasuhiro Ohshima

RH07 **10:24 – 10:25**
NUCLEAR DYNAMICS OF FLEXIBLE CYCLIC MOLECULES: CONFORMATIONAL SPACE, PSEUDOROTATIONAL AND ROTATIONAL MOTIONS OF DIOXOLANES, DITHIOLANES AND OXATHIOLANES, Lorenzo Paoloni, Sergio Rampino, Assimo Maris

RH08 **10:28 – 10:29**
ROTATIONAL AND VIBRATIONAL WAVE PACKET IMAGING SPECTROSCOPY: BROAD BANDWIDTH, HIGH-RESOLUTION SPECTRA AND DYNAMICS OF WEAKLY BOUND MOLECULAR DIMERS, Ar_2, $(N_2)_2$, AND $(CH_4)_2$, Kenta Mizuse, Hikaru Sato, Haruki Ishikawa, Yuhei Oyagi, Tomomi Murai, Genki Ishibashi, Yuya Tobata, Yasuhiro Ohshima

RH09 **10:32 – 10:33**
HIGH-RESOLUTION GAS PHASE THz SPECTROSCOPY OF THE CATECHOL LOW FREQUENCY MODES INVOLVING AN INTRAMOLECULAR HYDROGEN BOND , Jonas Bruckhuisen, Guillaume Dhont, Anthony Roucou, Atef Jabri, Hamdi Bayoudh, Thi Thanh Tran, Manuel Goubet, Marie-Aline Martin-Drumel, Arnaud Cuisset

RH10 **10:36 – 10:37**
HIGH RESOLUTION INFRARED SPECTROSCOPY OF OC-HOH TRAPPED IN SOLID PARAHYDROGEN: COHERENT TUNNELING IN A QUANTUM SOLID, Morgan E. Balabanoff, Aaron I. Strom, Kelly M. Olenyik, David T. Anderson

RH11 **10:40 – 10:41**
IN SEARCH OF VIBRATIONALLY EXCITED STATE MONODROMY IN NCNCS, Dennis W. Tokaryk, Stephen Cary Ross, Manfred Winnewisser, Brenda P. Winnewisser, Frank C. De Lucia, Brant E. Billinghurst

RI. Mini-symposium: Precision Spectroscopy for Fundamental Physics

Thursday, June 24, 2021 – 10:0 AM

Room: 2021 Online Everywhere

Chair: Alejandra Collopy, National Institute of Standards and Technology, Boulder, CO, USA

RI02 *Journal of Molecular Spectroscopy Review Lecture* **10:06 – 10:08**
SEARCHING FOR FUNDAMENTAL SYMMETRY VIOLATIONS WITH POLYATOMIC MOLECULES, Nicholas R Hutzler

RI03 **10:14 – 10:15**
USE OF MOLECULES TO SEARCH FOR NEW PHYSICS AND STUDY PROPERTIES OF THE NUCLEUS., Leonid V. Skripnikov

RI04 **10:18 – 10:19**
CALCULATION AND UNCERTAINTY EVALUATION OF THE P,T-ODD ENHANCEMENT FACTORS OF POLYATOMIC MOLECULES , Aleksandra A. Kyuberis, Anastasia Borschevsky, Lukáš Félix Pašteka

RI05 **10:22 – 10:23**
ANALYTIC RELATIVISTIC COUPLED-CLUSTER CALCULATIONS OF TIME-REVERSAL VIOLATING PARAMETERS, Chaoqun Zhang, Xuechen Zheng, Lan Cheng

RI06 **10:26 – 10:27**
ELECTRONIC STRUCTURE OF TRIATOMIC MOLECULES FOR SEARCH OF AXIONLIKE PARTICLES, Daniel E. Maison

RI07 **10:30 – 10:31**
A NEW EXPERIMENT TO TEST PARITY SYMMETRY IN COLD CHIRAL MOLECULES USING PRECISE MID-INFRARED SPECTROSCOPY, Mathieu Manceau, Louis Lecordier, Anne Cournol, Nicolas Cahuzac, Dang Bao An Tran, Rosa Santagata, Matthieu Pierens, Alexander Shelkovnikov, Andrei Goncharov, Olivier Lopez, Anne Amy-Klein, Sean Tokunaga, Benoit Darquie

RI08 **10:34 – 10:35**
SPECTROSCOPY ON ALUMINUM MONOCHLORIDE (ALCL) FOR LASER COOLING AND TRAPPING, John Daniel, Kayla Rodriguez, Taylor Lewis, Alexander Teplukhin, Chen Wang, Madhav Dhital, Brian K Kendrick, Christopher Bardeen, Shan-Wen Tsai, Boerge Hemmerling

RI09 **10:38 – 10:39**
OBSERVATION AND LASER SPECTROSCOPY OF YTTERBIUM MONOMETHOXIDE, $YbOCH_3$, Benjamin Augenbraun, Timothy Steimle, Zack Lasner, Alexander Frenett, Hiromitsu Sawaoka, Anh T. Le, John M. Doyle

RI10 **10:42 – 10:43**
SPECTROSCOPIC STUDIES OF ALUMINUM MONOFLUORIDE WITH RELEVANCE FOR LASER COOLING AND TRAPPING, Stefan Truppe, Silvio Marx, Sebastian Kray, Maximilian Doppelbauer, Simon Hofsäss, Christian Schewe, Nicole Walter, Jesús Pérez-Ríos, Boris Sartakov, Gerard Meijer

RI11 **10:46 – 10:47**
INVESTIGATION OF THE $b^3\Sigma^+, v = 0$ STATE IN ALUMINIUM MONOFLUORIDE, Maximilian Doppelbauer, Nicole Walter, Simon Hofsäss, Silvio Marx, Christian Schewe, Sebastian Kray, Jesús Pérez-Ríos, Boris Sartakov, Stefan Truppe, Gerard Meijer

RI12 **10:50 – 10:51**
SPECTROSCOPIC CHARACTERIZATION OF THE $\mathrm{A}^1\Pi, v = 6 \leftrightarrow \mathrm{b}^3\Sigma^+, v = 5$ INTERACTION OF ALUMINUM MONOFLUORIDE IN VIEW OF LASER COOLING AND TRAPPING EXPERIMENTS, Nicole Walter, Silvio Marx, Johannes Seifert, Boris Sartakov, Stefan Truppe, Gerard Meijer

RI13 **10:54 – 10:55**
FINE AND HYPERFINE INTERACTIONS IN ^{171}YbOH AND ^{173}YbOH, Nickolas H Pilgram, Arian Jadababaie, Yi Zeng, Nicholas R Hutzler, Timothy Steimle

RI14 **10:58 – 10:59**
$\mathcal{P}, \mathcal{T}$-ODD FARADAY EFFECT: A NEW APPROACH TO IMPROVE THE SENSITIVITY OF THE SEARCH FOR TIME-REFLECTION-NONINVARIANT INTERACTIONS IN NATURE, Dmitry Chubukov

RI15 **11:02 – 11:03**
ISOTOPE SHIFT IN OPTICAL SPECTRA OF MoO MOLECULE, Lei Zhang, Yao Yu, Jie Yang

RJ. Dynamics and kinetics

Thursday, June 24, 2021 – 10:0 AM

Room: 2021 Online Everywhere

Chair: Scott Kevin Cushing, Caltech, Pasadena, CA, USA

RJ01 **10:00 – 10:01**
ULTRAFAST EXCITED STATE DYNAMICS OF TWISTED AROMATICS, Mahesh Hariharan

RJ02 **10:04 – 10:05**
TRACKING THE REACTION COORDINATE OF ULTRAFAST SPIN-CROSSOVER IN Fe(II) COMPLEXES WITH FEMTOSECOND M-EDGE XANES, Ryan T Ash, Kaili Zhang, Josh Vura-Weis

RJ03 **10:08 – 10:09**
FEMTOSECOND PUMP-PROBE SPECTROSCOPY OF NEUTRAL Ni AND Cr OXIDE CLUSTERS , Jacob M Garcia, Scott G Sayres

RJ04 **10:12 – 10:13**
ELECTRONIC STATE-RESOLVED RELAXATION DYNAMICS IN METAL CLUSTERS STUDIED USING TWO-DIMENSIONAL ELECTRONIC SPECTROSCOPY, William R. Jeffries, Jordan Wallace, Kenneth L. Knappenberger, Jr.

RJ05 **10:16 – 10:17**
SIZE EFFECTS ON EXCITED STATE LIFETIMES OF TITANIUM OXIDE CLUSTERS, Lauren F Heald, Jacob M Garcia, Scott G Sayres

RJ06 **10:20 – 10:21**
ULTRAFAST REACTION DYNAMICS OF NEUTRAL ALUMINUM OXIDE CLUSTERS USING TWO COLOR FEMTOSECOND SPECTROSCOPY, Ananya Sen, Scott G Sayres

RJ07 **10:24 – 10:25**
PHOTOPHYSICS OF EXCITED STATES IN THE Co_4O_4 CUBANE CATALYST FOLLOWED VIA FEMTOSECOND $M_{2,3}$-EDGE ABSORPTION SPECTROSCOPY, Yusef A. Shari'ati, Josh Vura-Weis

RJ08 **10:28 – 10:29**
OPTICALLY PUMPED RESTSTRAHLEN BAND TUNING OF WIDE BANDGAP SEMICONDUCTORS, Elizabeth S Ryland, Vanessa M Breslin, Daniel C Ratchford, Jeff Owrutsky, Adam Dunkelberger

RJ09 **10:32 – 10:33**
MEASUREMENT AND EXCITED STATE PREDICTION OF PHOTOEXCITED ELECTRON AND HOLE DYNAMICS IN ZnTe WITH TRANSIENT ULTRAVIOLET REFLECTION SPECTROSCOPY, Hanzhe Liu, Jonathan M Michelsen, Isabel M Klein, Scott Kevin Cushing

RJ10 **10:36 – 10:37**
ULTRAFAST CARRIER SPECIFIC DYNAMICS AND BAND GAP RENORMALIZATION IN $CH_3NH_3PbBr_3$ UNDERSTOOD BY FEMTOSECOND TABLETOP EXTREME ULTRAVIOLET SPECTROSCOPY, Aastha Sharma, Josh Leveillee, Max A Verkamp, André Schleife, Josh Vura-Weis

RJ11 **10:40 – 10:41**
MONITORING PHOTOINDUCED AND PHOTOCATALYTIC SURFACE REACTIONS WITH TIME, MASS, AND ENERGY RESOLUTION, Mihai E Vaida

RJ12 **10:44 – 10:45**
X-RAY TRANSIENT ABSORPTION REVEALS THE ^1A_u ($n\pi^*$) STATE OF PYRAZINE IN ELECTRONIC RELAXATION, Valeriu Scutelnic, Shota Tsuru, Mátyás Pápai, Zheyue Yang, Michael Epshtein, Tian Xue, Eric Haugen, Yuki Kobayashi, Anna Krylov, Klaus Møller, Sonia Coriani, Stephen R. Leone

RJ13 **10:48 – 10:49**
CHARACTERIZATION OF THE $N_{6,7}$-EDGE AND $O_{2,3}$-EDGE OF Pt AND Ir COMPLEXES BY EXTREME ULTRAVIOLET SPECTROSCOPY, Clare Leahy, Josh Vura-Weis

RK. Structure determination

Thursday, June 24, 2021 – 10:0 AM

Room: 2021 Online Everywhere

Chair: Ha Vinh Lam Nguyen, Université Paris-Est Créteil, Créteil, France

RK01 **10:00 – 10:01**
MICROWAVE SPECTRA AND MOLECULAR STRUCTURES OF THE GAS-PHASE HOMOCHIRAL HOMODIMERS OF 3,3-DIFLUORO-1,2-EPOXYPROPANE AND 3-FLUORO-1,2-EPOXYPROPANE, Mark D. Marshall, Helen O. Leung

RK02 **10:04 – 10:05**
THE MICROWAVE SPECTRUM AND MOLECULAR STRUCTURE OF *TRANS*-2-FLUORO-3-(TRIFLUOROMETHYL)OXIRANE AND ITS COMPLEX WITH THE ARGON ATOM, Jordan M. Aucoin, Helen O. Leung, Mark D. Marshall

RK03 **10:08 – 10:09**
STRUCTURE AND INTERNAL MOTIONS OF THE PROPARGYL ALCOHOL-WATER COMPLEX, Sharon Priya Gnanasekar, Elangannan Arunan

RK04 **10:12 – 10:13**
ROTATIONAL SPECTRUM OF 2-AMINOACETOPHENONE AND ITS 1:1 WATER COMPLEX, Giovanna Salvitti, Assimo Maris, Susana Blanco, Juan Carlos Lopez

RK05 **10:16 – 10:17**
CHARACTERIZING HYDROGEN-BONDED SYSTEMS BY COLD-ION INFRARED ACTION SPECTROSCOPY: THE FORMIC ACID TRIMER CASE, Martín Taccone, Daniel A Thomas, Katja Ober, Gert von Helden, Gerard Meijer

RK06 **10:20 – 10:21**
IRMPD SPECTROSCOPY OF $CO_3^-(H_2O)_{1,2}$ AND $CO_4^-(H_2O)_{1,2}$, Maximilian G Münst, Milan Oncak, Martin K Beyer, Christian van der Linde

RK07 **10:24 – 10:25**
ROTATIONAL SPECTROSCOPY OF IMINE-BASED MOLECULAR SWITCHES: ISOLATED AND MICRO-SOLVATED, Nuno Campos, Pablo Pinacho, Corina H. Pollok, Christian Merten, Manuela Ramos Silva, Melanie Schnell, Sergio R. Domingos

RK08 **10:28 – 10:29**
INTRAMOLECULAR INTERACTIONS WITHIN 1- AND 2-NAPHTHOL: A ROTATIONAL SPECTROSCOPIC AND THEORETICAL STUDY, Arsh Singh Hazrah, Sadisha Nanayakkara, Nathan A. Seifert, Elfi Kraka, Wolfgang Jäger

RK09 **10:32 – 10:33**
MULTI-AGENT CONSENSUS EQUILIBRIUM (MACE) IN MOLECULAR AND ELECTRONIC STRUCTURE DETERMINATION, Jiayue Rong

RK10 **10:36 – 10:37**
THE SHAPES OF SULFONAMIDES: ROTATIONAL SPECTRA OF BENZENESULFONAMIDE, *ortho*-TOLUENSULFONAMIDE, *para*-TOLUENSULFONAMIDE AND SULFANILAMIDE, Sonia Melandri, Annalisa Vigorito, Assimo Maris, Camilla Calabrese, M. Eugenia Sanz, Donatella Loru, Isabel Peña

RK11 **10:40 – 10:41**
NEW INVESTIGATION OF THE ROTATIONAL SPECTRUM OF SABINENE, Mhamad Chrayteh, Therese R. Huet, Pascal Dréan

RK12 **10:44 – 10:45**
THE SHAPE OF LEVODOPA: A LASER ABALATION ROTATIONAL STUDY, Miguel Sanz Novo, Elena R. Alonso, Iker León, José L. Alonso

RK14 **10:52 – 10:53**
CONFORMERS OF VANILLIC ACID: A ROTATIONAL SPECTROSCOPIC AND THEORETICAL STUDY, Mohamad Al-Jabiri, Wolfgang Jäger

RK15 **10:56 – 10:57**
PROGRESS MADE TOWARDS CONTEXT-FREE MOLECULAR STRUCTURE DETERMINATION FROM ISOTOPOLOGUE ROTATIONAL SPECTROSCOPY, Lia Yeh, Dylan Finestone, Lincoln Satterthwaite, Jieyu Yan, David Patterson

RL. Electronic structure, potential energy surfaces

Thursday, June 24, 2021 – 10:0 AM

Room: 2021 Online Everywhere

Chair: Mallory Green, Fritz Haber Institute of the Max Planck Society, Berlin, Germany

RL01 **10:00 – 10:01**
LASER-INDUCED FLUORESCENCE (LIF) OF JET-COOLED SmO, Joel R Schmitz, Arianna Rodriguez, Michael Heaven

RL02 **10:04 – 10:05**
LASER-INDUCED FLUORESCENCE (LIF) OF JET-COOLED NdO AND NdO^+ , Joel R Schmitz, Arianna Rodriguez, Michael Heaven

RL03 ***Post-Deadline Abstract*** **10:08 – 10:09**
ELECTRONIC STRUCTURE OF THE GROUND AND EXCITED STATES OF RhO^{2+}: ITS ROLE IN THE C-H BOND ACTIVATION OF METHANE, Shahriar N Khan, Evangelos Miliordos

RL04 **10:12 – 10:13**
ELECTRONIC STRUCTURE ANALYSIS OF GROUND AND EXCITED STATES OF $MO^{2+/+/0/-}$ (M = Mo, Ru) AND THEIR WATER ACTIVATION STRENGTHS, Isuru R. Ariyarathna, Evangelos Miliordos

RL05 **10:16 – 10:17**
ADIABATIC MOLECULAR ORBITAL TRACKING IN AB INITIO MOLECULAR DYNAMICS, Asylbek A Zhanserkeev, Ryan P Steele

RL06 **10:20 – 10:21**
PROBING THE WAVELENGTH-DEPENDENT EXCITED-STATE DYNAMICS OF A PHOTOCHROMIC MOLECULAR SWITCH USING RESONANCE RAMAN SPECTROSCOPY, Kristen H. Burns, Christopher G. Elles

RL07 **10:24 – 10:25**
THE EFFECT OF THE SADDLE POINT POSITION AND THE OH-BONDING FORCE CONSTANT ON THE TRANSITION FREQUENCIES OF H-BOND OF NAPHTHAZARIN, Fatemeh Afshar Ghahremani, Mansoureh Zahedi-Tabrizi, Sayyed Faramarz Tayyari

RL08 **10:28 – 10:29**
VALENCE-HOLE ELECTRON CONFIGURATIONS: A NEW GLOBAL ELECTRONIC STRUCTURE PARADIGM FOR C_2 AND BEYOND , Jun Jiang, Timothy Schmidt, Klaas Nauta, Robert W Field

RL09 **10:32 – 10:33**
EXAMINING HYPERMETALLIC OXIDE MgOMg WITH LASER INDUCED FLUORESCENCE AND PHOTOIONIZATION SPECTROSCOPY , Thomas D. Persinger, Michael Heaven

RL10 **10:36 – 10:37**
STUDY OF LiMg AND $LiMg^+$ USING LASER INDUCED FLUORESCENCE AND TWO-PHOTON IONIZATION, Thomas D. Persinger, Jiande Han, Michael Heaven

RL11 **10:40 – 10:41**
INTERPRETING THE ELECTRONIC STRUCTURE OF SUPERATOMIC $AU_8(PPH_3)_7^{2+}$, Jonathan Wood Fagan, Christopher J. Johnson

RL12 **10:44 – 10:45**
SPECTROSCOPIC STUDIES OF SMALL POLYATOMIC MOLECULES NEAR ION-PAIR DISSOCIATION THRESHOLDS, Carla Kreis, Urs Hollenstein, Frédéric Merkt

RL14 **10:52 – 10:53**
DETAILED VIEW INTO THE Au_2^+ POTENTIAL ENERGY SURFACES, Marko Förstel, Kai Pollow, Taarna Studemund, Robert G. Radloff, Roland Mitric, Otto Dopfer

RM. Action spectroscopy (incl. PE, PD, PI, LIR)

Thursday, June 24, 2021 – 10:0 AM

Room: 2021 Online Everywhere

Chair: Michael D. Morse, University of Utah, Salt Lake City, UT, USA

RM01 **10:00 – 10:01**
OBSERVATION OF A DIPOLE-BOUND STATE IN THRESHOLD PHOTODETACHMENT SPECTROSCOPY OF THE INTERSTELLAR ANION C_3N^-, Malcolm James Simpson, Markus Nötzold, Tim Michaelsen, Robert Wild, Franco A. Gianturco, Roland Wester

RM02 *Post-Deadline Abstract* **10:04 – 10:05**
A GENERAL PATH TO INFRARED SPECTROSCOPY OF SINGLE MOLECULAR IONS , David Patterson

RM03 **10:08 – 10:09**
THE ZEEMAN EFFECT IN CO^+ OBSERVED WITH ROTATIONAL ACTION SPECTROSCOPY, Aravindh Nivas Marimuthu, Kim Steenbakkers, Britta Redlich, Sandra Brünken

RM04 **10:12 – 10:13**
STRUCTURE AND OPTICAL PROPERTIES OF THE $Si_4C_2^+$ CATION, Robert G. Radloff, Marko Förstel, Kai Pollow, Taarna Studemund, Otto Dopfer

RM05 **10:16 – 10:17**
PHOTODEPLETION SPECTROSCOPY OF IO^- WITHIN THE ACTINIC RANGE, Benjamin McKinnon, Samuel Marlton, Boris Ucur, Berwyck Poad, Stephen J. Blanksby, Evan Bieske, Adam J. Trevitt

RM06 **10:20 – 10:21**
HIGH-RESOLUTION PHOTODISSOCIATION SPECTROSCOPY OF N_2O^+, Anthony Roucou, Xavier Urbain, Clément Lauzin

RM07 **10:24 – 10:25**
ROVIBRATIONAL SPECTROSCOPY OF THE CH^+-He AND CH^+-He_4 COMPLEXES, Thomas Salomon, José Luis Doménech, Philipp C Schmid, Ernest A Michael, Stephan Schlemmer, Oskar Asvany

RM08 **10:28 – 10:29**
INFRARED SPECTROSCOPY OF THE $Co^+(H_2O)$ COMPLEX WITH He, Ne, AND Ar TAGGING., Joshua H Marks, Evangelos Miliordos, Michael A Duncan

RM09 **10:32 – 10:33**
AN ION MOBILITY MASS SPECTROMETRY CRYOGENIC ION TRAP INSTRUMENT COUPLED TO THE FRITZ HABER INSTITUTE INFRARED FREE ELECTRON LASER, Maike Lettow, Eike Mucha, Jan Horlebein, Gerard Meijer, Gert von Helden

RM10 **10:36 – 10:37**
CIVP SPECTROSCOPY OF PYRIDINIUM IONS: SURPRISING PERTURBATION BY TAG MOLECULES, Alexandra Tsybizova, Eno Paenurk, Vladimir Gorbachev, Peter Chen

RM11 **10:40 – 10:41**
OPTICAL SPECTRUM OF THE ADAMANTANE RADICAL CATION, Parker B. Crandall, David Müller, Marko Förstel, Otto Dopfer

RM12 **10:44 – 10:45**
DETERMINATION OF SPECTROSCOPICALLY-STRUCTURAL CONNECTION IN THE PYRIDINIUM SERIES TO PROBE LONDON DISPERSION FORCES, Vladimir Gorbachev, Alexandra Tsybizova, Larisa Miloglyadova, Peter Chen

RM13 **10:48 – 10:49**
TEMPERATURE DEPENDENCE IN RELATIVE POPULATIONS BETWEEN ISOMERS HAVING DISTINCT HYDROGEN BOND STRUCTURES OF PHENOL-METHANOL CLUSTER CATIONS, Masataka Orito, Masayoshi Ozeki, Haruki Ishikawa

RM14 **10:52 – 10:53**
DIRECT OBSERVATION OF IR INDUCED ISOMERIZATIONS OF HYDROGEN-BONDED PHENOL CLUSTER CATIONS, Masayoshi Ozeki, Masataka Orito, Kenta Mizuse, Haruki Ishikawa

RM15 *Post-Deadline Abstract* **10:56 – 10:57**
HIGH RESOLUTION ANION PHOTOELECTRON SPECTRA OF NDO^-, Mark C Babin, Martin DeWitt, Jessalyn A. DeVine, David C McDonald II, Nicholas S. Shuman, Albert Viggiano, Lan Cheng, Daniel Neumark

FA. Mini-symposium: Spectroscopy with Undergraduates

Friday, June 25, 2021 – 8:0 AM

Room: 2021 Online Everywhere

Chair: AnGayle (AJ) Vasiliou, Middlebury College , Middlebury , VT, USA

FA01 *INVITED TALK* **8:00 – 8:02**
RESEARCH WITH UNDERGRADUATES: SPECTROSCOPY IS JUST THE BEGINNING, Laura R. McCunn

FA02 **8:08 – 8:09**
OBSERVATION OF THE C_6H_7 RADICAL IN AN ARGON MATRIX USING MATRIX ISOLATION INFRARED SPECTROSCOPY, Jay C. Amicangelo, Lia Totleben, Jacob Oslosky, Yen Jui Su, Nicole Orwat

FA03 **8:12 – 8:13**
HELIUM NANODROPLETS AND LIQUID HOT NAGMA: WHAT STUDENTS CAN LEARN ABOUT THERMODYNAMICS FROM INFRARED SPECTROSCOPY AND A MODEL DIPEPTIDE, Alaina R. Gunn

FA04 **8:16 – 8:17**
WEAK HYDROGEN BONDING IN COMPLEXES OF SELENOPHENE AND WATER: A MATRIX ISOLATION FTIR AND COMPUTATIONAL STUDY, Josh Newby, Tiara Sivells

FA05 **8:20 – 8:21**
HELIUM NANODROPLET ISOLATION SPECTROSCOPY IN AN UNDERGRADUATE TEACHING LABORATORY, Paul Raston

FA06 **8:24 – 8:25**
COMPOSITIONAL ANALYSIS OF TITAN'S ATMOSPHERE USING SPITZER INFRARED SPECTROGRAPH DATA, Brandon Park Coy, Conor A Nixon, Naomi Rowe-Gurney

FA07 **8:28 – 8:29**
A BROADBAND ROTATIONAL SPECTROSCOPIC STUDY OF DIETHYL PHTHALATE, Raiden Speelman, Arsh Singh Hazrah, Nathan A. Seifert, Wolfgang Jäger

FA08 **8:32 – 8:33**
FABRICATION AND CHARACTERIZATION OF HIGHLY EFFICIENT DYE-SENSITIZED SOLAR CELL WITH COMPOSITED DYES, Garris H.C. Radloff, Feven M Naba, Dorothy B Ocran-Sarsah, Makenzie E Bennett, Kathryn M Sterzinger, Abigail T Armstrong, Nahom Zewde, Cameron Gray, Mahesh B. Dawadi

FA09 **8:36 – 8:37**
EFFICIENT COMPRESSION OF MOLECULAR LINE LISTS: APPLICATION OF 'SUPER-ENERGIES' TO THE EXOMOL DATABASE, Xudong Ke Lin, Samuel Wright, Alec Owens, Jonathan Tennyson, Sergei N. Yurchenko

FA10 **8:40 – 8:41**
INVOLVING HIGH-SCHOOL STUDENTS IN COMPUTATIONAL CHEMISTRY MOLECULAR DATA GENERATION FOR EXOPLANET SPECTROSCOPY, Laura K McKemmish, Anna-Maree Syme, Clara Sousa-Silva

FA11 **8:44 – 8:45**
EPR SPECTROSCOPY OF RUBY IN THE UNDERGRADUATE PHYSICAL CHEMISTRY TEACHING LABORATORY, Bryan Lynch

FA12 **8:48 – 8:49**
GUIDED-INQUIRY SPECTROSCOPIC PROJECTS IN THE PHYSICAL CHEMISTRY LAB, Steven Shipman

FA13 **8:52 – 8:53**
BUILDING A RESEARCH PROGRAM AT A PRIMARILY UNDERGRADUATE INSTITUTION, Jacob Stewart

FB. Clusters/Complexes

Friday, June 25, 2021 – 8:0 AM

Room: 2021 Online Everywhere

Chair: Daniel A. Obenchain, Georg-August-Universität Göttingen, Göttingen, Germany

FB01 **8:00 – 8:01**
HOW SOLVENTS CHANGE THE CONFORMATIONAL LANDSCAPE IN MOLECULES WITH WEAK INTRAMOLECULAR INTERACTIONS: METHYL 2-METHOXYBENZOATE, Alberto Macario, Juan Carlos Lopez, Susana Blanco

FB02 **8:04 – 8:05**
PROBING AZULENE-WATER INTERACTIONS AND AZULENE AGGREGATION BY BROADBAND ROTATIONAL SPECTROSCOPY, Shefali Saxena, Ecaterina Burevschi, Yang Zheng, Qian Gou, M. Eugenia Sanz

FB03 **8:08 – 8:09**
UNRAVELLING THE MICROSOLVATION FRAMEWORK AROUND PROTOTYPE POLYCYCLIC AROMATIC HYDROCARBON, NAPHTHALENE, BY HIGH-RESOLUTION INFRARED SPECTROSCOPY, Kuntal Chatterjee, Tarun Kumar Roy, Jai Khatri, Martina Havenith

FB04 **8:12 – 8:13**
MICROWAVE SPECTROSCOPY OF THE 2-METHYLAMINOETHANOL-WATER COMPLEX, DYLAN S VALENTE, Dinesh Marasinghe, Michael Tubergen

FB05 **8:16 – 8:17**
MICROWAVE SPECTRUM AND LARGE AMPLITUDE MOTION OF METHANESULFONIC ACID , Anna Huff, Nathan Love, Kenneth R. Leopold

FB06 **8:20 – 8:21**
MICROWAVE SPECTRUM OF THE METHANESULFONIC ACID – WATER COMPLEX, Anna Huff, Nathan Love, Kenneth R. Leopold

FB07 **8:24 – 8:25**
ATTENUATED STABILITY OF DEUTERIUM-BOUND COMPLEXES AT ROOM TEMPERATURE, Alexander Kjærsgaard, Emil Vogt, Henrik G. Kjaergaard

FB08 **8:28 – 8:29**
ROTATIONAL SPECTRA OF THE CH_3CN-CO_2 COMPLEX: OBSERVING A CARBON 'TETREL BOND', Sharon Priya Gnanasekar, Elangannan Arunan

FB09 **8:32 – 8:33**
BOUND STATE CALCULATIONS OF THE VAN DER WAALS NH_3−Ne COMPLEX AND FIRST MICROWAVE DETECTION OF THE MISSING $(para)$-NH_3−Ne NUCLEAR SPIN ISOMER, Leonid Surin, Ivan Tarabukin, Cristobal Perez, Melanie Schnell, Jerome Loreau, Ad van der Avoird

FB10 **8:36 – 8:37**
ETHANOL TRIMER CONFIGURATIONS REVEALED BY CP-FTMW SPECTROSCOPY AND COMPUTATIONAL CALCULATIONS, S. Indira Murugachandran, Isabel Peña, Al Mokhtar Lamsabhi, Manuel Yáñez, M. Eugenia Sanz

FB11 **8:40 – 8:41**
CONFORMATIONAL LANDSCAPES OF 2-FUROIC ACID MONOMERS AND DIMERS BY ROTATIONAL SPECTROSCOPY AND DFT CALCULATIONS, Qian Yang, FAN XIE, Wolfgang Jäger, Yunjie Xu

FB12 **8:44 – 8:45**
ROOM TEMPERATURE GAS-PHASE GIBBS ENERGIES OF WATER AMINE COMPLEXES, Emil Vogt, Alexander Kjærsgaard, Henrik G. Kjaergaard

FB13 **8:48 – 8:49**
MICROSOLVATION OF CARBENES IN SUPERFLUID HELIUM NANODROPLETS, Jai Khatri, Tarun Kumar Roy, Stefan Henkel, Kuntal Chatterjee, Gerhard Schwaab, Martina Havenith

FC. Astronomy

Friday, June 25, 2021 – 8:0 AM

Room: 2021 Online Everywhere

Chair: SERGIO IOPPOLO, Queen Mary University of London (QMUL), London, United Kingdom

FC01 **8:00 – 8:01**
SUBLIMATION OF LABORATORY ICES MILLIMETER/SUBMILLIMETER EXPERIMENT (SubLIME): IDENTIFICATION AND QUANTIFICATION OF ORGANIC SPECIES FROM A UV PHOTOLYZED METHANOL ICE, Katarina Yocum, Stefanie N Milam, Perry A. Gerakines, Susanna L. Widicus Weaver

FC02 **8:04 – 8:05**
REVEALING THE CHEMISTRY OF POLYCYCLIC AROMATIC HYDROCARBONS BY PLASMA SOURCES, Donatella Loru, Daniel Rap, Sébastien Gruet, Amanda Steber, Melanie Schnell

FC03 **8:08 – 8:09**
IR ABSORPTION AND CALCULATED FREQUENCIES OF FORMALDEHYDE DISSOLVED IN LIQUID Kr, Suresh Sunuwar, Carlos Manzanares

FC04 **8:12 – 8:13**
FORMATION OF PYRUVIC ACID AND 1,2-ETHENEDIOL IN INTERSTELLAR ANALOG ICES, N. Fabian Kleimeier, André K. Eckhardt, Peter R. Schreiner, Ralf Ingo Kaiser

FC05 **8:16 – 8:17**
SPECTROSCOPIC STUDIES OF METHYL FORMATE AND ITS FORMATION PATHWAYS IN SPACE UPON ION IRRADIATION, Alejandra Traspas Muiña , SERGIO IOPPOLO, Peter Herczku, Zoltan Juhász, Sándor T. S. Kovács, Duncan Mifsud, Zuzana Kaňuchová, Nigel Mason, Robert w McCullough, Béla Sulik

FC06 **8:20 – 8:21**
DISCOVERING NOVEL GAS-PHASE NITROGEN-HETEROCYCLE FORMATION PATHWAYS WITH AN AB INITIO NANOREACTOR, Sommer L. Johansen, Lisa Oh, Lee-Ping Wang, Kyle N. Crabtree

FC07 **8:24 – 8:25**
MEASURING THE DIFFERENCE IN COLLISIONAL INTERACTION OF HCN/HNC WITH He AT LOW TEMPERATURES USING THE CPUF TECHNIQUE, Brian M Hays, Theo Guillaume, Divita Gupta, Franck Thibault, François Lique, Ian R. Sims

FC08 **8:28 – 8:29**
LOW-TEMPERATURE KINETICS MEASUREMENTS OF THE GAS-PHASE REACTIONS BETWEEN AROMATIC SPECIES AND THE CN RADICAL , Divita Gupta, Ilsa Rose Cooke, Joseph P. Messinger, Mitchio Okumura, Ian R. Sims

FC09 **8:32 – 8:33**
REACTION RATE MODELING TO OPTIMIZE $O(^1D)$ INSERTION INTO METHYLAMINE FOR THE DETECTION OF AMINOMETHANOL , Hayley Bunn, Chase P Schultz, Christopher M Jernigan, Susanna L. Widicus Weaver

FC10 **8:36 – 8:37**
TESTING DUST-SURFACE FORMATION MODEL OF PREBIOTIC MOLECULE CH_3NCO IN STAR-FORMING CORE SAGITTARIUS B2(N1) BY ALMA, Kyoichi Izuoka, Mitsunori Araki, Yuki Ohno, Takahiro Oyama, Shuro Takano, Nobuhiko Kuze, Koichi Tsukiyama

FC11 **8:40 – 8:41**
REEVALUATION OF THE C_4H ABUNDANCE BASED ON THE REVISED DIPOLE MOMENT, Takahiro Oyama, Yoshihiro Sumiyoshi, Mitsunori Araki, Shuro Takano, Nobuhiko Kuze, Koichi Tsukiyama

FC12 **8:44 – 8:45**
ANALYSIS OF THE CH_2OH RADICAL SPECTRUM WITH AN IAM TUNNELING APPROACH, L. H. Coudert, Olivia Chitarra, Jean-Thibaut Spaniol, Marie-Aline Martin-Drumel, Olivier Pirali, J.-C. Loison

FC13 **8:48 – 8:49**
HIGH-LEVEL ROVIBRATIONAL CALCULATIONS ON KETENIMINE, Martin Tschöpe, Benjamin Schröder, Sebastian Erfort, Guntram Rauhut

FD. Small molecules

Friday, June 25, 2021 – 8:0 AM

Room: 2021 Online Everywhere

Chair: Qian Gou, Chongqing University, Chongqing , China

FD01 **8:00 – 8:01**
IN SEARCH OF PHOSPHORUS IN ASTRONOMICAL ENVIRONMENTS: THE REACTION BETWEEN THE CP RADICAL ($X^2\Sigma^+$) AND METHANIMINE, Silvia Alessandrini, Francesca Tonolo, Cristina Puzzarini

FD02 **8:04 – 8:05**
THE STRUCTURE OF ScC_2 ($\tilde{X}^2A_1$): A COMBINED FOURIER TRANSFORM MICROWAVE/MILLIMETER-WAVE SPECTROSCOPY AND COMPUTATIONAL STUDY, Mark Burton, Qianyi Cheng, DeWayne T Halfen, J. Hayden Lane, Nathan DeYonker, Lucy M. Ziurys

FD03 **8:08 – 8:09**
THE MILLIMETER WAVE SPECTRUM OF RARE IRON MONOXIDE ISOTOPOLOGUES: A MASS INDEPENDENT ANALYSIS, Björn Waßmuth, Alexander A. Breier, Guido W Fuchs, Thomas Giesen

FD04 **8:12 – 8:13**
HYPERFINE STRUCTURE OF NITROSYL IODIDE (INO), Akiko Nishitsunoi, Hiroyuki Ozeki, Kaori Kobayashi, Stephane Bailleux

FD06 **8:20 – 8:21**
HIGH-RESOLUTION ANALYSIS OF THE 83.3 μm TORSIONAL BANDS OF THE $ClONO_2$ MOLECULE, F. Kwabia Tchana, Anusanth Anantharajah, Jean-Marie Flaud, Laurent Manceron, Johannes Orphal

FD07 **8:24 – 8:25**
HIGH-RESOLUTION FAR INFRARED SPECTROSCOPY AND ANALYSES OF TRIOXANE, Cyril Richard, Vincent Boudon, Olivier Pirali, Pierre Asselin

FD08 **8:28 – 8:29**
HIGH RESOLUTION INFRARED SPECTRA OF THE LINEAR DIALUMINUM MONOXIDE Al-O-Al, Daniel Witsch, Eileen Döring, Jürgen Gauss, Thomas Giesen, Guido W Fuchs

FD09 **8:32 – 8:33**
SUB-DOPPLER DOUBLE-RESONANCE SPECTROSCOPY OF METHANE USING A FREQUENCY COMB PROBE, Vinicius Silva de Oliveira, Isak Silander, Alexandra C Johanssson, Ove Axner, Aleksandra Foltynowicz, Lucile Rutkowski, Grzegorz Soboń, Kevin Lehmann

FD10 **8:36 – 8:37**
NEW LINE POSITIONS ANALYSIS OF THE ν_3 BANDS OF $^{35}ClNO_2$ AND $^{37}ClNO_2$ AROUND 370 cm^{-1}, Anusanth Anantharajah, F. Kwabia Tchana, Jean-Marie Flaud, Laurent Manceron, Johannes Orphal

FD11 **8:40 – 8:41**
ISOTOPIC RELATIONS FOR TETRAHEDRAL AND OCTAHEDRAL MOLECULES, Michel Loete, Cyril Richard, Vincent Boudon

FD12 **8:44 – 8:45**
ROTATIONAL ANALYSIS OF A NEW [15.05] Ω=0^+ – $X\ ^3\Sigma(0^+)$ ELECTRONIC TRANSITION OF TUNGSTEN SULFIDE (WS) IN THE 14,900 - 16,100 cm^{-1} REGION OBSERVED USING ILS-FTS, Kristin N Bales, Jack C Harms, James J O'Brien, Leah C O'Brien

FD13 **8:48 – 8:49**
CHARACTERIZATION OF THE $A^2\Sigma^+$ STATE OF SH/SD RADICALS BY PHOTODISSOCIATION SPECTROSCOPY, Yuan Qin, Xianfeng Zheng, Yu Song, Ge Sun, Jingsong Zhang

FE. Atmospheric science

Friday, June 25, 2021 – 8:0 AM

Room: 2021 Online Everywhere

Chair: Hamzeh Telfah, University of Louisville, LOUISVILLE, KY, USA

FE01 **8:00 – 8:01**

COMPUTATIONAL KINETICS STUDY OF ATMOSPHERIC RING-CLOSURE AND DEHYDRATION REACTIONS OF 1,4-HYDROXYCARBONYLS IN THE GAS PHASE, Parandaman Arathala, Chanin B. Tangtartharakul, Amitabha Sinha

FE03 **8:08 – 8:09**

TEMPERATURE-DEPENDENT WATER UPTAKE BEHAVIOR OF CLUSTERS RELEVANT TO NEW PARTICLE FORMATION, John J. Kreinbihl, Nicoline C. Frederiks, Christopher J. Johnson

FE04 **8:12 – 8:13**

A SPECTROSCOPIC AND COMPUTATIONAL PEEK INTO THE STRUCTURE OF ATMOSPHERICALLY RELEVANT DRY AND HYDRATED AMMONIUM BISULFATE CLUSTERS, Nicoline C. Frederiks, John J. Kreinbihl, Christopher J. Johnson

FE05 **8:16 – 8:17**

LOW-PRESSURE YIELDS OF STABILIZED CRIEGEE INTERMEDIATES PRODUCED FROM OZONOLYSIS OF A SERIES OF ALKENES, Lei Yang, Mixtli Campos-Pineda, Jingsong Zhang

FE06 **8:20 – 8:21**

LONG-OPEN-PATH MONITORING OF GREENHOUSE GASES BY NEAR-IR SPECTROSCOPY, Hans A Schuessler, Jinbao Xia, carlos Rodriguez, Alexandre Kolomenskii

FE07 **8:24 – 8:25**

MULTICHARME : A NEW CHERNIN TYPE MULTIPASS CELL FOR LONG PATHLENGTH TERAHERTZ SPECTROSCOPY EXPERIMENTS IN AN ATMOSPHERIC SIMULATION CHAMBER., Jean Decker, Jonas Bruckhuisen, Eirc Fertein, Nicolas Houzel, Pierre Kulinski, Robin Bocquet, Francis Hindle, Guillaume Dhont, Gaël Mouret, Cécile Coeur, Arnaud Cuisset

FE08 **8:28 – 8:29**

MOLECULAR TRANSITION FREQUENCES OF CO_2 NEAR 1.6 μ WITH KHZ-LEVEL UNCERTAINTIES, Zachary Reed, Brian Drouin, David A. Long, Joseph T. Hodges

FE09 **8:32 – 8:33**

HIGH ACCURACY NEAR-INFRARED CARBON DIOXIDE INTENSITY MEASUREMENTS TO SUPPORT REMOTE SENSING, David A. Long, Zachary Reed, Adam J. Fleisher, Joseph Mendonca, Sebastien Roche, Joseph T. Hodges

FE10 **8:36 – 8:37**

DOPPLER-FREE SATURATED ABSORPTION SPECTROSCOPY OF CH_4 IN THE MID-INFRARED REGION USING A CONTINUOUS-WAVE OPTICAL PARAMETRIC OSCILLATOR, S M Shah Riyadh, Hamzeh Telfah, Meagan Nicole Haase, Brianna Paige Haase, Jinjun Liu, Cunfeng Cheng

FF. Spectroscopy as an analytical tool
Friday, June 25, 2021 – 8:0 AM
Room: 2021 Online Everywhere

Chair: Carlos Manzanares, Baylor University, Waco, TX, USA

FF01 **8:00 – 8:01**
GENERATIVE ADVERSARIAL LINEAR DISCRIMINANT ANALYSIS FOR DISTINGUISHING API POLYMORPHS BY RAMAN SPECTROSCOPY, Ziyi Cao, Casey J Smith, Youlin Liu, Alex M Sherman, Garth Simpson

FF02 **8:04 – 8:05**
IDENTIFYING UNKNOWN MOLECULES WITH PROBABILISTIC DEEP LEARNING AND ROTATIONAL SPECTROSCOPY, Kelvin Lee, Michael C McCarthy

FF03 ***Post-Deadline Abstract*** **8:08 – 8:09**
EXHAUSTIVE PRODUCT ANALYSIS OF THREE BENZENE DISCHARGES BY MICROWAVE SPECTROSCOPY, Michael C McCarthy, Kelvin Lee, Brandon Carroll, Jessie P Porterfield, Bryan Changala, James H. Thorpe, John F. Stanton

FF04 **8:12 – 8:13**
IS IT CHIRAL?TOWARDS IDENTIFYING CHIRALITY IN UNKNOWN SAMPLES WITHOUT PRIOR SPECTRAL ASSIGNMENT., Greta Koumarianou, Lincoln Satterthwaite, Irene Wang, David Patterson

FF05 **8:16 – 8:17**
TIME-RESOLVED ROTATIONAL SPECTROSCOPY OF CARBOXYLIC ACIDS. IDENTIFICATION AND QUANTIFICATION OF THE COMPONENTS FROM HEATING ADIPIC ACID., Pablo Pinacho, Wenhao Sun, Daniel A. Obenchain, Melanie Schnell

FF06 **8:20 – 8:21**
CHIRPED PULSE MILLIMETER WAVE SPECTROSCOPY OF COMPLEX MOLECULES, Marius Hermanns, Nadine Wehres, Bettina Heyne, Frank Lewen, Stephan Schlemmer

FF08 **8:28 – 8:29**
LASER SYNTHESIS AND SPECTROSCOPY OF PYRENE DIMERS, Ian Webster, Michael A Duncan

FF09 **8:32 – 8:33**
DEEP REPRESENTATION LEARNING OF SPECTROSCOPIC GRAPHS, Kelvin Lee, Christine Li, Brett A. McGuire, Kyle N. Crabtree

FF10 **8:36 – 8:37**
COMBINED ROTATIONAL AND VIBRATIONAL CARS SPECTRA OF O_2 FOR SIMULTAENOUS TEMPERATURE AND PRESSURE MEASUREMENTS, Aman Satija, Robert P. Lucht

FF11 **8:40 – 8:41**
USING ULTRAVIOLET LASER ABSORPTION SPECTROSCOPY TO MEASURE VIBRATIONAL TEMPERATURE TIME HISTORIES OF SHOCK-HEATED OXYGEN, Ajay Krish, Jesse William Streicher, Ron K Hanson

FF12 **8:44 – 8:45**
BROADBAND FREQUENCY COMB VERNIER SPECTROSCOPY IN THE MID-IR WITH VIDEO-RECORDING RETRIEVAL OF ABSORPTION SPECTRUM, Hans A Schuessler, James R Bounds, Alexandre Kolomenskii

FG. Plenary

Friday, June 25, 2021 – 9:0 AM

Room: 2021 Online Everywhere

Chair: Anthony Remijan, NRAO, Charlottesville, VA, USA

FG02 **9:03 – 9:43**

CHIRALITY RECOGNITION/TRANSFER/AMPLIFICATION: ROTATIONAL SPECTROSCOPIC AND CHIROPTICAL SPECTROSCOPIC STUDIES, Yunjie Xu

FH. Mini-symposium: Spectroscopy with Undergraduates

Friday, June 25, 2021 – 10:0 AM

Room: 2021 Online Everywhere

Chair: Jacob Stewart, Connecticut College, New London, CT, USA

FH01 *INVITED TALK* **10:00 – 10:02**
UNDERGRADUATE MOLECULAR SPECTROSCOPY APPROACHES IN RESEARCH AND TEACHING AS AN EXPERIENTIAL LEARNING ENTERPRISE AT MISSOURI S&T, G. S. Grubbs II

FH02 **10:08 – 10:09**
OODLES OF UNDERGRADS UNDERGROUND: CLASSROOM UNDERGRADUATE RESEARCH AT WIND CAVE NATIONAL PARK, Joshua A Sebree

FH03 **10:12 – 10:13**
USING COMPUTATIONAL TOOLS TO ENHANCE LEARNING IN AN UNDERGRADUATE MOLECULAR SPECTROSCOPY COURSE, M. Reza Poopari, Shyam Parshotam, Yunjie Xu

FH04 **10:16 – 10:17**
BIOMOLECULAR STRUCTURE OF TROPINE DETERMINED FROM QUANTUM CHEMISTRY SIMULATIONS OF VIBRATIONAL SPECTROSCOPY, Emily Lyn Yang, Ryan P Steele

FH05 **10:20 – 10:21**
AN EXOMOL LINE LIST FOR SO: ROVIBRONIC SPECTRUM OF SULFUR MONOXIDE, Ryan Brady, Gap-Sue Kim, Wilfrid Somogyi, Jonathan Tennyson, Sergei N. Yurchenko

FH07 **10:28 – 10:29**
COMPUTATIONAL SPECTROSCOPIC SIGNATURES OF PROTEINOGENIC GLUTAMIC ACID AND ITS ISOMERIC SPECIES OF ASTROPHYSICAL IMPORTANCE , Namrata Rani, Vikas

FH08 **10:32 – 10:33**
NARROWING DOWN THE POSSIBLE GEOMETRIES OF A MOLECULE FROM ISOTOPOLOGUE ROTATIONAL CONSTANTS WITH STRUCTURAL FILTERS, Jieyu Yan, David Patterson

FH09 **10:36 – 10:37**
USE OF STUDENT-SPECIFIC MOLECULES AND THEIR SPECTROSCOPIC PROPERTIES IN PHYSICAL CHEMISTRY COURSES, David E. Woon

FH10 ***Post-Deadline Abstract*** **10:40 – 10:41**
THE CHIRPED-PULSE CLUB: MICROWAVE SPECTROSCOPY RESEARCH IN HIGH SCHOOL, Josue Cervantes, Emily Geraghty, Anish Kanthamneni, Ziwei Liu, Shamitha Nandi, Elic Weeks, Garrett Youngblood, Gordon G Brown

FH11 **10:44 – 10:45**
EXPLAINER: EFFECTS OF NUCLEAR QUADRUPOLE COUPLING TENSOR MAGNITUDE, ASYMMETRY, AND ORIENTATION ON THE APPEARANCE OF ROTATIONAL HYPERFINE STRUCTURE, S. A. Cooke

FH12 **10:48 – 10:49**
IMPLEMENTING EXTENDED CROSS CORRELATION AS A TOOL FOR SEMI-AUTOMATED MICROWAVE SPECTROSCOPIC ANALYSIS OF WEAKLY BOUND CLUSTER SPECTRA, Hannah Fino, Rebecca A. Peebles, Sean A. Peebles, Channing West, Brooks Pate

FH13 **10:52 – 10:53**
ENGAGING UNDERGRADUATE STUDENTS IN SPECTROSCOPY RESEARCH VIA DEVELOPMENT AND INCORPORATION OF ADVANCED DATA ANALYSIS TECHNIQUES, Rebecca A. Peebles, Sean A. Peebles, Prashansa Kannangara, Hannah Fino

FI. Clusters/Complexes

Friday, June 25, 2021 – 10:0 AM

Room: 2021 Online Everywhere

Chair: Wenhao Sun, DESY, Hamburg, Germany

FI01 **10:00 – 10:01**
INFRARED SPECTRA OF $(CO_2)_n$ - (RARE GAS)$_m$ TRIMERS AND TETRAMER, (n, m) = (1,2), (1,3), (2,1), A. J. Barclay, A.R.W. McKellar, Andrea Pietropolli Charmet, Nasser Moazzen-Ahmadi

FI02 **10:04 – 10:05**
INFRARED SPECTROSCOPY OF $[H_2O\text{-}(Kr)_n]^+$ (n=1-3): HEMIBOND FORMATION WITH WATER, Tomoki Nishigori, Toshihiko Maeyama, Marusu Katada, Asuka Fujii, Jing-Min Liu, Jer-Lai Kuo

FI03 ***Post-Deadline Abstract*** **10:08 – 10:09**
NEUTRAL IRON (III) SPECIES OBSERVED BY SECOND HARMONIC GENERATION SPECTROSCOPY AT THE AQUEOUS INTERFACE, Ka Chon Ng, Heather C. Allen

FI04 **10:12 – 10:13**
A CLOSE COMPETITION BETWEEN OH-O AND OH-π HYDROGEN BONDING: IR SPECTROSCOPY OF ANISOLE-METHANOL COMPLEX IN HELIUM NANODROPLETS , Tarun Kumar Roy, Devendra Mani, Gerhard Schwaab, Martina Havenith

FI05 **10:16 – 10:17**
HIGH-RESOLUTION INFRARED STUDY OF THE C_3Te AND TeC_3Te CLUSTERS, Sven Thorwirth, Thomas Salomon, Sophia Burger, Jürgen Gauss, Stephan Schlemmer, John B Dudek

FI06 **10:20 – 10:21**
STRUCTURE AND INFRARED SPECTRA OF NEW AEROSOL PARTICLE FORMATION SEED CLUSTERS, Daniel P. Tabor, Jezrielle R. Annis, Nathanael M. Kidwell

FI07 **10:24 – 10:25**
AB INITIO STUDY ON THE VIBRATIONAL SIGNATURES OF Ar_nH^+ (n=2–3), Jake A. Tan, Jer-Lai Kuo

FI09 **10:32 – 10:33**
NEW INFRARED SPECTRA OF CO_2-Xe: MODELING Xe ISOTOPE EFFECTS, INTERMOLECULAR BEND AND STRETCH, AND SYMMETRY BREAKING OF THE CO_2 BEnd, A. J. Barclay, A.R.W. McKellar, Colin Western, Nasser Moazzen-Ahmadi

FI10 **10:36 – 10:37**
$Si_nO_m^+$ – OPTICAL ABSORPTION AND PHOTODISSOCIATION PROPERTIES, Taarna Studemund, Marko Förstel, Lars Dahllöf, Kai Pollow, Robert G. Radloff, Otto Dopfer

FI11 **10:40 – 10:41**
INFRARED SPECTRA OF $(CO_2)_2$-X, CO_2-X_2, AND CO_2-X_3, X = CO OR N_2, A. J. Barclay, A.R.W. McKellar, Andrea Pietropolli Charmet, Nasser Moazzen-Ahmadi

FI12 **10:44 – 10:45**
THE INFRARED SPECTRUM OF CO_2-Kr, INCLUDING THE INTERMOLECULAR BENDING MODE AND SYMMETRY BREAKING OF THE CO_2 BEND, Sye Ghebretnsae, A. J. Barclay, Nasser Moazzen-Ahmadi

FI13 **10:48 – 10:49**
TUNNELING DYNAMICS IN $N_2 - D_2O$ OBSERVED IN THE OD STRETCHING REGION, R. Glorieux, Clément Lauzin, A. J. Barclay, Michel Herman, Nasser Moazzen-Ahmadi

FJ. Photodissociation and photochemistry

Friday, June 25, 2021 – 10:0 AM

Room: 2021 Online Everywhere

Chair: Katharine Moore Tibbetts, Virginia Commonwealth University, Richmond, VA, USA

FJ01 **10:00 – 10:01**
DYNAMICAL SIGNATURES FROM COMPETING, NONADIABATIC FRAGMENTATION PATHWAYS OF S-NITROSOTHIOPHENOL, K. Jacob Blackshaw, Marcus Marracci, Andrew S. Petit, Nathanael M. Kidwell

FJ02 *Post-Deadline Abstract* **10:04 – 10:05**
THE PHOTOCHEMICAL PATHWAYS FOR THE NONREACTIVE ELECTRONIC QUENCHING OF NO ($A^2\Sigma^+$) BY CO AND H_2O, Jose Guardado Sandoval, Nathanael M. Kidwell, Andrew S. Petit

FJ03 **10:08 – 10:09**
UNIMOLECULAR DISSOCIATION OF PEROXYFORMIC ACID INITIATED BY VIBRATIONAL OVERTONE EXCITATION TO THE 6νOH STATE, Josue Emmanuel Perez, Madhusudan Roy, Amitabha Sinha

FJ04 **10:12 – 10:13**
ROTATIONAL COOLING DYNAMICS OF HOT TRAPPED OH^- IONS PROBED BY VMI PHOTOELECTRON SPECTROSCOPY, Abhishek Shahi, Saurabh Mishra, Dhanoj Gupta, Oded Heber, Daniel Zajfman

FJ05 **10:16 – 10:17**
BOND DISSOCIATION DYNAMICS AND THERMODYNAMICS OF NiO^+ AND NiS^+, Schuyler P Lockwood, Ricardo B. Metz

FJ06 **10:20 – 10:21**
SPECTROSCOPIC STUDIES OF TRANSITION METAL AND LANTHANIDE BORIDES WITH RESONANT TWO-PHOTON IONIZATION SPECTROSCOPY, Dakota M. Merriles, Kimberly H. Tomchak, Christopher Nielson, Erick Tieu, Michael D. Morse

FJ07 **10:24 – 10:25**
BOND DISSOCIATION ENERGIES OF DIATOMIC LANTHANIDE SULFIDES AND SELENIDES, Jason J Sorensen, Erick Tieu, Michael D. Morse

FJ08 **10:28 – 10:29**
EXOMOLHD: PHOTODISSOCIATION OF DIATOMIC MOLECULES, Marco Pezzella, Sergei N. Yurchenko, Jonathan Tennyson

FJ09 **10:32 – 10:33**
AB INITIO STUDY OF THE HIGHLY EXCITED ELECTRONIC STATES OF C_2 AND ITS PHOTODISSOCIATION, Zhongxing Xu, Lee-Ping Wang, Steven Federman, William M. Jackson, Cheuk-Yiu Ng, Kyle N. Crabtree

FJ10 **10:36 – 10:37**
PHOTOINDUCED CHARGE TRANSFER PROCESSES, Ethan M Cunningham, Christian van der Linde, Milan Oncak, Martin K Beyer

FJ11 **10:40 – 10:41**
PROTOMERS OF FLAVIN RADICAL ANIONS PROBED WITH PD ACTION SPECTROSCOPY, Samuel Marlton, Benjamin McKinnon, Boris Ucur, James P Bezzina, Stephen J. Blanksby, Adam J. Trevitt

FJ12 **10:44 – 10:45**
DELIBERATE FUNCTIONALIZATION AND THE CONSEQUENTIAL ELECTRONIC RELAXATION PATHWAYS OF THE PYRIMIDINE CHROMOPHORE, Sean J. Hoehn, Sarah E. Krul, Carlos E. Crespo-Hernández

FJ13 **10:48 – 10:49**
ELECTRONIC RELAXATION MECHANISM OF GUANINE DERIVATIVES IN SOLUTION, Sarah E. Krul, Sean J. Hoehn, Carlos E. Crespo-Hernández

FJ14 **10:52 – 10:53**
POTENTIAL DEPENDENT PLASMONIC CATALYZED CLEAVAGE OF C-BR BOND OF 8-BROMOADENINE ON SILVER ELECTRODES OF NANOSTRUCTURE, De-Yin Wu, Zhong-Qun Tian

FK. Structure determination

Friday, June 25, 2021 – 10:0 AM

Room: 2021 Online Everywhere

Chair: Helen O. Leung, Amherst College, Amherst, MA, USA

FK01 **10:00 – 10:01**
SEMI-EXPERIMENTAL EQUILIBRIUM STRUCTURE (r_e^{SE}) OF METHACRYLONITRILE(C_4H_5N), Houston H. Smith, Samuel M. Kougias, Danny J Lee, Brian J. Esselman, R. Claude Woods, Robert J. McMahon

FK02 **10:04 – 10:05**
SEMI-EXPERIMENTAL EQUILIBRIUM STRUCTURE OF 1H- AND 2H-1,2,3-TRIAZOLES ($C_2H_3N_3$), Maria Zdanovskaia, Brian J. Esselman, Samuel M. Kougias, John F. Stanton, R. Claude Woods, Robert J. McMahon

FK03 **10:08 – 10:09**
DETERMINATION OF SUBSTITUTION EFFECTS ON THE STRUCTURES OF 2-, 3-, AND 4-PICOLYLAMINE USING FOURIER TRANSFORM MICROWAVE SPECTROSCOPY, Ryan G Bird, Caleb B Shiery, Kaylee X Shook

FK04 **10:12 – 10:13**
OXAZOLE: PRECISE SEMI-EXPERIMENTAL EQUILIBRIUM STRUCTURE DETERMINATION BY ROTATIONAL SPECTROSCOPY, Taylor K. Adkins, Maria Zdanovskaia, Kaori Kobayashi, Shozo Tsunekawa, Brian J. Esselman, R. Claude Woods, Robert J. McMahon

FK05 **10:16 – 10:17**
PRECISE SEMI-EXPERIMENTAL EQUILIBRIUM STRUCTURE OF THIAZOLE (C_3H_3NS), Brian J. Esselman, Maria Zdanovskaia, John F. Stanton, R. Claude Woods, Robert J. McMahon

FK06 **10:20 – 10:21**
PROPANE ISOTOPOLOGUES: HIGH RESOLUTION SYNCHROTRON FAR-IR SPECTRA OF THE SYMMETRICALLY DEUTERATED SPECIES $CH_3CH_2CD_3$, $CD_3CH_2CD_3$ AND C_3D_8. FIRST EXPERIMENTALLY DETERMINED GROUND STATE CONSTANTS FOR THESE SPECIES, Stephen J. Daunt, Robert Grzywacz, Colin Western, Brant E. Billinghurst, Jianbao Zhao

FK07 **10:24 – 10:25**
SEMI-EXPERIMENTAL EQUILIBRIUM STRUCTURE DETERMINATION OF THIOPHENE (C_4H_4S), Vanessa L. Orr, Yotaro Ichikawa, Brian J. Esselman, Aatmik R. Patel, Samuel M. Kougias, Andrew N. Owen, Kaori Kobayashi, John F. Stanton, R. Claude Woods, Robert J. McMahon

FK08 **10:28 – 10:29**
IMPROVED SEMI-EXPERIMENTAL EQUILIBRIUM STRUCTURE DETERMINATION AND THEORETICAL PREDICTION OF PYRIDAZINE (o-$C_4H_4N_2$), AND THE IMPACT OF THE ISOTOPOLOGUE DATA SET, Andrew N. Owen, Maria Zdanovskaia, Brian J. Esselman, John F. Stanton, R. Claude Woods, Robert J. McMahon

FK09 **10:32 – 10:33**
MICROWAVE SPECTRUM AND IODINE NUCLEAR QUADRUPOLE COUPLING CONSTANTS OF 1,1-DIIODOETHANE, Michael J. Carrillo, Wei Lin, Yasuki Endo

FK10 **10:36 – 10:37**
A MICROWAVE STUDY OF THREE BROMINE-CONTAINING MOLECULES: CBr_2F_2, AgBr, and H_2-AgBr, Joshua A. Signore, Christopher Falls, Corey J Evans, Wallace C. Pringle, S. A. Cooke, Stewart E. Novick, Daniel A. Obenchain

FK11 **10:40 – 10:41**
STRUCTURE OF THE MODEL GRIGNARD-TYPE REAGENT $ClZnCH_3$ ($\tilde{X}^1A_1$) BY MILLIMETER-WAVE SPECTROSCOPY , Mark Burton, Nazifa Tabassum, Lucy M. Ziurys

FK12 **10:44 – 10:45**
RO-VIBRATIONALLY AVERAGED MOLECULAR STRUCTURE OF BENZENE I. ALMOST THE SAME BOND LENGTHS FOR THE C–H AND C–D BONDS., Masaaki Baba, Umpei Nagashima, Tsuneo Hirano

FK13 **10:48 – 10:49**
RO-VIBRATIONALLY AVERAGED MOLECULAR STRUCTURE OF BENZENE II. COMPUTATIONAL MOLECULAR SPECTROSCOPY STUDY., Tsuneo Hirano, Umpei Nagashima, Masaaki Baba

FK14 **10:52 – 10:53**
THE EQUILIBRIUM STRUCTURE OF SMALL RADICALS: THE SEMI-EXPERIMENTAL APPROACH AT WORK, Silvia Alessandrini, Mattia Melosso, Cristina Puzzarini

FL. Small molecules

Friday, June 25, 2021 – 10:0 AM

Room: 2021 Online Everywhere

Chair: Kyle N. Crabtree, University of California, Davis, CA, USA

FL01 **10:00 – 10:01**
THE (1,0) BAND OF THE [13.10] Ω=1 – X $^3\Sigma^-(0^+)$ TRANSITION OF TUNGSTEN SULFIDE, WS, OBSERVED BY ILS-FTS, Jack C Harms, Brendan M. Ratay, Kristin N Bales, James J O'Brien, Leah C O'Brien

FL02 **10:04 – 10:05**
DETECTION AND IDENTIFICATION OF PLATINUM FLUORIDE, PTF: ANALYSIS OF THE (0,0) BAND OF THE [15.3]Ω=3/2 – $X\ ^2\Pi_{3/2}$ TRANSITION USING INTRACAVITY LASER SPECTROSCOPY, Caroline A Welch, Jack C Harms, James J O'Brien, Leah C O'Brien

FL03 **10:08 – 10:09**
OBSERVATION AND SPECTRAL ANALYSIS OF THE A Ω=1 – X Ω=0^+ ELECTRONIC TRANSITION OF DIATOMIC PLATINUM SULFIDE, PtS, BY INTRACAVITY LASER ABSORPTION SPECTROSCOPY WITH FOURIER TRANSFORM DETECTION (ILS-FTS), Leah C O'Brien, Jack C Harms, James J O'Brien, Wenli Zou

FL04 **10:12 – 10:13**
DISPERSED LASER INDUCED FLUORESCENCE STUDY OF $CaNH_2$ AND CaSH , Timothy Steimle, Anh T. Le, Chaoqun Zhang, Lan Cheng, Benjamin Augenbraun, John M. Doyle

FL05 **10:16 – 10:17**
HIGH RESOLUTION LASER INDUCED FLUORESCENCE AND ZEEMAN EFFECT IN THE [18.6]1.5-$X^2\Sigma^+$ TRANSITION OF YbOH , Colan Linton, Timothy Steimle, Ephriem Tadesse Mengesha, Allan G. Adam, Anh T. Le

FL06 **10:20 – 10:21**
A COUPLED-CHANNELS POTENTIAL FIT DESCRIBING THE LOW-LYING $X^2\Delta$, $^2\Pi$ AND $^2\Sigma^+$ STATES OF NiH TO EXPERIMENTAL ACCURACY , Ilvie Havalyova, Ivayla BOZHINOVA, Asen Pashov, Amanda J. Ross, Patrick Crozet

FL07 **10:24 – 10:25**
PHOTOELECTRON VELOCITY MAP IMAGING SPECTROSCOPY OF THE BERYLLIUM TETRAMER ANION Be_4^- , Noah B Jaffe, Michael Heaven

FL08 **10:28 – 10:29**
HIGH-RESOLUTION LASER SPECTROSCOPY OF LEAD OXIDE (PbO) IN 400-450 NM, Katsunari Enomoto, Takehiro Suzuki, Masaaki Baba

FL09 **10:32 – 10:33**
EVOLUTION OF IRON AND CALCIUM MONOOXIDES' BANDS IN LASER PLASMA UNDEL LOW PRESSURE, Aleksandr Zakuskin, Babken Beglaryan, Timur A. Labutin

FL10 **10:36 – 10:37**
FREQUENCY COMB REFERENCED SPECTRA OF $A - X$ TRANSITIONS IN SH, Arthur Fast, Samuel Meek

FL11 **10:40 – 10:41**
REVIEW OF DIATOMIC SPECTROSCOPIC DATA, Laura K McKemmish

FL12 **10:44 – 10:45**
IR, VISIBLE, AND UV LINE LIST OF SILICON MONOXIDE (SiO) – A HACKATHON PROJECT, Ahmad Y. Adam, Victoria H.J. Clark, Bridgette Cooper, Pria Dobney, Shaun T. E. Donnelly, Maire N. Gorman, Anthony E. Lynas-Gray, Thomas Meltzer, Alec Owens, Qianwei Qu, Mikhail Semenov, Wilfrid Somogyi, Anna-Maree Syme, Jonathan Tennyson, Apoorva Upadhyay, Samuel Wright, Sergei N. Yurchenko, Juan C. Zapata Trujillo

FL13 **10:48 – 10:49**
HIGH RESOLUTION LASER SPECTROSCOPY OF RUTHENIUM MONOXIDE, Allan G. Adam, Geoffrey M. Chenard, Colan Linton, Dennis W. Tokaryk

FL14 **10:52 – 10:53**
EXPERIMENTAL AND THEORETICAL ANALYSIS OF THE INTER- AND INTRA-MOLECULAR DYNAMICS OF FORMYL RADICAL TRAPPED IN SOLID CO, Yurij Dmitriev, Aatto Laaksonen, Nikolas Ploutarch Benetis

FM. Chirality and stereochemistry

Friday, June 25, 2021 – 10:0 AM

Room: 2021 Online Everywhere

Chair: Guojie Li, University of Alberta, Edmonton, Canada

FM01 **10:00 – 10:01**
ASSESSING THE PERFORMANCE OF ROTATIONAL SPECTROSCOPY IN CHIRAL ANALYSIS, Sergio R. Domingos, Cristobal Perez, Mark D. Marshall, Helen O. Leung, Melanie Schnell

FM02 **10:04 – 10:05**
CHIRALITY RECOGNITION IN THE TERNARY AGGREGATES OF PROPYLENE OXIDE: EXPERIMENTALLY GUIDED THEORETICAL CONFORMATIONAL SEARCHES , Fan Xie, Marco Fusè, Arsh Singh Hazrah, Wolfgang Jäger, Vincenzo Barone, Yunjie Xu

FM03 **10:08 – 10:09**
CHIRAL TAG ROTATIONAL SPECTROSCOPY FOR CHIRAL ANALYSIS OF CARBOXYLIC ACIDS, Haley N. Scolati, Kevin J Mayer, Brooks Pate

FM04 **10:12 – 10:13**
REACTION CHEMISTRY OF EPOXIDES WITH FLUORINATED CARBOXYLIC ACIDS, Kevin J Mayer, Brooks Pate, Haley N. Scolati, Martin S. Holdren, Reilly E. Sonstrom, Channing West

FM05 **10:16 – 10:17**
A BROADBAND ROTATIONAL SPECTROSCOPIC AND THEORETICAL STUDY OF CIS AND TRANS (-)-CARVEOL, Arsh Singh Hazrah, Mohamad Al-Jabiri, Raiden Speelman, Wolfgang Jäger

FM06 **10:20 – 10:21**
CHIRAL MOLECULAR RECOGNITION TRENDS IN AROMATIC AND HELICAL SYSTEMS REVEALED WITH ROTATIONAL SPECTROSCOPY, Sergio R. Domingos, Cristobal Perez, Narcis Avarvari, Melanie Schnell

FM07 **10:24 – 10:25**
CHIRAL TAG ROTATIONAL SPECTROSCOPY FOR STRUCUTRE ANALYSIS OF CHIRAL METHYLPHENYL OXIRANE, Haley N. Scolati, Kevin J Mayer, Martin S. Holdren, Brooks Pate

FM08 **10:28 – 10:29**
MANIPULATION OF COLD CHIRAL MOLECULES USING ELECTRONIC AND ROTATIONAL SPECTROSCOPY, A. O. Hernandez-Castillo, Johannes Bischoff, Ju Hyeon Lee, Gerard Meijer, Sandra Eibenberger-Arias

FM09 **10:32 – 10:33**
EXPLORING CONFORMATIONAL SPACES AND AGGREGATION PREFERENCES OF SERINE-ASPARAGINE AND VALINE-ASPARAGINE DIMERS BY IRMPD SPECTROSCOPY AND QUANTUM CHEMISTRY , Matthias Heger, Haolu Wang, Mohamad Al-Jabiri, Yunjie Xu

FM10 **10:36 – 10:37**
CAN PHOTOELECTRON CIRCULAR DICHROISM WORK FOR CHIRAL ANIONS?, Mallory Green, Jenny Triptow, Gerard Meijer

FM11 **10:40 – 10:41**
MATRIX ISOLATION-VIBRATIONAL CIRCULAR DICHROISM SPECTROSCOPIC STUDY OF TETRAHYDRO-2-FUROIC ACID AND ITS AGGREGATES , Yanqing Yang, Joseph Cheramy, Yunjie Xu

FM12 **10:44 – 10:45**
COMPUTATIONAL INSIGHTS INTO THE CHIRAL SUM FREQUENCY GENERATION RESPONSE OF WATER SUPERSTRUCTURES SURROUNDING AN ANTIPARALLEL β-SHEET, Daniel Konstantinovsky, Ethan Alexander Perets, Sharon Hammes-Schiffer, Elsa Yan

FM13 **10:48 – 10:49**
CHIRAL SUM FREQUENCY GENERATION SPECTROSCOPY REVEALS HOW MIRROR-IMAGE β-SHEETS ORGANIZE WATER SUPERSTRUCTURES WITH OPPOSITE CHIRALITY, Ethan Alexander Perets, Daniel Konstantinovsky, Ty Santiago, Luis Velarde, Sharon Hammes-Schiffer, Elsa Yan

MA. Plenary
Monday, June 21, 2021 – 8:0 AM
Room: 2021 Online Everywhere

Chair: Cathy Murphy, University of Illinois at Urbana-Champaign, Urbana, IL, USA

Welcome **8:00**
Susan Martinis, Vice Chancellor for Research and Innovation
University of Illinois at Urbana-Champaign

MA01 **8:10 – 8:50**

PREBIOTIC ASTROCHEMISTRY IN THE "THz-GAP"

SUSANNA L. WIDICUS WEAVER, *Chemistry and Astronomy, University of Wisconsin-Madison, Madison, WI, USA.*

Small reactive organic molecules are key intermediates in interstellar chemistry, leading to the formation of biologically-relevant species as stars and planets form. These molecules are identified in space via their pure rotational spectral fingerprints in the far-IR or terahertz (THz) regime. Despite their fundamental roles in the formation of life, many of these molecules have not been spectroscopically characterized in the laboratory, and therefore cannot be studied via observational astronomy. The reason for this lack of fundamental laboratory information is the challenge of spectroscopy in the THz regime combined with the challenge of studying unstable molecules. Our laboratory research involves characterization of astrophysically-relevant unstable species, including small radicals that are the products of photolysis reactions, organic ions formed via plasma discharges, molecules released during UV and thermal processing of interstellar ice analogs, and small reactive organics that form via $O(^1D)$ insertion reactions. Our observational astronomy research seeks to examine the chemical mechanisms at play in a range of interstellar environments and to identify chemical tracers that can be used as clocks for the star-formation process. In this talk, I will present recent results from our laboratory and observational studies that examine prebiotic chemistry in the interstellar medium. I will discuss these results in the broader context of my integrative research program that encompasses laboratory spectroscopy, observational astronomy, and astrochemical modeling.

RAO AWARDS **8:55**
Presentation of Awards by Jennifer van Wijngaarden, University of Manitoba

2019 Rao Award Winners
Mark Babin, University of California Berkeley
Lidor Foguel, Yale University
Sommer Johansen, University of California Davis

MILLER PRIZE **9:05**
Introduction by Michael Heaven, Emory University

MA02 ***Miller Prize Lecture*** **9:50 – 10:05**

ENHANCING NONLINEAR OPTICAL RESPONSE IN ARTIFICIAL STACKED 2D MATERIALS

FANG LIU, *Department of Chemistry, Stanford University, Stanford, CA, USA.*

Two dimensional (2D) semiconductors and their artificial structures hold great promises for electronic, optoelectronic, and quantum devices. We developed a facile method to disassemble van der Waals (vdW) single crystals layer-by-layer into monolayers with near-unity yield, high quality, and macroscopic dimensions, and reassemble them into artificial stacked structures. With the stacked multilayers, we have enhanced nonlinear optical response in second harmonic generation and high harmonic generation. These findings reveal versatile optical responses of the 2D semiconductor systems that can be engineered on demand for future applications.

COBLENTZ AWARD **10:10**
Presentation of Award by Ellen Miseo, Coblentz Society

MA03 **10:15 – 10:55**

PARA-ORTHO HYDROGEN CONVERSION; SOLVING A 90-YEAR OLD MYSTERY

AD VAN DER AVOIRD, *Theoretical Chemistry, Radboud University, Nijmegen, Netherlands.*

It is well known among spectroscopists that hydrogen has two modifications: para-H_2 and ortho-H_2. Pure para-H_2 can be produced by leading "normal" H_2, a 3:1 ortho:para mixture, over a catalyst at low temperature. It is perhaps less well known that para-ortho H_2 conversion is also catalyzed by collisions with paramagnetic molecules, such as O_2.

Almost ninety years ago Farkas and Sachsse measured the rate coefficient of para-ortho H_2 conversion in gas mixtures with O_2.[1] In the same year, 1933, it was proposed by Wigner [2] that it is the magnetic dipole-dipole coupling between the electron spin of O_2 and the nuclear spins of the two protons in H_2 that is responsible for the conversion. In asymmetric collisions this coupling makes the two H-nuclei inequivalent and mixes the nuclear spin functions of para- and ortho-H_2, as well as their rotational states with even and odd j values. Another mechanism, suggested to be much more effective, was proposed later: the exchange interaction with the open-shell O_2 induces spin density into the electronic wavefunction of H_2. In most collisions the spin density is different at the two H-nuclei, which makes them inequivalent by different hyperfine interactions through the Fermi contact term.

An important application of para-H_2 is in NMR spectroscopy and its imaging variant, MRI. By adding para-H_2 to the sample the sensitivity of NMR can be increased by four orders of magnitude by a phenomenon called para-hydrogen induced polarization (PHIP). Para-ortho H_2 conversion by O_2 in the gas phase was remeasured in 2014 in view of this application. A detailed and quantitative understanding of the conversion process was still lacking, however.

We theoretically investigated the para-ortho H_2 conversion by collisions with O_2 in a first principles approach.[3] Both mechanisms were taken into account and the corresponding coupling terms were quantitatively evaluated as functions of the geometry of the O_2-H_2 collision complex by means of *ab initio* electronic structure calculations. Then they were included in nearly exact quantum mechanical coupled-channels scattering calculations for the collisions between O_2 and H_2, which yielded the para-ortho H_2 conversion cross sections and the rate coefficients for temperatures up to 400 K. The conversion rate and its temperature dependence are in good agreement with the values measured in H_2-O_2 gas mixtures. The calculations provide detailed insight into the conversion process.

[1] L. Farkas and H. Sachsse, Z. Phys. Chem. B **23**, 1 (1933). [2] E. Wigner, Z. Phys. Chem. B **23**, 28 (1933). [3] X. Zhang, T. Karman, G. C. Groenenboom, and A. van der Avoird, Nat. Sci. (2021); https://doi.org/10.1002/ntls.10002.

TA. Mini-symposium: Large Amplitude Motions

Tuesday, June 22, 2021 – 8:0 AM

Room: 2021 Online Everywhere

Chair: Sonia Melandri, University of Bologna, Bologna, Italy

TA01 *INVITED TALK* **8:00 – 8:02**

MOLECULES' ROTATION SIGNALS (AND THEIR OBSERVATION): TORSION, INVERSION, FLEXIBILITY, CHIRALITY, PHASE

JENS-UWE GRABOW, *Institut für Physikalische Chemie und Elektrochemie, Gottfried-Wilhelm-Leibniz-Universität, Hannover, Germany.*

All molecular system come with their own set of challenges for rotational spectroscopy, theoretically and experimentally: (Multiple) internal interactions might cause complicated energy level schemes and the resulting spectra will be rather difficult to predict theoretically. Experimentally, these spectra are difficult to assess and assign. With today's broad-band microwave (MW) techniques, finding and identifying such spectral features have lost their major drawback of being very time consuming for many molecules. The unrivalled resolution of advanced fast-passage spectrometers, previously only available for narrow-banded MW techniques, now also allows to tackle - at the highest precision – very subtle effects.

Historically, (very) low barriers to large amplitude motions leading to (very) large tunnelling splittings often prevented an experimental assessment or, if identified, their analysis to experimental accuracy. Barriers to large amplitude motions can not only be related to the local atom arrangement but also to the molecular orbital and electron density structure, e.g. chemical information relayed through conjugated π-systems, of the molecule. Theoretically, such systems require calculations at elevated levels, e.g. CCSD(T)/cc-pcVTZ or beyond, but quantitative predictions of the dynamical features often still fall behind those of equilibrium structures. Experimentally, the analysis might require the measurement of tunneling species (in the cm- and mm-wave regions) beyond the torsional ground state to reveal the origin of the observed spectrum and underlying hindering potential.

Furthermore - in the realm of barriers to large amplitude motions - details on internal dynamics and the (stereo-chemical) molecular structure encode their nature in the coherent signature of molecular rotation spectra obtained after single- and/or double-resonance excitation. Phase, indeed, provides pitfalls here and elsewhere. Current examples and new directions together with an outlook will be given.

TA02 **8:08 – 8:09**

BROADBAND MICROWAVE AND COMPUTATIONAL STUDY OF HEXAFLUORO-O-XYLENE: HIGHLY COUPLED CF3 ROTORS

SVEN HERBERS, SEAN FRITZ, PIYUSH MISHRA, YONGBIN KIM, LYUDMILA V SLIPCHENKO, TIMOTHY S. ZWIER, *Department of Chemistry, Purdue University, West Lafayette, IN, USA.*

The rotational constants and quartic centrifugal distortion coefficients of hexafluoro-o-xylene and all singly 13C isotopologues were precisely determined from the 8 to 18GHz gas phase microwave spectrum. A preliminary r0 structure was determined, reproducing the experimental rotational constants with deviations of no more than 15kHz. Interestingly, rather than the C2v symmetry structure expected intuitively, as in o-xylene, calculations with a variety of methods (B3LYP, CAM-B3LYP, ωB97XD, MP2, and CCSD(T)) predict a C2 symmetry structure in which the two CF3 groups rotate in opposite directions by about 16 degrees. Analysis of the interactions between the two CF3 groups using an effective fragment potential (EFP) approach identified two major contributions to their interaction, due to exchange repulsion and electrostatic repulsion, with electrostatic repulsion responsible for the barrier at the C2v geometry.

SH, SMF, PM and TSZ gratefully acknowledge support for this work from the Department of Energy Basic Energy Sciences Gas Phase Chemical Physics program under Grant No. DE-FG02-96ER14656. YK and LVS gratefully acknowledge support from the National Science Foundation (NSF CHE-1800505). Present address for TSZ: Combustion Research Facility, Sandia National Laboratory, Livermore, CA 94550.

TA03 **8:12 – 8:13**

2-PROPIONYLTHIOPHENE: PLANAR, OR NOT PLANAR, THAT IS THE QUESTION

CHRISTINA DINDIĆ, WOLFGANG STAHL[a], *Institute for Physical Chemistry, RWTH Aachen University, Aachen, Germany*; HA VINH LAM NGUYEN, *CNRS UMR 7583, Université Paris-Est Créteil, Université de Paris, Laboratoire Interuniversitaire des Systèmes Atmosphériques (LISA), Créteil, France.*

The molecular planarity of molecules that contain an alkyl group attached to a system with conjugated double bonds has posed a great challenge for both experiments and theory for a long time. This also holds true for the case of 2-propionylthiophene [1] where a propionyl group is attached at the second position of the planar, aromatic thiophene ring. Quantum chemical calculations performed at different levels of theory yield contradicting results on whether the ethyl group of the propionyl moiety is lying in-plane with the thiophene ring or slightly tilted out-of-plane.

In the microwave spectrum both *syn*-2PT and *anti*-2PT were assigned. For the energetically more favourable *syn*-conformer it was possible to observe several ^{13}C-isotopologues. This allowed the determination of a partial experimental heavy atom skeleton structure which revealed a tiny, but non-zero tilt angle of the ethyl group out of the thiophene plane, thereby convincingly confirming the non-planarity of 2-propionylthiophene. The results were further supported by inertial defects of both conformers calculated from the experimental rotational constants.

Aditionally, splittings arising from the internal rotation of the terminal methyl group were analysed, yielding torsional barriers of 806.94(54) cm^{-1} and 864.5(88) cm^{-1} for the two observed conformers, respectively.

[1] C. Dindić, W. Stahl, H.V.L. Nguyen, *Phys. Chem. Chem. Phys.*, 2020, **22**, 19704-19712.

[a]Posthumous Abstract

TA04 **8:16 – 8:17**

Ka BAND MICROWAVE SPECTRUM OF METHYL TERT-BUTYL ETHER

J. H. WESTERFIELD, KELLY S. MEYER, SOMMER L. JOHANSEN, KYLE N. CRABTREE, *Department of Chemistry, University of California, Davis, Davis, CA, USA.*

Methyl tert-butyl ether is a gasoline additive and a water pollutant. Its rotational spectrum was measured from 26.5 – 40 GHz using Chirped-Pulse Fourier Transform Microwave Spectroscopy. Measurements were conducted at low temperature via supersonic expansion with two different backing pressures as well as room temperature via static cell. The two different backing pressures provided spectra at $\sim$ 30 K and $\sim$ 40 K which allowed meaningful probing of the first excited vibrational state which lies below the first excited torsional state. The room temperature spectrum is highly congested due to low lying vibrational states as well as the torsionally excited states. The molecule was previous reported in Suenram et. al 1997 in a range of 9 – 18.6 GHz which fit 32 lines up to $J = 3$. This work expands that fit to over 400 transitions and converts it to the Rho Axis Method utilizing the program RAM36. The improved ground torsional state measurements as well as the room temperature data allowed for tentative assignments of torsionally excited and vibrationally excited transitions.

TA05 **8:20 – 8:21**

MENTHYL ACETATE. A NEW LINK IN THE CHAIN OF ACETATES STUDIED WITH ROTATIONAL SPECTROSCOPY

ANNA KRIN, PABLO PINACHO, CRISTOBAL PEREZ, MELANIE SCHNELL, *FS-SMP, Deutsches Elektronen-Synchrotron (DESY), Hamburg, Germany.*

Natural essential oils have nowadays a vast range of applications in different areas, from medicine and pharmacology, to food industry and cosmetics. They are composed of several, structurally often similar constituents. Due to the high relevance of essential oils in our everyday life it is of interest to obtain detailed structural and conformational information on their main constituents, to widen our knowledge of their unique properties. Rotational spectroscopy is a powerful technique to address these important questions in an accurate and precise manner.

Here we present a comprehensive conformational analysis of menthyl acetate, one of the constituents of peppermint oil (*Mentha x piperita*). Two conformers of menthyl acetate were observed in the broadband rotational spectrum in the 2-12 GHz frequency range. The structure of the lowest energy conformer was obtained experimentally, based on the assignment of the singly-substituted ^{13}C-isotopologues. Additionally, the internal rotation of the methyl top of the acetyl side group was characterized. The experimentally determined low barrier height is in line with previous rotational spectroscopy results for other acetates, for which barrier heights on the order of 1 kJ/mol were reported. A comparison to the other acetates will be discussed in the scope of this talk.

TA06 **8:24 – 8:25**

MICROWAVE SPECTRA OF A POTENTIAL FOUR-FOLD INTERNAL ROTOR, PHENYLSULFUR PENTAFLUORIDE

JOSHUA A. SIGNORE, CHRISTOPHER FALLS, *Department of Chemistry, Wesleyan University, Middletown, CT, USA*; SUSANNA L. STEPHENS, *School of Natural and Environmental Sciences, Newcastle University, Newcastle-upon-Tyne, UK*; DANIEL A. OBENCHAIN, *FS-SMP, Deutsches Elektronen-Synchrotron (DESY), Hamburg, Germany*; CARLOS A JIMENEZ-HOYOS, *Chemistry , Wesleyan University , Middletown, CT, USA*; S. A. COOKE, *Natural and Social Science, Purchase College SUNY, Purchase, NY, USA*; STEWART E. NOVICK, *Department of Chemistry, Wesleyan University, Middletown, CT, USA.*

We present the microwave spectra of the fourth molecule containing the four-fold rotor $-SF_5$, phenylsulfur pentafluoride, $c\text{-}C_6H_5\text{-}SF_4\text{-}F$ (PhSPF). The first three molecules in this series were vinylsulfur pentafluoride (VSPF), propen-1-ylsulfur pentafluoride (PSPF) and buten-1-ylsulfur pentafluoride (BSPF). VSPF exhibited splitting into the A, E, and B torsional states with 10's of MHz between the torsional transitions. PSPF exhibited the torsional splitting with 10's of kHz between transitions. BSPF exhibited no torsional splitting. Likewise, PhSPF shows no torsional splitting in the spectra. This phenomenon is mostly explained by the differences in the values of the four-fold barrier to internal rotation, V_4, in this series of molecules.

TA07 **8:28 – 8:29**

LOWERING THE TORSIONAL BARRIERS BY STERICAL HINDRANCE: MICROWAVE SPECTRUM OF THE THREE-TOP MOLECULE 2,6-DIMETHYLANISOLE

LYNN FERRES, JOSHUA SPAUTZ, WOLFGANG STAHL, *Institute for Physical Chemistry, RWTH Aachen University, Aachen, Germany*; HA VINH LAM NGUYEN, *CNRS UMR 7583, Université Paris-Est Créteil, Université de Paris, Laboratoire Interuniversitaire des Systèmes Atmosphériques (LISA), Créteil, France.*

The title molecule 2,6-dimethylanisole (26DMA) is one of the six isomers of dimethylanisole systematically studied by microwave spectroscopy. The spectrum of 26DMA was recorded using a pulsed molecular jet Fourier transform spectrometer. The experimental part was supported by quantum chemical calculations carried out at the B3LYP/6-311++G(d,p) level of theory. As calculated and experimentally proven for the three mono-methylanisoles (*o*-,[a] *m*-,[b] and *p*-methylanisole[c]) and three dimethylanisoles (2,3-DMA,[d] 3,4-DMA,[e] and 2,4-DMA[f]), the barrier to internal rotation of the methoxy methyl rotor surpasses 1000 cm^{-1}, causing unresolvable torsional splittings in the microwave spectrum.

With both ortho positions substituted by a methyl group in 26DMA, the methoxy part is highly sterically hindered. It is thus forced to tilt out of the plane spanned by the heavy atoms of the phenyl ring by an angle of 90°. Many experimental studies have shown that sterical hindrance often increases the barrier to internal rotation. Surprisingly, in the case of 26DMA, the torsional barrier decreases dramatically to about 460 cm^{-1}, leading to observable fine splittings in the microwave spectrum. Thus, 26DMA represents a three-top molecule, featuring two equivalent aryl methyl rotors and one methoxy methyl rotor.

[a]L. Ferres, H. Mouhib, W. Stahl, and H. V. L. Nguyen, *ChemPhysChem* **18**, 1855-1859, (2017).
[b]L. Ferres, W. Stahl, H. V. L. Nguyen, *J. Chem. Phys.* **148**, 124304, (2018).
[c]L. Ferres, W. Stahl, I. Kleiner, and H. V. L. Nguyen, *J. Mol. Spectrosc.* **343**, 44-49, (2018).
[d]L. Ferres, K-N. Truong, W. Stahl, H. V. L. Nguyen, *ChemPhysChem* **19**, 1781-1788, (2018).
[e]L. Ferres, J. Cheung, W. Stahl, H. V. L. Nguyen, *J. Phys. Chem. A* **123**, 3497-3503, (2019).
[f]L. Ferres, W. Stahl, H. V. L. Nguyen, *J. Chem. Phys.* **151**, 104310, (2019).

TA08 **8:32 – 8:33**

LOCAL AND GLOBAL APPROACHES TO TREAT THE TORSIONAL BARRIERS OF 4-METHYL-ACETOPHENONE USING MICROWAVE SPECTROSCOPY

SVEN HERBERS, SEAN FRITZ, PIYUSH MISHRA, *Department of Chemistry, Purdue University, West Lafayette, IN, USA*; HA VINH LAM NGUYEN, *CNRS UMR 7583, Université Paris-Est Créteil, Université de Paris, Laboratoire Interuniversitaire des Systèmes Atmosphériques (LISA), Créteil, France*; TIMOTHY S. ZWIER[a], *Department of Chemistry, Purdue University, West Lafayette, IN, USA.*

The Fourier transform microwave spectrum of 4-methylacetophenone recorded from 8 GHz to 18 GHz under jet-cooled conditions has revealed large tunneling splittings arising from a low barrier to internal rotation of the ring methyl group and small splittings from a high torsional barrier of the acetyl methyl group. The large splittings are especially challenging to model, while the small splittings are difficult to analyze due to the resolution limit of 120 kHz. The combination of two methyl groups undergoing internal rotations caused each rotational transition to split into five torsional species, which were resolved and fitted using a modified version of the *XIAM* code and the newly developed *ntop* code to a root-mean-square deviation close to measurement accuracy, providing an estimate of the V_3 potential barriers of about 22 cm^{-1} and 584–588 cm^{-1} for the ring and the acetyl methyl groups, respectively. The assignment was aided by separately fitting the five torsional species using odd-power order operators. Only one conformer in which all heavy atoms are located on a symmetry plane could be identified in the spectrum, in agreement with results from conformation analysis using quantum chemical calculations.

[a]Current address: Combustion Research Facility, Sandia National Laboratories, Livermore, CA 94551-0969, USA.

TA09 **8:36 – 8:37**

STERIC EFFECTS ON TWO METHYL INTERNAL ROTATIONS OF 2,6- AND 3,4-DIMETHYLFLUOROBENZENE

SAFA KHEMISSI, JULIE MELAN, HA VINH LAM NGUYEN, *CNRS UMR 7583, Université Paris-Est Créteil, Université de Paris, Laboratoire Interuniversitaire des Systèmes Atmosphériques (LISA), Créteil, France.*

The microwave spectra of two dimethylfluorobenzene isomers, 2,6- and 3,4-, were measured using two pulsed molecular jet Fourier transform microwave spectrometers operating in the frequency range from 2.0 to 40.0 GHz with the goal of quantifying the steric effects on the barriers to internal rotation of the two methyl groups. Due to the internal rotations of two equivalent methyl groups in 2,6-dimethylfluorobenzene[a] (26DMFB), all rotational transitions split into quartets, while quintets appear for 3,4-dimethylfluorobenzene[b] (34DMFB) because its two methyl groups are inequivalent. The splittings were analyzed and modeled to deduce a torsional barrier of 236.7922(21) cm^{-1} for the two methyl groups in 26DMFB and of 456.20(13) cm^{-1} and 489.78(15) cm^{-1} for the methyl groups at the *meta* and *para* positions, respectively, in 34DMFB. Each torsional species was fitted separately using odd power order parameters to check the correctness of the assignment. For both isomers, a global fit obtained with the program *XIAM*[c] has achieved a standard deviation close to the measurement accuracy. The experimental results are compared with the predicted values obtained by quantum chemical calculations and those of other toluene derivatives.

[a]S. Khemissi, H.V.L. Nguyen, ChemPhysChem 2020, 21, 1682-1687.
[b]J. Mélan, S. Khemissi, H.V.L. Nguyen, Spectro. Chem. Acta A 2021, 253, 119564.
[c]H. Hartwig, H. Dreizler, Z. Naturforsch. 1996, 51a, 923-932.

TA10 **8:40 – 8:41**

INTERNAL ROTATIONS OF METHYL PIVALATE BY ROTATIONAL SPECTROSCOPY

NOBUHIKO KUZE, YOSHIYUKI KAWASHIMA, *Department of Materials and Life Sciences, Sophia University, Tokyo, Japan.*

The rotational spectrum of methyl pivalate (t-BuC(O)OCH$_3$) in the ground vibrational state was observed by molecular beam-Fourier transform microwave spectroscopy. Observed spectral lines for normal species as well as five ^{13}C-isotopomers were mainly assigned to the *b*-type rotational transitions. Some high-K_a lines were found to be split and we have interpreted these splittings in terms of the internal rotation of the methyl group. Some forbidden transitions were also observed for normal species in case where $K_a = 2$ levels were involved in the internal rotation with E state. The analysis of the observed spectra was carried out by using the XIAM program and thus determined potential barrier V_3 to CH_3 internal rotation was 5.1 kJ mol^{-1}. Since gas electron diffraction study for this molecule shows the large-amplitude motion of the t-Bu group, we are observing the further spectral splittings from the rotational spectra. We are also trying to observe the ^{18}O-isotopomers.

TA11 **8:44 – 8:45**

CHARACTERIZATION OF *SEC*-BUTOXYTRIMETHYLSILANE BY CHIRPED-PULSE FOURIER TRANSFORM MICROWAVE SPECTROSCOPY

FREYA E. L. BERGGÖTZ, HIMANSHI SINGH, MELANIE SCHNELL, *FS-SMP, Deutsches Elektronen-Synchrotron (DESY), Hamburg, Germany.*

Silicon chemistry is an extensive research topic due to its importance for industry and technology, and because of its natural abundance on earth. Silicon is a versatile element, its applications range from pure silicon to compounds. To understand the physical and chemical properties of silicon-containing molecules it is essential to characterize the gas-phase structures.

The rotational spectrum and structural analysis of *sec*-butoxytrimethylsilane (sBT-Si) will be presented. The spectrum of sBT-Si has been recorded using the Hamburg COMPACT spectrometer, which is a chirped-pulse Fourier transform microwave spectrometer, in the 2 – 8 GHz frequency range. Quantum-chemical calculations have been carried out to study the conformational flexibility of sBT-Si, and the measured rotational spectrum was examined for the lowest energy conformers. The spectrum is complicated due to the fact that three of the five methyl groups in sBT-Si have a rotational barrier lower than 7 kJ/mol, leading to internal rotation splitting. Despite this, the lowest energy conformer is prominent in the spectrum and has been successfully assigned. Weak signals of the conformer second lowest in energy have also been assigned. In this talk, the conformational flexibility and internal motion of this molecule will be discussed and compared to related molecules.

TB. Instrument/Technique Demonstration

Tuesday, June 22, 2021 – 8:0 AM

Room: 2021 Online Everywhere

Chair: Anna C. Wannenmacher, University of California, Davis, Davis, CA, USA

TB01 **8:00 – 8:01**

MIXING SYNCHROTRON RADIATION AND LASER SOURCES: DUAL-COMB SPECTROSCOPY IN THE SUBMILLIMETER-WAVE REGION

FRANCIS HINDLE, GAËL MOURET, *Laboratoire de Physico-Chimie de l'Atmosphère, Université du Littoral Côte d'Opale, Dunkerque, France*; THOMAS SANDOW HEARNE, OLIVIER PIRALI, MARIE-ALINE MARTIN-DRUMEL, *Institut des Sciences Moléculaires d'Orsay, Université Paris Saclay, CNRS, Orsay, France*; ZACHARY BUCHANAN, *Department of Chemistry, The University of California, Davis, CA, USA*; SOPHIE ELIET, *Institut d'Electronique de Microélectronique et de Nanotechnologie, Université de Lille 1, Villeneuve d'Ascq, France*; JEAN-FRANÇOIS LAMPIN, *UMR CNRS 8520, Institut d'Electronique de Microélectronique et de Nanotechnologie, Villeneuve d'Ascq, France.*

On the AILES beamline of the SOLEIL synchrotron, the HEROES consortium is currently developing new spectrometers based on heterodyne mixing of the THz synchrotron radiation with dedicated laser sources. We report here the first results on one of these spectrometers that aims at exploiting the discrete nature of coherent synchrotron radiation (CSR) in the 100–1000 GHz region, revealed a few years ago by our team[a], to perform dual-comb THz spectroscopy. CSR generated by the so called low-α mode of the SOLEIL machine produces a relatively intense, offset-free, high density frequency-comb in the THz range (THz-FC). We will present the details of our preliminary experimental set-up mixing the THz-FC from SOLEIL with an optical comb from Menlo C-fiber femtosecond laser. Pure rotation absorption transitions of acetonitrile in the frequency domain (covering the 100–500 GHz range) as well as time-domain free induction decays (FIDs) were observed allowing to establish the performances of this new instrument.

[a]Tammaro, S., Pirali, O., Roy, P., Lampin, J.F., Ducournau, G., Cuisset, A., Hindle, F., Mouret, G. "High density terahertz frequency comb produced by coherent synchrotron radiation" Nature Communications., 6: art. 7733. (2015)

TB02 **8:04 – 8:05**

HIGH-RESOLUTION MICROSECOND-TIME-RESOLVED DUAL-COMB SPECTROSCOPY OF TRANSIENT INTERMEDIATES

PEI-LING LUO, *Institute of Atomic and Molecular Sciences, Academia Sinica, Taipei, Taiwan.*

We demonstrated high-resolution microsecond-time-resolved dual-comb spectroscopy of an important short-lived molecule, the simplest Criegee intermediate (CH_2OO). A dual-comb spectrometer with central wavelength near 8 μm was built by means of single-pass difference frequency generation between a near-infrared dual-comb source and a continuous-wave Tm-doped laser in an OP-GaP crystal[a]. By coupling the 8-μm dual-comb source into a multipass cell, the time-dependent absorption signals of CH_2OO and its reaction product (formaldehyde) can be simultaneously obtained upon 248-nm photolysis of the flowing mixtures of CH_2I_2/O_2. Furthermore, the pressure broadened spectra of CH_2OO were measured by employing spectrally interleaved dual-comb spectroscopy to derive the collisional broadening coefficient.

[a]Ref: Opt. Lett., 45, 6791 (2020)

TB03 **8:08 – 8:09**

DIRECT FREQUENCY COMB CAVITY ENHANCED SPECTROSCOPY FOR TRACE GAS DETECTION USING MID-INFRARED INTERBAND CASCADE LASERS

CHARLES R. MARKUS, TZULING CHEN, DOUGLAS OBER, *Division of Chemistry and Chemical Engineering, California Institute of Technology, Pasadena, CA, USA*; LUKASZ A. STERCZEWSKI, MAHMOOD BAGHERI, *Instruments Division, Jet Propulsion Laboratory/Caltech, Pasadena, CA, USA*; MITCHIO OKUMURA, *Division of Chemistry and Chemical Engineering, California Institute of Technology, Pasadena, CA, USA.*

Optical frequency combs provide broadband coverage while still being able to take full advantage of cavity-enhanced methods. The mid-infrared is highly desirable for molecular spectroscopy, where many strong fundamental vibrational bands exist. Optical frequency comb development in this region has lagged behind that of the near-IR. Interband Cascade Lasers are monolithic devices which can provide mid-infrared frequency combs in the C-H stretching region (3 μm) with high power per comb tooth and large repetition rates ($\sim$9 GHz). Although they lack the octave-spanning coverage of fiber-based mode locked lasers, they can still provide sensitive multi-species detection. We have investigated different cavity enhanced schemes with these devices, including Vernier spectroscopy where we were able to resolve the individual comb teeth without the use of any diffraction optics. Here we discuss the development of these devices and their application towards cavity enhanced detection of trace molecules.

TB04 **8:12 – 8:13**

HIGH-RESOLUTION SPECTROSCOPY OF COLD SAMPLES IN SUPERSONIC BEAMS USING A QCL DUAL-COMB SPECTROMETER

JOSEF A. AGNER, *Laboratorium für Physikalische Chemie, ETH Zurich, Zurich, Switzerland*; PITT ALLMENDINGER, *IRsweep AG, IRsweep AG, Stäfa, Switzerland*; URS HOLLENSTEIN, *Laboratorium für Physikalische Chemie, ETH Zurich, Zurich, Switzerland*; ANDREAS HUGI, *IRsweep AG, IRsweep AG, Stäfa, Switzerland*; KAREN KEPPLER, *Laboratorium für Physikalische Chemie, ETH Zurich, Zurich, Switzerland*; MARKUS MANGOLD, *IRsweep AG, IRsweep AG, Stäfa, Switzerland*; FRÉDÉRIC MERKT, MARTIN QUACK, *Laboratorium für Physikalische Chemie, ETH Zurich, Zurich, Switzerland.*

Optical frequency comb spectroscopy has proven a very useful tool for high resolution molecular spectroscopy. Frequency combs based on quantum cascade lasers (QCL) offer the possibility to easily explore the mid-infrared spectral range (4-12 μm), but suffer from very large repetition frequencies ($\sim$ 10 GHz) which make them seemingly unsuitable for high resolution spectroscopy.

Here, we present techniques to overcome this limitation. We have employed the combined advantages of high temporal (< 4 μs) and high spectral resolution to measure the IR spectra of CF_4 and $CHCl_2F$ in pulsed, skimmed supersonic beams. The low rotational temperature of the beams and the narrow expansion cone after the skimmer enabled the recording of spectra of cold samples with high resolution. The spectra cover the range from 1200 to 1290 cm^{-1} and the narrowest lines have a full width at half maximum of 15 MHz, limited by the Doppler effect. The results demonstrate the potential of QCL dual-comb spectroscopy for broadband (> 60 cm^{-1}) acquisition of spectra at high resolution (< 15 MHz) and high sensitivity in the mid-infrared range. The power of the new technology is demonstrated by comparison with previous results on these molecules obtained by FTIR and diode laser spectroscopy of seeded cw and pulsed supersonic jets.[a]

a) M. Snels and M. Quack, J. Chem. Phys.1991,95,6355, M.Snels, V. Horka-Zelenkova, H. Hollenstein, M. Quack ,'High resolution FTIR and diode laser spectroscopy of supersonic jets', in Handbook of High-resolution Spectroscopy, Eds.; M. Quack and F.Merkt , Vol. 2, pp. 1022-1067, Wiley, Chichester, 2011; M. Caviezel, V. Horka, Z. Guennoun , G. Seyfang, M. Quack, unpublished manuscript (in preparation for Mol Phys.)

TB05 **8:16 – 8:17**

HIGH-RESOLUTION COMB-BASED FOURIER TRANSFORM SPECTROSCOPY IN THE 3.3 μm AND 7.8 μm RANGE

ADRIAN HJÄLTÉN, MATTHIAS GERMANN, CHUANG LU, FRANCISCO SENNA VIEIRA, ALEKSANDRA FOLTYNOWICZ, *Department of Physics, Umea University, Umea, Sweden*; IBRAHIM SADIEK, *INP, Leibniz Institute for Plasma Science and Technology, Greifswald, Germany*; MICHAEL STUHR, *Institute of Physical Chemisty, University of Kiel, Kiel, Germany*; KAROL KRZEMPEK, ARKADIUSZ HUDZIKOWSKI, ALEKSANDER GLUSZEK, DOROTA TOMASZEWSKA, GRZEGORZ SOBOŃ, *Faculty of Electronics, Wrocław University of Science and Technology, Wrocław, Poland.*

We use Fourier transform spectrometers based on mid-infrared frequency combs to measure and analyze broadband spectra of molecules of environmental importance in the two water windows around 3.3 μm and 7.8 μm. Both comb sources are based on difference frequency generation (DFG) using signal and pump waves derived from a single femtosecond laser, and are therefore inherently carrier-envelope-offset-free, which simplifies their frequency stabilization [1,2]. We use the sub-nominal sampling-interleaving method to measure spectra with resolution limited by the comb-mode linewidth [3,4]. At 3.3 μm, we measured high-resolution spectra of multiple absorption bands of two halogenated volatile organic compounds, methyl iodide, CH_3I [5], and dibromomethane, CH_2Br_2. We assigned the ν_4 band of CH_3I with improved accuracy compared to previous work based on FTIR measurements [6]. At 7.8 μm, we measured the spectrum of the ν_1 band of $^{14}N_2{}^{16}O$ and retrieved line center frequencies with precision of the order of 100 kHz [7], in excellent agreement with previous high-accuracy measurement using a comb-referenced continuous wave quantum cascade laser [8].

[1] G. Sobon et al., Opt. Lett. 42, 1748 (2017). [2] K. Krzempek et al., Opt. Express 27, 37435 (2019). [3] P. Maslowski et al., Phys. Rev. A 93, 021802(R) (2016). [4] L. Rutkowski et al., J. Quant. Spectrosc. Radiat. Transf. 204, 63 (2018). [5] I. Sadiek et al., J. Quant. Spectrosc. Radiat. Transf. 255, 107263, 107263 (2020). [6] R. Anttila et al., J. Mol. Spectrosc. 119, 190 (1986). [7] A. Hjältén et al., in preparation. [8] B. AlSaif, et al., J. Quant. Spectrosc. Radiat. Transf. 211, 172 (2018).

TB06 **8:20 – 8:21**

HIGH-PRECISION MID-INFRARED SPECTROSCOPY WITH A WIDELY TUNEABLE SI-TRACEABLE FREQUENCY-COMB-STABILISED QCL

NICOLAS CAHUZAC, MATHIEU MANCEAU, DANG BAO AN TRAN, ROSA SANTAGATA, ETIENNE CANTIN, OLIVIER LOPEZ, *Laboratoire de Physique des Lasers, CNRS, Université Sorbonne Paris Nord, Villetaneuse, France*; DAN XU, MICHEL ABGRALL, YANN LE COQ, PAUL-ERIC POTTIE, RODOLPHE LE TARGAT, *LNE-SYRTE, Observatoire de Paris, PSL Research University, CNRS, Sorbonne Universités, UPMC Univ. Paris 06, Paris, France*; ANNE AMY-KLEIN, BENOIT DARQUIE, *Laboratoire de Physique des Lasers, CNRS, Université Sorbonne Paris Nord, Villetaneuse, France.*

There is an increasing demand for precise molecular spectroscopy, in particular in the mid-IR fingerprint window, whether it be for modelling our atmosphere, interpreting astrophysical spectra or testing fundamental physics.

Here, we present a new technology for ultra-high-resolution vibrational spectroscopy using quantum cascade lasers (QCLs) traceable to primary standards [a]. Using an optical frequency comb, a 10 μm QCL is stabilized at the sub-Hz level to an ultra-stable near infrared reference signal operated at the French metrology institute. This signal is calibrated there to some of the best atomic clocks and transferred through a noise-compensated 43-km long fiber cable. This results in a record 0.1 Hz QCL linewidth. We have also developed a method to continuously scan the stabilized QCL over 1.5 GHz at the precision of the frequency reference.

We have used the apparatus to carry out saturated absorption spectroscopy in a compact multipass cell. We have measured absolute frequencies (as well as frequency shifts and pressure broadening) of osmium tetroxyde, methanol, ammonia and trioxane, with record uncertainties, from 10 Hz to 10 kHz (depending on the species and the details of the apparatus). We were able to resolve yet unreported subtle structures in methanol (doublets and triplets induced by the combined effects of tunnelling and asymmetry).

We have recently added to our spectrometer a 3 meter-long Fabry-Perot resonator to perform cavity enhanced measurements in order to improve our resolution and extend saturated absorption spectroscopy to more complex molecules. First results will be presented.

---

[a] Santagata, R., et al., Optica 6, no. 4 (2019): 411-423.

TB07 **8:24 – 8:25**

TOWARDS REAL-TIME PROCESSING OF DUAL-COMB SPECTROSCOPY DATA WITH QUANTUM CASCADE LASERS

MICHELE GIANELLA, SIMON VOGEL, BÉLA TUZSON, AKSHAY NATARAJ, *Laboratory for Air Pollution / Environmental Technology, Empa, Dubendorf, Switzerland*; KENICHI KOMAGATA, STÉPHANE SCHILT, THOMAS SÜDMEYER, *Laboratoire Temps-Fréquence, Université de Neuchâtel, Neuchâtel, Switzerland*; ANDREAS HUGI, MARKUS MANGOLD, PIERRE JOUY, *IRsweep AG, IRsweep AG, Stäfa, Switzerland*; FILIPPOS KAPSALIDIS, JOHANNES HILLBRAND, MATTIAS BECK, JÉRÔME FAIST, *Institute for Quantum Electronics, ETH Zurich, Zurich, Switzerland*; LUKAS EMMENEGGER, *Laboratory for Air Pollution / Environmental Technology, Empa, Dubendorf, Switzerland.*

Dual-comb spectroscopy (DCS) with quantum cascade lasers (QCL) offers direct access to the mid-infrared region and, thus, to the strong and characteristic ro-vibrational absorption bands of many molecules of interest. In DCS, two frequency comb lasers with unequal repetition frequency produce an array of beat notes which carry the information about magnitude and phase of the optical frequency components that generate them. A large beat note spacing is a requisite if the two sources are free-running, since the beat notes will exhibit a width determined by the (uncorrelated) phase noise of the two lasers. This results in a relatively large acquisition bandwidth, and thus requires a correspondingly large sampling rate. Furthermore, since co-averaging of interferograms in free-running systems is not possible, data processing is computationally intensive, leading to a low duty cycle (time spent acquiring data versus total time) around 1%.

We have developed data processing routines that extract all the relevant spectroscopic information from the measured interferograms in less than the duration of the interferogram itself, paving the way for continuous acquisition with on-the-fly processing (100% duty cycle). The algorithm can equally handle static measurements, where all the comb line frequencies are constant over time, *step sweep* measurements, where the frequencies of the combs are shifted step-wise, and *rapid sweep* measurements, where the frequencies of the combs are shifted in a continuous and periodic fashion. In the last two approaches, the various offset spectra are interleaved to produce a composite spectrum with smaller point spacing. This algorithm represents an important advance towards high-sensitivity, high-resolution DCS measurements with QCLs, especially when combined with continuous scans and spectral interleaving, which produce large amounts of raw data.

TB08 **8:28 – 8:29**

TWO-COLOR, INTRACAVITY PUMP-PROBE, CAVITY RINGDOWN SPECTROSCOPY

JUN JIANG, A. DANIEL McCARTT, *Center for Accelerator Mass Spectrometry, Lawrence Livermore National Laboratory, Livermore, CA, USA.*

We report a proof-of-principle demonstration of intracavity pump-probe, cavity ringdown (CRD) detection in a three-mirror, traveling-wave cavity. With both cavity-enhanced pump $power$ and probe absorption $pathlength$, the technique is a generalized, high-sensitivity, high-selectivity trace detection method. In our experiments, the pump radiation is switched off during every other probe ringdown, which allows uncorrelated measurements of analyte and background cavity decay rates. The net, two-color signal from the difference between the pump-on and pump-off decay rates is immune to empty cavity ringdown fluctuations and spectral overlaps from non-target molecular transitions. The immunity to the ringdown fluctuations allows longer signal averaging, and thus higher detection sensitivity. The ability to compensate for the unwanted, background molecular absorption greatly enhances the detection selectivity in spectrally congested regions. While its application is not limited to a specific spectral range, the technique is well-suited for trace detection in the mid-IR region, where pump-probe schemes based on strong ro-vibrational transitions can be applied. In this work, our two-color CRD detection is implemented on a ladder-type, three-level system based on the N_2O, $\nu_3 = 1 \leftarrow 0$, P(19) (pump) and $\nu_3 = 2 \leftarrow 1$, R(18) (probe) ro-vibrational transitions. By frequency-locking two quantum cascade lasers to the p-polarization (pump, Finesse = 5280) and s-polarization (probe, Finesse = 67700) modes of the ring-cavity, we achieve high intracavity pump power (36 W) and high probe ringdown rates (>2 kHz). The observed two-color CRD spectra are simulated based on a density-matrix, three-level-system model which is solved under the constraints of the cavity resonance conditions. In addition to its background compensation capability, experimental flexibilities in the selection of pump-probe schemes and signal insensitivity to intracavity laser power are further features which enhance the general utility of our technique for mid-IR trace detection.

TB09 **8:32 – 8:33**

MEASURING ROTATIONAL SPECTRA IN EXCITED VIBRATIONAL MODES: A NEW TECHNIQUE BASED ON A QUANTUM CASCADE LASER-PUMPED MOLECULAR LASER

PAUL CHEVALIER, ARMAN AMIRZHAN, MARCO PICCARDO, FEDERICO CAPASSO, *Harvard John A Paulson School of Engineering and Applied Sciences, Harvard University, Cambridge, MA, USA*; HENRY O. EVERITT, , *Army Aviation and Missile RD&E, Redstone Arsenal, AL, USA*.

Measuring the rotational spectra of a molecule in excited vibrational modes can be challenging due to the low thermal population of these rotational levels and the weakness of the underlying absorption lines. We recently demonstrated a quantum cascade laser (QCL)-pumped molecular laser (QPML) concept in which virtually any rotational transition of any excited vibrational mode of virtually any molecule with a permanent dipole moment and a vapor pressure can be made to lase by pumping its corresponding ro-vibrational transition with a frequency-tunable QCL. Here, we show how the frequency of those QCL-pumped rotational transitions in excited vibrational modes may be measured with accuracy comparable to transitions in ground vibrational levels using high precision modulation spectroscopy techniques. We applied this concept to nitrous oxide (N_2O), and measured the individual frequencies of 20 lines in the v3 vibrational mode (2225 $\mathrm{cm}^{-1} \approx$ 10 kT) by means of heterodyne spectroscopy with an experimental uncertainty of 200 kHz when lasing and without modulation, improving to 50 kHz with QCL-enhanced absorption or amplification with modulation. We report the measured spectra and the fitted rotational constants B_3 and DJ_3 corresponding to this vibrational mode.

TB10 **8:36 – 8:37**

DEVELOPMENT OF A CBGB SOURCE AND A QCL LASER SYSTEM FOR STUDYING THE IR SPECTROSCOPY OF CLUSTERS

GREGORY T. PULLEN, *JILA, The University of Colorado, Boulder, CO, USA*; GARY E. DOUBERLY, *Department of Chemistry, University of Georgia, Athens, GA, USA*; HEATHER LEWANDOWSKI, *JILA and Department of Physics, University of Colorado, Boulder, CO, USA*.

We report progress on the construction and development of a cryogenic buffer gas beam (CBGB) instrument for studying the IR spectroscopy of atomic and molecular clusters. Clusters are produced via laser ablation of a solid target inside the CBGB cell, and the nascent clusters are quickly cooled to the buffer gas temperature before exiting the CBGB cell. Upon exiting the cell, the clusters are probed with $\sim$5 μm tunable light from a quantum cascade laser (QCL). Light from signal and reference beams each hit detectors, and the difference signal is collected using an autobalanced subtractor circuit to achieve shot-noise limited measurements. Recent developments in the construction of the instrument and spectra measured will be presented.

TB11 **8:40 – 8:41**

HIGH-TEMPERATURE HYPERSONIC LAVAL NOZZLE FOR NON-LTE CAVITY RINGDOWN SPECTROSCOPY

ESZTER DUDÁS, *Département "Physique Moléculaire", Univ Rennes, CNRS, IPR (Institut de Physique de Rennes) - UMR 6251, Rennes, France*; ROBERT GEORGES, ABDESSAMAD BENIDAR, *IPR UMR6251, CNRS - Université Rennes 1, Rennes, France*; SHUVAYAN BRAHMACHARY, VINAYAK KULKARNI, *Department of Mechanical Engineering, Indian Institute of Technology Guwahati, Guwahati, India*; SAMIR KASSI, *UMR5588 LIPhy, Université Grenoble Alpes/CNRS, Saint Martin d'Hères, France*; CHRISTINE CHARLES, *Research School of Physics, Australian National University, Canberra, ACT, Australia*; NICOLAS SUAS-DAVID, *Department of Chemistry, University of Missouri, Columbia, MO, USA.*

The SMAUG apparatus (Spectroscopy of Molecules Accelerated in Uniform Gas flows) was developed to produce hot spectra of various molecules of interest for hot astrophysical atmospheres, like the one surrounding hot Jupiters, reaching up to 2500 K. High-temperature IR spectroscopic data is needed to retrieve temperature and concentration profiles from astronomical spectra. A small dimension Laval nozzle connected to a compact high enthalpy source equipped with cavity ringdown spectroscopy (CRDS) is used to produce high-resolution infrared spectra of polyatomic molecules in the 1.67 μm region.[a]. The experimental setup can operate according to two complementary working regimes: non-local thermodynamic equilibrium (non-LTE) (vibrationally hot and rotationally cold) and LTE conditions, to interpret the complex pattern of highly-excited vibrational states. Two different gases, carbon monoxide (CO) and methane (CH_4) were used as test molecules. Using non-LTE conditions vibrational (T_{vib}) and rotational (T_{rot}) temperatures were extracted from the recorded infrared spectrum leading to T_{vib} = 1346(52) K and T_{rot} = 12(1) K for CO. A rotational temperature of 39(3) K was measured for CH4, while two vibrational temperatures were necessary to reproduce the observed intensities. The population distribution between vibrational polyads was correctly described with $T_{vib,I}$ = 825(50) K" , while the population distribution within a given polyad was modelled correctly by $T_{vib,II}$ = 39(5) K" , testifying to a more rapid vibrational relaxation between the vibrational energy levels constituting a polyad. Using a "post-shock CRDS" technique CO and CH_4 LTE spectra were recorded at 950 K and 1400 K.

[a]*E.Dudás* et al. *High-temperature hypersonic Laval nozzle for non-LTE cavity ringdown spectroscopy.* *J Chem Phys 2020;152:134201. https://doi.org/10.1063/5.0003886.*

TB12 **8:44 – 8:45**

INTRACAVITY LASER SPECTROSCOPY INTEGRATED WITH FOURIER TRANSFORM DETECTION

JACK C HARMS, JAMES J O'BRIEN, *Chemistry and Biochemistry, University of Missouri, St. Louis, MO, USA*; LEAH C O'BRIEN, *Department of Chemistry, Southern Illinois University, Edwardsville, IL, USA.*

Cavity enhancement of molecular absorption through laser action has made intracavity laser spectroscopy (ILS) a powerful tool for the detection of trace species and weakly absorbing molecules. The effective pathlength for ILS measurements is proportional to the speed of light, leading to a high degree of sensitivity for spectroscopic measurements, and effective pathlengths of up to 70,000 km have been demonstrated with this technique. Fourier-transform spectroscopy (FTS) is a powerful technique for detection of spectroscopic signals, benefitting both from Fellgett's advantage and inherent calibration derived from the interference zero crossings of a single frequency light source. The traditional dispersive ILS system at the University of Missouri – St. Louis has been integrated with a Bruker IFS-125M FTS spectrometer. The two time-based techniques are synchronized using a National Instruments field-programmable gate array (FPGA). The maximum instrumental resolution for the combined technique is improved by nearly an order of magnitude, from 0.02 cm^{-1}resolution for 2 m monochromator with 9th order diffraction to 0.0035 $\mathrm{cm}^{-1}$with the Bruker FTS. Similarly, the detection bandwidth (7 cm^{-1}per dispersed ILS spectrum) also has improved by an order of magnitude, enabling the collection of the entire broadband laser profile (50-100 cm^{-1}) in a single measurement. In addition, a 3-fold improvement in absolute wavenumber accuracy is achieved due to the internal calibration of the FTS detection. The improved resolving power of the integrated spectroscopic system enables Doppler-width limited detection of $5d$-metal diatomic molecules. These species are of fundamental interest for the quantitation of the relativistic effects that dominate their electronic energy structure, and newly observed transitions of platinum sulfide and tungsten sulfide have already been recorded and analyzed. Details of the instrumentation, integration method, and improved capabilities will be presented.

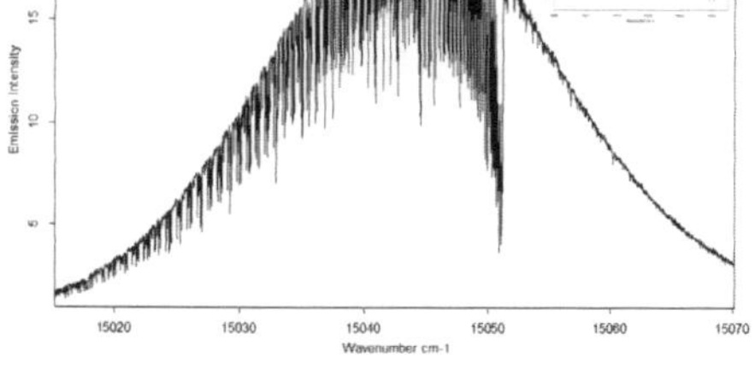

TB13 **8:48 – 8:49**

CHARACTERISATION OF A 17 μm QUANTUM CASCADE LASER AND SPECTROSCOPY OF THE ν_2 FUNDAMENTAL MODE OF N_2O

MATHIEU MANCEAU, *Laboratoire de Physique des Lasers, CNRS, Université Sorbonne Paris Nord, Villetaneuse, France*; THOMAS WALL, *Centre for Cold Matter, Imperial College London, London, United Kingdom*; HADRIEN PHILIPPE, *IES , University of Montpellier, CNRS, Montpellier , FRANCE*; ALEXEI BARANOV, *IES , University of Montpellier, CNRS , Montpellier , FRANCE*; MICHAEL TARBUTT, *Centre for Cold Matter, Blackett Laboratory, Imperial College London, London, United Kingdom*; ROLAND TEISSIER, *IES , University of Montpellier, CNRS, Montpellier , FRANCE*; BENOIT DARQUIE, *Laboratoire de Physique des Lasers, CNRS, Université Sorbonne Paris Nord, Villetaneuse, France.*

Owing to their narrow linewidth and broad tunability, continuous wave (CW) quantum cascade lasers (QCLs) have become ubiquitous for mid-infrared rovibrational molecular spectroscopy. However, while the 4-11 μm region is fairly well covered by available room-temperature QCLs, the extension to longer wavelengths is a challenge of great interest for molecular spectroscopy.

Here we present spectroscopy measurements using a newly fabricated room temperature CW QCL working at 17 μm, a new spectral region for QCLs [a], and delivering a few mWs of output power. We will describe our characterization of this laser, including measurements of its spectral range, frequency noise and linewidth. To do this, we park the laser on the side of a strong N_2O absorption line which we use as a frequency-to-intensity converter. The frequency noise spectrum of the source is deduced from the measured intensity fluctuations.

We have also demonstrated the QCL's capabilities by performing linear rovibrational absorption spectroscopy of the ν_2 fundamental mode of N_2O in a single-pass cell, covering the 580 to 582.5 cm^{-1} spectral region. Doppler-limited and pressure-broadened lines are measured with various N_2O pressures in the range from 1 to 500 Pa leading to a precise investigation of pressure broadening in this mode. We will finally discuss the potential of this source for precise measurements in ultra-cold diatomic species and for probing low energy vibrations in polyatomic molecules.

[a] H. Nguyen Van, et al., "Long Wavelength ($\lambda > 17$ μm) Distributed Feedback Quantum Cascade Lasers Operating in a Continuous Wave at Room Temperature", Photonics 6, 1, pp. 31 (2019).

TC. Dynamics and kinetics

Tuesday, June 22, 2021 – 8:0 AM

Room: 2021 Online Everywhere

Chair: Elsa Yan, Yale University, New Haven, CT, USA

TC01 *Coblentz Society Award Lecture* **8:00 – 8:02**

NONCOVALENT INTERACTIONS OF HYDRATED DNA AND RNA MAPPED BY 2D-IR SPECTROSCOPY

BENJAMIN P FINGERHUT, *Theory Department, Max Born Institute, Berlin, Germany.*

Biomolecules couple to their aqueous environment through a variety of noncovalent interactions. Local hydration structures at the surface of DNA and RNA are frequently determined by directed hydrogen bonds with water molecules, complemented by non-specific electrostatic and many-body interactions. I will present recent results from 2D-IR spectroscopy of sugar-phosphate backbone vibrations of native and artificial DNA and RNA, together with theoretical calculations of molecular couplings and molecular dynamics simulations. The results reveal the femtosecond fluctuation dynamics of the water shell, a short-range character of Coulomb interactions, and the strength and fluctuation amplitudes of interfacial electric fields [1,2]. Recent applications of phosphate vibrations [3,4,5] as probes for local hydration patterns and contact ion pair configurations hold strong potential for quantifying folding-induced changes of the ion distribution around DNA and RNA on a multitude of time scales.

References:

1. T. Siebert, B. Guchhait, Y. Liu, B. P. Fingerhut, T. Elsaesser, J. Phys. Chem. Lett. 7, 3131 (2016).
2. E. M. Bruening, J. Schauss, T. Siebert, B. P. Fingerhut, T. Elsaesser, J. Phys. Chem. Lett. 9, 583 (2018).
3. J. Schauss, F. Dahms, B. P. Fingerhut, T. Elsaesser, J. Phys. Chem. Lett. 10, 238 (2019).
4. A. Kundu, J. Schauss, B. P. Fingerhut, T. Elsaesser, J. Phys. Chem. B, 124, 2132 (2020).
5. J. Schauss, A. Kundu, B. P. Fingerhut, T. Elsaesser, J. Phys. Chem. B, 125, 740 (2021).

TC02 **8:08 – 8:09**

UREA-WATER DYNAMICS IN PROTEINS: AN ULTRAFAST SPECTROSCOPIC STUDY

SNEHA BANERJEE, RAPTI GOSWAMI, PANKAJ MANDAL, *Department of Chemistry, Indian Institute of Science Education and Research, Pune, Maharshtra, India.*

Water plays a vital role in many biological processes like enzyme activity, protein folding-refolding and denaturation. Interfacial water has a significant effect on the protein's internal structure and dynamics. It is essential to know the time scales characteristic of both, the local protein rearrangements and water dynamics within the solvation shell to understand the protein-water interactions. Urea is a chaotropic agent and a well-known denaturant for proteins. The molecular picture of the interaction of urea with the water hydrogen bond network and thereby, the chemical denaturation of the proteins is still ambiguous. Time-resolved Optical Kerr effect (OKE) spectroscopy is a powerful spectroscopic technique to study the hydrogen-bonded structure and dynamics of complex aqueous systems, in the picosecond time scales. In this study, we have investigated the mechanism behind urea denaturation of three proteins of different hydrophobicities- lysozyme, BSA and trypsin. The OKE data reveals the effect that different concentrations of urea have on the aqueous protein solutions. The temporal profiles of the aqueous protein solutions are almost indistinguishable from that of pure water. Resolving the data in the frequency domain and subtracting the solvent contribution gives us a better picture of the water and water-urea interactions with the protein. The spectral density (SD) obtained contains the α relaxation at the lowest frequencies corresponding to the orientational diffusion of the molecules, linked by the stretched β relaxation to the intermolecular librational modes at terahertz frequencies. The shape of the SDs resembles that of urea solutions; the addition of protein brings down the contribution from the α relaxation. At lower urea concentrations, this change is even more apparent. The OKE spectra of urea have a huge α contribution compared to that of water which masks the faster β dynamics. Removing the diffusive contributions in the time domain itself leaves us with the Reduced Spectral Densities (RSD). Preliminary analysis of the RSDs shows the β relaxation timescales of water changes on the addition of urea and the subtracted spectra for the urea denatured lysozyme shows two distinct β processes characteristic of water and water-urea dynamics. A detailed analysis of the changes in the line shapes of the RSDs is required to elucidate the effect urea has on the water hydrogen bond network and to map out the structural changes occurring in three different proteins on the addition of urea.

TC03 **8:12 – 8:13**

STRUCTURAL FLUCTUATIONS IN AN AZEOTROPE: UNDERSTANDING THE BENZENE-METHANOL AZEOTROPE

SNEHA BANERJEE, SOHINI SARKAR, PANKAJ MANDAL, *Department of Chemistry, Indian Institute of Science Education and Research, Pune, Maharshtra, India.*

The structure and dynamics of molecular liquids and their binary mixtures have been of interest for a long time. Azeotropes is a particular class of liquid mixture that boils at a constant temperature at a specific composition. Understanding of azeotropic systems at the molecular level is limited. In this study, we try to investigate this azeotropic non-ideality, using ultrafast Optical Kerr Effect (OKE) spectroscopy, broadband (1-10 THz) THz-Time domain spectroscopy (THz-TDS) along with temperature-dependent Nuclear Magnetic Resonance spectroscopy (NMR) of the azeotropic as well as mixtures of different compositions of benzene and methanol.

Vibrational and NMR spectroscopic studies show that the formation of the methanol-benzene azeotrope weakens the hydrogen bond network. Intermolecular forces between the benzene molecules are also reduced significantly. Methanol disrupts the stacking in benzene which is also evident from the depression in the boiling points. Ultrafast OKE spectroscopy is a powerful tool to probe both, the collective orientational diffusion and the intermolecular dynamics in liquids. The spectral density (SD) obtained by the Fourier deconvolution of the OKE time transients gives us information about the structural relaxation occurring in the liquid at the terahertz and sub terahertz frequencies. With the increase of methanol in the mixtures, the α relaxation timescales become faster. An azeotropic composition mixture was prepared at room temperature without further distillation. The spectral densities of this mixture and the azeotrope at frequencies pertaining to collective intermolecular dynamics were quite different from each other. All of benzene's entire rotational dynamics show up as molecular reorientation having contributions throughout the OKE spectra. The centre-of-mass translational part is only visible when it affects the interaction induced (I-I) part of the polarizability[a]. The addition of methanol decreases this contribution of the translations to the I-I term for benzene. A detailed analysis of the similarity of the azeotrope spectral density to benzene and how they differ from the other composition mixtures can give us useful insights into the structural fluctuations happening in the picosecond timescales in the benzene-methanol mixtures.

[a]Ryu, S.; Stratt, R. M. J. Phys. Chem. B 2004, 108, 6782.

TC04 **8:16 – 8:17**

ACOUSTIC STUDIES OF RELAXATION PROCESSES DUE TO CONFORMATIONAL TRANSITIONS OF FURFURAL MOLECULES

FARKHAD AKHMEDZHANOV, SIROJIDDIN ZAINIEVICH MIRZAEV, KAMOLIDDIN EGAMBERDIEV, *Department of thermophysics of Multiphase Systems, Institute of Ion-Plasma and Laser Technologies, Tashkent, Uzbekistan.*

The acoustic spectra of furfural were studied in the frequency range from 0.1 MHz to 150 MHz and at temperatures 303 - 333 K by the coaxial resonator method using two different cells to cover the whole frequency range. The temperature in the cells was controlled with an accuracy of 0.05 degrees. The accuracy of the determination of the attenuation of acoustic waves in liquid furfural was approximately 5%. The studies were shown that the obtained experimental data can be explained with help of two relaxation processes. One relaxation process is observed in the low-frequency range of frequencies (0.2 MHz), and the second relaxation process is observed in the frequency range of about 2 MHz. The process with a lower relaxation frequency can be associated with the internal rotation of the furfural molecules "X0-cis" and "X0-trans". The kinetic analysis of acoustic data about conformation processes for a low-frequency relaxation process in pure furfural was carried out by using Eyring relations. The relaxation parameters and the velocity of acoustic waves, as well as the contribution of the different factors to the attenuation of acoustic waves have been determined from experimental results.

TC05 **8:20 – 8:21**

DYNAMICS OF COPPER PHTHALOCYANINE MOLECULES INSIDE AN OPTICAL CAVITY REVEALED BY TWO-DIMENSIONAL ELECTRONIC SPECTROSCOPY (2DES)

TUPHAN DEVKOTA, KENNETH L. KNAPPENBERGER, JR., *Department of Chemistry, Pennsylvania State University, University Park, PA, USA.*

Polaritons are hybrid light-matter states that can be created by placing a molecule inside an optical cavity due to strong coupling between confined electromagnetic modes and optical transitions of the molecule, and can have different energies, coherence, and vibrational characteristics than the bare molecules outside of the cavity. The strong coupling results in new physicochemical properties of the hybrid system including their reactivity or charge and energy transfer characteristics and has recently gained significant research interest. We have used two-dimensional electronic spectroscopy (2DES) to study the dynamics of the copper phthalocyanine (CuPc) molecules placed inside an optical cavity. The 2DES is a powerful tool to investigate excited state dynamics that enables a direct correlation between excitation and detection energies of the system with ultrafast time resolution. We compare the dynamics of the CuPc molecules that are inside an optical cavity with that of the bare molecules outside the cavity under similar experimental conditions to understand how the optical cavity modifies the excited state dynamics of the molecules. The coupling between light and the optical transition of the material inside cavity can be controlled by changing the incident angle of the light. We demonstrate this by repeating 2DES experiments on a cavity sample at normal and 75 degree incidence of the pump pulse. The results show that the presence of an optical cavity can significantly modify the excited state dynamics of the molecules and enhance the coherence.

TC06 **8:24 – 8:25**

ULTRAFAST PUMP-PROBE PHOTODISSOCIATION DYNAMICS OF CO_2 FOR THE PRODUCTION OF MOLECULAR OXYGEN

JACOB M GARCIA, *School of Molecular Sciences and Biodesign Center for Applied Structural Discovery, Arizona State University, Tempe, AZ, USA*; SCOTT G SAYRES, *School of Molecular Sciences, Arizona State University, Tempe, AZ, USA.*

Molecules excited by strong-field laser pulses evolve through coupled nuclear and electronic motion over ultrafast timescales. Even simple molecules demonstrate a variety of characteristic dynamics, including vibrations, fragmentation, and ionization. The final products and their relative yields depend sensitively on details of these coupled processes that occur within the first few femtoseconds of interacting with the laser beam. Here, ultrafast pump-probe spectroscopy is applied to study the fragmentation and ionization dynamics of several molecules. Photodissociation of CO_2 proceeds via multiple pathways depending on available energy, but commonly into CO and O. Multiphoton excitation from a 35 fs pump laser impulsively transfers CO_2 from the ground to 1st excited state, preparing a bending vibrational wavepacket that influences its dissociation. Using mass spectrometry, we report changes in the fragmentation pattern as a function of time delay between the pump and probe laser pulses that reflect the vibrational motion. At well-defined time delays the dissociation oscillates between observable CO^+ and O_2^+ fragments. The state relaxes to the ground state through a conical intersection. Similar control over the fragmentation pathway and ion yields will be demonstrated for the excited state motions of ethanol and formic acid.

TC07 **8:28 – 8:29**

USING COMPUTATIONAL CHEMISTRY TO DESIGN A PUMP-PROBE SCHEME FOR MEASURING NITROBENZENE RADICAL CATION DYNAMICS

HUGO A. LÓPEZ PEÑA, DERRICK AMPADU BOATENG, SHANE L. McPHERSON, KATHARINE MOORE TIBBETTS, *Department of Chemistry, Virginia Commonwealth University, Richmond, Virginia, USA.*

Nitrobenzene is often used as a model molecule for the study of the dissociation dynamics of nitroaromatic energetic materials. The potential energy surfaces for the ground cationic state D_0 and the first ten excited states D_1 through D_{10} were calculated as a function of the C–NO_2 torsional angle using time-dependent density functional theory. These surfaces were employed in the prediction of the most efficient probe wavelength for femtosecond time-resolved mass spectrometry measurements. It was found that the $D_0 \rightarrow D_4$ transition in nitrobenzene cation has a geometry-dependent oscillator strength, reaching a maximum at 90° C–NO_2 torsional angle, with a corresponding energy gap of $\sim$2 eV. These results are consistent with the experimental observation of a vibrational wave packet along the C–NO_2 torsional mode in nitrobenzene cation. Time-resolved measurements using a probe wavelength of 650 nm, nearly resonant with the strong $D_0 \rightarrow D_4$ transition, result in enhanced ion yield oscillation amplitudes as compared to excitation with the nonresonant 800 nm wavelength. These results demonstrate that computational chemistry can predict the best choice of probe wavelength in time-resolved measurements of vibrational coherent states in molecular cations.

TC08 **8:32 – 8:33**

ULTRAFAST COULOMB EXPLOSION OF FORMIC ACID CLUSTERS AND PRODUCTION OF TRIPLY CHARGED CARBON MONOXIDE

SHAUN SUTTON, *School of Molecular Sciences and Biodesign Center for Applied Structural Discovery, Arizona State University, Tempe, AZ, USA*; SCOTT G SAYRES, TARAKESHWAR PILARISETTY, DANE MILLER, *School of Molecular Sciences, Arizona State University, Tempe, AZ, USA.*

Multiply charged diatomic molecules are exotic gas-phase species and require high amounts of energy to be produced. Fundamental questions regarding the structures, stabilities, and bonding schemes of small multiply charged ions tests our concepts of bonding. Although uncommon in most chemical settings, the conditions found within the Earth's ionosphere enable such species to be constantly produced, albeit for short periods of time, through the interaction between small atmospheric molecules and cosmic radiation in the extreme ultraviolet regime. We have performed laboratory experiments using intense laser pulses to investigate the stability and production of multiply charged ions from small atmospherically relevant molecules. I will present our recent work where femtosecond laser pulses are utilized to drive multiple ionization in molecular gas-phase formic acid dimers and studied using time-of-flight mass spectrometry. The interaction of formic acid dimer with 200 fs linearly polarized laser pulses of 400 nm with intensities up to $3.7\text{x}10^{15}$ W/cm^2 produces a carbon monoxide dication and trication. An enhanced ionization is observed in CO ions when the source analyte was switched from the molecular beam to formic acid clusters. Measurements of the kinetic energy release resulting from the Coulomb explosion of clusters are in excellent agreement with our simulations performed over the clusters observed in the mass spectra and suggest that almost no movement occurs during the ionization mechanism. Lastly, potential energy curves for CO^{n+}, for $n < 4$, have been calculated using high level theory, confirming the existence of a metastable state with a large potential barrier with respect to dissociation of several eV.

TC09 **8:36 – 8:37**

SITE-SPECIFIC CHARACTERIZATION OF P450CAM SUBSTRATE RECOGNITION *VIA* 2D IR SPECTROSCOPY

SASHARY RAMOS, CLAIRE C MAMMOSER, MEGAN THIELGES, *Department of Chemistry, Indiana University, Bloomington, IN, USA.*

Determining the mechanism by which Cytochrome P450s (P450s) can catalyze oxidation reactions of substrates with differing specificity and regioselectivity is crucial for aiding drug development and understanding drug metabolism. Cytochrome P450cam (P450cam), a model P450, catalyzes the hydroxylation of *d*-camphor to 5-exo-hydroxycamphor with high specificity and regioselectivity. P450cam can also act upon camphor-like analogs at the expense of regioselectivity. To investigate the contribution of conformational dynamics to varying regioselectivity of hydroxylation, we characterized specific locations throughout P450cam when the enzyme was in complex with camphor or norcamphor, substrates acted upon with 100% and 45% regioselectivity respectively. Linear and two-dimensional IR spectroscopy were applied to measure P450cam side-chain dynamics with high spatial and temporal resolution. Cyanophenylalanine was used as a vibrational probe and incorporated in five distinct locations of P450cam, three sites in the active site and two progressively distal from the active site. The results suggest norcamphor binding does not induce the same large-scale conformational change associated with the closed enzyme state found for the camphor-bound complex. Additionally, probes located in the active site of the enzyme report distinct, localized changes that, in some cases, can be directly correlated to hydroxylation product distribution. Overall, this study illustrates the utility of site-selective infrared spectroscopy to address questions of functional protein dynamics.

TC10 **8:40 – 8:41**

THE RISE OF THE EXCITON IN SOLID AMMONIA

ANDREW CASSIDY, *Department of Physics and Astronomy, University of Aarhus, Aarhus, Denmark*; RACHEL JAMES, ANITA DAWES, *Department of Physical Sciences, The Open University, Milton Keynes, United Kingdom*; DAVID FIELD, *Department of Physics and Astronomy, University of Aarhus, Aarhus, Denmark.*

We study the dynamics of a system searching for minutes to hours to establish a population of nuclei, which can then go on to create a phase change, following the rise of an exciton in thin films of solid ammonia with deposition temperatures T_d = 48 K, 50 K and 52 K. This behaviour is tracked by following the growth of the exciton, using vacuum ultraviolet absorption spectra of ices at 194.4 nm in the $\tilde{A}^1A_2$" ← $\tilde{X}^1$A' band. Absorbance is observed to increase through an order of magnitude between Td = 48K to 52K, through greater flexing of the solid state structure, as the size of crystallites expands from an average of 10± 2 unit cells at 48K to 34± 8 at 52K. Time delays, associated with nucleation, are encountered before the appearance of exciton absorption, varying between 7870 seconds at 48K to 120 seconds at 52K, with rates of subsequent exciton absorbance growth between 1.49 x 10^{-6} s^{-1} and 1.19 x 10^{-4} s^{-1}. Activation energies of 21.7± 0.2 kJ mol^{-1} for the nucleation process and 22.8± 0.2 kJ mol^{-1} for the phase change are derived, corresponding to the breaking of two to three hydrogen bonds. Results demonstrate a new means to track nucleation and recrystallization rates in polymorphic systems.

TC11 8:44 – 8:45

REIMAGINING OF OPTICAL KERR EFFECT SPECTROSCOPY: DEVELOPMENT OF A NEW SPECTROSCOPIC TECHNIQUE

MATTHEW M BRISTER, RICHARD THURSTON, *Chemical Science Division, Lawrence Berkeley National Laboratory, Berkeley, CA, USA*; LIANG Z. TAN, *Molecular Foundry Division, Lawrence Berkeley National Laboratories, Berkeley, CA, USA*; THORSTEN WEBER, *Chemical Science Division, Lawrence Berkeley National Laboratory, Berkeley, CA, USA*; NIRANJAN SHIVARAM, *Department of Physics, Purdue University, West Lafayette, IN, USA*; DANIEL S. SLAUGHTER, *Chemical Science Division, Lawrence Berkeley National Laboratory, Berkeley, CA, USA*.

Multidimensional nonlinear spectroscopic methods are powerful tools to investigate ultrafast vibrational dynamics and coherences. Several techniques that have recently been applied to excited electronic states require three or more ultrashort pulses to measure the nonlinear optical response. The additional beamsplitters, mirrors and optical delay stages in these techniques complicates their application in the extreme ultraviolet and X-ray regime, where reflectance is low except at grazing incidence. Optical Kerr effect spectroscopy is a traditional two-pulse technique to measure the 3rd-order nonlinear optical susceptibility of molecules in their ground electronic state. Ultrafast transient polarization spectroscopy (UTPS) is an extension of this technique to excited electronic states, enabling coupled electronic and nuclear dynamics to be investigated by the 3rd-order nonlinear optical susceptibility. In UTPS, a pump pulse excites a population, then a Kerr gate and probe pulse monitor the 3rd-order nonlinear response of excited-state molecules, as a function of delay between each of the three pulses. Two-photon absorption of femtosecond pump pulses populate the S_1 excited-state of nitrobenzene. We were able to extract a dephasing time that oscillates as function of the time delay after excitation. This dephasing time and supporting theoretical calculation allows for distinguishing between an intersystem crossing conical intersection and an internal conversion conical intersection on the same excited-state potential energy surface.

TC12 8:48 – 8:49

HIGH SENSITIVITY BROADBAND TRANSIENT ABSORPTION SPECTROSCOPY OF MOLECULAR BEAMS

MYLES C SILFIES, GRZEGORZ KOWZAN[a], NEOMI LEWIS, THOMAS K ALLISON, *Departments of Physics and Chemistry, Stony Brook University, Stony Brook, NY, USA*.

Molecules with ultrafast dynamics inherently have broad spectral features and modeling ultrafast spectroscopy data is a complex art. The complexity is reduced in the gas phase, however most ultrafast spectroscopies are limited to high-density samples such as liquids. By using a frequency comb laser and optical cavities, we present a technique for performing ultrafast optical spectroscopy with high sensitivity, enabling work in dilute gas-phase molecules and clusters[b]. This sensitivity enables ultrafast spectroscopy in dilute molecular beams, where cold isolated designer molecules, radicals, and clusters can be produced that do not exist in solution.

This new technique enables direct comparisons to well-established ultrafast techniques which can provide additional insight for theoretical models and molecular dynamics. In this talk we will introduce our broadband cavity-enhanced transient absorption spectrometer[c], which has a UV pump at 355 nm and a probe tunable from 450 to 700 nm, and discuss measurements of chemical dynamics of molecules in seeded molecular beams. Example systems discussed will include proton transfer in 1'-hydroxy 2'-acetonapthone and the effects of argon clustering on the internal conversion of salicylidene aniline.

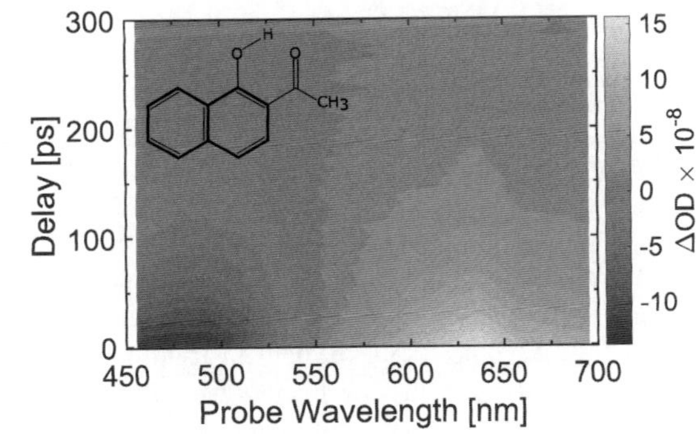

[a]Second affiliation: Institute of Physics, Faculty of Physics, Astronomy and Informatics, Nicolaus Copernicus University, Torun, Poland.

[b]M. A. R. Reber, Y. Chen, T. K. Allison, Optica 3, 311 (2016)

[c]M. C. Silfies, G. Kowzan, N. Lewis, and T. K. Allison, arXiv:2102.04981 (2021)

TD. Fundamental interest

Tuesday, June 22, 2021 – 8:0 AM

Room: 2021 Online Everywhere

Chair: Trevor Sears, Stony Brook University, Stony Brook, NY, USA

TD01 **8:00 – 8:01**

PERTURBATIONS OF THE A'$^1\Pi$ AND C$^1\Sigma^+$ STATES OF CaO

SEAN MICHAEL BRESLER, JOEL R SCHMITZ, *Department of Chemistry, Emory University, Atlanta, GA, USA*; ROBERT W FIELD, *Department of Chemistry, MIT, Cambridge, MA, USA*; MICHAEL HEAVEN, *Department of Chemistry, Emory University, Atlanta, GA, USA*.

The electronic structure of CaO is complex due to the large number of low-lying energy states and a multitude of rovibronic interactions among them. Several vibrionic bands of the $A'^1\Pi - X^1\Sigma^+$ CaO have been identified in the visible region using laser induced fluorescence. Analysis of these rotationally resolved data provides more accurate band origins and rotational constants for levels that were previously determined indirectly using perturbation data. Fluorescence decay lifetime measurements were used to determine the radiative decay rate for the A' state.

A previously noted homogeneous perturbation of the $C^1\Sigma^+$ state was examined to determine the identity of the perturbing state. Dispersed fluorescence spectra and fluorescence decay rate measurements were used to show that the perturbation results from the interaction with a state of $^3\Pi(0+)$ symmetry.

TD02 **8:04 – 8:05**

THE MOLECULAR CONSTANTS OF THE X2Σ+, A2Π, B2Σ+, AND C2Π ELECTRONIC STATES OF THE CALCIUM MONOHALIDE RADICALS

ROBERT W FIELD, *Department of Chemistry, MIT, Cambridge, MA, USA*; GUY TAIEB, *Institut des Sciences Moléculaires d'Orsay, Université Paris-Sud, Orsay, France*; CHIHEB BAHRINI, *Department of Physics, Tunis Preparatory Engineering Institute (IPEIT), Tunis, Tunisia*.

The alkaline earth monohalides are molecules of interest in fields such as astrophysics, high-temperature chemistry, chemiluminescent reactions, spectroscopy, computational chemistry, and cold molecule trapping. The electronic properties of the CaX molecules are well described by Ligand Field Theory. These properties include the relative energies of the X, A, B, and C states, their spin-orbit, spin-rotation, and lambda-doubling constants, and their spin-orbit and L-uncoupling perturbation matrix elements. In this talk we will present some Ligand Field Theory-based ideas: Schmidt orthogonalization, ligand-induced 4p-3d induced polarization, ligand-to-metal charge transfer, and molecular orbital-size based on effective principal quantum number 1/n*$^{(}$3) orbital radius scaling. This paper is dedicated to Joelle Rostas (deceased June 2019) who spent many years studying the alkaline earth monohalide molecules and discussing them with the authors of this talk.

TD03 **8:08 – 8:09**

A LIGAND FIELD THEORY VIEW OF THE ELECTRONIC STRUCTURE OF CaX (X=F, Cl, Br, I, AND O)

ROBERT W FIELD, CHRISTOPHER CUMMINS, *Department of Chemistry, MIT, Cambridge, MA, USA*; MICHAEL HEAVEN, *Department of Chemistry, Emory University, Atlanta, GA, USA*; GUY TAIEB[a], *Institut des Sciences Moléculaires d'Orsay, Université Paris-Sud, Orsay, France*.

The CaX family of diatomic molecules illustrates concepts developed by inorganic chemists to rationalize the properties of metal-centered complexes. The basic idea is that an atom or an atomic-ion is surrounded by ligands, and that the electronic properties of the complexes are dealt with in a model in which the central metal atom and the ligands are treated as retaining their separated atom or molecule properties perturbed by identifiable and quantifiable metal-ligand interactions. Ligand Field Theory is *semi-empirical* in the sense that it is a framework for building a systematic understanding of the properties of families of complexes from spectroscopic measurements of the properties of the separated species and the interactions between them. The electronic structures of the CaX molecules are described by atomic-ions-in-molecule ligand field models. The Ca atom is treated as Ca^+ with a single electron in the 4sσ , 4pσ or π, or 3dσ,π, or δ orbital For X=F, Cl, Br, and I, the ligand is a closed-shell halide ion. For X=O, the ligand is an open-shell O^- ion with a single hole in the pπ (π^{-1}) or $p\sigma$ (σ^{-1}) orbital. The building blocks of the electronic structure model are known by different names in the inorganic chemistry, small-molecule spectroscopy, and quantum chemistry communities. Fine structure (spin-orbit, spin-spin, spin-rotation, and lambda-doubling) and spectroscopic perturbation matrix elements (spin-orbit and L-uncoupling) report on the CaX electronic structure.

[a](ISMO-UMR 8214), Universite Paris Sud, Bat. 210

TD04 **8:12 – 8:13**

THE MOLECULAR CONSTANTS OF THE $X^2\Sigma^+$, $A^2\Pi$, $B^2\Sigma^+$, AND $C^2\Pi$ ELECTRONIC STATES OF THE CALCIUM MONOHALIDE RADICALS

CHIHEB BAHRINI, *Department of Physics, Tunis Preparatory Engineering Institute (IPEIT), Tunis, Tunisia*; ROBERT W FIELD, *Department of Chemistry, MIT, Cambridge, MA, USA*; GUY TAIEB, *Institut des Sciences Moléculaires d'Orsay, Université Paris-Sud, Orsay, France*.

The alkaline earth monohalides are molecules of interest in fields such as astrophysics, high-temperature chemistry, chemiluminescent reactions, spectroscopy, computational chemistry, and cold molecule trapping. The electronic properties of the CaX molecules are well described by Ligand Field Theory. These properties include the relative energies of the X, A, B, and C states, their spin-orbit, spin-rotation, and lambda-doubling constants, and their spin-orbit and L-uncoupling perturbation matrix elements. In this talk we will present some Ligand Field Theory-based ideas: Schmidt orthogonalization, ligand-induced 4p-3d induced polarization, ligand-to-metal charge transfer, and molecular orbital-size. The lambda doublings definitely prove that the spin-orbit splitting in the C-state is 1/2 below 3/2 (i.e. regular). Finally, the simultaneous use of both laser techniques Laser Induced Fluorescence (LIF) and Cavity Ring Down Spectroscopy (CRDS), allowed the extension of previous measurements to high vibrational levels and provided accurate vibrational parameters [a].

[a]This paper is dedicated to Joelle Rostas (deceased June 2019) who spent many years studying the alkaline earth monohalide molecules and discussing them with the authors of this talk.

TD05 **8:16 – 8:17**

THE DIATOMIC MOLECULAR SPECTROSCOPY DATABASE: DATA-SCIENCE DRIVEN APPLICATIONS

XIANGYUE LIU, STEFAN TRUPPE, GERARD MEIJER, JESÚS PÉREZ-RÍOS, *Department of Molecular Physics, Fritz-Haber-Institut der Max-Planck-Gesellschaft, Berlin, Germany.*

Spectroscopic constants of molecules characterize the unique fingerprints of molecules and atoms. In particular, for diatomic molecules, spectroscopic constants encapsulate essential information about different applications in atomic, molecular, and optical physics, such as laser cooling or quantum information. To help find molecules well-suited for a given application, we have developed a database linked to an interactive website.[a] The spectroscopic constants and Franck-Condon factors can be retrieved in useful formats from the website or via an application programming interface. New data can also be uploaded upon acceptance by the web managers.

By applying machine-learning approaches to this dataset, we show that the spectroscopic constants, including the equilibrium distance, harmonic vibrational frequency, and binding energy, are correlated and depend solely on the constituent's groups and periods. Based on these relationships, ground-state spectroscopic constants of polar diatomic molecules can be predicted with a relative error of $< 5\%$, whereas the same properties for the A-excited electron state are predicted with an error of $< 11\%$.[b] Anyone can make these predictions with access to our database, and it does not require any quantum chemistry knowledge.

Separately, we construct a database consisting of experimental electric dipole moments of 162 diatomic molecules. We show that the dipole moment of diatomic molecules is related to the constituent atoms' atomic properties, including electron affinity and ionization potential, and molecular properties that describe the force on the electrons at the equilibrium distance.[c]

[a] X. Liu, S. Truppe, G. Meijer and J. Pérez-Ríos, J. Cheminform. **12**, 31 (2020)
[b] X. Liu, G. Meijer and J. Pérez-Ríos, arXiv:2005.07913 (2020)
[c] X. Liu, G. Meijer and J. Pérez-Ríos, Phys. Chem. Chem. Phys. **22**, 24191 (2020)

TD07 **8:24 – 8:25**

NONLINEAR FOURIER-TRANSFORM SPECTROSCOPY OF SINGLE GOLD NANOPARTICLES

MEGAN A. STEVES, KENNETH L. KNAPPENBERGER, JR., *Department of Chemistry, Pennsylvania State University, University Park, PA, USA.*

Plasmonic metal nanoparticles exhibit strong and tunable light-matter interactions which have enabled a variety of applications. Alongside their strong linear extinction, plasmonic nanoparticles have also been noted for their nonlinear optical properties. Here we present a study of multiphoton absorption in plasmonic gold nanorods using Fourier-transform spectroscopy with nonlinear optical detection. The excitation spectra of single gold nanorods is retrieved from an interferometric multiphoton photoluminescence (MPPL) signal which is generated by a pair of phase-locked pulses with attosecond interpulse delay precision. The resulting Fourier-transform spectra reveal the two- and three-photon excitation pathways that lead to emission from gold nanorods. Investigation of the spectra demonstrates the connection between resonance frequency and nonlinear absorption cross-section in gold nanorods, which is attributed to the influence of gold's electronic structure.[a]

[a] This work was supported by the Air Force Office of Scientific Research, grant number FA-9550-18-1-0347, the National Science Foundation Graduate Research Fellowship Program under grant no. DGE1255832 and the National Science Foundation, award number CHE-1807999

TD08 **8:28 – 8:29**

A GENERALIZED BADGER'S RULE QUANTIFYING THE STRUCTURE-SPECTRA RELATIONSHIP FOR HYDROGEN-BONDED SYSTEMS

MARK A. BOYER, *Department of Chemistry, University of Washington, Seattle, WA, USA*; ONDREJ MARSALEK, *Faculty of Mathematics and Physics, Charles University, Prague, CZ*; JOSEPH P HEINDEL, *Department of Chemistry, University of Washington, Seattle, WA, USA*; THOMAS E MARKLAND, *Department of Chemistry, Stanford, Palo Alto, CA, USA*; ANNE B McCOY, *Department of Chemistry, University of Washington, Seattle, WA, USA*; SOTIRIS XANTHEAS, *Physical Sciences Division, Pacific Northwest National Laboratory, Richland, WA, USA*.

Badger's rule originally described a non-linear relationship between the equilibrium bond length and force constant for diatomic molecules. This rule has since become synonymous with many different relationships between molecular structure and the frequency of a corresponding molecular vibration. In this work we provide an intuitive and general rule describing the relationship between the OH equilibrium bond lengths, R_e, and the harmonic OH stretch frequencies, ω_e, as well as the vibrationally averaged OH bond lengths, R_0, and the anharmonic OH stretch frequencies, ν_0. We show that the same rule applies for hydrogen bonds of varying strengths and corresponding red shifts in the OH vibrations such as the ones in neutral water clusters, protonated water clusters, and aqueous halide clusters. Remarkably, we find a simple linear correlation between the changes in the covalent OH bond length and corresponding stretching frequency of -19 cm^{-1}/ 0.001 Å that holds for both the (ω_e vs R_e) and (ν_0 vs R_0) pairs. We provide physical insights regarding the origin of this linear correlation by modeling the covalent, hydrogen bonded OH bond via a Morse oscillator. In particular, we show that the electric-field-dependent frequency shift for the harmonic and anharmonic frequencies lies on the same line. More importantly, using this simple linear relationship and scaling factor obtained from the aqueous clusters, we are able to reproduce both the structure and the position of the OH vibrational band in liquid water using the OH bond length distribution obtained from an ab initio molecular dynamics simulation.

TD09 **8:32 – 8:33**

HIGH-SENSITIVITY FRANCK-CONDON FACTOR MEASUREMENTS ENABLED BY OPTICAL CYCLING

BENJAMIN AUGENBRAUN, ZACK LASNER, NATHANIEL VILAS, *Department of Physics, Harvard University, Cambridge, MA, USA*; TIMOTHY STEIMLE, *School of Molecular Sciences, Arizona State University, Tempe, AZ, USA*; JOHN M. DOYLE, *Department of Physics, Harvard University, Cambridge, MA, USA*.

Recent experiments have successfully laser cooled a variety of molecules, including diatomic, linear triatomic, and symmetric top species [1-3]. Laser cooling and trapping can require repeatedly scattering more than 10,000 photons per molecule, so all potential losses above the level of 1 part in 10^5 must be identified and repumped to mitigate losses. Here, we report on the use of optical cycling to measure vibrational branching ratios of laser-coolable polyatomic molecules. We achieve relative intensity sensitivities at the 10^{-5} level, approximately a factor of 100 more sensitive than previous dispersed fluorescence studies [4-6]. The apparatus described can be adapted to probe any molecule with a nearly-closed cycling transition by tuning two laser wavelengths. In addition, we discuss how these high-precision branching ratio measurements have allowed us to infer values for Renner-Teller parameters in CaOH and YbOH, and for pseudo-Jahn-Teller parameters in $CaOCH_3$.

[1] J. Barry, et al., Nature 512, 286 (2014).
[2] I. Kozyryev, et al., Phys. Rev. Lett. 118, 173201 (2017).
[3] D. Mitra, N. B. Vilas, et al., Science 369, 1366 (2020).
[4] I. Kozyryev, et al., New J. Phys. 21, 052002 (2019).
[5] A. C. Paul, et al., J. Chem. Phys. 151, 134303 (2019).
[6] E. T. Mengesha, et al., J. Phys. Chem. A 124, 3135 (2020).

TD10 **8:36 – 8:37**

HIGH-RESOLUTION AND HIGH-PRECISION LASER SPECTROSCOPY OF A-BENZANTHRACENE

MASAAKI BABA, *Division of Chemistry, Graduate School of Science, Kyoto University, Kyoto, Japan*; SHO YAMASAKI, *Applied Physics, Fukuoka University, Fukuoka, Japan*; AKIKO NISHIYAMA, *Institute of Physics, Faculty of Physics, Astronomy and Informatics, Nicolaus Copernicus University, Torun, Poland*; MASATOSHI MISONO, *Applied Physics, Fukuoka University, Fukuoka, Japan.*

The electronic excited states of polycyclic aromatic hydrocarbons (PAHs) are especially interesting and high-resolution laser spectroscopy is very powerful to elucidate molecular structure and excited-state dynamics. We observed and analyzed the high-resolution and high-precision spectrum of the $S_1 \leftarrow S_0$ 0-0 band of jet-cooled a-benzanthracene using a single-mode laser system precisely controlled by optical frequency comb [a]. There are two candidates for the S_1 state of planar PAHs with high symmetry such as naphthalene and anthracene, Ψ_A (HOMO $\rightarrow$ LUMO : strong transition and short fluorescence lifetime) and Ψ_B (HOMO $\rightarrow$ LUMO+1 and HOMO-1 $\rightarrow$ LUMO : weak transition and long fluorescence lifetime) [b]. The S_1 states of naphthalene and zigzag catacondenced PAHs are well expressed by Ψ_B, but The S_1 states of anthracene and linear catacondenced PAHs show typical properties of Ψ_A, srong fluorescence and short-lived. It is concluded that the S_1 state of a-benzanthracene is the mixture of Ψ_A and Ψ_B and shows an intermediate property because of its low symmetry.

[a]A. Nishiyama, K. Nakashima, A. Matsuba, and M. Misono, J. Mol. Spectrosc **318**, 40 (2010).
[b]M. Baba, T. Katori, M. Kawabata, S. Kunishige, and T. Yamanaka, J. Phys. Chem. A **117**, 13524 (2013).

TD11 **8:40 – 8:41**

HIGH-RESOLUTION LASER SPECTROSCOPY OF TRANS-STILBENE : NONPLANAR STRUCTURE IN THE GROUND STATE

AKIRA SHIMIZU, KOSUKE NAKAJIMA, *Graduate School of Science, Kobe University, Kobe, Japan*; SHUNJI KASAHARA, *Molecular Photoscience Research Center, Kobe University, Kobe, Japan*; MASATOSHI MISONO, *Applied Physics, Fukuoka University, Fukuoka, Japan*; MASAAKI BABA, *Division of Chemistry, Graduate School of Science, Kyoto University, Kyoto, Japan.*

Trans-stilbene os og great interest in the excited-state dynamics such as cis-trans isomerization in the electronic excited state. Zewail at al. reported the results of time-resolved spectroscopy and suggested its nonplanar structure in the ground S_0 state [a]. In contrast, Pratt et al. concluded that the molecule is essentially planar both in the S_0 and S_1 states by analyzing the rotationally resolved high-resolution speoctrum of the $S_1 \leftarrow S_0$ 0-0 band [b]. We observed the spectrum with much higher accuracy and quality, and re-determined the rotational constants. Although it is impossible to accurate determine the abosolute value of A for the a-type transition, We could conclude that trans-stilbene is nonplanar in the S_0 state. Theoretical calculation using WB97XD functional provided the nonplanar structure in which the phenyl rings are rotated around the C-C bond axis and take the C_2 symmetry. It suggests that steric repulsion between H atoms of *ortho*-position in a phenyl ring and in an ethylene part surpasses stabilization by π conjugation.

[a]J. A. Syage, P. M. Felker, and A. H. Zewail, J. Chem. Phys. **81**, 4685 (1984).
[b]D. W. Pratt, W. L. Meerts et al., J. Phys. Chem. **94**, 6 (1990).

TE. Comparing theory and experiment

Tuesday, June 22, 2021 – 8:0 AM

Room: 2021 Online Everywhere

Chair: Edwin Sibert, University of Wisconsin–Madison, Madison, WI, USA

TE01 **8:00 – 8:01**

ANALYSIS OF THE CORIOLIS- AND FERMI-COUPLED TRIAD NEAR 315 cm^{-1} OF BENZONITRILE (C_6H_5CN)

MARIA ZDANOVSKAIA, BRIAN J. ESSELMAN, R. CLAUDE WOODS, ROBERT J. McMAHON, *Department of Chemistry, University of Wisconsin-Madison, Madison, WI, USA*; ZBIGNIEW KISIEL, *ON2, Institute of Physics, Polish Academy of Sciences, Warszawa, Poland.*

We previously presented the least-squares fit of the benzonitrile (C_6H_5CN, C_{2v}, μ_a = 4.5 D) ground vibrational state, which was fit to a partial octic Hamiltonian, as well as the first analysis of its two Coriolis-coupled, lowest-energy fundamental states, ν_{22} and ν_{33}.[1] Herein, we present the continuation of this work: the analysis and fitting of the Coriolis- and Fermi-coupled triad of the overtone and combination states (ν_{22} = 2, ν_{33} = 2, and ν_{22} + ν_{33}) near 315 cm^{-1}. Approximately 3000 transitions are assigned for each state, including multiple resonances, and their least-squares fitting results in precise energy separations that are in agreement with those expected based on the energy separation determined for ν_{22} and ν_{33}.

1. Zdanovskaia, M. A.; Esselman, B. J.; Lau, H. S.; Bates, D. M.; Woods, R. C.; McMahon, R. J.; Kisiel, Z. The 103 - 360 GHz Rotational Spectrum of Benzonitrile, the First Interstellar Benzene Derivative Detected by Radioastronomy. *J.Mol.Spectrosc.* **2018**, 351, 39-48.

TE02 **8:04 – 8:05**

BRIEF SUMMARY OF THE MILLIMETER-WAVE ROTATIONAL SPECTRA OF 2-, 3-, AND 4-CYANOPYRIDINE: THEIR VIBRATIONAL GROUND STATES AND THE CORIOLIS-COUPLED DYADS OF THEIR LOWEST-ENERGY VIBRATIONALLY EXCITED STATES

P. MATISHA DORMAN, BRIAN J. ESSELMAN, R. CLAUDE WOODS, ROBERT J. McMAHON, *Department of Chemistry, University of Wisconsin-Madison, Madison, WI, USA.*

The rotational spectra of 2-, 3-, and 4-cyanopyridine ($C_6H_4N_2$) were recorded from 130 – 360 GHz, and an analysis of the ground vibrational state and two lowest-energy excited vibrational states for each isomer was completed. Each ground state was least-squares fit to a partial octic, distorted-rotor Hamiltonian with several thousand distinct transitions assigned (σ_{fit} < 50 kHz). The B3LYP/6-311+G(2d,p)-predicted quartic and sextic distortion constants are in excellent agreement with their experimentally determined values for all three isomers. Given the large dipole moments of 2-, 3-, and 4-cyanopyridine (μ = 5.8 D, 3.7 D, 2.0 D, respectively) and the astrochemical community's interest in detecting nitriles, the cyanopyridines are an attractive set of aromatic species for detection by radioastronomy. This work provides the fundamental constants needed to support an astronomical search of the cyanopyridine isomers in the interstellar medium. We also examined the two lowest-energy fundamentals of each isomer, which correspond to the in-plane and out-of-plane CN bending modes for all three species. These states are $\sim$ 150 cm^{-1}higher in energy than the ground state and are separated by less than 30 cm^{-1}, an energy separation small enough that each corresponding pair exhibits Coriolis coupling. The dyads display a-type Coriolis coupling for 4-cyanopyridine (C_{2v}) and both $a-$ and b-type Coriolis coupling in 2- and 3-cyanopyridine (C_s), resulting in both global and local perturbations to the rotational transitions. Each isomer required the inclusion of several coupling terms in the two-state least-squares fit in order to fit all observed rotational transitions, including numerous resonances. Fitting each dyad's spectroscopic parameters allowed for the precise experimental determination of each dyad's energy separation, the Coriolis coupling coefficients, and the deperturbed vibration-rotation interaction constants. Combined with the recently published work on the analogous dyad of benzonitrile, this coupling in the cyanopyridines provides an opportunity to compare the Coriolis interactions of cyano-substituted aromatic molecules in greater detail.

TE03 **8:08 – 8:09**

HIGH-RESOLUTION FTIR SPECTROSCOPY OF BENZALDEHYDE IN THE FAR-INFRARED REGION: PROBING THE ROTATIONAL BARRIER

YUE LIANG, YICHI ZHANG, *College of Chemistry and Chemical Engineering, Lanzhou University, Lanzhou, Gansu, China*; CSABA FÁBRI, *Laboratory of Molecular Structure and Dynamics, Eötvös University, Budapest, Hungary*; JIARUI MA, *College of Chemistry and Chemical Engineering, Lanzhou University, Lanzhou, Gansu, China*; JIANBAO ZHAO, BRANT E. BILLINGHURST, *EFD, Canadian Light Source Inc., Saskatoon, Saskatchewan, Canada*; ZIQIU CHEN, *College of Chemistry and Chemical Engineering, Lanzhou University, Lanzhou, Gansu, China.*

A discrepancy between theoretical and experimental values of the rotational barrier in benzaldehyde has been observed, which was attributed to inaccurate experimental results in part.[a] Here, we report results on the –CHO torsion of benzaldehyde (C_6H_5CHO) based on a high resolution spectroscopic investigation in the far-infrared range in an effort to remove the experimental ambiguity. The rotationally-resolved vibrational spectra were measured with an unapodized resolution of 0.00064 cm^{-1}using synchrotron-based Fourier transform infrared (FTIR) spectroscopy at the Canadian Light Source. The torsional fundamental ν_t = 109.415429(20) $\mathrm{cm}^{-1}$was unambiguously assigned via rovibrational analysis, followed by the tentative assignment of the first ($2\nu_t - \nu_t$) and second ($3\nu_t - 2\nu_t$) hot bands at 107.58 $\mathrm{cm}^{-1}$and 105.61 cm^{-1}, respectively, by comparison of the observed Q branch structures at high resolution with simulation based on a previous microwave study.[b] This assignment is different from any previous low resolution infrared studies in which the intensity patterns were misleading. The key result of the assignment of the first three transitions allowed for the determination of the barrier to internal rotation of (hc)1533.6 cm^{-1}(4.38 kcal mol^{-1}). When compared with calculated results from vibrational second-order perturbation theory (VPT2) and quasiadiabatic channel reaction path Hamiltonian (RPH), the experimental value is still too low and this suggests that the discrepancy between theory and experiment remains despite the best experimental efforts.

[a] I.A. Godunov, V.A. Bataev, A. V. Abramenkov, V.I. Pupyshev, *J. Phys. Chem.A*, **2014**, 118, 10159-10165, and references therein.
[b] R. K. Kakar, E. A. Rinehart, C. R. Quade and T. Kojima, *J. Chem. Phys*, **1970**, 52, 3803-3813

TE04 **8:12 – 8:13**

IMPROVED SEMI-EXPERIMENTAL EQUILIBRIUM STRUCTURE DETERMINATION AND THEORETICAL PREDICTION OF HYDRAZOIC ACID (HN_3)

ANDREW N. OWEN, *Department of Chemistry, University of Wisconsin-Madison, Madison, WI, USA*; NITAI P SAHOO, *Department of Chemistry, University of Florida, Gainesville, FL, USA*; BRIAN J. ESSELMAN, *Department of Chemistry, University of Wisconsin-Madison, Madison, WI, USA*; JOHN F. STANTON, *Quantum Theory Project, University of Florida, Gainesville, FL, USA*; R. CLAUDE WOODS, ROBERT J. McMAHON, *Department of Chemistry, University of Wisconsin-Madison, Madison, WI, USA.*

We conducted multiple high-level *ab initio* calculations to obtain improved semi-experimental equilibrium structures (${r_e}^{SE}$) of hydrazoic acid (HN_3) using previously reported experimental data and to obtain improved, purely theoretical predictions of the structure. For the ${r_e}^{SE}$ structures, we used the isotopologue-dependent vibrational corrections to the ground rotational constants obtained from anharmonic VPT2 calculations at CCSD(T) using cc-pVXZ and cc-pCVXZ basis sets (where $X = D, T, Q, 5$), as well as the isotopologue-dependent electron-mass corrections at the same level of theory, to carry out nonlinear least-squares fits of the experimentally determined rotational constants for all but two of the HN_3 isotopologues. The extent of corrections that were calculated allowed for extrapolation of the ${r_e}^{SE}$ structure to the complete basis set limit. To achieve an improved theoretical prediction, we obtained a CCSD(T)/cc-pCV6Z optimization and included corrections for extrapolation to the complete basis set limit, for effects of electron correlation, for relativistic effects, and for the Born-Oppenheimer approximation. The parameters of the resulting theoretical structure agrees to within the 2σ uncertainties of the ${r_e}^{SE}$.

TE05 **8:16 – 8:17**

UPDATES TO AUTOFIT: PROGRESS AND PROSPECTS

ARIANNA T RODRIGUEZ, *Division of Natural Sciences, New College of Florida, Sarasota, FL, USA*; STEVEN SHIPMAN, *Department of Chemistry, New College of Florida, Sarasota, FL, USA*.

Spectral complexity can prove to be a challenge when investigating the rotational spectra of complicated systems and developments in automated fitting tools can reduce the time spent fitting these spectra. In this talk, we discuss our progress on improving various aspects of Autofit (algorithmic, including incorporating double resonance information, and usability, e.g. improved graphical interface). Our main test cases are spectra collected from our lab of small molecules near room temperature where contributions from multiple vibrational states are present, but we will also discuss results from molecular beam spectra.

TE06 **8:20 – 8:21**

MOLECULES PROBED WITH A SLOW CHIRPED-PULSE EXCITATION: ANALYTICAL MODEL OF THE FREE-INDUCTION-DECAY SIGNAL

GUILLAUME DHONT, DANIELE FONTANARI, CÉDRIC BRAY, GAËL MOURET, ARNAUD CUISSET, FRANCIS HINDLE, ROBIN BOCQUET, *Laboratoire de Physico-Chimie de l'Atmosphère, Université du Littoral Côte d'Opale, Dunkerque, France*; KEVIN HICKSON, *Institut des Sciences Moléculaires, Université de Bordeaux, Talence, France*.

A chirped pulse experiment is a powerful means to rapidly obtain an high-resolution spectrum of molecules on a large frequency band. The theoretical paper from McGurk *et al.*[a] is the main reference paper to describe the polarization induced by fast chirped pulses generated with microwave sources.

We built a chirped pulse spectrometer operating at 200 GHz for astrophysical applications.[b] It works in the millimeter domain with slower chirped pulses. In such a situation, the paper of McGurk *et al.* does not capture all the physics involved in the polarization step. In particular, the intensity of a molecular transition is dependent on its temporal position inside the chirped pulse, as discovered by Abeysekera et al.[c]

A theoretical study of the polarization of molecules subjected to a slow chirped pulse is presented for three typical cases: the cell, the uniform flow and the molecular beam. Analytical expressions are proposed alongside the numerical solution and are used in the expression of the free induction decay signal. We test the analytical expression on the rotational emission spectra of OCS molecules. In the thermalized case, a relation between the pulse duration, the line position in the chirped pulse, and the signal amplitude is proposed to correct the line intensities.[d]

[a] J. C. McGurk, T. G. Schmalz, and W. H. Flygare, J. Chem. Phys. **60**, 4181 (1974).

[b] F. Hindle, C. Bray, K. Hickson, D. Fontanari, M. Mouelhi, A. Cuisset, G. Mouret and R. Bocquet, J. Infrared Millim. Te. **39**, 105 (2018).

[c] C. Abeysekera, L. N. Zack, G. B. Park, B. Joalland, J. M. Oldham, K. Prozument, N. M. Ariyasingha, I. R. Sims, R. W. Field, and A. G. Suits, J. Chem. Phys. **141**, 214203 (2014).

[d] D. Fontanari, C. Bray, G. Dhont, G. Mouret, A. Cuisset, F. Hindle, R. Bocquet, and K. M. Hickson, Phys. Rev. A **100**, 043407 (2019).

TE07 **8:24 – 8:25**

FREQUENCY COMB ASSISTED, CAVITY RING-DOWN, LAMB-DIP SPECTROSCOPY OF ACETYLENE AT 1.39 μm.

ANTONIO CASTRILLO[a], EUGENIO FASCI, STEFANIA GRAVINA, GIUSEPPE PORZIO, LIVIO GIANFRANI[b], *Dipartimento di Matematica e Fisica, Universitá della Campania Luigi Vanvitelli, Caserta, Italy.*

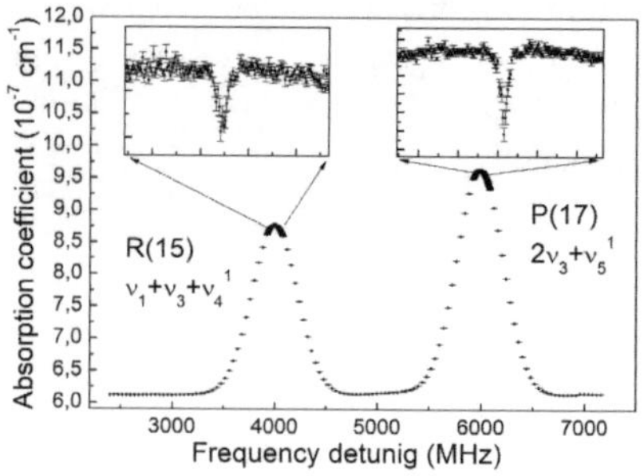

Doppler-free saturated-absorption Lamb dips were observed for weak vibration-rotation transitions of acetylene between 7167 and 7217 cm^{-1}, using frequency comb assisted cavity ring-down spectroscopy. We measured the absolute center frequency of 16 lines of the $2\nu_3+\nu_5{}^1$ band, targeting *ortho* and *para* states of the molecule. Line pairs of the P and Q branches were selected so as to form a V-scheme, sharing the lower energy level. Such a choice made it possible to determine the rotational energy separations of the excited vibrational state for J-values from 11 to 20. The spectrometer is an upgraded version of that described by Fasci *et al.*[c], the main novelty being the use of a BOA - Booster Optical Amplifier, to increase the optical power injected into the high-finesse cavity. Our data provide a very stringent test of the MARVEL analysis recently performed on acetylene[d]. Figure on the right reports an example of observed Lamb dips recorded in correspondence of the line doblet already exploited for low-uncertainty Doppler-broadening gas thermometry[e].

---

[a]antonio.castrillo@unicampania.it
[b]livio.gianfrani@unicampania.it
[c]E. Fasci *et al.*, Phys. Rev. A **98**, 022516, (2018).
[d]K.L. Chubb *et al.* J. Quant. Spectrosc. Radiat. Transfer **204**, 42–55, (2018).
[e]A. Castrillo *et al.* Phys. Rev. Appl. **11**, 064060, (2019)

TE08 **8:28 – 8:29**

THEORY OF INTRACAVITY NEAR-RESONANT TWO-PHOTON ABSORPTION

KEVIN LEHMANN, *Departments of Chemistry and Physics, University of Virginia, Charlottesville, VA, USA.*

I recently published a paper[1] that analyzed near-resonant two-photon absorption (TPA) spectra of polyatomic molecules excited in the vibrational fundamentals. For each molecule, a very small number of TPA lines are greatly enhanced due to near resonance. It is well known that TPA in a standing wave is dominated by a Doppler Free absorption.

In this talk, the theory will be summarised and extensions to the published paper will be presented, including: (1) Theory of high finesse optical cavities with TPA loss, including the peak transmission and spectral shape of cavity modes (which are not Lorenztian with TPA).[2] (2) Extension of the theory of saturation that includes the consequences of slow vibrational relaxation, which invalidates the traditional optical Bloch equations. (3) Theory of the TPA lineshape in the limit of low pressure such that the transition width is limited by the finite time of flight of the absorbers through the TEM_{00} mode of the cavity.[3]

1. K.K. Lehmann, J. Chem. Phys. **151**, 144201 (2019) 2. K.K. Lehmann, J. Opt. Soc. Am. A **37**, 3055 (2020). 3. K.K. Lehmann, to be published in J. Chem. Phys.

TE09 **8:32 – 8:33**

CAVITY RING-DOWN SPECTROSCOPY MEASUREMENTS OF RESONANCE-ENHANCED TWO-PHOTON ABSORPTION BY N_2O

GANG ZHAO, ADAM J. FLEISHER, D. MICHELLE BAILEY, JOSEPH T. HODGES, *Chemical Sciences Division, National Institute of Standards and Technology, Gaithersburg, MD, USA*; KEVIN LEHMANN, *Departments of Chemistry and Physics, University of Virginia, Charlottesville, VA, USA.*

As recently discussed by K.K. Lehmann in a theoretical analysis of two-photon absorption (TPA) [1], the combination of high circulating power and counterpropagating fields associated with the cavity ring-down spectroscopy (CRDS) technique can yield relatively prominent, two-photon, Doppler-free absorption features for near-resonant, three-level rovibrational systems. Here, we present CRDS measurements of TPA by N_2O near λ =4.5 μm. The experiment comprises a quantum cascade laser which is frequency-coupled to a high-finesse optical resonator through controlled optical feedback. Consistent with Lehmann's model, we observe CRDS decay signals that depend upon two characteristic decay rates: a constant single-photon value and an intracavity-power-dependent two-photon absorption rate. The resulting spectra exhibit strong Doppler-free features, saturation effects at low pressure, and TPA cross-section and collisional broadening coefficient consistent with theoretical predictions.

1. K.K. Lehmann, "Resonance enhanced two-photon cavity ring-down spectroscopy of vibrational overtone bands: A proposal," J Chem Phys **151**, 144201 (2019).

TE10 **8:36 – 8:37**

AN EDGE-SPECIFIC SCHEME FOR EQUATION-OF-MOTION COUPLED-CLUSTER CALCULATIONS OF X-RAY ABSORPTION SPECTRA

XUECHEN ZHENG, CHAOQUN ZHANG, LAN CHENG, *Department of Chemistry, Johns Hopkins University, Baltimore, MD, USA.*

We present an edge-specific scheme for calculating near edge x-ray absorption fine structure (NEXAFS) spectra using core-valence separated equation-of-motion coupled-cluster (CVS-EOM-CC) theory. [1,2] Standard correlation-consistent basis set for the atom where targeted core excitation takes place is systematically augmented with diffuse s-, p-, and d-type functions to accurately describe Rydberg-type core excitations with diffuse character. It is also shown that triple excitations in CVS-EOM-CC methods not only are important for obtaining accurate absolute values of core excitation energies, but also make significant contributions to relative shifts between local and Rydberg core excitations. Quadruples excitations are shown to be relevant when aiming at high-accuracy calculations of absolute values.

Reference

[1] L. S. Cederbaum, W. Domcke, J. Schirmer, and W. von Niessen, Phys. Scripta 21, 481 (1980).
[2] S. Coriani, and H. Koch, J. Chem. Phys. 143, 181103 (2015).

TE11 **8:40 – 8:41**

DENSITY DEPENDENCE OF SPECTRAL DETAIL IN PRESSURIZED AND SUPERCRITICAL CARBON DIOXIDE ELECTRONIC ABSORPTION SPECTRA

TIMOTHY W MARIN, *Physical Science, Benedictine University, Lisle, IL, USA*; IRENEUSZ JANIK, *Radiation Laboratory, University of Notre Dame, Notre Dame, IN, USA.*

The density dependence of pressurized and supercritical carbon dioxide (CO_2) electronic absorption spectra was explored by vacuum ultraviolet (VUV) spectroscopy over the wavelength range 1455-2000 Å. The peak energy position of the lowest absorption band of gaseous CO_2 does not change upon pressurizing up to and beyond the thermodynamic critical point (137 bar, 308 K). Upon increase of density, the known diffuse vibrational structure inherent to the VUV absorption spectrum of gaseous CO_2 gradually diminishes in magnitude and nearly disappears upon reaching a density of 0.767 g cm^{-3}. This loss of spectral detail cannot be explained solely by collisional broadening and/or dimerization. We suggest that perturbation of the monomer potential energy surfaces belonging to multiple upper electronic states leads to increased coupling between binding and dissociative states. This perturbation is caused by the near proximity of CO_2 molecules at high densities and a variety of orientations without the need for equilibrated dimers, and in turn gives rise to the observed spectral changes. Based on a high-quality CO_2 dimer potential energy surface, we estimate a critical radius of 4.1 +/- 0.2 Å between molecules necessary to cause such perturbations.

TE12 **8:44 – 8:45**

DYNAMICS OF NITRO-NITRITE REARRANGMENT IN NITROMETHANE RADICAL CATION

MI'KAYLA D WORD, HUGO A. LÓPEZ PEÑA, DERRICK AMPADU BOATENG, KATHARINE MOORE TIBBETTS, *Department of Chemistry, Virginia Commonwealth University, Richmond, Virginia, USA.*

Nitromethane, the smallest organic-nitro compound, is commonly studied to model ignition and detonation of energetic materials. Using pump-probe femtosecond laser photoionization mass spectroscopy, coupled-cluster theory, and ab initio molecular dynamics, we study nitromethane cation (NM^+) fragmentation into $CH_3{}^+$, $NO_2{}^+$, and NO^+. From theoretical analysis, $NO_2{}^+$ and $CH_3{}^+$ are formed through direct cleavage of the C-N bond, whereas NO^+ forms spontaneously upon nitro-nitrite rearrangement (NNR) of the NM^+ cation. Direct ionization into the electronically excited D_1 or D_2 states by the pump pulse provides sufficient excess energy to initiate the NNR pathway. With excess energy stored in the NNR transition state, molecular dynamics simulations indicate that NNR requires 660 ± 230 fs and is typically followed by rapid NO^+ loss 100-200 fs later. Experimentally, the fragmentation pathways to NO^+ and $CH_3{}^+$ are in competition, with associated decay timescale of $\sim 480 \pm 200$ fs that is similar to the computed NNR timescale. This result suggests that $CH_3{}^+$ is formed by further excitation of the NM^+ initially ionized into the D_1 or D_2 states before it undergoes NNR. Finally, the dissociation to $NO_2{}^+$ from NM^+ can be assigned to a $D_0 \rightarrow D_2$ transition.

TE13 **8:48 – 8:49**

TRAJECTORY-BASED SIMULATION OF FAR-INFRARED CIA PROFILES OF CH_4-N_2 FOR MODELING TITAN'S ATMOSPHERE

ARTEM FINENKO, IOULI E GORDON, EAMON K CONWAY, *Atomic and Molecular Physics, Harvard-Smithsonian Center for Astrophysics, Cambridge, MA, USA*; BRUNO BÉZARD, *LESIA, Observatoire de Paris, Université PSL, CNRS, Sorbonne Université, Université de Paris, Paris, France*; YULIA N KALUGINA, *Department of Optics and Spectroscopy, Tomsk State University, Tomsk, Russia*; DANIIL CHISTIKOV, SERGEI E LOKSHTANOV, SERGEY V PETROV, *Department of Chemistry, Lomonosov Moscow State University, Moscow, Russia*; ANDREI VIGASIN, *Laboratory of Atmospheric Spectroscopy, Obukhov Institute of Atmospheric Physics, Moscow, Russia.*

Far-infrared opacity of tropospheric and lower stratospheric layers in Titan's atmosphere is dominated by collision-induced absorption (CIA) in various molecular pairs containing N_2, CH_4, and H_2. The presently available spectra of these pairs are often insufficiently accurate for reliably analyzing observed Titan spectra. Analysis of emission spectra from Titan's atmosphere recorded with the Cassini Composite Infrared Spectrometer (CIRS)[a] suggests that the Borysow et al. model[b] for CH_4-N_2 CIA coefficients underestimates absorption by about 50%.

We present the trajectory-based study of the rototranslational CIA band in CH_4-N_2. Assuming rigid monomers, potential energy and induced dipole are characterized quantum-chemically at the CCSD(T)/CCSD(T)-F12b levels of theory. The Monte Carlo strategy is adopted to obtain the dipole autocorrelation function. The original procedure is employed to sample initial conditions throughout the phase space of a molecular pair. The autocorrelation function is derived from an ensemble of 5 to 10 million classical trajectories obtained through the solution of Hamilton equations in the space-fixed reference frame. The Fourier transform of the autocorrelation function yields the CIA band profile. We propose a new semiempirical model for CH_4-N_2 CIA that allows us to reproduce CIRS spectra recorded at low and high emission angles in the equatorial region[a].
This work is partially supported by RFBR-CNRS grant 18-55-16006 and NASA HITRAN grant.

[a]Bézard et al. (2020). Icarus. 344, 113261.
[b]Borysow, et al. (1993). Icarus. 105, 175.

TF. Linelists

Tuesday, June 22, 2021 – 8:0 AM

Room: 2021 Online Everywhere

Chair: Frances M Skinner, Harvard-Smithsonian Center for Astrophysics, Malden, MA, USA

TF01 **8:00 – 8:01**

HITRAN2020: ACT (ACCURACY, COMPLETENESS, TRACEABILITY)

IOULI E GORDON, LAURENCE S. ROTHMAN, ROBERT J. HARGREAVES, ROBAB HASHEMI, EKATERINA KARLOVETS, FRANCES M SKINNER, ARTEM FINENKO, EAMON K CONWAY, KYLE NELSON, TIJS KARMAN, *Atomic and Molecular Physics, Harvard-Smithsonian Center for Astrophysics, Cambridge, MA, USA*; YAN TAN, *Hefei National Laboratory for Physical Science at Microscale, University of Science and Technology of China, Hefei, China*; ROMAN KOCHANOV, *Laboratory of Quantum Molecular Mechanics and Radiation Processes, Tomsk State University, Tomsk, Russia*; CHRISTIAN HILL, *Atomic and Molecular Data Unit, International Atomic Energy Agency, Vienna, Austria.*

The HITRAN2020 database will be publicly released this year. It is a coordinated effort of experimentalists, theoreticians, atmospheric and planetary scientists who measure, calculate and validate the HITRAN data. The lists for most of the HITRAN molecules in the line-by-line section were updated in comparison with the previous compilation HITRAN2016[a]. The extent of the updates ranges from updating a few lines of certain molecules to complete replacements of the lists and introducing additional isotopologues. Six new molecules (SO, CH_3F, GeH_4, CS_2, CH_3I, and NF_3) were also added to HITRAN. In addition, the accuracy of the parameters for major atmospheric absorbers has been increased, often featuring sub-percent uncertainties. The number of parameters was also increased significantly, now incorporating, for instance, non-Voigt line profiles for many gases; broadening by water vapor[b]; update of collision-induced absorption sets[c].

The new edition will continue taking advantage of the modern structure and interface available at www.hitran.org and the HITRAN Application Programming Interface[d]. Their functionality has been extended for the new edition. This talk will provide a brief overview of HITRAN2020[e] and its main improvements with respect to the previous edition.

[a] Gordon et al., (2017). JQSRT. 203, 3–69.
[b] Tan et al., (2019) J. Geophys. Res. Atmos. 2019JD030929.
[c] Karman et al., (2019) Icarus 328, 160–175.
[d] Kochanov et al., (2016) JQSRT. 177, 15–30.
[e] This work is supported by NASA.

TF02 **8:04 – 8:05**

A URANIUM ATLAS IN ASCII FORMAT, 20000 – 27000 cm^{-1}

AMANDA J. ROSS, PATRICK CROZET, *Inst. Lumière Matière, Univ Lyon 1 & CNRS, Université de Lyon, Villeurbanne, France*; DENNIS W. TOKARYK, *Department of Physics, University of New Brunswick, Fredericton, NB, Canada*; ALLAN G. ADAM, *Department of Chemistry, University of New Brunswick, Fredericton, NB, Canada.*

This work was motivated by difficulties encountered while trying to calibrate laser excitation spectra, taken in short (1 cm^{-1}) scans around 438 nm, by matching optogalvanic transitions from a Uranium-Argon hollow cathode lamp to peaks listed in a widely-circulated 'informal report' on the Uranium spectrum (11000 –25900 cm^{-1}) from Los Alamos[a]. Short pieces of excitation spectra often fell between secure calibration lines, because many of the weaker features had been excluded from the printed linelist. To remedy this, we have re-recorded emission from a commercial Uranium hollow-cathode lamp 19800 – 27400 cm^{-1} on a Fourier transform spectrometer, at an instrumental resolution of at 0.04 cm^{-1}. The wavenumber scale was fine-tuned to match earlier reference data[abc] to within 0.003 cm^{-1}. This spectrum (together with its peak list) is proposed in ascii format[d] as a possible aid to calibration of laser excitation spectra in the blue, violet and near UV. It extends the spectrum reported by Sarmiento and co-workers[b] that focused on calibration of astronomical spectrographs in the near IR and visible.

[a] An atlas of uranium emission intensities in a hollow cathode discharge; Palmer, Keller & Engleman, Los Alamos report LA 8251-MS, (1980)
[b] Comparing the emission spectra of U and Th hollow cathode lamps, and a new U line list; Sarmiento *et al.*, A & A, 618, A118, (2018)
[c] Uranium and iodine standards measured by means of Fourier-transform spectroscopy; Gerstenkorn, *et al.*, A & A, 58, 255-66, (1977)
[d] A uranium atlas, from 365 to 505 nm; Ross *et al.* J Mol Spectrosc , 369, 111270, (2020)

TF03 **8:08 – 8:09**

THE ELECTRIC QUADRUPOLE SPECTRA OF DIATOMIC MOLECULES

WILFRID SOMOGYI, SERGEI N. YURCHENKO, *Department of Physics and Astronomy, University College London, London, UK.*

Owing to their molecular symmetry, many transitions of homonuclear diatomic molecules are forbidden in the electric dipole approximation. Instead their spectra are dominated by higher order transition moments, including the magnetic dipole moment and electric quadrupole moment. Here we present a new implementation of electric quadrupole transition moments in DUO[a]. The implementation is validated against the highly accurate linelist of Roueff et al. [b] for rovibrational transitions of the hydrogen molecule. We also perform ab initio calculations for potential energy curves (PECs), electric quadrupole moment curves (EQCs), and spin-orbit coupling curves (SOCs) and demonstrate rovibronic linestrength calculations for the three lowest lying states ($X^3\Sigma_g^-$, $a^1\Delta_g$ and $b^2\Sigma_g^+$) of molecular oxygen. Further demonstrations are provided for various other molecules of interest, including CO and HF as part of the ExoMol project [c]. Absorption cross-sections are calculated using the EXOCROSS program[d].

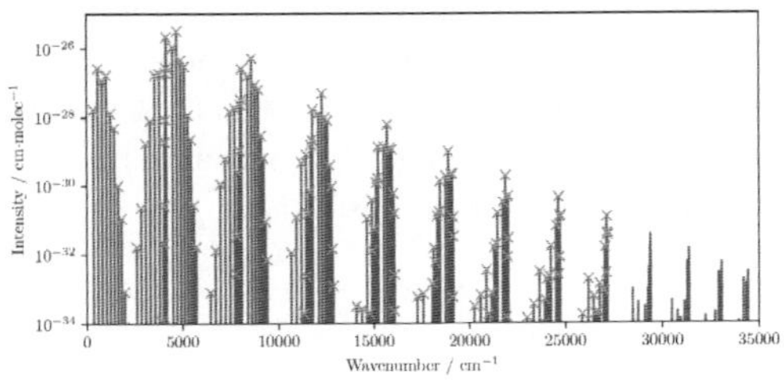

[a] S. N. Yurchenko, L. Lodi, J. Tennyson, A. V. Stolyarov, *Comput. Phys. Commun.*, 2016, **202**, 262 – 275; publicly available at *https://github.com/Trovemaster/Duo*.

[b] The full infrared spectrum of molecular hydrogen, Astron. Astrophys, 630 (2019)

[c] J. Tennyson et al. *J. Quant. Spectrosc. Radiat. Transf.*, 2020, **255**, 107228; *www.exomol.com*.

[d] S. N. Yurchenko, A. F. Al-Refaie, J. Tennyson, *Astron. Astrophys*;, 2018, **614**, A131; publicly available at *https://github.com/Trovemaster/ExoCross*.

TF04 **8:12 – 8:13**

EXOMOL ROVIBRATIONAL LINELIST FOR NaO

GEORGI B MITEV, JONATHAN TENNYSON, SERGEI N. YURCHENKO, *Department of Physics and Astronomy, University College London, London, UK*; ALEXEI BUCHACHENKO, *Center for Energy Science and Technology, Skolkovo Institute of Science and Technology, Skolkovo Innovation Center, Moscow 121205, Russia*; ANDREY STOLYAROV, *Department of Chemistry, Moscow State University, Moscow, Russia*; STEVEN TAYLOR, *Department of Physics and Astronomy, University College London, London, UK.*

Sodium oxide (NaO) is observed in airglows in the Earth's atmosphere and likely has astronomical importance. This study concerns the transitions with X $^2\Pi$ and and to the very low-lying ($T_0 < 2000$ cm^{-1}) A $^2\Sigma^+$ state. A line list consisting of energy levels, allowed transitions, Einstein coefficients, and a partition function are produced based on variational solution of the coupled rovibronic Schrödinger equations using program Duo[a]. Ab initio calculations which characterized the potential energy, spin-orbit, Λ-doubling and (transition) dipole moment curves were used as starting points to form the final model. Ab initio PECs were parameterized using Morse potentials and improved by least-squares fitting to experimental data on the rotational spectrum by Yamada et al [b] and the electronic spectrum by Joo et al [c]. A lack of data detailing the dissociation energies and vibrational structure of the X and A states prompts a request for further experimental study into the species which would allow further improvement of the model.

[a] S. Yurchenko, L. Lodi, J. Tennyson, A.V. Stolyarov, *Comput. Phys. Comm.*, 2016, **202**, 262-275

[b] C. Yamada, M. Fujitake, E. Hirota, *J. Chem. Phys*, 1989, **90**, 3033

[c] S. Joo, D.R. Worsnop, C.E. Kolb, S.K. Kim, D.R. Herschbach, *J. Phys. Chem.*, 1999, **103**, 3193-3199

TF05 **8:16 – 8:17**

AN *AB INITIO* STUDY OF ELECTRONICALLY EXCITED STATES OF SiN AND SO

GAP-SUE KIM, *Dharma College, Dongguk University, Seoul, Korea*; RYAN BRADY, NICHOLAS CLARK, WILFRID SOMOGYI, MIKHAIL SEMENOV, SERGEI N. YURCHENKO, *Department of Physics and Astronomy, University College London, London, UK.*

CASSCF + MRCI calculations for the diatomic molecules, SiN and SO, have been performed using the C_{2v} point group symmetry. For SiN, five lowest bound electronic have been were considered, $X\,^2\Sigma^+$, $A\,^2\Pi$, $B\,^2\Sigma^+$, $a\,^4\Pi$, $b\,^4\Sigma^+$, while for SO, 9 electronic states were selected, $X\,^3\Sigma^-$, $A\,^3\Pi$, $A'\,^3\Delta$, $A''\,^3\Sigma^+$, $B\,^3\Sigma^-$, $C\,^3\Pi$, $a\,^1\Delta$, $b\,^1\Sigma^+$ and $c\,^1\Sigma^-$, due to their importance for the spectroscopic applications in the IR, Visible and UV regions. For all the excited states potential energy, electronic angular momenta, spin orbit and (transition) dipole moment curves were generated. We use these *ab initio* curves to predict rovibronic spectra of SO and SiN as well as their lifetimes. We aim to construct accurate molecular line lists for these molecules, which will require an empirical refinement of the *ab initio* curves in order to improve the quality of the predictions of experimental spectra.

TF06 **8:20 – 8:21**

AB INITIO AND EMPIRICAL STUDIES OF ELECTRONICALLY EXCITED STATES OF PHOSPHOROUS MONONITRIDE (PN) AND ITS ROVIBRONIC SPECTROSCOPY

MIKHAIL SEMENOV, *Department of Physics and Astronomy, University College London, London, UK*; NAYLA EL-KORK, *Physics, Khalifa University, Abu Dhabi, United Arab Emirates*; SERGEI N. YURCHENKO, JONATHAN TENNYSON, *Department of Physics and Astronomy, University College London, London, UK.*

We report an *ab initio* study on the rovibronic spectroscopy of the open-shell diatomic molecule phosphorous mononitride, PN. The study considers nine lowest electronic states, $X^1\Sigma^+$, $A^1\Pi$, $C^1\Sigma^-$, $D^1\Delta$, $E^1\Sigma^-$, $a^3\Sigma^+$, $b^3\Pi$, $d^3\Delta$ and $e^3\Sigma^-$, using high level electronic structure theory and accurate nuclear motion calculations. Using the *ab initio* data for bond lengths ranging from 1 to 3.16Å, we compute 9 potential energy, 9 spin-orbit coupling, 7 electronic angular momentum coupling, 9 electric dipole moments, and 9 transition dipole moment curves. The Duo nuclear motion program [a] is used to solve the coupled nuclear motion Schrödinger equations for these nine electronic states. The spectra of $^{31}P^{14}N$ simulated for different temperatures are compared with several available high-resolution experimental studies. Lifetimes are calculated for all states and reported here with comparison to previous results in the literature. We then produce a separate line list for the $X^1\Sigma^+$, $A^1\Pi$, $E1\Sigma^-$ states, with the potential energy functions and some couplings being fitted the experimental energy values inverted using the MARVEL procedure.

[a] S. N. Yurchenko, L. Lodi, J. Tennyson, A. V. Stolyarov, *Comput. Phys. Commun.*, 2016, **202**, 262 – 275; see *https://github.com/exomol.*

TF07 **8:24 – 8:25**

SPEED-DEPENDENT VOIGT LINESHAPE PARAMETER DATABASE USING DUAL FREQUENCY COMB LASER ABSORPTION MEASUREMENTS OF PURE AND AIR-BROADENED H_2O FROM 6656-7540 CM^{-1} UP TO 1100 K

SCOTT C EGBERT, NATHAN A MALARICH, DAVID YUN, *Mechanical Engineering, University of Colorado at Boulder, Boulder, CO, USA*; KEEYOON SUNG, *Jet Propulsion Laboratory, California Institute of Technology, Pasadena, CA, USA*; SEAN COBURN, *Department of Mechanical Engineering, University of Colorado Boulder, Boulder, CO, USA*; BRIAN DROUIN, *Jet Propulsion Laboratory, California Institute of Technology, Pasadena, CA, USA*; GREGORY B RIEKER, *Department of Mechanical Engineering, University of Colorado Boulder, Boulder, CO, USA.*

We present broadband dual frequency comb laser measurements of pure and air-broadened H_2O absorption from 6656 to 7540 cm^{-1} (1326-1502 nm) with a spectral point spacing of 0.0068 cm^{-1}. Sample pressure and temperature were carefully controlled for each of the 56 datasets collected, with measured temperatures between 300 and 1100 K and pressures ranging from 0.5 to 16 Torr and 20 to 600 Torr for the pure H_2O and 2% H_2O in air, respectively.

We employ a multispectrum fitting routine based on the quadratic speed-dependent Voigt profile to extract self- and air-broadening and shift parameters, along with corresponding power-law temperature dependence exponents for the thousands of visible absorption features. These results are then compared against existing high temperature H_2O linelists.

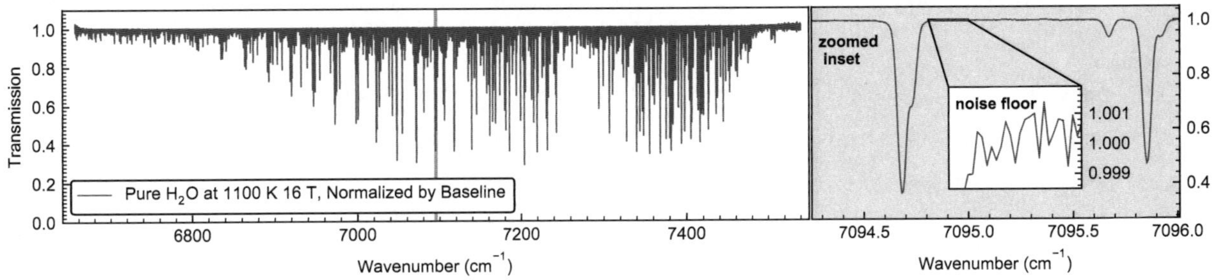

TF08 **8:28 – 8:29**

A THEORETICAL RO-VIBRATIONAL LINE LIST OF H2CS USING A NEW APPROACH TO CONSTRUCT THE EXACT KINETIC ENERGY OPERATOR

THOMAS MELLOR, *Physics and Astronomy , University College London, London, United Kingdom*; SERGEI N. YURCHENKO, *Department of Physics and Astronomy, University College London, London, UK.*

A procedure to generate the exact kinetic energy operator in valence coordinates, based on Sørensen's method for constructing non-rigid Hamiltonians, is presented. This method is currently being applied to the thioformaldehyde (H_2CS) molecule, where the TROVE program is used to compute ro-vibrational energy levels and transition intensities. Moreover, the *ab initio* PES is refined with the MARVEL approach. The exact kinetic energy operator itself is produced using the symbolic computation program *Mathematica* and acts as TROVE input.

TF10 **8:36 – 8:37**

MEASUREMENTS OF NEW LINE POSITIONS AND EFFECTIVE LINE INTENSITIES OF CIS-HONO OF THE ν_2 BAND AROUND 1660 cm^{-1}USING QUANTUM CASCADE LASER ABSORPTION SPECTROSCOPY

NHUT MINH NGO, *Laboratoire de Physico-Chimie de l'Atmosphère, Université du Littoral Côte d'Opale, Dunkerque, France*; QIAN GOU, *School of Chemistry and Chemical Engineering, Chongqing University, Chongqing, China*; NICOLAS HOUZEL, TONG NGUYEN-BA, CÉCILE COEUR, WEIDONG CHEN, *Laboratoire de Physico-Chimie de l'Atmosphère, Université du Littoral Côte d'Opale, Dunkerque, France.*

Observation of HONO concentration change in the atmosphere can improve our understanding of atmospheric chemistry details and their effects on the regional air quality and global climate [1]. However, highly desired spectral line parameters of the most intense bands of HONO in the mid-IR for optical sensing are not available in the common databases like the HITRAN or the GEISA. We report on recent investigation of about 60 new line positions and their effective line strengths of cis-HONO of the ν_2 band in the range of 1660.0-1662.2 cm^{-1}using direct quantum cascade laser absorption spectroscopy coupled to a multi-pass cell (L_{eff} =100 m). The HONO absorption frequencies were absolutely determined using a λ-meter with an accuracy of 0.002 cm^{-1}. The effective line intensities were determined by scaling the measured HONO absorption intensities to the line strengths of two previously reported HONO lines located in the same spectral region near 1659.85 cm^{-1}[2]. The experimental details and the preliminary results will be presented and discussed.

Acknowledgments. The authors thank the financial supports from the regional CPER CLIMIBIO program, the national ANR projects of Labex CaPPA (ANR-10-LABX005) and MULTIPAS-2 (ANR-16-CE04-0012).

References

[1] B.J. Finlayson-Pitts, and J.N. Pitts, Jr., Chemistry of the Upper and Lower Atmosphere, Academic Press, New York, 273–276 (2000).

[2] B.H. Lee, E.C. Wood, J. Wormhoudt, J.H. Shorter, S.C. Herndon, M.S. Zahniser, and J.W. Munger, Effective line strengths of trans-nitrous acid near 1275 $cm^{-1}$and cis-nitrous acid at 1660 cm^{-1}, J. Quant. Spectrosc. Radiat. Transfer 113 (2012) 1905-1912.

TF11 **8:40 – 8:41**

SHOCKGAS-IR: A HIGH-TEMPERATURE AND HIGH-PRESSURE ABSORPTION CROSS-SECTION DATABASE

CHRISTOPHER L STRAND, YIMING DING, SARAH E JOHNSON, WEY-WEY SU, RONALD K HANSON, *Mechanical Engineering, Stanford University, Stanford, CA, USA.*

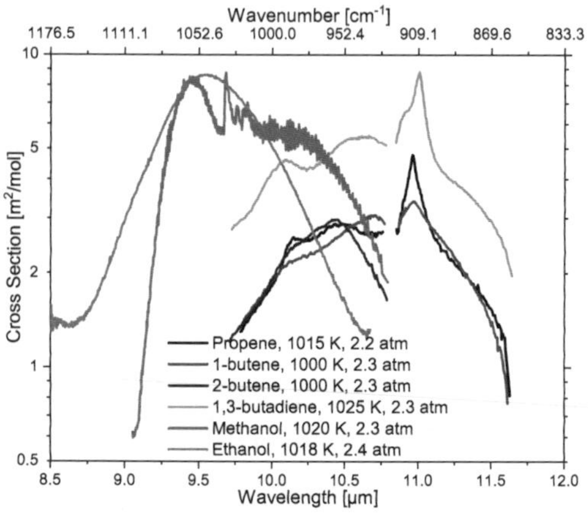

An infrared absorption cross-section database for gas-phase molecules at high-temperatures and high-pressures is under construction to address a growing cross-disciplinary need for experimental data at these conditions. Recently developed broad-scan, rapid-tuning external-cavity quantum cascade lasers (QCL) have enabled the application of shock tube facilities, commonly used to study high-temperature chemical kinetics, to the efficient acquisition of absorption spectra under short-duration shock-heated test gas conditions. Available shock tube facilities can produce temperatures from 500 to 10,000 K and pressures from 0.1 to 1000 atm with test time durations ranging from 500 μs to 50 ms. Uncertainties in the known thermodynamic conditions as low as $\pm 1\%$ can be achieved. Presently available laser systems enable the rapid acquisition ($<$ 10 ms) of approximately 300 cm^{-1} wide spectral regions at any location within the QCL-accessible wavelength region of 3.6 -11.7 μm (850 - 2800 cm^{-1}). The resulting spectra are composed of discrete data points at a spectral interval ranging from 0.3 - 0.6 cm^{-1} and an instrument broadening function defined by the laser linewidth ($\leq$ 0.0033 cm^{-1}).

Present efforts are focused on studying large polyatomic molecules (4+ atoms) dilute in a bath gas of argon under conditions for which dissociation is negligible and test time durations are favorable (T $<$ 1600K and P $<$ 5atm). The database currently includes ethylene, methanol, and ethanol with over a dozen more species measured and being prepared for inclusion soon. Database permanent URL: https://purl.stanford.edu/cy149sv5686

TF12 **8:44 – 8:45**

A NEW STRATEGY FOR COLLECTION OF HIGH-TEMPERATURE BROAD-BAND ABSORPTION SPECTRA FOR GAS-PHASE MOLECULES IN THE MID-INFRARED

YIMING DING, SARAH E JOHNSON, CHRISTOPHER L STRAND, RONALD K HANSON, *Mechanical Engineering, Stanford University, Stanford, CA, USA.*

To address the notable lack of knowledge on high-temperature absorption cross sections of important molecular species in combustion and exoplanets, a new strategy is proposed and deployed to collect broad-band absorption spectra in shock-heated gases. The methodology utilizes a broad-scan, rapid-tuning external-cavity quantum cascade laser in conjunction with a shock tube and is capable of providing quantitative spectroscopic information across full vibrational bands spanning over 200 cm^{-1}within 6 ms (> 30,000 cm^{-1}/s), with a spectral resolution between 0.3 – 0.6 cm^{-1}. This experimental approach is demonstrated with absorption spectra measurements on the ν_7 vibrational band of ethylene (C_2H_4) from 8.4 μm to 11.7 μm at temperature/pressure conditions between 800 – 1600 K, 1 – 5 atm. The measured spectra are compared against spectral simulations using existing spectroscopic databases, showing better agreement with the line list of Rey et al.[a] than of HITRAN 2016[b]. With the current set of instruments available, this methodology could be applied to numerous gas-phase molecules that have attractive absorption features in the spectral range of 3.6 – 11.7 μm and opens an efficient pathway towards improving knowledge on radiation absorption in the mid-infrared at high temperatures.

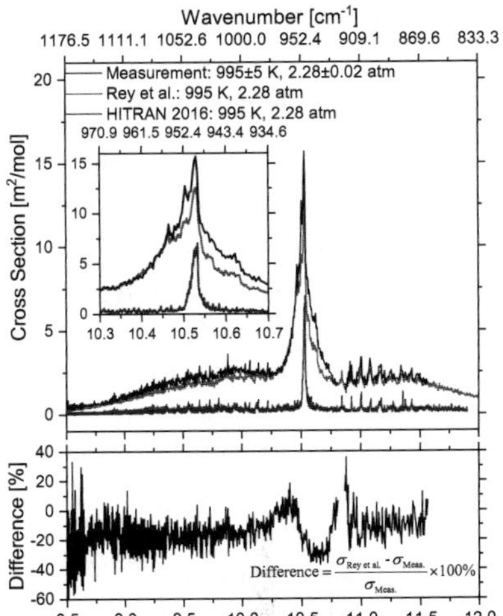

[a]M. Rey, T. Delahaye, A. V. Nikitin, and V. G. Tyuterev, "First theoretical global line lists of ethylene ($^{12}C_2H_4$) spectra for the temperature range 50-700 K in the far-infrared for quantification of absorption and emission in planetary atmospheres," Astron. Astrophys., vol. 594, pp. 1–16, 2016.

[b]I. E. Gordon et al., "The HITRAN2016 molecular spectroscopic database," J. Quant. Spectrosc. Radiat. Transf., vol. 203, pp. 3–69, 2017.

TG. Plenary
Tuesday, June 22, 2021 – 9:0 AM
Room: 2021 Online Everywhere

Chair: Robert W Field, MIT, Cambridge, MA, USA

TG02 **9:03 – 9:43**

IMAGING ROTATIONAL WAVE PACKETS IN MOLECULES AND CLUSTERS

YASUHIRO OHSHIMA, *Department of Chemistry, Tokyo Institute of Technology, Tokyo, Japan.*

Irradiation of ultrashort laser pulses onto a molecular ensemble inherently results in the creation of a quantum wave packet (WP), i.e., a coherent superposition of several (or sometimes many) eigenstates. It is an ultimate goal in modern molecular physics to establish the way for creating WPs as designed, and it is also essential for advanced WP manipulation to know how to characterize the WP experimentally.

Over the last two decades, intense nonresonant excitation has been extensively adopted to realize "nonadiabatic molecular alignment" or "nonadiabatic rotational excitation," where the impulsive torque due to anisotropic molecular polarizability instantaneously aligns the molecules and their rotation is coherently excited in the vibronic ground-state manifold.[a] Evolution of the rotational WP thus created can be tracked as a series of images for the time-dependent molecular orientational distribution, e.g., by implementing pump-probe Coulomb explosion ion-imaging measurements. We will represent some examples of such "molecular movies" taken with a newly developed imaging configuration,[b] which is capable to clearly capture the time-dependent nodal structures, instantaneous alignment, angular dispersion, and fractional revivals of the rotational WP while the molecular ensemble keeps rotating in one direction.[c]

Wave-packet imaging will also be developed as a new approach in molecular spectroscopy, since energy intervals between the eigenstates that constitute the WP are encoded in the molecular movies shoot by the method. We will show some recent results along this direction; rotational spectra have been successfully extracted for homodimers of nonpolar molecules, which have been scarcely investigated because of the difficulty in recording or analyzing their microwave or infrared spectrum.

[a]Y. Ohshima and Hasegawa, Int. Rev. Chem. Phys. **29**, 619 (2010).
[b]K. Mizuse, R. Fujimoto, and Y. Ohshima, Rev. Sci. Instrum. **90**, 103107 (2019).
[c]K. Mizuse, K. Kitano, H. Hasegawa, and Y. Ohshima, Sci. Adv. **1**, e1400185 (2015).

TH. Mini-symposium: Large Amplitude Motions

Tuesday, June 22, 2021 – 10:0 AM

Room: 2021 Online Everywhere

Chair: Kaori Kobayashi, University of Toyama, Toyama, Japan

TH01 *INVITED TALK* **10:00 – 10:02**

THE EXCEL-ERATION OF METHANOL SPECTROSCOPY: ISOTOPIC TUNING OF TORSION-VIBRATION INTERACTIONS

RONALD M. LEES, *Department of Physics, University of New Brunswick, Saint John, NB, Canada.*

One of the current "frontiers" in the spectroscopy of molecules with large amplitude motion is the extension of the analysis of excited vibrational states to move beyond the isolated state model to a more global treatment including several coupled vibrational modes. Before that, of course, one needs to explore the isolated states themselves, and there are still states even for small molecules like methanol, methyl mercaptan and methylamine whose structures have not yet been characterized in detail. In this task, the use of Loomis-Wood plots and Excel spreadsheets has proved to be very helpful, in conjunction with solid bases of ground-state energy term values provided by the pioneering work of the microwave and THz community. The Excel difference table approach relies on systematic trends in the J-dependence of the spectral sub-bands, and can be a sensitive pointer to perturbations arising from level-crossing resonances between interacting modes. The vibrational modes can also exhibit anharmonic resonances with the ground-state torsional manifold as it rises up through the vibrational regions. Isotopic substitution can then serve as a useful tool for tuning the resonances with two degrees of freedom, one along the energy axis by altering the relative energies of the coupled states, and a second along the K-axis by changing the value of the ρ parameter which governs the periodic K-dependence of the torsional energies. Examples will be presented of this "isotopic tuning" for isotopologues of methanol, along with discussion of features of the Excel spreadsheet approach. We will also illustrate how isotopic shifts may give insight into sub-band vibrational assignments from comparison of the torsion-vibration manifolds of the lower modes of normal CH_3OH and its O-18 relative.

TH03 **10:12 – 10:13**

A NEW PROGRAM FOR RADICALS WITH INTERNAL ROTATION

J. H. WESTERFIELD, KYLE N. CRABTREE, *Department of Chemistry, University of California, Davis, Davis, CA, USA.*

The presently available tools of rotational spectroscopy do not provide a meaningful way to treat small organic radicals with methyl groups. This in turn prevents astrochemical detection of these species as it is not possible to accurately predict rotational spectra complicated by both spin-rotation coupling and methyl torsions. This work presents a new program capable of treating these interactions in C_s molecules as well as a new operator to account for spin-torion interactions. The program, written in Julia, utilizes BELGI's two stage diagonalization process to address the torsions in the first stage with the spin-rotation and spin-torsion terms being added into the second diagonalization stage. SPCAT and PGOPHER were used to test just the spin-rotation implementation while BELGI was used to test the torsional-rotation implementation. This preliminary testing of the new program has shown initial agreement with the existing programs. The current status of the program and the next stages in its implementation will be discussed.

TH04 **10:16 – 10:17**

1- AND 2-DIMENSIONAL POTENTAL FUNCTIONS WHEN V_3 IS NOT THE BARRIER

PETER GRONER, *Department of Chemistry, University of Missouri - Kansas City, Kansas City, MO, USA.*

In simple cases of methyl group internal rotation, the barrier to internal rotation is equal to the V_3 coefficient in the standard equation of the potential function. In the past few years, methyl internal rotation potentials have been reported with significant V_6 contributions, of which p-toluic acid is just one example.[a] For $|V_6| << |V_3|$, the barrier is still $|V_3|$. However, if $0 < |V_3/V_6| < 4$, there are now two different barriers because there are two different potential minima (or maxima), and none of the barriers is equal to $|V_3|$ or $|V_6|$. Their difference is exactly $|V_3|$ but, for $V_3 > 0$ and $V_6 < 0$, the lower barrier is equal to $-V_6(1 + V_3/(4V_6))^2$. It is therefore incorrect to say that $|V_3|$ or $|V_6|$ is the barrier. Of course, corresponding effects are also present in systems with two or more internal rotors. However, in 2-D systems, additional minima and/or maxima may occur when potential interaction terms become significant, e.g. when V_{33} and/or V'_{33} have magnitudes similar to V_3 in a molecule like acetone (molecular symmetry group $G_{36} = [33]C_{2v}$). A number of examples for 1-D and 2-D systems are given and some consequences for the spectroscopy are discussed.

[a]E.G. Schnitzler, et al., J. Phys. Chem. A 121 (2017) 8625

TH05 **10:20 – 10:21**

GLOBAL ANALYSIS OF THE CD_2HOH MOLECULE ROTATION-TORSION SPECTRUM

L. MARGULÈS, R. A. MOTIYENKO, *UMR 8523 - PhLAM - Physique des Lasers Atomes et Molécules, University of Lille, CNRS, F-59000 Lille, France*; F. KWABIA TCHANA, *CNRS - Université de Paris - Université Paris Est Créteil , LISA, Créteil, France*; L. H. COUDERT, *Institut des Sciences Moléculaires d'Orsay, Université Paris Saclay, CNRS, Orsay, France.*

Doubly deuterated methanol CD_2HOH is a non-rigid molecule displaying internal rotation of its asymmetrical CD_2H methyl group. Like the isotopic species of methanol with a symmetrical CH_3 or CD_3 group, it displays a strong rotation-torsion Coriolis coupling. Unlike these species, it also displays a dependence of its generalized inertia tensor on the angle of internal rotation. Its complicated rotation-torsion spectrum was investigated in the microwave,[a] submillimeter-wave,[b,c] terahertz,[b] and FIR[b,c,d] domains. Although more than 3000 transitions have been assigned so far, no global analysis, like the one performed for the analogous species CH_2DOH,[e] has been carried out.

In this talk, new assignments in the terahertz and FIR spectra of CD_2HOH will be reported. Parallel and perpendicular transitions, characterized by a higher K-value than in our previous investigation,[b] could be identified up to $J = 35$ for the three lowest lying torsional states. Using the theoretical approach developed for CH_2DOH,[e] a global analysis of the available high-resolution data could also be carried out and parameters describing the hindering potential and the generalized inertia tensor[f] were determined. So far, this global analysis has been restricted to transitions with $K \leq 9$ as rotation-torsion levels with $K > 9$ are affected by a yet non-identified rotation-torsion couplings and cannot be properly modeled.

[a]Liu and Quade, *J. Mol. Spectrosc.* **146** (1991) 252; Su, Liu, and Quade, *J. Mol. Spectrosc.* **149** (1991) 557; Quade, Liu, Mukhopadhyay, and Su, *J. Mol. Spectrosc.* **192** (1998) 378; Su and Quade, *J. Chem. Phys.* **90** (1989) 1396

[b]Ndao, Tchana, Coudert, Motiyenko, Margulès, Barros, Manceron, and Roy, *J. Mol. Spectrosc.* **326** (2015) 136

[c]Mukhopadhyay, *Inf. Phys. Tech.* **75** (2016) 139; *ibid.* **76** (2016) 116

[d]Mukhopadhyay and Billinghurst, *Inf. Phys. Tech.* **113** (2021) 103563

[e]Coudert, Zemouli, Motiyenko, Margulès, and Klee, *J. Chem. Phys.* **140** (2014) 064307

[f]Liu and Quade, *J. Mol. Spectrosc.* **146** (1991) 238; El Hilali, Coudert, Konov, and Klee, *J. Chem. Phys.* **135** (2011) 194309

TH06 **10:24 – 10:25**

NEW MEASUREMENTS AND ASSIGNMENTS IN THE v_t = 0, 1, 2 TORSIONAL STATES OF CD_3OH AND CH_3OD: FROM MILLIMETER-WAVE TO FIR SPECTRA

V. ILYUSHIN, YAN BAKHMAT, E. A. ALEKSEEV, OLGA DOROVSKAYA, *Radiospectrometry Department, Institute of Radio Astronomy of NASU, Kharkov, Ukraine*; HOLGER S. P. MÜLLER, FRANK LEWEN, STEPHAN SCHLEMMER, *I. Physikalisches Institut, Universität zu Köln, Köln, Germany*; SIGURD BAUERECKER, CHRISTOF MAUL, *Institut für Physikalische und Theoretische Chemie, Technische Universität Braunschweig, Braunschweig, Germany*; K. BEREZKIN[a], *Research School of High-Energy Physics, National Research Tomsk Polytechnic University, Tomsk, Russia*; RONALD M. LEES, LI-HONG XU, *Department of Physics, University of New Brunswick, Saint John, NB, Canada.*

We present[b] the results of our new study of the torsion-rotation spectra of the two deuterated isotopologues of methanol: CD_3OH and CH_3OD. The new microwave measurements were carried out from the millimeter wave range (starting at 34 GHz) to the THz range (up to 1.1 THz) using spectrometers in Kharkiv and Köln. The new measurements in the FIR range were carried out in Braunschweig for CD_3OH from 20 to 900 cm^{-1}. In this work we significantly extend the rotational quantum number coverage for both isotopologues (from J_{up} = 26 [1] to J_{up} = 55 for CD_3OH and from J_{up} =21 [2] to J_{up} =40 for CH_3OD). The analysis is done using the rho axis method and the RAM36 program code. Our preliminary fits show that for both isotopologs the v_t = 2 torsional state is significantly affected by intervibrational interactions with non-torsional vibrational modes which propagate down through intertorsional interactions. At the same time, for CD_3OH we were able to get a fit within experimental error for v_t = 0, 1 states. For CH_3OD analysis is in progress now. In the talk the details of this new study will be discussed.

[1] A. Predoi-Cross, Li-Hong Xu, M.S. Walsh, R.M. Lees, M. Winnewisser, and H. Lichau J. Mol. Spectrosc.188, 94–101 (1998). [2] Y.-B. Duan, I. Ozier, S. Tsunekawa, and K. Takagi, J. Mol. Spectrosc. 218 (2003) 95–107.

[a]Current address: Institut für Physikalische und Theoretische Chemie, Technische Universität Braunschweig, D - 38106, Braunschweig, Germany

[b]This work was done under support of the Deutsche Forschungsgemeinschaft and Volkswagen foundation. The assistance of Science and Technology Center in Ukraine is acknowledged (STCU partner project P756).

TH07 **10:28 – 10:29**

A SIMULTANEOUS FIT OF THE TORSION-WAGGING-ROTATIONAL LEVELS FROM THE EXCITED (V_t = 0, 1 and 2) STATES OF METHYLAMINE USING A HYBRID (TUNNELING AND NON-TUNNELING) HAMILTONIAN FORMALISM

ISABELLE KLEINER, *Université Paris-Est Créteil et Université de Paris, Laboratoire Interuniversitaire des systèmes atmosphériques (LISA), CNRS UMR7583, Creteil, France*; IWONA GULACZYK, MAREK KREGLEWSKI, *Faculty of Chemistry, Adam Mickiewicz University, Poznan, Poland*; R. A. MOTIYENKO, PRAKASH GYAWALI, *UMR 8523 - PhLAM - Physique des Lasers Atomes et Molécules, University of Lille, CNRS, F-59000 Lille, France*; V. ILYUSHIN, *Radiospectrometry Department, Institute of Radio Astronomy of NASU, Kharkov, Ukraine.*

We used our hybrid program[a] to fit an extended dataset consisting of almost 30000 rotational-torsionial-wagging transitions in the MW and FIR of v_t = 0, 1 and 2 of CH_3NH_2. The program can fit rotational levels in molecules with one CH_3 internal-rotation large-amplitude motion, one NH_2 inversion large-amplitude motion. Our data set contains around 3000 MW and 26848 FIR transitions, which are fit to a weighted standard deviation of 1.75 using 102 parameters. Most of the FIR transitions are taken from recent measurements of the v_t = 1-0 band centered near 265 cm-1[b], and the ground torsional state transitions are from Motiyenko et al.[c]. Around new 340 and 176 microwave transitions were also assigned in the v_t = 1-1 and v_t = 2-2 states respectivelly. We hope to be able to fit all this data simultaneously with the far-infrared data from v_t = 2-1, 2-0 and 2-2[d].

[a]I. Kleiner and J. T. Hougen, J. Mol. Spectrosc., 368, 111255 (2020)

[b]I. Gulaczyk, M. Kreglewski, V.-M. Horneman, J. Mol. Spectrosc. 342 (2017) 25-30

[c]R.A. Motiyenko, V.V. Ilyushin, B.J. Drouin, S. Yu, L. Margulès, Astron.Astrophys. 563 (2014) A1

[d]Part of this work has been funded by the Programme National de Physique Chimie du Milieu Interstellaire (PCMI) and French ANR Labex CaPPA through the PIA under Contract No. ANR-11-LABX-0005-01

TH08 **10:32 – 10:33**

ULTRAHIGH-RESOLUTION LASER SPECTROSCOPY OF ACETALDEHYDE : TORSION-INVERSION-ROTATION INTERACTION IN THE EXCITED STATE

KOSUKE NAKAJIMA, AKIRA SHIMIZU, *Graduate School of Science, Kobe University, Kobe, Japan*; SHUNJI KASAHARA, *Molecular Photoscience Research Center, Kobe University, Kobe, Japan*; MASATOSHI MISONO, *Applied Physics, Fukuoka University, Fukuoka, Japan*; MASAAKI BABA, *Graduate School of Science, Kyoto University, Kyoto, Japan.*

Li-Hong Xu, Jon Hougen, Isabelle Kleiner, Jens-Uwe Grabow et al. beautifully analyzed ro-vibrational levels in the ground state of acetaldehyde taking CH_3-torsion rotation interaction into consideration [a b]. For the lowest electronic excited state S_1 $(n\pi^\star)$ state, the ro-vibrational level structure is much more complicated because of the out-of-plane distorsion in the CHO moiety (tunnel splitting due to double minimum potential) in addition to the profound level structure of CH_3 torsion [c d]. We observed and analyzed rotationally resolved ultrahigh-resolution spectra for the $S_1 \leftarrow S_0$ transition of jet-cooled aectaldehyde, of which the resolution was much higher than those reported previously [e f]. The effective rotational constant A_{eff} was found to be drastically different between the levels of below and above the barrier to CH_3 rotation. We well explained this fact by considering the mechanism of Coriolis interaction and estimating the interaction strength by a model calculation.

[a]L.-H. Xu, J. T. Hougen et al., J. Mol. Spectrosc. **214**, 175 (2002).
[b]I. Kleiner, J. T. Hougen, J.-W. Grabow et al., J. Mol. Spectrosc. **179**, 41 (1996).
[c]M. Baba, I. Hanazaki, and U. Nagashima, J. Chem. Phys. **82**, 3938 (1985).
[d]M. Baba, U. Nagashima, and I. Hanazaki, J. Chem. Phys. **83**, 3514 (1985).
[e]E. C. Lim, R. H. Judge, D. C. Moule et al., J. Mol. Spectrosc. **190**, 78 (1998).
[f]I.-C. Chen et al., J. Chem. Phys. **115**, 5089 (2001).

TH09 **10:36 – 10:37**

MULTI-DIMENSIONAL PROTON TUNNELING IN 2-METHYLMALONALDEHYDE

IWONA GULACZYK, MAREK KREGLEWSKI, *Faculty of Chemistry, Adam Mickiewicz University, Poznan, Poland.*

2-methylmalonaldehyde (2-MMA) has two large amplitude strongly coupled large amplitude vibrations (LAVs), internal rotation of the methyl group and proton tunneling between two equivalent oxygen atoms, which results in a multiple splitting of the ground vibrational state. Since the symmetry group of 2-MMA is G_{12} isomorphic to a point group C_{6v}, each vibrational level of LAV is split into nondegenerate (A_1, A_2, B_1, B_2) and degenerate (E_1, E_2) substates. In the present paper a four-dimensional model for 2-MMA is discussed where the out-of-plane vibrations are treated together with LAVs. In the standard approach the out-of-plane vibrations are handled as non-degenerate. In the non-rigid picture both out-of plane vibrations can be treated as a degenerate mode strongly coupled to LAVs and are also split into nondegenerate and degenerate substates. This effect is shown numerically using a simple harmonic model for out-of-plane degenerate mode. The results show that the out-of-plane vibrations are split into several components and their vibrational excitation should create a system of several transitions belonging to different species of the G_{12} symmetry group.

TH10 10:40 – 10:41

A UBIQUITOUS KINETIC COUPLING BETWEEN TORSION AND IN- AND OUT-OF-PLANE XH_3 WAGGING VIBRATIONS FOR AN $-XH_3$ GROUP ATTACHED TO A PLANAR FRAME

JASON R. GASCOOKE, WARREN D. LAWRANCE, *College of Science and Engineering, Flinders University, Adelaide, South Australia, Australia.*

As a large amplitude motion, the internal rotation of a methyl group, methyl torsion, is traditionally treated as being separate from the remaining small amplitude vibrations.[1] However, recent studies have shown that this is not the case in toluene,[2] several substituted toluenes[3,4] and *N*-methylpyrrole,[5] where methyl torsion interacts with vibrations involving out-of-plane wagging of the methyl group. Likewise, interaction between silyl torsion and the out-of-plane silyl wagging mode has been observed in phenylsilane.[6]

The origin of this interaction is discussed from a kinetic energy perspective in a curvilinear framework. The model considered consists of three vibrational motions when an XH_3 group is attached to a planar frame: the in-plane and out-of-plane wagging motions of the XH_3 group and XH_3 group internal rotation. Tilting of the XH_3 group relative to the frame is included. When the "equilibrium position" of the XH_3 group at each torsional angle involves it being tilted relative to the planar frame, the XH_3 wag vibrations kinetically couple with the torsional motion, with the coupling terms being linearly dependent on the magnitude of the respective XH_3 tilt angles. The coupling only vanishes when the tilt angle is zero. XH_3 tilt also leads to the $-XH_3$ group precessing relative to the frame during the torsional motion. Quantum chemistry calculations on a range of methylated molecules show the ubiquitous nature of in-plane and out-of-plane methyl group tilt, and hence the pervasive nature of the interaction between methyl torsion and in-plane and out-of-plane wag vibrations of the methyl group.

1. D. G. Lister, J. N. Macdonald and N. L. Owen, Internal rotation and inversion: an introduction to large amplitude motions in molecules. (Academic Press, London, 1978). 2. J. R. Gascooke, E. A. Virgo and W. D. Lawrance, J. Chem. Phys. 142, 024315 (2015). 3. J. R. Gascooke, L. D. Stewart, P. G. Sibley and W. D. Lawrance, J. Chem. Phys. 149, 074301 (2018). 4. L. D. Stewart, J. R. Gascooke and W. D. Lawrance, J. Chem. Phys. 150, 174303 (2019). 5. J. R. Gascooke and W. D. Lawrance, unpublished results. 6. M. Griggs, J. R. Gascooke and W. D. Lawrance, unpublished results.

TH11 10:44 – 10:45

ROTATIONALLY RESOLVED $S_1 \leftarrow S_0$ ORIGIN BANDS OF DIFFERENT METHYLINDOLES AND THEIR INTERNAL ROTATION EFFECTS

MARIE-LUISE HEBESTREIT, HILDA LARTIAN , HAJO BÖSCHEN, *Institut für Physikalische Chemie I, Heinrich-Heine-Universität, Düsseldorf, NRW, Germany*; W. LEO MEERTS, *Institute for Molecules and Materials (IMM), Radboud University Nijmegen, Nijmegen, Netherlands*; MICHAEL SCHMITT, *Institut für Physikalische Chemie I, Heinrich-Heine-Universität, Düsseldorf, NRW, Germany.*

We determined the electronic nature, the dipole moments and the torsional barriers in the ground and electronically lowest excited singlet state of substituted indoles using rotationally resolved laser induced fluorescence Stark spectroscopy. The electronic origin bands of 1-, 3- and 5-methylindole have been investigated before *via* high resolution spectroscopy and the perturbation by the hindered internal rotation of the methyl group was discussed in detail by the groups of Pratt and Meerts [1,2]. In general each spectrum consists of two overlapping subbands due to the $0a_1 \leftarrow 0a_1$ and $1e \leftarrow 1e$ torsional transitions. In 6-methylindole the difference of the torsional level splitting between the $0a_1$ and 1e levels in the ground and excited state is large enough, to have the two origins of the subbands shifted more than 90 GHz, i.e. completely separated. Both resulting spectra were evaluated *via* evolutionary algorithms and compared to the results of *ab initio* calculations. The rotational constants, the orientation of the transition dipole moment, the size and orientation of the permanent dipole moment, the torsional barrier heights and the orientation of the internal rotor axis in the ground and electronically excited states along with the fluorescence lifetime could be determined. Finally a comparison with the torsional barriers of other methylindoles is given in this presentation.

[1] T. M. Korter and D. W. Pratt, J. Phys. Chem. B **105**, 4010 (2001)
[2] K. Remmers, E. Jalviste, I. Mistrík, G. Berden, and W. L. Meerts, J. Chem. Phys. **108**, 8436 (1998)

TH12 **10:48 – 10:49**

STUDY OF LARGE AMPLITUDE MOTIONS OF METHYL GROUP IN 9-METHYLANTHRACENE BY HIGH-RESOLUTION SPECTROSCOPY

MASATOSHI MISONO, SHO YAMASAKI, *Applied Physics, Fukuoka University, Fukuoka, Japan*; SHUNJI KASAHARA, *Molecular Photoscience Research Center, Kobe University, Kobe, Japan*; AKIKO NISHIYAMA, *Institute of Physics, Faculty of Physics, Astronomy and Informatics, Nicolaus Copernicus University, Torun, Poland*; MASAAKI BABA, *Division of Chemistry, Graduate School of Science, Kyoto University, Kyoto, Japan.*

We study large amplitude motions of methyl group in 9-methylanthracene (9MA) by high-resolution spectroscopy. 9MA molecules are delivered in a supersonic beam and are excited by a single mode Ti:Sapphire laser. The frequency of the laser is controlled with reference to an Er doped fiber optical frequency comb.

The figure is the observed rovibronic spectra of $\mathrm{S}_1(0a_1') \leftarrow \mathrm{S}_0(0a_1')$ and $\mathrm{S}_1(1e'') \leftarrow \mathrm{S}_0(1e'')$ transitions. Although the two transitions are overlapped, the rotational lines are well resolved. Now we try to assign the rotational lines and to analyze interactions in the vibronic excited states.

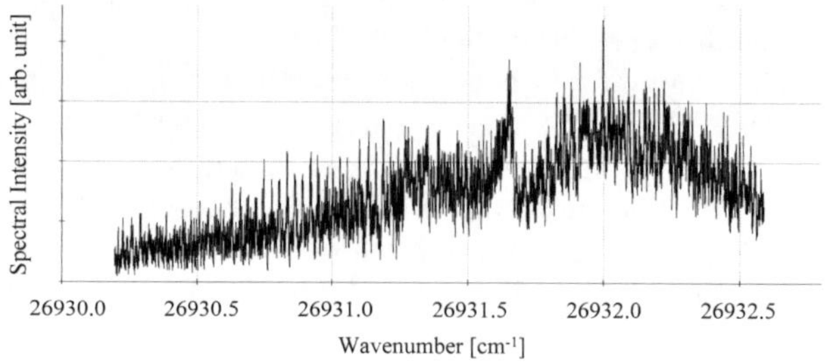

TI. Instrument/Technique Demonstration

Tuesday, June 22, 2021 – 10:0 AM

Room: 2021 Online Everywhere

Chair: Brant E. Billinghurst, Canadian Light Source Inc., Saskatoon, SK, Canada

TI01 **10:00 – 10:01**

THE HEROES OF TERAHERTZ SYNCHROTRON SPECTROSCOPY

THOMAS SANDOW HEARNE, OLIVIER PIRALI, MARIE-ALINE MARTIN-DRUMEL, *Institut des Sciences Moléculaires d'Orsay, Université Paris Saclay, CNRS, Orsay, France*; P. ROY, *AILES beamline, Synchrotron SOLEIL, Saint Aubin, France*; JEAN-FRANÇOIS LAMPIN, *UMR CNRS 8520, Institut d'Electronique de Microélectronique et de Nanotechnologie, Villeneuve d'Ascq, France*; MARIE-HÉLÈNE MAMMEZ, DOMINIQUE MAMMEZ, FRANCIS HINDLE, GAËL MOURET, *Laboratoire de Physico-Chimie de l'Atmosphère, Université du Littoral Côte d'Opale, Dunkerque, France.*

Technological innovation is a key driver in the field of molecular spectroscopy, and despite recent leaps forward with chirped-pulse spectroscopy, multiplication chains, dual-comb techniques, and mid-infrared lasers, there remains still a sizeable spectral gap, untouched by these innovations, from around 1 to 10 THz. In this terahertz gap it is still difficult to produce high-resolution broadband spectra. The HEROES project aims to fill the gap, by combining a new generation of far-IR molecular laser with synchrotron radiation.[a,b] The HEROES spectrometer uses heterodyne mixing of a far-IR laser, pumped by a quantum cascade laser, with broadband far-IR synchrotron radiation, within a hot electron bolometer to produce spectra from 1 to 5.5 THz with 5 GHz instantaneous bandwidth and 80 kHz resolution. This resolution is 375 times finer than the ultimate resolution available with the Bruker Fourier-transform infrared (FTIR) spectrometer installed on the AILES beamline at SOLEIL (30 MHz). This allows for far more precise determinations of transition energies, particularly important in the field of astrochemistry. Recent improvements to the HEROES spectrometer will be presented, along with a demonstration of its ability to resolve complicated spectral features, such as transitions in the rotational-torsional spectrum of methanol and its deuterated isotopologues. Further improvements to the technique will also be proposed.

[a] Lampin, J.-F. et al. Opt. Lett. (2019) 44, 20
[b] Paiges, A. et al. APL Photonics (2016) 1, 031302

TI02 **10:04 – 10:05**

CHARACTERIZATION OF A THZ ELECTRIC FIELD BY MOLECULAR ION SPECTROSCOPY

FLORIN LUCIAN CONSTANTIN, *UMR 8523 CNRS, Laboratoire PHLAM, Villeneuve d'Ascq, France.*

The Rydberg atom spectroscopy, exploited for SI-traceable electrometry, allowed to measure weak microwave electric fields at the μV/cm level. The Doppler-free spectroscopy methods allowed recently significant improvements of the resolution and precision of the measurements with cold trapped HD^+ molecular ions. The ab-initio molecular ion theory provided accurate predictions of the HD^+ energy levels and their shifts in external fields. This contribution proposes a new method to characterize a THz electric field that is off-resonantly coupled to the HD^+ energy levels based on the comparison of the measurements of the lighshifts induced on a two-photon rovibrational transition with the theoretical ab-initio predictions. Precisely, a THz-wave slightly detuned to the Zeeman subcomponents of the (v,L)=(0,0)-(0,1) transition may be characterized by measuring the lightshift of a Zeeman subcomponent of the (v,L)=(0,0)-(2,0) two-photon transition with potential Hz-level uncertainty limited by the molecular ion quantum projection noise. This method allows detecting a THz electric field at the μV/m level from a THz-wave optimally detuned to a hyperfine transition of HD^+. An algorithm is proposed to retrieve the amplitudes and the phases of a THz electric field in a Cartesian reference frame from six lightshift measurements using two orientations and three values of the static magnetic field in the ion trap. The Cartesian components of the electric field of a THz-wave, with an intensity of 1 W/m^2, circularly polarized, and detuned to a hyperfine transition of HD^+, may be characterized with mV/m-level uncertainties for the amplitudes, and 0.1 rad-level for the phases.

TI03 **10:08 – 10:09**

AN HETERODYNE SPECTROMETER FOR TERAHERTZ SPECTROSCOPY

DOMINIQUE MAMMEZ, MARIE-HÉLÈNE MAMMEZ, FRANCIS HINDLE, GAËL MOURET, *Laboratoire de Physico-Chimie de l'Atmosphère, Université du Littoral Côte d'Opale, Dunkerque, France*; THOMAS SANDOW HEARNE, MARIE-ALINE MARTIN-DRUMEL, OLIVIER PIRALI, *Institut des Sciences Moléculaires d'Orsay, Université Paris Saclay, CNRS, Orsay, France*; SOPHIE ELIET, JEAN-FRANÇOIS LAMPIN, *UMR CNRS 8520, Institut d'Electronique de Microélectronique et de Nanotechnologie, Villeneuve d'Ascq, France.*

The Terahertz (THz) region of the electromagnetic spectrum between the infrared to the microwave domains (0.1 – 10 THz) is often referred to as the "THz gap". Nevertheless, it has become widely accessible over the last decades by different sources, particularly with multiplication chains. In this context, the HEROES consortium has developed a heterodyne spectrometer based on a far-infrared (FIR) molecular laser pumped by a mid-infrared (MIR) quantum cascade laser (QCL) to address this spectral domain [a,b]. We present here a laboratory setup mixing on a hot electron bolometer (HEB) the FIR emission from the QCL-pumped molecular laser with a blackbody radiation transmitted by an single-path cell filled with a few μbar of the gaz under investigation. This setup enables to perform high resolution spectroscopy of rotational transitions of small molecules between 1 THz and 3.37 THz with a 5 GHz bandwidth and 80 kHz resolution. We will demonstrate these performances through absorption spectra of methanol at 1 THz and 2 THz along with emission spectra against a cold bakground of methanol and CD_3OD.

[a]Lampin, J.-F. et al. Opt. Lett. (2019) 44, 20
[b]Pagies, A. et al. APL Photonics (2016) 1, 031302

TI04 **10:12 – 10:13**

THZ FABRY-PEROT SPECTROMETER

FRANCIS HINDLE, CORALIE ELMALEH, *Laboratoire de Physico-Chimie de l'Atmosphère, Université du Littoral Côte d'Opale, Dunkerque, France*; FABIEN SIMON, *SATT-Nord, SATT-Nord, Lille, France*; A. PIENKINA, ROBIN BOCQUET, ARNAUD CUISSET, GAËL MOURET, *Laboratoire de Physico-Chimie de l'Atmosphère, Université du Littoral Côte d'Opale, Dunkerque, France.*

The development of Cavity-Enhanced Techniques and Cavity Ring Down Spectroscopy has allowed many sensitive infrared measurements to be undertaken. We have constructed a THz resonator with a high finesse to form the basis of a new instrument for sensitive cavity enhanced THz measurements. The resonator uses a low loss oversized corrugated waveguide and high reflectivity photonic mirrors. An effective path length of one kilometer is obtained for a device that is 50 cm in length. A significant sensitivity improvement has been evaluated at 620 GHz by the measurement of minority isotopologues of OCS[a]. The sensitivity achieved has allowed several centrifugal distortion-induced rotational lines of CF_4 to be recorded and its tetrahedral splitting to be resolved [b].

[a]Francis Hindle, Robin Bocquet, Anastasiia Pienkina, Arnaud Cuisset, and Gaël Mouret, Terahertz gas phase spectroscopy using a high finesse Fabry-Pérot cavity Optica (2019) vol 6, 1449-1454 DOI: 10.1364/OPTICA.6.001449

[b]Cuisset A, Hindle F, Mouret G, Bocquet R, Bruckhuisen J, Decker J, Pienkina A, Bray C, Fertein E, Boudon V. Terahertz Rotational Spectroscopy of Greenhouse Gases Using Long Interaction Path-Lengths Applied Sciences (2021) vol 11(3) p 1229. https://doi.org/10.3390/app11031229

TI05 **10:16 – 10:17**

TECHNICAL ENHANCEMENTS OF A SUBMILLIMETER-WAVE SPECTROMETER: LABORATORY DETECTION OF NEW LINES OF METHANOL RADICAL DERIVATIVES

JEAN-THIBAUT SPANIOL, OLIVIA CHITARRA, THOMAS SANDOW HEARNE, MARIE-ALINE MARTIN-DRUMEL, OLIVIER PIRALI, *Institut des Sciences Moléculaires d'Orsay, Université Paris Saclay, CNRS, Orsay, France.*

Detection of radicals in the interstellar medium, such as hydroxymethyl (CH_2OH) and methoxy (CH_3O), is a highly interesting tool for better understanding the formation of commonly observed complex organic molecules such as glycolaldehyde, ethanol, ethylene glycol, and dimethyl ether. In this context, improving the predictions of astronomical lines with a well-defined model, based on laboratory measurements, becomes decisive.

In an attempt to enrich models of CH_2OH [1] and CH_3O with new frequencies, we have re-investigated their pure rotational spectrum in the millimeter-wave domain. Both radicals were produced at room temperature by fluorine abstraction of hydrogene from methanol. We will report the technical improvements that have been made to increase both the sensitivity and the signal-to-noise ratio of our experimental set-up [1]. We suceeded to increase synthesis yield of both radicals by multiplying fluorine injections and we also further improved our optical set-up, now using a double passage of the beam in the cell. Finally, we wrapped an induction coil around the cell to create a magnetic field, in addition to the usual frequency modulation, allowing us to operate using double modulation detection scheme thus making us sensitive to species affected by Zeeman splitting. Both signals (single and double modulation) are recovered separately and displayed simultaneously on the measurement software. A strength of the double modulation scheme is that only lines arising from open-shell molecules, such as CH_2OH and CH_3O, are visible over a flat baseline (no residual Fabry-Perot interference fringes). These improvements significantly increase our sensitivity to short-lifetime species and grant a powerful tool for distinguishing radicals from stable molecules.

[1] O. Chitarra et al., Astronomy and Astrophysics (2020) 644, A 123

TI06 **10:20 – 10:21**

OPTICALLY-PUMPED AMMONIA TERAHERTZ LASER UP TO 5.5 THz

MARIE-HÉLÈNE MAMMEZ, FRANCIS HINDLE, GAËL MOURET, *Laboratoire de Physico-Chimie de l'Atmosphère, Université du Littoral Côte d'Opale, Dunkerque, France*; JEAN-FRANÇOIS LAMPIN, SOPHIE ELIET, STEFANO BARBIERI, *UMR CNRS 8520, Institut d'Electronique de Microélectronique et de Nanotechnologie, Villeneuve d'Ascq, France*; MARIE-ALINE MARTIN-DRUMEL, OLIVIER PIRALI, *Institut des Sciences Moléculaires d'Orsay, Université Paris Saclay, CNRS, Orsay, France*; P. ROY, *AILES beamline, Synchrotron SOLEIL, Saint Aubin, France.*

Optically-pumped molecular THz lasers are powerful and versatile sources. We have demonstrated a continuous wave molecular laser emission based on ammonia (NH_3) optically pumped by a quantum cascade laser at about 1 THz [a]. The purpose of this work is to investigate NH_3 laser transitions at higher frequencies. This molecule is pumped by the pump laser from the ground state to the $v_2 = 1$ vibrational state. Within the excited state, two types of THz transitions can occur in this molecule: pure inversion transitions and rotation-inversion transitions. Inversion motion is a particular quantum phenomenon of the NH_3 molecule that splits the energy levels: the N atom is able to tunnel through the potential barrier formed by the three H triangle. The inversion splitting is about 1 THz in the $v_2 = 1$ state but rotation-inversion transitions can be used to generate higher frequencies. The investigation of molecular laser shows a lack of available databases of potentially lasing transitions for users to exploit. We propose a molecule dependent figure of merit which enables to discriminate potentially lasing transitions by their lasing potential. We report here its use to predict lasing lines of ammonia. The demonstration of its pertinence is made by observing 32 lasing lines of $^{14}NH_3$ and 5 lines of $^{15}NH_3$ up to 5.5 THz. This work is supported by the ANR project HEROES (ANR-16-CE30-0020), the "Photonics for Society" CPER and the Interreg project TERAFOOD.

[a] A. Pagies, G. Ducournau, and J.-F. Lampin, "Low-threshold terahertz molecular laser optically pumped by a quantum cascade laser," APL Photonics, vol. 1, 031302, 2016.

TI07 **10:24 – 10:25**

CONSTRUCTION AND DEMONSTRATION OF A MICROWAVE THREE-WAVE MIXING SPECTROMETER AT THE MISSOURI UNIVERSITY OF SCIENCE AND TECHNOLOGY

NICOLE MOON, AMANDA DUERDEN, JOSHUA E. ISERT, G. S. GRUBBS II, *Department of Chemistry, Missouri University of Science and Technology, Rolla, MO, USA.*

Building off the previous works of Schnell, Patterson, and Pate, a new microwave three-wave mixing (M3WM) spectrometer was constructed and tested at the Missouri University of Science and Technology. This new instrument consists of a four-horn design, allowing traditional CP-FTMW experiments to be performed in addition to M3WM experiments. Within this presentation, the design, construction, and demonstration of the instrument's capabilities using carvone and preliminary work on 2-bromo-1,1,1,2-tetrafluoroethane will be discussed. Preliminary work on chirality detection and dipole forbidden transition analysis utilizing M3WM techniques will also briefly be presented.

TI08 **10:28 – 10:29**

TWO INSTRUMENTS IN ONE: A NEW CP-FTMW EXPERIMENTAL SETUP TO MEASURE MULTIPLE FREQUENCY BANDS SIMULTANEOUSLY

CRISTOBAL PEREZ, AMANDA STEBER, MELANIE SCHNELL, *FS-SMP, Deutsches Elektronen-Synchrotron (DESY), Hamburg, Germany.*

The introduction by Pate and coworkers[a] of broadband capabilities in rotational spectrometers revolutionized the field and widened the scope of applications of rotational spectroscopy.[b] Since its introduction, many different experimental setups have been reported depending on the end application. In most cases, the bandwidth is restricted to that of commercially available electronic components (mainly high-power amplifiers). The most common setups operate, thus, in limited bands of 2-8, 8-18, 18-26GHz, etc., and the collection in different bands entails the recording of the spectrum several times with the consequent increase in time and sample consumption. Here we present a new experimental approach that allows for the collection of two of those otherwise separate bands in a single measurement, which reduces the time and sample consumption by half. We use two dual-polarization broadband horn antennae to simultaneously polarize the molecular sample in the 2-8 GHz (horizontal polarization) and 8-12 GHz (vertical polarization). The molecular emission is then combined and directly collected on a fast oscilloscope as in a traditional broadband experiment. We will show the performance of this setup compared to separated measurements, which allows for a faster collection of the whole frequency range without compromising the sensitivity. This approach only requires minimal modifications to the current spectrometers.

---

[a] Brown, G. G.; Dian, B. C.; Douglass, K. O.; Geyer, S. M.; Shipman, S. T.; Pate, B. H. A Broadband Fourier Transform Microwave Spectrometer Based on Chirped Pulse Excitation. *Rev. Sci. Instrum.* **2008**, 79 (5), 053103. https://doi.org/10.1063/1.2919120.

[b] Park, G. B.; Field, R. W. Perspective: The First Ten Years of Broadband Chirped Pulse Fourier Transform Microwave Spectroscopy. *J. Chem. Phys.* **2016**, 144 (20), 200901. https://doi.org/10.1063/1.4952762.

TI09 **10:32 – 10:33**

IMPROVING THE SENSITIVITY OF CHIRPED-PULSE FOURIER TRANSFORM MM-WAVE DETECTION IN UNIFORM SUPERSONIC FLOWS

OMAR ABDELKADER KHEDAOUI, BRIAN M HAYS, ILSA ROSE COOKE, THOMAS SANDOW HEARNE, THEO GUILLAUME, DIVITA GUPTA, MYRIAM DRISSI, IAN R. SIMS, *CNRS, IPR (Institut de Physique de Rennes) - UMR 6251, Univ Rennes, F-35000 Rennes, France.*

The CPUF (Chirped Pulse in Uniform supersonic Flow) technique is a combination of the CRESU (Cinétique de Réaction en Ecoulement Supersonique Uniforme, or Reaction Kinetics in Uniform Supersonic Flow) technique to provide a very low temperature (down to 5 K) gas-phase collisional environment with chirped pulse Fourier transform mm-wave/microwave (CPFTMW) spectroscopic detection. The goal of the current CRESUCHIRP project is to determine branching ratios of astrochemically relevant bimolecular reactions at low temperatures using the CPUF technique. Two new CPFTMW spectrometers have been built and characterized in the Ka band (26.5-40 GHz) and the E-band (60-90 GHz). While reaction products have been successfully detected at temperatures down to 10 K in continuous CRESU flows in Rennes, the sensitivity of the CPFTMW technique is reduced by collisional broadening in the relatively high pressure CRESU flows. Reducing the collisional frequency rate is critical, and one of the methods that have been developed to achieve this aim is molecular beam sampling of the uniform flow via a skimmer to create an expansion into a much higher vacuum environment where both the temperature and pressure of the gas will be lowered, creating favorable conditions for the detection of the molecular signal. The latest results from these experiments will be presented.

TI10 **10:36 – 10:37**

A CHIRP PULSE FOURIER TRANSFORM MICROWAVE SPECTROMETER WITH MULTI-ANTENNA DETECTION (MAD-CP-FTMW)

AMANDA DUERDEN, NICOLE MOON, CHRISTIAN SWANSON, FRANK E MARSHALL, JOSHUA E. ISERT, KRISTEN DONNELL, G. S. GRUBBS II, *Department of Chemistry, Missouri University of Science and Technology, Rolla, MO, USA.*

At the 74th ISMS, our group showed that it is possible to detect microwave radiation in a CP-FTMW experiment that did not copropagate in the direction of incident radiation. In that talk, it was shown that this could be achieved with the broadcast antenna by the implementation of a circulator, switch, and low noise amplifier in order to also detect off of the same antenna. Coincidentally, the circulator that was utilized attenuated the input power below a level where this detection would be advantageous to the overall signal-to-noise ratio (SNR) of the collected free induction decays (FIDs). However, this discovery provided both the preliminary data and the impetus for a new hypothesis to be tested: Could FIDs be detected at other points not in the direct linear path of the incident microwaves? To address this, we utilized our new microwave three-wave mixing (M3WM) instrument based upon the four-antennae design of Pate in order to utilize the orthogonality of the setup for the purposes of CP-FTMW FID collection. The design of the new four-antennae MAD-CP-FTMW at Missouri S&T will be presented along with the exciting results of detection in traditional, 180 degree, and quadrature angles. Additional testing, done to mitigate the concern of reflection voiced in the original presentation, will also be discussed. Additional information concerning this spectrometer's design and functionality, as well as further details related to data processing, will be discussed in presentations given by Nicole Moon, and Christian Swanson, respectively.

TI11 **10:40 – 10:41**

A HEIGHT ADJUSTABLE LASER ABLATION SOURCE FOR A CP-FTMW SPECTROMETER AT THE MISSOURI UNIVERSITY OF SCIENCE AND TECHNOLOGY

JOSHUA E. ISERT, JOSIE GLENN, AMANDA DUERDEN, NICOLE MOON, FRANK E MARSHALL, G. S. GRUBBS II, *Department of Chemistry, Missouri University of Science and Technology, Rolla, MO, USA.*

While previous iterations of laser ablation designs have been attempted at Missouri S&T, none had the capability to adjust the location of the nozzle in relation to the horn antenna *in situ* without breaking vacuum. This design serves two purposes. The first is to optimize signal strength in real time and the second is to make improvements on spatial and mass efficiency. The source was designed as a prototype for current and future CP-FTMW instruments primarily concerned with studying metal-containing molecules. Aspects of the design as well as the implementation and viability of the source in one of the CP-FTMW instruments will be discussed.

TI12 **10:44 – 10:45**

MICROWAVE SPECTROSCOPY: LINESHAPE APPROXIMATION FOR SQUARE-WAVE FREQUENCY MODULATION

E. A. ALEKSEEV[a], V. ILYUSHIN, *Radiospectrometry Department, Institute of Radio Astronomy of NASU, Kharkov, Ukraine.*

To improve sensitivity of absorption spectrometers a source modulation with lock-in detection is usually employed. In the Kharkiv millimeter wave spectrometer we employ DDS based square-wave frequency modulation which is characterized by a high certainty of modulation parameters. Commonly applied approaches developed for a sine-wave frequency modulation (see for example [1]) are not able to fully account for all lineshape modifications due to the square-wave frequency modulation. That is why we have developed a new expression which allows us to take into account lineshape modification due to square-wave frequency modulation as well as well-known problem of lineshape distortions caused by presence of standing wave in an absorbing cell. Our approach reproduce well observed line profiles and as the result provides some improvement of measurement accuracy. In the talk the details of the new approach will be discussed.

[1] L. Dore, J. Mol. Spectrosc. 221, pp.93-98, 2003.

[a]Both authors are affiliated also with Quantum Radiophysics Department, V.N. Karazin Kharkiv National University, Kharkiv, Ukraine.

TI13 **10:48 – 10:49**

MILLIMETER-MILLIMETER-WAVE DOUBLE-MODULATION DOUBLE-RESONANCE SPECTROSCOPY

OLIVER ZINGSHEIM, LUIS BONAH, HOLGER S. P. MÜLLER, FRANK LEWEN, SVEN THORWIRTH, STEPHAN SCHLEMMER, *I. Physikalisches Institut, Universität zu Köln, Köln, Germany.*

Complex organic molecules (COMs) show regularly very rich spectra, sometimes at a line density close to the confusion limit. The plethora of lines often originates from the presence of different conformers and/or low-lying vibrational states. The analysis of spectra may considerably be further complicated by vibration-rotation or other interactions. However, accurate spectroscopic predictions in the millimeter-wave (MMW) region are essential for identifying molecules in space. Double-resonance techniques can help to solve these challenges.

We present first MMW−MMW double-resonance (DR) spectra to unambiguously assign weak and perturbed rotational lines of propanal (C_2H_5CHO). As already shown in chirped pulse Fourier transform microwave (CP-FTMW)[a] and in MW−MMW DR experiments,[b] the Autler-Townes splitting[c] allows for distinguishing between regressive or progressive energy level schemes. The Autler-Townes splitting is clearly visible in our 2D spectra. Furthermore, implementation of a double-modulation double-resonance (DM-DR) technique, pulse modulation of the pump and frequency modulation of the probe source, allows for confusion- and baseline-free spectra containing only the line(s) of interest. We discuss details of the observed Autler-Townes splitting, benefits of simplified spectra, and possible future applications, such as automatization.

[a]D. Schmitz et al., *J. Phys. Chem. Lett.* **6** (2015) 1493
[b]K. M. Roenitz et al., *J. Phys. Chem. A.* **122** (2018) 6321
[c]S. H. Autler and C. H. Townes, *Phys. Rev.* **100** (1955) 703

TI14 **10:52 – 10:53**

MILLIMETER-WAVE DETECTIONS OF LASER-ABLATED SALTS WITH A MINIATURE SPECTROMETER

ALEXANDER W RAYMOND, KELVIN LEE, MICHAEL C McCARTHY, ERIC MAZUR, *Center for Astrophysics , Harvard & Smithsonian, Cambridge, MA, USA*; BRIAN DROUIN, *Jet Propulsion Laboratory, California Institute of Technology, Pasadena, CA, USA.*

This presentation describes the application of a miniature millimeter-wave rotational spectrometer to the detection of laser-ablation products. The laboratory experiments we present are forerunners to possible future field- or space deployments. We focus on NaCl and KCl salts, which are interesting targets at the icy moons of the outer solar system. The laser-coupled spectrometer incorporates a collisional-cooling, pulsed carrier gas beam. We leverage the small size of the spectrometer cavity to probe the ablation product signal along the beam length. We find that the volatilized species are widely dispersed in the carrier-gas. Additionally, we present centimeter-wave rotational and mass spectroscopic measurements to help characterize the laser ablation process.

TJ. Astronomy

Tuesday, June 22, 2021 – 10:0 AM

Room: 2021 Online Everywhere

Chair: Brett A. McGuire, Massachusetts Institute of Technology, Cambridge, MA, USA

TJ01 **10:00 – 10:01**

METHYL-CARBON CHAIN CHEMISTRY IN TMC-1: THE FIRST INTERSTELLAR DETECTION OF METHYL-CYANOTRIACETYLENE (CH_3C_7N)

MARK A. SIEBERT, *Department of Astronomy, University of Virginia, Charlottesville, VA, USA*; ANTHONY REMIJAN, *NAASC, National Radio Astronomy Observatory, Charlottesville, VA, USA*; KELVIN LEE, *Center for Astrophysics , Harvard & Smithsonian, Cambridge, MA, USA*; ANDREW M BURKHARDT, *Smithsonian Astrophysical Observatory, Center for Astrophysics | Harvard & Smithsonian, Cambridge, MA, USA*; MICHAEL C McCARTHY, *Center for Astrophysics , Harvard & Smithsonian, Cambridge, MA, USA*; BRETT A. McGUIRE, *Department of Chemistry, Massachusetts Institute of Technology, Cambridge, MA, USA.*

Cold carbon chemistry in the interstellar medium is well-known for its efficient production of linear carbon chain molecules. Among the many variations on these species are the symmetric top methylpolyynes and methylcyanopolyynes ($CH_3C_{2n}H$ and $CH_3C_{2n-1}N$, where $n = 1, 2, 3...$). Despite their widespread presence in environments with rich carbon chemistry, the main formation mechanisms of these molecules are still not well understood. With the high sensitivity and broad frequency coverage obtained by the ongoing GOTHAM (Green Bank Telescope Observations of TMC-1: Hunting for Aromatic Molecules) survey of TMC-1, we have the opportunity to study the spectral signatures of these carbon chains in great detail. In this talk, we will present a rigorous study of the methyl carbon chains in TMC-1, in addition to the discovery of the largest interstellar symmetric top, methylcyanotriacetylene (CH_3C_7N). Making use of the second data release of GOTHAM in combination with Markov-Chain Monte Carlo simulation and spectral line stacking techniques, we detect statistically significant emission from the $K = 0$ and $K = 1$ components of this molecule, and derive its abundance and excitation conditions in TMC-1. Furthermore, by carrying out the same analysis for the many other methylpolyynes and methylcyanopolyynes that show emission lines in our data, and comparing our results with predictions of chemical models, we assess the chemistry governing the production of this class of molecules in this source and compare it with that of other carbon chain species.

TJ02 **10:04 – 10:05**

DETECTION OF CH_3NCO IN THE GALACTIC CENTER STAR-FORMING REGION SAGITTARIUS B2(M) BY RADIO ASTRONOMICAL OBSERVATIONS

YUKI OHNO, *Faculty of Science Division I, Tokyo University of Science, Tokyo , Japan*; MITSUNORI ARAKI, *Research Institute for Science and Technology, Tokyo University of Science, Noda, Japan*; YOSHIAKI MINAMI, *Faculty of Science Division I, Tokyo University of Science, Shinjuku-ku, Tokyo, Japan*; TAKAHIRO OYAMA, *Department of Materials and Life Sciences, Sophia University, Tokyo, Japan*; SHURO TAKANO, *College of Engineering, Nihon University, Fukushima, Japan*; NOBUHIKO KUZE, *Department of Materials and Life Sciences, Sophia University, Tokyo, Japan*; YOSHIHIRO SUMIYOSHI, *Division of Pure and Applied Science, Faculty of Science and Technology, Gunma University, Maebashi, Japan*; KOICHI TSUKIYAMA, *Faculty of Science Division I, Tokyo University of Science, Shinjuku-ku, Tokyo, Japan.*

Large difference of chemical compositions between molecular clouds and comets is a big question for astrochemistry. The case of a pre-biotic molecule CH_3NCO is one of them. The abundance ratio of [CH_3NCO]/[HNCO] is high in the comet 67P (> 4, [1]), although it is low ($0.02 - 0.3$, e.g., [2]) in molecular clouds. An abundance of CH_3NCO is expected to be held and/or increased during evolutionary process of a cloud. A pair of an old core and a young core having the similar chemical compositions needs to be investigated for this evolutionary process. In this work, we aimed to detect CH_3NCO in the middle (M) core, which is relatively older than the north (N) core, in the Galactic Center star-forming region Sagittarius B2 with the 45 m telescope of Nobeyama Radio Observatory. The rotational transitions of $J = 10 \rightarrow 9$ to $13 \rightarrow 12$ for CH_3NCO were detected in the $85 - 114$ GHz region. The column density and the rotational temperature are derived to be $N = (4.3 \pm 2.1) \times 10^{13}$ cm^{-2} and $T_{rot} = (32 \pm 9)$ K, respectively, assuming local thermal equilibrium. Similarly, an abundance of HNCO is estimated to be $N = (1.3 \pm 0.5) \times 10^{15}$ cm^{-2} ($T_{rot} = 21 \pm 2$ K), giving the ratio of [CH_3NCO]/[HNCO] = 0.032. Thus, as a simplest model, it is suggested that an abundance of CH_3NCO is held during evolutionary process of the Sagittarius B2 region.

[1] Goesmann et al., Science, 349, 689 (2015). [2] Halfen et al., ApJ, 812, L5 (2015).

TJ03 **10:08 – 10:09**

FIRST INTERSTELLAR DETECTION OF ISOCYANODIACETYLENE (HC_4NC), THE LARGEST ISOCYANIDE MOLECULE IN THE ISM

CI XUE, ERIC R. WILLIS, ERIC HERBST, *Department of Chemistry, The University of Virginia, Charlottesville, VA, USA*; ANTHONY REMIJAN, RYAN A LOOMIS, *NAASC, National Radio Astronomy Observatory, Charlottesville, VA, USA*; ANDREW M BURKHARDT, *Smithsonian Astrophysical Observatory, Center for Astrophysics | Harvard & Smithsonian, Cambridge, MA, USA*; KELVIN LEE, BRETT A. McGUIRE, *Department of Chemistry, Massachusetts Institute of Technology, Cambridge, MA, USA.*

The cyanide and isocyanide (-CN and -NC) pairs of isomers have been used regularly to probe the physical conditions and history of interstellar sources and to improve the accuracy and predictive power of astrochemical models. Two examples are the strong sensitivity of the HCN/HNC abundance ratio to the gas kinetic temperatures[a] and the dependence of the CH_3CN/CH_3NC abundance ratio to the cosmic-ray ionization rates[b]. Yet, despite the numerous detections of cyanides in astronomical environments, there have been very few confirmed detections of isocyanides. Alongside $C_nH_{2n+1}CN$, one of the most frequently observed families of cyanide species in cold sources are the cyanopolyynes ($HC_{2n}CN$). In contrast to their ubiquity, the only isocyanide version that had been successfully detected is HCCNC, the isomer of HC_3N. In this talk, we will present the first astronomical detection of the largest isocyanide molecule, isocyanodiacetylene (HC_4NC), using the data available from the GOTHAM (Green Bank Telescope Observations of TMC-1: Hunting for Aromatic Molecules) observational program of TMC-1[c]. Assisted by a cutting-edge application of spectral line stacking and matched filtering techniques, we determined the NC/CN isomeric intensity ratios of the $HC_{2n}NC/HC_{2n}CN$ family rigorously for n=1 and 2 toward TMC-1 and provided an upper limit of that for n=3. The abundance ratios derived from observations helped in constraining the interplay between -CN and -NC formation chemistry and their dependence on the physico-chemical history of the source. This work also demonstrated the need for a detailed investigation of the related formation pathways in the laboratory.

[a]A. Hacar, A. D. Bosman, and E. F. van Dishoeck, A&A 635, A4(2020)
[b]E. R. Willis, et al., A&A, 636, A29 (2020)
[c]B. A. McGuire, et al., ApjL, 900, L10 (2020)

TJ04 **10:12 – 10:13**

INDIVIDUAL DETECTIONS OF POLYCYCLIC AROMATIC HYDROCARBONS IN TMC-1

ANDREW M BURKHARDT, *Smithsonian Astrophysical Observatory, Center for Astrophysics | Harvard & Smithsonian, Cambridge, MA, USA*; KELVIN LEE, *Department of Chemistry, Massachusetts Institute of Technology, Cambridge, MA, USA*; BRYAN CHANGALA, *JILA, National Institute of Standards and Technology and Univ. of Colorado Department of Physics, University of Colorado, Boulder, CO, USA*; CHRISTOPHER N SHINGLEDECKER, *Department of Physics & Astronomy, Benedictine College, Atchison, KS, USA*; ILSA ROSE COOKE, *Institut de Physique de Rennes, Université de Rennes 1, Rennes, France*; RYAN A LOOMIS, *NAASC, National Radio Astronomy Observatory, Charlottesville, VA, USA*; HONGJI WEI, *Department of Physics & Astronomy, Benedictine College, Atchison, KS, USA*; STEVEN B CHARNLEY, *Astrochemistry, NASA Goddard Space Flight Center, Greenbelt, MD, USA*; ERIC HERBST, *Department of Chemistry, The University of Virginia, Charlottesville, VA, USA*; MICHAEL C McCARTHY, *Atomic and Molecular Physics, Harvard-Smithsonian Center for Astrophysics, Cambridge, MA, USA*; BRETT A. McGUIRE, *Department of Chemistry, Massachusetts Institute of Technology, Cambridge, MA, USA.*

Polycyclic Aromatic Hydrocarbons (PAHs) have long been invoked in the study of interstellar and protostellar sources, but the unambiguous identification of any single PAH has proven elusive until very recently. As a result, the formation mechanism for this important class of molecules remains poorly constrained. Here, we will discuss the dedicated and sustained effort to explore the aromatic content in the ISM at radio wavelengths with the GOTHAM (GBT Observations of TMC-1: Hunting for Aromatic Molecules) survey. We will focus on the first interstellar detection of a pure PAH, indene (C_9H_8), and how it fits within the context of the other recently detected cyclic molecules, including the cyanonaphthalenes (1- and 2-$C_{10}H_7CN$). Indene is found to be the most abundant organic ring detected in TMC-1 to date and is more abundant than predictions from astrochemical modeling with NAUTILUS by several orders of magnitude. This detection provides a new avenue of chemical inquiry where hydrocarbon abundances can now be directly compared to those of closely-related but CN-functionalized rings and creates a strong motivation to search for these species' cyano or pure ring counterparts.

TJ05 **10:16 – 10:17**

A SENSITIVE LINE SURVEY OF TMC-1: THE CHEMICAL COMPLEXITY OF A COLD DARK CLOUD

JOSE CERNICHARO, CARLOS CABEZAS, MARCELINO AGÚNDEZ, *Instituto de Fisica Fundamental, CSIC, Madrid, Spain*; BELÉN TERCERO, *OAN-IGN, Observatorio Astronómico Nacional, Madrid, Spain*; PABLO DE VICENTE, *Centro Astronómico de Yebes, Observatorio Astronómico Nacional, Yebes, Guadalajara, Spain*; NURIA MARCELINO, JUAN R. PARDO, *Instituto de Fisica Fundamental, CSIC, Madrid, Spain.*

We present a line survey of the cold dark core TMC-1 carried out with the YEBES 40m radio telescope in the Q-band. A new set of receivers have been installed in the telescope within the frame of the ERC synergy Nanocosmos project that allows to cover the whole 31-50 GHz band in dual polarization. The spectral resolution is 38.15 kHz. The sensitivity achieved so far varies between 0.3 and 1.5 mK, and allows to search for new molecules in a line by line (no stacking) detection procedure. These new data have permitted to detect the protonated species HC_5NH^{+}[a], HC_3O^{+}[b], HC_3S^{+}[c], and CH_3CO^{+}[d]. Each one of these species were detected first in TMC-1 by looking for unknown lines with harmonic frequency relations. All of them have been confirmed in the laboratory except HC_5NH^+, for which our identification is based in high-level of theory ab initio calculations.

Neutral molecules with low permanent dipole moment such as CH_2CHCCH[e], and $CH_2CCHCCH$[f] have been also detected with a very large abundance. In addition, nitrile anions such as C_3N^- and C_5N^- have been also detected confirming the previous assigment of C_5N^- reported in the carbon-rich star IRC+10216 (Cernicharo et al. 2008, ApJ, 688, L83).

[a]Marcelino et al. 2020, A.&A., 643, L6
[b]Cernicharo et al. 2020, A.&A., 642, L17
[c]Cernicharo et al. 2021, A.&A., 643, L3
[d]Cernicharo et al. 2021, A.&A., 646, L7
[e]Cernicharo et al. 2021, A.&A., in press; 2021arXiv210210920C
[f]Cernicharo et al., 2021, A.&A., in press

TJ06 **10:20 – 10:21**

IDENTIFICATION OF PHOSPHORUS MONOXIDE ($X^2\Pi_r$) IN THE ORION MOLECULAR CLOUD: FURTHER EVIDENCE FOR THE UBIQUITOUS P-O BOND

JACOB BERNAL, *Department of Chemistry and Biochemistry, University of Arizona, Tucson, AZ, USA*; LUCY M. ZIURYS, *Department of Chemistry and Biochemistry, Department of Astronomy, The University of Arizona, Tucson, AZ, USA*; LILIA KOELEMAY, *Department of Chemistry and Biochemistry, University of Arizona, Tucson, AZ, USA.*

The PO molecule has been identified towards the Orion-KL region based on a 3mm survey carried out with the ARO 12m. The J = 2.5-1.5 transition was observed, consisting of two lambda-doublets, both of which were detected. The PN ($X^1\Sigma$) J = 2-1 transition was also detected. Both PO and PN exhibited line profiles and LSR velocities characteristic of the Orion Plateau region, indicating that shocks are primarily responsible for their formation. A calculated PO/PN value of approximately 3 is similar to other molecular clouds where both species have been observed, suggesting that PO may be a relatively common molecule in star-forming regions.

TJ08 **10:28 – 10:29**

RADIAL LOCATION OF SGR B2 MEASURED FROM H_3^+ AND H_2O^+ ABSORPTION SPECTRA

TAKESHI OKA, *Department of Astronomy and Astrophysics and Department of Chemistry, The Enrico Fermi Institute, University of Chicago, Chicago, IL, USA*; THOMAS R. GEBALLE, , *Gemini Observatory, Hilo, HI, USA*.

The giant molecular cloud Sgr B2 in the $\sim$ 150 pc radius Central Molecular Zone (CMZ) of the Galactic center has played a central role in molecular radio astronomical observations. In spite of its large distance, over 70 molecules have been first detected in Sgr B2 since the discoveries of NH_3 and H_2O. Nevertheless there seems to be no consensus on the depth within the CMZ of this well observed cloud. It has not even been known whether Sgr B2, which is 101 pc distant on the plane of the sky from the central black hole Sgr A*, is to the front or the rear of Sgr A*. A trigonometric parallax measurement by Reid et al. (2009)[a] placed Sgr B2 130 pc in front of Sgr A* which would put it outside of the CMZ. Both Kruijssen et al. (2015) and Ridley et al. (2017) also placed Sgr B2 in front of Sgr A*. On the other hand Molinari et al (2011)[b] placed Sgr B2 about 70 pc behind Sgr A* based on their dust continuum measurements.

Recent observations of infrared lines of H_3^+ and CO [c] and the conclusion from the analysis of their velocity profiles that diffuse gas in the CMZ is expanding radially at a velocity of 150 km s^{-1} with the front of the expansion 150 pc from Sgr A* provides a useful tool for determining the location of Sgr B2 within the CMZ. Although currently there is no known infrared star usable for observations of H_3^+ toward Sgr B2, the star ι, 2M17470898-2829561, 16.6 pc to the west of the center of Sgr B2, is sufficiently close that it probes much of the same gas; the similarity of the velocity profile of the H_3^+ spectrum toward ι observed at the Gemini South Observatory and of H_2O^+ [d] by Herschel Observatory toward Sgr B2 attest to this. Using the velocity profiles of infrared absorption lines of H_3^+ toward the star ι and far infrared absorption lines of H_2O^+, both of which molecular ions reside in diffuse clouds, we conclude that Sgr B2 is behind Sgr A* by at least 70 pc.

[a]Reid, M. J., Menten, K. M., Zheng, X. W., Bunthaler, A. & Xu, Y. 2009, ApJ, 105, 7548
[b]Molinari, S., Bally, J., Noriega-Crespo, A. et al. 2011, ApJ, 735, L33
[c]Oka, T. & Geballe, T. R. 2020, ApJ, 902, 9
[d]Schilke, P., Comito, C. Müller, H. S. P., et al. 2010, A&A, 521, L11

TJ09 **10:32 – 10:33**

METHANOL AT THE EDGE OF THE GALAXY: NEW OBSERVATIONS TO CONSTRAIN THE GALACTIC HABITABLE ZONE

JACOB BERNAL, *Department of Chemistry and Biochemistry, University of Arizona, Tucson, AZ, USA*; LUCY M. ZIURYS, *Department of Chemistry and Biochemistry; Department of Astronomy, Arizona Radio Observatory, University of Arizona, Tuscon, AZ, USA*; CATHRYN SEPHUS, *Department of Molecular and Cellular Biology, University of Arizona, Tucson, AZ, USA*.

Searches have been conducted for various J=2-1 transitions of methanol at 3 mm in a sample of molecular clouds located 13-23.5 kpc from the Galactic Center, using the 12m telescope of the Arizona Radio Observatory (ARO). The sources are in the Cygnus arms, and typically are cold with T_K approximately 20 K. Multiple transitions of this organic molecule were detected in 19 clouds, including ones at distances of approximately 23.5 kpc. Typical abundances found for methanol are $1x10^9$. The results suggest that the Galactic Habitable Zone (GHZ) may exist much further from the Galactic Center than previously thought.

TJ10 **10:36 – 10:37**

PUSHING THE LIMITS OF MOLECULAR COMPLEXITY IN THE OUTER GALAXY - THE SEARCH FOR FORMAMIDE (NH_2CHO) AT VARIOUS GALACTOCENTRIC DISTANCES

MARYAM HAMI, *NAASC, National Radio Astronomy Observatory, Charlottesville, VA, USA*; ANTHONY REMIJAN, *ALMA, National Radio Astronomy Observatory, Charlottesville, VA, USA*.

Galactic Habitability is a concept of growing popularity. So far, research has been done in understanding the temporal and spatial evolution of a Galactic Habitable Zone (GHZ) based on parameters such as local SN rate, host star metallicity, and age of the system. However, the popular GHZ literature does not account for the potential influence of molecular complexity at different spatial locations in the Galaxy. With the high sensitivity of ALMA, we are interested in exploring molecular complexity of star-forming clumps in these different spatial locations of the Galaxy. In this work, we focus on one complex organic molecule - Formamide (NH_2CHO) - which recent literature has identified as a potential key precursor to prebiotic life. Using ALMA archival data, we examine the presence and abundance of formamide at various galactocentric distances in the Galaxy. Several archival surveys were utilized for the search. Most extensively, we used the ALMA Three-millimeter Observations of Massive Star-forming regions (ATOMS) survey, to search for 7(0,7) $\rightarrow$ 6(1,6) transition of Formamide.

TJ11 **10:40 – 10:41**

COMPLEX ENVELOPE CHEMISTRY AND DYNAMICS OF NML CYGNUS

AMBESH PRATIK SINGH, *Department of Molecular and Cellular Biology, University of Arizona, Tucson, AZ, USA*; JESSICA L EDWARDS, LUCY M. ZIURYS, *Department of Chemistry and Biochemistry, Department of Astronomy, The University of Arizona, Tucson, AZ, USA*.

Oxygen-rich supergiant stars undergo intense, sporadic mass loss often causing them to have highly directed, non-isotropic outflows. These outflows have been previously identified in the envelope of the supergiant VY CMa, both in the infrared and in molecular lines. In VY CMa, these flows are best traced by sulfur-bearing molecules SO_2 and SO. To further investigate the unusual properties of supergiant stars, we have conducted a 1 mm survey of another such object, NML Cyg. This survey revealed the presence of unusual species such as PO, AlO, NS, and PN in NML Cyg, as well as HCN, HCO+, CN, NaCl, SO, SiS, and SO_2 - an almost identical set of molecules as observed towards VY CMa. Two major asymmetric outflows have also been identified in the envelope of NML Cyg from the spectra of SO and SO_2, one blue-shifted and the other red-shifted. Spectral line analysis with the radiative transfer code ESCAPADE suggests that these two outflows are in random directions and are not bipolar in nature.

TJ12 **10:44 – 10:45**

RESOLVING THE NEW CHEMICALLY-ACTIVE OUTFLOW HH114

ADITYA POTHANABOYINA, *College of Information and Computer Sciences, University of Massachusetts Amherst, Amherst, MA, USA*; ANDREW M BURKHARDT, *Smithsonian Astrophysical Observatory, Center for Astrophysics | Harvard & Smithsonian, Cambridge, MA, USA*; QIZHOU ZHANG, *Radio and Geoastronomy Division, Harvard-Smithsonian Center for Astrophysics, Cambridge, MA, USA*.

Chemically-active protostellar outflows provide unique laboratories to study shock chemistry in relatively simple physical environments. However, only a small handful of these types of sources are currently known. Recently, Tafalla & Hacar (2013) discovered a chemically-active outflow HH114. Images obtained with the IRAM 30m Telescope revealed strong emission in SiO, HCO^+, HCN, CH_3OH, and CS in the redshifted and blueshifted lobes. Here we present SMA observations resolving the blue-shifted outflow of HH114. Leveraging the new wideband capabilities of the SMA, these new high-resolution maps reveal the rich chemistry displays complex morphologies coming from the shocked bullets and processing jet. We discuss the implications these observations can have on our understanding of shocked molecular outflows.

TJ13 **10:48 – 10:49**

MOLECULES IN OUTFLOW OF HIGH-MASS PROTOSTAR IRAS 20126-4104

BORE GAO, *Department of Physics, University of Illinois at Urbana-Champaign, Urbana-Champaign, IL, USA*; ANDREW M BURKHARDT, *Smithsonian Astrophysical Observatory, Center for Astrophysics | Harvard & Smithsonian, Cambridge, MA, USA*; QIZHOU ZHANG, *Radio and Geoastronomy Division, Harvard-Smithsonian Center for Astrophysics, Cambridge, MA, USA.*

Molecular outflows are crucial for us to understand not only the internal structure and conditions close to protostars, but also probe the morphology and the dynamics of the chemistry in the surrounding cloud. But, the relationship of the chemistry and physics within these outflows is complex and not well constrained. Isolated molecular outflows provide simplified environments to constrain the underlying processes. However, the majority of isolated outflows originate from low-mass protostars, which have distinct chemistry relative to high-mass. Here, we utilized archival SMA observations of the young and isolated high-mass protostar I20126+4104 in order to study the chemical diversity and differentiation of both the disc and the outflow. We found that there is complex chemistry by distinguishing molecules such as HCN, CH_3OH, SO_2. We also assessed the relative column densities for these molecules.

TJ14 **10:52 – 10:53**

ALMA CN ZEEMAN OBSERVATIONS OF AS 209: LIMITS ON MAGNETIC FIELD STRENGTH AND MAGNETICALLY DRIVEN ACCRETION RATE

RACHEL E. HARRISON, *Astronomy, University of Illinois at Urbana-Champaign, Urbana, IL, USA*; LESLIE LOONEY, *Department of Astronomy, University of Illinois at Urbana-Champaign, Urbana, IL, USA*; IAN STEPHENS, *Radio and Geoastronomy Division, Harvard-Smithsonian Center for Astrophysics, Cambridge, MA, USA*; ZHI-YUN LI, *Department of Astronomy, The University of Virginia, Charlottesville, VA, USA*; RICHARD TEAGUE, *Radio and Geoastronomy Division, Harvard-Smithsonian Center for Astrophysics, Cambridge, MA, USA*; RICHARD CRUTCHER, *Department of Astronomy, University of Illinois at Urbana-Champaign, Urbana, IL, USA*; HAIFENG YANG, *Institute for Advanced Study, Tsinghua University, Beijing, China*; ERIN GUILFOIL COX, *Center for Interdisciplinary Exploration and Research in Astrophysics (CIERA) , Northwestern University, Evanston, IL, USA*; MANUEL FERNANDEZ-LOPEZ, *Instituto Argentino de Radioastronomía, Centro Científico Tecnológico La Plata, Villa Elisa, Argentina*; HIROKO SHINNAGA, *Department of Physics and Astronomy, Kagoshima University, Kagoshima, Japan.*

Magnetic fields are thought to play a crucial role in the formation and evolution of protoplanetary disks by providing a means of angular momentum transport. However, finding observational evidence for the presence of magnetic fields in disks has proven difficult. Zeeman splitting observations offer a way to directly measure or put upper limits on line-of-sight magnetic field strengths in astronomical sources, as the circularly polarized signal produced by Zeeman splitting depends directly on the magnetic field strength along the line of sight. We present upper limits on the toroidal and vertical magnetic field strengths in the Class II protoplanetary disk AS 209 from ALMA observations of the CN 2-1 line. If magnetic disk winds are a significant mechanism of angular momentum transport in the disk, magnetic fields of a strength close to our upper limits would be sufficient to drive accretion at the rate previously inferred for regions near the protostar.

TJ15 **10:56 – 10:57**

A SEARCH FOR LIGHT HYDRIDES IN THE ENVELOPES OF EVOLVED STARS

MARK A. SIEBERT, *Department of Astronomy, University of Virginia, Charlottesville, VA, USA*; ANTHONY REMIJAN, *ALMA, National Radio Astronomy Observatory, Charlottesville, VA, USA*; BRETT A. McGUIRE, *NAASC, National Radio Astronomy Observatory, Charlottesville, VA, USA*; CHRISTOPHER N SHINGLEDECKER, *The Center for Astrochemical Studies, Max-Planck-Institut für extraterrestrische Physik, Garching, Germany*; ANDREW M BURKHARDT, *Smithsonian Astrophysical Observatory, Center for Astrophysics | Harvard & Smithsonian, Cambridge, MA, USA.*

Hydrides are important molecular constituents of the interstellar and circumstellar media, but there are still many questions regarding their variety and formation. In the envelopes of asymptotic giant branch and red supergiant stars, hydrides like silane SiH_4, phosphine PH_3, ammonia NH_3, and water H_2O are known to form, but have been observed in stark overabundance relative to predictions of chemical equilibrium models[a]. Diatomic hydrides (species with the form XH) are natural precursors to their more hydrogenated counterparts, and could therefore be crucial in constraining this puzzling chemistry. In this talk, I will present our search for the hydrides silicon monohydride (SiH), phosphinidene (PH), and iron hydride (FeH) using the Stratospheric Observatory for Infrared Astronomy (SOFIA). We used the German Receiver for Astronomy at Terahertz Frequencies (GREAT) instrument to search for rotational emission lines of these molecules along the line of sight toward the chemically rich circumstellar envelopes of the evolved stars IRC+10216 and VY Canis Majoris. In these spectra we detected high-energy ro-vibrational lines from over a dozen molecules, though no significant emission from our target molecules was found. We derive upper limits on their abundances in each source, discuss how these findings influence our understanding of hydride chemistry in circumstellar envelopes, and outline the observational steps needed to further constrain this chemistry.

---

[a] Agundez et al., A&A 637, A59 (2020)

TK. Comparing theory and experiment

Tuesday, June 22, 2021 – 10:0 AM

Room: 2021 Online Everywhere

Chair: Karl K. Irikura, National Institute of Standards and Technology, Gaithersburg, MD, USA

TK01 **10:00 – 10:01**

VAPOR-PHASE INFRARED AND RAMAN SPECTRA AND THEORETICAL INVESTIGATIONS OF π-TYPE INTRAMOLECULAR HYDROGEN BONDING IN 3-CYCLOPENTEN-1-OL AND 3-CYCLOPENTEN-1-AMINE

ESTHER JULIANA OCOLA, JAAN LAANE, *Department of Chemistry, Texas A & M University, College Station, TX, USA.*

The vapor-phase and Raman spectra of 3-cyclopenten-1-ol (3CPOL) and 3-cyclopenten-1-amine (3CPAM) have been recorded and analyzed. The spectra demonstrate the existence of six conformers for each molecule, two pairs of which are mirror images of each other and with equivalent vibrational modes. The conformational minima are achieved for selected values of the ring-puckering coordinate and the internal rotation coordinate of either the -OH or -NH2 group. Theoretical CCSD/cc-pVTZ computations for both molecules were carried out and their two-dimensional potential energy surfaces (PEFs) were calculated. The PEFs confirm the existence of all conformers and provide the relative energies for these. The structures with the π-type intramolecular hydrogen bonding are at the lowest calculated energies and 301 to 411 cm^{-1}lower than the other conformations for 3CPOL, and 165 to 197 cm^{-1}lower for 3CPAM.

TK02 **10:04 – 10:05**

VIBRATIONAL SPECIFICITY OF PROTON-TRANSFER DYNAMICS IN ELECTRONICALLY EXCITED 6-HYDROXY-2-FORMYLFULVENE

LIDOR FOGUEL, ZACHARY VEALEY, PATRICK VACCARO, *Department of Chemistry, Yale University, New Haven, CT, USA.*

The transduction of protons between distinct donor and acceptor sites, as often directed by attendant hydrogen bonds, is a ubiquitous chemical transformation essential for all of acid/base chemistry, yet the role of selective nuclear displacements in this deceptively simple process remains a topic of active investigation. Polarization-resolved degenerate four-wave mixing (DFWM) spectroscopy was employed to investigate the vibrational specificity of proton-transfer dynamics in the lowest-lying singlet excited state, $\tilde{A}^1B_2$ $(\pi^*\pi)$, of 6-hydroxy-2-formylfulvene (HFF), with judicious selection of incident and detected polarization geometries allowing for the extraction of refined rotation-tunneling parameters. While the zero-point level of the ground electronic state $[\tilde{X}^1A_1]$ straddles the barrier crest for hydron migration and thus affords a prototypical example of low-barrier hydrogen bonding,[a] a dramatic change in dynamics has been suggested to accompany $\pi^* \leftarrow \pi$ electron promotion, as reflected by a >1000-fold decrease in tunneling rate.[b] This talk will present complementary experimental and computational analyses of vibronic levels in the pertinent $\tilde{A}^1B_2$ $(\pi^*\pi)$ manifold designed to unravel the dependence of unimolecular reactivity on heavy atom motion and to elucidate the disparate behavior observed for analogous $\tilde{X}^1A_1$ features.

[a]Z. N. Vealey, L. Foguel and P. H. Vaccaro, *J. Phys. Chem. Lett.* **9**, 4949 (2018).
[b]Z. N. Vealey, L. Foguel and P. H. Vaccaro, *J. Phys. Chem. A.* **123**, 6506 (2019).

TK03 **10:08 – 10:09**

THE MYSTERIOUS CASE OF THE MISSING NH STRETCH TRANSITION

KARL N. BLODGETT, TIMOTHY S. ZWIER, *Department of Chemistry, Purdue University, West Lafayette, IN, USA*; EDWIN SIBERT, *Department of Chemistry, University of Wisconsin–Madison, Madison, WI, USA.*

The ground and excited state IR vibronic spectra of jet-cooled methyl anthranilate (MA) in the hydride stretch (2400-3800 cm^{-1} and mid-IR (1400-1800 cm^{-1}) regions have been recorded and many of the peaks have been assigned. The key exception, and the subject of this talk, is the H-bonded NH stretch on the S_1 excited surface. In contrast to the S_0 surface, where the NH stretches of -NH_2 can be modeled assuming symmetric and asymmetric stretch vibrations, on the S_1 surface only the free NH stretch is observed. Time-dependent density functional electronic structure calculations combined with both normal mode and VPT2 results predict an extremely bright transition between 2900 cm^{-1} and 3100 cm^{-1} depending on the level of theory for the hydrogen bonded NH stretch. No corresponding transition is observed experimentally. To explain the discrepancy between the experimental and calculated intensities of the dislocated NH stretch transition in the S_1 excited state a model is proposed based on the adiabatic separation of the NH stretch and other internal coordinates. In this model, the excitation of the NH stretch leads to dramatic structural reorganization, this leading to many Franck-Condon factors that, in turn, lead to substantial shared intensity of the initial bright state over hundreds a wavenumbers, thereby diluting the band sufficiently that it is no longer apparent in the spectra.

TK04 **10:12 – 10:13**

ABNORMAL RAMAN BANDS OF AROMATICAL AMINES AND BENZYL RADICALS ADSORBED ON METAL SURFACES

DE-YIN WU, ZHONG-QUN TIAN, *College of Chemistry and Chemical Engineering, Xiamen University, Xiamen, China.*

In the work we present our recent works focusing on the chemical enhancement effect of Raman cross section of the wagging vibrations in aromatic amines and benzyl radical adsorbed on metal surfaces. These molecules can display giant chemical enhancement effect in Raman intensity of the specific wagging vibrational modes. To understand the origin of the Raman intensity enhancement, we calculated the potential energy surfaces along the vibrational mode and analysed the change of polarizability due to the binding interaction. Our results also showed that the change of the polarizability derivatives is closely associated with the binding interaction and the orbital hybridization. Furthermore, we also analysed the anharmonicity of the potential energy surface and the vibrational coupling effect of the wagging vibration contributing to the Raman intensity. The Raman features of these special vibrational modes significantly change in vibrational frequency and the relative Raman signal. Finally, we further predict the contribution of the charge transfer state to the relative Raman intensity based on the density functional theoretical calculations.

TK06 **10:20 – 10:21**

CONFORMATIONAL ISOMERS OF NICOTINE, NORNICOTINE AND THEIR HYDRATED CLUSTERS

GARRETT D SANTIS, *Department of Chemistry, University of Washington, Seattle, WA, USA*; NAOYA TAKEDA, SHUN-ICHI ISHIUCHI, KAZUYA TSURUTA, MASAAKI FUJII, *Chemical Resources Laboratory, Tokyo Institute of Technology, Yokohama, Japan*; SOTIRIS XANTHEAS, *Physical Sciences Division, Pacific Northwest National Laboratory, Richland, WA, USA.*

Tobacco addiction plagues society and stems from the neuroactivity of nicotine, a natural compound that is abundant in tobacco leaves. Recent studies have determined that the protonation sites for nicotine are different in its gas (at the pyridine ring) and aqueous (at the pyrrolidine ring) states. These two different protonation sites are expected to trigger different biological activity in the native, anhydrous environment of the binding pocket of the human brain. Infrared (IR) spectroscopy is a powerful tool, which records the molecular vibrations associated with a specific bond and its environment. With the aid of first principles (ab-initio) electronic structure calculations, the IR spectra can be decoded and associated to underlying molecular structures. In this context, protonation in different sites is associated with spectral bands of different frequencies. We have relied on different hierarchical approximations of electronic structure methods, such as Density Functional Theory (DFT), Second Order Møller-Plesset Perturbation Theory (MP2) and Coupled Cluster Theory [CCSD(T)] to compute the IR spectra of nicotine, nornicotine, and their hydrated clusters to investigate the transition of the protonation site from the pyridine to the pyrrolidine rings with an increasing number of water molecules in the cluster. The experimentally observed stabilization of the pyrrolidine protonation site is facilitated by the formation of strong hydrogen bonds to both nitrogen centers, which requires multiple waters. The result is a strong red-shift in the acidic N-H vibrational bands. Notably, nicotine favors the pyrrolidine protonation site more than nornicotine at each hydration level. This increased stability of the pyrrolidine protonation in nicotine is suggested to support stronger binding of nicotine to tryptophan in the nicotinic acetylcholine receptor. The quantification of the incremental hydration for nicotine and nornicotine manifests the multiple energetically relevant hydrated states, which is currently considered in biological applications, such as binding strength to neuroreceptors.

TK07 **10:24 – 10:25**

TOWARD 0.1% UNCERTAINTY FOR CO_2 THEORETICAL IR INTENSTIES

XINCHUAN HUANG[a], *Carl Sagan Center, SETI Institute, Moutain View, CA, USA*; DAVID SCHWENKE, *NAS Facility, NASA Ames Research Center, Moffett Field, CA, USA*; TIMOTHY J. LEE, *Space Science and Astrobiology Division, NASA Ames Research Center, Moffett Field, CA, USA.*

After the first highly accurate IR intensity study on CO_2 20012-00001 band was published in 2015, [Polyansky et al, PRL 114,243001 (2015)], reliable intensity data have been accumulated experimentally for several other bands in the 2001x and 3001x series, with uncertainties less than 0.1-0.5%. Compared to these data, earlier published theoretical CO_2 IR intensities were found with deviations usually around 0.5-1%. To further reduce deviations and uncertainties in the theoretical IR intensities computed using the semi-empirically refined potential energy surfaces (PES) and ab initio dipole moment surfaces (DMS), we have carried out systematic studies to estimate the magnitude of various contributions from the PES, the DMS, and the experimental data. We will present the procedure through which we have achieved 0.2% uncertainty, and discuss why we may need an even more accurate PES, a carefully built (or selected) high quality DMS, and more consistent experimental data, to finally achieve 0.1% or better uncertainty.

[a]Government sponsorship acknowledged

TK08 **10:28 – 10:29**

ACCURATE PREDICTION OF VIBRONIC LEVELS AND BRANCHING RATIOS FOR LASER-COOLABLE LINEAR POLYATOMIC MOLECULES: APPLICATIONS TO CAOH, SROH, AND YBOH

CHAOQUN ZHANG, LAN CHENG, *Department of Chemistry, Johns Hopkins University, Baltimore, MD, USA.*

We report calculations of vibronic levels and branching ratios for laser-coolable linear polyatomic molecules to an accuracy and completeness to be useful to guide experimental studies. The present computational scheme consists of a multi-state quasidiabatic Hamiltonian with relevant perturbations such as Renner-Teller, linear vibronic, and spin-orbit coupling, coupled-cluster calculations for adiabatic potential energy surfaces and molecular parameters, and discrete variable representation calculations for vibronic levels and wave functions. The computed levels and branching ratios for the $A^2\Pi_{1/2} \rightarrow X^2\Sigma_{1/2}$ transitions of CaOH, SrOH, and YbOH show promising agreement with experimental measurements. Based on the computed branching ratios, laser-cooling SrOH requires fewer repumping lasers than CaOH. The calculations also elucidate intensity-borrowing mechanisms for nominally symmetry-forbidden transitions. A close inspection of computational results further reveals it beneficial to avoid Fermi resonances in designing laser-coolable molecules.

TK09 **10:32 – 10:33**

SPECTROSCOPIC-NETWORK-ASSISTED PRECISION SPECTROSCOPY AND ITS APPLICATION TO WATER: THE EXPERIMENT

ROLAND TÓBIÁS, TIBOR FURTENBACHER, ATTILA CSÁSZÁR, *MTA-ELTE Complex Chemical Systems Research Group, Laboratory of Molecular Structure and Dynamics, ELTE Eötvös Loránd University, Budapest, Hungary*; IRÉN SIMKÓ, *Institute of Chemistry, Eötvös Loránd University, Budapest, Hungary*; MEISSA DIOUF, FRANK M.J. COZIJN, EDCEL JOHN SALUMBIDES, WIM UBACHS, *Department of Physics and Astronomy, VU University , Amsterdam, Netherlands.*

Frequency combs and cavity-enhanced optical techniques have revolutionized molecular spectroscopy: their combination allows recording saturated Doppler-free lines with ultrahigh precision. Despite these advancements, precision spectroscopy has not been employed systematically to improve the quality of comprehensive spectroscopic databases as individual observations are often time consuming and lacks impact.

Here we present a new spectroscopic method using network theory, based on the generalized Ritz principle, which offers a powerful tool for the intelligent design and validation of precision-spectroscopy experiments and the subsequent derivation of accurate energy differences.

As a proof of concept, 351 carefully-selected near-infrared transitions (at 1.4 μm) are detected for both $H_2{}^{16}O$ [a] and $H_2{}^{18}O$ [b], two benchmark species of molecular spectroscopy. Transition frequencies of the Lamb-dips are measured up to kHz accuracy using our frequency comb referenced NICE-OHMS spectrometer. These measurements, augmented with extremely-accurate literature lines to ensure overall connectivity, allow the precise determination of the lowest *ortho*-energy and 348 energy levels of both isotopes with unprecedented accuracy. Based on the limited number of observed transitions, 2765 calibration-quality lines are obtained in a wide wavenumber interval. These can be used to improve spectroscopic information systems and applied to frequency metrology, astrophysics, atmospheric sensing, and combustion chemistry.

[a] R. Tóbiás *et al.*, Spectroscopic-network-assisted precision spectroscopy and its application to water, *Nature Comm.* **11**, 1708 (2020)

[b] M.L. Diouf *et al.*, Network-based design of near-infrared Lamb-dip experiments and determination of pure rotational energies of $H_2{}^{18}O$ at kHz accuracy, in preparation (2021)

TK10 **10:36 – 10:37**

SPECTROSCOPIC-NETWORK-ASSISTED PRECISION SPECTROSCOPY AND ITS APPLICATION TO WATER: THEORETICAL FRAMEWORK

ROLAND TÓBIÁS, TIBOR FURTENBACHER, ATTILA CSÁSZÁR, *MTA-ELTE Complex Chemical Systems Research Group, Laboratory of Molecular Structure and Dynamics, ELTE Eötvös Loránd University, Budapest, Hungary*; IRÉN SIMKÓ, *Institute of Chemistry, Eötvös Loránd University, Budapest, Hungary*; MEISSA DIOUF, FRANK M.J. COZIJN, EDCEL JOHN SALUMBIDES, WIM UBACHS, *Department of Physics and Astronomy, VU University , Amsterdam, Netherlands.*

Using the NICE-OHMS (noise-immune-cavity-enhanced optical-heterodyne-molecular spectroscopy) technique, a large number of rovibrational transitions have been observed in the 7000-7350 cm^{-1} window for $H_2^{16}O$ [Nat. Commun. 2020, 11, 1708.] and $H_2^{18}O$ [in preparation], at the kHz-accuracy level. This talk focuses on the theoretical methods that were applied in the design of high-precision NICE-OHMS experiments and the extraction of accurate spectroscopic information from the measured lines. In spectroscopic networks (SN), the vertices and edges are the energy levels and the transitions, respectively. We used the SNAPS (spectroscopic-network-assisted precision spectroscopy) method [Nat. Commun. 2020, 11, 1708.] to select the target lines for measurement and provide initial line positions. The internal consistency of the ultraprecise experimental transitions was verified using cycles of the SN, while paths allow to extract high-accuracy energy levels and derive benchmark-quality predicted lines. The SN of $H_2^{16}O$ and $H_2^{18}O$ consists of four subcomponents, corresponding to the *ortho* and *para* nuclear-spin isomers combined with even and odd parity. For a given nuclear-spin isomer, the levels with even and odd parity are not connected by the vibrational measurements, their connectivity relies on the inclusion of purely rotational transitions. No transitions connecting the *ortho* and *para* states have been observed. Thus, the *ortho* and *para* components of the SNs are not connected, and the energy of the *ortho* states is known only relative to the lowest *ortho* state and not to the *para* ground state. The energy of the lowest *ortho* state was determined in two ways: 1) an effective-Hamiltonian fit to a set of energy differences (taken from the literature and calculated from NICE-OHMS lines) within the ground vibrational band; 2) a network-based approach: paths of NICE-OHMS transitions augmented with diminishing *ortho-para* energy splittings obtained from first-principles quantum-chemical computations. Notably the quantum-chemical computations resulted in highly accurate splittings without the consideration of any experimental data.

TK11 **10:40 – 10:41**

VIBRATIONAL LAMB-DIP SPECTROSCOPY OF WATER ISOTOPOLOGUES: HYPERFINE STRUCTURE IN $H_2{}^{17}O$ AND PERTURBATIONS IN $HD^{16}O$

MEISSA DIOUF, FRANK M.J. COZIJN, EDCEL JOHN SALUMBIDES, WIM UBACHS, *Department of Physics and Astronomy, VU University , Amsterdam, Netherlands*; MATTIA MELOSSO, *Dept. Chemistry "Giacomo Ciamician", University of Bologna, Bologna, ITALY*; CRISTINA PUZZARINI, *Dep. Chemistry 'Giacomo Ciamician', University of Bologna, Bologna, Italy*; ROLAND TÓBIÁS, ATTILA CSÁSZÁR, *MTA-ELTE Complex Chemical Systems Research Group, Laboratory of Molecular Structure and Dynamics, ELTE Eötvös Loránd University, Budapest, Hungary.*

Doppler-free saturation techniques have revolutionized the precision and resolution of molecular spectroscopy. It sets the standard for improving the accuracy of the level structure of molecules by several orders of magnitude. In our studies we employ a NICE-OHMS setup for measuring spectra of water isotopologues in vibrational excitation to the 4th polyad, at a wavelength of 1.4 μm [a]. The high intra-cavity circulating laser power allows for saturating the vibrational lines producing Lamb dips at typical widths of 400 kHz.

Here we present our work on two different water isotopologues $HD^{16}O$ and $H_2{}^{17}O$, in which various physical effects significantly alter the ordinary saturated Lamb-dip. In $H_2{}^{17}O$, thanks to the spin of the ^{17}O, we resolve the hyperfine structure, which can be exploited to extract hyperfine constants from a rovibrational transition. In $HD^{16}O$, where the deuteron breaks the para/ortho symmetry, perturbed spectral line shapes are observed, in particular for lines that exhibit small K_c splittings between lines of opposite parity. It is hypothesized that AC Stark effects are the cause for breaking up the line into a multi-component structure.

[a] R. Tobias, T. Furtenbacher, I. Simko, A.G. Csaszar, M.L. Diouf, F.M.J. Cozijn, J.M.A. Staa, E.J. Salumbides, W. Ubachs, Spectroscopic-network-assisted precision spectroscopy and its application to water, Nature Comm. 11, 1708 (2020)

TK12 **10:44 – 10:45**

COUPLED-CLUSTER APPROACHES TO ELECTRIC POLARIZABILITIES FOR LONG-RANGE FORCE FIELDS

STEPHEN L COY, TIMOTHY J BARNUM, ROBERT W FIELD, *Department of Chemistry, MIT, Cambridge, MA, USA*; JOHN F. STANTON, *Physical Chemistry, University of Florida, Gainesville, FL, USA.*

Whether in ionic or covalent bonding, in weakly bound clusters, in liquids, or in solids, perturbed electronic structure contributes to spectroscopy, electromagnetic interactions and enhanced reactivity. For Rydberg states, effects of current interest include vibrational autoionization as discussed by Ed Eyler and by Timothy Barnum The range of importance of classical force fields extends through VdW clusters up to biological problems such as enhanced protein folding from fluorine-substitution in proteins. For smaller molecules and Rydberg ion cores such as NO+ or alkaline earth mono-halide cations, accurate coupled cluster methods are quite feasible at the CCSD(T) or CCSDT level, using augmented basis sets up to the quadruple-zeta level. These methods can be used in the CFOUR ab-initio suite to determine polarizability expansions giving the local force field out to quite high order. Several approaches will be described, including arrays of test-charges, the use of implemented analytical derivatives, and static field perturbations. This presentation will focus on results useful for modeling Rydberg vibrational autoionization in NO Rydberg states.

TK13 **10:48 – 10:49**

LONG-RANGE POLARIZATION MODEL OF VIBRATIONAL AUTOIONIZATION IN RYDBERG STATES OF NITRIC OXIDE

TIMOTHY J BARNUM, *Department of Chemistry, MIT, Cambridge, MA, USA*; GLORIA CLAUSEN, *Laboratorium für Physikalische Chemie, ETH Zurich, Zurich, Switzerland*; STEPHEN L COY, ROBERT W FIELD, *Department of Chemistry, MIT, Cambridge, MA, USA.*

In high angular momentum ($\ell \geq 3$) Rydberg states, the centrifugal barrier hinders close approach of the Rydberg electron to the ion-core. As a result, these core-nonpenetrating Rydberg states can be well described by a simplified model in which the Rydberg electron is only perturbed by the long-range electric properties of the ion-core. We have developed a long-range model to describe the vibrational autoionization dynamics of high-ℓ Rydberg states of nitric oxide. In particular, our model explains the extensive angular momentum exchange between the ion-core and Rydberg electron previously observed in vibrational autoionization of nf Rydberg states. In addition, we have measured total decay lifetimes of ng Rydberg states and find that the decay of ng states is dominated by autoionization rather than predissociation. We examine the predicted ion rotational state distributions generated by vibrational autoionization of ng states and discuss a potential application in the production of quantum state-selected molecular ions.

TL. Ions

Tuesday, June 22, 2021 – 10:0 AM

Room: 2021 Online Everywhere

Chair: Stephan Schlemmer, I. Physikalisches Institut, Köln, Germany

TL01 **10:00 – 10:01**

VIBRATIONAL SPECTROSCOPY OF H_2He^+ and D_2He^+

OSKAR ASVANY, STEPHAN SCHLEMMER, *I. Physikalisches Institut, Universität zu Köln, Köln, Germany*; AD VAN DER AVOIRD, *Institute for Molecules and Materials (IMM), Radboud University Nijmegen, Nijmegen, Netherlands*; TAMÁS SZIDAROVSZKY, ATTILA CSÁSZÁR, *Research Group on Complex Chemical Systems, MTA-ELTE, Budapest, Hungary*.

Vibrational modes of the relatively strongly bound H_2He^+ molecular ion and its deuterated congener D_2He^+ are investigated by low-resolution multi-photon photodissociation spectroscopy, using a combination of a 4 K cryogenic ion-trap machine and the free electron laser FELIX. The band origins obtained are fully explained by accurate variational calculations of the rovibrational states based on the three-dimensional potential energy surface of Koner *et al.* [Phys. Chem. Chem. Phys. **21** (2019) 24976]. Results from second-order vibrational perturbation theory, based on a linear H–H–He equilibrium structure, agree well with those of the variational calculations for energy levels up to about 1300 cm^{-1}. The low-resolution experiments corroborate the linear structure of the ions and identify the bright IR-active HH-stretch fundamental in H_2He^+ at about 1840 cm^{-1} and the DD-stretch fundamental in H_2He^+ at about 1309 cm^{-1}. The calculations also reveal the H_2^+–He bend and stretch fundamentals to be at 640 and 732 cm^{-1} and the D_2^+–He bend and stretch fundamentals at 478 and 641 cm^{-1}, respectively. A short outlook is given on future high-resolution experiments.

TL02 **10:04 – 10:05**

KINETIC AND SPECTROSCOPIC STUDIES OF C_2^- IN A CRYOGENIC WIRE TRAP

MARKUS NÖTZOLD, ROBERT WILD, CHRISTINE LOCHMANN, ROLAND WESTER, *Institute for Ion Physics and Applied Physics, University of Innsbruck, Innsbruck, Austria.*

The study of ion-molecule reactions plays a vital role in cold chemistry, thus implying the need of well-controlled ion ensembles in a cold environment. The internal and external degrees of freedom of molecular ions, trapped in multipole radio frequency ion traps, can be cooled via collisions with neutral atoms [1]. Usually the coolant undergoes collisions with a thermal shield mounted on a cryostat attaining temperatures of about 4 K. To overcome this lower temperature limit two approaches have been proposed. Firstly, using a laser-cooled buffer-gas localized at the center of the ion cloud [2]. Secondly, sympathetic cooling via a second laser cooled molecular anion like C_2^- [3]. This, in addition to its potential role in forming carbon chain anions in the interstellar medium, makes C_2^- an important molecule in anion research.

In this contribution we present a newly developed 16-pole cryogenic radio frequency wire trap for spectroscopic and kinetic studies of molecular anions. First results of quenching rates of the first excited vibrational level of C_2^- due to collisions with H_2 are presented. Furthermore, possible reaction pathways with H_2 are discussed and recent spectroscopic measurements of the second electronic excited state of C_2^- are presented.

References:

[1] R. Wester , J. Phys. B 42, 154001 (2009)

[2] B. Höltkemeier et al., Phys. Rev. A 94, 062703, (2016)

[3] P. Yzombard et al., Phys. Rev. Lett. 114, 213001 (2015)

TL03 **10:08 – 10:09**

THE SPECTRUM OF ν_3 BAND OF CH_3^+ IN HELIUM NANODROPLETS

SWETHA ERUKALA, DEEPAK VERMA, ANDREY VILESOV, *Department of Chemistry, University of Southern California, Los Angeles, CA, USA.*

CH_3^+ ions were produced upon electron impact ionization of the He droplets doped with methane molecules.The spectra was obtained by recording the intensity of ions detected based upon upon ejection from the droplet following absorption of multiple mid infrared photons[a]. Perpendicular ν_3 band of CH_3^+ in He droplets shows three prominent peaks which are assigned to partially resolved rotational structure. The results show that CH_3^+ retains the ability to rotate in liquid helium, however the decrement of rotational constants is larger than previously observed for neutrals. It was concluded that CH_3^+ in helium behaves as a prolate symmetric top, whereas the free ion is reported to be an oblate top [b].

[a]D. Verma, E.Swetha, A.F. Vilesov, Infrared Spectroscopy of Water and Zundel cations in Helium Nanodroplets, The Journal of Physical Chemistry A 124(34) (2020) 6207-6213.

[b]M.W. Crofton, M.F. Jagod, B.D. Rehfuss, W.A. Kreiner, T. Oka, Infrared-Spectroscopy of Carbo-Ions .III. ν_3 Band of Methyl Cation CH_3^+, Journal of Chemical Physics 88(2)(1988) 666-678

TL04 **10:12 – 10:13**

HIGH-RESOLUTION DOUBLE RESONANCE ACTION SPECTROSCOPY IN ION TRAPS: VIBRATIONAL AND ROTATIONAL FINGERPRINTS OF $CH_2NH_2^+$

CHARLES R. MARKUS, *Division of Chemistry and Chemical Engineering, California Institute of Technology, Pasadena, CA, USA*; SVEN THORWIRTH, OSKAR ASVANY, STEPHAN SCHLEMMER, *I. Physikalisches Institut, Universität zu Köln, Köln, Germany.*

Applying various action spectroscopic techniques in a 4 K cryogenic ion trap instrument, protonated methanimine, $CH_2NH_2^+$, has been investigated by high-resolution rovibrational and pure rotational spectroscopy for the first time. In total, 39 rovibrational transitions within the fundamental band of the ν_2 symmetric C-H stretch were measured around 3026 cm^{-1}, which were used to predict pure rotational transition frequencies of $CH_2NH_2^+$ in the ground vibrational state. Based on these predictions, nine rotational transitions were observed between 109 and 283 GHz using a novel double resonance method. This method consists of rotational excitation followed by vibrational excitation, which is finally detected as a reduction in the number of $CH_2NH_2^+$-He complexes formed in the 4 K He bath of the trap.

TL05 **10:16 – 10:17**

THE ν_1 VIBRATIONAL MODE OF HC_3O^+ OBSERVED AT HIGH SPECTRAL RESOLUTION

OSKAR ASVANY, *I. Physikalisches Institut, Universität zu Köln, Köln, Germany*; MICHAEL E. HARDING, *Institute of Nanotechnology, Karlsruhe Institute of Technology, Karlsruhe, Germany*; STEPHAN SCHLEMMER, SVEN THORWIRTH, *I. Physikalisches Institut, Universität zu Köln, Köln, Germany.*

Following-up on our recent infrared photodissociation (IRPD) spectroscopic detection of the linear Ne-tagged HC_3O^+ molecular ion,[a] the C-H stretching mode ν_1 of bare HC_3O^+ has now been studied at high spectral resolution. The spectrum was observed using a 4 K cryogenic ion trap apparatus at Cologne (COLtrap) and a cw optical parametric oscillator using the method of laser-induced inhibition of complex growth (LIICG) with helium as tagging agent. Fifteen rotational-vibrational transitions were observed, covering $P(8)$ to $R(6)$. The band origin is found at 3237.1 cm^{-1} and hence blueshifted by some 5 cm^{-1} compared to that of the HC_3O^+–Ne weakly bound complex probed earlier in the IRPD study.

[a]S. Thorwirth, M. E. Harding, O. Asvany, S. Brünken, P. Jusko, K. L. K Lee, T. Salomon, M. C. McCarthy, and S. Schlemmer 2020, Mol. Phys. 118, e1776409

TL06 **10:20 – 10:21**

NITROUS OXIDE IS NOTHING TO LAUGH ABOUT: $Au_2N_2O^+$

KAI POLLOW, MARKO FÖRSTEL, TAARNA STUDEMUND, ROBERT G. RADLOFF, OTTO DOPFER, *Institut für Optik und Atomare Physik, Technische Universität Berlin, Berlin, Germany.*

Nitrous Oxide is the third largest contributor to the greenhouse effect having a potency 300 times that of CO_2. Furthermore it is a metastable molecule that can be catalytically converted into harmless nitrogen and oxygen gas. Gold is an interesting candidate because small metal clusters could provide reaction pathways to enable this activation. Therefore we study the simple system $Au_2N_2O^+$. In this talk we will present the measured vibrationally-resolved optical photodissociation spectrum and compare the results to quantum-chemical calculations of different isomers and bare Au_2^+[1].

[1] M. Förstel et al., Angew. Chem. Int. Ed., 2020, 123, 21587-21592.

TL07 **10:24 – 10:25**

INFRARED SPECTROSCOPY OF SINGLE-TURN AND DOUBLE-TURN TETHERED ALPHA-HELICES IN THE GAS PHASE: DON'T LET YOUR LEFT HAND KNOW WHAT YOUR RIGHT HAND IS DOING.

JOHN T LAWLER, TIMOTHY S. ZWIER[a], *Department of Chemistry, Purdue University, West Lafayette, IN, USA.*

This talk will describe single-conformation IR and UV spectroscopy of a series of single-turn and double-turn alpha helices as cryo-cooled, gas phase ions. Synthesized samples of tethered pentapeptides are known to form single-turn alpha helices in aqueous solution. When L-amino acids are used, a right-handed single-turn helix is formed while D-amino acids produce a left-handed helix. Due to the tether, these structures are remarkably stable in aqueous solution over a wide range of temperatures, pH, and denaturant. They can be concatenated, making LL, DD, LD, and DL double-turn forms. When a methylated arginine is placed at the C-terminal end of the tethered peptide, single-turn helices are the most stable structure, and are observed exclusively. The spectra in the NH stretch and amide I regions show distinct effects that depend on position along the helix, and the presence or absence of a kink due to concatenation of two opposite-handed helices. We will discuss these spectra and the prospects they offer as scaffolds for studying a wide range of interesting structural and dynamical problems.

[a]Current address: Combustion Research Facility, Sandia National Laboratories, Livermore, CA 94551 U.S.A. Support for this research from the National Science Foundation through grant NSF CHE1714658. TSZ acknowledges support during the analysis phase of the work from the Department of Energy Basic Energy Sciences Gas Phase Chemical Physics program.

TL08 **10:28 – 10:29**

PROBING THE CONFORMATIONAL LANDSCAPE AND THERMOCHEMISTRY OF DINUCLEOTIDE ANIONS VIA HELIUM NANODROPLET INFRARED ACTION SPECTROSCOPY

DANIEL A THOMAS[a], RAYOON CHANG, EIKE MUCHA, MAIKE LETTOW, KIM GREIS, GERARD MEIJER, GERT VON HELDEN, *Department of Molecular Physics, Fritz-Haber-Institut der Max-Planck-Gesellschaft, Berlin, Germany.*

When molecules are captured in a helium nanodroplet, the rate of cooling to an equilibrium temperature of ca. 0.4 K is faster than the rate of isomerization, resulting in "shock-freezing" that kinetically traps molecules in the local conformational minimum. This unique property enables the study of temperature-dependent conformational equilibria via infrared spectroscopy without the deleterious effects of spectral broadening at higher temperatures.[b,c] We utilize this approach to explore the equilibrium conformer populations of deprotonated dinucleotides, which have been shown previously by ion mobility spectrometry to exhibit a strong temperature dependence.[d] Dinucleotide anion species were generated by electrospray ionization, confined in a helium-buffer-gas ion trap at temperatures between 90 and 350 K, and entrained in traversing helium nanodroplets. The infrared spectra of the dinucleotide ions captured in nanodroplets show a strong dependence on pre-pickup ion temperature, consistent with the preservation of conformer populations prior to cooling in the helium nanodroplet. Non-negative matrix factorization was utilized to identify component conformer infrared spectra and thereby determine temperature-dependent conformer populations. Relative enthalpies and entropies of conformers were subsequently obtained from a van 't Hoff analysis. These initial results demonstrate the promise of this technique to elucidate competing intramolecular interactions and experimentally measure thermochemical parameters for isolated biomolecular ions.[e]

[a]Present Address: University of Rhode Island, Department of Chemistry, Kingston, RI 02881
[b]D. S. Skvortsov, A. F. Vilesov, *J. Chem. Phys.* **2009**, *130*, 151101.
[c]C. M. Leavitt *et al.*, *J. Phys. Chem. A* **2014**, *118*, 9692-9700.
[d]J. Gidden, M. T. Bowers, *Eur. Phys. J. D* **2002**, *20*, 409-419.
[e]D. A. Thomas *et al.*, *Phys. Chem. Chem. Phys.* **2020**, *22*, 18400-18413.

TL09 **10:32 – 10:33**

DOUBLE-RESONANCE SPECTROSCOPY WITH A CONTINUUM: APPLICATION TO THE $Mg(3d_\delta)Ar^+$ $^2\Delta$ STATE OF $MgAr^+$

MATTHIEU GÉNÉVRIEZ, DOMINIK WEHRLI, THOMAS BERGLITSCH, FRÉDÉRIC MERKT, *Laboratorium für Physikalische Chemie, ETH Zurich, Zurich, Switzerland.*

Whereas the electronic ground states of a large number of small molecular cations have been spectroscopically characterized, much less is known concerning electronically excited states, in particular because of the low densities in which molecular ions can be formed and because of the high excitation energies required. Electronically excited states of molecular ions are commonly studied using resonance-enhanced multiphoton dissociation (REMPD) [1] or isolated-core multiphoton Rydberg dissociation (ICMRD) spectroscopy [2]. These techniques rely on the fact that the excited molecular ion either predissociates rapidly or can be efficiently excited to a dissociative state by further photoabsorption. The $Mg(3d_\delta)Ar^+$ $^2\Delta$ state of $MgAr^+$ is an example of an electronic state that does not fulfill these conditions and cannot be studied with conventional REMPD or ICMRD. We will report on the experimental study of this state using a double-resonance spectroscopic technique we have developed. With this technique, $MgAr^+$ molecules were prepared in their electronic ground state and then coupled, *via* an intermediate state, to *both* the $Mg(3d_\delta)Ar^+$ $^2\Delta$ state and a predissociation continuum. In contrast to double-resonance spectroscopy involving only bound states, the presence of a predissociation continuum leads to a rich variety of spectral lineshapes, which exhibit asymmetric profiles reminiscent of Fano lineshapes. We carried out detailed simulations of these lineshapes using a quantum-optics-based effective Hamiltonian and solving the time-dependent Schrödinger equation. Agreement with experimental spectra is excellent and shows that the lineshapes are the result of quantum interferences between the different photoexcitation pathways leading to dissociation. We will discuss how the lineshapes can be controlled with external parameters such as laser pulse energies and wavenumbers in order, *e.g.*, to facilitate spectroscopic analysis. The analysis of the rovibrational structure of the $Mg(3d_\delta)Ar^+$ $^2\Delta$ electronic state will be presented, with particular emphasis on the anomalous behavior of the splitting between its two spin-orbit components.

[1] P.O. Danis, T. Wyttenbach and J.P. Maier, J. Chem. Phys. **88**, 3451–3455 (1988)
[2] M. Génévriez, D. Wehrli and F. Merkt, Mol. Phys. **118**, e1703051 (2019)

TL10 **10:36 – 10:37**

VIBRONIC SPECTRA OF GROUP 13 METAL-PIPERIDINE COMPLEXES

MICHEAL OKEKE, DONG-SHENG YANG, *Department of Chemistry, University of Kentucky, Lexington, KY, USA.*

Group 13 (Al, Ga, and In)-piperidine complexes are produced in a pulsed metal-cluster beam source, observed by time-of-flight mass spectrometry, and characterized with pulsed-field-ionization zero electron kinetic energy spectroscopy. The spectrum of each complex exhibits several vibronic progressions associated with metal-ligand stretching, metal-ligand bending, or ligand-based vibrations. The Franck-Condon profile of the Al-piperidine spectrum is considerably shorter than those of Ga/In-piperidine, suggesting a larger charge effect on the structures of the heavier metal complexes. Electronic states, active vibrational modes, metal binding sites, and the conformation of the metal coordinated piperidine are identified by comparing the spectra of the three complexes and with theoretical calculations.

TL11 ***Post-Deadline Abstract*** **10:40 – 10:41**

INFRARED SPECTROSCOPIC OBSERVATION OF THE MCLAFFERTY REARRANGEMENT IN IONIZED 2-PENTANONE

YOSHIYUKI MATSUDA, RYO YASUMOTO, ASUKA FUJII, *Department of Chemistry, Tohoku University, Sendai, Japan.*

The McLafferty rearrangement is a well-known process in mass spectrometry. The Mclafferty rearrangement is dissociations of ionized ketones with accompanying hydrogen transfer on the gamma carbon atom to generate an enol cation. This reaction has undergone numerous mass spectrometric investigations but there has been no spectroscopic research to observe the intermediate enol cation. In this study, we have performed infrared spectroscopy of jet-cooled neutral and ionized 2-pentanone to investigate its isomerization process following photoionization. The OH stretch bands as well as CH stretch bands are observed in the spectrum of cationic 2-pentanone, while only CH stretch bands are observed for the neutral. These clearly indicate the enolization following hydrogen transfer from CH occurs in the ionized pentanone. The enolization of ionized 2-pentanone through hydrogen transfer from the gamma carbon is also supported by the theoretical reaction path search calculation.

TM. Lineshapes, collisional effects

Tuesday, June 22, 2021 – 10:0 AM

Room: 2021 Online Everywhere

Chair: Keeyoon Sung, Jet Propulsion Laboratory/Caltech, Pasadena, CA, USA

TM01 **10:00 – 10:01**

INVESTIGATION OF ZEEMAN STATE-TO-STATE COLLISION-INDUCED TRANSITIONS IN NITRIC OXIDE USING TWO-COLOR POLARIZATION SPECTROSCOPY

ZIQIAO CHANG, AMAN SATIJA, ROBERT P. LUCHT, *Mechanical Engineering, Purdue University, West Lafayette, IN, USA.*

Polarization spectroscopy (PS) is a nonlinear pump-probe technique that utilizes a change in the polarization of the probe beam, due to anisotropic Zeeman state populations created in the target molecule by the pump beam. The line strength and line shape of a PS signal is dependent on the structure and dynamics of the molecule. Here we present a two-color polarization spectroscopy (TCPS) technique, with independent spectral tuning of the pump and probe beams, for investigating collision induced transitions (CITs) in the $A^2\Sigma^+$-$X^2\Pi$ (0-0) band of nitric oxide (NO) at 295 K and 1 atm. We distinguish CITs from shared level transitions (SLTs), which occur when the transitions excited by pump and probe beams share a common upper and/or lower level. In TCPS, CITs only occur when Zeeman state anisotropy (ZSA) is preserved to some extent during state-to-state rotational transfer. In these NO TCPS studies, a circularly-polarized pump beam is tuned to create a ZSA in the NO molecules at either low or high J level. A weak probe beam is then scanned over a range of transitions close to the pump frequency in order to probe SLTs and CITs. Gas mixtures of 1% NO in the buffer gases He, N_2, and Ar were selected for the experiments to investigate the dependence of CIT on collision species. The strongest CITs were observed in the He buffer gas and the weakest CITs were observed in the Ar buffer gas. A time-dependent density matrix model incorporating a modified-exponential-gap-law-based collisional submodel was developed to investigate the state-to-state ZSA retention rate of NO with different colliding partners. A key result is that the spin-flip transition rate in the $A^2\Sigma^+$ level is significant at low J, while being almost zero at high J ($J > 10$). These results will provide useful information for comparison with ab initio potential energy surface collision studies.

TM02 **10:04 – 10:05**

LINE MIXING STUDY ON THE NITRIC OXIDE FUNDAMENTAL BAND NEAR 5.3 MICRONS

WEY-WEY SU, *Mechanical Engineering, Stanford University, Stanford, CA, USA*; CHRISTOPHER ALMODOVAR, *School of Engineering, Brown University, Providence, RI, USA*; YIMING DING, CHRISTOPHER L STRAND, RONALD K HANSON, *Mechanical Engineering, Stanford University, Stanford, CA, USA.*

We present absorbance measurements of the full fundamental ro-vibrational band of nitric oxide in nitrogen bath (NO/N_2) from 1700 to 2000 cm^{-1} at pressure and temperature conditions of 20-34 atm and 293-802 K, respectively. These measurements were taken with a narrow-linewidth, broad-scan EC-QCL laser aligned through a high-pressure, high-temperature static cell. The results were compared to a line mixing model utilizing relaxation matrix formalism and the modified exponential gap (MEG) fitting law that was previously developed using absorbance measurements limited to the R-branch[a]. Improved knowledge from full-band absorbance measurements, including the P and Q-branches, indicates the need to account for inter-branch line mixing effects which were omitted in the previous model. A modified MEG line mixing model is presented with additional inter-branch coupling transfer rates and their associated scaling factors, showing stronger agreement with the measured spectra.

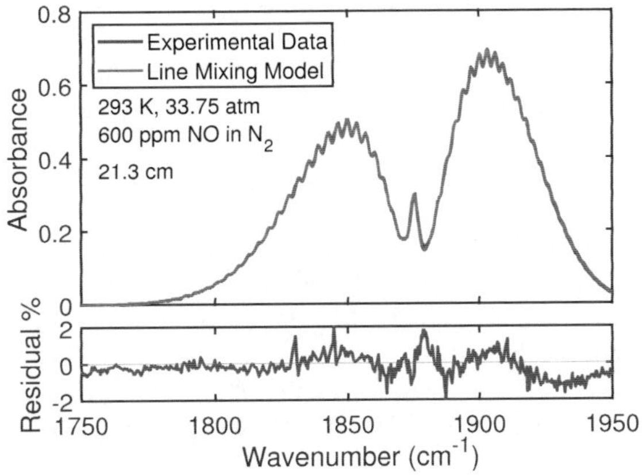

[a]Almodovar, C.A., "Infrared Laser Absorption Spectroscopy of Nitric Oxide for Sensing in High-Enthalpy Air," Ph.D. diss., (Stanford University, 2019)

TM03 **10:08 – 10:09**

AIR-BROADENING IN NEAR-INFRARED CARBON DIOXIDE LINE SHAPES: QUANTIFYING CONTRIBUTIONS FROM O_2, N_2, AND Ar

ERIN M. ADKINS, DAVID A. LONG, JOSEPH T. HODGES, *Material Measurement Laboratory, National Institute of Standards and Technology, Gaithersburg, MD, USA.*

Line-by-line spectroscopic databases containing CO_2, such as HITRAN, include so many transitions and bands that it is intractable to provide reference data for every transition and relevant collisional partner. To address this dilemma, theoretical line parameters enabling widespread coverage need to be validated in terms of accurate spectroscopic measurements having well-established uncertainties. In this work, we present frequency-agile, rapid scanning cavity ring-down spectroscopy (FARS) measurements of CO_2 (30012) $\leftarrow$ (00001) band transitions up to $J'' = 50$. These data correspond to foreign broadening by four gas mixtures: air, N_2, and two Ar-enriched synthetic air samples, with each sample containing CO_2 at a mole fraction near atmospheric levels. The measured O_2, N_2, and Ar foreign broadening parameters in addition to advanced line shape parameters were simultaneously determined using a multi-spectrum fitting algorithm which used constraints for pressure, temperature, and sample composition. These results were compared to theoretical and experimental broadener-specific line shape parameters from the literature. Additionally, requantized classical molecular dynamic simulation results were explored as constraints to enable differentiation between narrowing mechanisms in finite signal-to-noise ratio spectra.

TM04 **10:12 – 10:13**

REVISING THE LINESHAPE PARAMETERS FOR AIR- AND SELF- BROADENED CO_2 LINES AT A SUB-PERCENT LEVEL

ROBAB HASHEMI, IOULI E GORDON, *Atomic and Molecular Physics, Harvard-Smithsonian Center for Astrophysics, Cambridge, MA, USA*; THI NGOC HA TRAN, *Laboratoire de Meteorologie Dynamique, Ecole Polytechnique, University Paris Saclay and CNRS, Paris, France*; ROMAN V KOCHANOV, *Laboratory of Quantum Molecular Mechanics and Radiation Processes, Tomsk State University, Tomsk, Russia*; JULIEN LAMOUROUX, , *Independent Researcher, Paris, France*; YAN TAN, *Hefei National Laboratory for Physical Science at Microscale, University of Science and Technology of China, Hefei, China*; LAURENCE S. ROTHMAN, *Atomic and Molecular Physics, Harvard-Smithsonian Center for Astrophysics, Cambridge, MA, USA.*

Characterizing and modelling the atmospheric CO_2 with a sub-percent accuracy necessitates high-quality spectroscopic lineshape parameters. For this goal, we collected the best experimentally and theoretically measured lineshape coefficients of CO_2 lines broadened by air and CO_2 to create sets of semi-empirical models for updating all the transitions of the HITRAN database [1]. Based on the available data, we estimated the air- and CO_2- broadening coefficients, their associated temperature exponents, and the speed dependence of the broadening together with its temperature dependence for every transition in HITRAN. Furthermore, the semi-empirical approach proposed by Hartmann 2009 [2] (trained by most reliable experimental data) is used to calculate the line shifts of air- and self- broadened CO_2 absorption lines. The updated data will be provided on www.hitran.org and will be used in the next edition of HITRAN. It is notable that thanks to the relational structure of the HITRAN database we provide separate consistent and complete sets of parameters in Voigt and speed-dependent Voigt parametrizations. Finally, the updated lineshape parameters are used for calculating the first-order line mixing using the program developed by Lamouroux et al. [3] which will also be provided in HITRAN 2020. For verifying the semi-empirically calculated lineshape parameters, the laboratory spectra measured by Dr. Keeyoon Sung at the Jet Propulsion Laboratory (JPL) is used to compare with the calculation of the absorption coefficient by HITRAN Application Programming Interface (HAPI) [4] which is now equipped with necessary functionality. [1] JQSRT, 203 (2017) 3-69. [2]JQSRT, 110 (18) (2009) 2019-2026. [3] JQSRT, 151 (2015) 88-96. [4] JQSRT, 177 (2016) 15-30.

TM05 **10:16 – 10:17**

DUAL FREQUENCY COMB ABSORPTION SPECTROSCOPY OF CO_2 AT HIGH PRESSURE AND TEMPERATURE

RYAN K. COLE, NAZANIN HOGHOOGHI, GREGORY B RIEKER, *Department of Mechanical Engineering, University of Colorado Boulder, Boulder, CO, USA.*

Accurate absorption models for gases at high pressure and temperature are needed for applications in both planetary and combustion science. Absorption models for these conditions require complete databases of temperature-dependent line shape parameters as well as temperature-dependent models for higher-order collisional effects that manifest at high pressure (e.g. line mixing, collision-induced absorption, finite duration collisions). In support of this goal, we present new measurements of CO_2 at pressures up to 25 bar and temperatures up to 981 K recorded with a broadband, high-resolution dual frequency comb absorption spectrometer in a specialized gas cell. We analyze the measured spectra using a multispectrum fitting approach to extract temperature-dependent line shape parameters for bands in the 6800 – 7000 cm^{-1} range using both a Voigt and speed-dependent Voigt profile. We compare the new parameters to prior measurements and calculations, particularly those adopted for the HITRAN2020 database. Finally, using the new line shape parameters, we expand our absorption model to include line mixing effects, and discuss the performance of the line mixing model at high pressure and temperature. These results improve absorption models for CO_2 in high-pressure and -temperature conditions and, more broadly, inform strategies for modelling high-pressure, high-temperature spectra in combustion and planetary science.

TM06 **10:20 – 10:21**

ADAPTATION TO HIGH RESOLUTION OF AN ALGORITHM TO RETRIEVE THE INSTRUMENT LINE SHAPE OF A FOURIER TRANSFORM SPECTROMETER

THIBAULT BERTIN, JEAN VANDER AUWERA, *SQUARES, Université Libre de Bruxelles, Brussels, Belgium.*

Fourier transform spectra include the non negligible contribution of the instrumental line shape (ILS) of the spectrometer, even at high resolution. To avoid biasing the information retrieved from these spectra, an accurate modeling of the actual ILS of the spectrometer is required. Several methods have been developed to retrieve the ILS from Fourier transform spectra of isolated lines at low pressure, either partially[a] or completely,[b,c] including its wavenumber dependence for the ACE-FTS.[d]

The present method builds upon the work of Boone and Bernath.[5] It replaces the modeling of the wavenumber dependence of the ILS adapted to the ACE-FTS instrument, which turned out not to be appropriate for high resolution laboratory Fourier transform spectrometers, and accounts for the loss of information on the ILS resulting from the molecular line shape. The method, implemented in a simple python script, will be presented and its performance compared with `linefit`.[3]

Acknowledgements: *T. Bertin thanks the FRIA (Belgium) for a PhD fellowship. This work is financially supported by the "Fonds de la Recherche Scientifique"–FNRS (Belgium).*

[a] D. Jacquemart, M. Chaboud, J. Quant. Spectrosc. Radiat. Transf. 119 (2013) 95–103.
[b] F. Hase, T. Blumenstock, C. Paton-Walsh, Appl. Opt. 38 (1999) 3417–3422.
[c] C. Bernardo, D.W.T. Griffith, J. Quant. Spectrosc. Radiat. Transf. 95 (2005) 141–150.
[d] C.D. Boone, P.F. Bernath, J. Quant. Spectrosc. Radiat. Transf. 230 (2019) 1–12.

TM07 **10:24 – 10:25**

A POTASSIUM LINE SHAPE STUDY AT STELLAR ATMOSPHERIC TEMPERATURES OF BROWN DWARFS

YIMING DING, JOSHUA A VANDERVORT, CHRISTOPHER L STRAND, RONALD K HANSON, *Mechanical Engineering, Stanford University, Stanford, CA, USA.*

There is considerable ambiguity in the collisional broadening mechanism for the resonance doublets of alkali metals, e.g., potassium near 0.77 μm. The presence of alkali metals within stellar atmospheres of brown dwarfs calls for accurate modeling on the effect of collisional broadening to better interpolate the spectra measured by space telescopes. We present an easy approach to generate potassium vapor in the laboratory at conditions similar to the effective surface temperatures ($\sim$1000 K) of brown dwarfs.

High-temperature potassium/argon mixtures are produced in a shock tube via shock-heating seeded potassium chloride salts. This seeding approach is effective over 1100 - 1900 K and is very safe, compared with the handling of highly reactive potassium samples. The absorption line shapes of both K I resonance doublets (D1: 770 nm; D2: 767 nm) are studied with argon as the collisional partner. The measured spectra are well-modeled with Voigt profiles, and the measured broadening parameters, i.e., argon broadening coefficients and pressure shift coefficients, are well-fit with power-law relationships in the range of test temperatures.

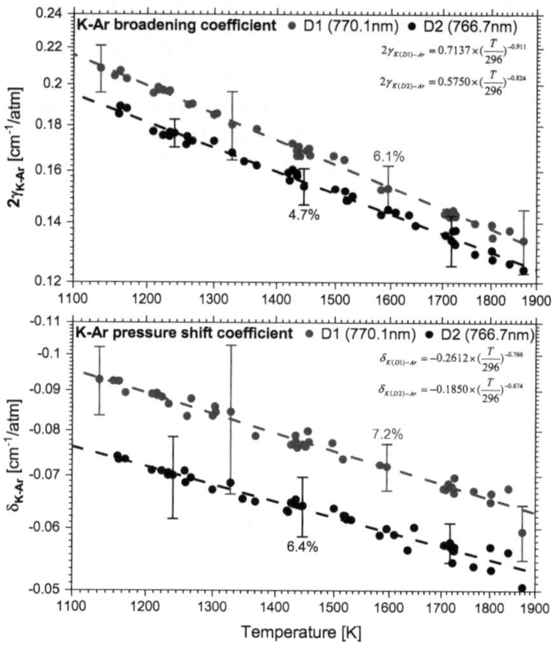

TM08 **10:28 – 10:29**

CONTINUING INVESTIGATIONS OF ORTHO-PARA-DEPENDENT PRESSURE BROADENING IN THE $\nu_1 + \nu_3$ BAND OF ACETYLENE

EISEN C. GROSS, KIMBERLY A TSANG, TREVOR SEARS, *Department of Chemistry, Stony Brook University, Stony Brook, NY, USA.*

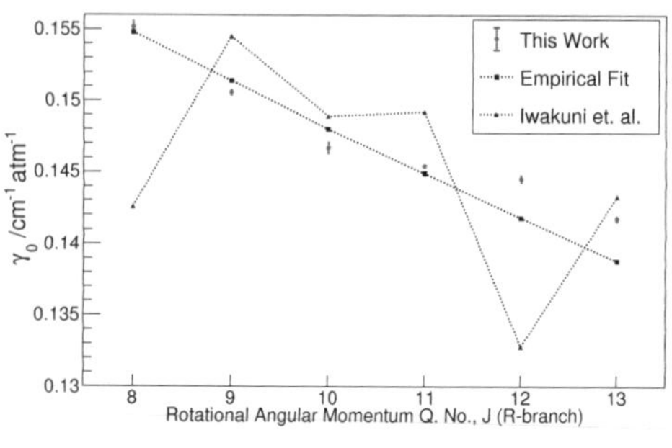

In 2016, Iwakuni et al.[1] measured the $\nu_1 + \nu_3$ vibrational combination band of acetylene using a dual-frequency comb based spectrometer. They reported an alternation in the self-pressure broadening coefficients of even and odd rotational levels, which correspond to the para- and ortho- nuclear spin states. This can occur if relaxation involving resonant energy transfer between molecules with common nuclear spin symmetry is important, because ortho-ortho collisions are statistically more probable than para-para ones. Subsequently several authors[2 3] have disputed these findings. Our recently published results, using a frequency-comb stabilized laser spectrometer found no experimental evidence of the reported effect in the R(8)−R(13) lines of the band.[4] Analysis of the data needed careful accounting of weak underlying absorptions due to hot-bands and lower abundance isotopomer lines. Detailed modeling of Iwakuni et al. results suggest the alternation is an artifact of the fits neglecting collisional narrowing in a strongly absorbing regime. Further low temperature measurements have been planned to try to limit influence of the hot-band lines.

1. K. Iwakuni, S. Okubo, K. M. T. Yamada, H. Inaba, A. Onae, F.-L. Hong, and H. Sasada, *Phys. Rev. Lett.* **117**, (2016).
2. K. K. Lehmann, *J. Chem. Phys.* **146**, 094309 (2017).
3. J.-M. Hartmann and H. Tran, *Phys. Rev. Lett.* **119**, (2017).
4. E.C. Gross, K. A. Tsang, and T.J. Sears, *J. Chem. Phys.* **154**, 054305 (2021).

TM09 **10:32 – 10:33**

CO_2 COLLISION-INDUCED LINE PARAMETERS IN THE ν_3 BAND OF CH_4

THIBAULT BERTIN, JEAN VANDER AUWERA, *SQUARES, Université Libre de Bruxelles, Brussels, Belgium.*

Methane is present in the atmosphere of a large number of objects in the Solar system and beyond. Probing CH_4 in these environments using optical remote sensing relies on the availability of appropriate information characterizing its spectrum. The present work aims to provide the spectroscopic information required to describe the effects of pressure on the infrared spectrum of methane in CO_2 dominated atmospheres, to compensate for the scarcity of the information currently available.[a,b,c,d,e,f] High resolution Fourier transform spectra of methane diluted in carbon dioxide at total pressures up to 800 hPa have been recorded at room temperature in the pentad region around 3.3 μm. Their analysis is being carried out using multi-spectrum fitting techniques[g] and a quadratic speed-dependent Rautian line shape model with line mixing. Results will be presented and discussed.

Acknowledgements: *T. Bertin thanks the FRIA (Belgium) for a PhD fellowship. This work is financially supported by the "Fonds de la Recherche Scientifique"–FNRS (Belgium).*

[a]M. Gharavi, S.G. Buckley, J. Mol. Spectrosc. 229 (2005) 78–88.
[b]L. Fissiaux *et al.*, J. Mol. Spectrosc. 297 (2014) 35–40.
[c]O.M. Lyulin *et al.*, J. Quant. Spectrosc. Radiat. Transf. 147 (2014) 164–170.
[d]E. Es-Sebbar, A. Farooq, J. Quant. Spectrosc. Radiat. Transf. 149 (2014) 241–252.
[e]J. Manne *et al.*, J. Quant. Spectrosc. Radiat. Transf. 191 (2017) 59–66.
[f]B. Vispoel *et al.*, J. Quant. Spectrosc. Radiat. Transf. 360 (2019) 1–6.
[g]D.C. Benner *et al.*, J. Quant. Spectrosc. Radiat. Transf. 53 (1995) 705–721.

TM11 **10:40 – 10:41**

COMB-ANCHORED, CAVITY RING-DOWN SPECTROSCOPY OF THE 1.27 μm BAND OF O_2

HELENE FLEURBAEY, ZACHARY REED, ERIN M. ADKINS, DAVID A. LONG, JOSEPH T. HODGES, *Material Measurement Laboratory, National Institute of Standards and Technology, Gaithersburg, MD, USA.*

New measurements of the $a^1\Delta_g \leftarrow X^3\Sigma_g^-$ band of oxygen ($^{16}O_2$) at 1.27 μm will be presented, improving on a previous study [Mendonca et al., Atmos. Meas. Tech. 12, 35-50 (2019)].

Spectra were acquired by frequency-stabilized cavity ring-down spectroscopy over a 160 cm^{-1} wave number range (7792 cm^{-1} to 7952 cm^{-1}). The frequency axis was anchored to a Cs-clock-referenced optical frequency comb through a heterodyne beat note between the comb and the probe laser at about 20 points across the wave number range. The probe laser was phase locked to the frequency comb prior to measuring the beat note frequency in order to improve the accuracy, yielding a 10-Hz uncertainty in the ring-down cavity free spectral range and a 50-kHz absolute frequency uncertainty for all mode orders. Six air-broadened spectra were recorded, at pressures ranging from 3.3 kPa to 100 kPa. They were analyzed with custom multi-spectrum fitting software based on the HAPI python library, using the speed-dependent Nelkin-Ghatak profile.

The resulting line shape parameters reveal important discrepancies with the HITRAN2016 values. These results will also be compared to those reported in recent studies by the Grenoble group [Konefał et al., JQSRT 241, 106653 (2020) and Tran et al., JQSRT 240, 106673 (2020)].

TM12 **10:44 – 10:45**

AB INITIO CALCULATIONS OF QUANTUM SCATTERING AND LINE-SHAPE PARAMETERS IN O_2 PERTURBED BY N_2

MACIEJ GRZEGORZ GANCEWSKI, HUBERT JÓŹWIAK, *Institute of Physics, Faculty of Physics, Astronomy and Informatics, Nicolaus Copernicus University, Torun, Poland*; FRANCK THIBAULT, *Institute of Physics of Rennes, Univ. Rennes, CNRS, Rennes, France*; ERNESTO QUINTAS SÁNCHEZ, RICHARD DAWES, *Department of Chemistry, Missouri University of Science and Technology, Rolla, MO, USA*; PIOTR WCISLO, *Institute of Physics, Faculty of Physics, Astronomy and Informatics, Nicolaus Copernicus University, Torun, Poland.*

The study and modelling of the N_2-perturbed lines in O_2 is of great importance for Earth's atmosphere studies. However, collisional systems with the ground-state molecular oxygen, O_2 $(X^3\Sigma_g^-)$, either as perturbing or active molecule, are difficult to handle because of its non-zero spin that needs to be taken into account in the description of quantum scattering. Here, we present the methodology as well as the results of our quantum scattering calculations and the line-shape parameters for the O_2 immersed in molecular nitrogen bath. It is the first theoretical *ab initio* investigation of this collisional system in the context of the shapes of molecular lines. The PES for this study was constructed automatically using the AUTOSURF code [a]. The data provided through this investigation is important for the terrestrial atmospheric measurements and can be used for populating the spectroscopic databases such as HITRAN or GEISA.

[a]Quintas-Sánchez, Ernesto, and Richard Dawes. "AUTOSURF: A freely available program to construct potential energy surfaces." Journal of chemical information and modeling 59, no. 1 (2018): 262-271

TM13 **10:48 – 10:49**

SUBPERCENT AGREEMENT BETWEEN AB INITIO AND EXPERIMENTAL COLLISION-INDUCED LINE SHAPES OF CARBON MONOXIDE PERTURBED BY ARGON

GRZEGORZ KOWZAN[a], *Institute of Physics, Faculty of Physics, Astronomy and Informatics, Nicolaus Copernicus University, Torun, Poland*; HUBERT CYBULSKI, *Institute of Physics, Kazimierz Wielki University, Bydgoszcz, Poland*; PIOTR WCISLO, MICHAŁ SŁOWIŃSKI, PIOTR MASLOWSKI, *Institute of Physics, Faculty of Physics, Astronomy and Informatics, Nicolaus Copernicus University, Torun, Poland*; ALEXANDRA VIEL, FRANCK THIBAULT, *Institute of Physics of Rennes, Univ. Rennes, CNRS, Rennes, France.*

We present fully ab initio calculations of second-overtone rovibrational line shapes of carbon monoxide perturbed by argon[b]. The quantum mechanical scattering problem between the CO molecule and the Ar atom is solved numerically for an ab initio interaction potential. We use the generalized Hess method[c] to determine the spectroscopic cross sections which describe the effect of collisions on spectral lines. These cross section are then used to determine line-shape parameters of the Hartmann-Tran profile, its β-corrected[d] version and the speed-dependent billiard ball profile (SDBBP). We compare the generated line shapes with high-quality experimental line profiles[e] obtained at five pressures between 0.01 and 1 atm and obtain subpercent agreement in the whole pressure range. We show that the remaining discrepancies are mostly due to residual errors of ab initio pressure broadening and shift. We use the P(9) line data to compare two potential energy surfaces. We explain the differences in obtained pressure broadening and shift coefficients based on the properties of the surfaces.

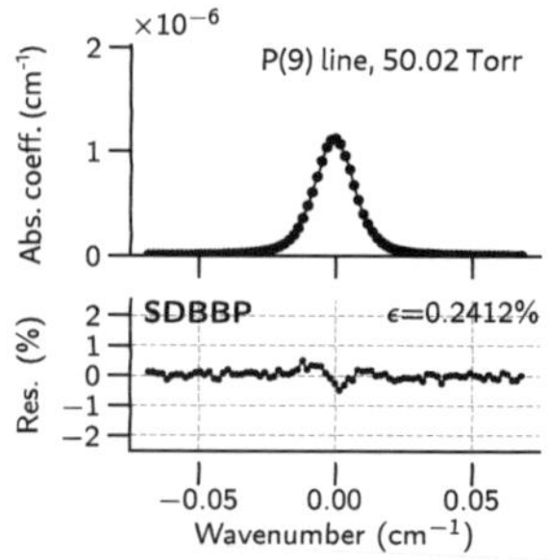

[a]Present address: Department of Chemistry, Stony Brook University, Stony Brook, NY, USA

[b]G. Kowzan, H. Cybulski, P. Wcisło, M. Słowiński, A. Viel, P. Masłowski, F. Thibault, PRA 102, 012821 (2020).

[c]L. Monchick and L. W. Hunter, JCP 85, 713 (1986).

[d]M. Konefał, M. Słowiński, M. Zaborowski, R. Ciuryło, D. Lisak, P. Wcisło, JQSRT 242, 106784 (2020).

[e]G. Kowzan, K. Stec, M. Zaborowski, S. Wójtewicz, A. Cygan, D. Lisak, P. Masłowski, R. S. Trawiński, JQSRT 191, 46 (2017).

TM14 *Post-Deadline Abstract* **10:52 – 10:53**

PREDICTION OF LINE-SHAPE PARAMETERS AND THEIR TEMPERATURE DEPENDENCES BY REQUANTIZED CLASSICAL MOLECULAR DYNAMICS SIMULATIONS

HA TRAN, *Laboratoire de Meteorologie Dynamique, Ecole Polytechnique, University Paris Saclay and CNRS, Paris, France*; NGOC HOA NGO, HUYEN TRANG NGUYEN, *Physics Department, Hanoi National University of Education, Hanoi, Vietnam.*

We show in this talk that requantized classical molecular dynamics simulations (rCMDSs) are capable of predicting various refined spectral-shape parameters of absorption lines of linear molecules such as CO2, N2O and O2 with high precision. Combining CMDSs and a requantization procedure, we computed the auto-correlation function of the dipole moment responsible for the absorption transition. Its Fourier-Laplace transform directly yields the spectrum. Calculations were made for various temperature conditions, at 1 atm and for a large range of Doppler widths, from the near-Doppler to the collision-dominant regimes. For each temperature and each line, the spectra calculated for various Doppler widths were simultaneously fit with a refined line-shape model. The latter takes into account the effects of the speed dependent collisional line broadening, the Dicke narrowing, and the collisional line mixing. The obtained parameters were then directly compared with those deduced from high-precision measurements. The results show very good agreements, even for those parameters whose influence on the spectra is very small. Good agreement is also obtained between measured and predicted temperature dependences of these parameters. This demonstrates that rCMDS is an excellent tool, highly competitive with respect to high quality measurements for precise line-shape studies.

WA. Mini-symposium: Large Amplitude Motions

Wednesday, June 23, 2021 – 8:0 AM

Room: 2021 Online Everywhere

Chair: R. A. Motiyenko, Université de Lille, Villeneuve d'Ascq, France

WA01 *INVITED TALK* **8:00 – 8:02**

AB INITIO CALCULATION APPLIED TO THE STUDY OF ORGANIC NON-RIGID MOLECULES WITH (AT LEAST) THREE TORSIONAL MODES

MARIA LUISA S SENENT, *Inst. Estructura de la Materia, IEM-CSIC, Madrid, Spain.*

Methods applicable to the spectroscopic study of non-rigid organic molecular species with various large amplitude motions (torsions and inversions), are shown. Recent studies of ethylene glycol, $C_3O_6H_6$ isomers, and other species containing C, H, O, and N are employed as examples.

Many organic molecules display non-rigidity. Vibrational modes (inversions and torsions) interconvert different conformers separated by relatively low barriers. Some conformers can be stabilized by the presence of hydrogen intermolecular bonds that can determine their geometry, symmetry, the shape of the potential energy surface and the internal dynamics. When a species displays three or more large amplitude motions, which cannot be separated because they interact strongly, the variational calculation of vibrational levels is complex and requires to search for ways reducing computational efforts. Especially tricky is the classification of the vibrational levels and their splittings.

WA02 **8:08 – 8:09**

CHALLENGES IN CONFORMATIONAL ANALYSIS OF FLEXIBLE MOLECULES

MALGORZATA BICZYSKO, *International Centre for Quantum and Molecular Structures, Shanghai University, Shanghai, China.*

The conformational analysis represents the first step toward a detailed characterization and understanding of the structure-function relationships of molecular systems. In this respect spectroscopic experiments on isolated bio- and organic-molecules allow detection of different binding schemes and three-dimensional (3D) conformations without perturbing effects of the environment. Detection of multiple 3D-geometries concomitantly present in an experimental mixture can be facilitated by "in situ" structural changes induced either by thermal variations, or the interaction with near-IR (NIR) to ultraviolet (UV) light.

These sophisticated experiments need to be supported by accurate and reliable computational studies allowing to link the rich experimental data to the desired information on the structure and properties of complex molecular systems. Therefore a reliable computational approach should be able to provide a balanced description of all interactions allowing for extended mapping of the whole conformational space, including the accurate prediction of equilibrium structures, their relative positions on the potential energy surface (PES), free energies corresponding to the specific experimental conditions and the spectroscopic properties.

Computations based on the second-order perturbation theory (VPT2) allow accounting for the anharmonicity of both wave function and properties. This results in a correct description of the intensity of non-fundamental transitions and more accurate band-shapes. Moreover, the same anharmonic force fields as employed in the determination of vibrational spectra allow considering vibrational corrections to molecular properties or thermodynamic functions. For flexible molecules, the large amplitude-motion (LAM) free approach, where all LAMs anharmonic constants are excluded, allows overcoming problems due to contaminating the overall VPT2 treatment and higher frequency vibrations.

The most reliable structural, spectroscopic and energetic results can be obtained combining various computational methods ranging from density functional theory (DFT) to coupled-cluster (CC), with the latter representing also references for the benchmarking of different DFT methodologies.

WA03 **8:12 – 8:13**

INTERNAL ROTATION AND CHLORINE NUCLEAR QUADRUPOLE COUPLING IN 2-CHLORO-4-FLUOROTOLUENE EXPLORED BY MICROWAVE SPECTROSCOPY AND QUANTUM CHEMISTRY

K.P. RAJAPPAN NAIR, SVEN HERBERS, DANIEL A. OBENCHAIN, JENS-UWE GRABOW, *Institut für Physikalische Chemie und Elektrochemie, Gottfried-Wilhelm-Leibniz-Universität, Hannover, Germany*; WILLIAM C. BAILEY, *Department of Chemistry-Physics, Kean University (Retired), Union, NJ, USA*; ALBERTO LESARRI, *Departamento de Química Física y Química Inorgánica, Universidad de Valladolid, Valladolid, Spain*; HA VINH LAM NGUYEN, *CNRS UMR 7583, Université Paris-Est Créteil, Université de Paris, Laboratoire Interuniversitaire des Systèmes Atmosphériques (LISA), Créteil, France.*

2-Chloro-4-fluorotoluene was investigated using a combination of molecular jet Fourier transform microwave spectroscopy in the frequency range from 5 to 21 GHz and quantum chemistry. The molecule experiences an internal rotation of the methyl group, which causes a fine splitting of all rotational transitions into doublets with separation on the order of a few tens of kHz. In addition, hyperfine effects originating from the chlorine nuclear quadrupole moment coupling its spin to the end-over-end rotation of the molecule are observed. The torsional barrier was derived using both the rho[a] and the combined-axis-method,[b] giving a value of 462.5(41) cm^{-1}. Accurate rotational constants and quadrupole coupling constants were determined for two ^{35}Cl and ^{37}Cl isotopologues and compared with Bailey's semi-experimental quantum chemical predictions.[c] The gas phase molecular structure was deduced from the experimental rotational constants supplemented with those calculated by quantum chemistry at various levels of theory. The values of the methyl torsional barrier and chlorine nuclear quadrupole coupling constants were compared with the theoretical predictions and with those of other chlorotoluene derivatives.

[a]A. Belloche, A.A. Mescheheryakov, R.T. Garrod, V.V. Ilyushin, E.A. Alekseev, R.A. Motiyenko, I. Margules, H.S.P. Müller, K.M. Menten, *Astron. Astrophys.* **601**, A49 (2017).
[b]H. Hartwig, H. Dreizler, *Z. Naturforsch.* **51a** 923 (1996).
[c]W.C. Bailey, *J. Mol. Spectrosc.* **209** 57 (2001).

WA04 **8:16 – 8:17**

GUIDED DIFFUSION MONTE CARLO APPROACHES FOR STUDIES OF WATER CLUSTERS: APPLICATIONS TO WATER HEXAMER

VICTOR G M LEE, MARK A. BOYER, ANNE B McCOY, *Department of Chemistry, University of Washington, Seattle, WA, USA.*

Water clusters provide an opportunity to explore the effects of nuclear quantum effects on the stability of hydrogen-bonded networks. Because of their well-defined size, such studies provide an opportunity to make detailed comparisons between experiment and calculation and explore experimental measurable consequences of nuclear quantum effects through explorations of changes in zero-point structures upon partial or full deuteration. Such studies are challenging due to the large number of relevant degrees of freedom, as the changes in the anharmonic frequencies of OH stretching vibrations upon hydrogen bond formation are comparable to the zero-point energy in the low-frequency intermolecular vibrations. This also makes these systems challenging for calculations by Diffusion Monte Carlo (DMC). Earlier studies indicated that ensemble sizes of upwards of 10^6 *walkers* are needed to obtain reliable energies.[a]

In this presentation, we will describe recent work in our group in developing a modified DMC approach in which guiding functions are used to improve the sampling of the high-frequency intramolecular vibrations (OH stretches and HOH bends). With this modification, the energies and wave functions can be obtained using ensembles that are more than an order of magnitude smaller compared to those used in earlier studies.[b] With this more efficient algorithm, we explore the effects of nuclear quantum effects on the relative energies of the low-energy prism and cage structures, as well as the relative energies of the partially deuterated $(H_2O)_5(D_2O)$ and $(H_2O)(D_2O)_5$ clusters.

[a]Mallory, J. D. and Mandelshtam, V. A., *J. Phys. Chem. A* (2015), **119**, 6504-6515.
[b]Lee, V. G. M.; Vetterli, N. J.; Boyer, M. A. and McCoy, A. B., *J. Phys. Chem. A* (2020), **124**, 6903-6912.

WA05 **8:20 – 8:21**

GUIDED DIFFUSION MONTE CARLO BASED ON BONDING ENVIRONMENT: AN EFFICIENT APPROACH FOR STUDYING MOLECULAR VIBRATIONS IN PATHOLOGICAL SYSTEMS

JACOB M FINNEY, ANNE B McCOY, *Department of Chemistry, University of Washington, Seattle, WA, USA.*

Diffusion Monte Carlo (DMC) is a technique that can be used to obtain the ground state energy and ground state wave function given a potential energy surface (PES) that fully describes the system of interest. However, one complication with this technique is that in order to obtain accurate results for molecular systems that have couplings between the high and low frequency vibrations, large ensemble sizes are needed. [a] One approach to combat these large ensemble sizes is to use a guiding function to describe the high-frequency vibrations. This approach has been applied to studies of neutral water clusters, protonated water clusters, and CH_5^+, where a significant reduction in the ensemble sizes that were needed in the simulations was achieved. [b] [c] An extension of this idea has been used to obtain excited state information in the coordinates described by the guiding functions.

In this work, I will describe the applications of this approach to systems with large coupling among the vibrational degrees of freedom. The use of a guiding function that describes the ground state wave function of the high-frequency vibrations allow us to use smaller ensemble sizes, while producing ground state energies and wave functions that are as accurate or more accurate than those obtained using traditional DMC approaches. By using an excited state guiding function in the degrees of freedom that are being excited, we can obtain the excited state energy and wave functions through fixed-node DMC. With these wave functions in hand, we can also obtain overlaps between the ground state and first excited state, allowing us to evaluate intensities. This approach provides accurate representations of the excited state energy and the intensity of the transition from the ground state as long as the guiding functions for the ground and excited states provide fairly accurate representations of the wave functions along the excited degree of freedom.

[a] Mallory, J. D. and Mandelshtam, V. A., *J. Phys. Chem. A* (2015), **119**, 6504-6515.
[b] Lee, V. G. M. and McCoy, A.B., *J. Phys. Chem. A* (2019), **123**, 37, 8063-8070.
[c] Finney, J. M., DiRisio, R. J., McCoy, A.B., *J. Phys. Chem. A* (2020), **124**, 45, 9567-9577.

WA06 **8:24 – 8:25**

LARGE AMPLITUDE MOTIONS AND π-HYDROGEN BONDING IN THE THIOPHENE–WATER COMPLEX CHARACTERIZED BY ROTATIONAL SPECTROSCOPY AND QUANTUM CHEMICAL CALCULATIONS

WESLLEY G. D. P. SILVA, JENNIFER VAN WIJNGAARDEN, *Department of Chemistry, University of Manitoba, Winnipeg, MB, Canada.*

The rotational spectrum of the thiophene–water (thiophene–w) complex was studied for the first-time using Fourier transform microwave (FTMW) spectroscopy from 7 to 20 GHz. Supported by density functional theory (DFT) calculations, transitions belonging to a single dominant conformer were observed in the spectrum. By comparing the experimentally derived spectroscopic parameters, which includes data for the singly substituted ^{18}O isotopic species, with the results from quantum chemical calculations at the B2PLYP-D3(BJ)/def2-TZVP level of theory, we show that the observed pattern of transitions is consistent with a structure that is highly averaged over a large amplitude rocking motion of the water. This effective geometry, stabilized via a primary O–H...π hydrogen bond, has the oxygen atom of water sitting above the plane of the thiophene molecule centered on the ring's σ_v plane of symmetry. The spectrum also reveals a tunneling splitting with a characteristic 3:1 intensity ratio that arises from a water-centered internal rotation about its C_2 axis which exchanges its hydrogen atoms with an estimated barrier of approximately 2.7 kJ/mol (B2PLYP-D3(BJ)/def2-TZVP). Based on symmetry-adapted perturbation theory (SAPT) calculations, electrostatic and dispersive interactions are shown to be the most stabilizing contributors behind the formation of thiophene–w.

WA07 **8:28 – 8:29**

VIBRATIONALLY AVERAGED STRUCTURE AND FREQUENCIES OF $(XeHXe)^+$: COMPUTATIONAL MOLECULAR SPECTROSCOPY STUDY

TSUNEO HIRANO, *Department of Chemistry, Ochanomizu University, Tokyo, Japan*; UMPEI NAGASHIMA, *Graduate school of Nanobioscience, Yokohama City University, Yokohama, Japan*; MASAAKI BABA, *Division of Chemistry, Graduate School of Science, Kyoto University, Kyoto, Japan.*

We have proposed that the ro-vibrationally averaged structure of a linear molecule is observed as being "bent."[a] To provide more evidence for this assertion, we here chose a linear molecule $(XeHXe)^+$. We expected: The Xe atoms at both ends are so heavy that they stand still during vibration, so that in the bending mode, the central H^+ atom inevitably moves perpendicularly against the a principal axis to give a "bent" ro-vibrationally averaged structure. The potential energy surface was calculated at the valence-CCSD(T)_DK3/[ANO-R3(Xe),cc-pV5Z-DK(H)] level, and ro-vibrational properties were calculated from the DVR3D wavefunctions in Discrete Variable Representation. The central H^+, which has +0.6 e charge, polarizes the Xe atoms by its reaction field, giving 136 kcal/mol of the heat of formation: $(XeHXe)^+$ is a stable cation. The equilibrium structure for Xe1–H–Xe2 has r_e(Xe1-H) = r_e(H–Xe2) = 1.8694 Å and ∠(Xe1–H–Xe2) = 180°, so that $(XeHXe)^+$ is a linear molecule. The ro-vibrationally averaged structure has $\langle r(\text{Xe1–H})\rangle_0 = 1.8913$ Å, $\langle r(\text{H–Xe2})\rangle_0 = 1.9017$ Å, and $\langle \angle(\text{Xe1–H–Xe2})\rangle_0 = 166.6°$, indicating a large amplitude bending motion.

The harmonic vibrational frequencies ω_1 (antisymmetric stretch), ω_2 (bending), and ω_3 (symmetric stretch) are 824, 562, and 149 cm^{-1}, respectively. The corresponding term values ν_1, ν_2, and ν_3 are 847, 545, and 143 cm^{-1}, respectively, to be compared with the values in *para*-H_2 matrix[b] $\nu_1 = 847.0$ cm^{-1} and $\nu_3 = 125.1$ cm^{-1}. The relation $\nu_1 > \omega_1$ is a typical feature for [(ultra)heavy–light–(ultra)heavy] system. In the antisymmetric stretch mode, the central H^+ moves back and forth between almost stand-still two Xe atoms just like a ball in catch-ball play, and hence the ν_1 value is not affected by matrix medium. On the other hand, the symmetric stretching mode should severely be affected by the mass of the matrix medium, as is reported,[b] since Xe atoms in this mode have to push out the cavity wall of the matrix.

[a]T. Hirano, U. Nagashima, P. Jensen, J. Mol. Spectrosc. **343**, 54 (2018); T. Hirano, U. Nagashima, M. Baba, J. Mol. Spectrosc. **369**, 111252 (2020); and references therein.
[b]M. Tsuge, J. Kalinowski, R.B. Gerber, Y-P. Lee, J. Phys. Chem. A **119**, 2651 (2015)

WA08 **8:32 – 8:33**

LARGE AMPLITUDE MOTIONS IN THE 1,1,1,3,3,3-HEXAFLUORO-2-PROPANOL BINARY WATER COMPLEX

BOWEI WU, *Department of Chemistry, University of Alberta, Edmonton, AB, Canada*; NATHAN A. SEIFERT, *Chemical Sciences and Engineering Division, Argonne National Laboratory, Lemont, IL, USA*; SOENKE OSWALD, *Institute of Physical Chemistry, Georg-August-Universität Göttingen, Göttingen, Germany*; YUNJIE XU, *Department of Chemistry, University of Alberta, Edmonton, AB, Canada.*

1,1,1,3,3,3-hexafluoro-2-propanol (hexafluoroisopropanol, HFIP) is an important solvent widely used in organic syntheses and biomatter treatments and is also considered as a greenhouse gas pollutant. The rotational spectrum of the most stable conformer of the HFIP—water complex, i.e. trans-HFIP—water, was reported before.[1]

In the current study, rotational spectra of HIFP with water were recorded using a broadband, chirped pulse Fourier transform microwave spectrometer. A less stable gauche-FIP–water complex was identified and its rotational spectrum assigned for the first time. Ab initio calculations including some multidimensional rigid potential energy surface (PES) scans of possible water rotational/wagging motions were carried out and were employed to characterize the large amplitude motions (LAM)s in the both HFIP–water conformers. Several deuterium Isotopic species were also studied to aid the analysis of the large amplitude motions. Furthermore, non-covalent interaction (NCI) analyses were carried out to characterized the hydrogen bonding interactions in HFIP—water.

[1] Shahi, A.; Arunan, E., Microwave spectroscopic and theoretical investigations of the strongly hydrogen bonded hexafluoroisopropanol-water complex. Physical Chemistry Chemical Physics 2015, 17 (38), 24774-24782.

WA09 **8:36 – 8:37**

LARGE AMPLITUDE MOTIONS IN 2,2,3,3,3-PENTAFLUOROPROPANOL AND ITS BINARY WATER COMPLEX

BOWEI WU, *Department of Chemistry, University of Alberta, Edmonton, AB, Canada*; NATHAN A. SEIFERT, *Chemical Sciences and Engineering Division, Argonne National Laboratory, Lemont, IL, USA*; SOENKE OSWALD, *Institute of Physical Chemistry, Georg-August-Universität Göttingen, Göttingen, Germany*; WOLFGANG JÄGER, YUNJIE XU, *Department of Chemistry, University of Alberta, Edmonton, AB, Canada.*

2,2,3,3,3-pentafluoropropanol (PFP) is an important solvent for organic syntheses. It is also considered to be a greenhouse gas pollutant because it is radiatively active in the mid-infrared region. Understanding properties of PFP and its hydrogen bonding interactions with water in the gas phase may help to develop more realistic estimate of its effects because of the abundance of water in the atmosphere. In the current study, we apply both rotational spectroscopy and ab initio calculations to characterize large amplitude motions in PFP and its water complex and also hydrogen bonding interactions between PFP with water. Their rotational spectra were recorded using a cavity-based and a chirped pulse Fourier transform microwave spectrometers. Two most stable PFP conformers, Pg+g+ and Ptg+ were identified. The rotational transitions of the latter exhibit tunneling splittings. Two PFP-H2O conformers were identified and both of them show tunneling splittings. Deuterated species of the water complex were also investigated to assist the identification of the tunneling paths, in addition to the theoretical calculations. The large amplitude motions responsible for these splittings will be discussed.

WA10 **8:40 – 8:41**

COUPLING OF TORSION AND OH-STRETCHING IN *TERT*-BUTYL HYDROPEROXIDE AND ITS RADICAL ANALOG, QOOH

RACHEL M. HUCHMALA, MARK A. BOYER, ANNE B McCOY, *Department of Chemistry, University of Washington, Seattle, WA, USA.*

Organic hydroperoxides and their radical products are important contributors to atmospheric chemistry, especially in atmospheric oxidation processes. Through understanding the vibrational spectroscopy of these compounds, we gain insights into their abundance in the atmosphere. The vibrational spectra of *tert*-butyl Hydrogen Peroxide (TBHP) and its radical product QOOH have been studied both experimentally and theoretically.[1] Due to their floppy nature and many low frequency degrees of freedom, standard methods such as harmonic treatments and second order vibrational perturbation theory are insufficient to fully characterize vibrational spectra of these molecules.

In this work, we introduce a reaction path model that is sufficient to explain the OH-stretching region of QOOH. Within this model, we perform an adiabatic separation of the OH-stretching and COOH-torsion modes and add a harmonic zero-point energy correction to account for the other vibrational degrees of freedom. In the process of developing this model, we first investigated the OH-stretching region of THBP.[2–3] Through this study, we discovered a strong contribution to the overall intensity in the v_{OH} + n_{tor} combination feature coming from the torsional dependence of the transition dipole moment. At low levels of vibrational excitation, the intensity of this feature reflects the torsion-dependence of the dipole function, while at higher levels of OH excitation (v_{OH} = 4 or 5) the intensity in this combination feature can be captured through a Franck-Condon treatment of the intensity. The transition from a mechanical to electrical origin to the intensity in this feature is discussed. Extension to QOOH will also be discussed.

[1] M. D. Likar, J. E. Baggott, and F. F. Crim, *J. Chem. Phys.* 90, 6266–6274 (1989).
[2] A. S. Hansen, R. M. Huchmala, E. Vogt, M. Boyer, T. Bhagde, M. F. Vansco, C. V. Jensen, A. Kjaersgaard, H. G. Kjaergaard, A. B. McCoy, and M. I. Lester, *J. Chem. Phys.* Submitted. 2021
[3] E. Vogt, R. M. Huchmala, C. V. Jensen, M. Boyer, Jens Wallberg, A. S. Hansen, A. Kjaersgaard, H. G. Kjaergaard, M. I. Lester, and A. B. McCoy, *J. Chem. Phys.* Submitted. 2021

WB. Instrument/Technique Demonstration

Wednesday, June 23, 2021 – 8:0 AM

Room: 2021 Online Everywhere

Chair: Marie-Aline Martin-Drumel, Université Paris Saclay, CNRS , Orsay Cedex, France

WB01 **8:00 – 8:01**

ENTANGLED PHOTON SPECTROSCOPY OF MOLECULES

SCOTT KEVIN CUSHING, *Chemistry and Chemical Engineering, California Institute of Technology, Pasadena, CA, USA.*

In this talk, I will discuss the growing field of entangled-photon spectroscopy as related to molecular systems. An entangled state is represented by a wavefunction, describing a group of particles, which cannot be factored into separate states of individual particles. For photons, these correlations lead to non-classical light-matter interactions, creating new opportunities for spectroscopic techniques. For example, second-order processes with two entangled photons, such as two-photon absorption or sum frequency generation, occur at a linear rate with a cross section that should be close to that of one-photon classical processes. However, early results in the field have produced conflicting measurements as to its magnitude. I will discuss the role of excited state dephasing and time-ordering for entangled photon interactions and their role in producing conflicting interaction cross sections for the same molecule on different experimental setups. I will also briefly remark on other interesting prospects of entangled photons, such as their ability to break the temporal-spectral Fourier transform limit. For instance, few-femtosecond spectroscopy is predicted to be possible with entangled light sources of MHz linewidths.

WB02 **8:04 – 8:05**

A NANOSECOND-RESOLVED ULTRAHIGH-DENSITY SPIN-POLARIZED HYDROGEN MAGNETOMETER

ALEXANDROS SPILIOTIS, MICHALIS XYGKIS, KONSTANTINOS TAZES, *Department of Physics, University of Crete, Heraklion, Greece*; GEORGE E. KATSOPRINAKIS, GIORGOS VASILAKIS, *IESL (Institute of Electronic Structure and Laser), FORTH (Foundation for Research and Technology Hellas), Heraklion, —, Greece*; T. PETER RAKITZIS, *Department of Physics, University of Crete, Heraklion, Greece.*

We introduce a novel and sensitive ns-resolved atomic magnetometer, which is at least three orders of magnitude faster than conventional magnetometers. The magnetic field dependence of hyperfine beating of high-density spin-polarized H atoms, produced from the rapid photodissociation of HCl gas with sub-ns laser pulses, results in a few nT sensitivity for a spin-projection limited sensor with 10 nl measurement volume after 1 ns measurement time. The magnetometer will allow ultrafast continuous B-field measurements in many fields, including spin chemistry, spin physics, and plasma physics.

WB03 8:08 – 8:09

POLARIZATION CONTROL OF ROTATIONALLY RESOLVED 2DIR SPECTROSCOPY

GRZEGORZ KOWZAN[a], MYLES C SILFIES, NEOMI LEWIS, THOMAS K ALLISON, *Departments of Physics and Chemistry, Stony Brook University, Stony Brook, NY, USA.*

Detection of trace amounts of molecules in multi-species mixtures is important for many purposes, ranging from chemical dynamics in complex environments to breath analysis. 2DIR spectroscopy is a powerful tool for studying both molecular structure and dynamics. It can provide better selectivity than linear spectroscopy due to the extra degrees of freedom for distinguishing the components of a complex mixture, but its application to trace-gas detection has been hindered by insufficient sensitivity and resolution of the technique. Cavity-enhancement methods for ultrafast nonlinear spectroscopy using frequency combs have the potential to overcome this problem[b].

In 2DIR spectroscopy of coupled vibrational modes, it is common to use specific beam polarization angles to suppress parts of the molecular response and simplify structure determination[c]. Here we show how to suppress parts of the rotational response of a single vibrational mode. We provide specific polarization angles that suppress diagonal or antidiagonal peaks, or the pathways with interstate coherences after the second excitation. We present simulations for carbon monoxide that demonstrate the effect of eliminating specific pathways on 2DIR rotationally-resolved spectra.

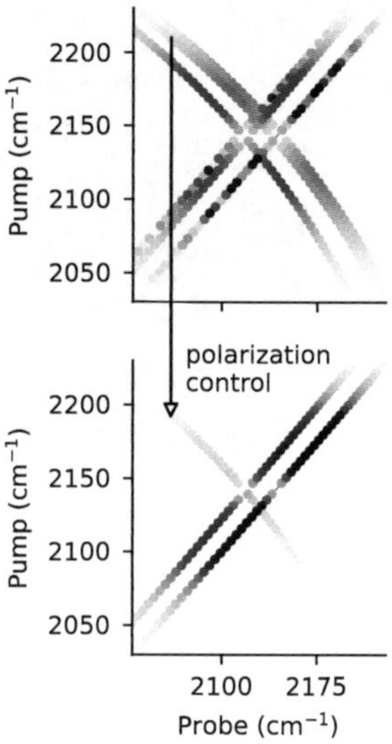

---

[a]Second affiliation: Institute of Physics, Faculty of Physics, Astronomy and Informatics, Nicolaus Copernicus University, Torun, Poland.

[b]T. K. Allison. J. Phys. B 50, 044004 (2017).

[c]M. T. Zanni, N. Ge, Y. S. Kim, R. M. Hochstrasser. Proc. Nat. Acad. Sci. 98, 11265 (2001).

[d]Supported by U.S. National Science Foundation award 1708743, U.S. Air Force Office of Scientific Research grant FA9550-20-1-0259. M. C. Silfies supported by the GAANN program of U.S. Dept. of Education. G. Kowzan supported by National Science Center, Poland scholarship 2017/24/T/ST2/00242.

WB04 8:12 – 8:13

HIGH RESOLUTION COHERENT MULTIDIMENSIONAL SPECTROSCOPY FOR OVERCOMING SEVERE SPECTRAL CONGESTION

PETER CHEN, *Department of Chemistry, Spelman College, Atlanta, GA, USA.*

High resolution coherent 2D and 3D spectroscopies are unusually powerful tools for overcoming problems of spectral congestion because they can 1) automatically sort peaks by rotational and vibrational quantum number, 2) spread out peaks into higher dimensions in order to improve resolution, and 3) limit the number of possible peaks that are produced at higher dimensions through the use of parametric and nonparametric four wave mixing processes. This talk will describe new multidimensional pattern recognition techniques that can be used with high resolution coherent multidimensional spectroscopy.

WB05 **8:16 – 8:17**

NOISE IMMUNE CAVITY ENHANCED OPTICAL HETERODYNE ZEEMAN MODULATION SPECTROSCOPY

ANNA C. WANNENMACHER, *Department of Chemistry, The University of California, Davis, CA, USA*; CHARLES R. MARKUS, *Division of Chemistry and Chemical Engineering, California Institute of Technology, Pasadena, CA, USA*; KYLE N. CRABTREE, *Department of Chemistry, The University of California, Davis, CA, USA*.

Of the roughly 210 species detected outside our Solar System, about a quarter of them are radicals. Radicals are sensitive probes of their chemical and physical environments and have been implicated in the formation of complex organic molecules (COMs). Astronomical observations of these species with mm-wave telescopes such as the Atacama Large Millimeter Array depend upon accurate rest frequencies of rotational transitions derived from laboratory spectroscopic measurements. Owing to uncertainties in theoretical rotational constants, centrifugal distortion, and angular momentum coupling, identification of a new radical from direct mm-wave spectroscopy is challenging in the absence of cm-band measurements at low J, requiring extensive frequency searches. We aim to determine mm-wave transition frequencies indirectly through rovibrational spectroscopy, which substantially alleviates the frequency search challenges of pure rotational spectroscopy in the mm-wave region. However, the much greater Doppler broadening at higher optical frequencies has traditionally prevented rovibrational spectroscopy from achieving the 1 MHz accuracy required for astronomical applications. To overcome this, we are combining cavity enhanced frequency modulation spectroscopy with an AC magnetic field generated by a solenoid to achieve a sensitive, radical-selective, and Doppler-free technique that we call NICE-OHZMS (Noise Immune Cavity Enhanced Optical Heterodyne Zeeman Modulation Spectroscopy). In conjunction with absolute frequency calibration afforded by an optical frequency comb, we expect to measure rovibrational transitions of radicals with an accuracy and precision of better than 1 MHz. Here, the status of the instrument and proof-of-concept measurements of the first overtone band of nitric oxide will be discussed.

WB06 ***Post-Deadline Abstract*** **8:20 – 8:21**

QUANTITY DETERMINTATION AND TRACEABILITY FOR SUPER-RESOLUTION MID-INFRARED LASER ABSORPTION SPECTROSCOPY

ZHENHUI DU, *Department of Precision Instrument , Tianjin University, Tianjin, China*.

Super-resolution spectroscopy is essential for the understanding of molecular fine structures, excited state population, distribution function of given energy states, and remote sensing applications. We addressed several key measures for achieving high performances of sprectral resolution and absorbance precision in a mid-infrared modulated laser spectrometer with a distributed feedback interband cascade laser, including linearization of laser scanning, suppression or deduction of optical fringe interferences, and internal calibration for baseline problems and nonlinear response of the photodiode used in the system. The performances of our modified spectrometer were verified with the spectral resolution in the order of 10^{-6} cm^{-1} ($\tilde{\text{h}}$undreds kHz) and absorbance uncertainty in the order of 10^{-3}. We provided a detailed error analysis with the uncertainty model of GUM, i.e. Guide to the expression of uncertainty in measurement. Further, we ensured the traceability of the spectrometer by linking a practical calibration reference standard. We measured the fundamental absorption of several organic molecules, e.g. dimethyl sulfide $(CH_3)_2S$), methyl mercaptan (CH_3SH) with our modified spectrometer. The recorded spectra were demonstrated to be similar to that in the Pacific Northwest National Laboratory (PNNL) database. These data have been used in our remote sensing applications.

WB07 **8:24 – 8:25**

THE FAR-INFRARED BEAMLINE AT THE CANADIAN LIGHT SOURCE

BRANT E. BILLINGHURST, *EFD, Canadian Light Source Inc., Saskatoon, Saskatchewan, Canada*.

The Far-Infrared beamline at the Canadian Light Source (CLS), provides access to High-Resolution Spectroscopy to researchers across Canada and around the world. The primary, instrument on the beamline is a Bruker IFS125HR Spectrometer capable of better than 0.001 cm^{-1} resolution. By exploiting the high brightness of the synchrotron source the beamline can achieve signal to noise levels up to 8 times better than that achievable using a thermal source. Equipped with a temperature-controlled, 2-meter multi-pass gas cell with a maximum pathlength of 72 meters, a 1.5-meter glow discharge cell, the Far-Infrared facility is well equipped for high-resolution molecular spectroscopy. A horizontal microscope is available for micro-spectroscopy experiments. This talk will provide details on the available equipment, techniques, and the methods of access at the Far-Infrared as well as some examples of recent research projects on the beamline.

WB08 **8:28 – 8:29**

NEAR-FOURIER-TRANSFORM-LIMITED LONG-PULSE YAG-PUMPED DYE LASER SYSTEM

HOLGER HERBURGER, URS HOLLENSTEIN, FRÉDÉRIC MERKT, *Laboratorium für Physikalische Chemie, ETH Zurich, Zurich, Switzerland.*

We demonstrate a laser system providing user-designed laser pulses with durations tunable from 10 ns to 1 μs and pulse energies up to 680 mJ at a repetition rate of 25 Hz and at a wavelength of 1064 nm. This radiation is frequency doubled in an LBO crystal yielding pulses of 532 nm radiation with pulse energies of 90 mJ. The frequency-doubled laser is used as a pump source for a dye amplification line seeded by the output of a commercial continuous-wave ring dye laser. This system enables us to generate 10 ns to 120 ns long pulses with a Gaussian temporal profile in the visible range of the electromagnetic spectrum with output energies of up to 5 mJ per pulse. We also generate long pulses of UV radiation (pulse energies up to 500 μJ, pulse length up to 85 ns) by frequency doubling in a BBO crystal.

The properties of the laser system are illustrated in measurements of the Rydberg spectrum of atomic argon in the $3p^5 4s[3/2]_2$ $^3P_2$ and $3p^5 4s'[1/2]_0$ $^3P_0$ metastable states. Metastable argon is generated in a supersonic beam using a dielectric barrier discharge. We have recorded spectra of Rydberg series of Ar below the $^2P_{3/2}$ and $^2P_{1/2}$ ionization thresholds. We use the long lifetimes of the former series to characterize the bandwith of the laser system and determine the autoionization linewidth and line shapes of the later series for comparison with earlier work.[a]

[a] V. L. Sukhorukov, I. D. Petrov, M. Schäfer, F. Merkt, M.-W. Ruf, and H. Hotop, *J. Phys. B: At. Mol. Opt. Phys.* **45**, 092001 (2012) and references therein.

WB09 **8:32 – 8:33**

DEVELOPING PROBABLISTIC MACHINE LEARNING MODELS FOR ION IMAGING ANALYSIS

G. STEPHEN KOCHERIL, *Department of Chemistry, Brown University, Providence, RI, USA*; KELVIN LEE, *Department of Chemistry, Massachusetts Institute of Technology, Cambridge, MA, USA.*

Since their inception, charged-particle imaging techniques have transformed how chemical reactions and dynamics are studied. Ion imaging is a powerful detection method for many as it allows for higher resolution measurements for photoion and photoelectron spectroscopic experiments and photodissociation dynamics. Although there have been many experimental innovations over the last two decades, major advancements in how we analyze these images are few and far between. A general weakness found in ion imaging experiments is low signal-to-noise ratios, which are intrisic to all single particle detection methods. Motivated by the development of convolutional neural networks (CNN) for general imaging applications, we explored the ability of using CNNs for ion imaging reconstruction with the goal to parametrize a neural network to learn the approximate mapping between the ion image projection and its central distribution. We demonstrate the effectiveness of our model to not only reduce noise in the reconstructed image but also produce sharp images. We also compare with standard image reconstruction methods to quantitatively show the improvements by our method on real spectroscopic images. We have also made the model publicly available on Github.

WB10 **8:36 – 8:37**

SPECTROSCOPICALLY IDENTIFYING FROM GAS-PHASE REACTIONS OF DISTONIC BENZONITRILEH$^+$ RADICAL IONS IN AN ION-TRAP MASS SPECTROMETER

OISIN J. SHIELS, SAMUEL MARLTON, P. D. KELLY, *School of Chemistry, University of Wollongong, Wollongong, New South Wales, Australia*; GABRIEL DA SILVA, *School of Chemistry, University of Melbourne, Melbourne, VIC, Australia*; STEPHEN J. BLANKSBY, *Central Analytical Research Facility, Queensland University of Technology, Brisbane, Queensland, Australia*; ADAM J. TREVITT, *School of Chemistry, University of Wollongong, Wollongong, New South Wales, Australia.*

Benzonitrile was recently detected in the interstellar medium and currently remains the largest aromatic molecule identified. Subsequent reactions with benzonitrile and related cations are good candidates to form polycyclic aromatic molecules (PAHs), potentially contributing to the UIB band. Previous investigations into the reactions of the three distonic radical isomers of the benzonitrile cation with ethylene and acetylene have identified that these reactions are barrierless and should proceed within the ultra-low temperatures of the interstellar medium – but what products do these reactions form?

Expanding on this previous work, the reactions of the 2-dehydrobenzonitrileH$^+$ distonic radical cation + propyne ($CHCCH_3$) were investigated using a combination of computational and experimental techniques. Experimental investigations, performed within the room temperature linear ion-trap reveal that multiple product channels arise, ranging from: C_3H_4 addition $[M + 40]^+$, C_2H_3 loss following C_3H_4 addition $[M + 40 - 27]^+$, double C_3H_4 addition $[M + 40 + 40]^+$, and H-atom loss following secondary C_3H_4 addition $[M + 40 + 40 - 1]^+$. Targeting the double C_3H_4 addition, calculations suggest that two tri-cyclic PAH isomers are energetically favourable products.

To assign these putative tri-cyclic PAHs, photodissociation action spectroscopy experiments were performed to structurally characterise these secondary addition products. Exploiting the ion trap, these reaction products can be selectively isolated, stored and then subjected to tunable laser photons. Photodissociation action spectra are recorded by tracking the yield of photoproduct ions as a function of photon energy. Spectra are compared to Franck-Condon simulations and good matches are found with the two tri-cylcic PAH products. These experiments allow us to definitely assign the reaction products, giving us a new measurement to benchmark calculations against.

WB11 **8:40 – 8:41**

A MODULAR DESIGN FOR REACTION TRAPS IN CRYOGENIC ION TRAP MASS SPECTROMETERS

GINA ROESCH, ETIENNE GARAND, *Department of Chemistry, University of Wisconsin–Madison, Madison, WI, USA.*

Innovations in cryogenic ion traps greatly enhance our ability to control ion-neutral chemistry and spectroscopically probe ionic species in real time. Currently, our lab studies microsolvated species and reaction intermediates using a home-built dual cryogenic ion mass spectrometer. The dual trap design allows for controlled ion manipulation and subsequent tagging in preparation for infrared action spectroscopy. The first trap, a liquid nitrogen cooled octupole "reaction trap", is used for the condensation of solvent molecules to the analyte or to perform temperature-controlled ion-neutral reaction chemistry to access unstable intermediates. The second "tagging" trap is held at 10K to cluster weakly perturbative tags such as D_2, which can serve as messengers for the subsequent action spectroscopy step.

Currently, the "reaction trap" is the sole location for ion manipulation which limits us to one chemical reaction or the addition of a single type of solvent molecules. To overcome these limitations, we have developed a mass selective, multi-reaction trap setup via a modular housing design. The modular design also reduces the cost and increases the adaptability. In addition, the ion traps utilize digital ion technology (DIT) to facilitate mass-selection, improve the signal-to-noise and increase the mass range for the study of larger clusters.

Preliminary results suggest that a prototype of a dual reaction trapping system can form clusters with two different solvents. For example, water clusters were made in the first trap, mass-selected and methanol was added to the cluster in the second trap. Thus, the multi-reaction trap design provides solvent position selectivity which is of great advantage for simulating more complex environments. Future plans for the multi-reaction trap CIVS instrument include characterizing a water network around an ion by inserting a D_2O as a spectroscopic molecular probe.

WB12 **8:44 – 8:45**

SOFTWARE IMPLEMENTATION OF A MULTI-CHANNEL, MULTI-FREQUENCY LOCK-IN AMPLIFIER

AMRUT NADGIR, DANIEL S. SLAUGHTER, RICHARD THURSTON, MATTHEW M BRISTER, *Chemical Science Division, Lawrence Berkeley National Laboratory, Berkeley, CA, USA*; NIRANJAN SHIVARAM, *Department of Physics, Purdue University, West Lafayette, IN, USA.*

Weak emission signals are usually measured and analyzed with one or more sensitive detectors, such as a photomultiplier tube, to obtain sufficient signal from fluorescent samples. Here we demonstrate the measurement of fluorescence from solutions of Rhodamine 6G in ethanol for optical excitation at 532 nm without a photomultiplier, but with a much less sensitive spectrometer (Ocean Optics OCEAN-FX-XR1-ES) and a Software Implementation of a Multi-Channel, Multi-Frequency Lock-in Amplifier (SILIA).

SILIA is a software implementation of a multi-channel, multi-frequency Lock-in Amplifier to extract modulated signals from noisy data with arbitrary dimensionality and number of channels. It emulates the functionality of a multi-channel, multi-frequency lock-in amplifier in a post-processing step following data acquisition. Unlike most traditional lock-in amplifiers, SILIA can work with any number of input channels and is especially useful to analyze data with high dimensionality. Since a photomultipler tube was not used, the observed spectrum contains spectral information from scatter photons of the pulsed 532 nm laser light and fluorescent signal of Rhodamine 6G onto the spectrometer. Without SILIA, this pollution renders the fluorescent signal indistinguishable from the background signal.

Present the methodology behind SILIA and demonstrate its application for extracting weak signals in spectroscopy. We also discuss more general applications and exhibit a method to automatically estimate error from a lock-in result.

WB13 **8:48 – 8:49**

LLWP - A NEW LOOMIS-WOOD SOFTWARE AT THE EXAMPLE OF PROPANONE-$^{13}C_1$

LUIS BONAH, OLIVER ZINGSHEIM, SVEN THORWIRTH, HOLGER S. P. MÜLLER, FRANK LEWEN, *I. Physikalisches Institut, Universität zu Köln, Köln, Germany*; J.-C. GUILLEMIN, *ENSC, Univ. Rennes, Rennes, France*; STEPHAN SCHLEMMER, *I. Physikalisches Institut, Universität zu Köln, Köln, Germany.*

Spectra of complex molecules are dense and complicated, especially if isotopologues, low-lying vibrationally excited states, hyperfine structure or other interactions are present. Analysis of these spectra can be difficult due to line confusion. One approach to accommodate this challenge are Loomis-Wood plots (LWPs), which are a visual aid for displaying series of transitions in a spectrum in order to ease assignments. Programs utilizing LWPs exist already in the literature, e.g. AABS [1], Pgopher [2] and LWW [3]. Here, we present a newly developed software which focuses on being intuitive and user friendly while simultaneously allowing for fast and confident assignments of molecular spectra. The software is called LLWP and is written in Python. The core functionality and selected features are presented on the example of first results of the analysis of isotopically enriched propanone-$^{13}C_1$ ($^{13}CH_3COCH_3$), which was synthesized as its signal at natural abundance only allowed for a very limited analysis [4, 5]. The software and its full documentation are available at ltotheois.github.io/LLWP.

[1] Z. Kisiel et al., J. Mol. Spectrosc. **233** (2005) 231 – 243.
[2] C. M. Western, J. Quant. Spectrosc. Radiat. Transf. **186** (2017) 221 – 242.
[3] W. Lodyga et al., J. Mol. Spectrosc. **243** (2007) 182 – 188.
[4] F. J. Lovas and P. Groner, J. Mol. Spectrosc. **236** (2006) 173.
[5] M. H. Ordu et al., Astron. Astrophys. **629** (2019) A72.

WB14 **8:52 – 8:53**

SPATIALLY ENHANCED ELECTRIC FIELD INDUCED SECOND HARMONIC (SEEFISH) GENERATION FOR MEASUREMENTS OF ELECTRIC FIELD DISTRIBUTIONS IN GASES AND PLASMAS

SAI RASKAR, KEEGAN ORR, IGOR V. ADAMOVICH, *Department of Mechanical and Aerospace Engineering, The Ohio State University, Columbus, OH, USA.*

The spatial resolution of the ps Electric Field Induced Second Harmonic (EFISH) generation has been enhanced by using a non-collinear laser beam phase matching geometry. This approach is similar to the one used in Unstable Resonator – Enhanced Detection Coherent Anti-Stokes Raman Scattering (USED CARS). Briefly, the pump laser beam (1064 nm, pulse duration 150 ps, pulse energy 20-35 mJ) is separated into two coaxial beams before the focusing lens. The two beams, with the combined pulse energy of 10-18 mJ, overlap only near the focal point, generating the Spatially Enhanced EFISH (SEEFISH) signal over a significantly shorter region compared to that in the collinear phase matching. The resulting SEEFISH signal is spatially isolated from the "conventional" EFISH signal and measured by a photomultiplier detector. Blocking of either of the two beams results in a complete suppression of the signal, demonstrating that it is generated by the superposition of the two beams overlapping near the focal point. Measurements of a known Laplacian field generated between two parallel cylinder electrodes in ambient air demonstrated that SEEFISH improves the spatial resolution of the measurements by well over a factor of 2. The spatial resolution is improved further by reducing the focal distance of the lens. As expected, the magnitude of the SEEFISH signal is lower compared to that of the "conventional" EFISH, by a factor of 2-10, depending on the lens focal distance. The estimated spatial resolution of the SEEFISH diagnostic is approximately 1 mm, in the direction of the laser beam. The SEEFISH spatial resolution can be improved further, potentially to $\sim$ 0.1 mm, by using two independently focused, crossed laser beams. However, this would result in a further reduction of the signal, which may necessitate the use of a fs pump laser. SEEFISH measurements of the electric field distribution in an atmospheric pressure argon plasma jet are underway.

WC. Dynamics and kinetics

Wednesday, June 23, 2021 – 8:0 AM

Room: 2021 Online Everywhere

Chair: Scott G Sayres, Arizona State University, Tempe, AZ, USA

WC01 **8:00 – 8:01**

TIME-RESOLVED CAVITY RINGDOWN MEASUREMENTS OF HO_2 RADICAL IN A HEATED PLASMA FLOW REACTOR

ELIJAH R JANS, *Department of Mechanical and Aerospace Engineering, The Ohio State University, Columbus, OH, USA*; IAN JONES, *Department of Chemistry, Ohio State University, Columbus, OH, USA*; XIN YANG, ANAM C. PAUL, *Department of Mechanical and Aerospace Engineering, The Ohio State University, Columbus, OH, USA*; TERRY A. MILLER, *Department of Chemistry and Biochemistry, The Ohio State University, Columbus, OH, USA*; IGOR V. ADAMOVICH, *Department of Mechanical and Aerospace Engineering, The Ohio State University, Columbus, OH, USA*.

Time-resolved, absolute HO_2 number density in diluted H_2-O_2-Ar, CH_4-O_2-Ar, and C_2H_4-O_2-Ar mixtures excited by a repetitive ns pulse discharge in a heated plasma flow reactor is measured by Cavity Ringdown Spectroscopy (CRDS). The experimental results are obtained at T=300-600 K and P=130 Torr, both during the discharge pulse burst and in the afterglow. The HO_2 number density is inferred from the CRDS data using a spectral model exhibiting good agreement with previous measurements of absolute HO_2 absorption cross sections. In the room-temperature H_2-O_2 mixture, as well as in CH_4-O_2 and C_2H_4-O_2 mixtures over the entire temperature range studied, HO_2 is generated only during the discharge burst and decays in the afterglow. However, in the H_2-O_2 mixture at elevated temperatures, T=400-600 K, HO_2 persists in the afterglow up to 10 ms after the discharge burst, comparable with the flow residence time in the reactor. Comparison with kinetic modeling shows that the sustained reactivity after the source of radicals is turned off is due to a chain propagation / hydrogen oxidation process, which dominates the radical recombination reactions. The kinetic modeling predictions are in good agreement with the relative HO_2 number density measured in all three mixtures, although the model unpredicts the absolute number densities in H_2-O_2 and CH_4-O_2 at T=400-600 K by up to a factor of two. Detection of the sustained low-temperature reactivity in H_2-O_2, initiated by the radical generation in the plasma, suggests that the plasma excitation may also affect kinetics of oxidation and reforming of fuels exhibiting low-temperature chemistry below hot ignition point. Development of a narrow linewidth optical parametric oscillator (OPO) for high-resolution, time-resolved HO_2 measurements during n-butane oxidation in a heated plasma flow reactor is underway.

WC02 **8:04 – 8:05**

MEASURING TIME-RESOLVED CONCENTRATIONS OF FREE RADICALS IN CHEMICAL REACTIONS WITH CAVITY RINGDOWN SPECTROSCOPY

IAN JONES, *Department of Chemistry, Ohio State University, Columbus, OH, USA*; ELIJAH R JANS, *Department of Mechanical and Aerospace Engineering, The Ohio State University, Columbus, OH, USA*; TERRY A. MILLER, *Department of Chemistry and Biochemistry, The Ohio State University, Columbus, OH, USA*; IGOR V. ADAMOVICH, *Department of Mechanical and Aerospace Engineering, The Ohio State University, Columbus, OH, USA*; JOHN F. STANTON, *Physical Chemistry, University of Florida, Gainesville, FL, USA.*

Numerous spectroscopic techniques have been used to follow the concentration of reactive intermediates, such as free radicals, during chemical reactions. However, it is often necessary to measure absolute concentrations to test proposed kinetic mechanisms. Such measurements have always posed more of a challenge because of the difficulty of experimentally measuring the required value of the dipole transition moment to whose square the absorption cross section is proportional. In the-just presented talk involving HO_2, the issue was partially resolved since an empirical value of the absorption cross section was available[1] for the $2\nu_2$ overtone band. However, the cross-section is temperature and pressure dependent and the kinetic experiment was performed at different conditions than the cross section measurements. To resolve this problem, we used the pGopher software[2] with the HO_2 molecular constants[3], μ, to simulate the HO_2 spectrum from which the cross sections were derived, and thereby get the transition moment, μ. A second simulation under the experimental conditions then determined the absolute HO_2 concentration. In addition, we carried out a quantum chemical calculation of μ using the CFOUR package. Despite the overtone nature of the transition, the calculation produced the same values of μ as our simulation, within experimental error. We are now investigating $C_2H_5O_2$ to compare experimental and calculated values of μ for its $\tilde{A} - \tilde{X}$ electronic transition. We hope to establish when it is reasonable to use calculated μ values instead of the difficult-to-measure, experimental ones, to determine concentrations of small, free radicals important in combustion and atmospheric reactions.

[1]Thiebaud, et. al, J. Phys. Chem. A 2007, 111, 6959-6966; [2] C. M. Western, J. Quant. Spectro. Rad. Tran., 186 221-242 (2017); [3]DeSain, et. al, J. Mol. Spectro. 219 (2003) 163–16.

WC03 **8:08 – 8:09**

SINGLE SUBSTITUTION KINETIC ISOTOPE EFFECT MEASUREMENTS FOR CH_4 + O(^{1}D) USING CAVITY RING-DOWN SPECTROSCOPY

DOUGLAS OBER, TZULING CHEN, *Division of Chemistry and Chemical Engineering, California Institute of Technology, Pasadena, CA, USA*; LINHAN SHEN, *Department of Geosciences, Princeton University, Princeton, USA*; THINH BUI, *Sensor Science Division, National Institute of Standards and Technology, Gaithersburg, MD, USA*; MITCHIO OKUMURA, *Division of Chemistry and Chemical Engineering, California Institute of Technology, Pasadena, CA, USA.*

As the most abundant atmospheric hydrocarbon and potent greenhouse gas, methane plays a major role in the chemistry of Earth's atmosphere. The study of kinetic isotope effects (KIEs) for H–D and ^{12}C–^{13}C substitutions on the reaction rates for methane is of importance for modelers, but is challenging because the effects are small, and producing methane oxidants results in a variety of secondary chemistry.

In this work, single and double substitution methane KIEs for $^{13}CH_4$ and CH_2D_2 and were produced using the flash photolysis of N_2O and the methane isotopic compositions were determined via frequency-stabilized cavity ring-down spectroscopy using a dual wavelength near-IR DBF laser system. The KIE of $^{13}CH_4$ was found to differ with the literature value at room temperature of 1.013 by a factor of two, and the H-D KIE of CH_2D_2 was measured for the first time to be 1.098(23). Further, the expected lack of a temperature-dependence of the KIE over the range 170 – 300 K was seen as expected.

WC04 **8:12 – 8:13**

PREDICTING FLUORESCENCE QUANTUMN YIELD of NO $A^2\Sigma^+$ VIA STATE-TO-STATE COLLISIONAL ENERGY TRANSFER MODEL

ZEYU YAN, SHENGKAI WANG[a], *State Key Laboratory for Turbulence and Complex Systems, College of Engineering,, Peking University, Beijing, China.*

NO LIF/PLIF has been used extensively in visualizing complex structures of turbulent, reactive, and compressible flows. However, its quantitative measurement capability has been historically limited by the uncertainty in NO fluorescence quantum yield (FQY). In this work, we present a generic model for the FQY of NO $A^2\Sigma^+$(v'=0) based on state-to-state collisional energy transfer calculation. Two energy transfer pathways were considered in this model, namely the collisional quenching/de-excitation of the $A^2\Sigma^+$(v'=0) system down to $X^2\Pi$(v"), and rotational energy transfer between various J levels (up to ΔJ = 30) within $A^2\Sigma^+$(v'=0). Their respective rate constants were modeled using empirical expressions determined from previous data in the literature. Vibrational energy transfer, on the other hand, was not included in the current model, since its rate constants were several orders of magnitude lower than that of collisional quenching and rotational energy transfer. Both steady-state and time-dependent transient analyses, which correspond to pulsed-laser excitation and CW-excitation, respectively, were performed by solving the master equation of quantum state population. The results were compared with direct spectroscopic measurements of NO FQY conducted in a heated gas cell with various collision partners, which in turn, allowed iterative optimization of the quenching and rotational energy transfer rate model. The current model should be useful in predicting NO FQY over a wide range of temperatures and pressures.

[a]Corresponding Email: sk.wang@pku.edu.cn

WC05 **8:16 – 8:17**

OBSERVING CHEMICAL REACTIONS IN LOW-TEMPERATURE SUPERSONIC FLOWS USING CHIRPED PULSE FOURIER TRANSFORM MILLIMETER WAVE SPECTROSCOPY

THEO GUILLAUME, DIVITA GUPTA, BRIAN M HAYS, ILSA ROSE COOKE, OMAR ABDELKADER KHEDAOUI, THOMAS SANDOW HEARNE, MYRIAM DRISSI, IAN R. SIMS, *CNRS, IPR (Institut de Physique de Rennes) - UMR 6251, Univ Rennes, F-35000 Rennes, France.*

The CPUF (Chirped Pulse in Uniform Flow) technique has been used previously in pulsed CRESU (Reaction Kinetics in Uniform Supersonic Flow) conditions to observe chemical reactions at low temperatures. We have adapted the technique to the continuous CRESU flows available in Rennes, and have observed the products of photolysis and chemical reactions using a chirped pulse Fourier transform millimeter wave spectrometer. We have characterized the flow conditions suitable for observing products of reactions and provide limits to the performance of these systems. In particular, pressure broadening is found to dominate these measurements, so steps had to be taken to resolve as much of the free induction decays as possible. We also observe the products of chemical reactions, particularly of CN radicals with hydrocarbons. The behavior of these products in CRESU environments as well as the results from these studies will be given and the application to observing the branching ratios of chemical reactions will be discussed.

WC06 **8:20 – 8:21**

SIGNATURES OF HYDROGEN ATOM QUANTUM DIFFUSION: H + N_2O REACTION IN SOLID PARAHYDROGEN

KELLY M. OLENYIK, FREDRICK M. MUTUNGA, AARON I. STROM, DAVID T. ANDERSON, *Department of Chemistry, University of Wyoming, Laramie, WY, USA.*

In 1969 A. F. Andreev and I. M. Lifshitz radically changed the way we think about diffusion in cryocrystals by predicting that at sufficiently low temperatures the probability of exchange tunneling of neighboring particles in quantum crystals becomes noticeable such that impurities can move freely through the crystal as narrow-band quasiparticles.[a] The term "quantum crystal" was introduced by de Boer in 1948 for substances in which the energy of the zero-point vibrations of the particles is comparable to the total energy of the crystal.[b] The main idea put forth by Andreev and Liftshitz is that the rate of quantum diffusion should increase with falling temperatures and should show an inverse dependence on the concentration of impurities. As we will show, the hydrogen atom (H-atom) trapped in a parahydrogen crystal is an ideal candidate for quantum diffusion owing to its small mass and neutral charge. In 2013 our group published a communication[c] on the kinetics of the H + N_2O reaction in solid parahydrogen that showed an anomalous temperature dependence. In these studies we generate the H-atoms as byproducts of the *in situ* photodissociation of N_2O and monitor the subsequent reaction kinetics using rapid scan FTIR. Specifically, if we photolyze N_2O doped parahydrogen solids with 193 nm UV radiation at 4.3 K, we observe little to no reaction; however, if we then slowly reduce the temperature of the sample, we observe an abrupt onset to the reaction at temperatures below 2.4 K. In a number of studies conducted since this original work we have come to a better understanding of the effect of temperature on the reaction and will show data that the rate constant for the H + N_2O reaction shows an inverse dependence on the N_2O concentration. These findings support previous ESR measurements of H-atom quantum diffusion in solid parahydrogen[d] and more importantly illustrate how H-atom quantum diffusion impacts the kinetics of these anomalous low temperature, condensed phase reactions.

[a] A. F. Andreev and I. M. Lifshitz, *Sov. Phys. JETP.* **29**, 1107-1113 (1969).
[b] J. de Boer, *Physica* **14**, 139-148 (1948).
[c] F. M. Mutunga, S. E. Follett, D. T. Anderson, *J. Chem. Phys.* **139**, 151104-4 (2013).
[d] T. Kumada et. al., *J. Chem. Phys.* **116**, 1109-1119 (2002).

WC07 **8:24 – 8:25**

N AND H TALIF MEASUREMENTS, $N_2(A^3\Sigma_u^+)$ TDLAS MEASUREMENTS, AND KINETIC MODELING OF NANOSECOND PULSE DISCHARGE PLASMAS IN N_2-H_2 MIXTURES

XIN YANG, CALEB RICHARDS, ELIJAH R JANS, SAI RASKAR, DIRK VAN DEN BEKEROM, IGOR V. ADAMOVICH, *Department of Mechanical and Aerospace Engineering, The Ohio State University, Columbus, OH, USA.*

Time-resolved, absolute number densities of ground state N atoms in nitrogen and H_2-N_2 plasmas, as well as ground state H atoms in H_2-N_2 plasmas, excited by a ns pulse discharge burst at P = 150 Torr, are measured by Two-Photon Absorption Laser-Induced Fluorescence (TALIF). Metastable $N_2(A^3\Sigma_u^+$,v=0,1) molecules and gas temperature in the discharge are measured at the same conditions by Tunable Diode Laser Absorption Spectroscopy (TDLAS). Both in pure nitrogen and in H_2-N_2 mixtures, the results show that the N atom number density does not decay on the time scale of 1 ms and is controlled only by the rate of N_2 dissociation in the plasma during the discharge burst. Both $N_2(A^3\Sigma_u^+$,v) populations and the rate of N generation decrease significantly during the ns pulse discharge burst (by a factor of 3-5), although the pulse energy coupled to the plasma and the number densities of $N_2(C^3\Pi_u)$ and $N_2(B^3\Pi_g)$ molecules remain approximately the same during the burst. Comparison of the measurement results and the modeling predictions indicates an additional major channel of N_2 dissociation in the plasma, by energy pooling in collisions of two $N_2(A^3\Sigma_u^+)$ molecules: $N_2(A^3\Sigma_u^+) + N_2(A^3\Sigma_u^+) \rightarrow N + N + N_2$. In H_2-N_2 mixtures, the N atom number density decreases significantly with the hydrogen mole fraction in the mixture, while the H atom number density is very high, up to 10^{16} cm^{-3} in a 1% H_2-N_2 mixture. Kinetic modeling suggests that a significant fraction of N atoms generated by electron impact in the plasma are formed in the excited electronic state, N(^{2}D). In pure nitrogen, the electronically excited N(^{2}D) atoms are quenched to the ground state, N(^{4}S), within $\sim$ 10 μs, while in H_2-N_2 mixtures, they react with H_2 to produce NH and H atoms, N(^{2}D) +H_2 $\rightarrow$ NH + H. Another major channel of H atom generation in the plasma is the reactive quenching of electronically excited nitrogen molecules by H_2, $N_2(C^3\Pi_u) + H_2 \rightarrow N_2 + H + H$. The rate of H atom generation remains nearly constant during the discharge pulse burst. The present work provides quantitative insight into the mechanism of radical species generation in N_2-H_2 plasmas, which is critical for understanding the kinetics of ammonia synthesis by non-thermal plasma-assisted catalysis.

WC08 **8:28 – 8:29**

CHARACTERIZATION OF HYBRID NS PULSE/RF PLASMAS AND ATMOSPHERIC PRESSURE PLASMA JETS

CALEB RICHARDS, ELIJAH R JANS, DIRK VAN DEN BEKEROM, DAVID KYLE MIGNOGNA, IGOR V. ADAMOVICH, *Department of Mechanical and Aerospace Engineering, The Ohio State University, Columbus, OH, USA.*

Strong vibrational nonequilibrium is sustained in nitrogen and nitrogen/carbon dioxide "hybrid" plasmas, generated by a ns pulse train overlapping with a sub-breakdown RF waveform. N_2 vibrational level populations in the plasma are measured by broadband Coherent Anti-Stokes Raman Spectroscopy (CARS). Vibrationally excited CO_2 and CO in the plasma are detected by Quantum Cascade Laser Absorption Spectroscopy (QCLAS). The plasma is generated using a custom-designed external circuit which overlaps a ns pulse train and a sine-wave RF waveform, generated by two different power supplies, in plane-to-plane, double dielectric barrier discharge configuration. The results show that the sub-breakdown RF waveform, which does not produce ionization but heats the electrons generated by the ns pulses, has a strong effect on vibrational excitation of molecules in the plasma. This enables isolating and quantifying the contribution of reactions of vibrationally excited molecules in plasmachemical and plasma-catalytic processes. Specifically, the effect of the excitation of CO_2 asymmetric stretch vibrational mode on the dissociation of carbon dioxide is studied by QCLAS measurements of CO_2 vibrational level populations and CO product. In a closely related study, a quasi-two-dimensional atmospheric pressure plasma jet in a noble gas/nitrogen mixture, impinging on a dielectric plate (glass or quartz), is interrogated by Coherent Anti-Stokes Raman Spectroscopy (CARS). The experiments are made in N_2/Ar, N_2/He, and N_2/Ne plasma jets powered by a ns pulse train or an RF waveform. Strong N_2 vibrational nonequilibrium is measured in the jet, and found to increase as the mole fraction of nitrogen in the mixture is reduced. This suggests that N_2 vibrational excitation is produced by the energy transfer from metastable electronically excited atoms to the nitrogen vibrational mode, possibly via the metastable excited electronic state, $N_2(A^3\Sigma_u^+)$. To quantify the role of electronically excited nitrogen in this energy transfer processes, the number density of $N_2(A^3\Sigma_u^+)$ molecules in the plasma is measured by Tunable Diode Laser Absorption Spectroscopy.

WC09 **8:32 – 8:33**

KINETICS OF $N_2(A^3\Sigma_u^+$,v) GENERATION AND DECAY IN REACTING GAS MIXTURES EXCITED BY NANOSECOND PULSE DISCHARGE PLASMAS

DAVID KYLE MIGNOGNA, ELIJAH R JANS, IGOR V. ADAMOVICH, *Department of Mechanical and Aerospace Engineering, The Ohio State University, Columbus, OH, USA.*

Absolute time-resolved populations of nitrogen molecules in a metastable excited electronic state, $N_2(A^3\Sigma_u^+)$, generated in a repetitive ns pulse discharge in reacting gas mixtures, have been measured by Tunable Diode Laser Spectroscopy (TDLAS). $N_2(A^3\Sigma_u^+$,v=0-1) population measurements are made in CO_2-N_2, CH_4-N_2, CH_4-CO_2-N_2, and C_2H_4-N_2 mixtures at a pressure of 150 Torr. The mixtures are excited in a diffuse plasma generated by a repetitively pulsed, double dielectric barrier, ns discharge across a 6 mm gap in a plane-to-plane geometry. The data are taken during the discharge bursts up to several tens of pulses long. The results show that the $N_2(A^3\Sigma_u^+)$ number density generated in the discharge, both by electron impact and by the cascade quenching of the higher energy excited electronic states, are significantly affected by the mixture components. In CO_2-N_2 mixtures, the effect on $N_2(A^3\Sigma_u^+$,v) populations is relatively minor, due to the relatively slow quenching rate. In CH_4-N_2 mixtures, the dominant effect is due to the vibrational energy transfer to methane, resulting in a rapid vibrational relaxation of $N_2(A^3\Sigma_u^+$,v=1 $\rightarrow$ v=0). In CH_4-CO_2-N_2 mixtures, $N_2(A^3\Sigma_u^+)$ quenching is also affected by the species generated in the plasma. The results are compared with kinetic modeling predictions, identifying the mechanisms of $N_2(A^3\Sigma_u^+)$ generation and decay during the discharge pulses and in the afterglow. The results demonstrate that high-pressure, high repetition rate, volume-scalable ns pulse discharges can be used for efficient generation of atomic and radical species for plasma chemical and plasma catalysis syntheses. $N_2(A^3\Sigma_u^+)$ measurements and kinetic modeling analysis can be used to quantify the amount of reactive species generated in the plasma.

WC10 **8:36 – 8:37**

THERMAL DECOMPOSITION OF CYCLOHEXANE BY FLASH PYROLYSIS VACUUM ULTRAVIOLET PHOTOIONIZATION TIME-OF-FLIGHT MASS SPECTROMETRY: A STUDY ON THE INITIAL UNIMOLECULAR DECOMPOSITION MECHANISM

KUANLIANG SHAO, *Department of Chemistry, University of California, Riverside, Riverside, CA, USA*; XINGHUA LIU, *School of Science, Hainan University, Haikou, Hainan, China*; PAUL JONES, GE SUN, *Department of Chemistry, University of California, Riverside, Riverside, CA, USA*; MARIAH GOMEZ, *Department of Chemistry and Biochemistry, University of California, Los Angeles, Los Angeles, CA, USA*; BLAKE RISER, *Department of Biochemistry, University of California, Riverside, Riverside, CA, USA*; JINGSONG ZHANG, *Department of Chemistry, University of California, Riverside, Riverside, CA, USA.*

Thermal decomposition of cyclohexane at temperatures up to 1310 K was performed using flash pyrolysis coupled with vacuum ultraviolet (118.2 nm) photoionization time-of-flight mass spectrometry. The experimental results revealed that the major initiation reaction of cyclohexane decomposition was C-C bond fission leading to the formation of 1,6-hexyl diradical. The 1,6-hexyl diradical could isomerize to 1-hexene and decompose into $\bullet C_3H_7$ + $\bullet C_3H_5$ and $\bullet C_4H_7$ + $\bullet C_2H_5$. The 1,6-hexyl diradical could also undergo direct dissociation; the C_4H_8 fragment via the 1,4-butyl diradical intermediate was observed, serving as evidence of the 1,6-hexyl diradical mechanism. Quantum chemistry calculations at UCCSD(T)/cc-pVDZ level of theory on the initial reaction pathways of cyclohexane were performed and found to be consistent with the experimental conclusions. Cyclohexyl radical was not observed as an initial intermediate in the pyrolysis. Benzene was produced from sequential H_2 eliminations of cyclohexane at high temperatures.

WC11 **8:40 – 8:41**

THE STUDY OF DIRECT D ATOM INCORPORATION IN RADICALS AT LOW TEMPERATURE PROBED BY CHIRPED PULSE mm-WAVE SPECTROSCOPY

NURESHAN DIAS, RANIL GURUSINGHE, BERNADETTE M. BRODERICK, ARTHUR SUITS, *Department of Chemistry, University of Missouri, Columbia, MO, USA.*

We are utilizing chirped pulse mm-wave spectroscopy in quasi-uniform supersonic flows at low temperature to probe isomer-specific product branching and kinetics. Earlier we have studied the photodissociation of the propargyl radical and monitored the branching between the three isomers of C_3H_2 and noted efficient conversion of H_2CCC and HCCCH to the cyclic form induced by H addition/elimination, a process termed H-catalyzed isomerization. We will show that by adding a D atom source to the flow we observe very efficient D atom enrichment in the products through an analogous process of D addition/H elimination to C_3H_2 isomers occurring at 40K or below. Cyclic C_3HD is the only deuterated isomer observed consistent with the expected addition/elimination yielding the lowest energy product. In the high-density region of the flow, we also observe singly deuterated propyne formed following stabilization of the D + C_3H_3 adduct, and both isotopomers CH_2DCCH and CH_3CCD are observed in nearly equal abundance. The implications of this for deuterium fractionation in astrochemical environments will be further discussed with the support of monodeuterated dark cloud model developed by Millar et al. Recent results for low temperature radical-radical reactions relevant to planetary atmospheres will also be highlighted.

WC12 **8:44 – 8:45**

REACTION DYNAMICS OF PROPARGYL + NH_2 PROBED USING CHIRPED PULSE ROTATIONAL SPECTROSCOPY IN A PULSED QUASI-UNIFORM FLOW (CPUF)

RANIL GURUSINGHE, NURESHAN DIAS, *Department of Chemistry, University of Missouri, Columbia, MO, USA*; ALEXANDER M MEBEL, *Department of Chemistry and Biochemistry, Florida International University, Miami, FL, USA*; ARTHUR SUITS, *Department of Chemistry, University of Missouri, Columbia, MO, USA.*

Reaction dynamics of the radical-radical reaction between the resonantly-stabilized propargyl radical with NH_2 and ND_2 were investigated using chirped-pulse rotational spectroscopy in a pulsed quasi-uniform flow. Propargyl, NH_2, and ND_2 radicals were produced by UV photodissociation of a mixture of propargyl bromide and ammonia in a low-temperature, helium Laval flow. The reaction products, HCN, HNC, HC_3N, DCN, DNC, and DC_3N, were simultaneously identified using their vibrational ground state rotational spectra in the 70 – 92 GHz region and product branching ratios were calculated. A theoretical analysis using RRKM calculations on an ab initio potential surface revealed diverse and complex reaction pathways and mechanisms that lead to the observed reaction products.

WC13 **8:48 – 8:49**

LASER INDUCED FLUORESCENCE MEASUREMENTS OF VIBRATIONALLY EXCITED OXYGEN PRODUCED BY RECOMBINATION OF O ATOMS

DIRK VAN DEN BEKEROM, KEEGAN ORR, ELIJAH R JANS, XIN YANG, ANAM C. PAUL, IGOR V. ADAMOVICH, *Department of Mechanical and Aerospace Engineering, The Ohio State University, Columbus, OH, USA.*

Vibrationally excited oxygen and nitrogen have been long recognized to be of critical importance in nonequilibrium high-enthalpy flows, primarily encountered behind hypersonic shock waves. To date, no direct experimental verification of vibrational state resolved dissociation rates predicted by different kinetic models has been undertaken, in large part due to the difficulty of measuring these rates directly. We present a framework where state specific recombination rates can be inferred from the time-resolved measurements of O_2 vibrational populations, such that the state specific dissociation rates can be obtained from the detailed balance. In the present approach, recombination reactions of atomic oxygen are monitored in the afterglow of a diffuse ns pulse discharge burst in an O_2-Ar mixture. The time evolution of O_2(v) populations in the recombining mixture are measured by ps Laser Induced Fluorescence (LIF) in the $O_2(B^3\Sigma_u^-$,v'=0 $\leftarrow X^3\Sigma_g^-$, v") Schumann-Runge bands, with absolute calibration by NO($A^2\Sigma^+$, v'=0 $\leftarrow X^2\Pi$, v"=0) LIF. By varying the output wavelength of the ps laser / Optical Parametric Oscillator (OPO) system used for the excitation in the 250-450 nm range, levels from v"=7 to 21 have been detected. Two-photon Absorption LIF (TALIF) at 226 nm has been used to measure the atomic oxygen concentration, with absolute calibration by Xe. Within $\sim$1 ms after the discharge burst, a rapid decay of O_2(v) is observed, indicating vibration-vibration (V-V) and vibration-translation (V-T) relaxation of vibrational states populated by electron impact and by quenching of the excited electronic states of Ar. After the rapid initial decay, the vibrational populations level off and remain nearly constant, or exhibit a transient rise, on the timescale of about 10 ms, suggesting the presence of a persistent source of vibrational excitation due to chemical reactions. In addition to O atom recombination to form vibrationally excited O_2 molecules, at low temperatures atomic oxygen may also recombine with O_2 and form ozone. The latter may well generate vibrationally excited O_2 in O + $O_3 \rightarrow O_2$ + O_2 reaction, which would therefore affect the present results. Ozone formation is controlled by preheating the excited mixture up to 600 K, as well as increasing the pressure and reducing the O_2 mole fraction, when the production of ozone is reduced significantly.

WD. Non-covalent interactions

Wednesday, June 23, 2021 – 8:0 AM

Room: 2021 Online Everywhere

Chair: Gang Feng, Chongqing University, Chongqing, China

WD01 **8:00 – 8:01**

MICROWAVE SPECTRUM OF TRIFLIC ACID DIHYDRATE AND TRIHYDRATE: EVIDENCE FOR COMPLETE PROTON TRANSFER IN A MICROSOLVATED SUPERACID

ANNA HUFF, NATHAN LOVE, KENNETH R. LEOPOLD, *Chemistry Department, University of Minnesota, Minneapolis, MN, USA.*

Microwave spectra have been observed for the dihydrate and trihydrate of triflic acid (CF_3SO_3H-$(H_2O)_2$ and CF_3SO_3H-$(H_2O)_3$). For the dihydrate, spectra for $CF_3{}^{34}SO_3H$-$(H_2O)_2$ and CF_3SO_3H-$(D_2O)_2$ were also identified. The fitted rotational constants for both the triflic acid dihydrate and trihydrate are in consistently good agreement with those derived from their respective global minimum structures calculated with various DFT methods. The two water molecules in the dihydrate bind to triflic acid in a cyclic arrangement to form an 8-membered ring, resembling an insertion of a second water molecule into the 6-membered ring of the triflic acid monohydrate. For the triflic acid trihydrate, however, rather than form a 10-membered ring via insertion of a third water molecule into the dihydrate geometry, the global minimum structure represents a hydronium triflate ion pair solvated by two water molecules (($CF_3SO_3{}^-H_3O^+$)-$(H_2O)_2$). This work represents direct experimental evidence in support of the predicted transition from hydrogen bonding to ion pair formation when triflic acid is solvated with only three water molecules.

WD02 **8:04 – 8:05**

EVIDENCE FOR SPONTANEOUS PROTON TRANSFER IN THE COMPLEX FORMED FROM TRIFLIC ACID AND TRIMETHYLAMINE: MICROWAVE SPECTRUM AND COMPUTATIONAL ANALYSIS OF THE TRIMETHYLAMMONIUM TRIFLATE ION PAIR

NATHAN LOVE, ANNA HUFF, KENNETH R. LEOPOLD, *Chemistry Department, University of Minnesota, Minneapolis, MN, USA.*

Gas phase trimethylammonium triflate, $(CH_3)_3NH^+$ - $^-OSO_2CF_3$, has been observed by microwave spectroscopy. The ion pair was produced by on-the-fly mixing of trimethylamine and the superacid triflic acid in a supersonic jet. An initial fit with unresolved ^{14}N hyperfine structure was obtained within several minutes from the chirped-pulse spectrum using a new fitting program for dense spectral, DAPPERS, and the nitrogen hyperfine structure was then measured by cavity FTMW spectroscopy. Rotational constants are in good agreement with those calculated at the MP2/6-311++G(df,pd) level, which indicate a covalent N-H bond distance. Moreover, the measured ^{14}N nuclear quadrupole coupling constants, together with those calculated at a series of N-H distances, provide definitive evidence of the transfer of a proton in this cold, 1:1 complex.

WD03 **8:08 – 8:09**

HOW INTERMOLECULAR INTERACTIONS EFFECT ESTERIFICATION REACTIONS? A MICROWAVE STUDY OF THE GAS-PHASE COMPLEXES OF FORMIC ACID WITH TWO METHANOL DERIVATIVES AND THEIR ESTERIFICATION PRODUCTS.

WENHAO SUN, MELANIE SCHNELL, *FS-SMP, Deutsches Elektronen-Synchrotron (DESY), Hamburg, Germany.*

Esterification is a reaction of great interest and importance in organic and biological chemistry, where typically an alcohol and a carboxylic acid react and form an ester as the product. Previously, by exploring gaseous mixtures of formic acid (FA) with various alcohols using rotational spectroscopy, it has been found that primary and secondary alcohols tend to readily form an ester by reacting with FA, whereas the tertiary alcohol-FA adduct remains unreacted.[a] Herein, we present the microwave spectroscopic study of FA with two primary alcohols, 3-methyl-3-oxetanemethanol (MOM) and cyclobutanemethanol (CBM), in the gas phase. The spectra in the frequency span of 18-26 GHz were collected on our newly built segmented chirped-pulse Fourier transform microwave (CP-FTMW) spectrometer.[b] Both of the esterification products have been unambiguously assigned with multiple structural conformations. Interestingly, their pre-reaction complexes, MOM-FA and CBM-FA, are observed in the spectra as well. Different from CBM-FA, whose ester product is more pronounced than the adduct in the spectrum, the reaction of MOM with FA seems to be more slowly. This could be attributed to the presence of relatively stronger intermolecular interactions in MOM-FA, compared to CBM-FA. Quantum-chemical calculations were performed to have a deeper insight into their reactivity.

[a] L. Evangelisti, L. Spada, W. Li, F. Vazart, V. Barone, and W. Caminati, Angew. Chem. Int. Ed. Engl. **56**, 3872-3875 (2017).
[b] M. Fatima, C. Pérez, B. E. Arenas, M. Schnell, and A. L. Steber, Phys. Chem. Chem. Phys. **22**, 17042-17051 (2020).

WD04 **8:12 – 8:13**

CONFORMATIONAL EQUILIBRIA BETWEEN ALDEHYDES AND ALCOHOLS: ROTATIONAL SPECTRA OF ACROLEIN-METHANOL AND ACROLEIN-ETHANOL COMPLEXES

DINGDING LV, WENTAO SONG, LUCA EVANGELISTI, ASSIMO MARIS, SONIA MELANDRI, *Dipartimento di Chimica G. Ciamician, Università di Bologna, Bologna, Italy.*

The rotational spectra of the acrolein-methanol and acrolein-ethanol complexes in gas phase were investigated with pulsed supersonic-jet Fourier-transform microwave spectroscopy and quantum mechanical calculations. Two complexes involving the s-*trans* acrolein and methanol were observed, identified by methanol oxygen interacting with methylenic or aldehydic hydrogen. Two complexes involving the s-*trans* acrolein and the *trans* and *gauche* conformations of ethanol were observed. The OD-substituted species of two conformations of s-*trans*-acrolein···methanol and the OD- and $^{13}C_1$-substituted species of the s-*trans*-acrolein···*trans*-ethanol were measured. Ab initio calculations run at the MP2/aug-cc-pVTZ level allowed to explore the conformational space of the acrolein-alcohols complexes. The complexes involving s-*cis* acrolein are less stable than those involving s-*trans* acrolein, according to the energy difference in the monomer. The three-fold barriers to internal rotation of the methyl group, V_3, in s-*trans*-acrolein···methanol-1 (2.629(5) kJ mol^{-1}) and s-*trans*-acrolein···methanol-2 (2.722(5) kJ mol^{-1}) were determined, which are smaller than the value in methanol monomer (4.462 kJ mol^{-1}). Two hydrogen bonds, a conventional O-H···O and a weak C-H···O hydrogen bond, forming a planar and ring-like structure were determined in s-*trans*-acrolein···methanol-1, s-*trans*-acrolein···methanol-2 and s-*trans*-acrolein···*trans*-ethanol. Both two molecules in each complex are acting as proton donor and acceptor. Another one weak C-H···O hydrogen bond was identified in conformation s-*trans* -acrolein···*gauche*-ethanol, in which the acrolein oxygen interacts with the methyl and hydroxyl hydrogen of ethanol at the same time.

WD05 **8:16 – 8:17**

ROTATIONAL SPECTROSCOPY AND CONFORMATIONAL SPACE OF GLYCEROL DIMERS

JIARUI MA, FAN XIE, *Department of Chemistry, University of Alberta, Edmonton, AB, Canada*; NATHAN A. SEIFERT, *Chemical Sciences and Engineering Division, Argonne National Laboratory, Lemont, IL, USA*; YUNJIE XU, *Department of Chemistry, University of Alberta, Edmonton, AB, Canada.*

Glycerol (CH2OHCHOHCH2OH) is a colorless, odorless, and viscous liquid with a sweet taste and is widely used in food and drug industry. This polyol compound with three hydroxyl groups is capable of taking on many different intra- and intermolecular hydrogen bonding topologies, leading to highly complex conformational spaces for its monomer and dimer. Rotational spectra of five of its monomeric conformers had been reported before.[1],[2] In the current study, we apply CREST, a conformer-rotamer ensemble sampling tool developed by the Grimme group,[3] together with DFT calculations to systematically explore the conformational spaces of its monomer and dimer. Rotational spectra of glycerol in the 1-12 GHz range were recorded using a chirped-pulse Fourier transform microwave spectrometer and analyzed. Rotational transitions of several conformers of the binary glycerol complex were assigned. The structure-energy relationships of the conformers of the glycerol dimer and the corresponding monomer will be discussed.

[1] V.V. Ilyushin, R.A. Motiyenko, F.J. Lovas, and D.F. Plusquellic, J. Mol. Spectrosc. 2018, 251,129.

[2] G. Maccaferri, W. Caminati and P.G. Favero, J. Chem. Spc., Faraday Trans., 1997, 93(23), 4115.

[3] S. Grimme, J. Chem. Theory Comput. 2019, 15, 2847.

WD06 **8:20 – 8:21**

INVESTIGATING INTERMOLECULAR INTERACTIONS WITHIN NAPHTHOL DIMERS USING BROADBAND ROTATIONAL SPECTROSCOPY

ARSH SINGH HAZRAH, *Department of Chemistry, University of Alberta, Edmonton, AB, Canada*; NATHAN A. SEIFERT, *Chemical Sciences and Engineering Division, Argonne National Laboratory, Lemont, IL, USA*; WOLFGANG JÄGER, *Department of Chemistry, University of Alberta, Edmonton, AB, Canada.*

Present in a variety of chemical systems, π-π stacking and hydrogen bonding are intermolecular forces critical to the formation and stabilization of various chemical structures. Within DNA these two forces work in unison to stabilize the infamous double helix structure;[1] however, these forces do not always act cooperatively and often compete with each other. This competition is clearly exhibited within the phenol dimer structure, where a predominance of hydrogen bonding over π-π stacking is observed.[2] However, it was unclear how the competition between of hydrogen bonding and π-π stacking would change as the size of the aromatic subunit increases. We use 1-naphthol and 2-naphthol, which can be considered analogues of phenol, as a tool to further understand the complex interplay between π-π stacking and hydrogen bonding Using chirped-pulse Fourier transform microwave spectroscopy, we detected pure rotational transitions of two conformers for both 1-naphthol and 2-naphthol. We additionally observed and subsequently assigned the dimers of 1-naphthol and 2-naphthol. The experimental identifications of the observed dimers were supplemented with a conformer search enabled by dispersion corrected DFT[3] and the CREST sampling program.[4] Through this study we find, somewhat surprisingly, that the structures of 1-naphthol and 2-naphthol are dictated mainly by π-π stacking, unlike the case of the phenol dimer. Furthermore, the dominance of the π -π stacking interactions not only provides information about 1-naphthol and 2-naphthol like structures, but also insights into the complicated and intricate dynamics of these intermolecular forces and the fine balance between them.

1. Ts'o, P. O., Elsevier: 2012; Vol. 2.; 2. Seifert, N. A., Steber, A. L., Neill, J. L., Pérez, C., Zaleski, D. P., Pate, B. H., Lesarri, A., Phys. Chem. Chem. Phys. 2013, 15 (27), 11468-11477.; 3. Becke, A. D., J Chem. Phys. 1992, 96 (3), 2155-2160.; 4. Pracht, P.; Bohle, F.; Grimme, S., Phys. Chem. Chem. Phys. 2020.

WD07 **8:24 – 8:25**

OBSERVATION OF 2-NAPHTHALENETHIOL HOMODIMER USING ROTATIONAL SPECTROSCOPY

RIZALINA TAMA SARAGI, MARCOS JUANES, ALBERTO LESARRI, *Departamento de Química Física y Química Inorgánica, Universidad de Valladolid, Valladolid, Spain*; LOURDES ENRIQUEZ, MARTIN JARAIZ, *Departamento de Electrónica, ETSIT, University of Valladolid, Valladolid, SPAIN.*

Following previous studies of gas-phase dimerization of sulfur-bearing aromatic thiols, like thiophenol[a], benzyl mercaptan[b] and 2-phenylethyl mercaptan[c], we conducted a structural investigation of 2-naphthalenethiol using chirped-pulse Fourier transform microwave spectroscopy in a jet-cooled expansion. Two conformers of the monomer have been observed in the frequency region 2-8 GHz. All monosubstituted (^{34}S and ^{13}C) isotopologues could also be observed. Finally, a single isomer of the homodimer of 2-naphthalenethiol was identified. The homodimer is stabilized by π-stacking interactions, with no hydrogen bond interaction between the two thiol groups. Supporting ab initio and DFT calculations will be presented.

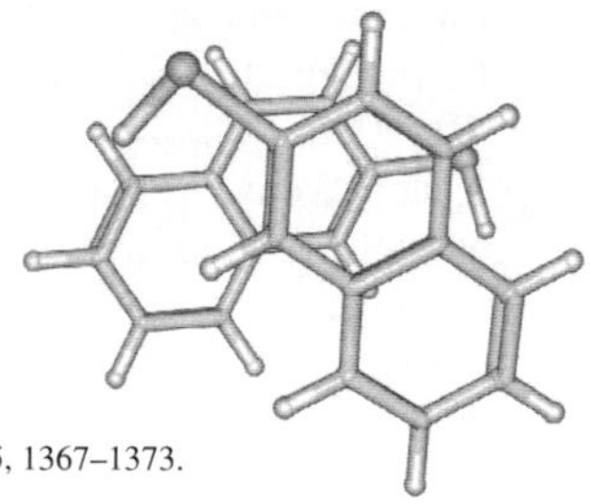

[a]R.T. Saragi, M. Juanes, C. Pérez, P. Pinacho, D.P. Tikhonov, W. Caminati, M. Schnell, A. Lesarri, *J. Phys. Chem. Lett.* 2021, 12, 5, 1367–1373.
[b]R.T. Saragi, et al., *in publication* 2021.
[c]R.T. Saragi, et al., *in publication* 2021.

WD08 **8:28 – 8:29**

INVESTIGATING SUBSTITUENT EFFECTS IN DISPERSION-CONTROLLED ACETOPHENONE-PHENOL BALANCES

C. ZIMMERMANN, MARTIN A. SUHM, *Institute of Physical Chemistry, Georg-August-Universität Göttingen, Göttingen, Germany.*

The carbonyl oxygen of the asymmetrically substituted ketone acetophenone exhibits two hydrogen bond docking sites, where in combination with a phenol molecule two competing isomers can be formed. The two conformers can be probed experimentally by analyzing the differences in the OH-stretching frequency via FTIR spectroscopy in a supersonic jet and determining their abundance ratio at low temperatures. [a] This allows for the experimental benchmarking of theoretically predicted relative conformational energies on a kJ mol^{-1} or even finer scale. [bc] By halogenating the second or fourth position in the phenyl-ring of the acetophenone molecule with fluorine, chlorine or bromine, six closely related systems are formed, allowing to probe the influence of substituent effects on the favored docking site in addition to the London dispersion attraction and steric hindrances.

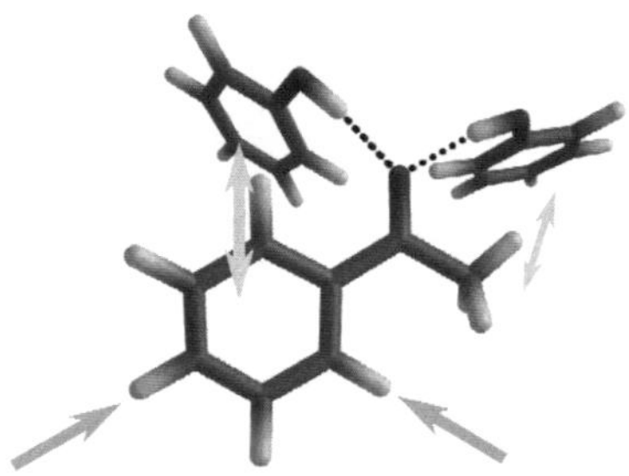

[a]C. Zimmermann et al., *Phys. Chem. Chem. Phys.*, **2020**, *22*, 2870.
[b]H. C. Gottschalk et al., *J. Chem. Phys.*, **2018**, *148*, 014301.
[c]A. Poblotzki et al., *J. Phys. Chem. Lett.*, **2017**, *8*, 5656.

WD09 **8:32 – 8:33**

BINDING SITES SWITECHED BY ALKYL SUBSTITUENTS: ROTATIONAL SIGNATURES OF $C_6H_5(CH_2)_nOH$-CO_2 (n = 0-2)

HAO WANG, JUNHA CHEN, QIAN GOU, *School of Chemistry and Chemical Engineering, Chongqing University, Chongqing, China.*

Noncovalent interactions topologies of $C_6H_5(CH_2)_nOH$-CO_2(n=0-2) complexes have been investigated by rotational spectroscopy complementary with quantum chemistry. Experimental evidences pointed out that with the extension of the alkyl chain, the primary binding sites are switched: phenol and CO_2 are linked through a dominant C···O tetrel bond and a secondary C-H···O weak hydrogen bond, while phenylmethanol and 2-phenylethanol link with CO_2 through a C···π(aromatic) interactions. In addition, the Symmetry-Adapted Perturbation theory analysis show that the dispersion term is the dominant force in such C···π(aromatic) complex, while the electrostatic term is dominating in phenol-CO_2.

WD10 **8:36 – 8:37**

P...N PNICOGEN BONDING INTERACTION IN PHOSPHORYL CHLORIDE...NITROGEN BASES: EVIDENCE FROM MATRIX ISOLATION INFRARED SPCTROSCOPY AND QUANTUM CHEMICAL CALCULATIONS

P K SRUTHI, NAGARAJAN RAMANATHAN, K SUNDARARAJAN, *Materials Chemistry and Metal Fuel Cycle Group, Indira Gandhi Centre for Atomic Research, Homi Bhabha National Institute, Kalpakkam, Tamilnadu, India.*

Pnicogen bonding emerged as an important interaction as ubiquitous hydrogen bonding, the study of interactions of simple molecular model systems involving pnicogen bonding can be a platform to understand the complex mechanisms controlled by these non-covalent interactions. In the present work matrix isolation spectroscopy in combination with quantum chemical computations were used to elucidate the structures of P...N pnicogen bonded dimers of phosphoryl chloride($POCl_3$) prototype with nitrogen-bases such as ammonia (NH_3), aniline (C_6H_7N), and pyridine (C_5H_5N), where phosphorus is predominantly present in pentavalent state.

The basicities of the interacting partner (NH_3,C_6H_7N,C_5H_5N) completely influences the geometrical preference of all these dimers. The $POCl_3$-NH_3 dimer is anticipated to have a hydrogen bonded geometry, however with hydrogen bonding, a P...N pnicogen bonding plays a definite and a non-trivial role in their overall stabilization. An interesting paradigm transformation was noticed in $POCl_3$-C_6H_7N and $POCl_3$-C_5H_5N heterodimers, where P...N pnicogen bonding was observed to completely dominate the hydrogen bonding. Furthermore, the characteristic interactions were investigated through electrostatic potential mapping, energy decomposition and non covalent interaction analyses.

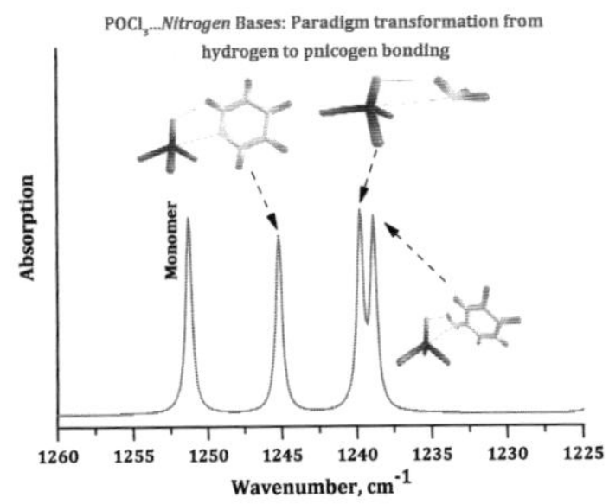

WE. Theory and Computation

Wednesday, June 23, 2021 – 8:0 AM

Room: 2021 Online Everywhere

Chair: Inga Ulusoy, Heidelberg University, Heidelberg, Germany

WE01 **8:00 – 8:01**

STACKED ENSEMBLE LEARNING FOR RANGE-SEPARATION PARAMETERS

CHENG-WEI JU, ETHAN FRENCH, *Department of Chemistry, University of Massachusetts, Amherst, MA, USA*; NADAV GEVA, *Advanced Micro Devices, Advanced Micro Devices, Boxborough, Massachusetts, USA*; ALEXANDER W. KOHN, *Cylance Inc., Cylance Inc., Irvine, California, USA*; ZHOU LIN, *Department of Chemistry, University of Massachusetts, Amherst, MA, USA*.

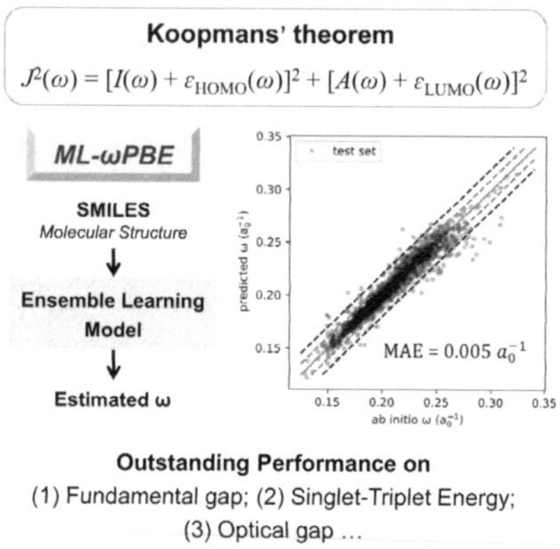

High-throughput quantum chemical calculations, especially those based on Kohn-Sham density functional theory (KS-DFT), have achieved tremendous success in materials discovery. However, due to the notorious self-interaction error, many popular exchange-correlation (XC) functionals suffer from catastrophic failures for molecules with delocalized electronic densities. As an effective but expensive solution to this problem, the optimally tuned range-separation hybrid functional utilizes a system-specific range-separation parameter (ω). [T. Stein, L. Kronik, and R. Baer, *J. Am. Chem. Soc.* **2009**, 131, 2818.] To accelerate the search for optimal ω and makes it practical for the high-throughput materials screening, we developed a stacked ensemble learning approach based on composite molecular descriptors, and assessed its accuracy and efficiency using the LRC-ωPBE functional and a diverse database of over 4,000 molecules that are equally divided into the training and test sets. Compared with the traditional optimal tuning method, our stacked ensemble learning algorithm reached a mean absolute error (MAE) of 0.005 a_0^{-1} in the values of ω while reducing the time cost by four orders of magnitude. In addition, the predictive power in essential properties such as fundamental and optimal band gaps were not compromised. Given sufficient diversity in the training set, stacked ensemble learning provides a promising alternative scheme to determine range-separation hybrid functional and eventually any system-specific XC functionals.

WE02 **8:04 – 8:05**

TOO MANY UNKNOWN MOLECULES IN THE LABORATORY ITSELF

KRISHNAN THIRUMOORTHY, *Department of Chemistry, School of Advanced Science, Vellore Institute of Technology, Vellore, Tamilnadu, India*; AMIR KARTON, *School of Molecular Sciences, The University of Western Australia, Perth, Western Australia, Australia*; NISHA JOB, *Department of Chemistry, School of Advanced Science, Vellore Institute of Technology, Vellore, Tamilnadu, India*; INGA ULUSOY, *Theoretical Chemistry Institute, University of Heidelberg, Heidelberg, Germany*; ANDREW L. COOKSY, VENKATESAN S. THIMMAKONDU, *Chemistry and Biochemistry, San Diego State University, San Diego, CA, USA.*

Over the last few years, we have generated considerable theoretical data on C_nH_2 (n = 5, 7, and 9)[a,b,c,d] and SiC_4H_2[e]isomers, in view of their astronomical relevance. An overview of these results will be discussed in this meeting. Although the potential target molecules have been theoretically identified, lack of their experimental data, especially the infrared and microwave spectra, is a serious concern. To unambiguously confirm molecules in astrophysical sources, precise laboratory rest frequencies will be required. To the best of our knowledge, all of the new isomers we theoretically identified so far remain elusive in the laboratory itself to date.

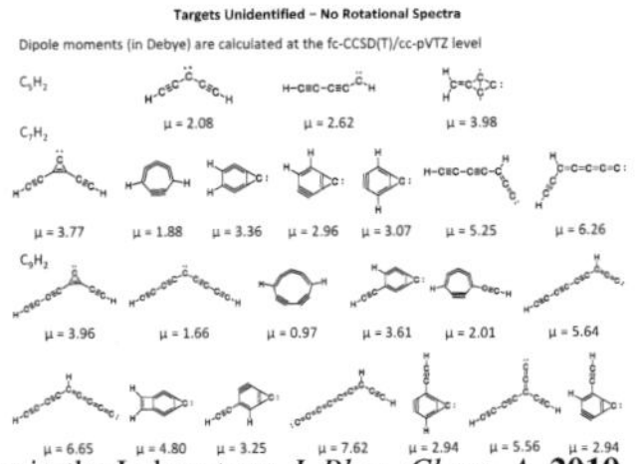

[a]Thimmakondu, V. S.; Ulusoy, I.; Wilson, A. K.; Karton, A. Theoretical Studies of Two Key Low-Lying Carbenes of C_5H_2 Missing in the Laboratory, *J. Phys. Chem. A*, **2019**, 123, 6618-6627.

[b]Thimmakondu, V. S.; Karton. A. Energetic and Spectroscopic Properties of the Low-Lying C_7H_2 Isomers: A High-Level Ab Initio Perspective, *Phys. Chem. Chem. Phys.*, **2017**, 19, 17685-17697.

[c]Thirumoorthy, K. and Karton, A. and Thimmakondu, V. S. From High-Energy C_7H_2 Isomers with A Planar Tetracoordinate Carbon Atom to An Experimentally Known Carbene, *J. Phys. Chem. A*, **2018**, 122, 9054-9064.

[d]Thirumoorthy, K.; Viji, M.; Pandey, A. P.; Netke, T. G.; Sekar, B.; Yadav, G.; Deshpande, S.; Thimmakondu, V. S. Many Unknowns Below or Close to the Experimentally Known Cumulene Carbene - A Case Study of C_9H_2 Isomers, *Chem. Phys.* **2019**, 527, 110496.

[e]Job, N. and Karton, A. and Thirumoorthy, K.; Cooksy, A. L.; Thimmakondu, V. S. Theoretical Studies of SiC_4H_2 Isomers Delineate Three Low-Lying Silylidenes Are Missing in the Laboratory, *J. Phys. Chem. A* **2020**, 124, 987-1002.

WE03 **8:08 – 8:09**

IMPROVING SPECTRAL SYNTHESIS PERFORMANCE BY UP TO 5 ORDERS OF MAGNITUDE WITH THE DISCRETE INTEGRAL TRANSFORM APPROACH

DIRK VAN DEN BEKEROM, *Department of Mechanical and Aerospace Engineering, The Ohio State University, Columbus, OH, USA*; PANKAJ MISHRA, *Electronics and Electrical Communication Engineering, Indian Institute of Technology, Kharagpur, India*; ERWAN PANNIER, *Laboratoire EM2C, CNRS UPR288, CentraleSupélec, Université Paris Saclay, Gif sur Yvette, France.*

The increasing number and size of large Line-By-Line (LBL)-databases, routinely exceeding hundreds of millions of lines, calls for spectral synthesis algorithms that can process these large number of lines efficiently. In the special case where the lineshape is identical for every line in the database, the spectrum can be rapidly synthesized by the convolution of a stick-spectrum and the constant lineshape. We propose an integral transform that extends this procedure to databases with unique lineshapes for each line, by generalizing the stick spectrum to a 3D "lineshape distribution function", which is a function of line position and Gaussian- & Lorentzian width axes.

A fast discrete version of the integral transform based on the Fast Fourier Transform (FFT) is formulated for which the computation time scales with $c_1 N_i + c_2 N_\nu \log N_\nu$ (where N_i is the number of lines, N_ν the number of spectral points, and c_1 and c_2 are small constants), which is much more efficient than the traditional $N_i \times N_\nu$ scaling. Furthermore, since the lineshape calculation is no longer a performance bottleneck, lineshapes such as exact Voigt profiles without cutoff can be computed with arbitrary precision. Our procedure can be implemented in existing spectral codes, providing a new level of accuracy and performance for high temperature, high resolution spectroscopy.

The procedure was benchmarked against traditional methods within the open source package RADIS: A benchmark HITEMP CO_2 spectrum consisting of 1.8M lines and 200k spectral points took 3.1s, an improvement of $\sim 300\times$. The new procedure has since been implemented as the default synthesis method for RADIS. The method's calculations can be easily divided up and are ideally suited for parallel computation. An experimental GPU procedure, also implemented in RADIS, was used to synthesize a CDSD-4000 CO_2 spectrum of 200M lines and 300k spectral points, which took only 150 ms per spectrum regardless of temperature (after an initialization of ~5 s), or $4 \cdot 10^{14}$ lines×spectral points/s – an improvement of 5 orders of magnitude compared to the state-of-the-art – with no appreciable loss in accuracy.

WE04 **8:12 – 8:13**

PARTICIPATION RATIO AND QUANTUM FIDELITY SUSCEPTIBILITY AS TOOLS TO CHARACTERIZE BENT-TO-LINEAR SHAPE TRANSITIONS

JAMIL KHALOUF-RIVERA, MIGUEL CARVAJAL, *Departamento de Ciencias Integradas, Universidad de Huelva, Huelva, Spain, Spain*; FRANCISCO CURRO PÉREZ-BERNAL, *Dpto. Fisica Aplicada, Unidad Asociada CSIC, Facultad de Ciencias Experimentales, Universidad de Huelva, Huelva, Spain.*

Molecular bending spectra can be broadly categorized into three physical cases, depending on the molecular equilibrium configuration: linear, bent, and nonrigid. We have studied the three cases in detail with an extended Hamiltonian (including up to four-body interactions) of the 2D limit of the Vibron Model (2DVM). We have obtained bending band origin predictions within experimental accuracy as well as the corresponding eigenstates for several molecules [a].

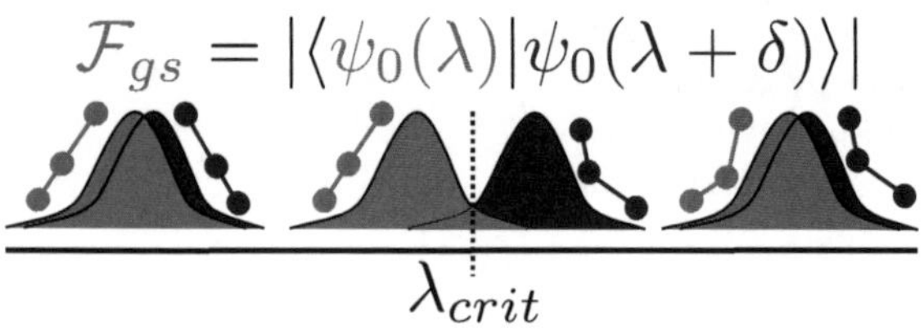

The particular spectroscopic signatures characterizing states that straddle the barrier to linearity in nonrigid molecules have been pinpointed with the quantum monodromy and the Birge-Sponer plots. In addition, we propose a characterization of the obtained bending eigenstates making use of the Participation Ratio and the Quantum Fidelity Susceptibility [b]. The first quantity has already proved useful in determining linearity barriers in molecular bent-to-linear transitions, as well as characterizing transition states in isomerization reactions, e.g., HCN-HNC bond-breaking system [c]. Besides, the second quantity allows us to determine in an elegant and basis-independent way the linear or bent character of any excited state.

As an application, we have studied, using the above mentioned quantities, the bending spectra of several molecules of interest in different fields: HNC, OCCCO, CH_3NCO, ClCNO, NCNCS, and Si_2C.

[a] J. Khalouf-Rivera, F. Pérez-Bernal, M. Carvajal, *J. Quant. Spectrosc. Radiat. Transfer* (2021) 261, 107436.
[b] J. Khalouf-Rivera, M. Carvajal, F. Pérez-Bernal, SciPost Physics (2021) submitted (arXiv:2102.12335).
[c] J. Khalouf-Rivera, M. Carvajal, L. F. Santos, F. Pérez-Bernal, J. Phys. Chem. A (2019) 123, 44, 9544-9551.

WE05 **8:16 – 8:17**

ASSIGNING THE COMPLICATED DISPERSED FLUORESCENCE SPECTRUM OF PhCCCN

JAMES H. THORPE, *Quantum Theory Project, University of Florida, Gainesville, FL, USA*; KHADIJA M. JAWAD, TIMOTHY S. ZWIER, *Department of Chemistry, Purdue University, West Lafayette, IN, USA*; JOHN F. STANTON, *Quantum Theory Project, University of Florida, Gainesville, FL, USA.*

The dispersed fluorescence spectrum from the S_1 origin of PhCCCN is reported. This molecule, which consists of a cyanoacetylene chain fused to an aromatic phenyl ring, is a potential candidate for astronomical detection. The high resolution spectrum was obtained under jet-cooled, gas-phase conditions with a rotational temperature of roughly 2 K, and appears to encode rich information about the vibronic coupling in this species. The experimentally observed peaks are assigned to emissions from the S_1 ($\tilde{A}\,^1B_2$) origin to a_1 vibrational levels of the ground state, which are dipole allowed and governed by FC factors, and to b_2 vibrational levels of the ground state, made possible by vibronic interactions between S_1 and S_2 ($\tilde{B}\,^1A_1$) states. The S_0 vibrational structure features a combined Fermi and Darling-Denison resonance near 950 cm^{-1}, which is accurately reproduced by diagonalization of an effective Hamiltonian containing the three a_1 states involved. A KDC Hamiltonian is employed to treat the vibronic b_2 features.

WE06 **8:20 – 8:21**

SUB-EV ACCURACY DELTA-COUPLED-CLUSTER CALCULATIONS FOR HETERO-SITE DOUBLE CORE-IONIZED STATES

XUECHEN ZHENG, JUNZI LIU, LAN CHENG, *Department of Chemistry, Johns Hopkins University, Baltimore, MD, USA*; GILLES DOUMY, LINDA YOUNG, *Chemical Sciences and Engineering Division, Argonne National Laboratory, Lemont, IL, USA.*

Benchmark scalar-relativistic delta-coupled-cluster calculations of hetero-site double core ionization energies of small molecules containing second-row elements are presented. This study has focused on high-spin triplet components of two-site double core-ionized states, which are single reference in character and consistent with the use of coupled-cluster methods. Contributions to computed double core ionization energies from electron-correlation and basis-set effects as well as corrections to the core-valence separation approximation have been analyzed. Based on systematic convergence of computational results with respect to these effects, delta-coupled-cluster calculations have been shown to be capable of providing accurate double core ionization energies with remaining errors estimated to be below 0.3 eV. The predictions for the double core ionization energies of CF_4, CH_3F, CH_3CF_3, and CH_2FCF_3 are reported. The perspective of these molecules to be used in the experimental studies of two-site double core-ionized states that are involved in x-ray pump/x-ray probe studies of electronic and molecular dynamics following inner shell ionization or excitation is discussed.

References

[1] X. Zheng, J. Liu, G. Goumy, L. Young, and L. Cheng, J. Phys. Chem. A Comput. **124**, 4413-4426 (2020).

WE07 **8:24 – 8:25**

MODELLING THE DIPOLE MOMENT FUNCTION OF CARBON MONOXIDE CAPABLE OF PREDICTING THE ROTATIONAL DISTRIBUTION IN THE 7-0 BAND

EMILE S. MEDVEDEV, VLADIMIR G. USHAKOV, *Theoretical Department, Institute of Problems of Chemical Physics, Russian Academy of Sciences, Chernogolovka, Moscow Region, Russia.*

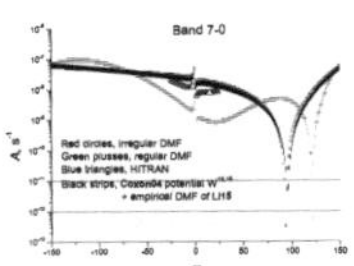

The rotational distributions of the intensities in the low-v vibrational bands are nearly insensitive to the specific forms of the PEFs and DMFs based on the experimental and/or *ab initio* data. This is not the case for the higher overtone bands. We discuss the problem: Which properties should the model PEF and DMF possess in order to be capable of predicting the intensities of the yet unobserved lines? Arguments are presented that the Born-Oppenheimer PEF and DMF should possess some features following from their properties as functions of the inter-atomic separation as a complex variable. In particular, they must contain branch points associated with the crossings between the ground and excited electronic states. This approach implies that both functions are to be fitted simultaneously to the common data set including both the line positions and the intensities. However, such a problem is very difficult to solve. Here and in Ref. (1), in application to CO, we assume that the PEF is given (2), and we develop an irregular DMF form containing two branch points corresponding to the expected crossings in the complex plane near 0.4 and 2.2 Å. We compare it with an alternative regular function (1) and find that the rotational distribution in the vibrational 7-0 band predicted by the former is very stable with respect to small variations in the data base, as opposed to the regular DMF showing strong instability. The predicted intensities (see figure) are stronger than the HITRAN values calculated by Li et al. (3) with a combined empirical/spline-interpolated *ab initio* DMF but are close to the ones calculated by us with the purely empirical DMF of Li et al. The irregular function is expected to provide for a reliable prediction of the ro-vibrational line intensities in the 7-0 band.

This work was performed in accordance with the state task, state registration No. AAAA-A19-119071190017-7.

(1) V. V. Meshkov, A. V. Stolyarov, A. Yu. Ermilov, E. S. Medvedev, V. G. Ushakov, I. E. Gordon, JQSRT (in preparation); (2) JQSRT 217 (2018) 262-273. (3) G. Li, I. E. Gordon, L. S. Rothman, Y. Tan, S.-M. Hu, S. Kassi, A. Campargue, E. S. Medvedev, Astrophys. J., Suppl. Ser. 216 (2015) 15.

WE08 8:28 – 8:29

GLOBAL ROVIBRATIONAL ANALYSIS FOR THE 20 LOWEST VIBRATIONAL BANDS OF HYDROGEN SULFIDE ($H_2^{32}S$)

MIGUEL CARVAJAL, *Dpto. Ciencias Integradas, Centro de Estudios Avanzados en Física, Matemáticas y Computación, Universidad de Huelva, Huelva, Spain*; JAMIL KHALOUF-RIVERA, *Departamento de Ciencias Integradas, Universidad de Huelva, Huelva, Spain, Spain*; FRANCISCO CURRO PÉREZ-BERNAL, *Dpto. Fisica Aplicada, Unidad Asociada CSIC, Facultad de Ciencias Experimentales, Universidad de Huelva, Huelva, Spain*; RENATO LEMUS, *Estructura de la Materia, Instituto de ciencias Nucleares, Mexico City, Mexico.*

The rovibrational energy structure of H_2S has been analysed simultaneously for the 20 lowest energy vibrational bands up to J=20. We have used a global analysis rovibrational algebraic approach of which the effective Hamiltonian interaction terms are constructed as products of powers of the angular momentum components and an algebraic realization of the vibrational interactions. The algebraic vibrational terms are obtained as a set of anharmonic Morse ladder operators based on the dynamical algebra U(2), one for every internal coordinate [a].

The parameters of the effective rovibrational Hamiltonian have been determined by a nonlinear least-squares fitting to the available experimental rovibrational energies [b]. More than 2500 experimental rovibrational energies, up to J=20 for the 20 lowest vibrational bands, have been fitted with a *rms* of the order of 10^{-3} cm^{-1}. In total, around 8000 rovibrational energy term values have been calculated.

[a] M. Carvajal, R. Lemus, *J. Phys. Chem.* **A** 119 (2015) 12823.
[b] K.L. Chubb *et al.*, *J. Quant. Spectrosc. Rad. Transf.* 218 (2018) 178–186.

WE09 8:32 – 8:33

COMPUTATIONAL NMR STUDY OF ION PAIRING OF 1-DECYL-3-METHYL-IMIDAZOLIUM CHLORIDE IN MOLECULAR SOLVENTS

DOVILE LENGVINAITE, VYTAUTAS KLIMAVICIUS, *Institute of Chemical Physics at Faculty of Physics, Vilnius University, Vilnius, Vilnius, Lithuania*; VYTAUTAS BALEVICIUS , KESTUTIS AIDAS, *Faculty of Physics, Vilnius University, Vilnius, Lithuania.*

Ionic liquids (ILs) are salts with a melting point below 100 °C and are typically composed of asymmetric organic cations and organic or inorganic anions. The modulate effect of the molecular solvent on the properties of ionic liquid thorough understanding of intermolecular interactions between the constituent ionic and molecular species is crucial. One of these effects is ion pairing at low concentrations of the ionic in the molecular solvent. Ion pairing was detected in nonpolar solvents at rather low concentrations of ionic while polar solvents demonstrate the capability of breaking ionic aggregate into separate ions.

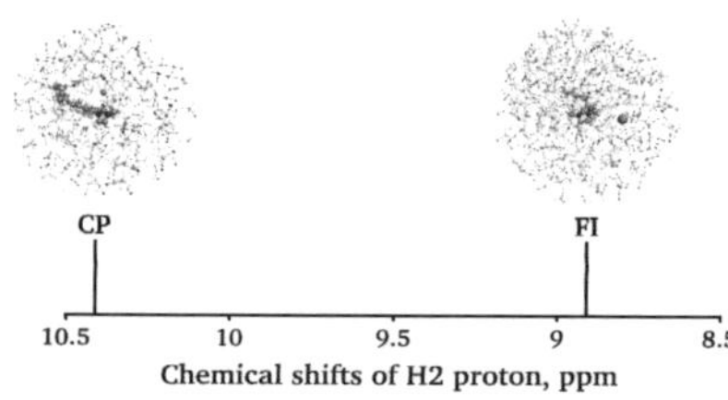

The ^1H NMR spectra of 10^{-5} mole fraction solutions of 1-decyl-3-methyl-imidazolium chloride ionic liquid in water, acetonitrile and dichloromethane have been measured. The chemical shift of the proton at position 2 in the imidazolium ring of 1-decyl-3-methyl-imidazolium is rather different for all three samples, reflecting the shifting equilibrium between the contact pairs and free fully solvated ions. Classical molecular dynamics simulations of the 1-decyl-3-methyl-imidazolium chloride contact ion pair as well as of free ions in three solvents have been conducted, and the quantum mechanics/molecular mechanics methods have been applied to predict NMR chemical shifts for the proton at position 2. By comparing experimental and computational results, we found that the ion pair breaks into free ions in an aqueous solution. Around 23% of the ion pairs were found to form contact pairs in acetonitrile. Ion-pairing breaking into free ions was predicted not to occur in dichloromethane.[a]

[a] D. Lengvinaite, V. Klimavicius, V. Balevicius, K. Aidas, J. Phys. Chem. B, 2020, 124, 47, 10776–10786.

WE10 **8:36 – 8:37**

XANES SPECTRA OF VANADIUM COMPLEXES CALCULATED BY TWO TDDFT METHODS

JUN YI, ZHOU LIN, *Department of Chemistry, University of Massachusetts, Amherst, MA, USA.*

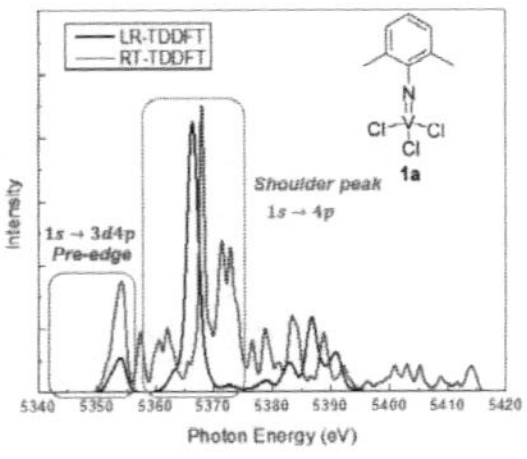

The K-edge of X-ray absorption near edge structure (XANES) spectra can provide in-situ geometric and electronic information about transition metal catalyst. Due to the complicated characters of the K-edge absorptions, theoretical studies are indispensable to extract such quantitative features. The present work focused on K-edge absorptions of a series of vanadium complex catalysts. The linear-response time-dependent density functional theory (LR-TDDFT) and real-time time-dependent density functional theory (RT-TDDFT) method have been used to calculate the K-edge XANES spectra. The pre-edge region can be well reproduced by LR-TDDFT. The peaks appearing in the pre-edge region were assigned to dipole-allowed transitions of $1s$ electrons to the $3d4p$ hybridized orbitals. However, the shoulder peak region located on the K-edge cannot be fully explained by LR-TDDFT calculation due to the complicated multiple excitations and large density rearrangement where the linear response approximation is no longer valid. The greatest strength of RT-TDDFT is that it can produce the entire broad-band spectrum within a single calculation, which happens to serve as a supplement to LR-TDDFT. Recently, Herbert et al. have developed and implement an efficient RT-TDDFT algorithm for computation of X-ray absorption spectra of small molecules. [J. Chem. Phys. 2018, 148, 044117] Herein, we have applied this RT-TDDFT algorithm to probe the absorption features on the raising K-edge. Based on our RT-TDDFT calculations, we have successfully assigned shoulder peaks on the K-edge and characterized the electronic properties of vanadium complexes.

WE11 **8:40 – 8:41**

COMPUTATIONAL INFRARED SPECTROSCOPY OF PHOSPHORUS-CONTAINING POTENTIAL BIOSIGNATURES

JUAN C. ZAPATA TRUJILLO, ANNA-MAREE SYME, *School of Chemistry, University of New South Wales, Sydney, NSW, Australia*; KEIRAN N. ROWELL, *School of Chemistry, University of Sydney, Sydney, NSW, Australia*; CLARA SOUSA-SILVA, , *Harvard-Smithsonian Center for Astrophysics, Cambridge, MA, USA*; LAURA K McKEMMISH, *School of Chemistry, University of New South Wales, Sydney, NSW, Australia.*

Phosphine is now well established as a biosignature, which has risen to prominence with its recent tentative detection on Venus. To follow up this discovery and related future exoplanet biosignature detections, it is important to spectroscopically detect the presence of phosphorus-containing (P-molecules) atmospheric molecules that could be involved in the chemical networks producing, destroying or reacting with phosphine. Here, we present a high-throughput approach utilising established computational quantum chemistry methods (CQC) to produce a database of approximate infrared spectra for 958 P-molecules that could be spectroscopically detected in planetary atmospheres. We performed the calculations with the strongly performing harmonic ωB97X-D/def2-SVPD model chemistry for all molecules and tested the more sophisticated and time-consuming GVPT2 anharmonic model for 250 smaller molecules. Limitations to our automated approach, particularly for the GVPT2 method, are considered along with pathways to future improvements. Our CQC calculations significantly improve on existing spectroscopic data by providing quantitative intensities, new data in the fingerprint and higher frequency regions, and improved data for fundamental transitions based on the specific chemical environment.

WE12 **8:44 – 8:45**

MOLECULAR FRAGMENT MACHINE LEARNING TRAINING TECHNIQUES TO PREDICT CLUSTER ENERGETICS AND FREQUENCIES IN BROWN CARBON AEROSOL CLUSTERS

EMILY E. CHAPPIE[a], *Department of Chemistry, College of William & Mary, Williamsburg, VA, USA*; DANIEL P. TABOR, *Department of Chemistry, Texas A & M University, College Station, TX, USA*; NATHANAEL M. KIDWELL, *Department of Chemistry, College of William & Mary, Williamsburg, VA, USA.*

Density functional theory (DFT) has become a popular method for computational work involving larger molecular systems as it provides accuracy that rivals ab initio methods while lowering computational cost. Nevertheless, computational cost is still high for systems greater than ten atoms in size, preventing their application in modeling realistic atmospheric systems at the molecular level. Newer machine learning techniques, however, show promise as cost-effective tools in predicting chemical properties when properly trained. In the interest of furthering chemical machine learning in the field of atmospheric science, we are developing a new training method to be used in the prediction of molecular characteristics for cyclic, nitrogen-based molecules that can undergo tautomerization within brown carbon aerosols. By creating a training dataset made of small molecule DFT calculations that supplement DFT cluster models of brown carbon molecules with hydration shells ranging from one to three waters, we hope to find a significant improvement in accuracy when predicting characteristics of brown carbon compounds while being computationally efficient.

[a] Additional affiliation with Texas A & M University as a Visiting Scholar

WE13 **8:48 – 8:49**

IMPROVING THE ROTATION VIBRATIONAL LINE LISTS FOR OZONE

APOORVA UPADHYAY, OLEG L. POLYANSKY, JONATHAN TENNYSON, ALEC OWENS, *Department of Physics and Astronomy, University College London, London, UK*; NIKOLAY F. ZOBOV, *Microwave Spectroscopy, Institute of Applied Physics, Nizhny Novgorod, Russia*; EAMON K CONWAY, *Atomic and Molecular Physics , Harvard-Smithsonian Center for Astrophysics, Cambridge, MA, USA.*

There are long running problems over the precise transition intensities and line positions for ozone[a,b]. In our work, state of the art, first principles quantum mechanical methods are being used to compute high accuracy transition intensities and line positions for the microwave and infrared regions of the spectrum of ozone. In this presentation I will discuss details of our most recent calculations of the ab initio dipole moment surface (DMS) and analysis of experimental ozone line positions using the MARVEL (Measured Active Rotation Vibration Energy Levels) technique[c]. To improve the quality of our current[d] DMS we are exploring the electronic structure model, finer grids and larger basis set sizes. The ozone MARVEL project currently involves the analysis of around 70 sources of scientific literature (we anticipate this number to increase). We will use the MARVEL energy levels to fit a new potential energy surface for ozone. We also intend to replace the calculated energy levels with MARVEL energy levels in our line lists. We hope the results of this study will be important for a range of atmospheric studies, such as self-consistency of ozone concentration retrievals in remote sensing techniques, and possible detections of ozone in exo-planetary atmospheres.

[a] M. A. H. Smith, V. M. Devi & D. C. Benner, "The quest for ozone intensities in the 9–11 μm region: a retrospective", Journal of Quantitative Spectroscopy and Radiative Transfer, **113(11)**, 825–828 (2012)

[b] A. Barbe et al, "Ozone spectroscopy in the electronic ground state: High-resolution spectra analyses and update of line parameters since 2003", Journal of Quantitative Spectroscopy and Radiative Transfer, **130**, 172–190 (2013)

[c] T. Furtenbacher, A. G. Császár & J. Tennyson, "MARVEL: measured active rotational–vibrational energy levels.", Journal of Molecular Spectroscopy, **245**, 115–125 (2007)

[d] O. L. Polyansky, N. F. Zobov, I. I. Mizus , A. A. Kyuberis, L. Lodi & J. Tennyson, "Potential energy surface, dipole moment surface and the intensity calculations for the 10 μm, 5 μm and 3 μm bands of ozone", Journal of Quantitative Spectroscopy and Radiative Transfer, **210**, 127–135 (2018)

WE14 **8:52 – 8:53**

NON-ADIABATIC CALCULATIONS OF SPECTRA OF OPEN-SHELL DIATOMIC MOLECULES

SERGEI N. YURCHENKO, *Physics and Astronomy , University College London, London, United Kingdom.*

Non-adiabatic couplings (NACs) or derivative couplings (DDRs) between nearly degenerate states can be significant or even divergent. NACs arise from nuclear gradients of electronic wave functions around avoided crossings between adiabatic potential energy curves. Large values of NACs result in strong interaction between corresponding adiabatic states, making the adiabatic approximation invalid. In this work we consider NACs in the case of diatomic open-shell molecules and implement a diabatizaton methodology in the variatonal code DUO.[a] The methodology is based on a unitary transformation to the so-called quasi-diabatic states defined to provide smooth (with respect to nuclear coordinates) behaviour of different properties, such as spin-orbit curves, (transition) dipole moment curves etc. As example, rovibronic calculations of the electronic spectra of yttrium oxide, YO,[b] in the quasi-diabatic representation will be presented.

[a] S. N. Yurchenko, L. Lodi, J. Tennyson, A. V. Stolyarov, *Comput. Phys. Commun.*, 2016, **202**, 262 – 275; publicly available at *https://github.com/ExoMol.*

[b] A. N. Smirnov, V. G. Solomonik, S. N. Yurchenko, J. Tennyson, *Phys. Chem. Chem. Phys.*, 2019, **21**, 22794–22810.

WF. Linelists

Wednesday, June 23, 2021 – 8:0 AM
Room: 2021 Online Everywhere

Chair: Amanda J. Ross, Universite de Lyon, Villeurbanne, France

WF01 — 8:00 – 8:01

LINE LISTS FOR HIGH RESOLUTION STUDIES OF EXOPLANETS

JONATHAN TENNYSON, SERGEI N. YURCHENKO, *Department of Physics and Astronomy, University College London, London, UK.*

The ExoMol project (www.exomol.com) provides comprehensive line lists for the study of exoplanets and other hot bodies. As part of the ERC-funded ExoMolHD project these line lists are being refactored to facilitate their use in characterization of exoplanets using high resolution Doppler shift spectroscopy. This technique is based the use of MARVEL (measured active rotation vibration energy level) to obtain empirical energy levels and illustrated by a recent study on formaldhyde (H_2CO).[a]

For formaldehyde we analysed of 16 596 non-redundant transitions from 43 experimental sources and resulted in the determination of 5029 empirical energy levels. As part of this work new measurements were performed in Bologna yielding high-accuracy rotational transitions within the ground, ν_3, ν_4 and ν_6 vibrational states, significantly improving the overall accuracy of the network. Eleven artificial transitions determined from effective Hamiltonian fits were added to the network to both fix the gap between ortho and para levels, and to join free-standing networks of transitions to the main network.

The empirical energies were used to update the AYTY ExoMol line list for formaldehyde. This yielded 367 779 transition frequencies determined using the empirical energy levels of which 183 673 lie above the dynamic HITRAN intensity cutoff, see the example in the figure.

The generation of line lists which combine empirically-determined transition wavenumbers with *ab initio* transition dipoles is suitable for high resolution studies of both the Earth's and exoplanetary atmospheres. High resoltion line lists for other molecules starting with AlO, VO and the isotopologues of H_3^+ are currently being prepared.

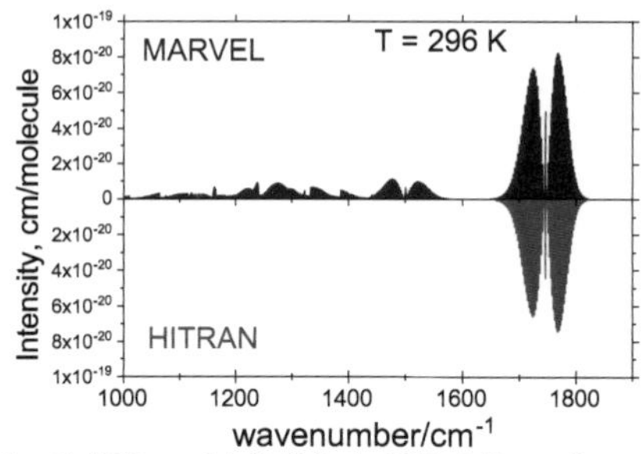

[a] A. R. Al-Derzi, S. N. Yurchenko, J. Tennyson, M. Melosso, Ningjing Jiang, C. Puzzarini, L. Dore, T. Furtenbacher, R. Tobias and A G. Császár, 2021, J. Quant. Spectrosc. Radiat. Transf., doi = 10.1016/j.jqsrt.2021.107563

WF02 — 8:04 – 8:05

EXPANSION OF THE HITEMP DATABASE

ROBERT J. HARGREAVES, *Atomic and Molecular Physics, Harvard-Smithsonian Center for Astrophysics, Cambridge, MA, USA*; EAMON K CONWAY, *Atomic and Molecular Physics , Harvard-Smithsonian Center for Astrophysics, Cambridge, MA, USA*; IOULI E GORDON, LAURENCE S. ROTHMAN, *Atomic and Molecular Physics, Harvard-Smithsonian Center for Astrophysics, Cambridge, MA, USA.*

The high-temperature molecular spectroscopic database, HITEMP [1], aims to provide line lists for use in the modeling of high-temperature environments. Usage can range from the sensing of specific transitions in combustion processes to simulating the broadband opacities of exoplanet atmospheres. One challenge has been to balance the substantial quantity of transitions necessary for high-temperature applications, while remaining practical for use in line-by-line radiative transfer calculations. For methane [2], a method was devised to compress the very weak intensities of the underlying *ab initio* transitions into "effective" lines, which can be used in regular radiative transfer calculations.

The HITEMP database currently constitutes line lists for eight molecules (H_2O, CO_2, N_2O, CO, CH_4, NO, NO_2, OH) and this talk will summarize the recent updates and additions to the HITEMP2010 data [2,3,4], including the new line list for water vapor [5]. A brief discussion of the remaining updates and proposed additions will also be included.

[1] L.S. Rothman, et al. (2010), *JQSRT* **111**, 2139-2150
[2] R.J. Hargreaves, et al. (2020), *ApJS* **247**, A55
[3] R.J. Hargreaves, et al. (2019), *JQSRT* **232**, 35-53
[4] G. Li, et al. (2015), *ApJS* **216**, A15
[5] E.K. Conway, et al. (2021), *JQSRT*, in prep

WF03 **8:08 – 8:09**

THE NON-LTE SPECTROSCOPY OF MOLECULAR REACTIONS USING THE EXOMOL DATABASE

VICTORIA H.J. CLARK, SERGEI N. YURCHENKO[a], JONATHAN TENNYSON, *Department of Physics and Astronomy, University College London, London, UK.*

This talk describes our recent development of two robust methods for calculating non-local thermal equilibrium (non-LTE) spectra of polyatomic molecules. Specifically, we look at molecules produced in reactive or dissociative environments, with vibrational populations outside local thermal equilibrium (LTE). The methodology is based on ExoMol's accurate and extensive ro-vibrational line lists containing transitions with high vibrational excitations and relies on the detailed ro-vibrational assignments. Two approaches for non-LTE vibrational populations of the product are introduced: a simplistic 1D approach based on the Harmonic approximation, and full 3D model incorporating accurate vibrational wavefunctions computed variationally with the TROVE (Theoretical ROVibrational Energy) program. The developed methodology is applied to two molecules, silylene (SiH_2) produced in a decomposition of disilane (Si_2H_6), and carbon monoxide (CO) produced by formamide (CH_3NO) glow discharge. We show how the two approaches compare well to each other and to experimentally obtained spectra, and how their non-LTE spectral signatures can be used to trace different reaction channels of molecular dissociations.

[a]s.yurchenko@ucl.ac.uk

WF04 **8:12 – 8:13**

EXOPLINES: MOLECULAR ABSORPTION CROSS-SECTION DATABASE FOR BROWN DWARF AND GIANT EXOPLANET ATMOSPHERES

EHSAN GHARIB-NEZHAD, *Space Science Division, NASA Ames Research Center, Moffett Field, CA, USA*; AISHWARYA IYER, MICHAEL R LINE, *School of Earth and Space Exploration, Arizona State University, Tempe, AZ, USA*; RICHARD S FREEDMAN, *Carl Sagan Center, SETI Institute, Moutain View, CA, USA*; MARK S MARLEY, NATASHA E BATALHA, *Space Science and Astrobiology Division, NASA Ames Research Center, Moffett Field, CA, USA.*

Stellar, substellar, and planetary atmosphere models are all highly sensitive to the input absorption cross-sections and subject to errors arising from incomplete line lists and the lack of appropriate pressure-broadening parameters. Generational differences between various state-of-the-art stellar and planetary models are primarily because of incomplete and outdated atomic and molecular line lists. Addressing this, here we present a database of pre-computed molecular absorption cross-sections for all isotopologues of key atmospheric absorbers relevant to late-type stellar, brown dwarf, and planetary atmospheres: MgH, AlH, CaH, TiH, CrH, FeH, SiO, TiO, VO, and H_2O. The pressure and temperature ranges of the computed data are between 10^{-6}–3000 bar and 75–4000 K, and their spectral ranges are 0.25–330 $\mathrm{cm}^{-1}$for many cases where possible.

Some details on absorption cross-sections such as wing cut-off and pressure broadening have been either ignored or forgotten even though they have an instrumental impact on radiative transfer atmospheric modelings. Furthermore, for most molecules such as TiO, VO, and H_2O, multiple sets of cross-section data exist which lead to extensive biases and inaccuracies on the interpretation of observational data including uncertainty in the C/O ratio, thermal structure, and composition of exoplanetary atmospheres. In sum, we present (1) a database of pre-computed molecular absorption cross-sections to mitigate shortcomings for pre-existing incomplete line lists, and (2) quantify biases that arise when characterizing substellar/exoplanet atmospheres due to line list differences.

Lastly, our team's endeavors at NASA Ames research center to leverage these disagreements and concerns on cross-section data and the lack of sufficient pre-computed and evaluated dataset will be addressed. Our comprehensive database platform, MAESTRO, will be introduced.

WF05 **8:16 – 8:17**

MODELING PLANETARY OPACITIES WITH HITRAN AND HAPI: TEST CASE OF AMMONIA MICROWAVE ABSORPTION SPECTRA UNDER JOVIAN CONDITION

FRANCES M SKINNER, *Atomic and Molecular Physics , Harvard-Smithsonian Center for Astrophysics, Cambridge, MA, USA*; ROBERT J. HARGREAVES, IOULI E GORDON, *Atomic and Molecular Physics, Harvard-Smithsonian Center for Astrophysics, Cambridge, MA, USA*.

The HITRAN (high-resolution transmission molecular spectroscopic database) is an international standard for reference molecular spectroscopy, particularly in simulating planetary and terrestrial atmospheric spectra [1]. HITRAN recently added new broadening parameters that are relevant to planetary atmospheres for many chemical species in the database. For NH_3, new broadening parameters include H_2, He, CO_2 [2] and H_2O [3]. These additional broadening parameters for NH_3 allowed for validations of HITRAN data with the HITRAN Application Programming Interface (HAPI) [4] against the NH_3 opacity models and laboratory data utilized by the Juno Mission. The Juno spacecraft carries with it a microwave radiometer which probes the atmospheric composition of Jupiter in the microwave range (0.02-0.73 cm^{-1}) [5,6]. At these frequencies, Jupiter's atmospheric spectra is dominated by the inversion of NH_3 and is broadened by H_2, He, and H_2O. This work required three new line shapes to be incorporated into HAPI in order to accurately compare to available laboratory data and standard NH_3 opacity models (the Ben-Reuven [7], Gross [8] and Van Vleck and Weisskopf [9] line shapes). The results of this work demonstrate that HAPI can be used with HITRAN data, to model NH_3 opacities under Jovian conditions in the microwave region. It also shows great promise to produce opacities for other species of interest to the planetary community.

References
[1] I. E. Gordon, et al. JQSRT, 203:3–69, 2017.
[2] J. S. Wilzewski, et al. JQSRT, 168:193–206, 2016.
[3] Y. Tan, et al. JGR (Atmospheres), 124(21): 11580–11594, 2019.
[4] R. V. Kochanov, et al. JQSRT, 177:15–30, 2016.
[5] M. A. Janssen, et al. Space Science Reviews, 213(1–4):139–185, 2017.
[6] S. J. Bolton, et al. Science, 356(6340):821–825, 2017.
[7] A. Ben-Reuven, Physical Review, 145:7–22, 1966.
[8] E. P. Gross, Physical Review, 97: 395–403, 1955.
[9] J. H. Van Vleck and V.F. Weisskopf, Review Modern Physics, 17:227–236, 1945.

WF06 **8:20 – 8:21**

MOLECULAR LINE LISTS FOR HOT ROCKY SUPER-EARTHS

ALEC OWENS, SERGEI N. YURCHENKO, JONATHAN TENNYSON, *Department of Physics and Astronomy, University College London, London, UK*.

The atmospheres of hot rocky super-Earths will have very different spectroscopic signatures compared to gas giants or cooler objects. Many of these exoplanets possess short orbital periods, hence hot atmospheres, and will have a lot in common with early Earth; the massive amounts of water and elevated temperatures are expected to turn the atmospheres into a (high pressure) steam bath containing the remains of melted rock.

We will present recent progress on the production of molecular line lists for hot rocky super-Earths. A number of molecules containing silicon, alkali and alkaline earth metals are to be included in the ExoMol database. For the temperature and wavelength ranges considered, line lists will have to come from rigorous, first-principles calculations. However, these species pose new challenges and there is a pressing need for laboratory observations to improve the accuracy of our spectroscopic models.

WF07 **8:24 – 8:25**

BUILDING A HIGH RESOLUTION LINE LIST FOR ALUMINIUM MONOXIDE

CHARLES A BOWESMAN, *Department of Physics and Astronomy, University College London, London, UK*.

Indications of aluminium monoxide (AlO) in the atmospheres of exoplanets are being reported and it is predicted to be an important source of opacity in hot Jupiters. Studies using high resolution spectroscopy should allow for a strong detection but require high accuracy reference data observed in a laboratory setting. A MARVEL (measured active rotational-vibrational energy levels) analysis is performed on the available, measured spectroscopic data for $^{27}Al^{16}O$: 22 679 validated transitions are used to determine 6 512 distinct energy levels. These empirical energy levels are used to provide an improved, spectroscopically accurate version of the ExoMol ATP line list for $^{27}Al^{16}O$; at the same time the accuracy of the line lists for the isotopically-substituted species $^{26}Al^{16}O$, $^{27}Al^{17}O$ and $^{27}Al^{18}O$ are improved by correcting levels in line with the corrections used for $^{27}Al^{16}O$. The four, newly updated line lists include full uncertainties and are made available via www.exomol.com as part of the ExoMol project.

WF08 **8:28 – 8:29**

LINE LIST FOR THE LOWEST FOUR STATES OF NO

QIANWEI QU, SERGEI N. YURCHENKO, JONATHAN TENNYSON[a], *Department of Physics and Astronomy, University College London, London, UK.*

We computed an accurate line list, called XABC, for nitric oxide (NO) which covers its pure rotational, vibrational and rovibronic spectra belonging to the lowest four electronic states of NO, i.e. $X\,^2\Pi$, $A\,^2\Sigma^+$, $B\,^2\Pi$ and $C\,^2\Pi$. XABC is a major extension and update of the ExoMol NOname line list which was calculated within the $X\,^2\Pi$ state of NO.

As first step we built a spectroscopic model which represents the rovibronic structure of $A\,^2\Sigma^+$, $B\,^2\Pi$, $C\,^2\Pi$ states of NO. Empirical energy levels for the three electronic states are determined using the a combination of the MARVEL procedure and *ab initio* calculations, and the available experimental data are critically evaluated. *Ab inito* methods which deal simultaneously with the Rydberg-like $A\,^2\Sigma^+$ and $C\,^2\Pi$, and the valence $B\,^2\Pi$ state are tested. Methods of modeling the sharp avoided crossing between the $B\,^2\Pi$ and $C\,^2\Pi$states are tested. A rovibronic Hamiltonian matrix is constructed using variational nuclear motion program DUO whose eigenvalues are fitted to the MARVEL energy levels. The matrix also includes coupling terms obtained from the refinement of the *ab initio* potential energy and spin-orbit coupling curves. Calculated and observed energy levels agree well with each other, validating the applicability of our method and providing a useful model for this open shell system. This part has been published in *J. Chem. Phys.* https://doi.org/10.1063/5.0038527.

A mixture of empirical and theoretical electronic transition dipole moments are used for the final calculation of NO rovibronic transitions belong to the $A\,^2\Sigma^+ - X\,^2\Pi$, $B\,^2\Pi - X\,^2\Pi$ and $C\,^2\Pi - X\,^2\Pi$ which correspond to the γ, β and δ band systems, respectively, as well as minor improvements to transitions within the $X\,^2\Pi$ ground state. Our model generates a high-accuracy NO ultraviolet line list covering the complicated regions where the $B\,^2\Pi$ -$C\,^2\Pi$ states interact. Technical details of this part are given in the XABC line list paper submitted to *Mon. Not. Roy. Astron. Soc.*.

XABC provides comprehensive data for $\lambda > 160$ nm ($\tilde{\nu} < 63000$ cm^{-1}) for the analysis of atmospheric NO on Earth, Venus or Mars, other astronomical observations and applications. It is available via www.exomol.com.

[a]j.tennyson@ucl.ac.uk

WF09 **8:32 – 8:33**

UPDATING CH_4 SPECTROSCOPIC MODELS FROM 6770-7630 CM^{-1} WITH DUAL FREQUENCY COMB ABSORPTION SPECTROSCOPY UP TO 1000 K

NATHAN A MALARICH, DAVID YUN, *Mechanical Engineering, University of Colorado at Boulder, Boulder, CO, USA*; KEEYOON SUNG, *Jet Propulsion Laboratory, California Institute of Technology, Pasadena, CA, USA*; SCOTT C EGBERT, *Mechanical Engineering, University of Colorado at Boulder, Boulder, CO, USA*; SEAN COBURN, *Department of Mechanical Engineering, University of Colorado Boulder, Boulder, CO, USA*; BRIAN DROUIN, *Jet Propulsion Laboratory, California Institute of Technology, Pasadena, CA, USA*; GREGORY B RIEKER, *Department of Mechanical Engineering, University of Colorado Boulder, Boulder, CO, USA.*

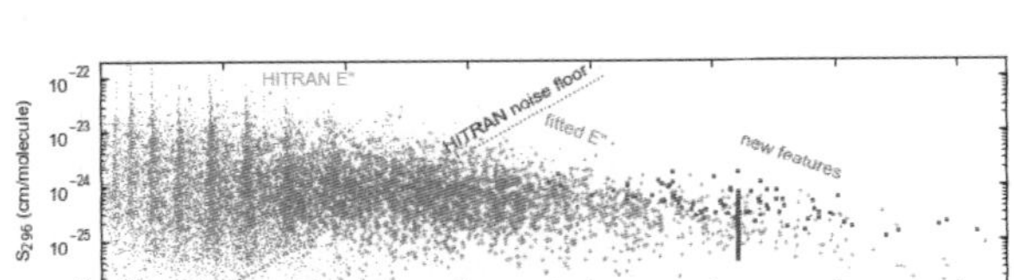

Accurate high-temperature methane spectroscopic models are needed to support the discovery and evaluation of methane in hot exoplanet atmospheres. We present data taken with dual frequency comb absorption spectroscopy with a 0.0067 cm^{-1} frequency point spacing of the methane icosad (6770-7630 cm^{-1}) of five temperatures up to 1000 K and three pressures up to 300 torr. A comparison of this data to HITRAN2016, HITEMP2020, and ExoMol reveals a best match with HITRAN2016 at room temperatures. However, there are significant mismatches with all three databases at elevated temperatures. Via a multispectrum fitting routine, we demonstrate that significant improvements can be made between HITRAN2016 high-temperature models and our data by updating several spectroscopic parameters. In particular, we update 4381 lower state energies, add 293 new hot absorption features, and apply band-wide changes to line-positions, self-widths, and temperature-dependence exponents for self-widths and self-shifts.

WF10 **8:36 – 8:37**

THE SECOND RESONANCE SYSTEM OF HC_3N. NEW RO-VIBRATIONAL GLOBAL ANALYSIS FOR ALL THE EXCITED STATES BELOW 1300 cm^{-1}.

LUCA BIZZOCCHI, *Scuola Normale Superiore, Scuola Normale Superiore, Pisa, Italy*; MATTIA MELOSSO, *Dept. Chemistry "Giacomo Ciamician", University of Bologna, Bologna, ITALY*; CRISTINA PUZZARINI, *Dep. Chemistry 'Giacomo Ciamician', University of Bologna, Bologna, Italy*; FILIPPO TAMASSIA, *Dipartimento di Chimica Industriale "Toso Montanari", Università di Bologna, Bologna, Italy*; ANDREA PIETROPOLLI CHARMET, *Dipartimento di Scienze Molecolari e Nanosistemi, Università Ca' Foscari, Venezia, Italy*; MARIE-ALINE MARTIN-DRUMEL, OLIVIER PIRALI, *Institut des Sciences Moléculaires d'Orsay, Université Paris Saclay, CNRS, Orsay, France*; BARBARA MICHELA GIULIANO, PAOLA CASELLI, *The Center for Astrochemical Studies, Max-Planck-Institut für extraterrestrische Physik, Garching, Germany*; J.-C. GUILLEMIN, *ISCR - UMR6226, Univ. Rennes. Ecole Nationale Supérieure de Chimie de Rennes, Rennes, France.*

The ro-vibrational spectrum of HC_3N has been recently the object of a comprehensive study[a] which put together new high-resolution mid-infrared measurements and all existing rotational data for the vibrationally excited states located below $\sim$ 1000 cm^{-1}. The resulting global analysis yielded accurate and physically sound spectroscopic parameters for 12 states, thanks to the careful treatment of the l-type resonance effects in bending states and the consideration of various anharmonic resonances, in particular those connecting the polyad of states $v_4 = 1$, $v_6 = 2$, $v_5 = v_7 = 1$, and $v_7 = 4$. Here, the extension of the study to the second polyad of interacting states is presented, they are: $v_4 = v_7 = 1$, $(v_6 = 2, v_7 = 1)$, $(v_5 = 1, v_7 = 2)$, and $v_7 = 5$, and are located in the energy interval 1100–1300 cm^{-1}. New far- and mid-infrared spectra have been recorded at SOLEIL, with a resolution of 0.001 cm^{-1}, and further measurements of the millimeter and sub-millimeter spectra of the four interacting states have been performed at Garching and Bologna. The results of a new global analysis including all the states below $\sim$ 1300 $cm^{-1}$are presented and discussed.

[a]L. Bizzocchi, F. Tamassia, et al., *Astoph. J. Supp. Ser.* 233:11, 2017

WF11 **8:40 – 8:41**

A RE-EXAMINATION OF THE QUANTITATIVE INFRARED ABSORPTION CROSS-SECTIONS OF ISOBUTANE

KENDALL D. HUGHEY, STEVEN W. SHARPE[a], ROBERT L. SAMS[b], TIMOTHY J. JOHNSON, TANYA L. MYERS, THOMAS A. BLAKE, *Chemical Physics and Analysis, Pacific Northwest National Laboratory, Richland, WA, USA.*

Recently published work[c] has called into question the absolute infrared absorption cross-section values for isobutane presented in the Northwest Infrared (NWIR) database. As a result, we have remeasured these cross-sections. In all, four data sets were acquired, analyzed and compared to the original NWIR database with excellent agreement. All new data sets were measured with a nominal pathlength of 20 cm and sample temperature of 25.0 °C. Three data sets were acquired using a Bruker IFS 125HR spectrometer equipped with a HgCdTe detector. Spectra were first recorded between 600 and 5000 cm^{-1}at 0.112 cm^{-1}instrument resolution using thirteen burdens of isobutane (0.3 to 22 Torr), each pressure-broadened to one atmosphere using N_2 gas. The second and third data sets were recorded using thirteen burdens of isobutane (0.1 to 23 Torr), at an instrument resolution of 0.01 cm^{-1}. A spectrum of each sample was recorded neat and then recorded pressure-broadened to one atmosphere using N_2 gas, producing two data sets. A fourth data set, using eleven burdens of neat isobutane (0.5 to 23 Torr) was recorded using a Bruker IFS 66v/S with a DTGS detector. Spectra were recorded between 400 and 6500 cm^{-1}at 2 cm^{-1}instrument resolution. Each of the four data sets was fitted using a weighted linear least squares algorithm and resulted in a "composite" $\log_{10}$ absorbance spectrum of isobutane with concentration-pathlength units of ppm^{-1} m^{-1}. The wavenumber axis is in units of cm^{-1}. For the 125HR data sets, the integrated band strengths for both the C-H stretch and CH_2 bend regions are within 2% of the original NWIR integrated band strengths, and the 66v/S integrated band strengths for both spectral regions are within 5% of the NWIR data. The agreement between the original and new cross-section data is close to the original experimental error, 3%, reported for the NWIR database.

[a]Retired.

[b]Retired.

[c]DM Hewett, PF Bernath, BE Billinghurst. 2019 "Infrared absorption cross sections of isobutane with hydrogen and nitrogen as broadening gases." *Journal of Quantitative Spectroscopy and Radiative Transfer* 227:226–229.

WF12 **8:44 – 8:45**

INFRARED ABSORPTION CROSS SECTIONS OF NEOPENTANE AND ETHANE

RANDIKA DODANGODAGE, *Physics, Old Dominion University, Norfolk, VA, USA*; PETER F. BERNATH, ANDY WONG, *Department of Chemistry and Biochemistry, Old Dominion University, Norfolk, VA, USA*; BRANT E. BILLINGHURST, JIANBAO ZHAO, *EFD, Canadian Light Source Inc., Saskatoon, Saskatchewan, Canada.*

Hydrocarbons are of considerable importance in studies of planetary atmospheres such as Titan and Giant Planets. In Titan, ethane (C_2H_6) is the second most abundant hydrocarbon and is also widespread in Giant Planets. Neopentane ($C(CH_3)_4$) may be detected in these planetary atmospheres. This talk will present the absorption cross sections of ethane and neopentane. Infrared absorption spectra of ethane and neopentane were recorded in the 2600-3300 cm^{-1} region by high resolution Fourier transform spectroscopy at the Canadian Light Source. Absorption cross sections for neopentane were obtained for pure samples and samples broadened by nitrogen. The data were taken at temperatures of 203 K, 232 K, 266 K and 293 K with broadening gas pressures of 10 Torr, 30 Torr and 100 Torr. Cross sections for ethane were obtained for pure samples and samples broadened by hydrogen and helium at the same temperatures and pressures. Calibration of cross sections for ethane was carried out using data from the Pacific Northwest National Laboratory (PNNL).

WF13 **8:48 – 8:49**

MEASUREMENT OF CROSS-SECTIONS AND PSEUDOLINE GENERATION FOR TOLUENE(C_7H_8) IN THE 7-15 μM REGION AT 240 – 298 K

KEEYOON SUNG, DEACON J NEMCHICK, GEOFFREY C. TOON, *Jet Propulsion Laboratory, California Institute of Technology, Pasadena, CA, USA*; CONOR A NIXON, *Planetary Systems Laboratory, NASA Goddard Space Flight Center, Baltimore, MD, USA.*

In search of elusive species that might be captured in the Cassini/CIRS and the JWST/MIRI spectral observations, high-precision laboratory spectroscopy constitutes a critical input to Titan atmospheric modeling emission features. For this, we have conducted a series of laboratory studies on hydrocarbons that are likely to be present in the Titan atmosphere (Sung et al. 2020, 2018, 2016, 2013). In this work, we report the measurements of temperature-dependent cross-sections of toluene in the mid-infrared (7-15 μ m) region. For this, we obtained 23 pure and N_2-mixture spectra at 240–298 K using a high-resolution Fourier transform spectrometer (Bruker IFS 125 HR) at the Jet Propulsion Laboratory. Moreover, we have generated empirical spectroscopic pseudoline parameters by fitting all the 23 laboratory spectra together. We observed that the pseudoline parameters (which consist of line position, intensities, and effective lower state energies) could reproduce most of the observed features within 3 % through line-by-line radiative transfer calculations, showing the pseudoline parameters are an excellent practical alternative until the line-by-line spectroscopic line parameters become available. We will present the results and comparisons to existing lower resolution spectra from the PNNL (Sharpe et al.2004).[a]

[a]Government support acknowledged.

WG. Plenary

Wednesday, June 23, 2021 – 9:0 AM

Room: 2021 Online Everywhere

Chair: Melanie Schnell, Deutsches Elektronen-Synchrotron (DESY), Hamburg, Germany

WG02 **9:03 – 9:43**

MOLECULAR COMPLEXES ON THE BRINK OF CHEMICAL CHANGE

KENNETH R. LEOPOLD, *Chemistry Department, University of Minnesota, Minneapolis, MN, USA.*

The study of weakly bound complexes has been a multidimensional endeavor for over forty years. In this talk, we focus on microwave spectroscopic studies of reactive complexes, i.e., those formed from molecules that would ordinarily react under bulk conditions but which may or may not yield products in a cold, isolated cluster. The work will be put in context with a brief review of partially bound Lewis acid-base complexes, highlighting the role of near-neighbor interactions in driving chemical bond formation. With that as an historical backdrop, we then describe the recent discovery of carboxylic sulfuric anhydrides, $RCOOSO_2OH$. These species are shown to form via a barrierless or nearly barrierless cycloaddition reaction between SO_3 and carboxylic acids within a putative SO_3-RCOOH complex. Results of statistical thermodynamic calculations are presented and the potential atmospheric significance of these species will be discussed. Finally, we consider the subject of spontaneous proton transfer in cold molecular complexes and the role of microsolvation in promoting chemical change. New work on the mono-, di-, and trihydrates of the superacid "triflic acid" (CF_3SO_2OH) demonstrates that only three water molecules are needed before acid ionization takes place. In contrast, with trimethylamine, no microsolvent is necessary for proton transfer and the 1:1 complex is best regarded as a trimethylammonium triflate ion pair. Simple energetic arguments rationalize these results.

WH. Mini-symposium: Large Amplitude Motions

Wednesday, June 23, 2021 – 10:0 AM

Room: 2021 Online Everywhere

Chair: Miguel Carvajal, Universidad de Huelva, Huelva, Spain

WH01 — 10:00 – 10:01

EXCITED TORSIONAL STATES OF DIMETHYLETHER $(CH_3)_2O$

V. ILYUSHIN, YAN BAKHMAT, E. A. ALEKSEEV, OLGA DOROVSKAYA, *Radiospectrometry Department, Institute of Radio Astronomy of NASU, Kharkov, Ukraine*; BRIAN DROUIN, *Jet Propulsion Laboratory, California Institute of Technology, Pasadena, CA, USA*; STEPHAN SCHLEMMER, *I. Physikalisches Institut, Universität zu Köln, Köln, Germany*; CHRISTIAN ENDRES, *The Center for Astrochemical Studies, Max-Planck-Institut für extraterrestrische Physik, Garching, Germany.*

Rotational transitions belonging to the three lowest torsional states of dimethylether (DME), $(CH_3)_2O$, have been analyzed using the recently developed model for molecules with two equivalent methyl rotors and C_{2v} symmetry at equilibrium (PAM_C2v_2tops program) [1]. Significant progress in fitting transitions within the first and second excited torsional states of DME has been achieved and the comprehensive dataset has been reproduced within experimental accuracy by our fit. The dataset comprises not only assignments from the literature and previous measurement campaigns (ground state [2], torsional excited states [3,4]), but also new measurements. These new measurements have been carried out using the Kharkiv spectrometer in the Institute of Radio Astronomy of NASU (Ukraine) from 49 GHz to 180 GHz and from 255 GHz to 400 GHz. Details of the experimental dataset, its analysis and the fit will be discussed[a].

[1] V.V. Ilyushin, J.T. Hougen, J. Mol. Spectrosc. 289, pp.41-49, 2013.
[2] C. P. Endres, B. J. Drouin, J. C. Pearson et al. A&A 504, 635–640 (2009).
[3] C.P. Endres, H.S.P. Müller, F. Lewen, et al., 65th ISMS, 2010 abstract id. FC01.
[4] S.E. Bisshop, P. Schilke, F. Wyrowski, et al., A&A 552, A122, 19 (2013).

[a] This work was done under support of the Volkswagen foundation. The assistance of Science and Technology Center in Ukraine is acknowledged (STCU partner project P686a).

WH02 — 10:04 – 10:05

FAR-INFRARED AND MICROWAVE SPECTROSCOPY OF $HCOOCH_3$ II.

KAORI KOBAYASHI, AKIO ITOH, *Department of Physics, University of Toyama, Toyama, Japan*; MASAHARU FUJITAKE, *Division of Mathematical and Physical Sciences, Graduate School of Natural Science & Technology, Kanazawa University, Kanazawa, Japan*; NOBUKIMI OHASHI, , *Kanazawa University, Kanazawa, Japan*; DENNIS W. TOKARYK, *Department of Physics, University of New Brunswick, Fredericton, NB, Canada*; BRANT E. BILLINGHURST, *EFD, Canadian Light Source Inc., Saskatoon, Saskatchewan, Canada.*

The known interstellar molecule, methyl formate ($HCOOCH_3$) has been studied by microwave spectroscopy since 1959 [a]. The laboratory spectra of methyl formate exhibit many unassigned transitions that are due to rotational transitions in the low-lying vibrational excited states. The first torsional excited state was reported in 2003 [b], and up to the second torsional excited state was identified in laboratory and in space. [c] [d]

Our laboratory microwave spectra include a series of unknown K_a=0,1 transitions. Based on relative intensities, we estimate that these transitions arise from an excited state about 300 cm^{-1} above the ground state. To facilitate identification, we have taken spectra of methyl formate in the 260-370 cm^{-1} range at Far-Infrared Beamline of the Canadian Light Source synchrotron. The resolution was instrument-limited to 0.00096 cm^{-1}. The spectra were very dense, and included the overlapping ν_{12} (C-O-C deformation) and ν_{17} (C-O torsion) modes. Conventional assignment proved very difficult, so we calculated a-type K_a =0, and 1 rotation-vibration spectra based on the unknown and ground-state microwave data, and gave them arbitrary origins near 300 cm^{-1}. By correlating them with the far-infrared spectrum, we were able to determine that the new series correspond to ν_{12} near 312 cm^{-1}.[e] We will report on our assignment technique and results, as well as any further developments we have made in extending the assignments of both the microwave and far-infrared spectra.

[a] R. F. Curl, *J. Chem. Phys.* **30**, 1529 (1959).
[b] H. Odashima, K. Ogata, K. Takagi, & S. Tsunekawa, *Molecules* **8**, 139 (2003).
[c] S. Takano, Y. Sakai, S. Kakimoto, M. Sasaki, & K. Kobayashi, *Publ. Astron. Soc. Jpn.* **64**, 89 (2012).
[d] K. Kobayashi, K. Takamura, Y. Sakai, S. Tsunekawa, H. Odashima, & N. Ohashi, *Astrophys. J. Suppl. Ser.* **205**, 9 (2013) and references therein.
[e] K. Kobayashi, Y. Sakai, M. Fujitake, D. W. Tokaryk, B. E. Billinghurst & N. Ohashi, *Can. J. Phys.* **98**, 551 (2020).

WH03 **10:08 – 10:09**

MICROWAVE SPECTRUM OF ACETIC ACID: THE THIRD AND FOURTH EXCITED TORSIONAL STATES

V. ILYUSHIN, YAN BAKHMAT, OLGA DOROVSKAYA, E. A. ALEKSEEV, *Radiospectrometry Department, Institute of Radio Astronomy of NASU, Kharkov, Ukraine.*

We present the first study of the millimeter and submillimeter wave spectra of the third and fourth excited torsional states of acetic acid (CH_3COOH). New measurements have been carried out in the 149-183 GHz and 255-420 GHz ranges using the millimeter wave spectrometer in the Institute of Radio Astronomy of NASU (Ukraine). Already published data [1] were combined with the new measurements and fitted using the rho-axis-method torsion–rotation Hamiltonian and RAM36 code [2]. The current fit uses 109 parameters to give an overall weighted root-mean-square deviation of 2.1 for the dataset consisting of 34799 transitions (which due to blending correspond to 21773 measured line frequencies), among which 2663 and 1243 transitions correspond to the third and fourth excited torsional states of CH_3COOH, respectively. The new dataset also contains numerous intertorsional transitions (2407) including those involving energy levels from the third and fourth torsional excited states that are observed due to intensity borrowing via avoided crossing interactions that provide a direct measure of torsional energy spacings associated with torsional potential barrier. In the talk the details of the experimental dataset and analysis will be given[a].

[1] V. V. Ilyushin, C. P. Endres, F. Lewen, S. Schlemmer, B. J. Drouin J. Mol. Spectrosc. 290, pp. 31 - 41, 2013.

[2] V. Ilyushin, Z. Kisiel, L. Pszczółkowski, H. Mäder, J. T. Hougen, J. Mol. Spectrosc. 259, pp. 26-38, 2010.

[a]This work was done under support of the Volkswagen foundation. The assistance of Science and Technology Center in Ukraine is acknowledged (STCU partner project P756).

WH04 **10:12 – 10:13**

EXTENDING THE MILLIMETER/SUBMILLIMETER ROTATIONAL SPECTRUM OF GROUND STATE PYRUVIC ACID

CONNOR J. WRIGHT, *Department of Chemistry, University of Wisconsin-Madison, Madison, WI, USA*; JAY A KROLL, *Department of Chemistry and Biochemistry, University of Colorado, Boulder, CO, USA*; SUSANNA L. WIDICUS WEAVER, *Chemistry and Astronomy, University of Wisconsin-Madison, Madison, WI, USA.*

Pyruvic acid ($C_3H_4O_3$, or $HOOCOCCH_3$) is one of the main reactants in the Krebs Cycle of biological systems where sugar is metabolized and glucose is converted to lactic acid. Its presence in carbonaceous meteorites has already been confirmed, and its abiotic formation in experimental ice analogs implies the potential for exogenous delivery to planets via comets and asteroids. Therefore, it is important to have a complete experimental spectrum within the same wavelengths of astronomical telescopes to facilitate detections of pyruvic acid. Previous work on pyruvic acid reported the spectrum from 160 GHz to 314 GHz. At room temperature, these measurements only cover part of the Boltzmann peak. Additionally, with the spectral coverage now available at telescopes ranging up to and beyond 1 THz, measurements covering a significantly broader region of the molecular spectrum are required. Newly-developed experimental capabilities and sensitivities have since allowed for more sensitive measurement of the rotational transitions in this same wavelength regime and beyond. This work remeasures and extends the spectrum of pyruvic acid from 90 GHz up to 1 THz. Spectral prediction and fitting was conducted using the ERHAM program based on the previous work. Reanalysis using XIAM was then performed due to key advantages and disadvantages in each program. The results of the spectral study and analysis of pyruvic acid from 90 GHz to 1 THz will be presented.

WH05 **10:16 – 10:17**

LARGE AMPLITUDE TORSIONS IN NITROTOLUENE ISOMERS STUDIED BY ROTATIONAL SPECTROSCOPY AND QUANTUM CHEMISTRY CALCULATIONS

ANTHONY ROUCOU[a], *Laboratoire de Physico-Chimie de l'Atmosphère, Université du Littoral Côte d'Opale, Dunkerque, France*; MANUEL GOUBET, SABATH BTEICH, *UMR 8523 - PhLAM - Physique des Lasers Atomes et Molécules, University of Lille, CNRS, F-59000 Lille, France*; ISABELLE KLEINER, *Université Paris-Est Créteil et Université de Paris, Laboratoire Interuniversitaire des systèmes atmosphériques (LISA), CNRS UMR7583, Creteil, France*; ARNAUD CUISSET, *Laboratoire de Physico-Chimie de l'Atmosphère, Université du Littoral Côte d'Opale, Dunkerque, France.*

The monitoring of gas phase mononitrotoluenes is crucial for defence, civil security and environmental interests since they are used as taggant for TNT detection. Rotational spectra of the three isomers of nitrotoluene have been recorded at low and room temperatures using a supersonic jet Fourier Transform microwave (MW) spectrometer and a millimeter-wave frequency multiplier chain, respectively. Supported by quantum chemistry calculations, the spectral analysis of pure rotation lines in the vibrational ground state has allowed to characterise the rotational energy, the hyperfine structure due to the ^{14}N nucleus and the internal rotation splittings arising from the methyl group. An anisotropic internal rotation of coupled -CH_3 and -NO_2 torsional motions was identified for the ortho isomer by quantum chemistry calculations and discussed from the results of its MW analysis. The study of the internal rotation splittings in the spectra of three NT isomers allowed to characterise the internal rotation potentials of the methyl group and to compare them with other mono-substituted toluene derivatives in order to study the isomeric influence on the internal rotation barrier. [b, c]

[a]Present address: Institut de la Matière Condensée et des Nanosciences (IMCN), Université catholique de Louvain, Louvain-la-Neuve, Belgium
[b]Roucou *et al., CHEMPHYSCHEM,* **21(22), 2523-2538, (2020).**
[c]Roucou *et al., CHEMPHYSCHEM,* **19, 1056-1067, (2018).**

WH06 **10:20 – 10:21**

NEXT LEVEL ACHIEVEMENT OF THE *XIAM* CODE IN MODELING MICROWAVE SPECTRA OF MOLECULES WITH VERY LOW TORSIONAL BARRIERS

HA VINH LAM NGUYEN, *CNRS UMR 7583, Université Paris-Est Créteil, Université de Paris, Laboratoire Interuniversitaire des Systèmes Atmosphériques (LISA), Créteil, France*; SVEN HERBERS, K.P. RAJAPPAN NAIR, JENS-UWE GRABOW, *Institut für Physikalische Chemie und Elektrochemie, Gottfried-Wilhelm-Leibniz-Universität, Hannover, Germany.*

The *XIAM* code is one of the most frequently used programs to treat the microwave spectra of molecules with up to three methyl internal rotors. *XIAM* is user-friendly and fast, but often shows difficulties in dealing with low torsional barriers. An example is the case of *m*-methylanisole where the methyl group attached at the *meta*-position of the ring undergoes internal rotation with a barrier height of about 56 cm^{-1} for the *cis* conformer and 37 cm^{-1} for the *trans* conformer.[a] The standard deviation obtained with *XIAM* is much larger than the measurement accuracy for both conformers. Recently, the code has been modified, and two higher order effective parameters connected to the potential term $\cos(3\alpha)$ were implemented, which reduced the standard deviations of the fits to almost measurement accuracy.[b] The $XIAM_{mod}$ code also succeeded in modeling the microwave spectra of 3-fluorotoluene, 3,4-dimethylfluorotoluene,[c] and 4-methylacetophenone[d] with torsional barriers of 17 cm^{-1}, 32 cm^{-1}, and 22 cm^{-1}, respectively, to measurement accuracy.

[a]L. Ferres, W. Stahl, H.V.L. Nguyen, *J. Chem. Phys.* **148**, 124304 (2018).
[b]S. Herbers, H.V.L. Nguyen, *J. Mol. Spectrosc.* **370**, 111289 (2020).
[c]K.P.R. Nair, S. Herbers, H.V.L. Nguyen, J.-U. Grabow, *Spectro. Chim. Acta A* **242**, 118709 (2020).
[d]S. Herbers, S.M. Fritz, P. Mishra, H.V.L. Nguyen, T.S. Zwier, *J. Chem. Phys.* **152**, 074301 (2020).

WH07 **10:24 – 10:25**

INTERNAL ROTATION OF THE ACETYL METHYL GROUP IN METHYL ALKYL KETONES: THE MICROWAVE SPECTRUM OF OCTAN-2-ONE

MAIKE ANDRESEN, DAMIAN SCHOENGEN, *Institute for Physical Chemistry, RWTH Aachen University, Aachen, Germany*; ISABELLE KLEINER, MARTIN SCHWELL, *Université Paris-Est Créteil et Université de Paris, Laboratoire Interuniversitaire des systèmes atmosphériques (LISA), CNRS UMR7583, Creteil, France*; WOLFGANG STAHL, *Institute for Physical Chemistry, RWTH Aachen University, Aachen, Germany*; HA VINH LAM NGUYEN, *CNRS UMR 7583, Université Paris-Est Créteil, Université de Paris, Laboratoire Interuniversitaire des Systèmes Atmosphériques (LISA), Créteil, France.*

Methyl *n*-alkyl ketones form a class of molecules with interesting internal dynamics in the gas-phase. They contain two methyl groups undergoing internal rotations. To explore the link between structure and barrier heights in ketones, investigations on a series of saturated methyl *n*-alkyl ketones were performed, i.e. pentan-2-one[a] hexan-2-one[b], heptan-2-one[c] and octan-2-one[d]. The molecular jet Fourier-transform microwave spectrum of octan-2-one was recorded between 2.0 and 40.0 GHz, revealing two conformers, one with C_1 and one with C_s symmetry. The barriers to internal rotation of the acetyl methyl group were determined to be 233.340(28) cm^{-1} and 185.3490(81) cm^{-1}, respectively, confirming the link between conformation and barrier height already established for other methyl alkyl ketones. The study combined high level *ab initio* calculations with experimentally dervived rotational and torsional parameters using the XIAM[e] and BELGI-C_1 (or BELGI-C_s)[f] codes. Results from the various fits will be presented. Finally comparisons to molecules in the literature and structural aspects of the conformers generally observed in methyl *n*-alkyl ketones will be reviewed.

---

[a]M. Andresen, I. Kleiner, M. Schwell, W. Stahl, H. V. L. Nguyen, J. Phys. Chem. A 2018, 122, 7071-7078
[b]M. Andresen, I. Kleiner, M. Schwell, W. Stahl, H. V. L. Nguyen, ChemPhysChem 2019, 20, 2063-2073
[c]M. Andresen, I. Kleiner, M. Schwell, W. Stahl, H. V. L. Nguyen, J. Phys. Chem. A 2020, 124, 1353-1361.
[d]M. Andresen, D. Schöngen, I. Kleiner, M. Schwell, W. Stahl, H. V. L. Nguyen, ChemPhysChem 2020, 21, 2206-2216
[e]H. Hartwig, H. Dreizler, Z. Naturforsch. 1996, 51a, 923-932
[f]I. Kleiner, J. T. Hougen, J. Chem. Phys. 2003, 119, 5505-5509.

WH08 **10:28 – 10:29**

COMBINATION OF IODINE QUADRUPOLE COUPLING AND ESSENTIALLY FREE METHYL INTERNAL ROTATION IN 3-IODOTOLUENE

JOSHUA A. SIGNORE, *Department of Chemistry, Wesleyan University, Middletown, CT, USA*; HA VINH LAM NGUYEN, *CNRS UMR 7583, Université Paris-Est Créteil, Université de Paris, Laboratoire Interuniversitaire des Systèmes Atmosphériques (LISA), Créteil, France*; WALLACE C. PRINGLE, *Department of Chemistry, Wesleyan University, Middletown, CT, USA*; S. A. COOKE, *Natural and Social Science, Purchase College SUNY, Purchase, NY, USA*; STEWART E. NOVICK, *Department of Chemistry, Wesleyan University, Middletown, CT, USA.*

Quadrupole coupling of an iodine nucleus with its coupling constants in the GHz order has always been a challenge in microwave spectroscopy. Methyl internal rotations with very low torsional barriers also often complicate the spectral analysis and modeling.[a] Here, we present the microwave spectrum of a molecule combining the two effects, 3-iodotoluene, observed using a Balle-Flygare Fourier transform microwave spectrometer. The A torsional state including the iodine hyperfine structure has been successfully assigned and fitted utilizing Pickett's *SPFIT/SPCAT*.[b] As expected, the assignment of E torsional state lines has been proven quite challenging due to the extremely low barrier to internal rotation in presence of the iodine hyperfine patterns. Currently, a tentative E state assignment exists and is checked by a separate fit which includes the odd power parameters D_a and D_b (multiplying the P_a and P_b operators) and their higher order parameters in the Hamiltonian. We believe that this is the first microwave report that investigates a molecular species possessing a very low barrier to internal rotation with an iodine embedded in its molecular framework.

---

[a]H.V.L. Nguyen and I. Kleiner, *Phys. Sci. Rev.* DOI: 10.1515/psr-2020-0037, in press.
[b]H.M. Pickett, *J. Mol. Spectrosc.* **148**, 371 (1991).

WH09 **10:32 – 10:33**

STRUCTURE AND DYNAMICS OF METHACRYLAMIDE

ASSIMO MARIS, SONIA MELANDRI, LUCA EVANGELISTI, *Dipartimento di Chimica G. Ciamician, Università di Bologna, Bologna, Italy*; CAMILLA CALABRESE, *Departamento de Química Física, Universidad del País Vasco (UPV-EHU), Bilbao, Spain.*

Methacrylamide (CH_2=C(CH_3)-$CONH_2$) is formed by an allyl non-polar frame and an amide polar frame connected by a rotatable bond. Despite the relatively reduced size of the molecule, the presence of four nearby functional groups causes complex internal dynamics. The underlying conformational space has been explored by quantum mechanical modeling and surveyed with millimeter-wave rotational spectroscopy using a Stark-modulated free-jet absorption spectrometer, in the 59.6-104 GHz frequency range. According to the relative orientation of the two unsaturated bonds (defined by the dihedral angle τ, C=C-C=O), two conformers were observed, namely s-$trans$ and s-cis. In the s-cis form, the methylene and carbonyl groups lie on the same side and the overall symmetry is C_s ($\tau = 0°$), whereas s-$trans$-methacrylamide consists of two equivalent non-planar minima ($\tau = \pm 151°$), which are enantiomers and are separated by a low energy barrier corresponding to a planar skeletal arrangement ($\tau = 180°$). From relative intensity measurements, s-cis-methacrylamide is estimated to lie 4(2) kJ mol^{-1} above s-$trans$-methacrylamide. The rotational spectra are characterized by a complex hyperfine structure which allowed the determination of the methyl internal rotation barrier and the ^{14}N nuclear quadrupole coupling constants for both conformers. Moreover, the tunneling spliting related to the double minimum potential of s-$trans$-methacrylamide was determined. A one-dimensional flexible model of the vibro-rotational interaction suggests that the corresponding interconversion barrier is about 2.4 kJ mol^{-1} and the first torsional quantum state lies 55 cm^{-1} above the ground state.

WH10 **10:36 – 10:37**

THE EFFECTS OF PROTON TUNNELLING, ^{14}N QUADRUPOLE COUPLING, AND METHYL INTERNAL ROTATIONS OF PLANAR SECONDARY AMINES

KENNETH J KOZIOL, WOLFGANG STAHL, *Institute for Physical Chemistry, RWTH Aachen University, Aachen, Germany*; HA VINH LAM NGUYEN, *CNRS UMR 7583, Université Paris-Est Créteil, Université de Paris, Laboratoire Interuniversitaire des Systèmes Atmosphériques (LISA), Créteil, France.*

The rotational spectra of three planar secondary amines diethylamine[a], ethylmethylamine[b] and dimethylamine[c] have been investigated. The hydrogen atom of the amino group performs an inversion tunnelling motion, causing splittings of all c-type transitions into doublets. The respective values of the splittings are 1521.54134(40) MHz[b] 1980.9176(62) MHz[c] and 2646.0 MHz[d]. The first microwave spectra of dimethylamine and ethylmethylamine have been recorded in 1967 and 1973[d], respectively, using Stark modulated spectrometers with a resolution of 25 kHz. The ^{14}N quadrupole hyperfine structure was reported to be resolved only for some transitions and the effects of internal rotation have not been mentioned.

In the present work, the spectra of N-ethylmethylamine and dimethylamine were remeasured using two molecular jet Fourier transform microwave spectrometers operating from 2 to 40 GHz. The proton tunnelling was analysed, taking into account Coriolis interactions which cause splittings in the order of about 0.2 to 1.2 MHz for all b-type transitions. Furthermore, hyperfine splittings due to the quadrupole coupling of the ^{14}N nucleus were fully resolved. The quadrupole coupling constants χ_{aa} and $\chi_{bb} - \chi_{cc}$ were determined with high accuracy and calculated well using Bailey's method[e]. Due to the difference in symmetry between ethylmethylamine and dimethylamine, quartets and triplets with splittings in the order of 150 kHz and 200 kHz, respectively, arising from internal rotations of two methyl groups, could be resolved. We observed that large amplitude motions such as internal rotation and/or proton tunnelling influence(s) the hyperfine patterns. Quantum chemical calculations carried out to support the experiment.

[a]H. V. L. Nguyen and W Stahl, *J. Chem. Phys.* **135**, 024310 (2011)
[b]K. J. Koziol, W. Stahl, H. V. L. Nguyen, *J. Chem. Phys* **153**, 184308 (2020)
[c]J. E. Wollrab and V. W. Laurie, *J. Chem. Phys.* **48**, 5058 (1968)
[d]R. E. Penn and J. E. Boggs, *J. Mol. Spectrosc.* **47**, 340 (1973)
[e]W. C. Bailey, *Chem. Phys.* **252**, 57, (2000)

WH11 **10:40 – 10:41**

ACCURATE TORSIONAL BARRIER HEIGHT OF TRIFLUROACETIC ACID

LUYAO ZOU, R. A. MOTIYENKO, L. MARGULÈS, *UMR 8523 CNRS - Université de Lille, Laboratoire PhLAM, Villeneuve d'Ascq, France.*

Trifluoroacetic acid (TFA, $CF_3C(O)OH$) is the final degradation product of many hydrochlorofluorocarbons (HCFCs), hydrofluorocarbons (HFCs), and hydrofluoroolifines (HFOs) in the troposphere. While a recent assessment of the TFA impact on the health of humans and the environment shows that its concentration is too small to be a risk, TFA still warrants continued attention, in part because of its very long environmental lifetime.[a] The ultimate sink of TFA is in surface waters in which it forms salts that are extremely stable and are likely to have half-lives of centuries. From the spectroscopic point of view, TFA is an interesting case of the internal rotation of a heavy C_{3v} top. The presence of the CF_3 internal rotor leads to relatively strong coupling between internal and overall rotation, $\rho = 0.68$. However, owing to the high mass of the top, the tunneling probability is low; the $A - E$ splittings are hardly observable in the rotational spectrum, despite relatively low barrier of about 230 cm^{-1}. In the previous studies, the splittings were observed only in the $v_t = 4$ excited torsional state,[b] and were not observed in the ground state using molecular beam Fourier transform microwave spectroscopy which typical resolution is few kHz.[c] We present new global analysis of the rotational spectrum of TFA using the rho axis method and RAM36 code. The rotational spectrum of TFA was recorded in the range from 50 to 330 GHz. The joint analysis of the v_t = 0, 1, and 2 states resulted in accurate determination of the V_3 and V_6 potential energy terms, 230.36(92) cm^{-1} and -4.736(82) cm^{-1} respectively. However, the potential energy terms are strongly correlated with the intrenal rotation constant F that is kept fixed in the fit. Up to now no $A - E$ splittings were observed in the Doppler-limited resolution spectra. The analysis will be extended to $v_t = 3$ and $v_t = 4$ states in which we expect to observe the splittings that will permit to remove the correlation between V and F terms. The latest results will be presented.

The present work was funded by the French ANR Labex CaPPA through the PIA contract ANR-11-LABX-0005-01

[a] Solomon, K. R., *et al.*, 2016, *J. Toxicol. Env. Health B*, **19**, 289.
[b] Stolwijk, W. M. and van Eijck, B. P., 1985, *J. Mol. Spec.*, **113**, 196.
[c] Antolinez, S., *et al.*, 1999, *Z. Naturforsch. A*, **54**, 524.

WI. Mini-symposium: Precision Spectroscopy for Fundamental Physics

Wednesday, June 23, 2021 – 10:0 AM

Room: 2021 Online Everywhere

Chair: Benoit Darquie, Laboratoire de Physique des Lasers, Villetaneuse, France

WI01 *INVITED TALK* **10:00 – 10:02**

PRECISION MEASUREMENTS IN FEW-ELECTRON ATOMS AND MOLECULES

FREDERIC MERKT, *Laboratorium für Physikalische Chemie, ETH Zurich, Zurich, Switzerland.*

Few-electron molecules are attractive systems for precision spectroscopy because their properties can be calculated with high accuracy by quantum-chemical methods (1-5). The measurements serve to test theoretical predictions, ideally at the level where their accuracy is limited by the uncertainties of the fundamental constants or by unrecognized physical effects. I will report on precision measurements of energy intervals in cold samples of He, H_2 and He_2. In particular, we determine their ionization energies with a precision ($\Delta\nu/\nu$) of 10^{-10} from high-resolution Rydberg spectra (6-8), approaching the level where uncertainties in the size of the nuclei and the nuclear-to-electron mass ratios would limit the accuracy of otherwise exact calculations and calibration requires the use of primary frequency standards. Comparison will be made to recent theoretical results in the context of more-than-100-year-long experimental and theoretical efforts invested in the accurate determination of the properties of fundamental few-electron atoms and molecules.

1.V. I. Korobov, L. Hilico and J.-P. Karr, Phys. Rev. Lett. 118, 23, 001 (2017). 2.M. Puchalski, J. Komasa, P. Czachorowski, and K. Pachucki, Phys. Rev. Lett. 122, 103003 (2019). 3.D. Ferenc, V. I. Korobov and E. Mátyus, Phys. Rev. Lett. 125, 213001 (2020). 4.V. A. Yerokhin, V. Patkóš, M. Puchalski, and K. Pachucki, Phys. Rev. A 102, 012807 (2020) 5.P. Danev, D. Balakov, V. I. Korobov, S. Schiller, Phys. Rev. A 103, 012805 (2021) 6.M. Beyer, N. Hölsch, J. A. Agner, J. Deiglmayr, H. Schmutz and F. Merkt, Phys. Rev. A 97, 012501 (2018). 7.N. Hölsch, M. Beyer, E. J. Salumbides, K. S. E. Eikema, W. Ubachs, Ch. Jungen, and F. Merkt, Phys. Rev. Lett. 122, 103002 (2019). 8.L. Semeria, P. Jansen, G.-M. Camenisch, F. Mellini, H. Schmutz, and F. Merkt, Phys. Rev. Lett. 124, 213001 (2020).

WI02 **10:08 – 10:09**

MEASUREMENTS OF np–2s TRANSITIONS IN THE HYDROGEN ATOM

SIMON SCHEIDEGGER, JOSEF A. AGNER, HANSJÜRG SCHMUTZ, FRÉDÉRIC MERKT, *Laboratorium für Physikalische Chemie, ETH Zurich, Zurich, Switzerland.*

Precision experiments in the hydrogen atom have a long tradition and extensive studies of transitions between low lying $n \leq 12$ states were carried out [a] [b] [c] [d] [e] [f]. These measurements can be used to determine values of the Rydberg constant and the proton charge radius. We present a new experimental approach to perform measurements of transition frequencies between the metastable 2s $^2S_{1/2}(F = 0, 1)$ state of H and highly excited Rydberg states with principal quantum number $n \geq 23$. We generate the hydrogen atoms by photodissociation of NH_3 in a capillary mounted at the orifice of a pulsed valve. The hydrogen atoms are entrained in supersonic expansions of a rare gas. The atoms enter a magnetically shielded region in which they are photoexcited to a specific hyperfine level of the metastable 2s $^2S_{1/2}$ state by a home-built frequency-tripled Fourier-transform-limited pulsed titanium sapphire laser (pulse length 40 ns). Transitions to np Rydberg states are then induced by a narrow-band frequency-doubled continuous-wave titanium sapphire laser, which is phase locked to an optically stabilized frequency comb and referenced to a Cs primary frequency standard. The highly excited Rydberg states are detected by pulsed-field ionization. We will report progress on our efforts to minimize uncertainties from stray electric fields and Doppler shifts and to obtain spectral lines with a FWHM below 10 MHz.

---

[a] J. C. Garreau *et al.*, J. Phys. France **51**, 2293 (1990).
[b] C. G. Parthey *et al.*, Phys. Rev. Lett. **107**, 203001 (2011)
[c] A. Beyer *et al.*, Science **358**, 79 (2017)
[d] H. Fleurbaey *et al.*, Phys. Rev. Lett. **120**, 183001 (2018)
[e] N. Bezginov *et al.*, Science **365**, 1007 (2019)
[f] A. Grinin *et al.*, Science **370**, 1061 (2020)

WI03 **10:12 – 10:13**

DETERMINATION OF THE IONIZATION ENERGY OF THE METASTABLE 2 $^1S_0$ STATE OF ^4He THROUGH RYDBERG-SERIES EXTRAPOLATION

GLORIA CLAUSEN, PAUL JANSEN, JOSEF A. AGNER, HANSJÜRG SCHMUTZ, FRÉDÉRIC MERKT, *Laboratorium für Physikalische Chemie, ETH Zurich, Zurich, Switzerland.*

Helium, as one of the simplest few-electron atoms, is well suited to test fundamental interactions and QED calculations with a high precision. Its importance is underlined by recent advances in the determination of particle properties such as the α-particle charge radius[a]. Yet, the most accurate theoretical[b,c] and experimental[d,e] data on the ionization energies of the low-lying electronic states show a significant discrepancy of more than 2 σ (about 3 MHz). We report on the determination of the ionization energy of the metastable 2 $^1S_0$ state of helium through Rydberg-series extrapolation with a relative uncertainty of 5×10^{-11} through the determination of 20 different np $\leftarrow$ 2 $^1S_0$ transition frequencies in the range of n from 24 to 102, yielding quantum-defect parameters for the np Rydberg states. A one-photon excitation scheme was employed, using the frequency-doubled output of a narrowband cw laser source (312 nm), calibrated to a frequency comb referenced to a GPS-disciplined Rb clock. The major sources of systematic uncertainties are minimized by (i) carrying out the experiment in a doubly skimmed, pulsed supersonic beam of metastable ^4He atoms to minimize the Doppler broadening, (ii) compensating electric stray fields to below 0.7 mV/cm, and (iii) cancelling the first-order Doppler shift by monitoring two Doppler components resulting from two counter-propagating laser beams. The effects of residual stray electric fields are included as DC-Stark shifts in the analysis. Our new value of the ionization energy of the 2 $^1S_0$ state of ^4He, with an absolute uncertainty better than 50 kHz, represents an improvement by a factor of about five in precision. It also allows for a purely experimental determination of the ionization energies of several other low-lying electronic states of ^4He, which were previously only accurately known through combination of measured and theoretical energy intervals.

[a]J. Krauth et al., Nature 589, 527531 (2021)
[b]K. Pachucki, V. Patkóš, and V. A. Yerokhin, Physical Review A 95, 062510 (2017)
[c]G. W. Drake and Z. C. Yan, Canadian Journal of Physics 86, 45 (2008)
[d]W. Lichten, D. Shiner, and Z.-X. Zhou, Physical Review A 43, 1663 (1991)
[e]C. J. Sansonetti and J. D. Gillaspy, Physical Review A 45, R1 (1992)

WI04 **10:16 – 10:17**

PHOTOLYSIS PRODUCTION AND PRECISION MEASUREMENT OF THE HIGHEST VIBRATIONAL STATES (v = 14) AND QUASI-BOUND RESONANCES IN $X^1\Sigma_g^+$ H_2

KIN FUNG LAI, MAXIMILIAN BEYER, EDCEL JOHN SALUMBIDES, WIM UBACHS, *Department of Physics and Astronomy, VU University , Amsterdam, Netherlands.*

Highly excited rovibrational states of H_2 in the X $^1\Sigma_g^+$ electronic ground state are prepared by two-photon photolysis of H_2S [1]. The highest vibrational levels $v = 14, J = 0 - 4$, with a dissociation energy of less than 100 cm^{-1}, and some long-lived quasi-bound resonances (v, J) = (7,21), (8,19), (9,17), and (10,15) are probed through Doppler-free two-photon spectroscopy of F $^1\Sigma_g^+$ - X $^1\Sigma_g^+$ transitions. By compensating AC-Stark shifts, absolute transition frequencies were determined with an accuracy on the order of 90 MHz. From combination differences of the F-X transitions the energy level splittings in the electronic ground state are determined and compared with *ab initio* calculations, including relativistic and QED effects. This study extends precision test of QED theory for the electronic ground state of the hydrogen molecule to the very highest bound level, and into the quasi-bound region.

[1] K.-F. Lai, M. Beyer, E.J.Salumbides, W. Ubachs, Photolysis production and spectroscopic investigation of the highest vibrational states in H2 ($X^1\Sigma_g^+$ $v = 13, 14$), J. Phys. Chem. A 125, 1221-1228 (2021)

WI05 **10:20 – 10:21**

IONIZATION ENERGIES OF PARA-H_2 FROM ZERO-QUANTUM-DEFECT POSITIONS

NICOLAS HÖLSCH, FRÉDÉRIC MERKT, *Laboratorium für Physikalische Chemie, ETH Zurich, Zurich, Switzerland.*

From the precise measurement of the ionization energy of H_2 its dissociation energy can be determined[a], which serves as a benchmark quantity for QED calculations[b]. Additionally, measurements of ionization energies corresponding to higher rovibrational levels of the ion enable the determination of rovibrational intervals in H_2^+[c]. These intervals can be calculated extremely precisely for one-electron systems, offering the prospect of improving the value of fundamental constants[d].

Until now, the most precise determinations of the ionization energies of molecular hydrogen have relied on the extrapolation of Rydberg series using multichannel quantum-defect theory (MQDT) and quantum defects extracted from high-precision measurements of Rydberg-Rydberg transitions using millimeter-wave (mmW) spectroscopy[e]. The uncertainty of these extrapolations are typically larger than 500 kHz, currently representing the dominant source of uncertainty in the determinations of ionization energies. Additionally, autoionization lifetimes impede mmW measurements above the lowest ionization threshold which renders accurate extrapolations to higher rovibrational levels of the ion difficult.

We present here a method to determine the binding energies of Rydberg states without having to resort to an extrapolation using MQDT. We carry out precision measurements of the linear Stark manifolds associated with near-degenerate high-l states by mmW spectroscopy in the presence of intentionally applied electric fields. Extrapolating the linear Stark manifold to zero field yields accurate values of the zero-quantum-defect positions, given by $-\mathcal{R}_{\mathrm{H}_2}/n^2$ relative to the ionization thresholds. This method will be illustrated for Rydberg states of H_2 above $n = 50$, circumventing the current bottlenecks and opening the route for order-of-magnitude improved ionization energies.

[a] N. Hölsch, M. Beyer, E.J. Salumbides, K.S.E. Eikema, W. Ubachs, Ch. Jungen, and F. Merkt, Phys. Rev. Lett., 122(10), 103003 (2019)
[b] M. Puchalski, J. Komasa, P. Czachorowski, and K. Pachucki, Phys. Rev. Lett., 122(10), 103003 (2019)
[c] C. Haase, M. Beyer, Ch. Jungen, and F. Merkt, J. Chem. Phys. 142(6), 064310 (2015)
[d] I.V. Kortunov, S. Alighanbari, M.G. Hansen, G.S. Giri, V.I. Korbov, and S. Schiller, Nat. Phys., 1-5 (2021)
[e] D. Sprecher, Ch. Jungen, and F. Merkt, J. Chem. Phys. 140, 104303:1-18 (2014)

WI06 **10:24 – 10:25**

PRECISION MEASUREMENT OF THE IONIZATION AND DISSOCIATION ENERGIES OF THE DEUTERIUM MOLECULE

JOËL HUSSELS, *Department of Physics and Astronomy, VU University , Amsterdam, Netherlands*; NICOLAS HÖLSCH, *Laboratorium für Physikalische Chemie, ETH Zurich, Zurich, Switzerland*; MAXIMILIAN BEYER, EDCEL JOHN SALUMBIDES, *Department of Physics and Astronomy, VU University , Amsterdam, Netherlands*; CHRISTIAN JUNGEN, *Department of Physics and Astronomy, University College London, London, UK*; FRÉDÉRIC MERKT, *Laboratorium für Physikalische Chemie, ETH Zurich, Zurich, Switzerland*; WIM UBACHS, *Department of Physics and Astronomy, VU University , Amsterdam, Netherlands.*

The hydrogen molecule is an important system for the development of molecular quantum mechanics. In particular, the dissociation energy is a benchmark quantity for ab initio calculations. Latest calculations including nonadiabatic QED corrections can now reach a precision of better than 1 MHz for the dissociation energy of molecular hydrogen (M. Puchalski et. al, Phys. Rev. Lett. 121, 073001 (2018)), opening up the prospect of contributing to the more accurate determination of the proton charge radius, if validated experimentally.

We present a spectroscopic determination of the ionization and dissociation energies of D_2 with an uncertainty below 1 MHz by combining separate measurements of the intervals between the X and GK states, and the GK and high-nf Rydberg states with MQDT-assisted extrapolation to the ionization limit.

The X-GK interval is measured by Doppler-free two-photon spectroscopy using 178 nm radiation, generated by frequency up-conversion using a KBBF crystal. The laser pulses are generated in a seeded, chirp-compensated, Ti:Sa oscillator-amplifier system where the seed is a Ti:Sa laser at 714 nm locked to a frequency comb. The GK-nf Rydberg state intervals are measured in a resonant three-photon excitation scheme, using pulsed VUV and VIS lasers to reach the intermediate GK state and a single-mode continuous-wave (cw) Ti:Sa laser for transitions to nf Rydberg states. The frequency of the cw laser was calibrated with a frequency comb referenced to an atomic clock. To reach an accuracy below 1 MHz, AC- and DC-Stark effects, as well as first- and second-order Doppler effects are analyzed and compensated.

WI07 **10:28 – 10:29**

PRECISE MEASUREMENT OF A FUNDAMENTAL VIBRATIONAL TRANSITION FREQUENCY IN HD

ARTHUR FAST, SAMUEL MEEK, *Precision Infrared Spectroscopy on Small Molecules, Max Planck Institute for Biophysical Chemistry, Göttingen, Germany.*

Precise measurements of vibrational transition frequencies in the isotopes of molecular hydrogen can provide a sensitive probe of fundamental physics. Because these transitions can be predicted with high-level *ab-initio* theory, comparisons between theory and experiment can be used to test quantum electrodynamics, search for new physics, and determine the nucleon-electron mass ratios more precisely. In this talk, I will present our measurement of the $1-0$ R(0) transition frequency in hydrogen deuteride (HD) using infrared-ultraviolet double resonance spectroscopy in a pulsed supersonic molecular beam.[a] HD molecules in the $v = 0$, $J = 0$ state are excited to $v = 1$, $J = 1$ using a tunable infrared laser stabilized to an optical frequency comb, and the excitation efficiency is determined by state-selectively ionizing the vibrationally-excited molecules using a pulsed UV laser. We have determined the absolute frequency of the transition with an uncertainty of 13 kHz (0.12 ppb relative uncertainty), limited primarily by the first order Doppler shift. Improvements in the compensation of this shift should make it possible to reduce the uncertainty by another order of magnitude.

[a] A. Fast and S. A. Meek., Phys. Rev. Lett. 125, 023001 (2020)

WI08 **10:32 – 10:33**

SUB-DOPPLER FREQUENCY METROLOGY IN HD FOR TESTS OF FUNDAMENTAL PHYSICS

FRANK M.J. COZIJN, MEISSA DIOUF, EDCEL JOHN SALUMBIDES, WIM UBACHS, *Department of Physics and Astronomy, VU University , Amsterdam, Netherlands.*

Molecular hydrogen has evolved into a benchmark quantum test system as highly accurate measurements can challenge the most accurate theoretical calculations, which allows for various tests of fundamental physics. Especially the rovibrational splitting serves as an excellent probe to put constraints on the strengths of putative fifth forces in nature.

Recent Doppler-free measurements in the (2,0) overtone band of the hydrogen deuteride molecule provided an ongoing stimulating debate on how to interpret the unusual line-shapes. The obtained saturated spectra differ significantly from an ordinary Lamb-dip, or even manifest itself as a 'Lamb-peak' for the P(1) line.

Here we present an overview of our latest work on the hydrogen deuteride molecule to provide insight in this conundrum. Doppler-free measurements were obtained with our frequency comb referenced NICE-OHMS spectrometer and carefully compared with numerical optical Bloch simulations to extract an accurate prediction of the hyperfineless transition frequency. This shows that levels of accuracy and resolution are reached where the hyperfine contribution cannot be neglected for accurate determination of rovibrational transitions in the hydrogen deuteride molecule and is the origin of the distinctively shaped Lamb-dips and peaks [a,b,c].

[a] F.M.J. Cozijn *et al.*, Sub-Doppler frequency metrology in HD for tests of fundamental physics, *Phys. Rev. Lett.* **120**, 153002 (2018)

[b] M.L. Diouf *et al.*, Lamb-dips and Lamb-peaks in the saturation spectrum of HD, *Opt. Lett.* **44**, 4733 (2019)

[c] M.L. Diouf *et al.*, Lamb-peak spectrum of the HD (2-0) P(1) line, *Phys. Rev. Res.* **2**, 023209 (2020)

WI09 **10:36 – 10:37**

COMB-CALIBRATED NONLINEAR SPECTROSCOPY OF THE Q(1) 1-0 LINE OF MOLECULAR HYDROGEN

MARCO LAMPERTI, *Department of Physics, Politecnico di Milano, Lecco, Italy*; LUCILE RUTKOWSKI, *IPR (Institut de Physique de Rennes)-UMR 6251, Univ Rennes, CNRS, Rennes, France*; DANIELE RONCHETTI, DAVIDE GATTI, RICCARDO GOTTI, *Department of Physics - Institute of Photonics and Nanotechnology, Politecnico di Milano, Lecco, Italy*; GIULIO CERULLO, *Dipartimento di Fisica, Politecnico di Milano, Milano, Italy*; FRANCK THIBAULT, *CNRS, IPR (Institut de Physique de Rennes) - UMR 6251, Univ Rennes, F-35000 Rennes, France*; HUBERT JÓŹWIAK, SZYMON WOJTEWICZ, PIOTR MASLOWSKI, PIOTR WCISLO, *Institute of Physics, Faculty of Physics, Astronomy and Informatics, Nicolaus Copernicus University, Torun, Poland*; DARIO POLLI, MARCO MARANGONI, *Dipartimento di Fisica, Politecnico di Milano, Milano, Italy.*

Molecular hydrogen is the subject of intensive theoretical and experimental studies because of its relevance to benchmark quantum electrodynamics models. We report an accurate study of the Q(1) 1-0 line of H_2 through a nonlinear spectroscopy setup based on Stimulated Raman Scattering (SRS) and comb calibration of the frequency axis. Systematic uncertainties affecting the apparatus, mainly due to pointing instabilities of pump and Stokes beams and to temperature drifts of the gas cell, have been reduced to about 200 kHz, which is comparable to statistical and systematic errors expected from the global fitting of multi-pressure SRS spectra. We performed measurements over two decades of pressure, from 0.05 to 5 bar, using low-pressure spectra to extrapolate the transition frequency of the isolated molecule, and high-pressure spectra to test collisional lineshape models. Our results are likely to be of relevance for a deeper understanding of H_2 physics and for bringing theory-vs-experiment comparison on the Q(1) 1-0 line-centre frequency below 1 MHz.

WI10 **10:40 – 10:41**

A WIDELY TUNABLE HIGH-POWER CONTINUOUS-WAVE OPTICAL PARAMETRIC OSCILLATOR (CW-OPO) SYSTEM FOR MID-INFRARED SPECTROSCOPY AND FREQUENCY METROLOGY

HAMZEH TELFAH, *Department of Chemistry, University of Louisville, Louisville, KY, USA*; S M SHAH RIYADH, *Department of physics and astronomy, University Of Louisville, Louisville, KY, USA*; JINJUN LIU, *Department of Chemistry, University of Louisville, Louisville, KY, USA*; DAVID B. FOOTE, WALTER HURLBUT, MATTHEW J. CICH, *TOPTICA Photonics, Inc, Farmington, NY, USA*; ULRICH EISMANN, *TOPTICA Photonics, Inc, Munich , Bavaria, Germany*; ADAM HEINIGER, CHRIS HAIMBERGER, *TOPTICA Photonics, Inc, Farmington, NY, USA.*

Continuous-wave optical parametric oscillators (CW-OPOs) can offer broad tuning with high resolution and high power in the mid-infrared (MIR) and have many important potential applications in precision spectroscopy. The widely tunable cw-OPO system (TOPO) developed by TOPTICA Photonics is capable of covering the wavelength range of 1.45-4.0 μm (with a degenerate gap between 2.07-2.19 μm) without optics or nonlinear optical crystal exchanges. A computer-controlled automation system has been developed to achieve a broad (up to 300 GHz) mode-hop-free (MHF) tuning range of the idler wavelengths and high output power (>1 W). Its narrow linewidth is demonstrated in the direct absorption measurements and the Doppler-free saturated absorption spectroscopy of atmospheric molecules. Furthermore, a much-improved frequency accuracy has been achieved by referencing the OPO to a frequency comb and creating a phase-coherent bridge between the NIR and MIR spectral ranges. Frequency noise from both the OPO cavity and the seed laser is eliminated by (i) beating the OPO signal output against the fundamental of the frequency comb and (ii) beating the seed laser against a 1064 nm comb extension. The TOPO system has been incorporated in the MIR cavity ring-down (CRD) system and the CRD-based two-photon spectroscopy system in our lab.

WI11 **10:44 – 10:45**

NARROW LINEWIDTH OPO LIGHT SOURCE FOR PRECISION SPECTROSCOPY

ZITAN ZHANG, CUNFENG CHENG, YU ROBERT SUN, SHUI-MING HU, *Hefei National Laboratory for Physical Science at Microscale, University of Science and Technology of China, Hefei, China.*

Precision spectroscopy of fundamental bands of molecules in the mid-infrared (MIR) region is of great interest in applications of trace detection and testing fundamental physics, where high-power and narrow-linewidth MIR lasers are needed. By controlling the phase noise of the signal and pump light of a continuous wave optical parametric oscillator (OPO), we established a broadly tunable MIR light source which has an output power of several hundred milliwatts and a linewidth of a few tens kilohertz. The long term frequency drift of the MIR laser was reduced and calibrated utilizing a near-infrared optical frequency comb. The performance of the light source was investigated and the laser system will be used for precision measurement of fundamental vibration of HD.

WI12 **10:48 – 10:49**

PRECISE FREQUENCY MEASUREMENTS OF THE $2\nu_3$ A_1 - ν_3 BAND TRANSITIONS OF METHANE WITH COMB-REFERENCED INFRARED-INFRARED DOUBLE-RESONANCE

HIROYUKI SASADA[a], *Department of Physics, Faculty of Science and Technology, Keio University, Yokohama, Japan*; SHO OKUBO, HAJIME INABA, *National Metrology Institute of Japan (NMIJ), Ntional Institute of Advanced Industrial Science and Technology (AIST), Tsukuba, Japan*; SHOKO OKUDA, *Department of Physics, Faculty of Science and Technology, Keio University, Yokohama, Japan.*

We have carried out infrared-infrared double-resonance spectroscopy of the $2\nu_3$ A_1 - ν_3 band of methane. The ν_3 band transitions are pumped using a 90.5 THz difference-frequency-generation (DFG) source frequency-controlled with an optical frequency comb (OFC), and ten tetrahedral components of the Q(1) to Q(4) transitions from the pumped levels are observed with a half-width at half maximum of 0.43 MHz using another 88.5 THz DFG source. The transition frequencies are determined with an uncertainty of 10 kHz using the OFC.

[a]National Metrology Insitute of Japan (NMIJ)

WI13 **10:52 – 10:53**

COMB-LOCKED CAVITY RING-DOWN SPECTROSCOPY FOR MOLECULAR TRANSITION FREQUENCY MEASUREMENTS BELOW 10^{-12} RELATIVE UNCERTAINTY

ZACHARY REED, DAVID A. LONG, HELENE FLEURBAEY, JOSEPH T. HODGES, *Material Measurement Laboratory, National Institute of Standards and Technology, Gaithersburg, MD, USA.*

The accurate determination of molecular transition frequencies can provide stringent tests and constraints on fundamental physics questions [1-3]. Here, we present recent work on a comb-locked cavity ring-down spectroscopy system which probes Doppler-broadened spectra in the linear absorption regime. These measurements have relative uncertainties in transition frequency below 10^{-12}, which are among the lowest values reported for optical molecular transition frequencies.

We use a probe laser which is phase-locked to a commercial optical frequency comb and subsequently coupled to a high-finesse optical cavity based on that of [4]. We observe stationary measurement statistics for measurements of more than 2000 spectra and find that measurements which are replicated in multiple experiments over several months are normally distributed. Single-spectrum signal-to-noise-ratios can exceed 50,000:1, with resulting line center uncertainties below 5 kHz. Because this method is based on linear absorption, it is an attractive alternative for the measurement of molecular transitions that cannot be probed by saturation-based Doppler-free spectroscopy. Furthermore, we demonstrate results having smaller systematic errors than those provided by more complicated nonlinear spectroscopy methods.

[1] F. M. J. Cozijn et. al. Phys. Rev. Lett. 120, 153002 (2018).
[2] H. Fleurbaey et. al. Phys. Rev. Lett. 120, 183001 (2018).
[3] J. Baron et. al. Science 343, 269-272 (2014).
[4] H. Lin et. al. J. Quant. Spectros. and Rad. Trans. 161, 11-20 (2015)

WI14 **10:56 – 10:57**

COMB-LOCKED CAVITY-ASSISTED DOUBLE RESONANCE (COCA-DR) SPECTROSCOPY OF MOLECULES WITH kHz ACCURACY

CHANGLE HU, *Hefei National Laboratory for Physical Science at Microscale, University of Science and Technology of China, Hefei, China*; VALERY PEREVALOV, *Laboratory of Theoretical Spectroscopy, Institute of Atmospheric Optics, Tomsk, Russia*; CUNFENG CHENG, TIAN-PENG HUA, AN-WEN LIU, YU ROBERT SUN, JIN WANG, YAN TAN, SHUI-MING HU, *Hefei National Laboratory for Physical Science at Microscale, University of Science and Technology of China, Hefei, China.*

Double resonance (DR) spectroscopy has been frequently applied in state-selective excitation and to reach energy levels forbidden to single-photon transitions. Due to the low cross section of two-photon transitions, usually high-power pulsed lasers are needed, which prevent high-precision measurements. Here we present a newly developed comb-locked cavity-assisted double resonance (COCA-DR) spectroscopy technique, which simultaneously lock two near-ir diode lasers to a high-finesse cavity and an optical frequency comb. Doppler-free spectra of molecules with selected speeds along the laser beam were observed, and the DR line positions were determined with a frequency accuracy of 3 kHz. The V and Λ type DR measurements of CO overtone transitions near 1.6 μm were used to verify the frequency accuracy of lines measured by COCA-DR. Transitions to the highly-excited (60025) ($v_{CO} = 8$) "dark" state of the CO_2 molecule were measured using the (30013) vibrational state as the intermediate. Rotational energies of the (60025) state were determined for the first time, and they were compared with the calculated values based on effective operators. The study paves the way to pump-probe measurements of molecules with unprecedented precision.

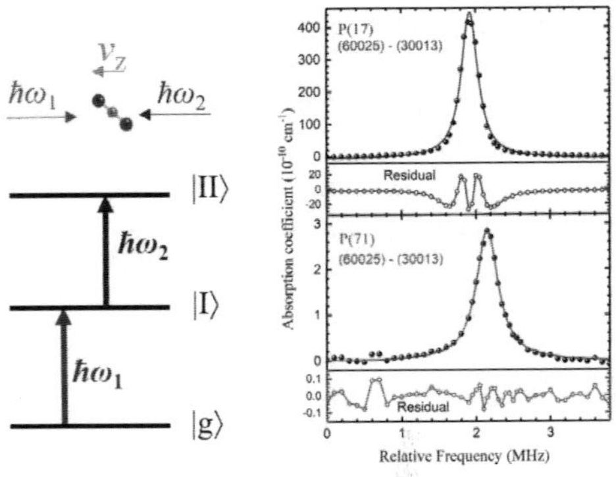

WJ. Astronomy
Wednesday, June 23, 2021 – 10:0 AM
Room: 2021 Online Everywhere

Chair: Harshal Gupta, National Science Foundation, Alexandria, VA, USA

WJ01 **10:00 – 10:01**

HIGH-RESOLUTION GIGAHERTZ AND TERAHERTZ SPECTROSCOPY OF THE ISOTOPICALLY CHIRAL MOLECULE TRANS-2,3-DIDEUTERO-OXIRANE(c-CHD-CHDO)

ZIQIU CHEN, *College of Chemistry and Chemical Engineering, Lanzhou University, Lanzhou, Gansu, China*; SIEGHARD ALBERT, KAREN KEPPLER, MARTIN QUACK, *Laboratory of Physical Chemistry, ETH Zurich, Zürich, Switzerland*; VOLKER SCHURIG, *Institute of Organic Chemistry, University of Tubingen, Tubingen, Germany*; OLIVER TRAPP, *Department of Chemistry, Ludwig Maximilians University, Munich, Germany.*

We report the observation and assignment of the rotational spectra of the isotopically chiral molecule, trans-2,3-dideutero-oxirane (c-CHD-CHDO) measured in the gigahertz range of 62-110 GHz and in the terahertz range, 25-80 cm^{-1}(instrumental resolution of 0.00052 cm^{-1}). Normal oxirane (c-C_2H_4O) has been detected by astrophysical spectroscopy in space.[a]A small number of lines of trans-2,3-dideutero-oxirane had been previously analyzed in the microwave region[b] up to 70 GHz. We have recently [c] measured and successfully analyzed the rotational spectrum of monodeutero-oxirane between 65 and 119 GHz using our GHz spectrometer,[d] and in the 0.75 to 2.5 THz range measured with our FTIR setup [e] at the Swiss Light Source.In the current work, we were able to assign and analyze more than 2500 rotational transitions of the vibronic ground state of trans-2,3-dideutero-oxirane up to J=65. The molecule is also of interest in the context of molecular parity violation, similar to the related molecules.[f] Our results are important in relation to isotopic chirality and parity violation,[g] and to the possible astrophysical observation of this molecule.

[a]J. E. Dickens, et al., *ApJ*, **1997**, 489, 753; M. Ikeda, et al., *ApJ*, **2001**, 560, 792; J. M. Lykke, et al., *A&A*,**2017**, 597, A53.

[b]C. Hirose, *Bull. Chem. Soc. Jap.*, **1974**, 47, 1311.

[c]S. Albert, Z. Chen, K. Keppler, Ph. Lerch, M. Quack, V. Schurig, O. Trapp, *Phys.Chem.Chem.Phys.*, **2019**, 21, 3669

[d]M. Suter, M. Quack, *Appl. Opt.*, **2015**, 54 (14), 4417; S. Albert, Z. Chen, C. Fabri, Ph. Lerch, R. Prentner, M. Quack, *Mol. Phys.*, **2016**, 114, 2751.

[e]S. Albert, Ph. Lerch, M. Quack, *ChemPhysChem*, **2013**, 14, 3204; S. Albert, K. K. Albert, Ph. Lerch, M. Quack, *Faraday Discuss.*, **2011**, 150, 71.

[f]M. Quack and G. Seyfang, *Tunnelling and parity violation in chiral and achiral molecules*, ch.6 in *Tunnelling in Molecules*, J.Kaestner and S. Kozuch eds.,pp 192-244, RSC publishing, Cambridge **2020**, and references cited therein.

[g]M. Quack, *Fundamental Symmetries and Symmetry Violations from High Resolution Spectroscopy*, in *Handbook of High-resolution Spectroscopy*, M. Quack and F. Merkt eds. , Vol.1 , pp. 659-722, Wiley, Chichester **2011**.

WJ02 **10:04 – 10:05**

MICROWAVE AND MILLIMETER WAVE SPECTRUM OF STYRENE OXIDE $C_6H_5C_2H_3O$

PASCAL STAHL, *Institute of Physics, University Kassel, Kassel, Germany*; BENJAMIN E ARENAS, SERGIO R DOMINGOS, *FS-SMP, Deutsches Elektronen-Synchrotron (DESY), Hamburg, Germany*; GUIDO W FUCHS, *Institute of Physics, University Kassel, Kassel, Germany*; MELANIE SCHNELL, *FS-SMP, Deutsches Elektronen-Synchrotron (DESY), Hamburg, Germany*; THOMAS GIESEN, *Institute of Physics, University Kassel, Kassel, Germany.*

Ever-increasingly complex molecules are being searched for in the interstellar medium, and following the detections of propylene oxide [a] and benzonitrile [b], chiral and aromatic molecules are becoming appealing targets for laboratory studies and interstellar searches. The chiral molecule styrene oxide ($C_6H_5C_2H_3O$), also known as phenyloxirane, is an epoxide ($R - C_2H_3O$) with a phenyl ring as the (-R) substituent. With a single conformer and a permanent dipole moment of about 1.8 Debye, styrene oxide emerges as an interesting chiral molecule for astrochemical investigations. We investigated the microwave and millimeter wave spectrum of styrene oxide and analysed the ground-state rotational spectrum as well as rotational transitions from low-energy vibrationally excited states. Chirped-pulse Fourier-transform microwave and millimeter-wave spectroscopy and frequency modulation absorption spectroscopy were used to record spectra in the regions of 2-12 GHz, 75-110 GHz, 170-220 GHz, and 260-330 GHz. From the spectral analysis, a set of precise rotational and centrifugal distortion parameters up to the sextic order was obtained. Our accurate predictions of styrene oxide into the (sub-)millimeter range are mandatory for radio astronomy searches with state-of-the-art observational facilities, such as ALMA. In addition, we assigned the spectra of all singly-substituted ^{13}C and ^{18}O isotopologues, which allowed us to determine the gas phase structure of the molecule experimentally.

[a]McGuire, B. A., Carroll, P. B., Loomis, R. A., et al. 2016, Science, 352, 1449

[b]McGuire, B. A., Burkhardt, A. M., Kalenskii, S., et al. 2018, Science, 359, 202

WJ03 **10:08 – 10:09**

THE PURE ROTATIONAL SPECTRUM OF THE HYDROXYMETHYL RADICAL REINVESTIGATED TO ENABLE ITS INTERSTELLAR DETECTION

OLIVIA CHITARRA, MARIE-ALINE MARTIN-DRUMEL, BÉRENGER GANS, OLIVIER PIRALI, *Institut des Sciences Moléculaires d'Orsay, Université Paris Saclay, CNRS, Orsay, France*; SILVIA SPEZZANO, VALERIO LATTANZI, *The Center for Astrochemical Studies, Max-Planck-Institut für extraterrestrische Physik, Garching, Germany*; HOLGER S. P. MÜLLER, *I. Physikalisches Institut, Universität zu Köln, Köln, Germany*; J.-C. LOISON, *Institut des Sciences Moléculaires, Université de Bordeaux, Talence, France.*

The hydroxymethyl (CH_2OH) and methoxy (CH_3O) radicals, products of CH_3OH photodissociation, are considered key reactive intermediates in the interstellar medium (ISM), and their recombination with other fragments is postulated to lead to the formation of commonly observed complex organic molecules (COMs) as glycolaldehyde, ethanol, ethylene glycol, and dimethyl ether. Interestingly, despite the recent first laboratory detection of CH_2OH pure rotational spectrum [1] and while this isomer is the most thermodynamically stable, only CH_3O has so far been detected in the ISM. A plausible explanation to this lack of interstellar detection is the non-observation in the laboratory of the most intense transitions at low temperature.

We have re-investigated the pure rotational spectrum of CH_2OH at room temperature in the millimeter-wave domain, using a frequency modulation submillimeter spectrometer, with emphasized searches for the fundamental b-type transitions and those intense at low temperature. The radical was produced by H abstraction from CH_3OH using F atoms produced by a microwave discharge. A combined fit of millimeter-wave lines from the literature and our new measurements using a rigid-rotor Hamiltonian yielded a large improvement in the spectroscopic parameters [2] values allowing now confident searches of CH_2OH in cold interstellar environments.

[1] C. Bermudez et al., Astronomy and Astrophysics (2017) 598, A 9

[2] O. Chitarra et al., Astronomy and Astrophysics (2020) 644, A 123

WJ04 **10:12 – 10:13**

SUBMILLIMETER WAVE INVESTIGATION OF TWO FORMAMIDE ISOMERS: FORMALDOXIME (CH_2NOH) AND NITROSOMETHANE (CH_3NO)

LUYAO ZOU, L. MARGULÈS, R. A. MOTIYENKO, *UMR 8523 - PhLAM - Physique des Lasers Atomes et Molécules, University of Lille, CNRS, F-59000 Lille, France*; J.-C. GUILLEMIN, *UMR 6226 CNRS - ENSCR, Institut des Sciences Chimiques de Rennes, Rennes, France.*

The knowledge of synthetic routes of complex organic molecules is still far to be fully understood. The creation of reliable models is particularly challenging. Hollis et al.[a] pointed out that the observations of molecular isomers provides an excellent tool to evaluate the hypothesis of the synthetic pathways. Formamide ($HC(O)NH_2$) is an abundant molecule in ISM detected in 1971 in SgrB2[b]. Since formaldoxime and nitrosomethane are two isomers of formamide, they are interesting ISM targets. Up to now the spectroscopic studies are only available up to 40 GHz[c d]. We reinvestigated the spectra of both isomers in the submillimeterwave domain in order to provide more accurate prediction to permit their possible detection in ISM. These two molecules are not commercially available and shoud be synthesized. The spectra were recorded in Lille from 150 to 660 GHz. In the region below 500 GHz we used the new Fourier transform millimeter-wave (FTmmW) spectrometer system based on DDS particulary suitable for unstable species[e]. Both analysis are not obvious, formaldoxime has a small dipole moment value: 0.2 Debye, giving weak transitions in the observed spectra. Concerning nitrosomethane, the methyl top internal rotation should be taken into account, therefore the analysis is performed using the version of RAM36 coded which includes the treatment of the nuclear quadrupole hyperfine structure[f]. The first spectroscopic results will be presented. *This work was supported by the CNES and the Action sur Projets de l'INSU, PCMI.*

[a] Hollis, J. M.; *et al.*, 2006, *ApJ* **642**, 933

[b] Rubin, R. H. ; *et al.*, 1971, *ApJ* **169**, L39

[c] Kaushik V. K. ; *et al.*, 1978, *J. Phys. Soc. Jap.* **45**, 1975

[d] Turner P. H. *et al.*, 1978, *J. Chem. Soc., Faraday Trans. 2* **74**, 533

[e] Zou L.; *et al.*, 2019, *74th ISMS, Champaign USA* **FB04**

[f] Ilyushin, V.V. *et al*, 2010, *J. Mol. Spectrosc.* **259**, 26

WJ05 **10:16 – 10:17**

A ROTATIONAL STUDY OF INTERSTELLAR ACETOHYDROXAMIC ACID, A GLYCINE ISOMER

MIGUEL SANZ NOVO, IKER LEÓN, SANTIAGO MATA, JOSÉ L. ALONSO, *Grupo de Espectroscopia Molecular, Lab. de Espectroscopia y Bioespectroscopia, Unidad Asociada CSIC, Universidad de Valladolid, Valladolid, Spain.*

The study of not only amino acids but its most essential isomers should be of crucial importance for revealing the chemical processes that may have led to life's origin. We here report the first structural characterization of acetohydroxamic acid ($CH_3CONHOH$), a glycine isomer, using a battery of state-of-the-art rotational spectroscopic techniques in the time domain. The ^{14}N nuclear quadrupole hyperfine structure and the A-E splittings due to the internal rotation have been observed and analyzed. Hence, a precise set of the rotational spectroscopic parameters have been determined for the two distinct structures, Z-amide and E-amide acetohydroxamic acid, which is the initial and prerequisite step of its radio astronomical search in low-frequency regions.

- **Acknowledgments:** The authors thank the financial fundings from Ministerio de Ciencia e Innovacion (CTQ2016-76393-P and PID2019-111396GB-I00), Junta de Castilla y Leon (VA077U16 and VA244P20) and European Research Council under the European Union's Seventh Framework Programme (FP/2007-2013) / ERC-2013-SyG, Grant Agreement n. 610256 NANOCOSMOS, are gratefully acknowledged. M.S.N. acknowledges funding from the Spanish "Ministerio de Ciencia, Innovación y Universidades" under predoctoral FPU Grant (FPU17/02987).

WJ06 **10:20 – 10:21**

MICROWAVE AND MILLIMETER WAVE SPECTRUM OF FIVE CONFORMERS OF CYSTEAMINE AND SEARCH IN SAGITTARIUS B2(N)

WENTAO SONG, ASSIMO MARIS, LUCA EVANGELISTI, DINGDING LV, SONIA MELANDRI, *Dipartimento di Chimica G. Ciamician, Università di Bologna, Bologna, Italy.*

Cysteamine ($NH_2CH_2CH_2SH$), is the precursor of cysteine (a sulfur-containing amino acid) in cell metabolism. As such it is interesting from the chemical and biochemical point of view and as a target interstellar molecule which could be a precursor of amino acid formation. Its rotational spectrum has already been investigated in the 18-40 GHz frequency region and two conformers and their vibrational satellites were characterized, but the sparse frequency coverage prevents their accurate predictions in higher frequency ranges. Moreover, conformational potential energy scans performed at the B3LYP-GD3(BJ)/def2-TZVP level of calculation suggest the existence of more stable conformers. To fill the lack of its spectroscopic knowledge, we have investigated the pure rotational spectrum of cysteamine by means of a Pulsed Jet Fourier transform microwave spectrometer and a Stark modulated free-jet millimeter-wave absorption spectrometer with frequency ranges of 6.5-18 GHz (46.12-16.66 mm) and 59.6-110.0 GHz (5.03-2.72 mm), respectively. According to theoretical predictions, five conformers, belonging to the *gauche* skeletal arrangement ($\angle$ NCCS $\approx 60°$) have been observed, and for three of them also the ^{34}S isotopologues were observed in natural abundance. Some of the detected lines shown a hyperfine structure ($\Delta\nu \leq 1$ MHz) due to the nuclear quadrupole interaction of the ^{14}N atom. Altogether, 336 transition lines of the five parent species and 63 lines of the three ^{34}S isotopologues conformers were assigned to fit the rotational constants, quartic centrifugal distortion constants and the ^{14}N nuclear quadrupole coupling constants. New laboratory data of cysteamine provided very precise values of the spectroscopic constants that can be used to search for cysteamine in astronomical surveys. As a first try, we have looked towards the north core of the giant molecular cloud Sagittarius B2 (N) (Sgr B2(N)), in the band 3 (3.6-2.6 mm), exploiting Belloche's data stored in the public available Atacama Large Millimeter/submillimeter Array (ALMA) archive (project 2016.1.00074.S).

WJ07 **10:24 – 10:25**

MILLIMETER-WAVE SPECTRA OF 5-METHYL HYDANTOIN IN ITS VIBRATIONALLY EXCITED STATES

MINAMI AWADU, HIROYUKI OZEKI, *Department of Environmental Science, Toho University, Funabashi, Japan*; KAORI KOBAYASHI, *Department of Physics, University of Toyama, Toyama, Japan*; SOICHIRO WATANABE, *Faculty of Science, Department of Biomolecular Science, Toho University, Funabashi, Japan.*

Pure rotational spectrum of 5-methyl hydantoin (5-methyl-imidazolidine-4-one, $C_4H_6N_2O_2$), known as a direct precursor of the simplest chiral amino acid Alanine, in its vibrationally excited states were measured in the frequency region of 90-180 GHz. So far, more than 500 spectral lines were recorded, and have been found to be attributed to 4 vibrational states. Guided with the results of density functional theory calculations as well as spectral intensities relative to that of the ground vibrational state, these 4 states can be assigned to fundamental bands and/or combination of these bands whose vibrational energies are considered to be less than 200 cm^{-1}. We also found that transition frequencies for one vibrational excited state can be explained within microwave spectroscopic precision by including the same set of centrifugal distortion constants as those for the ground vibrational sate. While the other spectral line frequencies showed sizeable deviations despite of inclusion of higher-order (up to the 10th order) centrifugal distortion constants. We are currently trying to conduct a perturbation analysis for these data.

WJ08 **10:28 – 10:29**

LABORATORY SPECTROSCOPY OF ALLYLIMINE AND ITS TENTATIVE DETECTION IN THE INTERSTELLAR MEDIUM

MATTIA MELOSSO, *Dept. Chemistry "Giacomo Ciamician", University of Bologna, Bologna, ITALY*; LUCA BIZZOCCHI, *Scuola Normale Superiore, Scuola Normale Superiore, Pisa, Italy*; NINGJING JIANG, *Dept. Chemistry "Giacomo Ciamician", University of Bologna, Bologna, ITALY*; DAVIDE ALBERTON, *Infrared/Submillimeter Group, Max Planck Institute for Extraterrestrial Physics, Garching, Germany*; PAOLA CASELLI, *The Center for Astrochemical Studies, Max-Planck-Institut für extraterrestrische Physik, Garching, Germany*; VICTOR MANUEL RIVILLA, *Departamento de Astrofísica, Centro de Astrobiología CAB, CSIC-INTA, Madrid, Spain*; ANDREA PIETROPOLLI CHARMET, *Dipartimento di Scienze Molecolari e Nanosistemi, Università Ca' Foscari, Venezia, Italy*; LUCA DORE, *Dept. Chemistry "Giacomo Ciamician", University of Bologna, Bologna, ITALY*; CRISTINA PUZZARINI, *Dep. Chemistry 'Giacomo Ciamician', University of Bologna, Bologna, Italy.*

The millimeter spectrum of allylimine has been recorded between 80 and 300 GHz with a frequency-modulation absorption spectrometer. Two conformers, *syn* and *anti*, have been observed in the gas-phase products of the pyrolysis of diallylamine at 500°C. The analysis of an extended data set allowed us to determine rotational constants and centrifugal distortion terms up to the sixth power of the angular momentum operators with high accuracy. The new set of spectroscopic constants has been used to search for allylimine signatures in the spectral survey of the quiescent giant molecular cloud G+0.693-0.027, nearby the Galactic center. A tentative detection of both allylimine conformers is reported.

WJ09 **10:32 – 10:33**

HIGH TEMPERATURE FOURIER TRANSFORM SPECTROSCOPY OF THE B $^1\Pi$ - X $^1\Sigma^+$ TRANSITION OF ZrO

JASON J SORENSEN, PETER F. BERNATH, *Department of Chemistry and Biochemistry, Old Dominion University, Norfolk, VA, USA.*

S-type stars are characterized by the presence of ZrO electronic transitions. Analysis of several ZrO band systems has, to date, relied upon data collected using photographic plates and has escaped a more modern spectral analysis made possible with programs such as PGOPHER. We present a re-analysis of a number of vibrational bands associated with the B $^1\Pi$ - X $^1\Sigma^+$ transition based on a high resolution (0.04 cm^{-1}) Fourier transform emission spectrum collected at the National Solar Observatory by S. Davis. The ZrO source was a carbon tube furnace at 2390 K. Updated spectroscopic constants are presented and discussed.

WJ10 **10:36 – 10:37**

THE PURE ROTATIONAL SPECTRUM OF THE SiP RADICAL ($X^2\Pi_i$)

MARK BURTON, *Department of Chemistry and Biochemistry, University of Arizona, Tucson, AZ, USA*; PHILLIP M. SHERIDAN, *Department of Chemistry and Biochemistry, Canisius College, Buffalo, NY, USA*; LUCY M. ZIURYS, *Department of Chemistry and Biochemistry; Department of Astronomy, Arizona Radio Observatory, University of Arizona, Tuscon, AZ, USA.*

The millimeter-wave spectrum of the SiP radical in its $X^2\Pi_i$ ground electronic state has been recorded using direct absorption spectroscopy in the frequency range 151 – 532 GHz. The species was synthesized in an AC discharge by the reaction of SiH_4 and red phosphorous, in argon carrier gas. Both lambda-doubling and hyperfine splittings, from the phosphorus nuclear spin (I = 1/2), were observed in both spin-orbit ladders, Ω = 3/2 and 1/2. The Ω =1/2 ladder appears to be perturbed, presumably by the nearby $A^2\Sigma$ state, as suggested by previous optical data. The data were analyzed with a Hund's case (a) Hamiltonian, establishing global spectroscopic constants. A deperturbation analysis was also conducted, further refining the Π-Σ interaction.

WJ11 **10:40 – 10:41**

HIGH RESOLUTION INFRARED SPECTROSCOPY OF CYANO-OXIRANE (c-C_2H_3OCN)

SIEGHARD ALBERT, *Physical Chemistry, ETH Zurich, Zurich, Switzerland*; ZIQIU CHEN, *College of Chemistry and Chemical Engineering, Lanzhou University, Lanzhou, Gansu, China*; KAREN KEPPLER, *Physical Chemistry, ETH Zurich, Zurich, Switzerland*; PHILIPPE LERCH, *Swiss Light Source, Paul Scherrer Institute, Villigen, Switzerland*; CARINE MANCA TANNER, MARTIN QUACK, *Physical Chemistry, ETH Zurich, Zurich, Switzerland*; JÜRGEN STOHNER, *ICBT Institute for Chemistry and Biotechnology, ZHAW Zurich University for Applied Sciences, Wädenswil, Switzerland.*

Oxiranecarbonitrile (cyano-oxirane, c-C_2H_3OCN) is of interest as a possible chiral precursor molecule of evolution[a]. We have calculated parity violation in this molecule in view of possible experiments and biomolecular homochirality[b]. Its spectrum has been investigated in the millimeter, submillimeter[c] and terahertz[d] regions. We have recorded its infrared spectrum at 295K with resolution 0.0011 cm^{-1}using the Zurich Prototype ZP 2001 FTIR spectrometer [e]. We report here the results of the rovibrational analysis transitions associated with the ν_{12} (915.3 cm^{-1}) and ν_{13} (848.2 cm^{-1}) fundamentals using a Watson Hamiltonian and the WANG program[f], including molecular parameters and ground state energies from our work in the THz region[d]. Simulations performed using the parameters reproduce the observed spectrum well. The results are discussed in relation to astrophysical spectroscopic searches and the evolution of biomolecular homochirality[g].

[a]M. Bolli, R. Micura, A. Eschenmoser, *Chem. Biol.*, **1997**, 4, 309 (and refs. cited therein).

[b]R. Berger, M. Quack, G. Tschumper, *Helv. Chim. Acta.*, **2000**, 83, 1919; M. Quack, *Chem. Phys. Lett.* **1986**, 132, 147; M. Quack, *Angew. Chem. Intl. Ed.*, **2002**, 41, 4618.

[c]M. Behnke, I. Medvedev, M. Winnewisser, F. C. De Lucia, and E. Herbst, *ApJ. Supplement Series*, **2004**, 152, 97.

[d]S. Albert, Ph. Lerch, K. Keppler and M. Quack, *Proceedings of the XX. Symposium on Atomic, Cluster and Surface Physics 2016, (SASP 2016)*, Innsbruck University Press (2016), pp. 165-168 (and refs. cited therein).

[e]S. Albert, K. Albert and M. Quack, *Trends in Optics and Photonics*, **2003**, 84, 177; "Handbook," Vol. 2, pp. 965-1019 (see also *f*).

[f]D. Luckhaus and M. Quack, *Mol. Phys.*, **1989**, 68, 745; S. Albert, K. Keppler Albert, H. Hollenstein, C. Manca Tanner, M. Quack in "Handbook of High-Resolution Spectroscopy," M. Quack and F. Merkt, Eds., 2011, Vol. 1, Chapter 3, pp. 117-173, Wiley, Chichester.

[g]M. Quack, *Adv. Chem. Phys.*, **2014**, 157, 249 (and refs. cited therein); M. Quack and G. Seyfang, in "Molecular Spectroscopy and Quantum Dynamics," R. Marquardt and M. Quack, Eds., 2020, Ch. 7, pp. 231-282, Elsevier, Amsterdam, see also www.ir.ETHz.CH

WJ12 **10:44 – 10:45**

HIGH-RESOLUTION INFRARED SPECTROSCOPY OF DC_3N IN THE STRETCHING REGION

NINGJING JIANG, MATTIA MELOSSO, *Dept. Chemistry "Giacomo Ciamician", University of Bologna, Bologna, ITALY*; FILIPPO TAMASSIA, *Dipartimento di Chimica Industriale "Toso Montanari", Università di Bologna, Bologna, Italy*; LUCA BIZZOCCHI, *The Center for Astrochemical Studies, Max-Planck-Institut für extraterrestrische Physik, Garching, Germany*; LUCA DORE, *Dept. Chemistry "Giacomo Ciamician", University of Bologna, Bologna, ITALY*; ELISABETTA CANÈ, *Dipartimento di Chimica Industriale "Toso Montanari", Università di Bologna, Bologna, Italy*; DAVIDE FEDELE, *Osservatorio Astrofisico di Arcetri, INAF , Firenze, Italy*; J.-C. GUILLEMIN, *ISCR – UMR6226, Université de Rennes, 35000 Rennes, FRANCE*; CRISTINA PUZZARINI, *Dep. Chemistry 'Giacomo Ciamician', University of Bologna, Bologna, Italy.*

Interstellar deuterated cyanoacetylene (DC_3N) has been identified in a vast variety of astronomical sources thanks to the emission of its rotational transitions. To date, the rotational spectrum of DC_3N has been accurately studied in laboratory, while the high-resolution infrared spectrum is limited to the low frequency range (200–1100 cm^{-1}). In order to support the identification of DC_3N in different spectral regions, we have investigated the infrared spectrum of DC_3N in the stretching region (1500–3500 cm^{-1}). The ν_1, ν_2, and ν_3 fundamentals as well as their hot-bands were recorded at 0.004 cm^{-1} resolution using a Fourier transform infrared spectrometer. Additional pure rotational spectra in the $v_3 = 1$, $v_2 = 1$, and $v_3 = v_7 = 1$ vibrational excited states were observed between 243 and 295 GHz with a frequency-modulation millimeter/submillimeter-wave spectrometer equipped with an electric furnace. The precision of the pure rotational lines, intrinsically much higher than ro-vibrational data, allowed us to improve the accuracy of the upper state spectroscopic parameters. The rotational and ro-vibrational data of DC_3N were combined into a single fit from which a consistent set of spectroscopic constants has been determined. In addition, the ro-vibrational features of its parent species (HC_3N) have been analyzed as well because HC_3N is observed as a by-product in the same spectra. The result of the combined analysis provides a highly-precise rest-frequency catalog that can be used to model the infrared spectra of DC_3N and HC_3N.

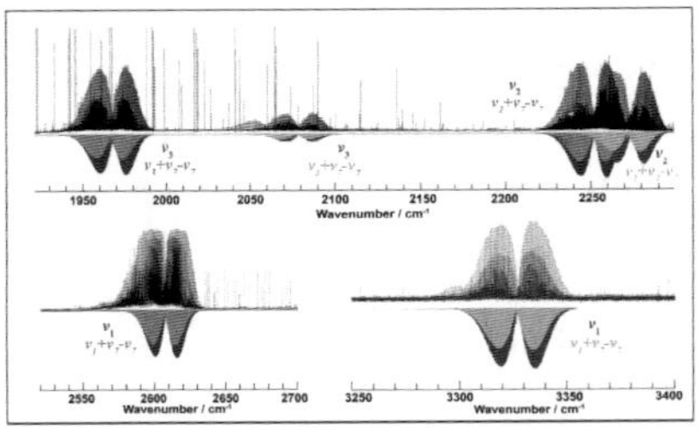

Figure 1: Portions of the recorded MIR spectra (black traces): 1930-2300 cm^{-1}, 2500-2700 cm^{-1} and 3250-3400 cm^{-1}. Spectral simulations based on the spectroscopic constants for both DC_3N (violet traces) and HC_3N (green traces)

WJ13 **10:48 – 10:49**

STUDIES OF IRON MONODEUTERIDE, FeD, VIA LASER EXCITATION SPECTROSCOPY AND DISPERSED FLUORESCENCE SPECTROSCOPY

DENNIS W. TOKARYK, *Department of Physics, University of New Brunswick, Fredericton, NB, Canada*; ALLAN G. ADAM, *Department of Chemistry, University of New Brunswick, Fredericton, NB, Canada*; RYAN A. R. HARVEY, *Department of Physics, University of New Brunswick, Fredericton, NB, Canada.*

Iron monohydride, FeH, is an important astrophysical molecule observed in the cool outer layers of stellar atmospheres. It has a strong magnetic response, which leads to pronounced Zeeman splitting of its spectral lines. Such splitting is observed in spectra of FeH taken above sunspots on the Sun, where magnetic fields are strong. Therefore, a thorough understanding of the structure of FeH and of its Zeeman response provides a way to make excellent measurements of the Sun's magnetic field in the region of sunspots.

The parent isotopologue FeH has been extensively studied, notably by the group of J. M. Brown (see J. Chem. Phys. **121** (2004) 7335 and references therein). However, the deuterated isotopologue, FeD, has received scant attention. We have undertaken a series of experiments on FeD, which we create from the reaction of Ar+D_2 discharge products with iron pentacarbonyl, $Fe(CO)_5$. The FeD molecules are probed with light from a scanning cw ring dye laser with laser excitation spectroscopy. Furthermore, with the laser frequency fixed to excite a single upper-state level we also dispersed the fluorescence at high resolution with a Bomem Fourier transform spectrometer. We have been able to characterize 5 excited electronic states of FeD for the first time. The new data greatly extend our understanding the FeH/FeD system as a whole.

WJ14 **10:52 – 10:53**

IMPROVED CENTRIFUGAL AND HYPERFINE ANALYSIS OF ND_2H AND NH_2D AND ITSAPPLICATION TO THE SPECTRAL LINE SURVEY OF L1544

MATTIA MELOSSO, *Dept. Chemistry "Giacomo Ciamician", University of Bologna, Bologna, ITALY*; LUCA BIZZOCCHI, *The Center for Astrochemical Studies, Max-Planck-Institut für extraterrestrische Physik, Garching, Germany*; LUCA DORE, *Dept. Chemistry "Giacomo Ciamician", University of Bologna, Bologna, ITALY*; ZBIGNIEW KISIEL, *ON2, Institute of Physics, Polish Academy of Sciences, Warszawa, Poland*; NINGJING JIANG, *Dept. Chemistry "Giacomo Ciamician", University of Bologna, Bologna, ITALY*; JÜRGEN GAUSS, *Institut für Physikalische Chemie, Universität Mainz, Mainz, Germany*; CRISTINA PUZZARINI, *Dep. Chemistry 'Giacomo Ciamician', University of Bologna, Bologna, Italy.*

Quantifying molecular abundances of astrochemical species is a key step towards the understanding of the chemistry occurring in the interstellar medium. This process requires a profound knowledge of the molecular energy levels, including their structure resulting from weak interactions between nuclear spins and the molecular rotation. With the aim of increasing the quality of spectral line catalogs for the singly- and doubly-deuterated ammonia (NH_2D and ND_2H), we have revised their rotational spectra by observing many hyperfine-resolved lines and more accurate high-frequency transitions. The measurements have been performed in the submillimeter-wave region (265-1565 GHz) using a frequency modulation submillimeter spectrometer and in the far-infrared domain (45-220 cm^{-1}) with a synchrotron-based Fourier-transform interferometer. The analysis of the new data, with the interpretation of the hyperfine structure supported by state-of-the-art quantum-chemical calculations, led to an overall improvement of all spectroscopic parameters. Moreover, the effect of the inclusion of deuterium splittings in the analysis of astrophysical NH_2D emissions at millimeter wavelengths has been tested using recent observations of the starless core L1544, an ideal astrophysical laboratory for the study of deuterated species. Our results show that accounting for hyperfine interactions leads to a small but significant change in the physical parameters used to model NH_2D line emissions.

WK. Theory and Computation

Wednesday, June 23, 2021 – 10:0 AM
Room: 2021 Online Everywhere

Chair: John F. Stanton, University of Florida, Gainesville, FL, USA

WK01 **10:00 – 10:01**

UTILIZATION OF NEURAL NETWORKS FOR GPU-ACCELERATED DIFFUSION MONTE CARLO FOR VIBRATIONAL PROBLEMS

FENRIS LU, RYAN J. DIRISIO, ANNE B McCOY, *Department of Chemistry, University of Washington, Seattle, WA, USA.*

In recent years, there has been increasing interest in combining machine learning with computational chemistry. Many machine learning applications in theoretical chemistry have focused on the development of potential energy surfaces (PES) based on *ab initio* data points[a]. Another computational resource that has gained popularity in recent years is the use of Graphics Processing Units (GPUs) to accelerate calculations such as molecular dynamics simulations [b]. In this work, we take advantage of the knowledge gained from both of these areas, and apply these approaches to the evaluations of the potential energy for Diffusion Monte Carlo (DMC) calculations. Diffusion Monte Carlo is a stochastic simulation approach through which an ensemble of localized functions (walkers) converges to the ground state vibrational wave function at long propagation times. This is accomplished through the ensemble randomly sampling a potential energy surface. These calculations require on the order of 10^8 to 10^10 potential energy evaluations, making the call to a potential energy surface the most expensive part of these calculations.

To this end, we have developed a general technique for "learning" already existing potential energy surfaces using neural networks, which can then easily be evaluated on GPUs using TensorFlow. The technique entails running a small-scale DMC simulation to collect training data, coordinates and energies, and using this data to fit a subspace of the potential energy surface that is relevant for the DMC simulations. We find that using the neural network potential energy surface maintains the fidelity of the wave function while also enabling the use of ensemble sizes orders of magnitude larger than previously used for the same amount of wall time. We test this method on small systems such as CH5+, H2O, and water dimer.

[a]Manzhos, S.; Carrington, T. Chem. Rev. Article ASAP. https://doi.org/10.1021/acs.chemrev.0c00665
[b]Abraham, M. J.; Murtola, T.; Schulz, R.; Páll, S.; Smith, J. C.; Hess, B.; Lindahl, E. SoftwareX 2015, 1–2, 19–25

WK02 **10:04 – 10:05**

DIFFUSION MONTE CARLO USING MACHINE LEARNING POTENTIAL ENERGY SURFACES

RYAN J. DIRISIO, MARK A. BOYER, JACOB M FINNEY, FENRIS LU, ANNE B McCOY, *Department of Chemistry, University of Washington, Seattle, WA, USA.*

Diffusion Monte Carlo (DMC) is a technique for obtaining the ground-state solution to the vibrational time-independent Schrödinger equation based on a stochastic sampling of an electronic potential energy surface (PES). Ideally, the electronic energies used in DMC are calculated at the CCSD(T) level of theory. Recently, Tom Miller's group at Caltech has developed a technique for calculating accurate CCSD(T) corrections to the electronic energy at the cost of a standard Hartree-Fock calculation using Gaussian process regression, a machine learning technique[ab]. DMC is a well-suited technique to validate these PESs, referred to as MOB-ML surfaces, since DMC samples the entire region of the PES in which the vibrational ground state wave function has amplitude. Despite the speed of these MOB-ML PESs relative to an *ab initio* calculation, calculating the Hartree-Fock energy for every one of thousands of DMC configurations over tens of thousands of time-steps makes the use of these surfaces computationally challenging.

To this end, we combined two techniques to bring these calculations into computational feasibility. First, we implemented a DMC algorithm to take advantage of massively parallel high performance computing environments. Second, we use this DMC code to collect training data for a neural network (NN). We use a generic algorithm to train the NN to learn the MOB-ML surface based on the points sampled by the DMC. Using TensorFlow, the evaluation of the NN can then easily be done using graphics processing units (GPUs). We have performed small-scale DMC calculations on H2O and CH5+ using these MOB-ML surfaces, and have also run large-scale NN+MOB-ML DMC simulations to obtain a high resolution ground state vibrational wave function and measure of the zero-point energy. Due to the generality of both the MOB-ML surface generation and the NN fitting workflow, we can easily extend this work to larger systems, such as large ion-water clusters or a Criegee intermediate, where running the DMC with traditional electronic structure would be intractable.

[a]Welborn, M. , Cheng, L., Miller, T. M. JCTC. 2018 14 (9), 4772-4779
[b]Cheng, L., Kovachki, N. B., Welborn, M., Miller, T. M. JCTC. 2019 15 (12), 6668-6677

WK03 **10:08 – 10:09**

PHYSICS-GUIDED CURVE FITTING FOR POTENTIAL-ENERGY FUNCTIONS OF DIATOMIC MOLECULES

KARL K. IRIKURA, *Chemical Sciences Division, National Institute of Standards and Technology, Gaithersburg, MD, USA.*

In ab initio calculations of diatomic spectroscopy, discrete points are typically computed along the potential energy curve. The points are fitted to a continuous function, such as a polynomial, a Morse function, or a spline, so that ro-vibrational energy levels can be computed and conventional constants extracted. The choice of fitting function is arbitrary and affects the results, which is undesirable in predictive work. Here we suggest using lower-level theory to create a dense, high-resolution grid, to be used as a guide. Instead of fitting the sparse, high-level data directly, the energy differences between the high-level points and the guiding potential are fitted. This simple strategy reduces the uncertainty from the choice of fitting function, yielding more precise predictions.

WK04 **10:12 – 10:13**

JIM WATSON AND THE THEORY OF VIBRATION-ROTATION INTERACTION

TAKESHI OKA, *Department of Astronomy and Astrophysics and Department of Chemistry, The Enrico Fermi Institute, University of Chicago, Chicago, IL, USA.*

Based on the the Coriolis interaction conceived by Teller and Tisza (1932), the fundamental Wilson-Howard Hamiltonian (WHH), formulated in 1936[a], includes everything about the vibration-rotation interaction. Enormous technical advances followed both in vibrational and rotational spectroscopy and have produced extremely rich data. Then God sent us the genius Jim Watson to deeply study the WHH and harvest all its fruits in the most sublime and direct manner.

Out of the many jewels Watson left us I single out three works.

(1) The theory of the centrifugal distortion of asymmetric-top molecules (1966)[b]: To solve the indeterminacy of centrifugal distortion constants of non-planar asymmetric tops, Watson discovered an angular momentum operator $P_xP_yP_z + P_zP_yP_x$ which commutes with the rotational Hamiltonian and produces an additional relation between centrifugal constants making the solutions possible. This is the most frequently quoted paper in the field of molecular spectroscopy.

(2) Simplification of the WHH (1968)[c]: For the first term of rearranged WHH $H = 1/2\Sigma(\Pi_\alpha-\pi_\alpha)\mu_{\alpha\beta}(\Pi_\beta-\pi_\beta)$ Watson discovered commutation relation $[\pi_\alpha, \mu_{\alpha\beta}]=0$. using absolutely beautiful tensor algebra, thus simplifying the Hamiltonian. This is the most fundamental work in the field of molecular spectroscopy and represents the triumph of tensor algebra.

(3) Forbidden rotational transitions (1971)[d]: The $\Delta K=0$ selection rule of a symmetric top molecule corresponds to cylindrical symmetry. Since the actual symmetry is C_3 rather than cylindrical for say NH_3, $\Delta K=3$ forbidden transitions are weakly allowed. Watson's theory showed that non-polar molecules such as CH_4 and H_3^+ are polar in some rotational levels and undergo forbidden rotational transitions. This theory has greatly influenced molecular astrophysics. [e]

[a] Wilson, Jr., E. B. & Howard, J. B. 1936 J. Chem. Phys. 4, 260

[b] Watson, J. K. G. 1966 J. Chem. Phys. 45, 1360; 46, 1935; 1968 J. Chem. Phys. 48, 4517

[c] Watson, J. K. G. 1968 Mol. Phys. 15, 479

[d] Watson, J. K. G. 1971 J. Mol. Speectrosc. 40, 536

[e] e.g. Oka, T., Geballe, T. R., Goto, M., Usuda, T., McCall, B. J., & Indriolo, N. 2019 ApJ, 883, 54

WK05 **10:16 – 10:17**

A SPARSE LINEAR ALGEBRAIC APPROACH TO ARBITRARY-ORDER VIBRATIONAL PERTURBATION THEORY

MARK A. BOYER, ANNE B McCOY, *Department of Chemistry, University of Washington, Seattle, WA, USA.*

Vibrational perturbation theory is a commonly-used method for obtaining anharmonic corrections to harmonic zero-order wave functions and energies. The method comes in two main variants, canonical Van Vleck perturbation theory, which has been used extensively by Sibert and coworkers[a] and Rayleigh-Schrödinger perturbation theory, which was used by Nielsen to derive analytic corrections up through second-order.[bc] In this work, we introduce an adaption to the Rayleigh-Schrödinger formalism. This approach, which is a generalization of approaches found in the physics literature,[d] provides a simple route to obtain high-order corrections to the vibrational energies and wave functions for a system. The intensive symbolic algebra required in both the Van Vleck and Nielsen approaches is replaced by a sparse, numerical linear algebra for which efficient libraries already exist. This approach is formally equivalent to standard methods and admits a straight-forward approach to account for degeneracies. We apply this method to obtaining 4th and higher order corrections to the vibrational energies of a series of water clusters making use of curvilinear internal coordinates.

[a]Sibert, E. L. J. Chem. Phys. 88, 4378-4390 (1987).
[b]Nielsen, H. H. Phys. Rev. 60, 794-810 (1941).
[c]Nielsen, H. H. Rev. Mod. Phys. 23, 90-136 (1951).
[d]Sakurai, J. J.; Liboff, R. L. Modern Quantum Mechanics. Am. J. Phys. (1986).

WK06 ***Post-Deadline Abstract*** **10:20 – 10:21**

RECONSTRUCTION OF TERM DIAGRAMS WITHOUT USING A MODEL HAMILTONIAN

STEFAN BRACKERTZ, SVEN KRISTKEITZ, OSKAR ASVANY, STEPHAN SCHLEMMER, *I. Physikalisches Institut, University of Cologne, Cologne, Germany.*

The fundamental Ritz combination principle [1] originally found for atoms has also been applied to molecules as a method to reconstruct the energy states from measured lines without relying on any model Hamiltonian. In 2006 Nesbitt and coworkers [2] proposed to apply it to protonated methane, CH_5^+, which was first done in 2015 [3] and extended in 2017 [4] by our group. Currently, we are elaborating this method to a universal, easy to use tool which can be used for arbitrary spectra. Essentials of the program and examples, including the floppy He-H_3^+ system, will be discussed.

[1] W. Ritz, On a new law of series spectra, Astrophys. J. 28 (1908), p. 237.
[2] C. Savage, F. Dong, D.J. Nesbitt, Toward a quantum-mechanical understanding of the high-resolution infrared spectrum of CH_5^+, in: Contribution TA05, 61st International Symposium on Molecular Spectroscopy, Columbus, OH, USA, 2006.
[3] Oskar Asvany, Koichi M. T. Yamada, Sandra Brünken, Alexey Potapov, Stephan Schlemmer. Experimental ground-state combination differences of CH_5^+. Science, 347 (2015), pp. 1346-1349.
[4] S. Brackertz, S. Schlemmer, O. Asvany, Searching for new symmetry species of CH_5^+ – From lines to states without a model, J. Mol. Spectrosc. 342 (2017), p. 73-82.

WK07 **10:24 – 10:25**

A DISCRETE VARIABLE APPROACH FOR INVESTIGATING TUNNELING SPLITTINGS AND VIBRATIONAL WAVE FUNCTIONS IN RARE GAS-ASYMMETRIC TOP HETERODIMERS

EZRA ARUMI ALEXANDER, MARK D. MARSHALL, HELEN O. LEUNG, *Chemistry Department, Amherst College, Amherst, MA, USA.*

A three dimensional discrete variable representation (DVR) is developed for the general case of a rare gas atom interacting with an asymmetric top molecule and applied to the case of argon-haloethylene heterodimers. The position of the rare gas is specified relative to the principal inertial axis system (in a I^r representation) by the spherical polar coordinates (r, θ, ϕ). While the DVR for r is straightforward, those for θ and ϕ presented particular challenges, which are discussed. In common with all DVR approaches, the present DVR is well suited for systems where the intermolecular potential is calculated on a grid of discrete points and provides easy access to the wave functions in the DVR coordinates. The method is applied to the well-characterized argon-*cis*-1,2-difluoroethylene system and used to predict the tunneling splitting and argon-molecule vibrational wave functions in argon-vinyl chloride for which the molecular structure and rotational spectrum remain a puzzle.

WK08 **10:28 – 10:29**

VARIATIONAL ROVIBRATIONAL CALCULATION FOR LINEAR TETRAATOMIC MOLECULES: I. THE C8V4 APPROACH

BENJAMIN SCHRÖDER, *Institut für Theoretische Chemie, Universität Stuttgart, Stuttgart, Germany.*

Variational rovibrational calculations for small molecules with up to 3 atoms are nowadays a routine task.[a] By employing accurate potential energy surfaces it is possible to achieve so called "spectroscopic accuracy" of 1 cm^{-1} for small linear molecules.[b] However, rovibrational calculations for linear molecules with more than 3 atoms are still rather scarce.[c] A new variational method (C8v4) will be presented that is able to obtain rovibrational term energies and wave functions of tetraatomic linear molecules based on Watsons isomorphic Hamiltonian for linear molecules.[d] The rovibrational wavefunction is expanded in (symmetrized) products of harmonic oscillator (1D and 2D) and rigid-rotor functions. The intricacies related to the vibrational angular momentum in linear molecules require a careful study of symmetry properties. Kinetic energy matrix elements in the chosen basis set can be evaluated in a fast mixed numerical/analytical fashion. The main computational bottlenecks are the integration of the potential energy matrix and the diagonalisation of the rovibrational Hamiltonian. An efficient hybrid MPI/OMP parallelization has been implemented, exploiting the block structure of the Hamiltonian, that yields a significant reduction of the computational time. The diagonalization employs a K-contraction scheme that reduces the number of basis functions in the final rovibrational Hamilonian by at least an order of magnitude. Example benchmark calculations for acetylene (HCCH) are presented. The converged ($N_{\text{vib}} = 2785$) results for HCCH up to $J_{\text{max}} = 2$ accurately reproduce earlier variational calculations[e] in both g and u symmetry.

[a] Tennyson, *J. Chem. Phys.* **145**, 120901 (2016).
[b] Schröder and Sebald, *J. Chem. Phys.* **144**, 044307 (2016); Makhnev *et al.*, *J. Phys. Chem. A* **122**, 1326 (2018).
[c] Mladenović, *J. Chem. Phys.* **141**, 224304 (2014); Chubb *et al.*, *J. Chem. Phys.* **149**, 14101 (2018).
[d] Watson, *Mol. Phys.* **14**, 465 (1970).
[e] Bramley and Handy, *J. Chem. Phys.* **98**, 1378 (1993).

WK09 **10:32 – 10:33**

VARIATIONAL ROVIBRATIONAL CALCULATION FOR LINEAR TETRAATOMIC MOLECULES: II. THE B11244 STORY RETOLD

BENJAMIN SCHRÖDER, *Institut für Theoretische Chemie, Universität Stuttgart, Stuttgart, Germany*; PETER SEBALD, *Institut für Physikalische Chemie, Georg-August-Universtität Göttingen, Göttingen, Germany.*

The linear propynylidynium l-C_3H^+ ($X^1\Sigma^+$) is part of the select group of interstellar cations. Its discovery was accompanied by a controversy in the astrophysical community.[a] Following its initial detection, theoretical calculations questioned the assignment based on 2nd order vibrational perturbation theory (VPT2) calculations. The matter was ultimately resolved by laboratory rotational spectra.[b] The failure of VPT2 was subsequently attributed to a shallow CCC bending potential.[c] Discrete Variable Representation (DVR) calculations[d] later confirmed the D_0/D_e ratio but resulted in a large sextic centrifugal distortion constant H_0 exceeding the astronomical value by an order of magnitude.

Using a new variational method for tetraatomic linear molecules (C8v4; see also P5277), based on Watsons isomorphic Hamiltonian for linear molecules, theory and experiment are reconciled. The C8v4 calculations confirm the small size of H_0 obtained in previous experimental studies. A high-level composite *ab initio* potential energy function (PEF) has been developed, combining explicitly correlated coupled-cluster results with corrections for core-valence correlation, scalar relativistic effects and higher-order correlation as well as the diagonal Born-Oppenheimer correction. Large scale C8v4 calculations using this PEF show excellent agreement with the available experimental rotational[a,c] and vibrational parameters.[e] The presented rotational spectroscopic parameters of excited vibrational states should facilitate forthcoming experimental spectroscopic studies on l-C_3H^+.

[a] Pety *et al.*, *Astron. Astrophys.* **548**, 68 (2012); Huang *et al.*, *Astrophys. J. Lett.* **768**, 25 (2013).
[b] Brünken *et al.*, *Astrophys. J. Lett.* **783**, 36 (2014).
[c] Botschwina *et al.*, *Astrophys. J.* **787**, 72 (2014).
[d] Mladenović *J. Chem. Phys.* **141**, 224304 (2014).
[e] Brünken *et al.*, *J. Phys. Chem. A* **123**, 8053 (2019).

WK11 ***Post-Deadline Abstract*** **10:40 – 10:41**

SIMULATION OF THE ABSORPTION SPECTRUM OF CHLORINE PEROXIDE (ClOOCl)

MEGAN R BENTLEY, *Chemistry, University of Florida, Gainesville, FL, USA*; JOHN F. STANTON, *Quantum Theory Project, University of Florida, Gainesville, FL, USA*.

Chlorine oxides, namely chlorine monoxide (ClO) and its head-to-tail dimer (ClOOCl), are thought to be important participants in the catalytic destruction of ozone in the Antarctic polar vortex. Chlorine peroxide photolysis is the crucial step in the ozone-depleting mechanism, requiring accurate measurements of absorption cross sections to estimate the amount of ozone destroyed by this process in the polar stratosphere. However, there are large inconsistencies in previous experimental determinations of absorption cross sections in the longer wavelength tail region, where chlorine peroxide photolysis is atmospherically relevant. We have used a model based upon Condon's reflection principle to construct a simulated absorption spectrum for dissociative excited states, as is the case for chlorine peroxide. The simulated spectrum uses oscillator strengths and excitation energies generated from equation-of-motion coupled-cluster (EOM-CC) techniques that include effects of triple excitations and agrees well with experimental spectra. This method shows promise in elucidating semi-quantitative features of the absorption cross sections without encountering common experimental complications.

WK12 **10:44 – 10:45**

VIBRONICALLY COUPLED STATES: COMPUTATION AND CHARACTERIZATION OF VIBRONIC AND ROVIBRONIC SPECTROSCOPIC PARAMETERS

KETAN SHARMA, TERRY A. MILLER, *Department of Chemistry and Biochemistry, The Ohio State University, Columbus, OH, USA*; JOHN F. STANTON, *Physical Chemistry, University of Florida, Gainesville, FL, USA*.

The importance of the breakdown of the Born-Oppenheimer (BO) approximation in the vicinity of a conical intersection has spurred the recent development of computational approches that involve vibronic coupling between electronic states. Computational chemistry has mainly focused on conical intersections along reaction paths. Jahn-Teller type conical intersections offer a spectroscopically accessible alternative that can be used for benchmarking these calculations. The presence of Jahn-Teller and pseudo-Jahn-Teller couplings not only leads to additional terms in the rotational Hamiltonian but also modify how well known terms like Coriolis coupling and spin-rotation coupling are computed. In this talk we build upon the general quantum chemical method pioneered by Köppel, Domcke and Cederbaum[a] to tackle molecules with vibronic coupling wherein ab initio electronic structure calculations in the adiabatic limit are used as the starting point for calculating properties of molecules in the regime where the BO approximation breaks down. A model vibronic Hamiltonian is parameterized using derivatives of adiabatic potential energy surfaces. Vibronic eigenvectors are obtained from this model Hamiltonian that allow the calculation of parameters in the rotation-spin Hamiltonian that can be determined experimentally from high resolution spectroscopy.

[a]H. Köppel and W. Domcke and L. S. Cederbaum Multimode Molecular Dynamics Beyond the Born-Oppenheimer Approximation. *Adv. Chem. Phys.* *57*, (1984), 59-246

WK13 **10:48 – 10:49**

VIBRONIC AND SPIN ANGULAR MOMENTUM IN ROTATIONALLY RESOLVED SPECTRA OF JAHN-TELLER ACTIVE MOLECULES

KETAN SHARMA, TERRY A. MILLER, *Department of Chemistry and Biochemistry, The Ohio State University, Columbus, OH, USA*; JOHN F. STANTON, *Physical Chemistry, University of Florida, Gainesville, FL, USA.*

Effects due to vibronic and spin angular momentum have long been observed in rotationally resolved spectra of Jahn-Teller active molecules. The breakdown of the Born-Oppenheimer approximation in these molecules leads to complications in their vibronic spectra. The molecular picture is further complicated due to the coupling of spin angular momenta with rotational and vibronic angular momentum. Values of these coupling constants have been determined by many high resolution rotationally resolved spectroscopic experiments. However, the presence of a conical intersection in the adiabatic potential energy surfaces has made getting a reliable quantum chemistry calculation of these terms challenging. In this talk we present methods that have been developed to make first principles calculations of vibronic angular momenta and Coriolis coupling constants from quantum chemistry. Further methods have been developed to calculated spin related terms (spin-orbit quenching and spin rotation coupling), using ab initio methods and model vibronic hamiltonian. We report a comparision of calculations of these parameters with corresponding results determined from high resolution spectroscopy for molecules like methoxy radical and cyclopentadienyl radical.

WK14 **10:52 – 10:53**

ACCURATE PREDICTION OF VIBRONIC LEVELS AND BRANCHING RATIOS FOR LASER-COOLABLE LINEAR POLYATOMIC MOLECULES: THE CONSTRUCTION OF THE QUASIDIABATIC HAMILTONIAN

CHAOQUN ZHANG, LAN CHENG, *Department of Chemistry, Johns Hopkins University, Baltimore, MD, USA.*

The vibronic structures of the low-lying electronic states in linear polyatomic molecules, which are utilized to construct closed optical cycling, play crucial roles in the laser-cooling processes. The construction of a multi-state Köeppel-Domcke-Cederbaum (KDC) quasidiabatic Hamiltonian with spin-orbit coupling, linear vibronic coupling, and Renner-Teller effects taken into account is reported aiming to obtain accurate vibronic levels and wave functions for laser-coolable triatomic molecules. The parameters for this KDC Hamiltonian were obtained from relativistic equation-of-motion coupled-cluster singles and doubles (EOM-CCSD) calculations. Discrete variable representation (DVR) calculations were then carried out to obtain the vibronic levels and wave functions. The accuracy of the present parametrization for the KDC Hamiltonian is demonstrated with calculations for vibronic levels of the $X^2\Sigma$ and $A^2\Pi$ states of the SrOH molecule.

WL. Large molecules

Wednesday, June 23, 2021 – 10:0 AM

Room: 2021 Online Everywhere

Chair: Etienne Garand, University of Wisconsin-Madison, Madison, WI, USA

WL01 **10:00 – 10:01**

ELECTRONIC AND INFRARED PHOTODISSOCIATION SPECTROSCOPY OF THE GREEN FLUORESCENT PROTEIN CHROMOPHORE IN VACUO

WYATT ZAGOREC-MARKS, *JILA and the Department of Chemistry, Universityy of Colorado, Boulder, CO, USA*; MADISON M. FOREMAN, J. MATHIAS WEBER, *JILA and Department of Chemistry, University of Coloroado, Boulder, CO, USA*.

The Green Fluorescent Protein (GFP) is one of the most widely used fluorescent markers in bioimaging, and much work has been dedicated to understanding the electronic structure of its anionic chromophore in solution, protein, and in vacuo. A model for this chromophore (deprotonated p-hydroxybenzylidene-2,3-dimethylimidazolinone, HBDI , see Figure 1) contains the complete conjugated system, and replaces the linkers to the protein structure with methyl groups. Previous work by many groups has established that the initial photophysics of the chromophore upon excitation is likely to be similar in the protein and in vacuo, but quite different from aqueous solution.[a,b] All previous spectroscopy in vacuo has been performed at room temperature, which introduces spectral congestion through hot bands. By studying this chromophore as a cryogenically prepared, mass-selected ion, we are able to provide unprecedented resolution in the electronic band origin region of the $S_1 \leftarrow S_0$ electronic transition.

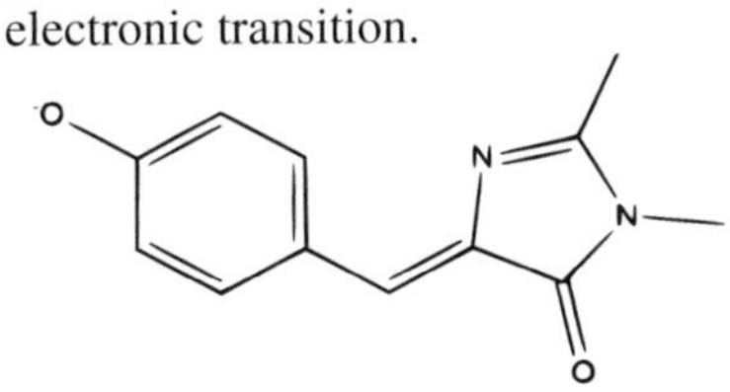

Figure 1: Structure of $HBDI^-$.

[a] S. Brøndsted Nielsen, A. Lapierre, J. U. Andersen, U. V. Pedersen, S. Tomita, L.H. Andersen, Phys. Rev. Lett. 87 (2001) 228102

[b] W. Zagorec-Marks, M. M. Foreman, J. R. R. Verlet, J. M. Weber, J. Phys. Chem. Lett. 10 (2019) 7817-7822

WL02 **10:04 – 10:05**

MICROSOLVATION OF THE GREEN FLUORESCENT PROTEIN CHROMOPHORE ONE WATER MOLECULE AT A TIME

WYATT ZAGOREC-MARKS, *JILA and the Department of Chemistry, Universityy of Colorado, Boulder, CO, USA*; MADISON M. FOREMAN, J. MATHIAS WEBER, *JILA and Department of Chemistry, University of Coloroado, Boulder, CO, USA*.

Solvation plays an important role in the function of fluorescent proteins. Many of these proteins contain a functional water molecule in the chromophore pocket, which can influence the electronic properties of the chromophore. In the case of the Green Fluorescent Protein (GFP), a single water molecule is coordinated to the phenolate group of the chromophore, raising questions about the effect this has on the electronic spectrum of GFP. Here, we present the electronic and infrared spectra of a model system for the GFP chromophore in complexes with up to two water molecules.

WL03 **10:08 – 10:09**

LOST AND BOUND: UNDERSTANDING THE ELECTRON DETACHMENT PATHWAYS OF THE TETRACENYL ANION ISOMERS

COLE R SAGAN, ETIENNE GARAND, *Department of Chemistry, University of Wisconsin–Madison, Madison, WI, USA.*

Polycyclic aromatic hydrocarbons (PAH) are some of the most abundant complex molecules in the interstellar medium. In their anionic forms, these molecules can exist either as a radical anion or a singly deprotonated species. These deprotonated varieties have been proposed as key intermediates in the formation of much larger interstellar molecules such as C60. Previous work has used anion slow-electron velocity map imaging (SEVI) to study the naphthyl and anthracenyl anions and the corresponding neutral radical[ab]. Here, we extend this work to the larger tetracenyl anions and radical. For the 9-tetracenyl radical, we report an electron affinity value of 1.8457(5)eV which differs from the previously published result of 2.6(2)eV[c], but is more consistent with the values for the smaller deprotonated PAHs. We also report the first anion photoelectron spectra of 1 and 2-tetracenyl isomers, yielding electron affinity values of 1.623(2) and 1.547(2) eV, respectively. Interestingly, the ordering of electron affinities of these isomers differs from the anthracenyl radical. The most active vibrations in these spectra involve displacements near the deprotonation site. In order to explain high intensity of very low kinetic energy electrons in multiple SEVI images, we have acquired the action photoelectron spectra of the 9-tetracenyl radical. This spectrum reveals an anion excited state about 2000 cm^{-1}above the detachment threshold with peak widths that suggest lifetimes on the order of 4.5ps. The primary pathway to detachment from this anion excited state is via thermionic emission, in agreement with previously published results. Implications for possible detection in astrochemical data will be discussed.

[a]J. Am. Chem. Soc. 2015, 137, 4, 1420–1423
[b]PNAS February 16, 2016 113 (7) 1698-1705
[c]Phys. Chem. Chem. Phys., 2015,17, 32464-32471

WL04 **10:12 – 10:13**

LABORATORY IR SPECTRA OF PROTONATED FULLERENES

JULIANNA PALOTÁS, *FELIX Laboratory, Institute for Molecules and Materials (IMM), Radboud University, Nijmegen, Netherlands*; JONATHAN K MARTENS, *Institute for Molecules and Materials (IMM), Radboud University Nijmegen, Nijmegen, Netherlands*; GIEL BERDEN, *FELIX Laboratory, Institute for Molecules and Materials (IMM), Radboud University, Nijmegen, Netherlands*; JOS OOMENS, *FELIX Laboratory, Radboud University, Nijmegen, The Netherlands.*

With the detection of C_{60}, C_{70} and C_{60}^{+}, the fullerenes constitute by far the largest molecular species individually identified in the interstellar medium (ISM). Proton affinities of C_{60} and C_{70} are significant which support the hypothesis that protonated fullerenes may also be abundant in the ISM.

We present the experimental vibrational spectra of gaseous $C_{60}H^{+}$ and $C_{70}H^{+}$. Protonation of the highly symmetrical molecules causes a drastic symmetry lowering resulting in a rich vibrational spectrum. As compared to C_{60}, where all C-atoms are equivalent due to the icosahedral symmetry, C_{70} belongs to the D_{5h} point group and has five non-equivalent C-atoms, which are available as protonation sites. Combined analysis of the experimental spectrum and spectra computed at the density functional theory level enables us to evaluate the protonation isomers being formed. We compare the IR spectra of $C_{60}H^{+}$ and $C_{70}H^{+}$ to IR emission spectra from planetary nebulae, which suggests that a mixture of these fullerene analogues could contribute to their IR emission.

WL05 **10:16 – 10:17**

ELECTRONIC AND INFRARED PHOTODISSOCIATION SPECTROSCOPY OF PROTOPORPHYRIN IN VACUO

WYATT ZAGOREC-MARKS, MADISON M. FOREMAN, J. MATHIAS WEBER, *JILA and Department of Chemistry, University of Coloroado, Boulder, CO, USA.*

Porphyrins are ubiquitous macrocycles in biology, where they perform a variety of functions ranging from behaving as chromophores in proteins to molecular/electron shuttles. Porphyrins often incorporate a metal center and have substituents on the macrocycle periphery to allow this versatility. These species have been studied for decades, using many techniques primarily focused on solution and solid phase environments. While such techniques yield much useful information, the chemical environment and the temperatures involved in such studies usually lead to solvatochromic shifts, broadening of spectral lines, and spectral congestion. Even spectra obtained in cryogenic matrices exhibit shifts whose magnitude and even direction are hard to predict. As a consequence, the intrinsic photophysical properties of these molecules, i.e., in the absence of effects caused by chemical environments, have been elusive. We are able to circumvent these difficulties by studying cryogenically prepared, mass selected ions. Here we report the electronic and infrared spectra of metal free protoporphyrin mono- and dianions. We interpret the experimental data in the framework of quantum chemical calculations.

WL06 **10:20 – 10:21**

STRUCTURAL CHARACTERIZATION OF METAL BIPYRIDINE COMPLEXES VIA CRYOGENIC ION SPECTROSCOPY

MADISON M. FOREMAN, WYATT ZAGOREC-MARKS, J. MATHIAS WEBER, *JILA and Department of Chemistry, University of Coloroado, Boulder, CO, USA.*

Catalytic reduction of CO_2 to produce chemical fuels is a viable strategy for meeting the growing demand for renewable energy, but better catalysts are needed to perform this chemistry on an industrial scale. The first step in designing improved catalysts is understanding key molecular properties of existing catalysts, which includes characterizing the structures and intramolecular forces of species in the catalytic cycle. Metal bipyridine complexes have been shown to efficiently reduce CO_2 with long catalyst lifetimes[a]. We prepared gas-phase ions of metal centers (Ni, Co, Cu) coordinated with substituted bipyridine ligands and a formate adduct. Infrared photodissociation spectroscopy was performed on each complex, and DFT calculations were carried out to assign peaks in the IR spectra.

[a]Inorg. Chem. 2010, 49, 9283–9289

WL07 **10:24 – 10:25**

THE ROTATIONAL SPECTRA OF FLAVONE AND FLAVANONE: LASER ABLATION AND HEATING METHODS FOR VAPORIZATION.

SUSANA BLANCO, ALBERTO MACARIO, JUAN CARLOS LOPEZ, *Departamento de Química Física y Química Inorgánica, Universidad de Valladolid, Valladolid, Spain.*

Flavonoids constitute a family of natural compounds found in a large number of fruits and vegetables being responsible for many of their vivid colours. Flavonoids are the largest group of phytonutrients, with more than 6,000 types. Flavone (2-Phenylchromone) and flavanone (2,3-Dihydroflavone) define the basic units for whole families of these compounds, anthoxantines and flavanones respectively. Due to their biological activity, their structure–activity relationships are of interest also for medicine and biochemistry. In this work, we present the first study of the microwave spectra of both flavone and flavanone. The spectra of these two molecules have been observed using a CP-FTMW spectrometer with two vaporization methods: conventional heating and a laser ablation (LA) system recently implemented. A conformational search was done for each compound using DFT, corrected with empirical dispersion terms, and MP2 methods. We have observed only one conformer of each system and their monohydrated complexes. Flavanone is a case where DFT and MP2 methods diverge in predicting the global minimum being the experimental data in agreement with the DFT predictions.

WL09 **10:32 – 10:33**

A ROTATIONAL STUDY OF 1-SUBSTITUTED BARBARALONES

MAURO MATO, *(ICIQ), Institute of Chemical Research of Catalonia , Tarragona, Spain*; MIGUEL SANZ NOVO, IKER LEÓN, *Grupo de Espectroscopia Molecular, Lab. de Espectroscopia y Bioespectroscopia, Unidad Asociada CSIC, Universidad de Valladolid, Valladolid, Spain*; ELENA R. ALONSO, *Departamento de Química Física, Universidad del País Vasco (UPV-EHU), Bilbao, Spain*; ANTONIO M ECHAVARREN, *(ICIQ), Institute of Chemical Research of Catalonia , Tarragona, Spain*; JOSÉ L. ALONSO, *Grupo de Espectroscopia Molecular, Lab. de Espectroscopia y Bioespectroscopia, Unidad Asociada CSIC, Universidad de Valladolid, Valladolid, Spain.*

The phenomena of valence tautomerism consists in a particular intramolecular process involving just one reactive species where an intramolecular bond migrates raising to a sometimes different, but not always, molecular structure. In this context, barbaralones, widely well-known fluxional molecules, have been deeply ingrained in the understanding of the phenomena of valence tautomerism. They can undergo low energy [3, 3]-sigmatropic process, where the number of constitutional isomers depends on the presence and chemical nature of any possible substituent that induces isomerization restrictions. We have laser-ablated 1-(4-tert-Butyl)phenyl)tricyclo[3.3.1.0^{2,8}]nona-3,6-dien-9-one, a large fluxional molecule that is central to the understanding of the phenomena of valence tautomerism, and one conformer has been characterized using chirped-pulse Fourier transform microwave LA-CP-FTMW spectroscopy. This precise structural data should be useful in future studies as a reference point in the characterization of new fluxional molecules.

- **Acknowledgments:** The authors thank the financial fundings from Ministerio de Ciencia e Innovacion (CTQ2016-76393-P and PID2019-111396GB-I00), Junta de Castilla y Leon (VA077U16 and VA244P20) and European Research Council under the European Union's Seventh Framework Programme (FP/2007-2013) / ERC-2013-SyG, Grant Agreement n. 610256 NANOCOSMOS, are gratefully acknowledged. E.R.A. acknowledges MINECO for a Juan de la Cierva postdoctoral fellowship and the Fundación Biofísica Bizkaia (Spain). M.S.N. acknowledges funding from the Spanish "Ministerio de Ciencia, Innovación y Universidades" under predoctoral FPU Grant (FPU17/02987).

WL10 **10:36 – 10:37**

DAPPERS: A NEW PROGRAM FOR THE RAPID ASSIGNMENT AND FITTING OF DENSE ROTATIONAL SPECTRA BASED ON SPECTRAL PROGRESSIONS

NATHAN LOVE, ANNA HUFF, KENNETH R. LEOPOLD, *Chemistry Department, University of Minnesota, Minneapolis, MN, USA.*

We describe a new interactive program (DAPPERS: Data Analysis Package for Productive and Enthusiastic Rotational Spectroscopists) for the rapid processing of dense rotational spectra of asymmetric rotors. DAPPERS is based on an intelligent algorithm that quickly and accurately locates spectral progressions with user-identified quantum number identities and then seamlessly integrates with Pickett's SPCAT and SPFIT programs to allow complete assignment and fitting. The program has been shown to be proficient across the full range of asymmetry parameters and can produce final fits containing hundreds of transitions of any type (*a*, *b*, or *c*) or branch (P, Q, or R) in just a few minutes. The software interacts with the user through a simple graphical user interface, and includes a peak-finder with adjustable baseline drift compensation, as well as a number of visualization features. It is designed for easy installation and use, with special attention given to the design of a single executable file platform. It is available for download, together with extensive documentation, at www.chem.umn.edu/groups/kleopold.

WL11 **10:40 – 10:41**

A MICROWAVE AND COMPUTATIONAL STUDY OF CARBOXYLIC ACID ANHYDRIDES

NATHAN LOVE, ANNA HUFF, KENNETH R. LEOPOLD, *Chemistry Department, University of Minnesota, Minneapolis, MN, USA.*

Microwave spectra for a series of carboxylic acid anhydrides derived from acetic acid, pivalic acid, benzoic acid, and trifluoroacetic acid are reported. All semi-rigid rotor spectra, including those of the A states of species with a single methyl rotor, were quickly assigned using the new rotational spectral fitting program, DAPPERS. The observed internal rotor states of the single-rotor anhydrides and the double rotor spectra of parent and D-6 acetic anhydride were fit using XIAM. The aid of closed loops in the assignment of the acetic anhydride spectrum will be briefly discussed along with remaining challenges in the spectral analysis. The heavy atom structure of pivalic anhydride and pivalic trifluoroacetic anhydride were determined through isotopic substitution and Kraitchman analysis. Trends of the dihedral angle between anhydride carbonyls are studied through an analysis of M06-2X/6-311++G(d,p) computational values, which are shown to be in good agreement with those experimentally determined for pivalic and pivalic trifluoroacetic anhydrides. The V_3 barriers measured for acetic anhydride, acetic trifluoroacetic anhydride, and acetic pivalic anhydride are compared with those for a wide variety of molecules exhibiting methyl group internal rotation in an acetate functionality. A straightforward synthesis for mixed carboxylic anhydrides will also be described.

WL12 **10:44 – 10:45**

MICROWAVE AND COMPUTATIONAL STUDIES OF HYDRATED ACID ANHYDRIDES: CAPTURING A LOCAL POTENTIAL ENERGY MINIMUM AND EXPLORING THE EFFECT OF $C(CH_3)_3$ AND CF_3 SUBSTITUENTS

NATHAN LOVE, ANNA HUFF, KENNETH R. LEOPOLD, *Chemistry Department, University of Minnesota, Minneapolis, MN, USA.*

Microwave studies of hydrated acid anhydrides (RCOOCOR-H_2O) provide an interesting venue for characterizing local minima on the potential energy landscape of reactive systems. This talk reports the microwave spectra of the monohydrates of pivalic anhydride (R = R' = $C(CH_3)_3$), trifluoroacetic anhydride (R = R' = CF_3), and the mixed pivalic-trifluoroacetic anhydride (R = $C(CH_3)_3$, R' = CF_3). While the ultimate fate of these species in bulk aqueous solution is hydrolysis to form the parent acids, this work captures the precursor complexes and investigates the effect of R and R' on the geometry of the monohydrate. Microwave spectra of the parent species and their D_2O and DOH isotopologues are reported, as is an in-depth computational analysis at different levels of theory. Calculated structures show varying degrees of hydrogen bonding and electrophilic-nucleophilic interaction, depending on the particular combination of R and R' groups. Additionally, closely spaced pairs of tunneling states arising from internal water motion were observed in the monohydrate spectra except in the case where R = R' = CF_3.

WL13 *Post-Deadline Abstract* **10:48 – 10:49**

CHEMO-DYNAMICAL MODELING OF CHA-MMS1 TO PREDICT NEW SOLID-PHASE SPECIES FOR DETECTION WITH JWST

MIWHA JIN, *Department of Chemistry, University of Virginia, Charlottesville, VA, USA*; KAHO LAM, *Department of Astronomy, University of Virginia, Charlottesville, VA, USA*; JEROEN TERWISSCHA VAN SCHELTINGA, *Leiden Observatory, Laboratory for Astrophysics, Universiteit Leiden, Leiden, Netherlands*; ROBIN T. GARROD, *Departments of Chemistry and Astronomy, The University of Virginia, Charlottesville, VA, USA*; ZHI-YUN LI, *Department of Astronomy, The University of Virginia, Charlottesville, VA, USA*; MELISSA K McCLURE, *Leiden Observatory, Laboratory for Astrophysics, Universiteit Leiden, Leiden, Netherlands*; ADWIN BOOGERT, *W. M. Keck Research Laboratory in Astrochemistry, University of Hawaii at Manoa, Honolulu, HI, USA*; ERIC HERBST, *Department of Chemistry, The University of Virginia, Charlottesville, VA, USA*.

Chemical models and experiments indicate that interstellar dust grains and their ice mantles play an important role in the production of complex organic molecules (COMs). The meeting of chemical species adsorbed from the gas phase onto the grain/ice surface allows reactions to occur efficiently, and leads to the emergence of the ice mantles as a major reservoir of volatile species. To date, the most complex solid-phase molecule detected with certainty in the ISM is methanol (CH_3OH), but it is hoped that the upcoming James Webb Space Telescope (JWST), aided by new laboratory data, will be able to identify yet larger organic species. In this study, we use a coupled chemo-dynamical model to predict new candidate species for JWST detection toward the young star-forming core Cha-MMS1, combining the gas-grain chemical kinetic model MAGICKAL with a 1-D radiative hydrodynamics (RHD) simulation. The abundances of the main ice constituents with respect to water in the model match well with observational values. The model also predicts high solid-phase abundances of intermediate radicals associated with the hydrogenation of CO to methanol (> 0.1 % with respect to water ice). Four oxygen-bearing COMs (ethanol C_2H_5OH, dimethyl ether CH_3OCH_3, methyl formate CH_3OCHO, and acetaldehyde CH_3CHO) as well as formic acid (HCOOH), show abundances as high as > 0.01 % with respect to water ice. N-bearing COMs are generally less abundant than O-bearing ones, suggesting methylamine (CH_3NH_2) as the only N-bearing solid-phase COM candidate for JWST detection.

WM. Radicals

Wednesday, June 23, 2021 – 10:0 AM

Room: 2021 Online Everywhere

Chair: Mitchio Okumura, California Institute of Technology, Pasadena, CA, USA

WM01 **10:00 – 10:01**

MEASUREMENT OF THE $\tilde{A}\leftarrow\tilde{X}$ BAND OF 1- AND 2-METHYLALLYL RADICALS USING CAVITY RINGDOWN SPECTROSCOPY

CHARLES R. MARKUS, WEN CHAO, GREGORY H JONES, MITCHIO OKUMURA, *Division of Chemistry and Chemical Engineering, California Institute of Technology, Pasadena, CA, USA.*

The reduced reactivity of resonance-stabilized hydrocarbon radicals allows for them to reach higher concentrations in harsh environments such as flames or planetary atmospheres. Reactions between them remain rapid and could explain the formation of aromatics in aliphatic flames and molecular growth in soot formation processes. Here, we have measured the $\tilde{A}\leftarrow\tilde{X}$ bands of the resonance-stabilized 1- and 2-methylallyl radicals near 410 nm using cavity ringdown spectroscopy. Although the absorption cross sections are relatively small, the extended lifetimes of the excited states allows for resolved vibronic structure of both C_4H_7 isomers. The transition has both $n \leftarrow \pi$ and $\pi^* \leftarrow n$ character, which we analyze using quantum chemical calculations. We also discuss how these results can be employed in chemical kinetics experiments.

WM02 **10:04 – 10:05**

HIGH-RESOLUTION INFRARED SPECTROSCOPY OF JET COOLED HCBr SINGLET BROMOCARBENE DIRADICAL

YA-CHU CHAN, *JILA and the Department of Chemistry, University of Colorado Boulder, Boulder, CO, USA*; ANDREW KORTYNA, *JILA, National Institute of Standards and Technology and Univ. of Colorado, Boulder, CO, USA*; DAVID NESBITT, *Department of Chemistry, JILA CU-NIST, Boulder, CO, USA.*

First high-resolution mid infrared rovibrational spectral data on jet cooled bromocarbene (HCBr) diradical are obtained using quantum shot noise limited laser absorption methods. The HCBr diradical is generated by coflowing bromoform ($HCBr_3$) in a mixture of Ne, He, and H_2 through a pulsed slit discharge beam source and is subsequently cooled down to approximately 40 K in a slit-jet supersonic expansion. Interestingly, optimization of the HCBr radical requires the presence of H_2, presumably due to decomposition of $HCBr_3$ by H atom chemistry in the discharge. Rotationally resolved absorption spectra of the CH stretch $\nu_1 = 1 \leftarrow 0$ fundamental are analyzed, resulting in precise determination of ground and excited state rovibrational constants for both ^{79}Br and ^{81}Br isotopologues. The results for the ground state are in good agreement with previous high resolution near IR electronic studies in the Sears group[a]. The ν_1 band origin is now unambiguously assigned at 2799 cm^{-1}, which agrees well with previous LIF/dispersed fluorescence studies of Reid and coworker[b].

[a] Journal of Molecular Spectroscopy 202, 131–143 (2000)

[b] J. Chem. Phys. 124, 134302 (2006)

WM03 **10:08 – 10:09**

INFRARED SPECTRUM OF THE 1-IODOPROPYL RADICAL PRODUCED FROM REACTION OF I + PROPENE IN SOLID PARA-HYDROGEN

WEI LIN, *Department of Chemistry, University of Texas Rio Grande Valley, Brownsville, TX, USA*; HUEI-RU TSAI, YU-HSUAN CHEN, *Department of Applied Chemistry, National Yang Ming Chiao Tung University, Hsinchu, Taiwan*; YUAN-PERN LEE, *Applied Chemistry, National Yang Ming Chiao Tung University, Hsinchu, Taiwan, Institute of Atomic and Molecular Sciences, Academia Sinica, Taipei, Taiwan.*

The addition reactions of iodine atom with propene in solid para-hydrogen (p-H_2) matrices were investigated with infrared (IR) absorption spectroscopy. Mixtures of propene and I_2 seeded in p-H_2 were co-deposited at 3.3 K for 7 to 8 hours, followed by irradiations with ultraviolet lights at various wavelengths to study the reaction of I atoms with propene. Quantum chemical calculations were carried out at the B3LYP/aug-cc-pVTZ-pp level in order to determine the relative energies, vibrational wavenumbers and IR intensities of 1-iodopropyl and 2-iodopropyl radicals. The transitions belong to I_2-propene complex, 1-iodopropyl radical, and the anti conformer of 1,2-diiodopropane were recorded and assigned. The assignments were based on expected reaction, the vibrational wavenumbers and IR intensities from theoretical calculations, and secondary photolysis behavior. The observation of 1-iodopropyl radical, the isomer with the least energy, indicates that the addition of iodine atom occurs at the terminal carbon atom. The role of the p-H_2 matrices, the difference between this reaction and the previously reported Cl + propene reaction will be discussed.

WM04 **10:12 – 10:13**

INFRARED SPECTRA OF GASEOUS (Z)-3-IODO-BUT-2-EN-1-YL [$C_2H_3C(CH_3)I$] RADICAL, METHYL VINYL KETONE OXIDE [$C_2H_3C(CH_3)OO$] CRIEGEE INTERMEDIATE, AND $C_2H_3CI(CH_3)OO$ PEROXY RADICAL PRODUCED UPON PHOTODISSOCIATION OF (Z)-1,3-DIIODO-BUT-2-ENE [$(CH_2I)HC{=}C(CH_3)I$] IN OXYGEN

YUAN-PERN LEE, *Applied Chemistry, National Yang Ming Chiao Tung University, Hsinchu, Taiwan, Institute of Atomic and Molecular Sciences, Academia Sinica, Taipei, Taiwan*; CHEN-AN CHUNG, *Department of Applied Chemistry, National Yang Ming Chiao Tung University, Hsinchu, Taiwan.*

Methyl vinyl ketone oxide [MVKO, $C_2H_3C(CH_3)OO$], an important Criegee intermediate in ozonolysis of isoprene, was recently identified in laboratories with near infrared action spectrum (to produce OH) using photolysis of a gaseous mixture of 1,3-diiodo-but-2-ene [$(CH_2I)HC{=}C(CH_3)I$] and O_2,[a] but its mid-infrared spectrum and the detailed mechanism of its formation remains unexplored. We employed a step-scan Fourier-transform infrared spectrometer to investigate the reaction intermediates. Upon irradiation at 248 nm of gaseous (Z)-1,3-diiodo-but-2-ene, the (Z)-3-iodo-but-2-en-1-yl [$C_2H_3C(CH_3)I$] radical was observed, indicating the fission of the terminal allylic C-I bond, not the central vinylic C-I bond. This radical is characterized by infrared absorption bands at 1406, 1261, 1109, 1019, 925, and 873 cm^{-1}. Upon irradiation at 248 nm of a gaseous mixture of (Z)-1,3-diiodo-but-2-ene and O_2 at 35 Torr, the Criegee intermediate MVKO, characterized by infrared absorption bands at 1416, 1383, 1346, 1060, 987, 948, and 908/916 cm^{-1}, was observed. At pressure 236 Torr, the reaction adduct 3-iodo-but-1-en-1-yl-peroxy [$C_2H_3CI(CH_3)OO$] radical, characterized by infrared absorption bands at 1375, 1213, 1108, 1063, 986, and 885 cm^{-1}, was observed. These new spectra of $C_2H_3C(CH_3)I$, $C_2H_3C(CH_3)OO$, and $C_2H_3CI(CH_3)OO$ provide valuable information for the understanding of the formation mechanism of the Criegee intermediate MVKO from the source reaction of photolysis of $(CH_2I)HC{=}C(CH_3)I$ in O_2 in laboratories. If time permits, we will discuss the formation kinetics and self-reaction of MVKO using a quantum-cascade laser.

[a]V. P. Barber, S. Pandit, A. M. Green, N. Trongsiriwat, P. J. Walsh, S. J. Klippenstein, M. I. Lester, *J. Am. Chem. Soc.* **140**, 10866 (2018).

WM05 **10:16 – 10:17**

PRODUCTION OF $HOCH_2CO$, HOCHCHO, AND HOCHCO IN THE REACTION H + GLYCOLALDEHYDE ($HOCH_2CHO$) IN SOLID p-H_2 AND ITS IMPLICATION IN ASTROCHEMISTRY

PRASAD RAMESH JOSHI, *Department of Applied Chemistry, National Yang Ming Chiao Tung University, Hsinchu, Taiwan*; YUAN-PERN LEE, *Applied Chemistry, National Yang Ming Chiao Tung University, Hsinchu, Taiwan, Institute of Atomic and Molecular Sciences, Academia Sinica, Taipei, Taiwan.*

Glycolaldehyde ($HOCH_2CHO$) has been detected in the interstellar medium; it is considered to play an important role in the formation of complex organic molecules, especially higher sugars. We took the advantages of unique properties of *para*-hydrogen (p-H_2), which serves as a quantum-solid matrix host and a medium for efficient hydrogen-atom reaction, to investigate the reaction between $HOCH_2CHO$ and H atoms. H atoms were generated on photolysis at 365 nm of a co-deposited mixture of $HOCH_2CHO$/p-H_2 and Cl_2 and subsequent IR irradiation for promoting the Cl + H_2 (ν = 1) $\rightarrow$ H + HCl reaction. Based on the orientation of O-H and C=O bonds, $HOCH_2CHO$ has 4 conformers; *cis-cis* conformer is found to have the least energy among all due to the intramolecular H-bonding. In the reaction H + $HOCH_2CHO$ at 3.2 K, 5 lines in the first group and 6 lines in the second group are assigned to $HOCH_2CO$ and HOCHCHO radicals, products of the first H-abstraction from -CHO and -CH_2 groups, respectively. In addition, 2 lines were assigned to HOCHCO, a product of the second H-abstraction. IR irradiation employed during H-atoms generation was also responsible for the conformational conversion of $HOCH_2CHO$, cc $\rightarrow$ *tt*; which intricates the H + *cc*-$HOCH_2CHO$ reaction to some extent. Since photolysis at 266 nm also promotes this conversion; we photolyzed the *cc*-$HOCH_2CHO$ at 266 nm prior to 365 nm/IR irradiation for complete conversion to the *tt*-form to facilitate the H + *tt*-$HOCH_2CHO$ reaction. Four lines in one group and 3 lines in the second group, those differ from their *cc*-form analogs, were assigned to the *tt*-$HOCH_2CO$ and *tt*-HOCHCHO radicals, respectively; 2 lines in the third group were assigned to HOCHCO. Besides these assignments, a line at 2079.3 $cm^{-1}$was tentatively assigned to the OCHCO radical, a product of the third H-abstraction. The assignments of all these products agree satisfactorily with vibrational wavenumbers predicted with the B3LYP/aug-cc-pVTZ method. The PES of H + *cc*- and *tt*-$HOCH_2CHO$ reactions reveal the feasibility of H-abstraction processes for $HOCH_2CO$, HOCHCHO, HOCHCO, and OCHCO formations after sequential H-abstractions from the CHO, CH_2, CH_2/CHO, and OH moieties, respectively.

WM06 **10:20 – 10:21**

AB INITIO SPECTROSCOPIC PARAMETERS OF PYRIDYL RADICALS

KELLY S. MEYER, SOMMER L. JOHANSEN, J. H. WESTERFIELD, ANAHUT SANDHU, JASMINE KEANE, KYLE N. CRABTREE, *Department of Chemistry, University of California, Davis, Davis, CA, USA.*

Nitrogen-substituted polycyclic aromatic hydrocarbons (PANHs) are fundamental species important in biological molecules, astrochemistry, and combustion. They have been detected on meteorites with non-terrestrial isotopic abundances, potentially play a role in prebiotic chemistry, and have been observed in the atmosphere of Titan. They are suggested to be responsible for some of the unidentified infrared (UIR) emission bands in the interstellar medium and have been identified as intermediates in the combustion of biomass. Pyridine is a prototypical nitrogen-containing aromatic molecule, and recent studies suggest that the pyridyl radicals are key intermediates to the formation of PANHs. However, no high-resolution spectra or coupled-cluster calculations of the pyridyl radicals are available. To complement our search for the pyridyl radicals with rotational spectroscopy, we calculated the equilibrium geometries, relative energies, and spectroscopic parameters for the three pyridyl radicals at the CCSD(T) level of theory. In addition, anharmonic vibrational frequencies were evaluated using second-order vibrational perturbation theory. We will discuss the results of our calculations and our progress to measure the rotational spectra of the pyridyl radicals using Fourier transform microwave spectroscopy.

WM07 **10:24 – 10:25**

COUPLED CLUSTER CHARACTERIZATION OF 1-, 2-, AND 3-PYRROLYL FOR VIBRATIONAL AND ROTATIONAL SPECTROSCOPY

SOMMER L. JOHANSEN, ZHONGXING XU, J. H. WESTERFIELD, ANNA C. WANNENMACHER, KYLE N. CRABTREE, *Department of Chemistry, University of California, Davis, Davis, CA, USA.*

A wide variety of nitrogen-containing heterocycles have been detected on meteorites with non-terrestrial isotopic abundances, indicative of an interstellar origin. However, no N-heterocycles have been detected in space and their formation pathways are unclear. Experimental work has shown that N-heterocycles can likely form through barrierless radical-neutral gas-phase reactions, which are feasible in the low temperature environments of cold molecular clouds and the outer regions of protoplanetary disks. Astronomical searches and laboratory studies of potential precursors and depletion products are critical to determining if such mechanisms play a role in N-heterocycle formation. Pyrrolyl is both a photodissociation product of the N-heterocycle pyrrole (C_4H_5N) and a potential astrophysical precursor to larger N-heterocycles. Furthermore, pyrrolyl is a known intermediate in the combustion of biomass and was tentatively detected in Titan's atmosphere by the Cassini-Huygens mission. Here, the first treatment of 1-, 2-, and 3-pyrrolyl at the CCSD(T) level of theory and progress towards the first experimental detection in the cm-wave region will be discussed. Equilibrium geometries were optimized at CCSD(T)/cc-pwCVTZ and quadratic, cubic, and partial quartic force constants were evaluated at CCSD(T)/ANO0 in order to obtain harmonic and anharmonic vibrational frequencies. Additional parameters for vibrational and rotational spectroscopy were calculated at similar levels of theory. This work will enable astronomical searches, laboratory spectroscopy, and kinetics and dynamics studies.

WM08 **10:28 – 10:29**

ELECTRONIC SPECTROSCOPY OF *CIS*- AND *TRANS-META*-VINYLBENZYL RADICALS

SEDERRA D. ROSS, JONATHAN FLORES, DANIEL M. HEWETT, NEIL J. REILLY, *Department of Chemistry, University of Massachusetts Boston, Boston, Massachusetts, USA.*

The electronic spectra of the resonance-stabilized radical C_9H_9 isomers *cis*- and *trans-meta*-vinylbenzyl (MVB), generated in a supersonically cooled discharge of *m*-vinyltoluene, have been investigated using resonant two-colour two-photon ionization (R2C2PI) and laser-induced fluorescence. The $D_0 - D_1$ band origins of the *cis* and *trans* conformers are at $19037\,\mathrm{cm}^{-1}$ and $18939\,\mathrm{cm}^{-1}$, respectively. Adiabatic ionization energies near 7.17 eV were determined for both conformers from two-colour ion-yield scans. Dispersed fluorescence (DF) was used to conclusively identify the *cis* conformer: ground-state *cis*-MVB eigenvalues calculated from a Fourier series fit of a computed (B3LYP/6-311G++(d,p) vinyl torsion potential are in excellent agreement with torsional transitions observed in the $19037\,\mathrm{cm}^{-1}$ DF spectrum. Features arising from *cis*- or *trans*-MVB in the R2C2PI spectrum were distinguished by optical-optical holeburning spectroscopy and vibronic assignments were made with guidance from DFT and TDDFT calculations. There is a notable absence of mirror symmetry between excitation and emission spectra for several totally symmetric modes, whereby a' fundamentals that are conspicuous in emission are nearly absent in excitation, and *vice-versa*. This effect is largely ascribed to interference between Franck-Condon and Herzberg-Teller contributions to the electronic transition moment, as the former is carried with a different sign in excitation *vs.* emission, while the latter is not. Rampant HT activity among a' modes is attributed to the low symmetry (C_s) of the molecule, which permits intensity-borrowing from several relatively bright electronic states of A'' symmetry.

WM09 **10:32 – 10:33**

THE GROUND AND EXCITED STATES OF AROMATIC OXIDE RADICALS VIA ANION PHOTOELECTRON SPECTROSCOPY

STEVEN J. KREGEL, ETIENNE GARAND, *Department of Chemistry, University of Wisconsin–Madison, Madison, WI, USA.*

Aromatic oxide free radicals play an important role in atmospheric and combustion chemistry, where they are involved in the formation of secondary organic aerosols and soot. The oxygen atom lone pairs can readily mix with the aromatic system giving rise to extensive electronic delocalization and influencing molecular reactivity. The oxygen atom also imparts a significant dipole moment to the radical system, which supports low-lying resonance and dipole bound states. We probed three cryogenically cooled aromatic oxide radicals (phenoxy, 1-naphthoxy, 2-naphthoxy) via Slow Electron Velocity Map Imaging (SEVI) to unravel their electronic and vibrational structure. We determined electron affinities and excited state energies for the three systems, and observed numerous active vibrational modes. Resonant photoexcitation to the dipole bound state was found to drastically alter the observed vibrational structure, and care was taken to avoid these resonances during direct photodetachment studies.

WM10 **10:36 – 10:37**

VIBRATIONAL ANALYSIS OF DF SPECTRUM OF THE NO_3 $\tilde{B}\ ^2E' - {}^2A_2'$ SYSTEM (II): COMBINED ANALYSIS WITH CRYO-SEVI PE SPECTRUM OF NO_3^-

MASARU FUKUSHIMA, *Information Sciences, Hiroshima City University, Hiroshima, Japan.*

We are currently studying the $\tilde{B}\ ^2E' - \tilde{X}\ ^2A_2'$ system of jet cooled NO_3 via laser induced fluorescence (LIF) spectroscopy. The dispersed fluorescence (DF) spectrum from the vibrationless level of the upper electronic state suggests the existence of two closely lying vibrational levels in the ν_1 fundamental region, $\sim$ 1050 cm^{-1}[a]. Recently, Babin et al. reported the high resolution photo-electron (PE) spectrum of NO_3^- measured by a spectroscopic method, slow photo-electron velocity-map imaging of cryogenically cooled anion (cryo-SEVI)[b], but unfortunately, the cryo-SEVI PE spectrum does not resolve the two levels in the ν_1 fundamental region. In the report, it is also shown that the PE band intensities depend on the excess kinetic energy of PE by the photo-detachment light source. This dependence is also reported in their spectra measured by traditional PE spectroscopy[c]. By combining results from these two methodologies, we have analyzed the excess energy dependence of the PE bands, and found that there are two components with different excess energy dependence in the ν_1 fundamental region. The two components can be attributed two vibrational levels, consistent with our DF results. The dependence of one of the two components corresponds to that of the vibrationless band (vibrationally a_1'), while the other does not agree with that of the ν_4 fundamental (e'), $\sim$ 350 cm^{-1}.

[a] M. Fukushima and T. Ishiwata, ISMS2013, paper WJ03 (2013).

[b] M. Babin, J. A. DeVine, M. DeWitt, J. F. Stanton, and D. M. Neumark, J. Phys. Chem. Lett. 11, 395 (2019)

[c] A. Weaver, D. W. Arnold, S. E. Bradforth, and D. M. Neumark, J. Phys. Chem. 94, 1740 (1991)

WM11 **10:40 – 10:41**

GATEWAY STATES OF THE $1^2\Delta$ STATE OF CaH.

SHOTA YAGURAMAKI, JIN FURUTA, KAORI KOBAYASHI, YOSHIKI MORIWAKI, *Department of Physics, University of Toyama, Toyama, Japan*; STEPHEN CARY ROSS, *Department of Physics, University of New Brunswick, Fredericton, NB, Canada.*

Calcium monohydride CaH is found in the Sun and other stars. Indeed, its A-X electronic spectrum has been a useful probe for stellar classification.[a] We have been working on this molecule in the visible and ultraviolet regions. Using Laser Induced Fluorescence (LIF) we have identified many new vibrational levels of the A, B/B′, and $1^2\Delta$ states. Our primary interest has been the detailed investigation of the B/B′ state which has a double-minimum potential energy function. We have previously studied vibrational levels lying both below and above the potential energy barrier between the two wells.[b,c] In that work, we were able to confirm the strong irregularity in the vibrational energy spacings that had been predicted by the quantum chemical study of Carlsund-Levin *et al.*[d]

We previously reported the first experimental observation of the direct, but forbidden, excitation $1^2\Delta \leftarrow X^2\Sigma$.[e] This was done using LIF. This excitation is possible due to interaction of levels of the $1^2\Delta$ state with nearby levels of states for which excitation from the ground state is not forbidden, so called "gateway" states. By studying the ensuing relaxation from the $1^2\Delta$ state we have now identified some of the gateway levels involved.

[a]For example, J.E. Gizis, *Astron. J.* **113**, 806 (1997).

[b]K. Watanabe, N. Yoneyama, K. Uchida, K. Kobayashi, F. Matsushima, Y. Moriwaki, S. C. Ross, *Chem. Phys. Lett.* **657**, 1 (2016).

[c]K. Watanabe, I. Tani, K. Kobayashi, Y. Moriwaki, S. C. Ross, *Chem. Phys. Lett.* **710**, 11 (2018).

[d]C. Carlsund-Levin, N. Elander, A. Nunez, A. Scrinzi, *Phys. Scripta* **65**, 306 (2002).

[e]J. Furuta, K. Watanabe, I. Tani, K. Kobayashi, Y. Moriwaki, S. C. Ross, *74th International Symposium on Molecular Spectroscopy*, **TI06**, (2019).

WM12 **10:44 – 10:45**

ELECTRONIC STRUCTURE AND VIBRATIONAL SIGNATURES OF THE DELOCALIZED RADICAL IN HYDRATED CLUSTERS OF COPPER ("II") HYDROXIDE, CUOH+(H2O)0-2

ELIZABETH G. CHRISTENSEN, *Department of Chemistry, Physical Chemistry, University of Utah, Salt Lake City, UT, USA*; KEVIN T LUTZ, *Chemistry, University of Utah, Salt Lake City, UT, USA*; RYAN P STEELE, *Department of Chemistry, University of Utah, Salt Lake City, UT, USA.*

The copper hydroxide ion, CuOH+ , serves as the catalytic core in several recently developed water-splitting catalysts, and an understanding of its chemistry is critical to determining viable catalytic mechanisms. In spite of its importance, the electronic structure of this open-shell ion has remained ambiguous in the literature. The source of this ambiguity is demonstrated to be the propensity of this ion to exist between traditional Cu(I) and Cu(II) oxidation-state limits. The spin density of the radical is shown to delocalize between the metal center and surrounding ligands, and increasing hydration serves to exacerbate this behavior. Equation-of-motion coupled-cluster methods were needed for spectral simulations, as well as direct simulation of the role of the deuterium "tag" molecules that are used in modern predissociation spectroscopy experiments. This nominally benign tag molecule underwent direct complexation with the open-valence metal ion, thereby forming a species akin to known metal- complexes and strongly impacting the resulting spectrum. Thermal populations of this configuration and other more traditional non-covalently bound isomers led to considerable broadening of the spectral lineshapes. Therefore, at least for the hydrates, these ions serve as a cautionary tale for the spectroscopy community, wherein the role of the tag is far from benign.

WM13 **10:48 – 10:49**

CHIRPED-PULSE MILLIMETER-WAVE SPECTROSCOPY OF ASTROPHYSICAL RADICALS IN A PULSE JET DISCHARGE EXPERIMENT

OLIVIA CHITARRA, BÉRENGER GANS, OLIVIER PIRALI, MARIE-ALINE MARTIN-DRUMEL, *Institut des Sciences Moléculaires d'Orsay, Université Paris Saclay, CNRS, Orsay, France.*

A decade ago, the advent of broadband chirped-pulse Fourier-transform microwave spectrometers revolutionized rotational spectroscopy in the centimeter-wave region [1]. Commercial solution are available in the millimeter-wave region, and new molecular spectroscopy investigations can now be undertaken.

Motivated by the prospect of enabling new interstellar detections, we have developed a new set-up associating a broadband chirped-pulse Fourier-transform millimeter-wave (W-band) spectrometer and a supersonic jet chamber. Radicals are produced by an electric discharge in the high pressure part of the jet and reactive species are directly probed by the radiation at temperatures as low as few Kelvin.

Using different organic precursors such as acetonitrile (CH_3CN), methanol (CH_3OH) or allene (C_3H_4), we were able to study rich discharge mixtures. Among others, we were able to produce and detect the cyanomethyl radical (CH_2CN) [2], the methoxy radical (CH_3O) [3] and cyclopropenylidene ($c - C_3H_2$) [4] in the vibrational ground state and in several vibrational excited states. In the presentation, technical details of the set-up will be provided, together with the preliminary results we obtained.

[1] Brown, G. G et al., Review of Scientific Instruments, 79, 053103 (2008)
[2] Saito, S. and Yamamoto, S., The Journal of Chemical Physics, 107, 1732 (1997)
[3] Endo, Y. et al., The Journal of Chemical Physics, 81, 122-135 (1984)
[4] Thaddeus, P. et al., The Astrophysical Journal, 299, L63-L66 (1985)

WM14 ***Post-Deadline Abstract*** **10:52 – 10:53**

HIGH RESOLUTION ANION PHOTOELECTRON SPECTRA OF CRYOGENICALLY COOLED SILICON CARBIDES

MARK C BABIN, *Department of Chemistry, University of California - Berkeley, Berkeley, CA, USA*; MARTIN DeWITT, *Chemistry, University of California, Berkeley, Berkeley, CA, USA*; MARISSA L. WEICHMAN, *Department of Chemistry, Princeton Unviersity, Princeton, NJ, USA*; JESSALYN A. DeVINE, *Dynamics at Surfaces, Max Planck Institute for Biophysical Chemistry, Göttingen, Germany*; DANIEL NEUMARK, *Department of Chemistry, The University of California, Berkeley, CA, USA.*

High-resolution anion photoelectron spectra of cryogenically cooled Si_3C^-, $Si_2C_2^-$, and SiC_3^- obtained using slow photoelectron velocity-map imaging (cryo-SEVI) are presented, providing insight into the geometries, energetics, and vibronic structure of the anionic and the neutral clusters. These spectra yield accurate vibrational frequencies for the neutral clusters. They also yield refined adiabatic detachment energies (ADEs) for the ground states of Si_3C^- and $Si_2C_2^-$ of 1.5374(6) eV and 1.9019(4) eV, respectively, while the ADE of a low-lying isomer of SiC_3^- is found to be 1.9050(7) eV. The cryo-SEVI spectra show that the ground state of $Si_2C_2^-$ is a distorted trapezoid, and represent the first confirmation of the distorted trapezoid structure of $Si_2C_2^-$, the only low-lying isomer of this cluster with a permanent dipole moment. Additional transitions are observed from two low-lying anion isomers: a linear structure and a rhombus. The spectrum of SiC_3^-, in combination with electronic structure calculations, suggests that the true ground state of SiC_3 is a ring structure with a transannular C–C bond, addressing a longstanding controversy surrounding this cluster. All three spectra exhibit Franck-Condon forbidden transitions; these are attributed to Herzberg-Teller coupling in Si_3C and SiC_3 and autodetachment from an excited electronic state of $Si_2C_2^-$.

RA. Rotational structure/frequencies

Thursday, June 24, 2021 – 8:0 AM

Room: 2021 Online Everywhere

Chair: G. S. Grubbs II, Missouri University of Science and Technology, Rolla, MO, USA

RA01 **8:00 – 8:01**

THE 130-360 GHZ ROTATIONAL SPECTRUM OF THE CHLORINE ISOTOPOLOGUES OF CHLOROBENZENE AND ITS EXCITED VIBRATIONAL STATES

P. MATISHA DORMAN, BRIAN J. ESSELMAN, R. CLAUDE WOODS, ROBERT J. McMAHON, *Department of Chemistry, University of Wisconsin-Madison, Madison, WI, USA.*

We collected the rotational spectrum of chlorobenzene (C_6H_5Cl, μ = 1.7117(14) D) in the frequency range of 130 – 360 GHz. For the [^{35}Cl]- and [^{37}Cl]- isotopologues, the ground states and a total of at least 15 excited vibrational states have been analyzed and fit as distorted rotors to sextic, A-reduced Hamiltonians with low-errors ($\sigma_{fit} < 50$ kHz). This analysis allowed for precise determination of the vibration-rotation interaction constants for each vibrationally excited state and demonstrated these constants are in quite close agreement with their predicted (B3LYP/6-311+G(2d,p)) values. For the lowest-energy vibrational states, transitions with high K_a and low J include hyperfine-resolved transitions of sufficient intensity to determine the quadrupole coupling constants. These data provide an exhaustive analysis of all accessible vibrational states in our frequency region and expand upon previously measured microwave transitions of chlorobenzene.

RA02 **8:04 – 8:05**

MILLIMETER-WAVE SPECTROSCOPY OF THE EXCITED VIBRATIONAL STATES OF THIOPHENE (C_4H_4S)

VANESSA L. ORR, BRIAN J. ESSELMAN, *Department of Chemistry, University of Wisconsin-Madison, Madison, WI, USA*; YOTARO ICHIKAWA, KAORI KOBAYASHI, *Department of Physics, University of Toyama, Toyama, Japan*; R. CLAUDE WOODS, ROBERT J. McMAHON, *Department of Chemistry, University of Wisconsin-Madison, Madison, WI, USA.*

Thiophene is a five-membered, aromatic heterocycle with C_{2v} symmetry and a moderate dipole (C_4H_4S, μ_a = 0.55 D). A number of fundamental states of thiophene had previously been investigated through ro-vibrational studies in the infrared, but pure rotational spectroscopy had not extended beyond the ground state. We have measured and assigned transitions for 19 excited states by rotational spectroscopy, three of which are the IR inactive, A_2 symmetry states, and several of which are overtones or combination states. The new mm-wave data (40 - 360 GHz) and the previously published high resolution IR data are combined in a global least-squares fit. The interactions between the states permit the determination of several precise fundamental frequencies beyond those previously directly measured by high-resolution IR. The vibrationally excited states treated here are connected by a Fermi interaction and complex set of multiple Coriolis couplings, many of which are determined by the global fit. Several of these states may be treated as isolated vibrational states, but other states are involved in a pentad, a triad, and at least three dyads.

RA03 **8:08 – 8:09**

THE ROTATIONAL ANALYSES OF 2-CYANOPYRIMIDINE ($C_5H_3N_3$) AND 2-CYANOPYRAZINE ($C_5H_3N_3$): VIBRATIONAL GROUND STATES AND DYAD OF LOWEST-ENERGY VIBRATIONALLY EXCITED STATES

HOUSTON H. SMITH, BRIAN J. ESSELMAN, R. CLAUDE WOODS, ROBERT J. McMAHON, *Department of Chemistry, University of Wisconsin-Madison, Madison, WI, USA.*

2-Cyanopyrimidine and 2-cyanopyrazine are attractive molecules for interstellar detection via radioastronomy because they are the pyrimidine and pyrazine analogs of the detected interstellar molecule, benzonitrile, and have substantial dipole moments (μ_a = 6.47 D and μ_a = 4.22 D, respectively). In the present work, we have analyzed and assigned the rotational spectrum of 2-cyanopyrimidine ($C_5H_3N_3$) and 2-cyanopyrazine ($C_5H_3N_3$) for the first time. Using data in the 130 – 360 GHz frequency region, the vibrational ground states of 2-cyanopyrimidine and 2-cyanopyrazine have been least-squares fit to partial octic, distorted-rotor Hamiltonians ($N_{lines} \sim 4000$, σ = 40 kHz, and $N_{lines} \sim 3900$, σ = 39 kHz, respectively). The resulting spectroscopic constants are sufficient for spectral prediction outside of the studied frequency range and enable, for the first time, radioastronomical searches for these molecules. Work currently continues on the least-squares fit of the Coriolis-coupled dyad of the two lowest-energy vibrationally excited states for each molecule. The progression of each least-squares fit will be presented along with a comparison between the two isomers. The complete analysis of these states is expected to yield a highly precise energy separation between these vibrationally excited states, along with an interesting comparison to the analogous dyads of benzonitrile and the cyanopyridines.

RA04 **8:12 – 8:13**

ANALYTICAL QUARTIC CENTRIFUGAL DISTORTION CONSTANTS BY FOURTH-ORDER RAYLEIGH SCHRÖDINGER PERTURBATION THEORY

PETER R. FRANKE, *Department of Chemistry, University of Florida, Gainesville, FL, USA*; JOHN F. STANTON, *Physical Chemistry, University of Florida, Gainesville, FL, USA.*

Recent advances in microwave spectroscopy, allowing for the measurement and fitting of thousands of spectral lines for a given chemical system, have prompted a need for high accuracy predictions of spectroscopic constants. The quartic Centrifugal Distortion (CD) constants are derived at fourth-order in Rayleigh-Schrödinger Vibrational Perturbation Theory (VPT4). Analytical expressions are presented. The constants are implemented in the CFOUR software package in both an explicit sum-over-states form and the analytical (i.e., algebraic) form. The expression for VPT4 quartic CD can be broken into ten distinct contributions, involving products of force constants, Coriolis constants, and coefficients in the expansion of the inverse moment of inertia tensor. It is considerably more complicated than the VPT2 vibration-rotation interaction constants and the VPT4 sextic CD constants. The quartic CD constants first appear at VPT2. The VPT4 level of approximation introduces corrections that are linear in the vibrational quantum numbers. Approximately linear relationships have been identified in analyses of microwave spectra, which allow for direct comparison with the computed CD constants. The VPT4 quartic CD constants require a partial quartic force field, containing all force constants except those for which all indices are different (i.e., ϕ_{ijkl}). As this truncation of quartic force field is usually computed for VPT2 vibrational frequencies, it will be possible to obtain the CD constants alongside routine VPT2 frequencies with negligible added cost.

RA05 **8:16 – 8:17**

PHASE DETERMINATION IN MULTI-ANTENNA DETECTION CHIRPED-PULSE MICROWAVE SPECTROSCOPY

CHRISTIAN SWANSON, NICOLE MOON, AMANDA DUERDEN, JOSHUA E. ISERT, G. S. GRUBBS II, *Department of Chemistry, Missouri University of Science and Technology, Rolla, MO, USA.*

In the last year, a paper was published by our group describing a multi-antenna detection, chirped-pulse Fourier transform microwave (MAD-CP-FTMW) spectrometer. A talk will also be given at this conference regarding this instrument and its design. The major unique aspect of the spectrometer, though, is that it possesses antennae in the traditional (0 degrees), quadrature (two at 90 degrees), and broadcast (180 degrees from the traditional antenna) locations. It was discovered that signal could be detected on the antennae that were not in line with the excitation. Because signal was able to be collected from nontraditional locations, the determination of the phase differences in the free induction decays from differing detection locations has become very important. The methods used to determine the phase shift of collected data, as well as the methods of shifting the data will be discussed.

RA06 **8:20 – 8:21**

MICROWAVE STUDY COMPLEMENTED WITH COMPUTATIONAL DATA OF MONO-CHLOROBENZALDEHYDES

MARIA DOHMEN, *Institute of Physical Chemistry, Georg-August-Universität Göttingen, Göttingen, Germany*; SEAN ARNOLD, *Department of Science and Mathematics, Coker College, Hartsville, SC, USA*; PABLO PINACHO, *FS-SMP, Deutsches Elektronen-Synchrotron (DESY), Hamburg, Germany*; GORDON G BROWN, *Department of Science and Mathematics, Coker College, Hartsville, SC, USA*; MELANIE SCHNELL, *FS-SMP, Deutsches Elektronen-Synchrotron (DESY), Hamburg, Germany*; DANIEL A. OBENCHAIN, *Institute of Physical Chemistry, Georg-August-Universität Göttingen, Göttingen, Germany.*

The coupling of the quadrupolar moment of a nucleus to the molecular rotation causes hyperfine splitting of the rotational transitions, which provides important information about electronic environment and therefore chemical properties. It occurs when the molecular rotation couples with the nuclear spin. Since the coupling is highly sensitive to the electric field gradient, it is useful for structure determination and cross-validation of predicted electric field gradients by quantum chemical calculations.

The series of mono-halogenated benzaldehydes containing fluorine has already been studied [a,b]. We expand on the series by replacing fluorine with a quadrupolar halogen atom ($I(\mathrm{Cl}) = \frac{3}{2}$), presenting broadband [c] and cavity microwave spectroscopy results of *ortho-*, *meta-*, and *para*-chlorobenzaldehyde. The quadrupolar coupling of the chlorine nucleus acts as a local probe for changes of the electric field gradient between the different isomers. The quadrupolar coupling constants are used to benchmark the description of the electric field gradient through dispersion corrected quantum chemical calculations. These studies serve as a baseline for future gas-phase complex studies involving chlorobenzaldehyde and analogue molecules with the heavier halogens, which have more complex spectra.

---

[a] W. Sun, I.B. Lozada, J. van Wijngaarden, *J. Phys. Chem. Chem. A*, **2018**, *122*, 2060.
[b] J. L. Alonso, R. M. Villamañán, *J. Chem. Soc., Faraday Trans. 2*, **1989**, *85*, 137-149.
[c] S. Arnold, J. Garrett, G. Brown, *68. Symposium ISMS*, RK15, **2013**.

RA07 **8:24 – 8:25**

CYCLOHEXANE VIBRATIONS: HIGH RESOLUTION SPECTRA AND ANHARMONIC LOCAL MODE CALCULATIONS

PETER F. BERNATH, *Department of Chemistry and Biochemistry, Old Dominion University, Norfolk, VA, USA*; EDWIN SIBERT, *Department of Chemistry, University of Wisconsin–Madison, Madison, WI, USA.*

High resolution infrared absorption spectra of cyclohexane (C_6H_{12}) have been recorded from 1100 to 4000 cm^{-1} at room temperature and 241 K. Cyclohexane is an oblate symmetric top with D_{3d} symmetry. A rotational analysis was obtained for the ν_{27} (e_u) and ν_{14} (a_{2u}) CH_2 scissor modes at 1452.9 cm^{-1} and 1456.4 cm^{-1}, respectively. Several combination modes were also assigned and rotationally analyzed. The C-H stretching modes are perturbed by overtone and combination modes of the CH_2 scissor vibrations, and an anharmonic local mode calculation was needed to interpret the spectra. The 4 main strong allowed C-H stretching modes appear as two e_u a_{2u} pairs near at 2862 cm^{-1} and 2933 cm^{-1}. The Fermi-resonance local mode model coupling terms give physical insight into the effects that organize the cyclohexane vibrational energy levels. The unstrained cyclohexane molecule is a useful paradigm for six-membered rings in larger chemical and biological systems.

RA08 **8:28 – 8:29**

SPECTROSCOPIC CHARACTERIZATION OF *E*- AND *Z*-PHENYLMETHANIMINE[a]

ALESSIO MELLI[b], LORENZO SPADA, VINCENZO BARONE, *Scuola Normale Superiore, Scuola Normale Superiore, Pisa, Italy*; SVEN HERBERS, KEVIN G. LENGSFELD, JENS-UWE GRABOW, *Institut für Physikalische Chemie und Elektrochemie, Gottfried-Wilhelm-Leibniz-Universität, Hannover, Germany*; MATTIA MELOSSO, LUCA DORE, *Dept. Chemistry "Giacomo Ciamician", University of Bologna, Bologna, ITALY*; CRISTINA PUZZARINI, *Dep. Chemistry 'Giacomo Ciamician', University of Bologna, Bologna, Italy.*

The two isomers (*E* and *Z*) of the aromatic imine phenylmethanimine (PMI) have been investigated by means of a multidisciplinary approach involving organic synthesis, nuclear magnetic resonance and rotational spectroscopy, supported and guided by computational chemistry. The choice of this molecule has been driven by its twofold relevance in chemistry, in the fields of organic synthesis and astrochemistry.

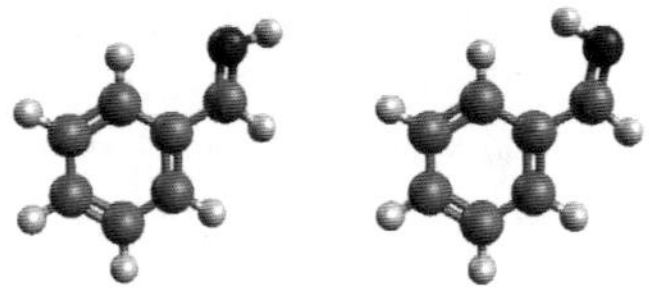

To face both aspects, an accessible synthetic approach to generate stable imine-intermediates in the gas phase and in solution has been introduced. Exploiting this formation pathway (which is based on the thermal decomposition of hydrobenzamide, HBA) and thanks to a state-of-the-art computational characterization of PMI, we laid the foundation for its first laboratory observation by means of rotational spectroscopy. At first, the 3-26 GHz range has been investigated for *E*- and *Z*-PMI using a Fourier-transform microwave spectrometer. Successively, the measurements have been extended in the 83-100 GHz range for *E*-PMI exploiting a frequency-modulation millimeter-wave spectrometer. Both isomers have been accurately characterized, thus providing a reliable basis to guide future astronomical observations. Furthermore, the feasibility of this synthetic approach in solution has been assessed by nuclear magnetic resonance spectroscopy. Finally, the temperature dependence as well as possible mechanisms of the thermolysis process have been examined exploiting both NMR and rotational spectroscopy techinques.

[a] A. Melli et al., *Chem. Eur. J.* **2020**, 26, 15016-15022.
[b] Also affiliated at Università di Bologna, Dept. Chemistry "Giacomo Ciamician", Bologna, Italy.

RA09 **8:32 – 8:33**

THE MILLIMETER/SUBMILLIMETER SPECTRUM OF 2-CHLOROETHANOL

HAYLEY BUNN, *Department of Chemistry, University of Wisconsin-Madison, Madison, WI, USA*; SUSANNA L. WIDICUS WEAVER, *Chemistry and Astronomy, University of Wisconsin-Madison, Madison, WI, USA.*

2-chloroethanol, the simplest chlorohydrin, is known to exist in 5 distinct conformers. The lowest energy conformer is gauche-gauche, designating the internal rotation around the C-C bond and the C-O bond, respectively. High resolution microwave[a] and far-infrared[b] spectra of the gauche-gauche conformer have been reported in the literature. 2-choloroethanol may play a role in interstellar chemistry. Since HCl constitutes at least 90% of the chlorine in the interstellar medium and its reaction with other known interstellar constituents (i.e., oxirane or ethylene glycol) is predicted to form 2-chloroethanol. However, attempts at its detection towards Sgr B2(N) have been unsuccessful. It is not clear if the lack of detection arises from its lack of presence in this sightline, its weak spectrum, or whether the extrapolated spectral information for 2-cholorethanol is not of sufficient accuracy to guide astronomical searches. Therefore, we have measured the spectrum of 2-chloroethanol in the millimeter/submillimeter region to further improve the constants and provide spectral frequencies directly comparable to telescopes such as ALMA. In this talk we will report on the experimental results and the progress on analysis of the 2-chloroethanol spectrum.

[a] R. G. Azark, E. B. Wilson, J. Chem. Phys., 52, 5299 (1970)
[b] R. M. Soliday, H. Bunn, I. Sumner, P. L. Raston, J. Phys. Chem., 123, 1208-1216 (2019)

RA10 **8:36 – 8:37**

ROTATIONAL SPECTRUM OF 2-CYCLOPROPYLIDENEACETONITRILE - A NEW ISOMER OF PYRIDINE

BRIAN J. ESSELMAN, SAMUEL M. KOUGIAS, R. CLAUDE WOODS, ROBERT J. McMAHON, *Department of Chemistry, University of Wisconsin-Madison, Madison, WI, USA.*

2-Cyclopropylideneacetonitrile (C_5H_5N, C_s, μ_a = 4.4 D, μ_b = 1.2 D) is a nitrile-containing structural isomer of pyridine. While pyridine has not been detected in the interstellar medium, its nitrile-containing isomers remain attractive targets for spectroscopists and radioastronomers. We have recently generated 2-cyclopropylideneacetonitrile via a two-step synthesis and obtained its rotational spectrum from 130 – 360 GHz. We have assigned and least-squares fit several thousand observed transitions to A- and S-reduced, octic Hamiltonians with low statistical uncertainty (σ less than 50 kHz). The work has yielded precise rotational constants that are in good agreement with their B3LYP and CCSD(T) values. The spectra of several vibrationally excited states have also been observed and assigned using their computed vibration-rotation interaction constants (A_0-A_v).

RA11 ***Post-Deadline Abstract*** **8:40 – 8:41**

CHEMICAL DISTRIBUTION OF ACETALDEHYDE IN ORION KL

MIWHA JIN, *Department of Chemistry, University of Virginia, Charlottesville, VA, USA*; ANTHONY REMIJAN, *ALMA, National Radio Astronomy Observatory, Charlottesville, VA, USA*; ROBIN T. GARROD, *Departments of Chemistry and Astronomy, The University of Virginia, Charlottesville, VA, USA.*

Despite the chemical richness of Orion KL, one of the ubiquitous aldehydes – acetaldehyde (CH_3CHO; AA) – has been only tentatively identified toward this region. We have investigated an extensive ALMA archive dataset of which frequency coverage spreads between 142 GHz - 355 GHz to search for AA and other unexplored aldehydes. Four emission components of AA are clearly identified toward Orion KL, showing its main emission peak towards hot core-SW (HC-SW). The column densities of AA and its kinetic temperatures is estimated toward this main emission region, assuming molecular excitation under local thermodynamic equilibrium conditions. The distribution of acetaldehyde is compared with the other aldehyde-like (CHO-bearing) species from the literatures such as methyl formate (CH_3OCHO;MF), glycolaldehyde (CH_2OHCHO;GA) and formic acid (HCOOH;FA). AA shows the abundance and the spatial distribution similar to that of FA, implying the chemical relation between them. The relative abundance ratios between the aldehyde-like species (hereafter, relative aldehydes ratios) towards HC-SW are investigated with a chemical model. The model shows that relatively longer collapsing timescale and the MF binding energy similar to water are needed to explain the observation. The relative aldehydes ratios estimated from the model sensitively depend on the assumed kinetic temperature. This explains the high spatial variability of the relative aldehydes ratios from the observations.

RA12 **8:44 – 8:45**

THE MILLIMETER- AND SUBMILLIMETER-WAVE SPECTROSCOPY OF ISOPRENE.

DANIEL J TYREE, IVAN MEDVEDEV, *Department of Physics, Wright State University, Dayton, OH, USA.*

Isoprene also known as 2-methyl-1,3-butadiene (CH_2=C(CH_3)-CH=CH_2) is a biologically important unsaturated hydrocarbon produced by many plants and animals. For example, it is present in exhaled human breath at a few hundred part per billion level of volumetric dilution. It is also thought to be contributing to the infrared spectra of interstellar carbonaceous dust, and thus can be relevant for analysis of interstellar gas clouds. In this presentation we report on our recent analysis of the rotational spectra of isoprene in its vibrational ground state recorded in 210 – 500 GHz spectral range.

RA13 **8:48 – 8:49**

THE MILLIMETER/SUBMILLIMETER SPECTRUM OF DIACETYL

JONATHAN REBELSKY, *Department of Chemistry, University of Wisconsin Madison, Madison, WI, USA*; CHASE P SCHULTZ, *Department of Chemistry, University of Wisconsin-Madison, Madison, WI, USA*; SUSANNA L. WIDICUS WEAVER, *Chemistry and Astronomy, University of Wisconsin-Madison, Madison, WI, USA*.

Diacetyl is a common food flavoring, used most commonly in microwave popcorn. In addition to being a molecule of culinary significance, diacetyl is also a molecule of atmospheric interest, as it is an important source of HO_x in the atmosphere. Of specific interest to astronomy, diacetyl was recently made in an interstellar ice analogue. Despite the number of studies on its vibrational characteristics, there have been no rotational studies done on this molecule. In this talk we will present the experimental results and preliminary assignment of the diacetyl rotational spectrum from 20-1000 GHz. This spectrum will allow for the potential detection of this molecule in the interstellar medium.

RA14 **8:52 – 8:53**

INVESTIGATION OF PURE ROTATIONAL SPECTROSCOPY OF ETHYNYLBENZONITRILE ISOMERS USING CHIRPED-PULSE W-BAND SPECTROSCOPY

JEAN-THIBAUT SPANIOL, *Institut des Sciences Moléculaires d'Orsay, Université Paris Saclay, CNRS, Orsay, France*; KELVIN LEE, *Department of Chemistry, MIT, Cambridge, MA, USA*; OLIVIER PIRALI, MARIE-ALINE MARTIN-DRUMEL, *Institut des Sciences Moléculaires d'Orsay, Université Paris Saclay, CNRS, Orsay, France*.

Simple aromatic molecules may be precursors for polycyclic aromatic hydrocarbons in space, and some of the simplest ones are now detected in the earliest stages of star formation [1]. Evidence of benzonitrile (C_6H_5–CN) in the interstellar medium [2] questions the presence of related aromatic nitriles and their ring-chain derivatives. In light of previous work [3] on phenylpropiolonitrile (C_6H_5–C_3N), we are investigating, by laboratory high-resolution studies, its ethynylbenzonitrile (HCC–C_6H_4–CN) derivatives where a –CN and a –CCH groups lie in ortho (2-ETB), meta (3-ETB) or para (4-ETB) positions.

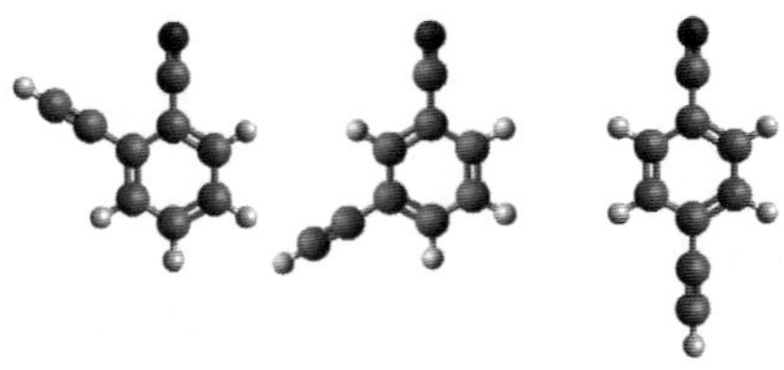

The pure rotational spectrum of these compounds has been recorded at room temperature in the millimeter-wave domain using a chirped-pulse W-band (75–110 GHz) spectrometer. To facilitate spectral assignments, quantum chemical calculations have been performed using density functional theory at the ωB97X-D/cc-pVQZ level of theory (geometry optimization, harmonic frequencies).

We will report a description of the experimental set-up and of our assignment procedure.

[1] A.Burkhardt et al., Nature Astronomy 5, 181-187 (2021)
[2] McGuire et al., Science 359, 202-205 (2018)
[3] Z.Buchanan et al., Journal of Molecular Spectroscopy, in press (2021)

RB. Mini-symposium: Precision Spectroscopy for Fundamental Physics

Thursday, June 24, 2021 – 8:0 AM

Room: 2021 Online Everywhere

Chair: Andrew Jayich, University of California, Santa Barbara, , USA

RB01 *INVITED TALK* **8:00 – 8:02**

SPECTROSCOPY OF SHORT-LIVED RADIOACTIVE MOLECULES

RONALD FERNANDO GARCIA RUIZ , *Department of Physics, MIT, Cambridge, MA, USA.*

Molecules containing heavy and octupole deformed radioactive nuclei are predicted to provide enhanced sensitivity to investigate the violation of fundamental symmetries and to search for physics beyond the Standard Model of particle physics. However, experimental measurements of such radioactive systems are scarce. Octupole deformed nuclei are very rare in nature or do not occur naturally. Thus, their study requires to overcome major experimental challenges. This contribution will discuss the recent achievements in laser spectroscopy of radioactive molecules at CRIS, ISOLDE-CERN. This talk will discuss recent spectroscopy measurements of short-lived radium fluoride molecules (RaF) alongside future perspectives in the study of other radioactive molecules. The impact of these developments in fundamental physics research will be discussed.

RB02 **8:08 – 8:09**

THEORETICAL STUDY OF PROPERTIES OF RADIUM MONOFLUORIDE

ALEKSANDRA A. KYUBERIS, ANASTASIA BORSCHEVSKY, *Van Swinderen Institute, Universiteit Groningen, Groningen, Netherlands*; LUKÁŠ FÉLIX PAŠTEKA, *Department of Experimental Physics, Comenius University, Bratislava, Slovakia.*

Heavy diatomic molecules are currently considered to be among the most sensitive systems used in the search for the eEDM and in probing of the Standard Model of particle physics. In certain molecules effects resulting from both parity violation and time-reversal violation (P,T- odd effects) are considerably enhanced with respect to atomic systems. The strength of these interactions grows with atomic number, nuclear spin and nuclear deformation. RaF is of particular interest because it is predicted to have an electronic structure appropriate for laser cooling and also being sensitive to the new phenomena[a]. The suitability of RaF for laser-cooling depends critically on its energy levels structure, lifetimes of its excited states, vibrational branching ratios and electronic transition probabilities. Although experimental knowledge of radioactive molecules is scarce, a recent work[b] presented an approach for performing laser spectroscopy of short-lived radioactive molecules, using the highly sensitive collinear resonance ionization method. As an example of the novel technique RaF was used. This work aims to determine properties at the highest possible level of computational accuracy, following the procedure from our earlier work[c], to conclude on the suitability of RaF for laser-cooling and compare with existing experimental data. We present high-accuracy relativistic Fock-Space coupled cluster calculations of the potential energy curves and the spectroscopic constants of the ground state and the lower excited states of RaF. The ionization potential of RaF was calculated and the Franck-Cordon factors were obtained, based on calculated potential energy curves. We have also calculated the TDMs of different transitions using multireference configuration interaction approach. Based on defined TDMs and experimental transitions, lifetimes of the excited states in RaF were determined. The new results are compared with existing theoretical and experimental data.

[a] L.V. Skripnikov. J. Chem. Phys. 153, 114114, 2020

[b] R.F. Garcia Ruiz et al. Nature, 581, 396-400, 2020

[c] Y. Hao et al. J. Chem . Phys. 151, 034302, 2019

RB03 **8:12 – 8:13**

INFLUENCE OF VIBRATIONS ON THE SENSITIVITY OF RAOH AND YBOH MOLECULES TO THE P, T-VIOLATION

ANNA ZAKHAROVA, ALEXANDER PETROV, *Division of Innovations, NRC "Kurchatov Institute" PNPI, Gatchina, Leningrad region, Russia.*

To find a new physics beyond the Standard Model (SM), it is necessary to investigate effects that violate the invariance with respect to spatial reflections and time reversal, such as the electric dipole moment of an electron (eEDM) and the scalar-pseudoscalar electron-nuclear interaction. Triatomic molecules that we study in this paper combine the advantages of the opposite parity closely spaced levels (l-doublets) and the possibility of laser cooling that makes them promising species for high-precision experiments. The average value of the operators responsible for the violation of spatial and temporal parity can be affected by the vibrational modes of molecules, which were not previously taken into account in theoretical calculations. We computed the parameters of $\mathcal{P}$, $\mathcal{T}$-odd interactions of E_{eff} and E_s for nonlinear configurations of the RaOH [a] and YbOH molecules with subsequent averaging over the vibrational wave function. We also obtained the value of l-doubling, that determines the value of the external field necessary for the maximum sensitivity of the molecule to $\mathcal{P}$, $\mathcal{T}$-odd effects. We obtained molecular orbitals by the Dirac-Hartree-Fock method implemented in Dirac 19 software package. Potential surfaces were calculated by the coupled cluster method taking into account triple excitations (CCSD(T)). To describe the electronic structure of heavy atoms, we used a generalized effective core potential with the restoration of the correct behavior of four-component spinors in the core region. This method was extended by us to complex molecular spinors. The vibrational wave functions were obtained in the Born-Oppenheimer approximation by the coupled channel method.

[a] A. Zakharova, A. Petrov, P,T-odd effects for RaOH molecule in the excited vibrational state, arXiv:2012.08427 [physics.atom-ph]

RB04 ***Post-Deadline Abstract*** **8:16 – 8:17**

CALCULATION OF THE CORRECTION ON THE MAGNETIZATION DISTRIBUTION IN THE NUCLEUS TO THE HYPERFINE STRUCTURE OF HEAVY ATOMS

SERGEY PROSNYAK, *Division of Innovations, NRC "Kurchatov Institute" PNPI, Gatchina, Russia*; LEONID V. SKRIPNIKOV, *Division of Innovations, NRC "Kurchatov Institute" PNPI, Gatchina, Leningrad region, Russia*; DANIEL E. MAISON, *Division of Innovations, NRC "Kurchatov Institute" PNPI, Gatchina, Russia.*

To reproduce accurately experimental values of hyperfine spliting of heavy atoms one have to take into account the corrections for the distribution of charge (the Breit-Rosenthal effect[a]) and magnetization (the Bohr-Weisskopf effect[b]) over the nucleus. In the presented study, a program was written to calculate the Bohr-Weisskopf correction in the one-particle model of the nucleus, in which the distribution of the valence nucleon is found from the solution of the Schrödinger equation with the Woods-Saxon potential. It was used to calculate the hyperfine structure of a neutral Tl atom, as well as a hyperfine magnetic anomaly - a special combination of hyperfine interaction constants and g factors of two different isotopes, which is quite sensitive to differences in the magnetization distribution. By comparing the results obtained with the model of a uniformly magnetized ball[c], it was shown that, with a sufficient accuracy, the ratio of anomalies for two electronic states is stable with respect to the choice of the nuclear model and its parameters[d]. This fact is important because it is used to predict the magnetic moments of short-lived nuclei. In addition, the differential hyperfine anomaly was calculated in the above mentioned nuclear models and the results obtained were compared with experimental data.

Calculations of the electronic structure were carried out with the support of the grant of the Russian Science Foundation (project 19-72-10019). The calculation of the correction for the Breit interaction in the Gaunt approximation was carried out with the support of the RFBR grant (project 20-32-70177).

[a] M. Crawford, Phys. Rev. 76, 1310 (1949).
[b] A. Bohr and V. Weisskopf, Physical Review 77, 94 (1950).
[c] Prosnyak, S. D., Maison, D. E., Skripnikov, L. V., The Journal of Chemical Physics, 152(4), 044301. (2020).
[d] S. Schmidt, J. Billowes, M. Bissell, K. Blaum, R. G. Ruiz, H. Heylen, S. Malbrunot-Ettenauer, G. Neyens, W. Nörtershäuser, G. Plunien, et al., Phys. Lett. B 779, 324 (2018).

RB05 **8:20 – 8:21**

SEARCH FOR PARITY VIOLATION USING ^{177,179}HFF^{+} CATIONS

IGOR KURCHAVOV, ALEXANDER PETROV, *Division of Innovations, NRC "Kurchatov Institute" PNPI, Gatchina, Leningrad region, Russia.*

Considering the great potential for investigations of T, P-violating effects on HfF^{+} ions [1], it was proposed in Ref. [2] to use ^{177}Hf^{19}F^{+} and ^{179}Hf^{19}F^{+} ions to measure nuclear magnetic quadrupole moment (MQM) of ^{177}Hf and ^{179}Hf nuclei which have spins $I = 7/2$ and $I = 9/2$ respectively.

The important characteristic of the experiments on HfF^{+} is that *rotating* magnetic and electric fields are used to trap ions [1]. In this case, the magnetic field, in contrast to experiments in static fields, is not an auxiliary tool, but should ensure a nonzero energy shift due to possible T, P-odd effects [3]. To completely polarize the molecule and to access the maximum T, P-odd effect both rotating electric and magnetic fields should be large enough. The saturating value of the magnetic field is strongly depends on the considered Zeeman sublevel of the ion. These values are required to plan the experiment and their calclation is the main aim of the work.

To populate the required levels in experiments one needs to know energy levels structure. This problem is especially important for ^{177,179}HfF^{+} since it has dense spectrum due to high nuclear spins of ^{177,179}Hf. Further, the knowledge of g-factors helps to control and suppress systematic effects due to stray magnetic field therefore calculations of these properties in external fields are also made in our work [4].

[1] W. B. Cairncross, D. N. Gresh, M. Grau, K. C. Cossel, T. S. Roussy, Y. Ni, Y. Zhou, J. Ye, and E. A. Cornell, Phys. Rev. Lett.**119**, 153001 (2017)

[2] V. V. Flambaum, D. DeMille, and M. G. Kozlov, Phys. Rev. Lett. **113**, 103003 (2014)

[3] A. N. Petrov, Phys. Rev. A **97**, 052504 (2018).

[4] I. P. Kurchavov and A. N. Petrov, Phys. Rev. A, **102**, 032805 (2020)

RB06 **8:24 – 8:25**

TANTALUM OXIDE SPECTROSCOPY TO FACILITATE EXPLORING NEW PHYSICS BEYOND THE STANDARD MODEL

TIMOTHY CHUNG, MATTHEW CHARLES COOPER, *Physics, University of Nevada, Las Vegas, Las Vegas, Nevada, USA*; YAN ZHOU, *Department of Physics and Astronomy, University of Nevada, Las Vegas, Las Vegas, NV, USA.*

The molecular ion TaO^{+} is a promising candidate to explore new physics beyond the Standard Model in both the leptonic and hadronic sectors via precision measurements of the electron's Electric Dipole Moment (eEDM) and Nucleus Magnetic Magnetic Quadrupole Moment (NMQM) [citation]. Similar to ThF^{+} that is under active investigation[citation], the eEDM sensitive state of TaO^{+}, $^{3}\Delta_1$, is predicted to be the ground state that facilitates a long coherent measurement[citation]. Although TaO^{+} has a smaller effective electric field (20.2 GV/cm) than ThF^{+} (35.2 GV/cm), it has a non-zero nuclear spin ($I = 7/2$) for which the latter is 0, allowing for studies of symmetry break in the nucleus, such as the NMQM, in a single experimental system. To perform the above mentioned precision measurements, the first step is to create TaO^{+} in the rovibraonic ground state ($^{3}\Delta_1$, v^{+}=0, and J^{+}=1). We plan to implement Resonant Enhanced Multiphoton Ionization (REMPI) method to create TaO^{+} from its neutral precursor TaO in a supersonic cooled molecular beam. To locate an appropriate intermediate electronic state for the REMPI scheme, we perform laser induced fluorescence spectroscopy of TaO in the regime of 30,000-45,000 cm^{-1} that is unexplored. Preliminary results of the survey spectroscopy and experimental design of the precision measurements will be discussed in this presentation.

RB07 **8:28 – 8:29**

TAO$^+$ CATION FOR THE STUDY OF QUADRUPLE NEUTRON DISTRIBUTION IN NUCLEI

GLEB OLEGOVICH PENYAZKOV, LEONID V. SKRIPNIKOV, *Division of Innovations, NRC "Kurchatov Institute" PNPI, Gatchina, Leningrad region, Russia.*

Studying the effects of spatial parity (P) nonconservation of fundamental interactions in atoms and molecules, it is possible to refine the parameters of the standard model in laboratory conditions, as well as to set constraints on the parameters of its extensions. Such experiments [1] were most successfully carried out for the Cs atom. Using the expression for the P-odd electron-nuclear weak interaction and expanding it in a series in terms of the multipole moments of the nuclear density, one can obtain the quadrupole term [2,3]. Since the weak charge of the neutron considerably exceeds the weak charge of the proton, the main contribution to the considered interaction is due to the neutron subsystem of the nucleus. Therefore, by studying the interaction of this type, it is possible (for the first time) to study the quadrupole distribution of neutrons in a nucleus. Using a two-step method for calculating the properties of atoms in compounds of heavy elements [4], we study the P-odd tensor interaction of the electron subsystem with the neutron quadrupole moment of the nucleus in the TaO^+ cation. We also study a possible contribution of the P-odd interaction of electrons with the Tl anapole moment. Finally, the energy levels of the TaO^+ molecule are predicted. The study was supported by a grant from the Russian Science Foundation (project No. 19-72-10019).

1. C. S. Wood, S. C. Bennett, D. Cho, B. P. Masterson, J. L. Roberts, C. E. Tanner, and C. E. Wieman, Science 275, 1759 (1997).

2. V.V. Flambaum, V.A. Dzuba, C. Harabati, Phys. Rev. A 96, 012516 (2017).

3. L.V. Skripnikov, A. N. Petrov, A. V. Titov, V. V. Flambaum, Phys. Rev. A 99, 012517 (2019).

4. A. V. Titov, N. S. Mosyagin, A. N. Petrov, T. A. Isaev, D. P. DeMille, Progr. Theor. Chem. Phys. 15, 253 (2006).

RB08 **8:32 – 8:33**

ACCURATE PREDICTION OF CLOCK TRANSITIONS IN A HIGHLY CHARGED ION WITH COMPLEX ELECTRONIC STRUCTURE

CHARLES CHEUNG, MARIANNA SAFRONOVA, SERGEY PORSEV, *Department of Physics and Astronomy, University of Delaware, Newark, DE, USA*; MIKHAIL KOZLOV, *Kurchatov Institute, Petersburg Nuclear Physics Institute of NRC, Gatchina, Russia*; ILYA TUPITSYN, *Institute of Physics, St. Petersburg State University, St.Petersburg, Russia*; ANDREY BONDAREV, *Center for Advanced Studies, Peter the Great St. Petersburg Polytechnic University, St. Petersburg, Russia.*

It was recently shown that coupling of ultralight scalar dark matter to the standard model leads to oscillations of fundamental constants and, therefore, may be observed in clock-comparison experiments. Highly charged ions such as Ir^{17+} allow for the development of novel atomic clocks with high sensitivity to the variation of the fine-structure constant and, therefore, dark matter searches. The clock transitions are weak and very difficult to identity without accurate theoretical predictions. In the case of Ir^{17+}, even stronger electric-dipole (E1) transitions eluded observations despite years of effort raising the possibility that theory predictions are grossly wrong. In this work, we have developed a broadly-applicable approach that drastically increases the ability to accurately predict properties of complex atoms and applied it to Ir^{17+} providing accurate predictions of transition wavelengths and E1 transition rates. Our results explain the lack of observation of the E1 transitions and provide a pathway towards detection of clock transitions. Computational advances demonstrated in this work are widely applicable to most elements in the periodic table and will allow to solve numerous problems in atomic physics, astrophysics, and plasma physics. We are currently developing an online portal with access to a database of high-precision atomic properties and a package of atomic codes that can be used to compute these properties.

RB09 **8:36 – 8:37**

QUANTUM LOGIC CONTROL AND SPECTROSCOPY OF A SINGLE MOLECULAR ION

ALEJANDRA COLLOPY, *Time and Frequency Division, National Institute of Standards and Technology, Boulder, CO, USA*; DAVID LEIBRANDT, *Time and Frequency Division; Department of Physics, National Institute of Standards and Technology; University of Colorado, Boulder, CO, USA*; DIETRICH LEIBFRIED, CHIN-WEN CHOU, *Time and Frequency Division, National Institute of Standards and Technology, Boulder, CO, USA.*

Pure quantum states of charged molecules can now be prepared, coherently manipulated, and efficiently detected in high-resolution spectroscopy experiments by employing quantum-logic spectroscopy, an action spectroscopy at the single quantum level. The coupled harmonic motion of co-trapped ions can be utilized to transfer action information from a "spectroscopy" molecular ion to an easily manipulated and detected atomic "logic" ion. With this technique and precise characterization of the systematic effects of the trap RF electric field on molecular levels, we demonstrate hertz-level resolution in terahertz-scale rotational spectroscopy of a single CaH^+ molecule using a Ca^+ logic ion. Precision measurements of molecular transitions can be used to determine molecular properties, and here we experimentally determine the CaH^+ dipole moment for the first time. In addition to detecting departure from the initial state, we can also detect arrival into the final state, facilitating confirmation of transition assignment in cases where the spectrum is congested or a priori information is limited. Because all of our laser operations on the molecule are driving stimulated Raman transitions with the lasers far detuned from molecular transitions, the techniques should be generalizable to a wide variety of charged molecules.

–A.L. Collopy et al., in preparation
–Chou, C-W. et al., Science 367, 6485 (2020)
–Lin, Y. et al. Nature 581, 273–277(2020)

RB10 **8:40 – 8:41**

SPECTROSCOPIC CHARACTERIZATION OF A THERMODYNAMICALLY STABLE DOUBLY CHARGED DIATOMIC MOLECULE: $MgAr^{2+}$

DOMINIK WEHRLI, MATTHIEU GÉNÉVRIEZ, FRÉDÉRIC MERKT, *Laboratorium für Physikalische Chemie, ETH Zurich, Zurich, Switzerland.*

Although numerous doubly positively charged diatomic molecules (diatomic dications) are known from investigations using mass spectrometry and *ab-initio* quantum chemistry, only three of them, NO^{2+}, N_2^{2+} and DCl^{2+}, have been studied using rotationally resolved optical spectroscopy[a] and only about a dozen by vibrationally resolved double-ionization methods [b]. So far, no thermodynamically stable diatomic dication has been characterized spectroscopically, primarily because of experimental difficulties associated with their synthesis in sufficient densities in the gas phase. Indeed, such molecules typically involve, as constituents, rare-gas, halogen, or chalcogen, and metal atoms. We report on a new approach to study molecular dications based on high-resolution PFI-ZEKE photoelectron spectroscopy of the singly charged parent molecular cation and present the first spectroscopic characterization of a thermodynamically stable diatomic dication, $MgAr^{2+}$. We have observed the partially resolved rotational structure of several vibrational levels of the ground electronic state of $MgAr^{2+}$ using a resonant (1+1'+1") three-photon excitation scheme. From the analysis of the photoelectron spectra of $^{24}MgAr^+$ and $^{26}MgAr^+$ we have determined the potential-energy function of the electronic ground state of $MgAr^{2+}$, its dissociation (binding) energy ($D_0 = 10690(3)$ cm^{-1}), and its harmonic ($\omega_e(^{24}MgAr^{2+}) = 327.02(11)$ cm^{-1}) and anharmonic ($\omega_e x_e(^{24}MgAr^{2+}) = 2.477(15)$ cm^{-1}) vibrational constants. The analysis enables us to explain quantitatively how the strong bond arises in this dication despite the fact that Ar and Mg^{2+} both have a full-shell rare-gas electronic configuration.

[a] P. C. Cosby, R. Möller, and H. Helm, Phys. Rev. A **28**, 766 (1983), D. Cossart, M. Bonneau, and J. M. Robbe, J. Mol. Spectrosc. **125**, 413 (1987), S. G. Cox, A. D. J. Critchley, P. S. Kreynin, I. R. McNab, R. C. Shiell, and F. E. Smith, Phys. Chem. Chem. Phys. **5**, 663 (2003)

[b] J. H. D. Eland and R. Feifel, *Double Photoinisation Spectra of Molecules* (Oxford University Press, 2018)

RB11 **8:44 – 8:45**

HYBRID LINE LIST AND SPECTROSCOPIC MODEL FOR CN

ANNA-MAREE SYME, LAURA K McKEMMISH, *School of Chemistry, University of New South Wales, Sydney, NSW, Australia.*

Accurate line lists are important for the description of the spectroscopic nature of small molecules. Given the significant role played by the CN radical in the chemical and astrophysical sciences, we present the process of creation for a new line list, from the collation of experimental data to the production of a hybrid line list. 8083 empirical rovibronic energy levels with uncertainties are determined for 8 doublet states of CN using the MARVEL (Measured Active Rotational-Vibrational Energy Levels) algorithm from 40,333 transitions. These empirical energy levels are utilised in a fitting process to create a spectroscopic model of the three lowest electronic states, using the nuclear motion program; DUO. A final Hybrid line list (up to $60,000\ \mathrm{cm}^{-1}$) has been created with the addition of results from a pre-existing model Hamiltonian line list (MoLList). Applications of the Spectroscopic Model are explored for the calculation of sensitivities to a variation of the proton-to-electron mass ratio.

RB12 **8:48 – 8:49**

VIBRATIONAL BENDING MODES METROLOGY IN THE 670-720 cm^{-1}RANGE

MARCO LAMPERTI, RICCARDO GOTTI, DAVIDE GATTI, *Department of Physics - Institute of Photonics and Nanotechnology, Politecnico di Milano, Lecco, Italy*; MOHAMMAD KHALED SHAKFA, *Clean Combustion Research Center, King Abdullah University of Science and Technology (KAUST), Thuwal, Saudi Arabia*; ELISABETTA CANÈ, FILIPPO TAMASSIA, *Dipartimento di Chimica Industriale "Toso Montanari", Università di Bologna, Bologna, Italy*; PAOLO LAPORTA, *Dipartimento di Fisica, Politecnico di Milano, Milano, Italy*; P. G. SCHUNEMANN, , *BAE Systems, Nashua, NH, USA*; AAMIR FAROOQ, *Clean Combustion Research Center, King Abdullah University of Science and Technology (KAUST), Thuwal, Saudi Arabia*; MARCO MARANGONI, *Dipartimento di Fisica, Politecnico di Milano, Milano, Italy.*

We introduce a comb-referenced optical spectrometer operating in the long-wavelength (LW) part of the mid-infrared (MIR) region. It is based on an innovative laser source based on difference frequency generation between two MIR lasers, namely a cw DFB-QCL and a CO_2 laser, which produces widely tunable light from 12.1 to 14.8 μm with optical power up to 110 μW and MHz-level linewidth. We exploit it to give the first evidence of bending modes metrology in this region, with the assessment of several CO_2-based frequency benchmarks with uncertainties down to 30 kHz, and the accurate study of the ν_{11} band of benzene, which is a significant testbed for the resolution of the spectrometer. These results foster optical metrology in a region not explored so far and pave the way for accurate rotationally-resolved studies of the energy structure of large molecules, such as aromatic hydrocarbons.

RB13 **8:52 – 8:53**

MULTISPECTRUM ROTATIONAL STATES DISTRIBUTION THERMOMETRY

RICCARDO GOTTI, MARCO LAMPERTI, DAVIDE GATTI, *Department of Physics - Institute of Photonics and Nanotechnology, Politecnico di Milano, Lecco, Italy*; SZYMON WOJTEWICZ, *Institute of Physics, Faculty of Physics, Astronomy and Informatics, Nicolaus Copernicus University, Torun, Poland*; THOMAS PUPPE, YURIY MAYZLIN, *Frequency Combs Research and Development, TOPTICA Photonics AG, Gräfelfing, Germany*; BIDOOR ALSAIF, *Clean combustion research center, King abdullah university for science and technology, Thuwal, Saudi arabia*; JULIAN ROBINSON-TAIT, FELIX ROHDE, RAFAL WILK, PATRICK LEISCHING, WILHELM KAENDERS, *Frequency Combs Research and Development, TOPTICA Photonics AG, Gräfelfing, Germany*; PAOLO LAPORTA, MARCO MARANGONI, *Dipartimento di Fisica, Politecnico di Milano, Milano, Italy*.

We introduce Multispectrum Rotational states Distribution Thermometry (MRDT) as a new optical method for primary thermometry that relies on the global fitting of multiple molecular absorption lines of the same band at different pressures. This allows leveraging the temperature-dependence of the Doppler width and also of the distribution of line intensities across the ro-vibrational band, provided a sufficiently accurate line-strength model is available. We give a preliminary demonstration of the method with a comb-locked frequency-swept cavity-ring-down spectrometer operated on the $3\nu_1+\nu_3$ band of CO_2 located around 1577 nm, which stands out among other spectroscopic samples for the availability of several line intensity models of both experimental and theoretical origin. The spectra signal-to-noise ratio represents the main limitation to a combined uncertainty to 530 ppm, but the comparative analysis between different line-strength models shows promise to reduce the error budget to 33 ppm. As compared to Doppler-broadening-thermometry, an advantage of the approach is the reduced impact of a wrong modelling of the absorption line-shapes. In a reversed approach, MRDT can be applied on a gas of known temperature to set an upper limit to the accuracy of a given line intensity model.

RC. Astronomy
Thursday, June 24, 2021 – 8:0 AM
Room: 2021 Online Everywhere

Chair: Mitsunori Araki, Tokyo University of Science, Shinjuku-ku, Tokyo, Japan

RC01 **8:00 – 8:01**

A STATUS REPORT ON THE COLOGNE DATABASE FOR MOLECULAR SPECTROSCOPY, CDMS

HOLGER S. P. MÜLLER, P. SCHILKE, STEPHAN SCHLEMMER, *I. Physikalisches Institut, Universität zu Köln, Köln, Germany.*

The CDMS[a] was founded more than 20 years ago to provide in its catalog section line lists of mostly molecular species which were or may be detected in space by radio astronomical means.[b] The line lists are generated by fitting critically evaluated experimental data, mostly from laboratory spectroscopy, to established Hamiltonian models. The assessment of the experimental data and of the Hamiltonian model is very important[c] and will be discussed in some detail. There are 1051 entries in the CDMS catalog as of end of Feb. 2021.

A large fraction of the contribution will deal with recent entries and with potential laboratory needs which are often linked to Atacama Large Millimeter/submillimeter Array projects such as (R)EMoCA[d], PILS[e], and ATOMIUM.[f] These include numerous diatomics, frequently containing metals, with highly excited states and isotopic species for several molecules already detected in space for the last project and excited states or isotopic species of known interstellar organic molecules, but also several new ones for the other projects.

Other sections of the classical CDMS include a page on Molecules in Space and a help page for users of Pickett's SPFIT/SPCAT programs. There is also a VAMDC compatible incarnation of the CDMS which is linked to a plethora of other spectroscopic, collisional, and kinetic databases via the Vitual Atomic and Molecular Data Centre portal.[g]

[a] Shortcut: cdms.de; web address: https://cdms.astro.uni-koeln.de/. The CDMS is supported by the Verbundforschung Physik of the BMBF (German Ministry of Science and Education), project ID 05A17PK1.

[b] H. S. P. Müller et al., Astron. Astrophys. 370 (2001) L49.

[c] e.g., C. P. Endres et al., J. Mol. Spectrosc. 327 (2016) 95.

[d] (Re-) Exploring Molecular Complexity with ALMA, A. Belloche et al., Astron. Astrophys. 587 (2016) A91 & 628 (2019) A10.

[e] The ALMA Protostellar Interferometric Line Survey, J. K. Jørgensen et al., Astron. Astrophys. 595 (2016) A117.

[f] ALMA Tracing the Origins of Molecules forming dust In oxygen-rich M-type stars, L. Decin et al., Science 369 (2020) 1497.

[g] http://www.vamdc.org/

RC03 **8:08 – 8:09**

ASTROCHEMICAL FORECASTING WITH MACHINE LEARNING

KELVIN LEE, *Department of Chemistry, MIT, Cambridge, MA, USA*; ANDREW M BURKHARDT, *Smithsonian Astrophysical Observatory, Center for Astrophysics | Harvard & Smithsonian, Cambridge, MA, USA*; MICHAEL C McCARTHY, *Atomic and Molecular Physics, Harvard-Smithsonian Center for Astrophysics, Cambridge, MA, USA*; BRETT A. McGUIRE, *Department of Chemistry, Massachusetts Institute of Technology, Cambridge, MA, USA.*

Since the first molecules were detected in space, we have now reached a point where chemical and physical complexity in the interstellar medium reaches the boundaries of what human expertise and intuition alone can achieve. With every new molecule we discover, the question "What comes next?" grows more and more difficult to answer as more possibilities emerge. Conventionally, we turn to chemical models for guidance; this may be complicated when considering complex, non-LTE processes such as shocks, radiation, and grain-surface chemistry. Moreover, expansion of chemical networks typically requires hand-picked reactions and species, requiring an exhaustive knowledge of chemical and astrophysical literature, and can impose human bias on which reactions and molecules are important. As a complimentary approach to conventional chemical models, we have developed an unsupervised machine learning pipeline for predicting molecular abundances in a non-parametric fashion. Leveraging tools originally developed in high throughput drug discovery and data science, our pipeline captures and uses millions of molecules from various databases to create chemically descriptive vector representations for quantitative comparison. These representations are subsequently used to predict molecular properties in a given environment; as a proof-of-concept, we use the well-characterized chemical inventory of TMC-1, including the latest discoveries from the GOTHAM collaboration. We show that the model can be successfully conditioned on an inventory, able to reproduce column densities of unseen molecules to within an order of magnitude without any tuning parameters. Simultaneously, we are able to use the model to predict column densities of hundreds of thousands of molecules not yet detected in space, as a way to guide efforts, as well as provide a robust statistical baseline for expected abundances.

RC04 **8:12 – 8:13**

LABORATORY ICE ASTROCHEMISTRY AT LARGE FACILITIES

SERGIO IOPPOLO, *School of Electronic Engineering and Computer Science, Queen Mary University of London, London, GREATER LONDON, United Kingdom.*

To date, many fundamental questions on the physico-chemical origin of the observed molecular complexity in space and its link to life on Earth still remain unanswered. Field work at large facilities such as free-electron lasers, synchrotrons and ion accelerators can help investigating the surface formation of biologically relevant species with unprecedented detail. During my talk, I will present recent work carried-out at FELIX Laboratory (Netherlands), $ASTRID^2$ (Denmark) and ATOMKI (Hungary) on surface molecular formation. The unique characteristics of each facility allows for the investigation of different processes occurring on interstellar and Solar System ice analogues. For instance, at FELIX Laboratory, selective IR/THz radiation spectroscopy is used to study molecular diffusion, reaction, desorption, and energy relaxation processes in ices; at $ASTRID^2$, VUV-UV-vis spectroscopy combined to 1 keV electron exposure of ices is performed in support of space missions like JUICE that are looking for traces of life-related molecules in the Solar System; and at ATOMKI, a suite of different ions and energies (200 keV - 6 MeV) are employed to bombardment space relevant ices to induce molecular synthesis in the solid phase. Results will be discussed in light of present and future observations of ice molecules in the interstellar medium and Solar System.

RC05 **8:16 – 8:17**

SPECTROMETER USING SUPERCONDUCTOR MIXER RECEIVER (SUMIRE) FOR MICROWAVE SPECTROSCOPY OF MOLECULES IN ASTRONOMICAL INTERESTS

YOSHIMASA WATANABE, *Material Science and Engineering, Shibaura Institute of Technology, Saitama, Saitama, Japan*; AKEMI TAMANAI, NAMI SAKAI, *Cluster for Pioneering Research, RIKEN, Saitama, Japan.*

In radio astronomy, accurate rest frequencies of molecular transitions are indispensable for secure identification of molecular species and accurate analyses of Doppler shifts caused by motions of target sources. In observations, we have seriously realized the importance of the accurate rest frequencies of molecular transitions. For rare isotopic species lines and weak vibrational satellite lines, the situation is more serious. To overcome such a situation, an emission-type millimeter-wave spectrometer utilizing state-of-the-art radio-astronomical technologies is developed. The spectrometer is equipped with a 200 cm glass cylinder cell, a two sideband (2SB) Superconductor-Insulator-Superconductor (SIS) receiver in the 215-265 GHz band, and wide-band auto-correlation digital spectrometers. By using the four 2.5 GHz digital spectrometers, a total instantaneous bandwidth of the 2SB SIS receiver of 8 GHz can be covered with a frequency resolution of 88.5 kHz. This wide bandwidth allows us to measure relative intensities of lines which fall into the 8 GHz range. Spectroscopic measurements of HDO, CH_3CN, and CH_3OH are carried out in the 230 GHz band so as to examine frequency accuracy, stability, and sensitivity, as well as intensity calibration accuracy of our system. We confirm that the frequency accuracy for lines detected with a sufficient signal-to-noise ratio is better than 1 kHz, when the high-resolution spectrometer having a channel resolution of 17.7 kHz is used. Following this successive development of the spectrometer, we are measuring spectral lines of various isotopic species of molecules in astronomical interests.

RC06 **8:20 – 8:21**

THE 2021 CENSUS OF INTERSTELLAR, CIRCUMSTELLAR, EXTRAGALACTIC, PROTOPLANETARY DISK, AND EXOPLANETARY MOLECULES: WHAT ARE THE PRESSING SPECTROSCOPIC NEEDS FROM THE LABORATORY?

BRETT A. McGUIRE, *Department of Chemistry, Massachusetts Institute of Technology, Cambridge, MA, USA.*

To date, 220 individual molecular species, comprised of 19 different elements, have been detected in the interstellar and circumstellar medium by astronomical observations. In this talk, I will provide a 30,000 foot view of the demographics of this inventory, the history and lessons learned from where these molecules were first detected, and discuss interesting trends that may help guide future observations. Most importantly, I will identify critical gaps in our knowledge of this inventory, and the areas in which spectroscopic investigations in the laboratory might be most efficiently used to continue driving the ever increasing pace of molecular discovery in the ISM.

RC07 **8:24 – 8:25**

A RIGOROUS K/KA-BAND HUNT FOR AROMATIC MOLECULES (ARKHAM): UBIQUITOUS AROMATIC CARBON CHEMISTRY AT THE EARLIEST STAGES OF STAR FORMATION

ANDREW M BURKHARDT, *Smithsonian Astrophysical Observatory, Center for Astrophysics | Harvard & Smithsonian, Cambridge, MA, USA*; RYAN A LOOMIS, *NAASC, National Radio Astronomy Observatory, Charlottesville, VA, USA*; CHRISTOPHER N SHINGLEDECKER, *Department of Physics & Astronomy, Benedictine College, Atchison, KS, USA*; KELVIN LEE, *Department of Chemistry, Massachusetts Institute of Technology, Cambridge, MA, USA*; ANTHONY REMIJAN, *NAASC, National Radio Astronomy Observatory, Charlottesville, VA, USA*; MICHAEL C McCARTHY, *Atomic and Molecular Physics, Harvard-Smithsonian Center for Astrophysics, Cambridge, MA, USA*; BRETT A. McGUIRE, *Department of Chemistry, Massachusetts Institute of Technology, Cambridge, MA, USA.*

Benzonitrile (C_6H_5CN), a polar proxy for benzene (C_6H_6), has the potential to serve as a highly convenient radio probe for aromatic chemistry, provided this ring can be found in other astronomical sources beyond the molecule-rich prestellar cloud TMC-1 where it was first reported by McGuire et al. (2018). Here we present radio astronomical evidence of benzonitrile in four additional pre-stellar, and possibly protostellar, sources: Serpens 1A, Serpens 1B, Serpens 2, and MC27/L1521F. These detections establish benzonitrile is not unique to TMC-1; rather aromatic chemistry appears to be widespread throughout the earliest stages of star formation, likely persisting at least to the initial formation of a protostar. The abundance of benzonitrile far exceeds predictions from models which well reproduce the abundances of carbon chains, such as HC_7N, a cyanopolyyne with the same heavy atoms, indicating the chemistry responsible for planar carbon structures (as opposed to linear ones) in primordial sources is favorable but not well understood. The abundance of benzonitrile relative to carbon-chain molecules displays sizable variations between sources within the Taurus and Serpens clouds, implying the importance of physical conditions and initial elemental reservoirs of the clouds themselves.

RC08 **8:28 – 8:29**

SPECTRAL STACKING AND MATCHED FILTERING AS A RIGOROUS DETECTION TECHNIQUE FOR INTERSTELLAR MOLECULES

RYAN A LOOMIS, *NAASC, National Radio Astronomy Observatory, Charlottesville, VA, USA*; KELVIN LEE, *Department of Chemistry, Massachusetts Institute of Technology, Cambridge, MA, USA*; CI XUE, *Department of Chemistry, The University of Virginia, Charlottesville, VA, USA*; ANDREW M BURKHARDT, *Smithsonian Astrophysical Observatory, Center for Astrophysics | Harvard & Smithsonian, Cambridge, MA, USA*; CHRISTOPHER N SHINGLEDECKER, *Department of Physics & Astronomy, Benedictine College, Atchison, KS, USA*; STEVEN B CHARNLEY, MARTIN CORDINER, *Astrochemistry, NASA Goddard Space Flight Center, Greenbelt, MD, USA*; ERIC HERBST, *Department of Chemistry, The University of Virginia, Charlottesville, VA, USA*; SERGEI KALENSKII, *Astro Space Center, Lebedev Physical Institute, Russian Academy of Sciences, Moscow, Russia*; BRETT A. McGUIRE, *Department of Chemistry, Massachusetts Institute of Technology, Cambridge, MA, USA*; MICHAEL C McCARTHY, *Center for Astrophysics , Harvard & Smithsonian, Cambridge, MA, USA*; ANTHONY REMIJAN, *NAASC, National Radio Astronomy Observatory, Charlottesville, VA, USA.*

As the inventory of interstellar molecules continues to grow, the gulf between small species, whose individual rotational lines can be observed with radio telescopes, and large ones, such as polycyclic aromatic hydrocarbons (PAHs) best studied in bulk via infrared and optical observations, is slowly being bridged. Understanding the connection between these two molecular reservoirs is critical to probing topics such as the interstellar carbon cycle, but will require pushing the boundaries of how far we can probe molecular complexity while still retaining observational specificity.

Toward this end, we have developed a method for detecting and characterizing new molecular species in single-dish observations toward sources with sparse line spectra. Application of this method to data from the ongoing GOTHAM (GBT Observations of TMC-1: Hunting Aromatic Molecules) Green Bank Telescope (GBT) large program has resulted in ten new interstellar species detections thus far. In this talk, I present an overview of the method and demonstrate that it is a robust detection technique, highlighting both its strengths and limitations.

RC09 **8:32 – 8:33**

LABORATORY SPECTROSCOPY FOR ASTROCHEMISTRY: A ROTATIONAL INVESTIGATION OF 3-AMINO-2-PROPENENITRILE

DAVIDE ALBERTON, VALERIO LATTANZI, CHRISTIAN ENDRES, PAOLA CASELLI, *The Center for Astrochemical Studies, Max-Planck-Institut für extraterrestrische Physik, Garching, Germany*; LUCA BIZZOCCHI, *Scuola Normale Superiore, Scuola Normale Superiore, Pisa, Italy.*

In order to unveil how chemistry complexity build up in space, Complex Organic Molecules (COMs) are receiving more and more attention from the astrochemical and astrobiological community. Nowadays, especially after the glycine detection in the 67P/C-G comet, there is a strong interest to detect amino acids and their precursors in space, with the aim of gaining understanding in their formation process. The most promising pathways to the synthesis of amino acids, namely photochemically and through the Strecker synthesis, include in their final step the hydrogenation of an aminonitrile molecule. It's in this context that the importance of 3-amino-2-propenitrile (APN) makes its appearance. This aminonitrile is simply obtained in gas phase or in solution by mixing cyanoacetylene (HCCCN) and ammonia (NH_3), both largely present in the Universe.

Therefore, starting from previous work taken as reference, the APN spectrum has herein collected and characterised using the MPE's CASAC (Center of Astrochemical studies Absorption Cell). Here the frequency modulated signal of synthesiser, locked to a Rb atomic clock, is multiplied several times to cover a possible frequency range from 40 GHz to 1.6 THz. The interaction of the radiation source with the molecular sample is hence acquired by a InSb hot electron bolometer detector, and demodulated by a lock-in amplifier.

The unprecedented level of detail in the data has therefore allowed the characterisation of the rotation and distortion constants of the APN at a deeper standard, providing a new level of precision for the hunt of this molecule in space with the highest level of confidence since now.

RC10 **8:36 – 8:37**

HIGH-RESOLUTION, ROTATIONALLY-RESOLVED FTIR SPECTRUM OF THE 3300 cm^{-1} TRANSITION OF ASTROPHYSICALLY-RELEVANT HCN

JESSICA PALKO, THOMAS HOWARD, LEAH G DODSON, *Department of Chemistry and Biochemistry, University of Maryland, College Park, MD, USA.*

Hydrogen cyanide (HCN) is ubiquitous in the interstellar medium, especially in the dying carbon star IRC+10216, where its abundance and reactivity are of great astrophysical relevance. We have developed a safe, robust synthesis and storage procedure for pure HCN gas, which is necessary for carrying out further studies on the reactivity of HCN in the gas phase. We present the high-resolution, rotationally-resolved vibrational spectrum of gaseous HCN obtained with a Nicolet iS50 Fourier transform IR (FTIR) spectrometer. Line-by-line frequency and spectral intensity data from the HITRAN database were used to fit the experimental FTIR spectra for the ν_3 ro-vibrational transition (C-H stretch at 3300 cm^{-1}) of HCN. We will describe the current state of knowledge for this transition and compare our findings with the HITRAN database.

RC11 **8:40 – 8:41**

COMPREHENSIVE ROTATIONAL SPECTROSCOPY OF METHYL CYANOACETATE FOR ASTRONOMICAL SEARCHES

GAYATRI BATRA, PABLO PINACHO, AMANDA STEBER, MELANIE SCHNELL, *FS-SMP, Deutsches Elektronen-Synchrotron (DESY), Hamburg, Germany.*

Out of the more than 200 individual molecular species already identified in the ISM, nearly 16% of the molecules contain a cyano functional group (see www.astro.uni-koeln.de/cdms/molecules). An interesting extension to this is studying molecules that contain an additional functional group. We present a comprehensive study on methyl cyanoacetate (MCA) whose condensed formula is $NCCH_2COOCH_3$. It is a molecule whose two functional groups (cyano, -CN, and ester, -$COOCH_3$) have already been identified individually in the ISM.

The rotational spectrum of MCA was obtained in the frequency range of 2-26 GHz using two chirped-pulse Fourier transform microwave (CP-FTMW) spectrometers, namely the COMPACT spectrometer and the 18-26 GHz spectrometer. The ^{14}N nucleus (I=1) in the cyano group, is responsible for the observation of the nuclear quadrupole hyperfine splitting (HFS) of rotational transitions. The ester functional group contains a methyl top that rotates with respect to the molecular frame and couples with the overall rotation (computed barrier height for internal rotation, V_3 is 309 cm^{-1}), giving rise to further splitting of each transition into A and E states. Both the nuclear quadrupole HFS and the methyl internal rotation splitting were resolved, and it was possible to obtain a single fit for all the rotational parameters using the XIAM program.[1]

This study of MCA in the 2-26 GHz region would provide insights into how the barrier height is affected by the presence of electron-withdrawing/donating moieties attached to the ester group. For example, in methyl carbamate,[2] V_3 is 352 cm^{-1}, while in methyl acetate,[3] V_3 is 425 cm^{-1}. Furthermore, the experimental data obtained from this study can facilitate searches for this molecule with various radio observatories, for example, the Jansky Very Large Array (JVLA) and the Radio Telescope Effelsberg.

(1) H.Hartwig and H.Dreizler, Z. Naturforsch 51a, 923-932 (1996) (2) J. Sheridan et al. J. Mol. Spectrosc. 80, 1-11 (1980) (3) B. Bakri et al. J. Mol. Spectrosc. 215, 312–316 (2002)

RC12 **8:44 – 8:45**

LINE LISTS FOR THE $b^1\Sigma^+ - X^3\Sigma^-$ AND $a^1\Delta - X^3\Sigma^-$ TRANSITIONS OF SO

PETER F. BERNATH, *Department of Chemistry and Biochemistry, Old Dominion University, Norfolk, VA, USA*; RYAN JOHNSON, *Physics Department, Old Dominion University, Norfolk, VA, USA*; JACQUES LIÉVIN, *Service de Chimie Quantique et Photophysique, Université Libre de Bruxelles, Brussels, Belgium.*

SO is an important radical found in many astronomical sources such as the atmosphere of Io and the atmosphere of Venus. In order to create more complete line lists, we fit spectroscopic data on SO from the literature using PGOPHER. The fits covered v=0 to v=6 for the $X^3\Sigma^-$ state, v=0-5 for the $a^1\Delta$ state and v=0-2 for $b^1\Sigma^+$ state. The B_v and G_v polynomial coefficients for each state were input into LeRoy's RKR program to produce pointwise potential energy curves. High level *ab initio* calculations, including spin-orbit coupling, were carried out to obtain the electric transition dipole moment functions for the nominally forbidden $b^1\Sigma^+-X^3\Sigma^-$ and $a^1\Delta-X^3\Sigma^-$ transitions. The RKR potentials and transition dipole moment points were input into LeRoy's LEVEL program to calculate the transition dipole matrix elements for all possible b-X and a-X bands. For the $b^1\Sigma^+-X^3\Sigma^-$ transition, the electric and magnetic transition dipole matrix elements were scaled using the experimental values of μ_0 = 0.0107 D, μ_1 = -0.0119 D and M = 0.16 μ_B obtained by Setzer *et al.*[a] for the 0-0 band. The transition dipole moment matrix elements were used in PGOPHER to produce our line lists for the $b^1\Sigma^+-X^3\Sigma^-$ and $a^1\Delta-X^3\Sigma^-$ transitions.

[a] K.D. Setzer, E.H. Fink, and D.A. Ramsay, High-resolution Fourier transform study of the $b^1\Sigma^+-X^3\Sigma^-$ and $a^1\Delta-X^3\Sigma^-$ transitions of SO, *J. Mol. Spectrosc.* **198**, 163-174 (1999).

RC13 **8:48 – 8:49**

HIGH-TEMPERATURE SPECTROSCOPIC DATA FOR EXO-PLANETARY STUDIES: THE e-PYTHEAS PROJECT

VINCENT BOUDON, *Laboratoire ICB, CNRS/Université de Bourgogne, DIJON, France*; ATHENA COUSTENIS, *LESIA, Observatoire de Paris / CNRS / UPMC, Meudon, France*; ALAIN CAMPARGUE, *UMR5588 LIPhy, Université Grenoble Alpes/CNRS, Saint Martin d'Hères, France*; ROBERT GEORGES, *IPR UMR6251, CNRS - Université Rennes 1, Rennes, France*; VLADIMIR TYUTEREV, *Laboratoire GSMA, CNRS / Université de Reims Champagne-Ardenne, REIMS, France*.

The e-PYTHEAS project combines theoretical and experimental work with exoplanet modelling applications. Our approach is to use theoretical research validated by laboratory experiments and to then inject it into models of the atmospheres of the giant gaseous planets in the solar system and other planetary systems. Our consortium of five French laboratories and associated partners proposes to improve the existing high-temperature spectroscopy data for several molecular species detected in exoplanets. More in detail, the goals are to: (1) Generate experimental and synthetic spectra in the 1–17 μm wavelength region for hydrocarbons and their isotopologues such as $^{12}CH_4$, $^{13}CH_4$, CH_3D, C_2H_2, C_2H_4 and C_2H_6 up to 2500 K. (2) Produce complete line lists without the current limitations in frequency and temperature ranges. (3) Record new absorption and emission spectra at high temperature by unique techniques developed by IPR, LIPhy and GSMA. (4) Produce global *ab initio* spectra predictions. (5) Validate and empirically correct them using spectra measurements. (6) Use the generated spectroscopic data to enhance the output of radiative transfer codes and improve our understanding of the processes involved in hot gaseous environments thanks to the analysis of a large amount of observations. (7) Determine the role of the target species on the thermal structure of hot exoplanets and hence to a new understanding of the origin and evolution of exoplanetary atmospheres. The results will help to analyze data and address essential questions on the formation and evolution of planetary systems, such as retrieved by ESA's M4 space mission ARIEL in 2029. See the project's website: `http://e-pytheas.cnrs.fr`

RD. Non-covalent interactions

Thursday, June 24, 2021 – 8:0 AM

Room: 2021 Online Everywhere

Chair: Malgorzata Biczysko, Shanghai University, Shanghai, China

RD01 **8:00 – 8:01**

IMAGING THE NONREACTIVE COLLISIONAL QUENCHING DYNAMICS OF NO ($A^2\Sigma^+$) RADICALS WITH O_2 ($X^3\Sigma_g{}^-$)

K. JACOB BLACKSHAW, NAA-KWARLEY QUARTEY, DAVID J. HOOD, CHRISTIAN D. HETTWER, NATHANAEL M. KIDWELL, *Department of Chemistry, College of William & Mary, Williamsburg, VA, USA.*

Nitric oxide (NO) radicals are ubiquitous chemical intermediates present in the atmosphere and in combustion processes, where laser-induced fluorescence is extensively used on the NO ($A^2\Sigma^+ \leftarrow X^2\Pi$) band to report on fuel-burning properties. However, accurate fluorescence quantum yields and NO concentration measurements are impeded by electronic quenching of NO ($A^2\Sigma^+$) to NO ($X^2\Pi$) with colliding atomic and molecular species. To improve predictive combustion models and develop a molecular-level understanding of NO ($A^2\Sigma^+$) quenching, we report the velocity map ion images and product state distributions of NO ($X^2\Pi$, v"=0,1, J", F_n, Λ) following nonreactive collisional quenching of NO ($A^2\Sigma^+$) with molecular oxygen, O_2 ($X^3\Sigma_g{}^-$). A novel dual-flow pulse valve nozzle is constructed and implemented to carry out the NO ($A^2\Sigma^+$) electronic quenching studies and to limit NO_2 formation. The isotropic ion images reveal that the NO–O_2 system evolves through a long-lived NO_3 collision complex prior to formation of products. Furthermore, the corresponding total kinetic energy release distributions support that O_2 collision coproducts are formed primarily in the $c^1\Sigma_u{}^-$ electronic state with NO ($X^2\Pi$, v"=0, J", F_n, Λ). The product state distributions also indicate that NO ($X^2\Pi$) is generated with a propensity to occupy the Π(A") Λ-doublet state, which is consistent with the NO π^* orbital aligned perpendicular to nuclear rotation. The deviations between experimental results and statistical phase space theory simulations illustrate the key role that the conical intersection plays in the quenching dynamics to funnel population to product rovibronic levels.

RD02 **8:04 – 8:05**

N_2O-AR AND N_2O-KR: SYMMETRY BREAKING OF INTRAMOLECULAR BENDING MODE OF N_2O IN THE PRESENCE OF A RARE GAS

CHRIS GERGESS, M. DEHGHANY, *Department of Chemistry and Physics, Mount Royal University, Calgary, AB, Canada*; A. J. BARCLAY, *Department of Physics and Astronomy, University of Calgary, Calgary, AB, Canada*; A.R.W. McKELLAR, *Steacie Laboratory, National Research Council of Canada, Ottawa, ON, Canada*; NASSER MOAZZEN-AHMADI, *Department of Physics and Astronomy, University of Calgary, Calgary, AB, Canada.*

Rotationally-resolved infrared spectra of the bending modes of N_2O-Ar and N_2O-Kr van der Waals clusters have been studied in the region of the N_2O ν_1 fundamental vibration ($\approx$ 2224 cm^{-1}), using a tunable quantum cascade laser source to probe complexes generated in pulsed supersonic jet expansion. The assigned vibrational transitions are hot bands (1, 1^1, 0)$\leftarrow$ (0, 1^1, 0) observed under supersonic conditions. In the presence of Argon/Krypton atom, the doubly-degenerate ν_2 bending mode of the N_2O monomer splits to two modes, in-plane and out-of-plane of the complex, with A' and A'' symmetry, respectively. These two infrared bands are heavily linked by Coriolis interaction.

Analysis of the two bands for N_2O-Ar, located about 2209.8 $cm^{-1}$with a splitting of $\sim$0.1 cm^{-1}between the in-plane and out-of-plane intramolecular bending modes, yields experimental values ξ_a= 0.04215and ξ_b =0.13646 for a- and b-type Coriolis interaction parameters for the lower state. For the N_2O-Kr, these values are found to be ξ_a= 0.04205 and ξ_b =0.09212. The two bands for this complex are located about 2209.5 $cm^{-1}$and with a splitting of $\sim$0.4 cm^{-1}. Contrary to CO_2 containing complexes, the sign of splitting cannot be determined. This is due to lower symmetry of the N_2O-rare gas complexes.

Coriolis interaction parameters found in these analyses, along with that of the previously-reported bands for CO_2-Ar[a] and CO_2-N_2[b] complexes, offer important information for testing the accuracy of theoretical calculation toward a better understanding of intermolecular interactions.

[a]T.A. Gartner, A.J. Barclay, A.R.W. McKellar, and N. Moazzen-Ahmadi, Phys. Chem. Chem. Phys. 22, 21488-21493 (2020).

[b]A.J. Barclay, A.R.W. McKellar, and N. Moazzen-Ahmadi, J. Chem. Phys. 153, 014303 (2020).

RD03 **8:08 – 8:09**

THE 4.2 MICRON SPECTRA OF CO_2-CO DIMER FOR BOTH THE C- AND O-BONDED ISOMERS, INCLUDING SPLITTING OF THE DEGENERATE ν_2 BEND IN THE PRESENCE OF CO

PRAVEEN WAKWELLA, *Physics and Astronomy, University of Calgary, Calgary, AB, Canada*; A. J. BARCLAY, *Department of Physics and Astronomy, University of Calgary, Calgary, AB, Canada*; BOB McKELLAR, *Steacie Laboratory, National Research Council of Canada, Ottawa, ON, Canada*; NASSER MOAZZEN-AHMADI, *Physics and Astronomy/Institute for Quantum Science and Technology, University of Calgary, Calgary, AB, Canada.*

CO_2-CO dimer was previously observed by high-resolution microwave and infrared spectroscopy in the form of a planar T-shaped C-bonded structure.[a,b] More recently, spectra of a second isomer were observed in the stretching region of carbon monoxide.[c] This isomer has also a planar T-shaped structure, but with the CO flipped by 180°. Moreover, two intermolecular frequencies were measured for each isomer. These are in very good agreement with recent high level theoretical calculations. Here, CO_2-CO dimer is observed in the carbon dioxide ν_3 asymmetric stretch region ($\sim$2350 cm^{-1}). Both C-bonded and O-bonded isomers are analyzed for the normal isotopologue as well as for $^{13}CO_2$-CO and $^{16}O^{13}C^{18}O$-CO, the latter being the first observation of an asymmetrically substituted form for which all values of K_a are allowed. Combination bands involving the lowest in-plane intermolecular mode are also observed yielding frequencies of 24.51 $cm^{-1}$for the C-bonded form and 14.37 $cm^{-1}$for the O-bonded form. In addition, two weak bands near 2337 $cm^{-1}$are assigned to CO_2 hot band transitions (01^11) - (01^10), yielding the splitting of the degenerate CO_2 bend into in-plane and out-of-plane components due to the presence of the CO. This splitting has rather different values for the C- and O- bonded isomers, 4.56 and 1.59 cm^{-1}, respectively, with the out-of-plane mode higher in energy than the in-plane for both cases.

[a] A.C. Legon, A.P. Suckley, *Journal of Chemical Physics* **91** 4440 (1989).
[b] R.W. Randall, J.P.L. Summersgill, B.J. Howard, *Journal Chemical Society Faraday Transactions 86* 1943 (1990).
[c] S. Sheybani-Deloui, A.J. Barclay, K.H. Michaelian, A.R.W. McKellar, N. Moazzen-Ahmadi, *Journal of Chemical Physics* **143** 121101 (2015).

RD04 **8:12 – 8:13**

INFRARED SPECTROSCOPY OF TITANIUM CATION ACETYLENE COMPLEXES: CATION-π COMPLEXES VS REACTED STRUCTURES

ANNA G BATCHELOR, JOSHUA H MARKS, MICHAEL A DUNCAN, *Department of Chemistry, University of Georgia, Athens, GA, USA.*

Titanium cation-acetylene complexes are investigated with infrared photodissociation spectroscopy to study latent reactivity. $Ti^+(C_2H_2)_n$ complexes are produced via laser vaporization of a titanium rod in a supersonic expansion of argon containing acetylene. Argon-tagged complexes are mass selected in a time-of-flight mass spectrometer and their spectra are measured in the C-H stretching region with infrared laser photodissociation. These spectra are assigned with the aid of B3LYP/Def2TZVP computations. The presence of reacted structures and cation-π structures is investigated by comparing experiment to theory.

RD05 **8:16 – 8:17**

SPECTROSCOPIC CHARACTERIZATION OF PSEUDOCARBYNES: INTERACTION BETWEEN –C≡C– CHAINS AND METAL CLUSTERS

HYUNSUB KIM, SCOTT G SAYRES, *School of Molecular Sciences, Arizona State University, Tempe, AZ, USA.*

Pseudocarbynes are a new class of molecules/materials that we define as finite sp-hybridized carbon chains stabilized through non-covalent interactions with metal clusters. These exciting and innovative materials are expected to approach the unprecedented strength, elastic modulus, and stiffness of carbyne, which has defied isolation and characterization for over a century. We optimized a procedure to synthesize pseudocarbynes via the finely controlled laser ablation of a liquid/metal interface, where clusters and one-dimensional carbon chains self-assemble from colloidal solutions into new mesomaterials that bridge the molecular and materials realms. I will present our spectroscopic results demonstrating the non-covalent interaction between –C≡C– chains and small metal clusters as characterized by strong signatures in UV-vis, Raman, and infrared spectroscopies.

RD06 **8:20 – 8:21**

INFRARED SPECTRA OF THE METHYLAMINE DIMER AND METHYLAMINE-WATER COMPLEXES IN SOLID NEON BETWEEN 80 AND 5500 cm^{-1}

PASCALE SOULARD, BENOÎT TREMBLAY, *MONARIS, Sorbonne Université, CNRS, Paris, France.*

For the first time the investigation of water molecule complexed with methylamine (CH_3NH_2) in solid neon was performed from the far to the near infrared using FTIR spectroscopy. By comparison with other hydrogen-bonded complexes and with the help of theoretical results we have identify several vibrational transitions for CH_3NH_2 dimer, CH_3NH_2-H_2O, and CH_3NH_2–$(H_2O)_2$ complexes. Theoretical calculations at the MP2 level have been performed to obtain their equilibrium geometries and vibrational spectra at the harmonic level and comparison with experimental data allows us to give structures of observed complexes. For the CH_3NH_2-H_2O complex, the infrared spectral changes (frequencies as well as intensities) indicate that the water plays the role of the proton donor, in agreement with the previous theoretical works. Careful examination of the far infrared allows the assignment of several intermolecular modes, confirmed by the observation of combinations of intra+intermolecular transitions. All of these results significantly increase the number of one and, especially, two quanta vibrational transitions for these complexes. This study shows the high sensibility of the solid neon isolation to the spectroscopy of the hydrogen-bonded complexes since two quanta transitions can't be easily observed in gas phase.

RD07 **8:24 – 8:25**

WETTING TRIACETONE TRIPEROXIDE ALLOWS ITS DETECTION BY MICROWAVE SPECTROSCOPY

SUSANA BLANCO, ALBERTO MACARIO, *Departamento de Química Física y Química Inorgánica, Universidad de Valladolid, Valladolid, Spain*; JOSÉ GARCÍA-CALVO, ANDREA REVILLA-CUESTA, TOMÁS TORROBA , *Departamento de Química, Universidad de Burgos, Burgos, Spain*; JUAN CARLOS LOPEZ, *Departamento de Química Física y Química Inorgánica, Universidad de Valladolid, Valladolid, Spain.*

Triacetone triperoxide (TATP) is a known peroxide-based explosive frequently used by terrorists in improvised devices due to its ease of synthesis and detection difficulty. Here we propose microwave spectroscopy as a highly selective detection method. The main conformer of TATP (95%) has D_3 symmetry and thus it has no dipole moment. However, TATP-water adducts are polar species and their microwave observation could open a way to detect TATP in the gas-phase. In this work we have observed the spectrum of TATP-H_2O and TATP-$(H_2O)_2$ which, on the other hand, have revealed the interesting properties of TATP. In TATP-H_2O water lies close to the C_3 axis and rotates around it. As a result, the ground state rotational constants average to those of a symmetric top. The complex exhibits a four center trifurcated O_w-H···O hydrogen bond further stabilized by a weak four center C-H···O_w chelated interaction. To our knowledge, those kinds of interactions have not been observed previously in the gas phase. The anomalous large O-H···O distances associated to the main hydrogen bond interaction evidences that TATP oxygen atoms are to some extent encapsulated by their hydrocarbon environment. The dihrydated cluster can be envisaged as formed from the TATP-H_2O adduct with the second water molecule acting as double hydrogen bond donor to the first water molecule and the closest TATP endocyclic oxygen atom.

RD08 **8:28 – 8:29**

A BROADBAND MICROWAVE STUDY OF ISOLATED α-METHOXY PHENYLACETIC ACID: STRUCTURE, INTERNAL ROTATION, AND MICRO-SOLVATION

HIMANSHI SINGH, PABLO PINACHO, *FS-SMP, Deutsches Elektronen-Synchrotron (DESY), Hamburg, Germany*; DANIEL A. OBENCHAIN, *Institute of Physical Chemistry, Georg-August-Universität Göttingen, Göttingen, Germany*; MARÍA MAR QUESADA-MORENO, MELANIE SCHNELL, *FS-SMP, Deutsches Elektronen-Synchrotron (DESY), Hamburg, Germany.*

Mandelic acid and its derivatives are useful as chiral synthons in the chemical and pharmaceutical industry because of their versatility. Their wide use in organic reactions makes them an important case to study solute-solvent interactions. In this work, we study the structure of α-methoxy phenylacetic acid (AMPA), a mandelic acid derivative, and its solute-solvent interaction in a weakly bound complex with the solvent dimethylsulfoxide (DMSO). This system can serve as a model to characterize the non-covalent interactions of such chiral solutes with different solvents. Rotational spectroscopy studies of weakly bound complexes are able to accurately reveal the structures and internal dynamics of molecules and complexes isolated in the gas phase.

We present a conformational study of AMPA and its 1:1 complex with dimethylsulfoxide (DMSO) using chirped-pulse Fourier transform microwave (CP-FTMW) spectroscopy in the 2-8 GHz range. Two conformers of AMPA were identified in the rotational spectrum. Splitting patterns arising from internal motions in the molecule are observed and will be analyzed. The computational structures of AMPA determined from its singly-substituted ^{13}C-isotopologues are in good agreement with the two lowest energy conformers observed in experiments. However, in the 1:1 lowest energy complex with DMSO, the structure of AMPA does not correspond to the lowest energy conformation of the monomer. This showed the influence of solvent over the conformational landscape of the solute. The preferred intra- and intermolecular interactions, as well as the observed structural changes upon complexation, will be discussed.

RD09 **8:32 – 8:33**

EXPLOITING F LONE PAIR$\cdots\pi_{AROMATIC}$-HOLE INTERACTION BETWEEN BENZALDEHYDE AND TETRAFLUOROMETHANE

HAO WANG, JUNHA CHEN, QIAN GOU, *School of Chemistry and Chemical Engineering, Chongqing University, Chongqing, China.*

An unexpected dominating F lone pair$\cdots\pi_{aromatic}$-hole interaction has been found to characterize the complex formed between benzaldehyde and tetrafluoromethane by exploring rotational spectroscopy which yields spectral feature with splittings originated from the internal rotation of -CF_3 around the F$\cdots\pi$ direction. Complemented with theoretical analyses, it pointed out irrefutably that benzaldehyde reveals an aromatic π^*character which is ready to link with F lone pair.Secondary F$\cdots\pi$-hole$_{-C=O-}$ and C σ-hole$_{CF4}\cdots\pi_{aromatic}$ interactions are also contributive to the configuration pereference. In the comparison with the complex about C_6F_6-CF_4, C_6H_6-CF_4, it implies that, the aromatic π^* antibonding orbital can be active not only by the substituents with electron withdrawing but also by the partner molecule with high electronegativity like CF_4, in participate the LP$\cdots\pi$-hole interaction.

RD10 ***Post-Deadline Abstract*** **8:36 – 8:37**

STRUCTURE AND NON-COVALENT INTERACTIONS OF THE BENZOFURAN-FORMALDEHYDE COMPLEX EXPLORED BY MICROWAVE SPECTROSCOPY AND QUANTUM-CHEMICAL CALCULATIONS

XIAOLONG LI, *School of Chemistry and Chemical Engineering, Chongqing University, Chongqing, China*; SILVIA ALESSANDRINI, *Dipartimento di Chimica G. Ciamician, Università di Bologna, Bologna, Italy*; YANG ZHENG, *School of Chemistry and Chemical Engineering, Chongqing University, Chongqing, China*; LORENZO SPADA, *Dep. Chemistry 'Giacomo Ciamician', University of Bologna, Bologna, Italy*; KEVIN G. LENGSFELD, JENS-UWE GRABOW, *Institut für Physikalische Chemie und Elektrochemie, Gottfried-Wilhelm-Leibniz-Universität, Hannover, Germany*; CRISTINA PUZZARINI, *Dep. Chemistry 'Giacomo Ciamician', University of Bologna, Bologna, Italy*; GANG FENG, *School of Chemistry and Chemical Engineering, Chongqing University, Chongqing, China*; VINCENZO BARONE, *Scuola Normale Superiore, Scuola Normale Superiore, Pisa, Italy.*

The rotational spectrum of the benzofuran-formaldehyde complex has been investigated by high resolution Fourier transform microwave spectroscopy. In addition to the parent species, the rotational spectra of all mono-substituted ^{13}C isotopologues and the complex with $H_2C^{18}O$ have been also measured. This extensive set of rotational constants for isotopic species allowed an accurate structural determination exploiting the so-called "semi-experimental" approach.

In the observed isomer, the two subunits orient themselves almost parallel to each other. The non-covalent bonding distance between the carbon atom of formaldehyde and the nearest carbon atom of benzofuran has been found to be well within the sum of van der Waals radius of carbon. The joint experimental and computational study pointed out that the two moieties are linked through a π-π interaction. The interaction energy is calculated to be about 20 kJ mol^{-1} and, according to a SAPT analysis, is dominated by dispersion.

RD11 **8:40 – 8:41**

COLD ION SPECTROSCOPY OF B_{12} DERIVATIVES: STRETCHING THE LIMITS OF THEORETICAL INTERPRETATION

ALEXANDRA TSYBIZOVA, LARISA MILOGLYADOVA, PETER CHEN, *Department of Chemistry and Applied Biosciences, ETH Zurich, Zurich, Switzerland.*

Aryl-corrins is a class of B_{12} derivatives that embodies "antivitamin" properties and represents a biologically important class of compounds that hence demands investigation. In our previous study, we experimentally determined bond strength in a series of aryl-corrins by the threshold CID experiments and compared these BDE's with those calculated with DFT.[1] We found that the computed BDEs were very much dependent on the chosen structure. Given that aryl-cobinamides have many side chains that increase their conformational space, and that the question of a specific structure, measured in the gas phase was important for further evaluation of our T-CID experiment, we proceeded to analyze structural properties of aryl-cobinamides using CIVP spectroscopy. We explored BOMD simulations with the semi-empirical GFN-xTB methods[2-3] for interpretation of experimental spectra in these conformationally flexible systems.

References:

[1] A. Tsybizova, C. Brenig, C. Kieninger, B. Kräutler, and P. Chen, Chem. Eur. J., in press. (DOI: 10.1002/chem.202004589)
[2] S. Grimme, C. Bannwarth, and P. Shushkov, J. Chem. Theory Comput. 13, 1989 (2017).
[3] C. Bannwarth, S. Ehlert, and S. Grimme, J. Chem. Theory Comput. 15, 1652 (2019).

RE. Atmospheric science

Thursday, June 24, 2021 – 8:0 AM

Room: 2021 Online Everywhere

Chair: Christopher J. Johnson, Stony Brook University, Stony Brook, NY, USA

RE01 **8:00 – 8:01**

WATER VAPOR NEAR-UV ABSORPTION: LABORATORY SPECTRUM, FIELD EVIDENCE, AND ATMOSPHERIC IMPACTS

LEI ZHU, LINSEN PEI, *Wadsworth Center, New York State Department of Health, Albany, NY, USA*; QILONG MIN, *Atmospheric Sciences Research Center, University at Albany, SUNY, Albany, NY, USA*; YUYI DU, *Atmospheric Sciences Research Center, University at Albany, Albany, NY, USA*; ZHE-CHEN WANG, *Wadsworth Center, New York State Department of Health, Albany, NY, USA*; BANGSHENG YIN, *Atmospheric Sciences Research Center, University at Albany, Albany, NY, USA*; KAI YANG, *Dept. of Atmospheric and Oceanic Science, University of Maryland, College Park, MD, USA*; PATRICK DISTERHOFT, *Global Monitoring Division, NOAA Earth System Research Laboratory, Boulder, CO, USA*; THOMAS J PONGETTI, *Jet Propulsion Laboratory, California Institute of Technology, Pasadena, CA, USA.*

Absorption of solar radiation by water vapor in the near-UV region is a poorly-understood but important issue in atmospheric science. To better understand water vapor near-UV absorption, we constructed a cavity ring-down spectrometer with a bandwidth comparable to those of field UV spectrometers and determined water vapor absorption cross-sections at 1 nm increments in the 290-350 nm region. We also measured water vapor absorption cross-sections at 0.05 nm intervals surrounding major absorption bands. We provide field evidence to support laboratory water vapor near-UV absorption measurements. Field UV residual spectra not only exhibited increased attenuation at higher atmospheric water vapor loadings but also showed structures suggested by the laboratory water vapor absorption spectrum. Spaceborne UV radiance spectra have spectral structures resembling the differential cross-section spectrum constructed from the laboratory wavelength-dependent water vapor absorption cross-sections. We incorporated water vapor absorption cross-section data into a radiative transfer model and obtained estimated energy budget of such absorption for the standard US atmosphere and for the tropics. We conclude that water vapor near-UV absorption is a significant contributor for climate simulation and ozone retrievals.

RE02 **8:04 – 8:05**

TRENDS IN ATMOSPHERIC COMPOSITION FROM THE ATMOSPHERIC CHEMISTRY EXPERIMENT (ACE) SATELLITE

PETER F. BERNATH, *Department of Chemistry and Biochemistry, Old Dominion University, Norfolk, VA, USA*; CHRIS BOONE, JEFF CROUSE, *Department of Chemistry, University of Waterloo, Waterloo, ON, Canada.*

After almost 18 years in low-Earth orbit, the ACE satellite is making near-real time measurements of numerous trace gases, thin clouds, aerosols and temperature by solar occultation. The primary instrument is a high-resolution (0.02 cm^{-1}) infrared Fourier transform spectrometer (FTS) operating in the 750–4400 cm^{-1} region, which provides data for the vertical distribution of trace gases.

Our current version of ACE-FTS processing, v.4.1, retrieves an unprecedented 44 molecules (H_2O, O_3, N_2O, NO, NO_2, HNO_3, N_2O_5, H_2O_2, HO_2NO_2, O_2, N_2, SO_2, HCl, HF, ClO, $ClONO_2$, CFC-11, CFC-12, CFC-113, COF_2, $COCl_2$, COFCl, CF_4, SF_6, CH_3Cl, CCl_4, HCFC-22, HCFC-141b, HCFC-142b, HFC-134a, HFC-23, CO, CH_4, CH_3OH, H_2CO, HCOOH, C_2H_2, C_2H_6, OCS, HCN, $CH_3C(O)CH_3$, CH_3CN, PAN ($CH_3C(O)OONO_2$), high and low altitude CO_2 as well as 24 additional isotopologues. ACE monitors the Montreal Protocol on substances that deplete the ozone layer, and all of the main greenhouse gases, including CO_2. Altitude-latitude distributions and trends in atmospheric abundance will be presented for a subset of the ACE molecules including new research retrievals for HOCl. See http://www.ace.uwaterloo.ca for more information.

RE03 **8:08 – 8:09**

SULFUR DIOXIDE FROM THE ATMOSPHERIC CHEMISTRY EXPERIMENT (ACE) SATELLITE

WILLIAM D CAMERON, *Physics, Old Dominion University, Norfolk, VA, USA*; PETER F. BERNATH, *Department of Chemistry and Biochemistry, Old Dominion University, Norfolk, VA, USA*; CHRIS BOONE, *Department of Chemistry, University of Waterloo, Waterloo, ON, Canada.*

The version 4.0 dataset from the Atmospheric Chemistry Experiment – Fourier Transform Spectrometer (ACE-FTS) on SCISAT, released in March of 2019, has sulfur dioxide (SO_2) volume mixing ratio (VMR) profiles as a routine data product. From this dataset, global SO_2 distributions between the altitudes of 10.5 km and 23.5 km are analyzed. The global distribution of all SO_2 VMR data by altitude is divided into 30° and 5° latitude zones. Seasonality of global SO_2 distribution is explored. Volcanic SO_2 plumes are isolated in the dataset and compared with aerosol extinction data from the ACE-FTS Imager. SO_2 is converted to sulfate aerosols on a timescale of about one month. Sulfate aerosols increase the Earth's albedo and cool the surface.

RE04 **8:12 – 8:13**

ABSORPTION COEFFICIENT (ABSCO) TABLES FOR THE ORBITING CARBON OBSERVATORIES

VIVIENNE H PAYNE, BRIAN DROUIN, FABIANO OYAFUSO, LE KUAI, BRENDAN M FISHER, KEEY-OON SUNG, DEACON J NEMCHICK, TIMOTHY J. CRAWFORD, MIKE SMYTH, DAVID CRISP, *Jet Propulsion Laboratory, California Institute of Technology, Pasadena, CA, USA*; ERIN M. ADKINS, JOSEPH T. HODGES, DAVID A. LONG, *Material Measurement Laboratory, National Institute of Standards and Technology, Gaithersburg, MD, USA*; ELI J MLAWER, , *Atmospheric and Environmental Research, Lexington, MA, USA*; ARONNE MERRELLI, *Space Science and Engineering Center, University of Wisconsin, Madison, WI, USA*; ELIZABETH M LUNNY, *Division of Chemistry and Chemical Engineering, California Institute of Technology, Pasadena, CA, USA.*

The accuracy of atmospheric trace gas retrievals depends directly on the accuracy of the molecular absorption model used within the retrieval algorithm. For remote sensing of well-mixed gases, such as carbon dioxide (CO_2), where the atmospheric variability is small compared to the background, the quality of the molecular absorption model is key. Recent updates to oxygen (O_2) absorption coefficients (ABSCO) for the 0.76 μm A-band and the water vapor (H_2O) continuum model within the 1.6 μm and 2.06 μm CO_2 bands used within the Orbiting Carbon Observatory (OCO-2 and OCO-3) algorithm are described here. Updates in the O_2 A-band involve the inclusion of new laboratory measurements within multispectrum fits to improve relative consistency between oxygen line shapes and collision-induced absorption (CIA). The H_2O continuum model has been updated to MT_CKD v3.2, which has benefited from information from a range of laboratory studies relative to the model utilized in the previous ABSCO version. Impacts of these spectroscopy updates have been evaluated against ground-based atmospheric spectra from the Total Carbon Column Observing Network (TCCON) and within the framework of the OCO-2 algorithm, using OCO-2 soundings covering a range of atmospheric and surface conditions. The updated absorption coefficients (ABSCO version 5.1) are found to offer improved fitting residuals and reduced biases in retrieved surface pressure relative to the previous version (ABSCO v5.0) used within B8 and B9 of the OCO-2 retrieval algorithm and have been adopted for the OCO B10 Level 2 algorithm.

RE05 **8:16 – 8:17**

THE MICROWAVE SPECTRUM OF 2-CHLOROETHYL RADICAL, CH_2ClCH_2

MICHAEL J. CARRILLO, WEI LIN, *Department of Chemistry, University of Texas Rio Grande Valley, Brownsville, TX, USA*; YASUKI ENDO, *Department of Applied Chemistry, National Yang Ming Chiao Tung University, Hsinchu, Taiwan.*

The pure rotational spectrum of 2-chloroethyl radical, CH_2ClCH_2, has been observed for the first time using a cavity-based Fourier-transform microwave spectrometer in the frequency region of 10 GHz – 34 GHz. The radical was generated through electric discharge by applying a 1 kV voltage to the precursor molecule of either 1, 2-dichloroethane, CH_2ClCH_2Cl, or 1-chloro,2-iodoethane, CH_2ClCH_2I, where the latter gave 2-3 times stronger signal. Nine rotational transitions, both a-type and b-type, have been measured with resolved fine and hyperfine components for both ^{35}Cl and ^{37}Cl isotopic species in the ground vibrational state. The spectrum is highly congested due to the interactions of the electron spin, nuclear spin of chlorine atom, and nuclear spins of four hydrogen atoms. To aid in our analysis of the spectrum, we performed CCSD(T) calculation on the geometry optimization of the radical and a single point calculation at MP2 level to obtain the fine and hyperfine constants. We will present and discuss the corresponding assignments of features in the spectrum.

RE06 **8:20 – 8:21**

DETAILED ANALYSIS OF THE INFRARED SPECTRUM OF SiF_4: AN UPDATE

VINCENT BOUDON, *Laboratoire ICB, CNRS/Université de Bourgogne, DIJON, France*; LAURENT MANCERON, *Synchrotron SOLEIL, CNRS-MONARIS UMR 8233 and Beamline AILES, Saint Aubin, France.*

Silicon tetrafluoride (SiF_4) should be a normal trace component of volcanic gases. However, a better knowledge of spectroscopic parameters is needed for this molecule in order to derive accurate concentrations.

As explained last year, we undertook an extensive high-resolution study of its infrared absorption bands, for the there isotopologues in natural abundance: $^{28}SiF_4$ (92.23 %), $^{29}SiF_4$ (4.67 %) and $^{30}SiF_4$ (3.10 %). We present here an update of this study. It includes a new global fit with consistent parameter sets for the ground and excited states (the Figure on the right presents the ν_4 bending fundamental region). In particular, all existing rotational line data have been included. The $2\nu_4$ band of $^{28}SiF_4$ could also be analyzed in detail. A first rough estimates of the dipole moment derivative for the ν_3 band has been performed, leading to to an integrated band intensity which is consistent with literature values, around 680 km/mol. The isotopic dependance of band centers and Coriolis parameters has been studied, thanks to the formula presented in talk P4363.

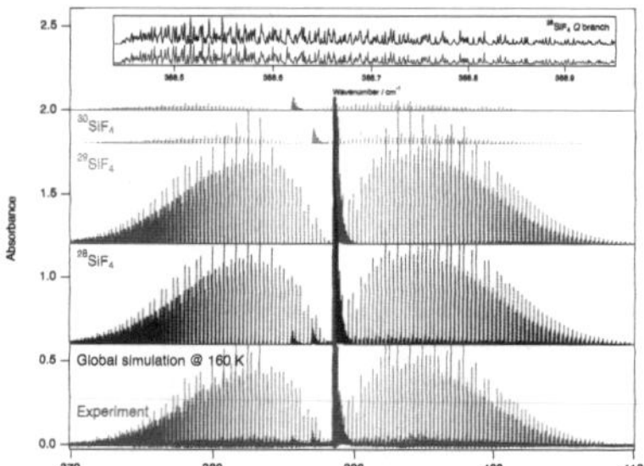

RE07 **8:24 – 8:25**

MICROWAVE SPECTROSCOPY STUDY SUPPORTED BY QUANTUM CHEMISTRY CALCULATIONS OF LIMONA KETONE, A KEY OXIDATION PRODUCT OF LIMONENE

NOUREDDIN OSSEIRAN, ANNUNZIATA SAVOIA, PASCAL DRÉAN, MANUEL GOUBET, THERESE R. HUET, *UMR 8523 - PhLAM - Physique des Lasers Atomes et Molécules, University of Lille, CNRS, F-59000 Lille, France.*

Vegetation is a major source of emission of Biogenic Volatile Organic Compounds (BVOCs), which play an important role in atmospheric chemistry. Apart from methane and isoprene, monoterpenes ($C_{10}H_{16}$) are emitted in significant amounts by plants. Among these, α-pinene, β-pinene, and limonene are the predominant species[a]. Recently, limonene and limonene oxide have been studied extensively with Fourier transform microwave spectroscopy (FTMW)[b,c]. Limona ketone ($C_9H_{14}O$) is a major oxidation product of limonene, and it was shown that it is considered as precursor of Secondary Organic Aerosol (SOA) formation[d]. Thus, BVOCs have considerable impact on numerous environmental processes, climate, and health, and it is important to determine their gas phase structure and to predict their interaction sites and patterns with surrounding molecular systems. Within this context, the rotational spectrum of limona ketone was recorded and analyzed over the 3.8-19.3 GHz range using FTMW spectrometer[e]. The rotational spectrum analysis was supported by quantum chemical calculations, and transitions were assigned to the most stable equatorial conformer. The spectrum showed clearly that the lines were split. This splitting is due to internal rotation of methyl group, where the A and E states lines were assigned and fitted at instrumental accuracy, and the experimental barrier of the methyl torsion was determined.

[a]P. S. Monks et al., Atmospheric Composition Change – Global and Regional Air Quality. Atmos. Environ. 2009, 43 (33), 5268–5350.

[b]J.R. Moreno et al., Conformational Relaxation of S-(+)-Carvone and R-(+)-Limonene Studied by Microwave Fourier Transform Spectroscopy and Quantum Chemical Calculations. Struct. Chem. 2013, 24 (4), 1163–1170.

[c]D. Loru et al., Conformational Flexibility of Limonene Oxide Studied By Microwave Spectroscopy. ChemPhysChem 2017, 18 (3), 274–280.

[d]N.M. Donahue et al., Secondary Organic Aerosol from Limona Ketone: Insights into Terpene Ozonolysis via Synthesis of Key Intermediates. Phys. Chem. Chem. Phys. 2007, 9 (23), 2991–2998.

[e]M. Tudorie et al., Magnetic Hyperfine Coupling of a Methyl Group Undergoing Internal Rotation: A Case Study of Methyl Formate. J. Chem. Phys. 2011, 134 (7), 074314.

RE08 **8:28 – 8:29**

REVEALING LONG-RANGE SUBSTITUENT EFFECTS IN THE LASER-INDUCED FLUORESCENCE AND DISPERSED FLUORESCENCE SPECTRA OF JET-COOLED $CH_XF_{3-X}CH_2O$ (X = 1, 2, 3) RADICALS

BENEDEK KONCZ, *Institute of Chemistry, Eotvos University, Budapest, Hungary*; GABOR BAZSO, *Institute of Chemistry, Eötvös Loránd University, Budapest, Hungary*; MD ASMAUL REZA, HAMZEH TELFAH, *Department of Chemistry, University of Louisville, Louisville, KY, USA*; KRISTOF HEGEDUS, *Institute of Organic Chemistry, Research Center for Natural Sciences, Budapest, Hungary*; JINJUN LIU, *Department of Chemistry, University of Louisville, Louisville, KY, USA*; GYORGY TARCZAY, *Institute of Chemistry, Eotvos University, Budapest, Hungary.*

The $\tilde{B}$ - $\tilde{X}$ laser-induced fluorescence (LIF) and dispersed fluorescence (DF) spectra of the atmospherically important β-monofluoro ethoxy (MFEO), β,β-difluoro ethoxy (DFEO), and β,β,β-trifluoro ethoxy (TFEO) radicals were recorded with vibronic resolution under jet-cooled conditions. To simulate the spectra, Franck-Condon factors were obtained from quantum chemical computations carried out at the CAM-B3LYP/6-311++G(d,p) level of theory. The simulations reproduce well both the LIF and DF spectra. Both conformers (G and T) of MFEO and one (G) of the two conformers of DFEO contribute to the LIF spectrum. A comparison between the experimental and calculated spectra confirms the expected long-range field effects of the CH_XF_{3-X} group on electronic transition energies and bond strengths, especially in the excited electronic ($\tilde{B}$) state. Although TFEO has only one conformer, its LIF spectrum is highly congested, which is attributed to the interaction between CO stretch and the -CF_3 internal rotation.

RE09 **8:32 – 8:33**

SENSITIVE INFRARED SPECTROSCOPY OF ISOPRENE AT THE PART PER BILLION LEVEL

JACOB STEWART, JACOB BELOIN, MELANIE JEAN FOURNIER, GRACE KOVIC, *Department of Chemistry, Connecticut College, New London, CT, USA.*

Isoprene (C_5H_8) is an important molecular target in trace gas sensing due to its presence in Earth's atmosphere and human breath. Isoprene is the most abundant of the so-called biogenic volatile organic compounds (BVOCs) emitted naturally into the atmosphere by plants, and so plays an important role in the chemistry of the troposphere. Isoprene is also one of the most abundant hydrocarbons present in human breath, and there is interest in measuring isoprene in breath as a way to perform noninvasive monitoring of patients. In both of these settings, isoprene is present as a trace gas at a concentration of parts per billion (ppb), making its detection quite challenging. We have used a quantum cascade laser-based infrared spectrometer to perform sensitive spectroscopy of isoprene down to the ppb level. We have used the strong Q-branch of the ν_{26} band of isoprene near 992 $\mathrm{cm}^{-1}$to monitor its concentration and achieved a minimum noise-equivalent concentration for our spectrometer of 3 ppb at an optimal averaging time of 25 s. We have also demonstrated the potential real-world applications of our approach by directly measuring the isoprene concentration in a breath sample from a volunteer.

RE10 **8:36 – 8:37**

A COLLISIONAL TRANSFER MECHANISM FOR SULFUR MASS INDEPENDENT FRACTIONATION IN WEAKLY INTERACTING EXCITED ELECTRONIC STATES OF S_2

ALEXANDER W HULL, *Department of Chemistry, MIT, Cambridge, MA, USA*; SHUHEI ONO, *Earth, Atmospheric, and Planetary Sciences, MIT, Cambridge, MA, USA*; ROBERT W FIELD, *Department of Chemistry, MIT, Cambridge, MA, USA.*

The Great Oxygenation Event, the introduction of O_2 into the Earth's atmosphere approximately 2.5 billion years ago, is a critical stage in the development of life on Earth. The exact timing of this event is thought to be correlated with the disappearance of sulfur isotope anomalies, called "Sulfur Mass Independent Fractionation" (S-MIF), in the rock record. However, the mechanism for the generation of S-MIF in a reducing atmosphere is still unknown. This talk explores the B-X system of S_2 where the short-lifetime B state is extensively perturbed by a long-lifetime B" state. We employ a master equation model that calculates rotationally and electronically inelastic collisional transfer rates between the B and B" states. For weakly perturbed B/B" level crossings (matrix element less than 1 cm^{-1}), these collisional transfer processes can generate significant isotope effects, where one isotopologue has a larger enhancement of excited state population than another. We discuss the effects of mass-dependent vibrational level shifts and nuclear permutation symmetry on this isotopic fractionation, and propose a possible mechanism for the S-MIF pattern observed in the rock record.

RF. Spectroscopy as an analytical tool

Thursday, June 24, 2021 – 8:0 AM

Room: 2021 Online Everywhere

Chair: David A. Long, National Institute of Standards and Technology, Gaithersburg, MD, USA

RF01 *Post-Deadline Abstract* **8:00 – 8:01**

MICRO-PARTICLES IMMUNOASSAYS FOR EARLY DETECTION OF OVARIAN CANCER USING LASER INDUCED BREAKDOWN SPECTROSCOPY.

ROBINSON KARUNANITHY, P SIVAKUMAR, TORREY E. HOLLAND, *Physics, Southern Illinois University Carbondale, Carbondale, IL, USA.*

Detecting cancer cells before any symptoms appear is essential for successful treatment, especially for epithelial ovarian cancer (EOC) with few or no symptoms at the early stages. Although there are methods that have been developed to identify the cancer cells, scientists are looking for other novel promising methods to detect that early stage, also cheap and user-friendly. Here, we cross-link elemental particles to a specific functional group of the targeted biomolecules based on a covalent and non-covalent linking chemistry to improve the sensitivity and the selectivity of biomarker detection. In this presentation, we look into the sandwich type of micro-particle immunoassay with pair of Fe3O4 and silicon micro-particles used for highly-selective detection of specific cancer antigen human epididymis protein-4 (HE4) in which U.S. Food and Drug Administration (FDA) accepted recently as a biomarker for monitoring EOC patients. The cancer biomarkers are quantified via detecting the silicon using Laser-induced breakdown spectroscopy (LIBS).

RF02 *Post-Deadline Abstract* **8:04 – 8:05**

LASER INDUCED BREAKDOWN SPECTROSCOPY FOR DETECTION OF HEAVY METALS IN CANCEROUS AND HEALTHY COLON TISSUES

MOHAMMED A GONDAL, *Department of Physics, King Fahd University of Petroleum and Minerals, Dhahran, Saudi Arabia.*

Cancer mortalities are common due to the lack of diagnostic at the early stages in many countries. Recent studies discovered that the heavy metals in the human colon could cause the colon cancer. The conventional cancer detection techniques suffer from the insensitiveness, imprecision, slowness, cumbersomeness of sample preparation, and some time show conflicting results. Hence an accurate, reliable, and rapid detection technique is essential for the early diagnostic and prevention of heavy metals accumulation induced colon cancers. In this work, calibration-free laser-induced breakdown spectrometer (LIBS) was applied on several cancerous and normal colon tissues collected from the colon cancer infested patients aged 40 — 60 years. The results showed the presence of carcinogenic heavy metals including lead (Pb), chromium (Cr), and mercury (Hg) in the malignant colon tissues, while the healthy tissues were devoid of these elements. The accuracy of the LIBS results was validated by comparing the results obtained using a standard inductively coupled plasma atomic emission spectroscopy (ICP-OES). This study demonstrated that LIBS technique is very effective for rapid, precise early detection of the heavy metals accumulation in malignant colon tissues.

RF03 **8:08 – 8:09**

STUDY OF MOLECULAR BAND PRESENT IN THE LASER-INDUCED PLASMA OF CHOLESTEROL GALLSTONE

ZAINAB GAZALI, *Department of Physics, Allahabad University, Allahabad, India*; PRADEEP KUMAR RAI, *, Opal Hospital, Varanasi, India*; SURYA NARAYAN THAKUR, *Department of Physics, Banaras Hindu University, Varanasi, Uttar Pradesh, India*; A. K. RAI, *Department of Physics, Allahabad University, Allahabad, India.*

Gallbladder cancer is associated with high death rates due to its no effective treatment. Gallstones are the most common risk factor for gallbladder cancer. Continuous efforts have been made to understand the morphology, development, and compositions of gallstones, but to the best of our knowledge, the mechanism of their formation is not properly known. In the present work, the spectral lines of elements and molecular bands in cholesterol gallstone have been monitored using laser-induced breakdown spectroscopy (LIBS). The LIBS spectra of cholesterol gallstone exhibit spectral lines of inorganic (Ca, Mg, Na, Al, K) and organic (C, H, N, O) elements as well as electronic spectra of CN Violet band, NH band, and C_2 Swan band. We have also recorded the Fourier transform infrared (FTIR) spectra of cholesterol gallstone, which show vibrational bands of CN, NH, and C_2 molecules. These studies are likely to reveal the mechanism of gallstone formation.

RF04 **8:12 – 8:13**

COMPOSITIONAL ANALYSIS OF GREEN TEA LEAVES USING LASER INDUCED BREAKDOWN SPECTROSCOPY (LIBS)

TEJMANI KUMAR, ABHISHEK DWIVEDI, ZAINAB GAZALI, *Department of Physics, Allahabad University, Allahabad, India*; ABHISHEK RAI, *Department of Earth and Planetary Science, University of Allahabad, Prayagraj, Uttar Pradesh, India*; A. K. RAI, *Department of Physics, Allahabad University, Allahabad, India.*

Green tea is a type of tea made from the leaves and buds of Camellia sinensis. To ensure the interests of Green Tea producers and consumers the precise identification of tea varieties is of great significance. Thus, Laser-induced breakdown (LIB) Spectra of Green tea have been recorded for the its compositional analysis.LIB Spectra of the sample shows the presence of molecular bands of CN and C_2 molecule in addition to the spectral signature of the elements like Carbon(C), Manganese (Mn), Magnesium (Mg), Iron (Fe), Aluminium (Al) etc. The concentration of C and N is corelated to the atomic lines of C and N and molecular band of CN and C_2. Thus, the results of present work reveal that LIBS technique is a direct, straight forward and easy method for detection of elements and some specified molecule present in the sample.

RF05 **8:16 – 8:17**

COMPOSITIONAL ANALYSIS OF AYURVEDIC MEDICINE USING LIBS ALONG WITH PAS TECHNIQUES[a]

RESHU KUMARI, ZAINAB GAZALI, ABHISHEK DWIVEDI, A. K. RAI, *Department of Physics, Allahabad University, Allahabad, India.*

In the present work, elemental and molecular compositions of Ayurvedic medicine have been performed using Photoacoustic Spectroscopy (PAS) and Laser-Induced Breakdown Spectroscopy (LIBS) techniques. The molecular bands of Protein, Carbohydrate, Flavonoid, and Chlorophyll, etc., have been observed using the PAS technique. PAS is based on the detection of photon-induced acoustic (PA) signals generated via non-radiative transition processes. The spectral lines of organic elements (C, H, N, and O) as well as the spectral lines of minerals (Al, Ca, Fe, Mg, Na, Si, and Sr) have been observed in the Laser-induced Breakdown (LIB) spectrum of the medicine. The presence of the spectral lines of organic elements is due to the photo fragments of the organic compounds present in the medicine. The molecular band of CN molecule in the LIB spectrum of the medicine further confirms the medicines' organic compound. Thus, along with LIBS, PAS is a suitable technique for the complete compositional analysis of Ayurvedic medication.

[a]THE AUTHOR IS GRATEFUL TO THE COUNCIL OF SCIENTIFIC & INDUSTRIAL RESEARCH (CSIR) FOR FINANCIAL SUPPORT AS A SENIOR RESEARCH FELLOW.

RF06 **8:20 – 8:21**

LOOKING FOR CACAO IN ALL THE WRONG PLACES: AN ANALYSIS OF MAYA POTTERY WITH 2-PHOTON RESONANCE SPECTROSCOPY

ANN WILLIAMS , MATTANJAH DE VRIES, *Chemistry and Biochemistry, UCSB, Santa Barbara, CA, USA.*

Cacao, a mesoamerican beverage similar to modern hot chocolate, is believed by archaeologists to have been drunk by the ancient Maya elite. Past analysis has often focused on highly decorative vessel forms that were only found in large sites with a social elite. We analyzed common drinking vessels for cacao to question if it was only the socially elite who had access to cacao. Focusing on the region of El Pillar, Belize in the Late Classical Period, we analyzed 35 archaeological sherds from 6 different regions, including sites with and without an elite population. The identification of cacao in ancient pottery sherds is dependent on the presence of the biomarkers theobromine, theophylline, and caffeine. Biomarkers are molecules that exist in high concentrations in the compound of interest, will survive burial, and are unique to that one compound. Samples of pottery are tested for presence of theobromine, theophylline and caffeine and if found to have measurable amounts of theobromine are considered indicative of cacao. Analysis is done by grinding off all outside surfaces to reduce contamination, pulverizing the inner clay matrix, extracting the biomarkers, and concentrating the extractions. These concentrated extractions are then most often analyzed via UPLC-MS. In order to obtain especially high selectivity and low limits of detection, our study utilized the novel technique of resonance enhanced multi-photon Ionization (REMPI) coupled with laser-desorption jet-cooling mass spectrometry. This technique isolates molecules in the cold gas phase where they can be selectively ionized through a two photon resonant process. We found evidence of cacao in samples from sites both with and without an elite.

RF07 **8:24 – 8:25**

DEVELOPMENT OF A SUPERSONIC WIND TUNNEL FOR A CAVITY RINGDOWN SPECTROMETER

ELIJAH R JANS, *Department of Mechanical and Aerospace Engineering, The Ohio State University, Columbus, OH, USA*; TERRY A. MILLER, *Department of Chemistry and Biochemistry, The Ohio State University, Columbus, OH, USA*; IGOR V. ADAMOVICH, *Department of Mechanical and Aerospace Engineering, The Ohio State University, Columbus, OH, USA.*

A cavity ringdown spectrometer with a supersonic wind tunnel for measurements of excited species and radicals at low pressures and temperatures has been developed. The spectrometer has been used for measurements of metastable nitrogen molecules in the lowest excited electronic state, $N_2(A^3\Sigma_u^+)$, in the supersonic test section of the wind tunnel. The tunnel has been operated in nitrogen at plenum pressure of P_0 = 200-250 Torr, with the flow expanding through a two-dimensional contoured nozzle to the Mach number of M = 3.6-4.6. The steady-state run time of the tunnel is approximately 10 s. The flow in the tunnel is excited by a repetitive ns pulse discharge operated in the plenum or in the nozzle throat. In the supersonic test section, absolute $N_2(A^3\Sigma_u^+$,v=0-2) populations at P = 0.8 Torr and T = 70 K are measured by Cavity Ring Down Spectroscopy (CRDS), using a tunable pulsed laser system operated at 10 Hz. During each run, 50 single-shot ring down traces are acquired, demonstrating good shot-to-shot reproducibility. The results demonstrate that the cavity ring down time is not affected by the supersonic flow. Further measurements of more complex radicals, such as HO_2, using a narrow linewidth tunable optical parametric oscillator (OPO) coupled to the supersonic wind tunnel, are currently under development.

RF08 **8:28 – 8:29**

OPTICALLY-SWITCHED DUAL-WAVELENGTH CAVITY RING-DOWN SPECTROMETER FOR HIGH-PRECISION ISOTOPIC RATIO MEASUREMENTS OF METHANE δD and ^{13}C IN THE NEAR-INFRARED

TZULING CHEN, DOUGLAS OBER, *Division of Chemistry and Chemical Engineering, California Institute of Technology, Pasadena, CA, USA*; ROBIN MIRI, *École Normale Supérieure de Cachan and Univerité de Sorbonne, Sorbonne Université, Paris, France*; THINH BUI, *Sensor Science Division, National Institute of Standards and Technology, Gaithersburg, MD, USA*; LINHAN SHEN, *Department of Geosciences, Princeton University, Princeton, USA*; MITCHIO OKUMURA, *Division of Chemistry and Chemical Engineering, California Institute of Technology, Pasadena, CA, USA.*

We report a spectrometer employing optically-switched dual-wavelength cavity ring-down spectroscopy (OSDW-CRDS) for high-precision measurements of methane isotopic ratios. A wave-guide optical switch rapidly alternated between two wavelengths to detect absorption by two isotopologues using near-infrared CRDS. This approach alleviated common-mode noise that originated primarily from temperature and frequency fluctuations. We demonstrated the measurement of δD in natural abundance methane to a precision of 0.23 ‰, despite the lack of active temperature or frequency stabilization of the cavity. The ability of alternating OSDW-CRDS in improving isotope precision were measured by Allan deviation as varying switching time intervals (0.1 Hz$\sim$10 Hz) and the use of frequency-stabilizing cavity length. This system can be extended to a wide variety of applications such as isotope analysis of other species, kinetic isotope effects, *ortho-para* ratio measurements, and isomer abundance measurements. Furthermore, our technique can be extended to multiple isotopic analysis through the use of multi-port optical switches.

RF09 **8:32 – 8:33**

HIGH RESOLUTION INFRARED CAVITY ENHANCED ABSORPTION AT LOW TEMPERATURES

CARLOS MANZANARES, SURESH SUNUWAR, *Department of Chemistry and Biochemistry, Baylor University, Waco, TX, USA.*

A high-resolution cavity enhanced absorption spectroscopy (CEAS) technique is presented for infrared absorption studies at temperatures between 77K and 300 K. An optical cavity with a pathlength of several kilometers is attached to a low temperature cryostat. The spectra are obtained with a tunable diode laser with resolution 0.0003 cm^{-1}. The output of the laser is modulated with an electro-optic modulator and coupled to an optical cavity. To illustrate the use of the technique, the first overtone of carbon monoxide at 298 K and 80 K and the first overtone transition of the acetylenic C-H stretch of propyne will be presented. The experiments are performed at pressures from 70 mTorr to 1 Torr. The combination of low pressures and temperatures makes this technique ideal for studies related to astrochemistry. The experimental set up will be used to simulate in the laboratory the kinetics and spectroscopy of molecules in the atmosphere of planets and satellites of the outer solar system.

RF10 **8:36 – 8:37**

SPECTROSCOPIC DETECTION OF METHANE AT A PPT SENSITIVITY LEVEL IN MID-IR WITH A LONG-PATH MULTIPASS CELL

HANS A SCHUESSLER, *Department of Physics and Astronomy, Texas A&M University, College Station, TX, USA*; JINBAO XIA, *State Key Laboratory of Crystal Materials, Shandong University, Jinan, China*; CARLOS RODRIGUEZ, *Department of Physics and Astronomy, Texas A & M University, college station, TX, USA*; JAMES R BOUNDS, ALEXANDRE KOLOMENSKII, *Department of Physics and Astronomy, Texas A&M University, College Station, TX, USA.*

Highly sensitive detection of methane is important for biomedical applications, environmental monitoring, and the detection of leaks in the gas and oil industry. An ultra-high sensitivity sensor employing a mid-IR (MIR) interband cascade laser (center wavelength of 3.37 micron) and a multi-pass cell (MPC) was developed for methane detection. The ultra-high sensitivity is achieved due to the high absorbance in the MIR, a long interaction path length, and the implementation of a wavelet denoising processing algorithm. The long interaction path of 580 m was achieved with a confocal MCP and the distance between the mirrors of 1 m. The performance of the sensor was tested in two measuring modes: direct absorption spectroscopy (DAS) and wavelength modulation spectroscopy (WMS). For the sensor working in the DAS measurement mode the optimal set of sub-wavelet functions was determined and utilized for denoising and the minimum of the Allan deviation of the sensor of 3 ppb was achieved with an averaging time of 200 s. For the WMS measuring mode the sensor detection limit for methane of 560 ppt with 290 s averaging time was determined from the Allan deviation analysis. The developed sensor is suitable for a compact and portable design and has broad applicability in the high-sensitivity measurements of methane and other trace gases. This work was supported by the Robert A Welch Foundation, grant No A1546 and the T3 grant from Texas A and M University and Open Fund of State Key Laboratory of Applied Optics (SKLA02020001A12).

[1] Jinbao Xia et al. A sensitive methane sensor of a ppt detection level using a mid-infrared interband cascade laser and a long-path multipass cell, Sensors and Actuators B: Chemical, 334, 129641 (2021). [2] Jinbao Xia: State Key Laboratory of Applied Optics, Changchun Institute of Optics, Fine Mechanics and Physics, Chinese Academy of Sciences Changchun, 130033, China

RF11 **8:40 – 8:41**

A PHOTONIC GAS SENSOR FOR THE MID-INFRARED

TRAVIS A GARTNER, *Department of Physics and Astronomy, University of Calgary, Calgary, AB, Canada*; PAUL BARCLAY, NASSER MOAZZEN-AHMADI, *Physics and Astronomy/Institute for Quantum Science and Technology, University of Calgary, Calgary, AB, Canada.*

The mid-infrared (MIR) contains the strong absorption signatures of many molecules, such as Methane and Carbon Dioxide, that are of extreme interest in real-world sensing applications. The miniaturization of spectroscopic sensing equipment made possible by engineered silicon photonics has the potential to revolutionize the way we conduct emissions sensing in the MIR. Nanophotonic devices have greatly benefited from telecommunication technology in the near infrared (NIR) region. The industry has reached a level of maturity where high volume production of integrated circuitry can be done at low cost. Advances in materials engineering have shown that silicon based photonic devices can support optical propagation in the MIR past 8 microns with losses approaching those of the telecommunications band [a] making the region attractive for nanoscale sensor development. Absorption sensing with photonic devices has been demonstrated in silicon on sapphire [b], silicon nitride [c], and metal assisted silicon on insulator [d] platforms, among others. These methodologies have demonstrated the ability to sense analyte concentrations as low as 5000 ppmv (parts per million by volume), which is the workplace limit in many North American constituencies.

We present our current state of research on the development of a high-quality factor MIR silicon-on-sapphire (SOS) photonic gas sensor for use in lab-on-a-chip sensing applications. An optical parametric oscillator (OPO) will be used as a MIR source to pump a grating coupled SOS ring cavity immersed in a controlled CO_2 environment. The cavity will be geometrically engineered to allow for high sensitivity spectroscopy of the CO_2 fundamental at 2350 cm^{-1}via absorption of the cavity evanescent field. Design and optimization is conducted through the use of COMSOL Multiphysics and Lumerical software suites.

[a] R. Shankar, I. Bulu, M. Loncar, *Applied Physics Letters*, **102**, 051108, 2013.
[b] C. Smith, R. Shankar, M. Laderer, M. Frish, M. Loncar, M. Allen, *Optics Express*, **23** 5491, 2015.
[c] C. Ranacher, C. Consani, N. Vollert, A. Tortschanoff, M. Bergmeister, T. Grille, B. Jakoby, *IEEE Photonics Journal*, **10** 2018.
[d] C. Ranacher, C. Consani,, A. Tortschanoff, R. Jannesari, M. Bergmeister, T. Grille, B. Jakoby, *Sensors and Actuators A: Physical*, **277**, 117, 2018.

RF12 **8:44 – 8:45**

MEASURING ACCURATE STIMULATED RAMAN SCATTERING CROSS-SECTIONS OF LIQUIDS

PRASENJIT SRIVASTAVA, KRISTEN H. BURNS, CHRISTOPHER G. ELLES, *Department of Chemistry, University of Kansas, Lawrence, KS, USA.*

Nonlinear spectroscopy provides important information about chemical systems that is not available from linear spectra alone. However, nonlinear spectroscopies have rarely been used for quantitative measurements due to the difficulty in obtaining accurate cross-sections. To overcome this limitation, we have been developing new methods to obtain accurate two-photon absorption (2PA) and stimulated Raman scattering (SRS) cross-sections of liquids and liquid solutions using ultrafast pump-probe spectroscopy. Here, we describe recent advances in measuring absolute SRS cross-sections of common liquid solvents based on a simple setup using single-wavelength pump and broadband probe pulses derived from a tunable repetition rate Yb:KGW laser. We obtain a two-dimensional transient absorption spectrum that is integrated over the time delay between the pump and the probe to obtain the Raman response as a frequency-dependent SRS spectrum. We model the overlap between the pump and probe beams in terms of the beam diameter, crossing angle, and refractive index of the solvent in order to determine accurate values for the SRS cross-sections based on the pump-probe signal strength. Specifically, we report absolute cross-sections for the C–H stretching modes of cyclohexane, dimethyl sulfoxide, acetonitrile, methanol, benzene, and toluene using Raman excitation wavelengths of 1030 nm (anti-Stokes), 515 nm (Stokes and anti-Stokes), and 343 nm (Stokes). The measured cross-sections follow the expected $\sim \nu^4$ frequency dependence. Our measurements also allow for direct comparison of the absolute SRS cross-sections for Stokes and anti-Stokes scattering from a single (515 nm) Raman excitation laser, which may be important for quantitative measurements using coherent nonlinear spectroscopies. For example, the SRS cross-sections that we measure for these solvents provide valuable internal reference standards for the determination of accurate 2PA cross-sections of solutes.

RG. Plenary

Thursday, June 24, 2021 – 9:0 AM
Room: 2021 Online Everywhere

Chair: Martin Gruebele, University of Illinois at Urbana-Champaign, Urbana, IL, USA

RG02 **9:03 – 9:43**

INFLUENCE OF NATURALLY-OCCURRING AND SYNTHETIC MODIFICATIONS ON THE STRUCTURES AND GLYCOSIDIC BOND STABILITIES OF DNA AND RNA NUCLEOSIDES

M T RODGERS, RANRAN WU, YANLONG ZHU, LUCAS HAMLOW, CHENCHEN HE, ZACHARY J DEVEREAUX, HARRISON ROY, ERIK O SOLEY, CHASE LESLIE, *Department of Chemistry, Wayne State University, Detroit, MI, USA*; GIEL BERDEN, JOS OOMENS, *FELIX Laboratory, Radboud University, Nijmegen, The Netherlands.*

The chemical and structural diversity and the extent of post-transcriptional modification of RNA are remarkable! Currently there are more than 163 naturally-occurring modified nucleosides known. Modified nucleosides have also been a target for pharmaceutical application as potential anticancer and antiviral agents such that many more synthetically-modified nucleosides have been studied. While the biochemical and physiological roles of modified nucleosides have been elucidated in some cases, their importance to RNA biochemistry is still largely unknown and underappreciated. Thus, comparative studies of the canonical versus naturally-occurring and synthetically-modified nucleosides to elucidate changes in structure and glycosidic bond stability arising from modifications are important to understanding their mechanisms of action. Synergistic tandem mass spectrometry and computational chemistry approaches are used to characterize the structures and relative glycosidic bond stabilities of the protonated and sodium cationized forms of the canonical DNA and RNA nucleosides and a wide variety of naturally-occurring and synthetic nucleosides. Vibrational frequency-resolved infrared multiple dissociation (IRMPD) action spectroscopy experiments coupled with spectral analyses of the stable low-energy conformers and their predicted linear IR spectra are used to elucidate the gas-phase conformations of these nucleosides. The stable structures of the nucleosides, their relative stabilities, and predicted linear IR spectra are determined using ab initio and density functional theory methods. Energy-resolved collision-induced dissociation (ER-CID) experiments coupled with survival yield analyses are used to elucidate the relative glycosidic bond stabilities of the nucleosides. Differences in structure induced by modifications and trends in the relative glycosidic bond stabilities of the canonical versus modified nucleosides are examined in detail. Implications of nucleoside modifications on structure-function relationships are discussed.

RH. Mini-symposium: Large Amplitude Motions

Thursday, June 24, 2021 – 10:0 AM

Room: 2021 Online Everywhere

Chair: Arnaud Cuisset, Université du Littoral Côte d'Opale, Dunkerque, France

RH01 **10:00 – 10:01**

MOLECULAR ROTATION IN FLOPPY MOLECULES: HE-H_3^+

THOMAS SALOMON, OSKAR ASVANY, *I. Physikalisches Institut, Universität zu Köln, Köln, Germany*; DIETER GERLICH, *Institut für Physik, Technische Universität Chemnitz, Chemnitz, Germany*; IGOR SAVIC, *Department of Physics, University of Novi Sad, Novi Sad, Serbia*; AD VAN DER AVOIRD, *Institute for Molecules and Materials (IMM), Radboud University Nijmegen, Nijmegen, Netherlands*; MICHAEL E. HARDING, *Institute of Nanotechnology, Karlsruhe Institute of Technology, Karlsruhe, Germany*; FILIPPO LIPPARINI, *Dipartimento di Chimica e Chimica Industriale, Università di Pisa, Pisa, Italy*; JÜRGEN GAUSS, *Institut für Physikalische Chemie, Universität Mainz, Mainz, Germany*; STEPHAN SCHLEMMER, *I. Physikalisches Institut, Universität zu Köln, Köln, Germany.*

The ro-vibrational predissociation spectrum of He-H_3^+ has been recorded via excitation of the ν_2 vibrational mode of the H_3^+ sub-unit in a cold 22-pole ion trap. The spectrum for the bare H_3^+ consists of only a few ro-vibrational lines each for the para and ortho nuclear spin configuration, respectively. Instead, the spectrum of the complex is very rich (several hundred lines) even at the low temperature (4 K) of the trap experiment. Part of this complexity is associated with the (almost) free internal rotation of H_3^+. The experimental results are compared to theoretical predictions of ro-vibrational spectra on the basis of ab-initio calculations of the He-H_3^+ potential energy surface. The energy levels result in transitions which agree in many cases with experimental results within a few wavenumbers. In particular the typical band structures of a P- and R-branch associated with an effective *diatomic* complex seen in the experimental and predicted spectrum help in assigning the rich spectrum. Moreover, an experimental energy term diagram is reconstructed from the observed transitions which can be compared to the rather accurate theoretical predictions. Despite of the floppiness of the complex rotational constants for the effective *diatomic* complex can be derived and match to the term diagram of a prolate, slightly asymmetric rotor. The influence of the Coriolis interaction resulting from the H_3^+ internal rotation in a rotating He-H_3^+ frame shall be discussed.

RH02 ***Post-Deadline Abstract*** **10:04 – 10:05**

SYMMETRIES of CH_5^+

STEFAN BRACKERTZ, *I. Physikalisches Institut, University of Cologne, Cologne, Germany*; BENJAMIN NUKIC, *University of Cologne, I. Physikalisches Institut, Koeln, Germany*; PER JENSEN, *Faculty of Mathematics and Natural Sciences, University of Wuppertal, Wuppertal, Germany*; STEPHAN SCHLEMMER, *I. Physikalisches Institut, University of Cologne, Cologne, Germany.*

Some time ago we developed a five dimensional SO(5) superrotor model [1] which describes the energy term diagram of the lowest energy states of CH_5^+ surprisingly well [2]. The basis for this model lies in the S_5 permutation symmetry of the five identical protons in this molecule. In this contribution we discuss possible sub-group structures, in particular the embedded $S_4 \otimes S_2 \subseteq S_5 \subset SO(5)$, which potentially simplifies the current model and more importantly can be associated with the internal motions (vibration/rotation/internal-rotation) of the molecule. As a result the ad-hoc SO(5) model motivated by the simple super-rotor energies can be replaced by a model justified by the underlying physics.

[1] H. Schmiedt, P. Jensen, S. Schlemmer, Rotation-vibration motion of extremely flexible molecules – the molecular superrotor, Chem. Phys. Lett. 672 (2017), p. 34-46

[2] O. Asvany, K. M. T. Yamada, S. Brünken, A. Potapov, S. Schlemmer, Experimental ground-state combination differences of CH_5^+, Science, 347 (2015), pp. 1346-1349

RH03 **10:08 – 10:09**

$^{14}NH_3$ ROVIBRATIONAL IR ANALYSIS AT 6000 CM^{-1}

XINCHUAN HUANG[a], *Space Science and Astrobiology Division, NASA Ames Research Center, Moffett Field, CA, USA*; KEEYOON SUNG[b], *Jet Propulsion Laboratory, California Institute of Technology, Pasadena, CA, USA*; TIMOTHY J. LEE, *Space Science and Astrobiology Division, NASA Ames Research Center, Moffett Field, CA, USA*; DAVID SCHWENKE, *NAS Facility, NASA Ames Research Center, Moffett Field, CA, USA*; GEOFFREY C. TOON, *Jet Propulsion Laboratory, California Institute of Technology, Pasadena, CA, USA*.

Ammonia is an important "weed" molecule in interstellar medium, planetary and exoplanetary atmosphere studies. In last ten years, new experimental IR analysis have been reported in the extended region between 5000 cm^{-1}(or 2 μm) and 10,000 cm^{-1}(or 1 μm). But before 2020, there was not a reliable NH_3 line list for the 6000 cm^{-1}(or 1.63 μm) region. We combined the line position predicted on our Ames-Pre3 potential energy surface and the 296K intensity predicted in the UCL-C2018 line list [Coles et al JQSRT (2018) 219, 199-212], to analyze the Kitt Peak FTS spectra archived at JPL. More than 1300 transitions (J=0-10) have been assigned to following bands in the range of 5700 - 6200 cm^{-1}: ν_2+ν_3+ν_4 (0111), ν_1+ν_2+ν_4 (1101), 3ν_2+ν_3 (0310), ν_1+3ν_2 (1300), and a "hot" band 2ν_2+ν_3+ν_4 (0211) – ν_2 (0100). The combination difference for the determined experimental energy levels are about 1E-3 cm^{-1}, close to the resolution of lab measurements. The Ames-Pre3 based line positions are usually found to be accurate within $\pm$ 0.05-0.10 cm^{-1}. Assignments and derived rovibrational levels will be compared to those reported recently in Cacciani et al [JQSRT (2021) 258, 107334].

[a]Government sponsorship acknowledged
[b]Government sponsorship acknowledged

RH04 **10:12 – 10:13**

THE BENDING-ROTATION APPROACH APPLIED TO THE METHYLENE RADICAL CH_2

L. H. COUDERT, *Institut des Sciences Moléculaires d'Orsay, Université Paris Saclay, CNRS, Orsay, France.*

Quasi-linear molecules display a large amplitude bending mode allowing them to sample their linear configuration. This leads to a strong coupling between the overall rotation and the bending mode and to a singularity in their Hamiltonian. Quasi-linearity has been extensively studied in many species including the closed shell water molecule and the open shell amidogen (NH_2) and methylene (CH_2) radicals. For these three species, the barrier to linearity ranges from 12 000 cm^{-1} for NH_2 to less than 2000 cm^{-1} for CH_2.[a] Their rovibrational energy levels can be computed with almost spectroscopic accuracy using variational approaches or, if a higher accuracy is required, with reduced dimensionality models such as the effective Bending-Rotation approach,[b] already applied to treat the anomalous centrifugal distortion of the water molecule[b] and of the amidogen radical.[c]

In this talk, the Bending-Rotation approach[b] is extended, adding the spin-rotation and spin-spin fine couplings, so as to be used in the case of the methylene radical. The new approach is applied to the fitting of high-resolution data pertaining to this species. In addition to the ground state data previously analyzed,[d] the data set includes FIR transitions belonging to the ν_2 band.[e] 336 transitions were reproduced with a standard deviation of 1.3 using 42 spectroscopic parameters.[f] In the talk, the results of this analysis will be reported and the dependence on the bending angle retrieved for the spin-rotation and spin-spin fine couplings will be discussed. We will also try to see if the analysis results[f] can be further improved.

[a]Jungen, Hallin, and Merer, *Molec. Phys.* **40** (1980) 25; Bunker, Jensen, Kraemer, and Beardsworth, *J. Chem. Phys.* **85** (1986) 3724; Partridge and Schwenke, *J. Chem. Phys.* **106** (1997) 4618
[b]Coudert, Marin-Drumel, and Pirali, *J. Mol. Spectrosc.* **303** (2014) 36
[c]TD03, Martin-Drumel, Pirali, and Coudert, 72nd ISMS, Urbana-Champaign, June 19–23, 2017
[d]Brünken, Müller, Lewen, and Giesen, *J. Chem. Phys.* **123** (2005) 164315
[e]Sears, Bunker, and McKellar, J. Chem. Phys. **77** (1982) 5363; McKellar, Yamada, and Hirota, *J. Chem. Phys.* **79** (1983) 1220; and Marshall and McKellar, *J. Chem. Phys.* **85** (1986) 3716
[f]Coudert, *J. Chem. Phys.* **153** (2020) 144115

RH05 **10:16 – 10:17**

TUNNELING AND RING OPENING IN THE CYCLOPROPYL RADICAL AND CATION

NADAV GENOSSAR, *Chemistry, Ben-Gurion University of the Negev, Beer-Sheva, Israel*; BRYAN CHANGALA, *Atomic and Molecular Physics, Harvard-Smithsonian Center for Astrophysics, Cambridge, MA, USA*; MARIE-ALINE MARTIN-DRUMEL, BÉRENGER GANS, *Institut des Sciences Moléculaires d'Orsay, Université Paris Saclay, CNRS, Orsay, France*; J.-C. LOISON, *Université de Bordeaux, Institut des Sciences Molécualires, Bordeaux, France*; JOSHUA H BARABAN, *Chemistry, Ben-Gurion University of the Negev, Beer-Sheva, Israel.*

We report spectroscopic studies of the cyclopropyl radical and cation ($c\text{-}C_3H_5$). The cation especially is unstable towards ring-opening to allylic geometries, and the radical exhibits tunneling splitting due to inversion tunneling by the α-H atom that lies out of the C-C-C ring plane[1]. These large amplitude motion phenomena complicate the photoionization (and other) spectra and the determination of properties that are of interest due to ring strain in this fundamental cyclic radical. Through a multiscale reduced-dimension *ab initio* description of the potential energy surfaces of both the radical and the cation, the rotational and ionization spectra of the radical are simulated using advanced perturbative and variational rovibrational treatments. The results are compared with experimental photoionization data from the literature and new measurements[2].

[1] Dong *et al.*; J. Phys. Chem. A; 2006; 110; 3059-3070.
[2] Dyke *et al.*; J. Chem. Soc., Faraday Trans. 2; 1985; 81; 1573-1586.

RH06 **10:20 – 10:21**

STATE-DISTRIBUTION CONTROL OF LARGE AMPLITUDE VIBRATION IN SUBSTITUTED BIPHENYLS WITH INTENSE LASER PULSES

MAKOTO NIKAIDO, KENTA MIZUSE, YASUHIRO OHSHIMA, *Department of Chemistry, Tokyo Institute of Technology, Tokyo, Japan.*

With recent advances in ultrashort laser technology, many studies using intense nonresonant laser fields have been conducted to control vibrational or rotational wave packets. In particular, control of large-amplitude low-frequency vibration is important because such vibration may cause a substantial change in molecular structure. For instance, torsional motion of biphenyl has deserved much attention since chirality and physical properties of the molecule depend on its torsional angle. In this study, we coherently excite torsional vibration of substituted biphenyl derivatives by the interaction with ultrashort laser fields and the resultant vibrational excitation is monitored by recording resonant two-photon ionization (R2PI) spectrum. We further adopt double-pulse excitation to control vibrational state distribution via wave-packet interference.

Adiabatically cooled molecular sample of 2-fluorobiphenyl is irradiated by the fundamental output from a fs Ti:Sapphire laser. This pump pulse induces vibrational excitation through impulsive Raman process. With an appropriate delay after the pump-pulse irradiation, the S_1-S_0 excitation spectrum of the molecules is recorded via R2PI with the doubled output of a nanosecond dye laser ($\sim$280 nm). A progression with almost constant spacings appears in the R2PI spectrum without the pump pulse. It has been assigned to that of the torsional mode from vibrational ground state, *i.e.*, $v = 0$ (v being the quantum number of the torsional mode in the electronic ground state).[a] When the pump pulse is introduced, the intensity of each band is reduced and new bands appear. These bands are assigned to the progression from $v = 1$. These observations indicate that impulsive Raman excitation of torsional vibration is realized. We also conduct a double-pump pulse experiment, where a pair of pulses are implemented for excitation. In this experiment, we succeeded in controlling the state distribution of torsional vibration by adjusting the time delay between the two pump pulses.

[a] H. S. Im and E. R. Bernstein, J. Chem. Phys. **88**, 7337 (1988).

RH07 **10:24 – 10:25**

NUCLEAR DYNAMICS OF FLEXIBLE CYCLIC MOLECULES: CONFORMATIONAL SPACE, PSEUDOROTATIONAL AND ROTATIONAL MOTIONS OF DIOXOLANES, DITHIOLANES AND OXATHIOLANES

LORENZO PAOLONI, *Dipartimento di Fisica e Astronomia, Università degli studi di Padova, Padova, Italy*; SERGIO RAMPINO, *Scuola Normale Superiore, Scuola Normale Superiore, Pisa, Italy*; ASSIMO MARIS, *Dipartimento di Chimica G. Ciamician, Università di Bologna, Bologna, Italy.*

In this contribution, an application of the ring puckering coordinates (originally devised by Cremer and Pople) to the construction of one dimensional and two dimensional (2D) cuts of the potential energy surfaces (PESs) and to the characterisation of pseudorotational and rotational motions of five-term ring systems is proposed.

Firstly, an analysis of 2D-PESs is presented. Special care is devoted to the aspect of symmetry in such 2D-PESs, and analytical formulations of the computed 2D-PESs using suitable functional forms with a limited set of parameters are provided.

Secondly, solutions of each of the time-independent nuclear Schrödinger equations associated with the pseudorotational motions of three five-term ring systems are illustrated and discussed. In order to take into account the interplay between pseudorotational and rotational motions, the nuclear hamiltonian matrices are formulated for the azimuthal quantum numbers $J = 0$ and $J = 1$. The nuclear hamiltonian matrices are constructed and diagonalized using a Python program developed by the authors.

RH08 **10:28 – 10:29**

ROTATIONAL AND VIBRATIONAL WAVE PACKET IMAGING SPECTROSCOPY: BROAD BANDWIDTH, HIGH-RESOLUTION SPECTRA AND DYNAMICS OF WEAKLY BOUND MOLECULAR DIMERS, Ar_2, $(N_2)_2$, AND $(CH_4)_2$

KENTA MIZUSE[a], HIKARU SATO, HARUKI ISHIKAWA, *Department of Chemistry, School of Science, Kitasato University, Sagamihara, Japan*; YUHEI OYAGI, TOMOMI MURAI, GENKI ISHIBASHI, YUYA TOBATA, YASUHIRO OHSHIMA, *Department of Chemistry, Tokyo Institute of Technology, Tokyo, Japan.*

We have developed a wave packet imaging-based, broad bandwidth, high-resolution spectroscopic method for weakly bound molecular dimers. In the present method, rotational and intermolecular vibrational wave packet motion is induced in the molecular dimer, via impulsive stimulated Raman scattering upon femtosecond, broad bandwidth pulse irradiation. The subsequent rotational/vibrational motion is observed as a molecular movie, utilizing time-resolved Coulomb explosion imaging. Rotational and vibrational Raman spectra are obtained as Fourier transform of the observed time-dependent image parameters. In our present setup, 80 MHz frequency resolution and $>$1 THz bandwidth are achieved simultaneously. We have measured high-resolution spectra of Ar_2, $(N_2)_2$, and $(CH_4)_2$, while all of them are difficult targets for microwave spectroscopy due to their no or small permanent dipole. All measured spectra in the region of rotational transitions ($<$150 GHz) show well-resolved structures. In the case of $(N_2)_2$ and $(CH_4)_2$, in which monomer units can rotate almost freely in the dimer, rotational constants vary with internal rotational states. This suggests internal motions govern the effective structures of the dimers. In addition to the rotational structure, the spectrum of $(N_2)_2$ shows a 250 GHz oscillation, which can be attributed to the fundamental band of an intermolecular vibration. These results indicate that the present approach is a powerful approach to study large-amplitude intermolecular dynamics. Details of the experimental setup and spectral analyses will be presented.

[a]Kitasato Univ. and Tokyo Institute of Technology

RH09 **10:32 – 10:33**

HIGH-RESOLUTION GAS PHASE THz SPECTROSCOPY OF THE CATECHOL LOW FREQUENCY MODES INVOLVING AN INTRAMOLECULAR HYDROGEN BOND

JONAS BRUCKHUISEN, GUILLAUME DHONT, ANTHONY ROUCOU, ATEF JABRI, HAMDI BAYOUDH, THI THANH TRAN, *Laboratoire de Physico-Chimie de l'Atmosphère, Université du Littoral Côte d'Opale, Dunkerque, France*; MANUEL GOUBET, *Laboratoire PhLAM, UMR 8523 CNRS - Université Lille 1, Villeneuve d'Ascq, France*; MARIE-ALINE MARTIN-DRUMEL, *CNRS, Institut des Sciences Moleculaires d'Orsay, Orsay, France*; ARNAUD CUISSET, *Laboratoire de Physico-Chimie de l'Atmosphère, Université du Littoral Côte d'Opale, Dunkerque, France.*

1,2-Benzenediol, commonly known as catechol, was investigated, an ortho substituted aromatic volatile organic compound (VOC) with two hydroxyl groups which, due to tunneling between two symmetrically equivalent structures, can interchangeably act as donor and acceptor in a weak hydrogen bond [a] . Catechol displays appreciable gas-phase reactivity and its monitoring in the atmosphere via rovibrational spectroscopy has a strong interest. We performed a rotationally resolved analysis of the "free" and "bonded" –OH torsion modes of the intramolecular H-bond using synchrotron-based FT-Far-IR spectroscopy at the AILES beamline of SOLEIL[b]. High level of theory anharmonic quantum chemistry calculations were required for the rovibrational assignement. Numerous series of hot bands involving the lowest vibrational energy modes are observed and a set of anharmonic parameters is proposed. Finally, using a millimeter-wave spectrometer,[c] the room temperature Doppler limited rotational spectrum of catechol has been measured in the 70-220 GHz frequency range. Pure rotational lines belonging to the ground and the four lowest energy vibrationally excited states have been assigned. Splitting due to the tunneling were resolved for the free –OH torsion state and a global fit gathering the far-IR and millimeter-wave data provides the rotational parameters of the low-energy far-IR modes, especially those involving the intramolecular hydrogen bond.

[a]W. Caminati, S. Di Bernardo, *J. Mol. Struct.*, **240**, 263-274 (1990).
[b]J.B. Brubach, L. Manceron, M. Rouzieres, O. Pirali, D. Balcon, F. K. Tchana, V. Boudon, M. Tudorie, T. Huet, A. Cuisset, P. Roy, *AIP Conf. Proc.* **1214**, 81–84 (2009).
[c]G. Mouret, M. Guinet, A. Cuisset, L. Croizé, S. Eliet, R. Bocquet, F. Hindle, *IEEE Sens. J.* **13**, 133-138 (2013).

RH10 **10:36 – 10:37**

HIGH RESOLUTION INFRARED SPECTROSCOPY OF OC-HOH TRAPPED IN SOLID PARAHYDROGEN: COHERENT TUNNELING IN A QUANTUM SOLID

MORGAN E. BALABANOFF, AARON I. STROM, KELLY M. OLENYIK, DAVID T. ANDERSON, *Department of Chemistry, University of Wyoming, Laramie, WY, USA.*

One of the main objectives in the study of weakly bound complexes is to provide a quantitative description of the (ro)vibrational dynamics which can be dominated by nuclear quantum effects. For example, water and carbon monoxide form a weakly bound complex where the H_2O moiety can undergo a large-amplitude tunneling motion within the complex that exchanges the free and bound hydrogen atoms in the intermolecular bond. The exchange symmetry of identical particles entangles the spin and spatial quantum states of H_2O such that in the ground vibrational state, the symmetric tunneling state A correlates with para-H_2O (I=0), while the antisymmetric tunneling state B correlates with ortho-H_2O (I=1). The gas phase water-CO complex has been extensively studied by microwave[ab] and IR spectroscopy[cde] and when compared with full-dimensional quantum bound state calculations on a nine-dimensional potential energy surface, the agreement is very good.[f] We have completed analogous IR studies of the tunneling splittings of the water-CO complex when the complex is isolated in a parahydrogen quantum solid. We can estimate the tunneling splittings in the ground and excited (CO stretch, water stretch, and water bend) vibrational states to see how the tunneling motion is perturbed by the presence of the quantum solid. Furthermore, we can examine the nuclear spin conversion kinetics between the two tunneling levels in the ground vibrational state by rapidly changing the temperature of the sample. Nuclear spin conversion has not been reported in the previous gas phase studies and thus these are the first results for this water-CO complex.

[a]D. Yaron, K. I. Peterson, D. Zolandz, W. Klemperer, F. J. Lovas, R. D. Suenram, *J. Chem. Phys.* **92**, 7095 (1990).
[b]R. E. Bumgarner, S. Suzuki, P. A. Stockman, P. G. Green, G. A. Blake, *Chem. Phys. Lett.* **176**, 123 (1991).
[c]M. D. Brookes, A. R. W. McKellar, *J. Chem. Phys.* **109**, 5823 (1998).
[d]L. Oudejans, R. E. Miller, *Chem. Phys. Lett.* **306**, 214 (1999).
[e]A. J. Barclay, A. van der Avoid, A. R. W. McKellar, N. Moazzen-Ahmadi, *Phys. Chem. Chem. Phys.* **21**, 14911 (2019).
[f]P. M. Felker, Z. Bacic, *J. Chem. Phys.* **153**, 074107 (2020).

RH11 **10:40 – 10:41**

IN SEARCH OF VIBRATIONALLY EXCITED STATE MONODROMY IN NCNCS

DENNIS W. TOKARYK, STEPHEN CARY ROSS, *Department of Physics, University of New Brunswick, Fredericton, NB, Canada*; MANFRED WINNEWISSER, BRENDA P. WINNEWISSER, FRANK C. DE LUCIA, *Department of Physics, The Ohio State University, Columbus, OH, USA*; BRANT E. BILLINGHURST, *EFD, Canadian Light Source Inc., Saskatoon, Saskatchewan, Canada.*

At previous ISMS meetings we have reported on the effects of monodromy on the ν_7 bending mode of NCNCS. The presence of monodromy was established directly from experimental data collected at the Canadian Light Source. To aid that work we assigned some of the spectrum of the ν_7 manifold built on the ν_3 stretching mode. In this talk we will discuss a more complete assignment of the ν_3+ν_7 spectrum. One of our goals is to consider the impact of stretching on the monodromy of the ν_7 mode. We will attempt to use the same Generalized SemiRigid Bender model as was applied to the pure ν_7 mode.

RI. Mini-symposium: Precision Spectroscopy for Fundamental Physics

Thursday, June 24, 2021 – 10:0 AM

Room: 2021 Online Everywhere

Chair: Alejandra Collopy, National Institute of Standards and Technology, Boulder, CO, USA

RI02 *Journal of Molecular Spectroscopy Review Lecture* **10:06 – 10:08**

SEARCHING FOR FUNDAMENTAL SYMMETRY VIOLATIONS WITH POLYATOMIC MOLECULES

NICHOLAS R HUTZLER, *Division of Physics, Mathematics and Astronomy, California Institute of Technology, Pasadena, CA, USA.*

The fact that the universe is made entirely out of matter, and contains no free anti-matter, has no physical explanation. The unknown process that created matter in the universe must violate a number of fundamental symmetries, including those that forbid the existence of certain electromagnetic moments of fundamental particles – moments which are amplified by the large internal fields in polar molecules. We discuss spectroscopic and theoretical investigations into polyatomic molecules that uniquely combine multiple desirable features for precision measurement, such as high polarizability through symmetry-lowering mechanical motions, laser-coolable electronic structures, and exotic nuclei.

RI03 **10:14 – 10:15**

USE OF MOLECULES TO SEARCH FOR NEW PHYSICS AND STUDY PROPERTIES OF THE NUCLEUS.

LEONID V. SKRIPNIKOV, *Division of Innovations, NRC "Kurchatov Institute" PNPI, Gatchina, Leningrad region, Russia.*

Molecular spectroscopy is one of the leading tools to search for the manifestation of New Physics. It can also provide accurate information about the nucleus properties, such as its magnetic moment. The existence of interactions that violate the combined CP-symmetry of fundamental interactions inside the nucleus can lead to a non-zero Schiff moment that corresponds to the electric field directed along with the nuclear spin. This moment is strongly enhanced in deformed nuclei. In molecules, an additional enhancement with respect to atoms occurs due to the existence of closely-lying opposite parity states. Using a combination of direct and two-step theoretical relativistic approaches, we study the electronic structure of heavy-atom molecules. We predict Schiff moment enhancement and other properties of ^{227}AcF, ^{227}AcN, ^{227}AcO^{+}, ^{229}ThO, ^{153}EuO^{+}, and ^{153}EuN molecules containing f-elements with deformed nuclei as well as the TlF molecule. It is shown that experiments with these molecules should be very sensitive to New Physics [1]. The developed theoretical methods are applied to related problems. One of them is the test of theoretical predictions of the molecular parameters used to interpret experiments to measure the electron electric dipole moment. For this, we study a hyperfine structure of a molecule. In this study, we consider the effect of the finite nuclear magnetization distribution. Usually, this effect is considered only in atoms, but it is demonstrated that it should be treated in precise studies of molecules [2]. Finally, we show how accurate molecular electronic structure's description can be used to solve the discrepancy between the theoretical and experimental data on the hyperfine structure of highly charged ions [3,4]. Research has been supported by the Russian Science Foundation Grant No. 19-72-10019.

1. L.V. Skripnikov, N.S. Mosyagin, A.V. Titov, V.V. Flambaum, Phys. Chem. Chem. Phys., 22, 18374 (2020).
2. L.V. Skripnikov, J. Chem. Phys. 153, 114114 (2020).
3. L.V. Skripnikov, S. Schmidt, J. Ullmann, et al, Phys. Rev. Lett., 120, 093001 (2018).
4. V. Fella, L.V. Skripnikov, W. Nörtershäuser, et al, M. Vogel, Phys. Rev. Res. 2, 013368 (2020).

RI04 **10:18 – 10:19**

CALCULATION AND UNCERTAINTY EVALUATION OF THE P,T-ODD ENHANCEMENT FACTORS OF POLYATOMIC MOLECULES

ALEKSANDRA A. KYUBERIS, ANASTASIA BORSCHEVSKY, *Van Swinderen Institute, Universiteit Groningen, Groningen, Netherlands*; LUKÁŠ FÉLIX PAŠTEKA, *Department of Physical and Theoretical Chemistry, Faculty of Natural Sciences, Comenius University, Bratislava, Slovakia.*

The Standard Model of particle physics (SM) is the most complete theory nowadays; this model predicts all known fundamental particles and explains their interactions unifying three of the four fundamental forces. There are still many open questions that cannot be explained by the SM, such as the matter-antimatter asymmetry. The electron electric dipole moment (eEDM) is one of the most sought-after phenomena as a non-zero value violates Parity and Time Reversal Symmetries and could provide a clue to the origin of the matter-antimatter assymetry. Experiments searching for the eEDM have been performed over the last 50 years and the latest upper limit was determined on ThO molecule[a]. Spectroscopy with high resolution and high sensitivity has developed enormously over the past years, enabling the observation of tiny optical effects induced by novel interactions. Now the focus of interest is shifting to polyatomic molecules. In this work we perform computational investigations of polyatomic molecules in the context of the search for the eEDM, using as the example $AcOH^+$ and $AcOCH_3^+$. The aim of this work is to provide values of effective electric field (E_{eff}- system-dependent relativistic enhancement factor that describes the interaction of the EDM of the unpaired electron with the molecular internal electric field) of $AcOH^+$ and $AcOCH_3^+$ on the highest level of theory currently available for heavy many-electron systems. Additionally we performed investigation of the influence of various computational parameters on the results. We analyzed the influence of the basis sets[b] by checking the description of the valence and core regions and varying amount of diffuse or tight functions. Separately we investigated the effects of the electron correlation, like limiting number of active and virtual orbitals and the influence of perturbative triple excitations. Based on these calculations we are able to assign uncertainties on our predictions.

[a]Andreev V. et al. Nature, 562, 355-360, 2018.
[b]Dyall K.G. The Journal of Phys. Chem. A. 113, 12638-12644, 2009.

RI05 **10:22 – 10:23**

ANALYTIC RELATIVISTIC COUPLED-CLUSTER CALCULATIONS OF TIME-REVERSAL VIOLATING PARAMETERS

CHAOQUN ZHANG, XUECHEN ZHENG, LAN CHENG, *Department of Chemistry, Johns Hopkins University, Baltimore, MD, USA.*

We report an analytic scheme for relativistic exact two-component coupled-cluster singles and doubles with a noniterative triples [X2C-CCSD(T)] calculations of electric effective field, ε_{eff}, a time-reversal symmetry-violating parameter that plays a key role in the interpretation of experimental precision measurement of paramagnetic atoms and molecules for electron electric dipole moment (eEDM) search. Benchmark X2C-CCSD(T) calculations for the ε_{eff} values of twenty-one heavy-metal containing small molecules demonstrate the efficacy and accuracy of the present scheme. The computational results show that metal methoxides including $BaOCH_3$, $YbOCH_3$, and $RaOCH_3$ possess large ε_{eff} values similar to those of the corresponding fluorides and hydroxides, supporting the recent proposal of using nearly degenerate rotational states of these symmetric-top molecules to enhance the sensitivity of eEDM measurement. The present analytic scheme enables fast and reliable initial screening of candidate molecules for the eEDM search.

RI06 **10:26 – 10:27**

ELECTRONIC STRUCTURE OF TRIATOMIC MOLECULES FOR SEARCH OF AXIONLIKE PARTICLES

DANIEL E. MAISON, *Institute of Physics, St. Petersburg State University, St.Petersburg, Russia.*

One of the great mysteries of modern cosmology is the unknown nature of dark matter. A popular candidate for the dark matter component is the axion – the hypothetical pseudoscalar particle. Despite numerous attempts, the axion or axionlike particles have not been reliably detected.

We study axion-mediated exchange between the atomic nucleus and electrons, which can induce a permanent electric dipole moment of the whole molecule. Therefore, axion properties can be measured indirectly in the experiments, which are aiming to search for the electron electric dipole moment (eEDM) and other spatial and time-invariance violation effects.

We consider the ytterbium monohydroxide molecule (YbOH) and calculate the corresponding electronic structure parameter, which is necessary for the interpretation of experimental data. The dependence of the axionlike particle mass is studied extensively. We estimate the expected energy shift due to this interaction; it is shown that it is the same order of magnitude as eEDM contribution, so, these effects should be taken into account simultaneously.

Electronic structure calculations have been supported by the Russian Science Foundation Grant No. 19-72-10019. Calculations of the interaction potential matrix elements were supported by the foundation for the advancement of theoretical physics and mathematics “BASIS” grant according to Project No. 20-1-5-76-1. Calculation of the Gaunt contribution has been supported by the Russian Foundation for Basic Research Grant No. 20-32-70177.

RI07 **10:30 – 10:31**

A NEW EXPERIMENT TO TEST PARITY SYMMETRY IN COLD CHIRAL MOLECULES USING PRECISE MID-INFRARED SPECTROSCOPY

MATHIEU MANCEAU, LOUIS LECORDIER, ANNE COURNOL, NICOLAS CAHUZAC, DANG BAO AN TRAN, ROSA SANTAGATA, MATTHIEU PIERENS, ALEXANDER SHELKOVNIKOV, ANDREI GONCHAROV, OLIVIER LOPEZ, ANNE AMY-KLEIN, SEAN TOKUNAGA, BENOIT DARQUIE, *Laboratoire de Physique des Lasers, CNRS, Université Sorbonne Paris Nord, Villetaneuse, France.*

We are building a new-generation mid-infrared spectrometer specifically designed for precision vibrational spectroscopy of cold complex polyatomic molecules in the gas phase. The proposed technology is at the forefront of cold molecule research and frequency metrology, and opens possibilities for using polyatomic molecules to perform tests of fundamental physics and explore the limits of the standard model. The apparatus will be used in the first place for parity violation (PV) measurements in chiral molecules, i.e. for measuring the tiny energy difference between enantiomers induced by electroweak interactions.

We will present our ongoing work towards developing the technologies needed for measuring PV in chiral molecules via Ramsey interferometry in the mid-infrared[a]. This includes amongst other things developing frequency stabilised quantum cascade lasers calibrated to some of the world's best frequency standards[bc] and producing gases of organo-metallic species cooled to a few kelvin in cryogenic buffer-gas cells[d]. We will also present the results of preliminary investigations conducted on various promising heavy metal complexes exhibiting intense signatures in different regions of the mid-infrared[ef].

[a] A. Cournol et al, Quantum Electron. 49, 288 (2019)
[b] R. Santagata et al, Optica 6, 411 (2019)
[c] B. Argence et al, Nature Photon. 9, 456 (2015)
[d] S.K. Tokunaga et al, New J. Phys. 19, 053006 (2017)
[e] P. Asselin et al, Phys. Chem. Chem. Phys. 19, 4576 (2017)
[f] N. Saleh et al, Chirality 30, 147 (2018)

RI08 **10:34 – 10:35**

SPECTROSCOPY ON ALUMINUM MONOCHLORIDE (ALCL) FOR LASER COOLING AND TRAPPING

JOHN DANIEL, KAYLA RODRIGUEZ, *Physics and Astronomy, University of California, Riverside, Riverside, CA, USA*; TAYLOR LEWIS, *Department of Chemistry, University of California, Riverside, Riverside, CA, USA*; ALEXANDER TEPLUKHIN, *Theoretical Division, Los Alamos National Laboratory, Los Alamos, NM, USA*; CHEN WANG, *Physics and Astronomy, University of California, Riverside, Riverside, CA, USA*; MADHAV DHITAL, *Physics, University of California, Riverside, Riverside, California, USA*; BRIAN K KENDRICK, *Theoretical Division, Los Alamos National Laboratory, Los Alamos, NM, USA*; CHRISTOPHER BARDEEN, *Department of Chemistry, University of California, Riverside, Riverside, CA, USA*; SHAN-WEN TSAI, BOERGE HEMMERLING, *Physics and Astronomy, University of California, Riverside, Riverside, CA, USA*.

Cooling atoms to the ultracold regime has allowed for studies of physics, ranging from many-body physics of quantum degenerate gases, quantum computing, precision measurements and tests of fundamental symmetries. Extending these experiments to polar molecules has the prospect of enhancing the sensitivity of such tests and of enabling novel studies, such as cold controlled chemistry. However, applying traditional laser cooling techniques to molecules is rendered difficult due their additional degrees of freedom which result in a limited photon scattering budget. Here we study aluminum monochloride (AlCl) as a promising candidate for laser cooling and trapping. The cooling transition at 261 nm ($A^1\Pi - X^1\Sigma^+$) has a theoretical Franck-Condon factor of 99.88% which allows for scattering 800 photons with a single laser before the molecule enters an excited vibrational state. We use a frequency-tripled (SHG + SFG) Titanium-Sapphire laser and generate AlCl via laser ablation in a cryogenic helium buffer gas beam source. We will present our spectroscopy results on AlCl and the measured molecular constants of the $A^1\Pi$ state and compare them with ab-initio calculations. We will also discuss our estimates on the Franck-Condon factors.

RI09 **10:38 – 10:39**

OBSERVATION AND LASER SPECTROSCOPY OF YTTERBIUM MONOMETHOXIDE, $YbOCH_3$

BENJAMIN AUGENBRAUN, *Department of Physics, Harvard University, Cambridge, MA, USA*; TIMOTHY STEIMLE, *School of Molecular Sciences, Arizona State University, Tempe, AZ, USA*; ZACK LASNER, ALEXANDER FRENETT, HIROMITSU SAWAOKA, *Department of Physics, Harvard University, Cambridge, MA, USA*; ANH T. LE, *School of Molecular Sciences, Arizona State University, Tempe, AZ, USA*; JOHN M. DOYLE, *Department of Physics, Harvard University, Cambridge, MA, USA*.

We describe a laser spectroscopic study of ytterbium monomethoxide, a species of interest to search for time-reversal symmetry violation using laser-cooled molecules. We have performed measurements of vibrational structure in the low-lying electronic states, vibrational branching ratios for several electronically excited vibronic states, and radiative lifetimes of low-lying electronic states. Both laser-induced fluorescence and dispersed fluorescence spectra have been recorded and analyzed. In addition, we have recorded the rotationally-resolved high-resolution excitation spectrum of the $\tilde{A}\,^2E_{1/2} \leftarrow \tilde{X}\,^2A_1$ band. *Ab initio* calculations aided the assignment of vibronic emission bands and provide insight into the electronic and vibrational structure. We compare the structure of $YbOCH_3$ to the isoelectronic species YbF and YbOH, as well as to the previously studied alkaline-earth monomethoxides. Finally, we discuss how our results open a path to increased sensitivity to P- and/or T-violating physics in future measurements.

RI10 **10:42 – 10:43**

SPECTROSCOPIC STUDIES OF ALUMINUM MONOFLUORIDE WITH RELEVANCE FOR LASER COOLING AND TRAPPING

STEFAN TRUPPE, SILVIO MARX, SEBASTIAN KRAY, MAXIMILIAN DOPPELBAUER, SIMON HOFSÄSS, CHRISTIAN SCHEWE, NICOLE WALTER, JESÚS PÉREZ-RÍOS, *Department of Molecular Physics, Fritz-Haber-Institut der Max-Planck-Gesellschaft, Berlin, Germany*; BORIS SARTAKOV, *Prokhorov General Physics Institute, Russian Academy of Sciences, Moscow, Russia*; GERARD MEIJER, *Department of Molecular Physics, Fritz-Haber-Institut der Max-Planck-Gesellschaft, Berlin, Germany.*

Aluminum monofluoride (AlF) is an excellent candidate for laser cooling on any Q-line of the $A^1\Pi$ - $X^1\Sigma$ transition and trapping at high densities.[a]
In preparation for cooling and manipulation experiments, it is necessary to know the detailed energy structure of the involved states, as well as their lifetimes, dipole moments and the Franck-Condon factors of their transitions.
The metastable $a^3\Pi$ state is the ideal starting point for extensive spectroscopic investigations. Therefore, this presentation will focus on the $a^3\Pi \leftarrow X^1\Sigma^+$ transition. The energy levels in the $X^1\Sigma^+, v''=0$ state and within each Ω manifold of the $a^3\Pi, v'=0$ state were determined with a relative accuracy of a few kHz, using laser-radio-frequency multiple resonance and ionization detection schemes in a jet-cooled, pulsed molecular beam. All spectroscopic parameters relevant for describing the rotational and hyperfine structure were determined by fitting the eigenvalues of the molecular Hamiltonian to the data. With this knowledge, the measured hyperfine structure in the $A^1\Pi$ state could be assigned. The dipole moments of the $X^1\Sigma^+$, $A^1\Pi$ and $a^3\Pi$ states were determined by recording cw excitation spectra in electric fields up to 150 kV/cm.
The $A^1\Pi$ - $a^3\Pi$ band was observed for the first time. Measurements on the transition strength showed that it is no significant loss channel for the $A^1\Pi$ - $X^1\Sigma$ laser cooling transition.

[a]Truppe et al., Phys. Rev. A 100, 052513 (2019)

RI11 **10:46 – 10:47**

INVESTIGATION OF THE $b^3\Sigma^+, v=0$ STATE IN ALUMINIUM MONOFLUORIDE

MAXIMILIAN DOPPELBAUER, NICOLE WALTER, SIMON HOFSÄSS, SILVIO MARX, CHRISTIAN SCHEWE, SEBASTIAN KRAY, JESÚS PÉREZ-RÍOS, *Department of Molecular Physics, Fritz-Haber-Institut der Max-Planck-Gesellschaft, Berlin, Germany*; BORIS SARTAKOV, *Prokhorov General Physics Institute, Russian Academy of Sciences, Moscow, Russia*; STEFAN TRUPPE, GERARD MEIJER, *Department of Molecular Physics, Fritz-Haber-Institut der Max-Planck-Gesellschaft, Berlin, Germany.*

The aluminium monofluoride (AlF) molecule is a promising candidate for laser cooling and trapping experiments[a]. Here, we describe experiments studying the hyperfine structure of the $b^3\Sigma^+, v=0$ state[b]. We first determined its radiative lifetime in a pulsed excitation – delayed ionization scheme and measured the rotational structure using (1+2)-REMPI.
We recorded laser-induced fluorescence spectra of the $b^3\Sigma^+, v'=0 \leftarrow X^1\Sigma^+, v''=1$ transition of AlF molecules from a bright buffer gas source. The fluorescence detection works background-free because visible photons are emitted after UV excitation. From the obtained line positions, we determined the relevant fine- and hyperfine structure parameters. In a next step, laser-induced fluorescence spectra were recorded after excitation on the $b^3\Sigma^+, v'=0 \leftarrow a^3\Pi_\Omega, v''=0$ transition; we use all three spin-orbit ($\Omega=0,1,2$) manifolds of the $a^3\Pi$ state. These spectra were used to improve the uncertainty of our previous measurement of the spin-orbit coupling parameters in the $a^3\Pi, v=0$ state by almost two orders of magnitude.
We observed the $b^3\Sigma^+, v'=0 \rightarrow X^1\Sigma^+, v''$ bands, which are result of the spin–orbit coupling of the $b^3\Sigma^+, v=0$ state with the nearby $A^1\Pi$ state.

[a]Truppe et al., Phys. Rev. A 100, 052513 (2019)
[b]Doppelbauer et al., Mol. Phys. 119:1-2, e1810351 (2020)

RI12 **10:50 – 10:51**

SPECTROSCOPIC CHARACTERIZATION OF THE $A^1\Pi, v = 6 \leftrightarrow b^3\Sigma^+, v = 5$ INTERACTION OF ALUMINUM MONOFLUORIDE IN VIEW OF LASER COOLING AND TRAPPING EXPERIMENTS

NICOLE WALTER, SILVIO MARX, JOHANNES SEIFERT, *Department of Molecular Physics, Fritz-Haber-Institut der Max-Planck-Gesellschaft, Berlin, Germany*; BORIS SARTAKOV, *Prokhorov General Physics Institute, Russian Academy of Sciences, Moscow, Russia*; STEFAN TRUPPE, GERARD MEIJER, *Department of Molecular Physics, Fritz-Haber-Institut der Max-Planck-Gesellschaft, Berlin, Germany.*

Aluminum monofluoride (AlF) is an excellent candidate for laser cooling.[a] All Q-lines of the strong $A^1\Pi \leftarrow X^1\Sigma^+$ transition are rotationally closed and thereby suitable for the main cooling cycle, while the spin-forbidden $a^3\Pi \leftarrow X^1\Sigma^+$ transition can be used to achieve final temperatures in the μK range. In view of cooling and trapping experiments, it is essential to have a detailed insight into the energy structure of the directly and indirectly involved states.

The $A^1\Pi, v = 6, J = 1$ and the $b^3\Sigma^+, v = 5, N = 2$ levels are very nearly iso-energetic and strongly interact.[b] Consequently, these levels have a mixed singlet and triplet character. The triplet character of the $A^1\Pi$ state causes a loss from the main laser cooling cycle that has been studied previously.[c] Furthermore, these states with their mixed character are particularly suited as doorway states between the singlet and the triplet manifold for ultracold experiments on AlF.

We completed an extensive rotationally resolved spectroscopic investigation of energy levels in this perturbed range using optical-optical double resonance ionization, followed by mass-selective ion detection. Subsequently, we performed hyperfine resolved excitation with a cw laser, using laser induced fluorescence for detection. Both measurement schemes were employed on a supersonic, pulsed molecular beam. The lifetimes of the perturbed levels cover two orders of magnitudes (about $2 - 200$ ns), which requires different experimental techniques to determine their exact values. Lifetimes of selected levels have been measured using e.g. time delayed ionization and Lamb-dip experiments. The fine- and hyperfine structure parameters as well as the spin-orbit interaction parameter are determined from the experimental data.

[a] Truppe et al., Physical Review A 100, 052513 (2019)
[b] Barrow et al., Physica Scripta 10, 86 (1974)
[c] Doppelbauer et al., Molecular Physics 119(1-2), e1810351 (2020)

RI13 **10:54 – 10:55**

FINE AND HYPERFINE INTERACTIONS IN ^{171}YbOH AND ^{173}YbOH

NICKOLAS H PILGRAM, ARIAN JADABABAIE, YI ZENG, NICHOLAS R HUTZLER, *Division of Physics, Mathematics and Astronomy, California Institute of Technology, Pasadena, CA, USA*; TIMOTHY STEIMLE, *School of Molecular Sciences, Arizona State University, Tempe, AZ, USA.*

The odd isotopologues of ytterbium monohydroxide, ^{171,173}YbOH, have been identified as promising molecules in which to measure parity (P) and time reversal (T) violating physics. We report on the prerequisite characterization of the $\tilde{A}^2\Pi_{1/2}(0,0,0) - \tilde{X}^2\Sigma^+(0,0,0)$ band near 577 nm for these odd isotopologues. Both laser-induced fluorescence (LIF) excitation spectra of a supersonic molecular beam sample and the absorption spectra of a cryogenic buffer-gas cooled sample were recorded. Additionally, a novel spectroscopic technique based on laser-enhanced chemical synthesis is demonstrated and utilized in the absorption measurements. This technique was critical as it enabled the disentangling of the congested isotopologue structure. An effective Hamiltonian model is used to extract the fine and hyperfine parameters for the $\tilde{A}^2\Pi_{1/2}(0,0,0)$ and $\tilde{X}^2\Sigma^+(0,0,0)$ states. A comparison of the determined $\tilde{X}^2\Sigma^+(0,0,0)$ parameters with recently predicted values [a] is made. The measured hyperfine parameters also provide experimental confirmation of the computational methods used to compute the P,T-violating coupling constants, W_d and W_M, theoretical constants needed to correlate the P,T-violating physics to the corresponding P,T-violating energy shifts in the molecule. The dependence of the fine and hyperfine parameters for both the even and odd isotopologues for both the $\tilde{A}^2\Pi_{1/2}(0,0,0)$ and $\tilde{X}^2\Sigma^+(0,0,0)$ states for YbOH and isoelectronic YbF are discussed.[b]

[a] M. Denis et al, J. Chem. Phys. 152, 084303 (2020), K. Gaul and R. Berger, Phys. Rev. A 101, 012508 (2020), J. Liu et al, J. Chem. Phys. 154, 064110 (2021)
[b] This work was supported by the Heising-Simons Foundation, NSF CAREER, and NIST Precision Measurement Grant

RI14 **10:58 – 10:59**

$\mathcal{P}, \mathcal{T}$-ODD FARADAY EFFECT: A NEW APPROACH TO IMPROVE THE SENSITIVITY OF THE SEARCH FOR TIME-REFLECTION-NONINVARIANT INTERACTIONS IN NATURE[a]

DMITRY CHUBUKOV, *St. Petersburg State University Division of Quantum Mechanics, St. Petersburg, NRC "Kurchatov Institute" PNPI, Division of Innovations, Gatchina, Leningrad region, , Russia.*

A search for the time-noninvariant ($\mathcal{T}$-odd) interactions is one of the most fundamental not yet resolved problems in physics. The existence of the electric dipole moment (EDM) for any particle violates both $\mathcal{P}$- and $\mathcal{T}$-invariances ($\mathcal{P}$ is the space parity). The search for the EDMs continues for more than half a century without any success. The present constraint on the $\mathcal{P}$- and $\mathcal{T}$-violating effects is based on the observation of the electron-spin precession in an external electric field using the ThO molecule (ACME collaboration, USA). This experiment sets the upper bound for the electron EDM (eEDM) $d_e < 1.1 \times 10^{-29}$ e cm (e is the electron charge)[b]. An accurate evaluation of the eEDM within the standard model is still absent. The maximum estimated value is $d_e \sim 10^{-38}$ e cm[c]. No signs of "new physics" inside this gap between the theory and experiment have not yet been found. This encourages to suggest the new, more sensitive methods for observation of the eEDM in low-energy physics. We suggest considering the $\mathcal{P}, \mathcal{T}$-odd Faraday effect (rotation of the polarization plane for the light propagating through a medium in presence of an external electric field). The experiment is assumed to be performed with the modern intra-cavity/cavity-enhanced absorption spectroscopy techniques in combination with a molecular beam crossing the cavity[d]. Theoretical simulations of the proposed experiment with the PbF and ThO molecular beams together with accurate molecular structure calculations show that the present constraint on the eEDM in principle can be improved by a few orders of magnitude. An advantage of the $\mathcal{P}, \mathcal{T}$-odd Faraday experiment is that the $\mathcal{P}, \mathcal{T}$-odd effect is cumulated on the light, while in the ACME-like experiment it is cumulated on the molecules. For the shot-noise limited measurement, it is much easier to have a larger number of photons than a larger number of molecules.

[a]This work was supported by RFBR Grant No. 20-32-70177 as well as the RSF Grant No. 17-12-01035.

[b]V. Andreev et al. (ACME collaboration), Nature **562**, 355 (2018)

[c]M. Pospelov, I. Khriplovich, Sov.Nucl.Phys. **53**, 638 (1991)

[d]D.V. Chubukov, L.V. Skripnikov, L.N. Labzowsky, JETP Letters **110**, 382 (2019); D.V. Chubukov, L.V. Skripnikov, A.N. Petrov, V.N. Kutuzov, L.N. Labzowsky, PRA (2021) [Accepted, to be published; Preprint: arXiv:2102.05157]

RI15 **11:02 – 11:03**

ISOTOPE SHIFT IN OPTICAL SPECTRA OF MoO MOLECULE

LEI ZHANG, YAO YU, JIE YANG, *Atomic Physics Center, Institute of Modern Physics, Chinese Academy of Sciences, Lanzhou, CHINA.*

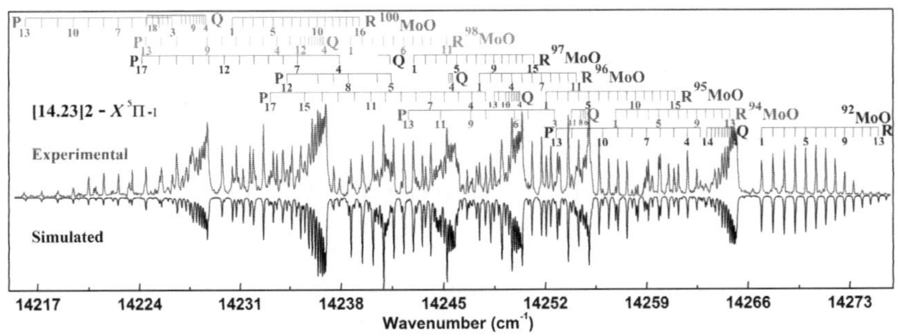

The jet-cooled molybdenum monoxide (MoO) molecule involving seven natural isotopologues from ^{92}MoO (14.5%), ^{94}MoO (9.2%), ^{95}MoO (15.8%), ^{96}MoO (16.7%), ^{97}MoO (9.6%), ^{98}MoO (24.4%), and ^{100}MoO (9.8%), have been investigated with the laser-induced fluorescence (LIF) excitation spectra and the single vibronic level (SVL) emission spectra in the energy range from 13 800 to 16 500 cm^{-1}. Four rotationally resolved transition bands near 14 107, 14 144, 14 237, and 15 034 cm^{-1} have been observed, and exhibit extremely large isotope shifts, in which the largest shift is 53 cm^{-1} for $\nu(^{92}\text{MoO}) - \nu(^{100}\text{MoO})$. By rotational analysis, the four bands all originate from the $X\,^5\Pi_{-1}$ ground state, and are assigned as the $6-0$, $7-0$, $6-0$, and $9-0$ (v$'$ – v$''$) bands of the $\Omega' = 2 \leftarrow \Omega'' = -1$ transition according to the vibrational isotope shift. In addition, the isotopologues-resolved SVL emission spectra have been obtained by fixing the excitation laser at Q-branch bandhead of the transition. The isotope shifts in the vibrational v$'' = 0, 1, 2$, and 3 levels of the $X^5\Pi_{-1}$ ground state have been observed and show well agreement with the calculation from the model of harmonic vibration. The solid experimental results are consistent with the theoretical prediction, which indicates that the works on MoO are of great benchmark to reveal the role of the isotope shift in the vibrational levels of simple molecules.

RJ. Dynamics and kinetics

Thursday, June 24, 2021 – 10:0 AM

Room: 2021 Online Everywhere

Chair: Scott Kevin Cushing, Caltech, Pasadena, CA, USA

RJ01 **10:00 – 10:01**

ULTRAFAST EXCITED STATE DYNAMICS OF TWISTED AROMATICS

MAHESH HARIHARAN, *School of Chemistry, IISER Thiruvananthapuram, Trivandrum, Kerala, India.*

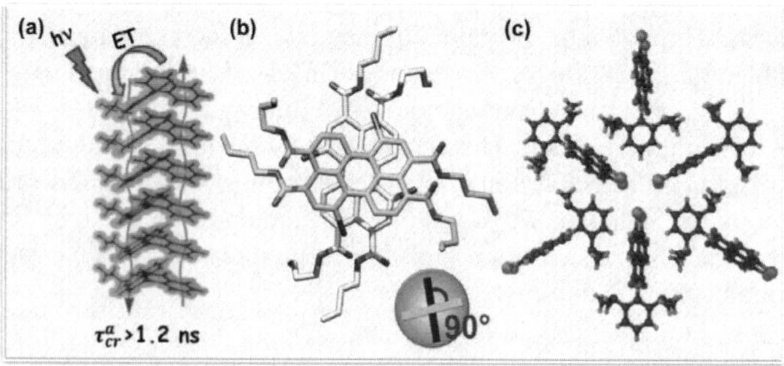

Figure. Representative strategies adopted in our group to spatially organize organic chromophores for emergent properties.

Self-assembling of organic chromophoric systems into elegant supramolecular architectures with emergent properties has received prodigious attention in recent years.[1] In the first example (Figure), a naphthalene-naphthalimide donor-acceptor (D-A) dyad assembled into segregated D-A stacks in the crystalline state. The photo-induced charge separated state in the aggregate state lasts 10,000 times longer than the monomeric dyad. The femtosecond transient absorption spectra depicted the spectroscopic signature for naphthalene dimer radical cation indicating the migration of charges through the stacks.[1] In the second example, we report the crystalline evidence for Greek cross-dipole (α=90°) stacking of 1,7-dibromoperylene-3,4,9,10-tetracarboxylic tetrabutylester (PTE-Br2) displaying null excitonic coupling and thereby monomeric optical behavior.[2] In the third example, we showcase a radial assembly of 1,8-dibromonaphthalene(2,6-diisopropylphenyl)imide (NIBr2) in crystalline phase driven by hexabromine synthon.[4] NIBr2 exhibits ultrafast intersystem crossing[3−5] and solid-state room temperature phosphorescence. References: [1] A. R. Mallia, P. S. Salini, M. Hariharan, J. Am. Chem. Soc., 137 (2015) 15604. [2] E. Sebastian, A. M. Philip, A. Benny, M. Hariharan, Angew. Chem., Int. Ed., 57 (2018) 15696. [3] M. A. Niyas, R. Ramakrishnan, V. Vijay, E. Sebastian, M. Hariharan, J. Am. Chem. Soc, 141 (2019) 4536. [4] K. Nagarajan, A. R. Mallia, K. Muraleedharan, M. Hariharan, Chem. Sci., 8 (2017) 1776. [5] M. P. Lijina, A. Benny, R. Ramakrishnan, N. Nair, M. Hariharan, J. Am. Chem. Soc. 41 (2020), 17393.

RJ02 **10:04 – 10:05**

TRACKING THE REACTION COORDINATE OF ULTRAFAST SPIN-CROSSOVER IN Fe(II) COMPLEXES WITH FEMTOSECOND M-EDGE XANES

RYAN T ASH, KAILI ZHANG, JOSH VURA-WEIS, *Department of Chemistry, University of Illinois at Urbana-Champaign, Urbana, IL, USA.*

Designing earth-abundant photosensitizers to replace rare-earth complexes is of high importance for the efficient collection and utilization of solar energy. The primary obstacle to using first-row transition metal complexes is the ultrafast dissipation of collected energy due to low energy metal-centered states.

Here, we study a series of Fe(II) complexes with different ligand frameworks in hopes to alter the intersection between various metal-centered states. Using femtosecond M-edge XANES, the involvement of triplet and quintet metal-centered states are identified. By decoupling the axial and equatorial stretching modes of an Fe(II) complex, we find that the lifetime of a triplet metal-centered state is significantly increased due to Jahn-Teller distortion in the excited state. This behavior is not observed in prototypical Fe(II) polypyridyl complexes, and provides a method to reduce energy losses in earth-abundant photosensitizers.

RJ03 **10:08 – 10:09**

FEMTOSECOND PUMP-PROBE SPECTROSCOPY OF NEUTRAL Ni AND Cr OXIDE CLUSTERS

JACOB M GARCIA, *School of Molecular Sciences and Biodesign Center for Applied Structural Discovery, Arizona State University, Tempe, AZ, USA*; SCOTT G SAYRES, *Biodesign Center for Applied Structural Discovery, Arizona State University, Tempe, AZ, USA.*

The ultrafast electron dynamics of transition metal oxide clusters provides information about the stability and reactivity of their bulk material counterparts. Nickel and chromium oxides are widely used catalytic materials which may be improved with the detailed atomic precision of their stable conformations and low energy electron properties. In our experiments, neutral Ni_nO_m and Cr_nO_m clusters are produced with small amounts of oxygen and their mass spectra show a primary stable stoichiometry of m = n - 1 for Ni clusters and m = 2n - 2 for Cr clusters. I will present our ultrafast pump-probe spectroscopy measurements on the direct ionization, dissociation, formation, and excitation-relaxation properties for these metal oxide cluster systems extending up to n = 9. Nickel oxides show an increase in the lifetime with the decrease in oxygen content, owing to the change in geometry and increase in relaxation pathways. In contrast, chromium oxides generally show a decreased lifetime with less oxygen atoms from the stoichiometric $(CrO_2)_n$ cluster. In both cluster systems, long-lived lifetimes (over 2 ps) are observed in the suboxide clusters. Overall, it is shown that the ultrafast dynamics observed for these clusters depend strongly on their metal composition, size, and oxidation state.

RJ04 **10:12 – 10:13**

ELECTRONIC STATE-RESOLVED RELAXATION DYNAMICS IN METAL CLUSTERS STUDIED USING TWO-DIMENSIONAL ELECTRONIC SPECTROSCOPY

WILLIAM R. JEFFRIES, *Chemistry, The Pennsylvania State University, University Park, Pennsylvania, USA*; JORDAN WALLACE, *Chemistry, Pennsylvania State University, University Park, Pennsylvania, USA*; KENNETH L. KNAPPENBERGER, JR., *Department of Chemistry, Pennsylvania State University, University Park, PA, USA.*

Monolayer protected nanoclusters (MPCs) are structurally-precise, quantum-confined metal nanostructures that include three structural components that influence their optical and electronic properties. These components include (i) an all-metal atom core, (ii) an organometallic semiring of alternating Au-S staples, and (iii) organic passivating ligands. The high degree of structural precision afforded by MPCs provides a well-defined platform to investigate structure-dependent energy relaxation in quantum-confined metals. In this presentation, ultrafast electronic relaxation and charge transfer dynamics will be described. Femtosecond two-dimensional electronic spectroscopy (2DES) provides spectrally resolved excitation-detection correlation maps while preserving the high time resolution of ultrafast spectroscopy by spreading the excitation-detection transient signals over two frequency axes. Here, 2DES was used to distinguish multiple electronic fine-structure states that comprise a charge-transfer resonance excited using laser pulses spanning 1.85 to 2.10 eV. These results show that electronically excited charge carriers relax through internal conversion via intramolecular vibrational relaxation (IVR) processes within 200 fs. The IVR process manifests as spectral diffusion in $Au_{38}(SC_6H_{13})_{24}$ nanoclusters, which was monitored by resolving the excitation-detection frequency-frequency correlation function (FFCF) decay obtained from the 2DES measurements. The 2DES-detected FFCF method was applied to understand solvent dependences of the charge carriers, which undergo interfacial ligand-to-metal charge transfer, prior to thermalization. The effects of different ligands were also investigated. These results demonstrate the ability of 2DES combined with FFCF to map energy flow through nearly degenerate states, and quantify rapid internal conversion of excited charge carriers in structurally-precise metal clusters.

RJ05 **10:16 – 10:17**

SIZE EFFECTS ON EXCITED STATE LIFETIMES OF TITANIUM OXIDE CLUSTERS

LAUREN F HEALD, JACOB M GARCIA, SCOTT G SAYRES, *School of Molecular Sciences and Biodesign Center for Applied Structural Discovery, Arizona State University, Tempe, AZ, USA.*

Transition metal oxides are widely used as catalysts for industrial processes. Notably, TiO_2 is used in applications such as water splitting, photovoltaics, and environmental degradation of organic pollutants. Despite the wide usage of TiO_2, there is not a clear understanding of the mechanism that underpins its reactivity. The study of ultrafast excitation/relaxation dynamics in neutral titanium oxide clusters offers atomic level insight into the driving forces in bulk reactions. Specifically, we utilize pump-probe spectroscopy to reveal the influence of both size and oxidation affect the excited state lifetimes of neutral metal oxides. All clusters exhibit a rapid relaxation lifetime of 30 fs, followed by a sub-picosecond lifetime that we attribute to carrier recombination. The excited state lifetimes oscillate with size in agreement with the cluster stability, coordination of metal atoms, and localization of electron excitation. These experimental results, when paired with TD-DFT, demonstrate the importance of subtle changes in the atomic positions and geometry over the cluster dynamics. Such revelations relate directly to the significance of defect sites in bulk materials. This presentation will focus on both experimental and computational analysis of sub-nanometer TiO_2 clusters and how the lifetimes of excited states can be understood through analysis of electron/hole dynamics. A thorough discussion of how properties of neutral clusters change with the addition or subtraction of a single atom will be used to provide insight into the properties that make TiO_2 such a favorable material.

RJ06 **10:20 – 10:21**

ULTRAFAST REACTION DYNAMICS OF NEUTRAL ALUMINUM OXIDE CLUSTERS USING TWO COLOR FEMTOSECOND SPECTROSCOPY

ANANYA SEN, *School of Molecular Sciences, Arizona State University, Tempe, AZ, USA*; SCOTT G SAYRES, *School of Molecular Sciences and Biodesign Center for Applied Structural Discovery, Arizona State University, Tempe, AZ, USA.*

Ultrafast relaxation dynamics of neutral aluminum oxide clusters (Al_nO_m, n,m $<=$ 20) in the gas phase were studied by combining two-color femtosecond spectroscopy and time-of-flight mass spectrometry. The clusters are pumped using the second harmonic of a Ti:Sapphire femtosecond (fs) laser system (400 nm = 3.1eV) and subsequently ionized through strong field ionization of the the fundamental beam (800 nm = 1.55 eV) with a time resolution of $<$ 35 fs. The excited states explored here are high binding energy excited states, which are mainly of oxygen 2p character into the Al sp-type orbitals. Changes in the ultrafast dynamics are observed to be strongly influenced by the stoichiometry and size of these clusters. Neutral clusters are ideal mimics of the true active sites of condensed phase and surface chemistry. We have developed an approach that involves the calculation of several topological descriptors to interpret the influence of the structural differences between clusters on the excited state lifetimes. Time-dependent density functional theory (TDDFT) calculations reveal the energies and structures of the excited states at both ground and excited state structure. These studies on molecular scale clusters provide an ideal arena for probing chemical activities and mechanisms in an unperturbed environment that can assist in the analysis of condensed phase catalysis systems. Using the atomic precision of clusters, we identify preferred bonding arrangements, electronic structure, and oxidation states that lead to increased excited state lifetimes and therefore enhance photochemical transformation.

RJ07 **10:24 – 10:25**

PHOTOPHYSICS OF EXCITED STATES IN THE Co_4O_4 CUBANE CATALYST FOLLOWED VIA FEMTOSECOND $M_{2,3}$-EDGE ABSORPTION SPECTROSCOPY

YUSEF A. SHARI'ATI, *Chemistry, University of Illinois at Urbana-Champaign, Urbana, IL, USA*; JOSH VURA-WEIS, *Department of Chemistry, University of Illinois at Urbana-Champaign, Urbana, IL, USA.*

The Co_4O_4 cubane and its oxidized derivatives are molecular models of heterogeneous cobalt-based oxygen evolution reaction catalysts and are structural cognates of the oxygen evolving center in plant life. Insight into these latter systems is garnered through study of the high-valent states achieved in oxidized cubane. The oxidized cubane species is generated transiently through photoinduced electron transfer to a laser-excited pendant perylene bisimide chromophore and interrogated via extreme ultraviolet (XUV) spectroscopy. The XUV probe effects transitions at the $M_{2,3}$ edge (3p→3d) in the cobalt centers and is sensitive to changes in e.g. oxidation and spin states. However, spectroscopic characterization of the high-valent states achieved in through this charge separation is hindered by the concurrent population of metal-centered excited states via energy transfer. Once populated, these states undergo further evolution via intersystem crossing and/or relaxation back into the charge separated state, imparting significant ambiguity into the observed XUV signals. This work clarifies these results through further studies into the ultrafast dynamics of excited cubane molecules, as well as synthetic strategies toward manipulation of the electronics and energetics of the pendant chromophore. As probed by our tabletop high-harmonic generation (HHG) XUV instrument, the excitation energy in this system is followed as it cascades through metal-centered states in the cubane manifold vs. the formation of charge separated states.

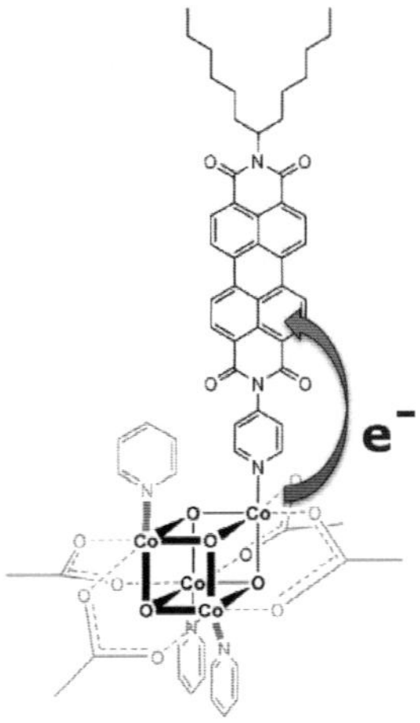

RJ08 **10:28 – 10:29**

OPTICALLY PUMPED RESTSTRAHLEN BAND TUNING OF WIDE BANDGAP SEMICONDUCTORS

ELIZABETH S RYLAND[a], VANESSA M BRESLIN[b], DANIEL C RATCHFORD, JEFF OWRUTSKY, ADAM DUNKELBERGER, *Chemistry Division, Code 6111, U.S. Naval Research Laboratory, Washington, DC, USA.*

Photoinjection studies of two wide bandgap semiconductors, 4H-SiC and GaN, are conducted with fs infrared reflectivity measurements in order to characterize how the relative penetration depths of UV-pump/IR-probe light affects the modulation of the IR reflectivity spectrum. The infrared spectrum of these materials is dominated by the high reflectivity reststrahlen band region that occurs between the longitudinal optical and transverse optical phonons. The injection of free carriers shifts this metal-like region to higher frequencies via coupling of the longitudinal optical phonon to the free carrier plasma (LOPC effect). The result of this LOPC active tuning is strongly perturbed by the charge carrier spatial distribution, and is thus highly sensitive to the means of carrier generation. We probe the effects of charge carrier spatial distribution on the photomodulated reflectivity of two promising wide bandgap semiconductors, indirect bandgap 4H-SiC and direct bandgap GaN, by comparing the transient reflectivity following photoexcitation with light of short and long penetration depths relative to the IR probe depth. This work shows sensitivity of bulk electronic properties to the charge carrier distribution that is critical to understanding the contributions of these materials to complex nanophotonic devices.

[a]NRC RAP Postdoctoral Associate
[b]NRC RAP Postdoctoral Associate

RJ09 **10:32 – 10:33**

MEASUREMENT AND EXCITED STATE PREDICTION OF PHOTOEXCITED ELECTRON AND HOLE DYNAMICS IN ZnTe WITH TRANSIENT ULTRAVIOLET REFLECTION SPECTROSCOPY

HANZHE LIU, JONATHAN M MICHELSEN, ISABEL M KLEIN, SCOTT KEVIN CUSHING, *Chemistry and Chemical Engineering, California Institute of Technology, Pasadena, CA, USA.*

Transient extreme ultraviolet (XUV) spectroscopy is becoming well developed for the study of transition metal oxides like those used in solar fuel generation. Si and Ge compounds, other popular solar energy semiconductors, have been used as test cases for the ab-initio prediction of XUV edges and their photoexcited change. Here, we use transient XUV spectroscopy to study the ultrafast carrier dynamics of ZnTe, both as a CO_2 reduction material of interest to the LiSA (Liquid Sunlight Alliance) initiative as well as a test of our group's ab-initio methods. XUV spectra were taken in a grazing reflection geometry to enhance the sensitivity to carrier dynamics at the ZnTe surface. The Te 4d core-to-valence transition is then measured after broad and narrow band excitation replicating solar or UV light, respectively. Electron and hole energies are observed as a function of time by state-filling effects. A fast electronic response is observed within the ZnTe bandgap and is compared to theoretical signatures of photoexcited renormalization or surface states.

RJ10 **10:36 – 10:37**

ULTRAFAST CARRIER SPECIFIC DYNAMICS AND BAND GAP RENORMALIZATION IN $CH_3NH_3PbBr_3$ UNDERSTOOD BY FEMTOSECOND TABLETOP EXTREME ULTRAVIOLET SPECTROSCOPY

AASTHA SHARMA, *Department of Chemistry, University of Illinois at Urbana-Champaign, Urbana, IL, USA*; JOSH LEVEILLEE[a], *Department of Materials Science and Engineering, University of Illinois at Urbana-Champaign, Urbana, IL, USA*; MAX A VERKAMP[b], *Department of Chemistry, University of Illinois at Urbana-Champaign, Urbana, IL, USA*; ANDRÉ SCHLEIFE, *Department of Materials Science and Engineering, University of Illinois at Urbana-Champaign, Urbana, IL, USA*; JOSH VURA-WEIS, *Department of Chemistry, University of Illinois at Urbana-Champaign, Urbana, IL, USA.*

Hybrid organic-inorganic halide perovskites, such as $CH_3NH_3PbBr_3$ ($MAPbBr_3$) have emerged as outstanding light absorbing and emitting materials. $MAPbBr_3$ has a bandgap around 2.3 eV and a high open circuit voltage, making it suitable for tandem solar cell applications. However, detailed studies on photoexcited carrier dynamics of $MAPbBr_3$ are limited compared to its iodine counterpart. We show that tabletop high-harmonic extreme ultraviolet (XUV) transient absorption spectroscopy measures transition from Br $3d_{5/2}$ and $3d_{3/2}$ to the valence and conduction band of photoexcited $MAPbBr_3$ perovskite, enabling us to observe carrier specific dynamics. Taking advantage of a straightforward, simple parabolic model incorporating band filling and band gap renormalization, we also study the time evolution of the band gap renormalization effect. Our work highlights the application of femtosecond XUV spectroscopy for understanding non-equilibrium ultrafast photophysics of complex semiconductor materials by distinguishing competing processes: carrier cooling, band gap renormalization, band filling and recombination.

[a]Current address: Center for Quantum Materials Design, University of Texas at Austin, Austin, TX, USA
[b]Current address: Department of Chemistry, University of Texas at Austin, Austin, TX, USA

RJ11 **10:40 – 10:41**

MONITORING PHOTOINDUCED AND PHOTOCATALYTIC SURFACE REACTIONS WITH TIME, MASS, AND ENERGY RESOLUTION

MIHAI E VAIDA, *Department of Physics, University of Central Florida , Orlando, FL, USA.*

Breaking and making of chemical bonds in molecules attached to a substrate constitute the elementary steps of a surface chemical reaction and occur on the ultrafast time scale of nuclear motion. Monitoring these elementary steps is crucial for a detailed understanding of the mechanism of surface photoinduced and photocatalytic reactions. In this work, an experimental methodology that combines surface mass spectrometry with femtosecond pump-probe technique and ultraviolet multiphoton or extreme ultraviolet single photon ionization is employed to decipher the mechanism of surface photoinduced and photocatalytic reactions. The technique relies on the detection of highly unstable intermediate species and final products with time-, mass-, and energy resolution. In the first part of the talk, the photoinduced reaction dynamics of methyl iodide adsorbed on an amorphous cerium oxide ultrathin film is investigated to understand the effect of a non-crystalline surface on the reaction dynamics. In the second part of the talk, the reaction dynamics that leads to the formation of methane and methanol from methyl iodide and water co-adsorbed on a TiO2(110) surface will be presented. The results presented here demonstrate the viability of the employed experimental methodology to decipher complex surface photoinduced and photocatalytic reaction mechanisms.

RJ12 **10:44 – 10:45**

X-RAY TRANSIENT ABSORPTION REVEALS THE ^1A_u (nπ*) STATE OF PYRAZINE IN ELECTRONIC RELAXATION

VALERIU SCUTELNIC[a], *Department of Chemistry, University of California, Berkeley, Berkeley, CA, USA*; SHOTA TSURU, MÁTYÁS PÁPAI, *Chemistry, Technical University of Denmark, Kongens Lyngby, Denmark*; ZHEYUE YANG, MICHAEL EPSHTEIN, TIAN XUE, ERIC HAUGEN, YUKI KOBAYASHI, *Department of Chemistry, University of California, Berkeley, Berkeley, CA, USA*; ANNA KRYLOV, *Department of Chemistry, University of Southern California, Los Angeles, CA, USA*; KLAUS MØLLER, *Chemistry, Technical University of Denmark, Kongens Lyngby, Denmark*; SONIA CORIANI, *Department of Chemistry, Technical University of Denmark, Kgs. Lyngby, Denmark*; STEPHEN R. LEONE, *Department of Chemistry, The University of California, Berkeley, CA, USA.*

X-rays promote electrons from the core levels to vacant valence orbitals, thus endowing them with a unique element specificity. Moreover, the core level transitions can easily sense the shifts in the electron density in the proximity of the probed element. We produce soft X-rays around 280 eV driving high harmonics in a helium gas target with 1470 nm pulses. This table-top broad band X-ray source allows us to investigate the ultrafast dynamics in photoexcited pyrazine ($C_4H_4N_2$) with a new view of the electronic states involved. In addition to the previously characterized $^1B_{2u}$ ($\pi\pi$*) (S_2) and $^1B_{3u}$ (nπ*) (S_1) states, the participation of the optically dark ^1A_u (nπ*) state is assigned by a combination of experimental X-ray core-to-valence spectroscopy, electronic structure calculations and nonadiabatic dynamics simulations. The ^1A_u (nπ*) state is populated about 200 femtoseconds after electronic excitation and plays a key role in the relaxation of pyrazine to the ground state.

[a] V.S. gratefully acknowledges the Swiss National Science Foundation (P2ELP2_184414).

RJ13 **10:48 – 10:49**

CHARACTERIZATION OF THE $N_{6,7}$-EDGE AND $O_{2,3}$-EDGE OF Pt AND Ir COMPLEXES BY EXTREME ULTRAVIOLET SPECTROSCOPY

CLARE LEAHY, JOSH VURA-WEIS, *Department of Chemistry, University of Illinois at Urbana-Champaign, Urbana, IL, USA.*

Third-row transition metal complexes, particularly those containing platinum and iridium, are ubiquitous photosensitizers and catalysts, and transient x-ray absorption near edge structure (XANES) spectroscopy at the metals' L-edges has been increasingly used to study their photodynamics. While synchrotron XANES provides high photon flux and ultrafast time resolution, beamtime is unfortunately limited. We have examined 5d metal complexes using a tabletop XANES spectrometer which generates femtosecond XUV pulses (30-100 eV, 30 fs IRF) via high-harmonic generation (HHG), where the $N_{6,7}$-edge (4f-5d) and $O_{2,3}$-edge (5p-5d) of these metals appear. We show the ground state N-edge and O-edge XUV spectra of several platinum and iridium complexes. We will use transient XUV spectroscopy to demonstrate that these edges can be used to track oxidation state changes at the metal center after excitation of a MLCT transition in $Ir(ppy)_3$. Overall, this will provide information on the metal electronic structure and allow for parsing out the impact of metal vs ligands in the excited states when combined with other transient spectroscopies.

RK. Structure determination

Thursday, June 24, 2021 – 10:0 AM

Room: 2021 Online Everywhere

Chair: Ha Vinh Lam Nguyen, Université Paris-Est Créteil, Créteil, France

RK01 **10:00 – 10:01**

MICROWAVE SPECTRA AND MOLECULAR STRUCTURES OF THE GAS-PHASE HOMOCHIRAL HOMODIMERS OF 3,3-DIFLUORO-1,2-EPOXYPROPANE AND 3-FLUORO-1,2-EPOXYPROPANE

MARK D. MARSHALL, HELEN O. LEUNG, *Chemistry Department, Amherst College, Amherst, MA, USA.*

Density functional theory is used to examine the possible conformations of both homochiral (RR or SS) and heterochiral (RS or SR) homodimers of 3,3-difluoro-1,2-epoxypropane and 3-fluoro-1,2-epoxypropane as a guide in the search for their microwave spectra. Similar to the analogous homodimers of 3,3,3-trifluoro-1,2-epoxypropane, the lowest energy heterochiral dimers of these species contain an inversion center and are microwave silent. However, spectra are obtained for the lowest energy conformers of the homochiral dimers. Analysis of the spectra confirms the theoretically predicted geometries.

RK02 **10:04 – 10:05**

THE MICROWAVE SPECTRUM AND MOLECULAR STRUCTURE OF *TRANS*-2-FLUORO-3-(TRIFLUOROMETHYL)OXIRANE AND ITS COMPLEX WITH THE ARGON ATOM

JORDAN M. AUCOIN, HELEN O. LEUNG, MARK D. MARSHALL, *Chemistry Department, Amherst College, Amherst, MA, USA.*

Structurally similar to previously characterized chiral tagging candidates, *trans*-2-fluoro-3-(trifluoromethyl)oxirane (tFTFO) is investigated, both theoretically and experimentally, as a potential chiral tagging molecule. With a strong, simple rotational spectrum, tFTFO shows promise for applications in chiral analysis through the conversion of enantiomers into spectroscopically distinct diastereomeric species through noncovalent attachment. Fourier transform microwave spectroscopy from 5.6 to 18.1 GHz is used to obtain the rotational spectrum of five isotopologues of tFTFO and four isotopologues of its heterodimer with the argon atom. Analysis of these spectra allows the determination of the structures for both species. Initial results show that the structure of the argon complex is distinct from the structures previously described for the 3,3,3-trifluoro-, 3,3-difluoro-, and 3-fluoro-1,2-epoxypropane species, suggesting that the addition of the fluorine atom to the ring carbon alters bonding in the epoxy moiety.

RK03 **10:08 – 10:09**

STRUCTURE AND INTERNAL MOTIONS OF THE PROPARGYL ALCOHOL-WATER COMPLEX

SHARON PRIYA GNANASEKAR, ELANGANNAN ARUNAN, *Department of Inorganic and Physical Chemistry, Indian Institute of Science, Bangalore, India.*

The rotational spectra of the propargyl alcohol (PA)–water complex has been studied using a pulsed nozzle Fourier transform microwave spectrometer. PA is multifunctional molecule having a hydroxyl group and an acetylenic moiety. We have observed a cyclic hydrogen bonded structure. The alcohol donates an H-bond to water and the acetylenic moiety accepts a weak O-H-π H-bond from water. Calculations show that the two lowest energy structures have this same structural motif and differ only in the position of the non-bonded H atom of water. Several isotopic substitutions were carried out to ascertain the position of the non-bonded hydrogen of H_2O. Rotational spectroscopy helps to differentiate between these two similar structures. Splitting of the rotational transitions was also observed, indicating the presence of internal motions of the H_2O fragment. The observed global minimum structure is compared with earlier results from IR spectroscopy in matrix[a] and helium nanodroplet[b]. We also compare the global minima of several alcohol-water complexes to understand the donor-acceptor capabilities of the OH groups in alcohol-water complexes.

[a]Saini, J.; Viswanathan, K. S. J. Mol. Struct. 2016, 1118, 147–156.

[b]Mani, D.; Pal, N.; Smialkowski, M.; Beakovic, C.; Schwaab, G.; Havenith, M. Phys. Chem. Chem. Phys. 2019, 21, 20582–20587.

RK04 **10:12 – 10:13**

ROTATIONAL SPECTRUM OF 2-AMINOACETOPHENONE AND ITS 1:1 WATER COMPLEX

GIOVANNA SALVITTI, ASSIMO MARIS, *Dipartimento di Chimica G. Ciamician, Università di Bologna, Bologna, Italy*; SUSANA BLANCO, JUAN CARLOS LOPEZ, *Departamento de Química Física y Química Inorgánica, Universidad de Valladolid, Valladolid, Spain.*

2-aminoacetophenone is a grape sweet odorant and foxy natural occurring compound. It can be found in fruits, milk and white wines for which it is responsible for a characteristic flavor within a few months of storage. It has also been found in some animal secretions and it plays a role in the metabolism of some bacteria.

Literature survey reveals that to the best of our knowledge no rotational investigations of aminoacetophenone in the isolated phase have been reported so far. So we investigated this system by supersonic jet broadband using chirped-pulse Fourier transform microwave spectroscopy (2-8 GHz).

Over 140 μ_a and μ_b transitions, ranging from J_{up}=1 to 6, were assigned to the monomer using a Watson S-reduced Hamiltonian implemented by the ^{14}N nuclear hyperfine Hamiltonian. Rotational transitions of ^{13}C and^{15}N isotopologues have been observed in natural abundance, allowing for the determination of the molecular structure. Other lines in the spectrum revealed the presence of a water complex and its isotopologues.

The monomer structure is consistent with a planar molecule, except for the methyl CH bonds contribution, with an intermolecular O—HN hydrogen bond, while the structure of the complex involves one water molecule coordinated with the acetyl group through a OH–O hydrogen bond and secondary interaction between oxigen lone pair and methyl group.

Experimental results are in agreement with quantum mechanical calculations carried out at B3LYP and MP2 levels of theory.

RK05 **10:16 – 10:17**

CHARACTERIZING HYDROGEN-BONDED SYSTEMS BY COLD-ION INFRARED ACTION SPECTROSCOPY: THE FORMIC ACID TRIMER CASE

MARTÍN TACCONE, *Department of Molecular Physics, Fritz-Haber-Institut der Max-Planck-Gesellschaft, Berlin, Germany*; DANIEL A THOMAS, *Department of Chemistry, University of Rhode Island, Kingston, RI, 02881*; KATJA OBER, GERT VON HELDEN, GERARD MEIJER, *Department of Molecular Physics, Fritz-Haber-Institut der Max-Planck-Gesellschaft, Berlin, Germany.*

Over the years, great effort has been made in understanding small hydrogen-bonded systems due to their relevance in biological sciences, among others. In particular, the formic acid dimer has been long investigating because it represents a suitable model system to gain information about the proton donor-acceptor interactions. Very recently, the ground-state structure of the proton-bound formate dimer was characterized in helium nanodroplets by Thomas et al.[a] showing that the lowest energy structure corresponds to a symmetrical motif in which the proton is equally shared between the carboxylates. Nevertheless, no reports are found for bigger hydrogen-bonded carboxylate complexes like trimers or tetramers.

Here we report the spectrum of the anion formic acid trimer complex in the gas phase, utilizing vibrational spectroscopy of ions trapped in helium nanodroplets in the 400-2000 cm^{-1} region. Isotopic labeling and anharmonic frequency calculations indicate that among several conformers a *C2* symmetry motif may be the prevalent structure found in the gas phase.

[a] *Angew. Chem. Int. Ed.* **2018**, 57, 10615 – 10619

RK06 **10:20 – 10:21**

IRMPD SPECTROSCOPY OF $CO_3^-(H_2O)_{1,2}$ AND $CO_4^-(H_2O)_{1,2}$

MAXIMILIAN G MÜNST, MILAN ONCAK, MARTIN K BEYER, CHRISTIAN VAN DER LINDE, *Institute for Ion Physics and Applied Physics, University of Innsbruck, Innsbruck, Austria.*

The hydrated radical anions $CO_3^-(H_2O)_{1,2}$ and $CO_4^-(H_2O)_{1,2}$ are important anions in the atmosphere. Quantitative models predict the steady state fractional abundance of $CO_3^-(H_2O)_{0,1}$ to be in the range of 0.3–2.3 % of the total negative ion inventory, with $CO_3^-(H_2O)$ being predicted to be dominating up to an altitude of 11 km [1]. Direct sampling of ions in the boreal forest confirmed the presence of $CO_3^-(H_2O)_{0,1}$ [2]. The CO_4^- ion is another radical anion that is derived from CO_2 and found with a fractional abundance of about 0.01 % [2]. The reactivity often depends strongly on the number of solvating water molecules [3], and therefore the hydration structure is key to understand their reactivity. Infrared multiphoton dissociation (IRMPD) spectroscopy is an excellent tool to collect information on the structure of ions. The spectra were measured in both the C-O and O-H stretch region at ion trap temperatures of 295 K and approx. 80 K [4]. The O-H stretching region exhibits broad spectra with additional maxima and shoulders beside the free O-H stretch frequency for all ions. Clear absorptions are observed in the C-O stretching region, but dissociation of $CO_3^-(H_2O)_{1,2}$ was surprisingly inefficient, probably due to radiative cooling. While $CO_3^-(H_2O)_{1,2}$ and $CO_4^-(H_2O)$ lose water upon dissociation, $CO_4^-(H_2O)_2$ exhibits an additional dissociation channel with loss of CO_2. All experimentally measured infrared spectra are compared to calculated spectra within harmonic approximation and from analysis of molecular dynamics (MD) simulations. The comparison of experiment and theory indicates that multiple isomers contribute to the observed spectrum at finite temperatures.

[1] H. Kawamoto and T. Ogawa, Planet. Space Sci. 34, (1986) 1229.
[2] M. Ehn, et al., Atmos. Chem. Phys. 10, (2010) 8513.
[3] C. van der Linde et al., Phys. Chem. Chem. Phys. 20 (2018) 10838.
[4] M. G. Münst et al., J. Chem. Phys. 154, (2021) 084301.

RK07 **10:24 – 10:25**

ROTATIONAL SPECTROSCOPY OF IMINE-BASED MOLECULAR SWITCHES: ISOLATED AND MICRO-SOLVATED

NUNO CAMPOS, *CFisUC, Department of Physics, University of Coimbra, Coimbra, Portugal*; PABLO PINACHO, *FS-SMP, Deutsches Elektronen-Synchrotron (DESY), Hamburg, Germany*; CORINA H. POLLOK, CHRISTIAN MERTEN, *Physikalische Chemie II, Ruhr University Bochum, Bochum, Germany*; MANUELA RAMOS SILVA, *CFisUC, Department of Physics, University of Coimbra, Coimbra, Portugal*; MELANIE SCHNELL, *FS-SMP, Deutsches Elektronen-Synchrotron (DESY), Hamburg, Germany*; SERGIO R. DOMINGOS, *CFisUC, Department of Physics, University of Coimbra, Coimbra, Portugal.*

Imine-based molecular motors and switches[a] have been recently developed, and many of their properties remain largely unexplored. With potential to perform multi-step unidirectional rotations, these systems are an important addition to the existing nano-motor toolbox.[b] Their photochemically-induced switching processes foresee applications in the regulation of chemical reactions, as well as performing mechanical functions. Previous condensed-phase studies show that the energetic balance between isomers of such a molecular switch can be markedly different to that predicted from quantum chemistry calculations.[c] Micro-solvation studies in supersonic jet conditions are thus an appealing route to investigate the origin of these population manoeuvres. Rotational spectroscopy allows us to study the 3D structure and conformational heterogeneities of these systems and their micro-solvated counterparts with great precision, since we can relate the pattern of rotational frequencies to the structure through the moments of inertia.[d] Experiments using chirped-pulse Fourier transform microwave spectroscopy in the 2-8 GHz range are ongoing. Preliminary results of our study will be presented and discussed.

[a] L. Greb, A. Eichhöfer, J.-M. Lehn, *Angew. Chem. Int. Ed.*, **2015**, 54, 14345-14348
[b] S. Kassem, T. van Leeuwen, A. S. Lubbe, M. R. Wilson, B. L. Feringa, D. A. Leigh, *Chem. Soc. Rev.*, **2017**, 46, 2592-2621
[c] C. H. Pollok, T. Riesebeck, C. Merten, *Angew. Chem. Int. Ed.*, **2017**, 56, 1925-192
[d] S. R. Domingos, A. Cnossen, W. J. Buma, W. R. Browne, B. L. Feringa, M. Schnell, *Angew. Chem. Int. Ed.*, **2017**, 56, 11209-11212

RK08 **10:28 – 10:29**

INTRAMOLECULAR INTERACTIONS WITHIN 1- AND 2-NAPHTHOL: A ROTATIONAL SPECTROSCOPIC AND THEORETICAL STUDY

ARSH SINGH HAZRAH, *Department of Chemistry, University of Alberta, Edmonton, AB, Canada*; SADISHA NANAYAKKARA, *Chemistry, Southern Methodist University, Dallas, TX, USA*; NATHAN A. SEIFERT, *Chemical Sciences and Engineering Division, Argonne National Laboratory, Lemont, IL, USA*; ELFI KRAKA, *Chemistry, Southern Methodist University, Dallas, TX, USA*; WOLFGANG JÄGER, *Department of Chemistry, University of Alberta, Edmonton, AB, Canada.*

1- and 2-naphthol, hydroxy-derivatives of naphthalene, the simplest polycyclic aromatic hydrocarbon, are used as precursors in the dye, perfume, insecticide, and pharmaceutical industries.[1] Recently polyaromatic hydrocarbons (PAHs) such as naphthol have been examined for their complex intermolecular interplay within dimer structures.[2] To further build on previous PAHs studies we present a combined spectroscopic and theoretical study of 1- and 2-naphthol. The microwave spectra of the 1-naphthol and 2-naphthol monomers were measured using a chirped-pulse Fourier transform microwave spectrometer in the 2-6 GHz range. Spectroscopic assignments of the cis- and trans-conformers of 1-naphthol and 2-naphthol are supported by results from electronic structure calculations. Spectra of ten ^{13}C isotopologues were identified and analyzed for all four species. This allowed for the determination of substitution structures and so-called semi-experimental effective structures. The theoretical results show that the OH group of cis-1-naphthol points 6° out of plane, which is consistent with the difference in inertial defect between cis- and trans-1-naphthol. For cis-1-naphthol, NCI[3] and QTAIM[4] analyses resulted in a bond critical point between the hydroxyl group H-atom and the close H-atom in the neighbouring ring, suggesting a bonding interaction. To confirm or deny this hypothesis, local mode analyses were carried out to obtain a more in-depth assessment of the O-H bond strengths. Compared to trans-1-naphthol, the strength of the O-H bond is much stronger in cis-1-naphthol. This is reflected in a blue shift of the O-H stretching frequency and is consistent with the traditional notion of a steric repulsion rather than a bonding interaction.

1. H. Shindy, Chem. Int, 2016, 2, 2016.; 2. N. A. Seifert, A. S. Hazrah and W. Jäger, J. Phys. Chem. Lett., 2019, 10, 2836-2841.; 3. E. Johnson, S. Keinan, P. Mori-Sánchez and J. Contreras-García, J. Am. Chem. Soc., 2010, 2010, 132.; 4. R. F. Bader, Chemical Reviews, 1991, 91, 893-928.

RK09 **10:32 – 10:33**

MULTI-AGENT CONSENSUS EQUILIBRIUM (MACE) IN MOLECULAR AND ELECTRONIC STRUCTURE DETERMINATION

JIAYUE RONG, *Department of Chemistry, Purdue University, West Lafayette, IN, USA.*

MACE is demonstrated for the integration of experimental observables as constraints in molecular structure determination and for the systematic merging of multiple computational architectures. MACE is founded on simultaneously determining the equilibrium point between multiple experimental and/or computational agents; the returned state description (e.g., atomic coordinates for molecular structure) represents the intersection of each manifold and is not equivalent to the average optimum state for each agent. The moment of inertia, determined directly from microwave spectroscopy measurements, serves to illustrate the mechanism through which MACE evaluations merge experimental and quantum chemical modeling. MACE results reported combine gradient descent optimization of each ab initio agent with an agent that predicts chemical structure based on root-mean-square deviation of the predicted inertia tensor with experimentally measured moments of inertia. Successful model fusion for several small molecules was achieved as well as the larger molecule solketal. Fusing a model of moment of inertia, an underdetermined predictor of structure, with low cost computational methods yielded structure determination performance comparable to standard computational methods such as MP2/cc-pVTZ, and greater agreement with experimental observables.

RK10 **10:36 – 10:37**

THE SHAPES OF SULFONAMIDES: ROTATIONAL SPECTRA OF BENZENESULFONAMIDE, *ortho*-TOLUENSULFONAMIDE, *para*-TOLUENSULFONAMIDE AND SULFANILAMIDE

SONIA MELANDRI, ANNALISA VIGORITO, ASSIMO MARIS, *Dipartimento di Chimica G. Ciamician, Università di Bologna, Bologna, Italy*; CAMILLA CALABRESE, *Departamento de Química Física, Universidad del País Vasco (UPV-EHU), Bilbao, Spain*; M. EUGENIA SANZ, DONATELLA LORU, ISABEL PEÑA, *Department of Chemistry, King's College London, London, United Kingdom.*

The effects of substitution were investigated for the sulfonamides class of molecules, in particular those which contain the benzosulfonamide functional group. This group of molecules is of extreme interest in the biological field since many of them are active against a variety of diseases. In this work, structural investigations on the pharmacophoric group benzensulfonamide and the substitution effects have been performed through the studies of its derivatives benzensulfonamide itself, *para*-toluensulfonamide, *ortho*-toluensulfonamide and the bioactive molecule sulfanilamide. In all compounds, but in *ortho*-toluensulfonamide, the amino group lies perpendicular to the benzene plane with the amminic hydrogens eclipsing the oxygen atoms. In *ortho*-toluensulfonamide where a weak attractive interaction between the nitrogen lone pair and the methyl hydrogen atoms takes place, the amino group lies in the *gauche* orientation. These results show that such weak non-covalent interactions are able to change the conformational preferences of the pharmacophoric group. For all species, the ^{14}N quadrupolar hyperfine analysis has been performed. This has provided crucial information for the unambiguous identification of the observed conformation and the structural parameters related to the position of the nitrogen atom. In addition, for *ortho*-toluensulfonamide, the vibration-rotation hyperfine structure related to the methyl torsion has been analyzed and the methyl group rotation barrier was determined.

RK11 **10:40 – 10:41**

NEW INVESTIGATION OF THE ROTATIONAL SPECTRUM OF SABINENE

MHAMAD CHRAYTEH, THERESE R. HUET, PASCAL DRÉAN, *UMR 8523 - PhLAM - Physique des Lasers Atomes et Molécules, University of Lille, CNRS, F-59000 Lille, France.*

Sabinene ($C_{10}H_{16}$-4-methylene-1-(1-methylethyl)bicyclo[3.1.0]hexane) is a bicyclic monoterpene with an exocyclic double bond. It is one of the main biogenic volatile organic compound. In Europe, it is emitted in the troposphere by trees such as *Quercus ilex*, *Betula pendula*, and *Fagus sylvatica* with an estimated flux of 20 Tg.yr^{-1}. It acts as precursor of secondary organic aerosols through several oxidation reactions. A first investigation of the low resolution rotational spectrum of sabinene was performed 40 years ago leading to the determination of the $(B + C)$ combination of rotational constants of the parent species.[1] From this unique data, and within numerous assumptions, the dihedral angle ϕ defining the boat arrangement of the five-membered ring was determined (55°), but it is not in agreement with the typical values observed in molecules based on bicyclo[3.1.0]hexane.[2] In this work, the rotational spectrum of sabinene along with its gas phase structure were reinvestigated theoretically and experimentally employing a combination of quantum chemical calculations and Fourier transform microwave spectroscopy coupled to a supersonic jet expansion in the 2-20 GHz frequency region. The spectra of the parent species and of all singly substituted ^{13}C isotopologues have been analysed in natural abundance. The 11 sets of rotational constants allowed to determine the partial substitution and effective structures of sabinene. They are in fair agreement with the optimized ones at the B3LYP, M06-2X and MP2 levels associated with the 6-311++G(d,p) basis set. The dihedral angle ϕ was determined to be 26.9°.

[1] Z. Kisiel, A. C. Legon, Conformations of some bicyclic monoterpenes based on bicyclo [3.1.0] hexane from their low-resolution microwave spectra, J. Am. Chem. Soc. 100 (1978) 8166–8169.

[2] E. J. Ocola, L. A. Wieding, S. Adams, J. Laane, Theoretical study of structures and ring-puckering potential energy functions of bicylo [3.1.0] hexane and related molecules, J. Phys. Chem. A 122 (2018) 5970–5977.

The present work was funded by the French ANR Labex CaPPA through the PIA under contract ANR-11-LABX-0005-01, by the Regional Council Hauts de France, by the European Funds for Regional Economic Development (FEDER), and by the French Ministère de l'Enseignement Supérieur et de la Recherche. It is a contribution to the CPER research Project CLIMIBIO.

RK12 **10:44 – 10:45**

THE SHAPE OF LEVODOPA: A LASER ABALATION ROTATIONAL STUDY

MIGUEL SANZ NOVO, *Grupo de Espectroscopia Molecular, Lab. de Espectroscopia y Bioespectroscopia, Unidad Asociada CSIC, Universidad de Valladolid, Valladolid, Spain*; ELENA R. ALONSO, *Departamento de Química Física, Universidad del País Vasco (UPV-EHU), Bilbao, Spain*; IKER LEÓN, JOSÉ L. ALONSO, *Grupo de Espectroscopia Molecular, Lab. de Espectroscopia y Bioespectroscopia, Unidad Asociada CSIC, Universidad de Valladolid, Valladolid, Spain.*

The rotational spectrum of neutral levodopa (L-dopa), an aminoacid precursor of neurotransmitters dopamine [a], norepinephrine (noradrenaline) and epineophrine (adrenaline), has been investigated for the first time using a broadband chirped pulse FTMW spectrometer coupled with a laser ablation source (LA-CP-FTMW). The spectroscopic parameters derived from the analysis of the spectrum conclusively identify the existence of three conformers of levodopa. The ^{14}N nuclear quadrupole coupling constants have been analyzed, probing the existence of stabilizing N-H-π interactions for the observed structures.

- **Acknowledgments:** The authors thank the financial fundings from Ministerio de Ciencia e Innovacion (CTQ2016-76393-P and PID2019-111396GB-I00), Junta de Castilla y Leon (VA077U16 and VA244P20) and European Research Council under the European Union's Seventh Framework Programme (FP/2007-2013) / ERC-2013-SyG, Grant Agreement n. 610256 NANOCOSMOS, are gratefully acknowledged. E.R.A. acknowledges MINECO for a Juan de la Cierva postdoctoral fellowship and the Fundación Biofísica Bizkaia (Spain). M.S.N. acknowledges funding from the Spanish "Ministerio de Ciencia, Innovación y Universidades" under predoctoral FPU Grant (FPU17/02987).

[a]C. Cabezas, I. Pena, J. C. Lopez and J. L. Alonso, J. Phys. Chem. Lett., 2013, 4, 486–490.

RK14 **10:52 – 10:53**

CONFORMERS OF VANILLIC ACID: A ROTATIONAL SPECTROSCOPIC AND THEORETICAL STUDY

MOHAMAD AL-JABIRI, WOLFGANG JÄGER, *Department of Chemistry, University of Alberta, Edmonton, AB, Canada.*

Vanillic acid is produced in significant quantities in forest fires and is used as a biomass burning tracer for softwood and hardwood combustion events. Vanillic acid has also been found in secondary organic aerosol and can be oxidized in aqueous atmospheric processes to humic-like substances. Hydrates of vanillic acid play undoubtedly important roles in the processes involved, and we present here a study of conformers of the vanillic acid monomer to lay the groundwork for subsequent studies of the mono- and di-hydrates.

Computationally, 12 conformers were found within an energy range of 51 kJ/mol using the Conformer–Rotamer Ensemble Sampling Tool (CREST).[1] The two lowest energy conformers could then be identified in the spectrum recorded with a chirped pulse Fourier transform microwave spectrometer in the 2-6 GHz range. The deviation between experimental and theoretical rotational constants determined at the MP2/aug-cc-pVTZ and DFT B3LYP-D3(BJ)/def2-TVPZ levels of theory is less than 1%. No tunnelling splitting was observed which suggests a relatively high barrier to methyl internal rotation, in agreement with other, previously studied vanillin derivatives. Furthermore, no c-type transitions could be observed in agreement with computed zero c-dipole moment component of the lowest energy structures. From the theoretical structures, it is apparent that intra-molecular hydrogen bonds play a significant role in stabilizing the lowest energy conformers. To further explore the intra-molecular interactions in vanillic acid, QTAIM and NCI analyses were performed.

[1]P. Pracht, F. Bohle, S. Grimme, Phys. Chem. Chem. Phys. 22, 7169-7192 (2020).

RK15 **10:56 – 10:57**

PROGRESS MADE TOWARDS CONTEXT-FREE MOLECULAR STRUCTURE DETERMINATION FROM ISOTOPOLOGUE ROTATIONAL SPECTROSCOPY

LIA YEH, DYLAN FINESTONE, *Physics, University of California, Santa Barbara, CA, USA*; LINCOLN SATTERTHWAITE, *Chemistry and Biochemistry, UCSB, Santa Barbara, CA, USA*; JIEYU YAN, DAVID PATTERSON, *Physics, University of California, Santa Barbara, CA, USA*.

Recent algorithms[ab] have demonstrated context-free assignment of rotational constants—needing no knowledge of the chemical species other than the rotational spectrum. Efforts to date to subsequently determine molecular structure require further information including assignment of singly-substituted isotopologues[cd], mass spectroscopy, and data mining[e]. We investigate two methodologies to resolve sign ambiguities of Kraitchman's substitution coordinates. The first methodology requires candidate rotational constants of doubly-substituted isotopologues. Given many such candidates, we have worked out how to determine 1) which candidates for singly- and doubly-substituted isotopologues are most probable, and 2) doubly-substituted atoms' relative position octant. This is realizable given resolution of doubly-substituted species in natural abundance, which is 10-100x order of magnitude above our instrument's present signal to noise.

The second methodology requires precision measurement of the electric dipole moments and magnetic g-factors of both the parent and singly-substituted isotopologues. The magnetic g-factor is measured via application of a large magnetic field to our microwave spectrometer, as done by Flygare et. al. (1969). For a 6 carbon molecule, this could be realized given the ability to resolve a $\approx 10^{-5}$ percent difference between magnetic g-factors of the parent and singly-substituted isotopolog species, as well as resolve the electric dipole moment to 4 or 5 significant figures. Improving the capabilities of microwave spectrometers to within these thresholds would therefore enable context-free molecular structure determination.

[a] N.A. Seifert et. al., Journal of Molecular Spectroscopy 312, 13 (2015).
[b] L. Yeh, L. Satterthwaite, and D. Patterson, The Journal of Chemical Physics 150, 204122 (2019).
[c] J. Yan and D. Patterson. Submitted to the 75th International Symposium on Molecular Spectroscopy (2021).
[d] K. Mayer et. al., Proceedings of the 74th International Symposium on Molecular Spectroscopy (2019).
[e] M. Muckle, A. Mikhonin, D. McDaniel, and/or J. Neill, Proceedings of the 74th International Symposium on Molecular Spectroscopy (2019).

RL. Electronic structure, potential energy surfaces

Thursday, June 24, 2021 – 10:0 AM

Room: 2021 Online Everywhere

Chair: Mallory Green, Fritz Haber Institute of the Max Planck Society, Berlin, Germany

RL01 **10:00 – 10:01**

LASER-INDUCED FLUORESCENCE (LIF) OF JET-COOLED SmO

JOEL R SCHMITZ, ARIANNA RODRIGUEZ, MICHAEL HEAVEN, *Department of Chemistry, Emory University, Atlanta, GA, USA.*

The chemi-ionization reactions of atomic lanthanides $M + O \rightarrow MO^+ + e^-$ are currently being investigated as a method to artificially increase the localized electron density in the ionosphere for uniform radio wave propagation. Recent experiments involving the release of atomic samarium (Sm) into the upper atmosphere have resulted in the production of a cloud with blue and red emissions[1]. Spectroscopic characterization of both SmO and its cation SmO^+ is required to accurately determine the fraction of SmO^+ present in the release cloud. While the low-lying states of SmO have been previously spectroscopically characterized, the analysis was hindered due to the production of SmO under high temperature conditions[2,3]. In this experiment, SmO was jet-cooled to 70K and laser-induced fluorescence (LIF) spectra were obtained over the range from 15,000-16,000 cm^{-1}. Dispersed laser-induced fluorescence (DLIF) spectra were also obtained for vibrational characterization of the ground and low-lying states. Fluorescence lifetime measurements have been used to determine Einstein *A* coefficients. Data and analysis of ground and low-lying excited states of SmO will be presented.

[1] Ard, S.G. et al. J. Chem. Phys.2015, 143, 204303.
[2] Hannigan, M. C. J. Mol. Spec. 1983, 99, 235-238.
[3] Linton, C. et al. J. Mol. Spec. 1987, 126, 370-392.

RL02 **10:04 – 10:05**

LASER-INDUCED FLUORESCENCE (LIF) OF JET-COOLED NdO AND NdO^+

JOEL R SCHMITZ, ARIANNA RODRIGUEZ, MICHAEL HEAVEN, *Department of Chemistry, Emory University, Atlanta, GA, USA.*

The chemi-ionization reactions of atomic lanthanides $M + O \rightarrow MO^+ + e^-$ are currently being investigated as a method to artificially increase the ion density in the ionosphere for uniform radio wave propagation. Recent experiments involving the release of atomic neodymium (Nd) into the upper atmosphere have resulted in the production of a cloud with green emission[1]. Based on the cloud emission, it is believed that NdO was the primary product, but spectroscopic characterization of NdO and NdO^+ is needed to properly identify the emitting species. While NdO is well characterized above 590 nm, little spectroscopic data exits at emission wavelengths below 590 nm[2,3]. Recently, the ionization energy of NdO was determined by REMPI and PIE methods[4], as well as the ion ground state vibrational separation $\Delta G_{1/2}{}^+$ but there exists no experimental rotational characterization of the low-lying states of NdO^+. In this experiment, NdO was supersonically expanded and then ionized at 193 nm. Laser-induced fluorescence (LIF) spectra of both NdO and NdO^+ was obtained at 16,650-20,000 cm^{-1}. Electronic states were vibrationally characterized using dispersed laser induced fluorescence (DLIF) techniques. Data and analysis of the ground and low-lying states of NdO and NdO^+ will be presented.

[1] Ard, S.G. et al. J. Chem. Phys.2015, 143, 204303.
[2] Kaledin, L.A. et al. Acta Physica Hungarica 1983, 54, 189-212.
[3] Linton, C. et al. J. Mol. Spec. 2004, 225, 132-144.
[4] VanGundy, R.A. et al. J. Chem. Phys. 2019, 114302

RL03 ***Post-Deadline Abstract*** **10:08 – 10:09**

ELECTRONIC STRUCTURE OF THE GROUND AND EXCITED STATES OF RhO^{2+}: ITS ROLE IN THE C-H BOND ACTIVATION OF METHANE

SHAHRIAR N KHAN, EVANGELOS MILIORDOS, *Chemistry and Biochemistry, Auburn University, Auburn, AL, USA.*

In this project, we have studied the electronic structure of RhO^{2+} using high level quantum mechanical calculations. Multireference method (MRCI) has been employed in combination with large basis sets to construct the potential energy profiles of the ground and excited states of RhO^{2+} with different spin multiplicities. Spectroscopic constants have been tabulated for 20 states along with the spin-orbit calculation for a few low-lying states. The ground state of RhO^{2+} is $^2\Pi$ followed by $^4\Delta$ and $^2\Delta$. The equilibrium bond lengths for these states are between 1.594-1.752 Åand the electronic structure is in situ $Rh^{4+}O^{2-}$ that corresponds to an oxo moiety. The next state is $^6\Sigma^+$ with an equilibrium bond length of 2.161 Åand possesses an in situ electronic structure of $Rh^{3+}O^-$ that corresponds to oxyl character with one unpaired electron on oxygen. Further investigation reveals that $^6\Sigma^+$, which is 19.6 kcal/mol higher in energy than the $^2\Pi$ (ground state), has the potency to activate C-H bond of methane with higher efficiency. Finally, from the spin-orbit calculations, the ground state of RhO^{2+} is assigned $^2\Pi_{1/2}$ followed by the state $^4\Delta_{7/2}$. In future, this project is going to probe the effect of ligands in the electronic structure of RhO^{2+}.

RL04 **10:12 – 10:13**

ELECTRONIC STRUCTURE ANALYSIS OF GROUND AND EXCITED STATES OF $MO^{2+/+/0/-}$ (M = Mo, Ru) AND THEIR WATER ACTIVATION STRENGTHS

ISURU R. ARIYARATHNA, *Chemistry, Auburn University, Auburn, Alabama, USA*; EVANGELOS MILIORDOS, *Chemistry and Biochemistry, Auburn University, Auburn, AL, USA.*

Production of H_2 gas via water splitting reactions facilitated by solar light harvesting, can be a solution to the constant increase of energy demand. Water splitting is an endothermic process which requires about 2.69 eV per water molecule. High endothermicity of this process can be overcome by exploiting the sun light and using a suitable catalyst. Transition metal oxide (MO) catalysts are promising candidates for this process because of their multiple low-lying electronic states.

The rate determining step in the water splitting reactions is often the activation of the O-H bonds. Here we have tested water activation strengths of several neutral and charged MOs computationally. The complicated electronic structures of these MOs forced us to perform multi-reference calculations. For these MOs the water activation process can be partitioned into three major processes. 1) Formation of the H_2O...OM interacting complex. 2) Surpass the transition state barrier which involve H-O bond cleavage of metal bound water. 3) HO-M-OH product formation.

Due to the multiple low-lying excited states of these species, spin crossovers and electron excitation from ground to higher states are expected. Among the considered H_2O+$[MoO]^{-/+/2+}$ reactions, the anionic system is the best candidate for the water activation, which has a lower activation energy barrier and create a more stabilized product than interacting complex. On the contrary, $MoO^{2+/+}$ stabilizes the $MoO^{2+/+}$...H_2O interacting complex over products. A similar pattern was observed for the H_2O+$[RuO]^{-/0/+/2+}$ reactions. The suitability of RuO species for the water activation vary in RuO^{2+} $< RuO^+ < RuO < RuO^-$ order.

RL05 **10:16 – 10:17**

ADIABATIC MOLECULAR ORBITAL TRACKING IN AB INITIO MOLECULAR DYNAMICS

ASYLBEK A ZHANSERKEEV, RYAN P STEELE, *Department of Chemistry, University of Utah, Salt Lake City, UT, USA.*

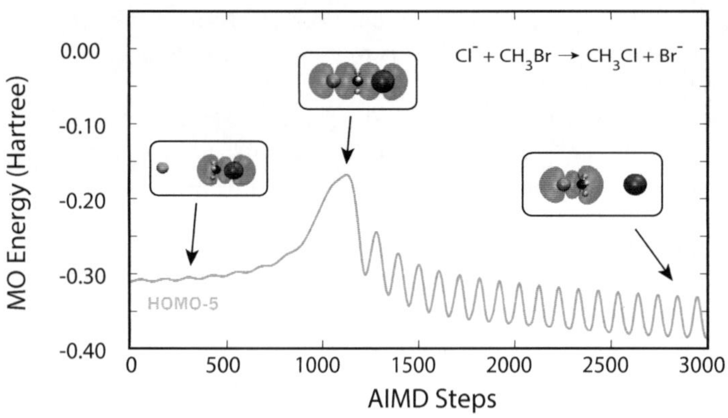

The ab initio molecular dynamics (AIMD) method provides a computational route for the real-time simulation of reactive chemistry and spectroscopy. An often-overlooked capability of this approach is the opportunity to examine the electronic evolution of a chemical system, including chemical bond formation and electrical responses to radiation.

For AIMD trajectories based on Hartree-Fock or density functional theory (DFT) methods, the real-time evolution of orbitals can provide detailed insights into the time-dependent electronic structure of a complex. However, the molecular orbital character, ordering, and associated phase are not preserved throughout the trajectory, due to the presence of different electronic Hamiltonians at each time step. By exploiting the similarity in neighboring timesteps' electronic structure, an algorithm has been developed that allows for reliably tracking the character of molecular orbitals throughout an AIMD trajectory, including cases of orbital crossing and degeneracy.

In this presentation, examples of the results of this tool will be shown, including reactive trajectories. These examples will also highlight the adiabatic character of the evolution of molecular orbitals. The utility of this approach for both educational purposes and analysis of trajectories will be demonstrated. Possibilities for extension to diabatic analyses will also be discussed.

RL06 **10:20 – 10:21**

PROBING THE WAVELENGTH-DEPENDENT EXCITED-STATE DYNAMICS OF A PHOTOCHROMIC MOLECULAR SWITCH USING RESONANCE RAMAN SPECTROSCOPY

KRISTEN H. BURNS, CHRISTOPHER G. ELLES, *Department of Chemistry, University of Kansas, Lawrence, KS, USA.*

Diarylethene (DAE) derivatives are an important class of photochromic molecular switches that undergo ring-opening and ring-closing reactions following excitation with visible or UV light, respectively. Here, we use resonance Raman spectroscopy to examine the wavelength-dependence of the cycloreversion (ring-opening) reaction following excitation into the two lowest electronic absorption bands of a common DAE derivative. Resonance Raman spectroscopy reveals the initial dynamics on the excited-state potential energy surface based on mode-specific enhancements of the vibrational spectrum that depend on the electronic resonance condition. Although the vibrational frequencies report on the ground-state structure of the molecule, the relative intensities of the Raman transitions reflect the initial motion immediately following excitation to the upper electronic state. Specifically, we report stimulated resonance Raman spectra and Raman gain profiles for excitation into two separate absorption bands centered near 560 nm and 370 nm. Although excitation into either band results in the cycloreversion reaction with similar $\sim 2\%$ quantum yield, the resonance Raman spectra indicate that the initial dynamics are different for the two excited states. Excitation into the lower energy absorption band reveals resonance enhancement of a 986 cm^{-1} mode that corresponds to a ring breathing mode of the central cyclohexadiene ring, and likely represents motion directly along the ring-opening reaction coordinate. In contrast, excitation into the higher energy absorption band results in resonance enhancement for 1400 $cm^{-1}$and 1600 cm^{-1} modes that represent ethylenic stretching along the conjugated backbone of the molecule and of the peripheral phenyl rings, respectively, and probably do not map directly onto the reaction coordinate. These observations provide key information for understanding the reactivity of DAE derivatives following excitation in the visible and near-UV.

RL07 **10:24 – 10:25**

THE EFFECT OF THE SADDLE POINT POSITION AND THE OH-BONDING FORCE CONSTANT ON THE TRANSITION FREQUENCIES OF H-BOND OF NAPHTHAZARIN

FATEMEH AFSHAR GHAHREMANI, MANSOUREH ZAHEDI-TABRIZI[a], *Department of Chemistry, Alzahra University, Tehran, Iran*; SAYYED FARAMARZ TAYYARI, *Department of Chemistry, Ferdowsi University, Mashhad, IRAN.*

The structure of Naphthazarin (NZ) has been considered in spectroscopic for a long time. However, there are some ambiguity in spectroscopic data up to now. In this work, an easy and feasible method has been introduced for studying the proton tunneling in NZ to assess symmetry. For this purpose, a two-dimensional potential energy surface which has been capable to explain the movement of hydrogen atom with high accuracy has been used. This potential energy function, which couples OH stretching with in-plane bending modes has been applied on a fixed skeleton geometry of NZ calculates the tunneling splitting, OH stretching, and in-plane bending frequencies. To study the effect of the saddle point and the bending force constant of OH on transition frequencies of hydrogen bond, a differentiation was applied on two dimensional function towards X and Y, respectively. The tunneling splitting of 15.3 and 0.8$\mathrm{cm}^{-1}$and the barrier height of 65.3 and 127.3 kJ/mol for stepwise and concerted proton transfer, respectively, indicate that both proton transfers are probable to happen, but NZ of $\mathrm{D}{-}2h$ symmetry will last for the longer time. In addition, as the saddle point position and the bending force constant increase, the tunneling frequency increases. It seems that the interaction between these two modes (the bending force constant) is responsible for higher OH stretching and lower OH bending frequencies in the bent hydrogen bonded systems compared to those in linear hydrogen bonded systems. This coupling, also, predicts a strong fermi resonance between OH stretching and the second overtone of OH bending modes in NZ and explains the cause of broading for OH stretching frequency in the bent H-bonded systems such as those in the enol form of β-diketones.

---

[a]*

RL08 **10:28 – 10:29**

VALENCE-HOLE ELECTRON CONFIGURATIONS: A NEW GLOBAL ELECTRONIC STRUCTURE PARADIGM FOR C_2 AND BEYOND

JUN JIANG, *Center for Accelerator Mass Spectrometry, Lawrence Livermore National Laboratory, Livermore, CA, USA*; TIMOTHY SCHMIDT, KLAAS NAUTA, *School of Chemistry, UNSW, Sydney, NSW, Australia*; ROBERT W FIELD, *Department of Chemistry, MIT, Cambridge, MA, USA.*

The global electronic structures of $C_2\,{}^1\Pi_g$ and ${}^3\Pi_g$ states, up to the energy of the first symmetry-allowed C(2s2p^3)+C(2s^{2}2p^2) dissociation channel, are modeled using a diabatic state interaction picture. The experimental observations (v=0-8 of $C^1\Pi_g$; v=0-12 of $d^3\Pi_g$ and $e^3\Pi_g$, and five v levels of the coupled $3,4^3\Pi_g$ states) are reproduced with an average residual of $0.3\,\mathrm{cm}^{-1}$. The key concept behind the diabatization is the valence-hole electron configurations, for which an electron in the anti-bonding $2\sigma_u$ orbital is excited to a higher energy orbital. For C_2, when this electron is excited to a bonding orbital (i.e. $3\sigma_g/2\pi_u\leftarrow 2\sigma_u$), the valence-hole configuration is the lowest energy configuration within a given symmetry manifold. These valence-hole configurations have a nominal bond-order of three, and correlate to the excited C(2s2p^3)+C(2s^{2}2p^2) channel with 2p←2s electron promotion in one of the carbon fragments. A *diabatic* valence-hole state with bond-order of three is expected to have a high dissociation energy, and in our model, it dissociates into the lowest symmetry-allowed C(2s2p^3)+C(2s^{2}2p^2) channel. As R increases, this deeply-bound valence-hole state crosses several other low-lying electronic states (derived from the $2\sigma_u^2 2\sigma_g^2$ configuration), all of which dissociate into the low-energy C(2s^{2}2p^2)+C(2s^{2}2p^2) channels without 2p←2s promotion. The curve-crossings between the valence-hole and the $2\sigma_u^2 2\sigma_g^2$-type states in C_2 are analogous to the ionic (A^+B^-)/covalent (AB) curve crossings in more ionic species. In both cases, the electronic structure landscape of the low-lying valence states is systematically disrupted due to their curve crossings with a single diabatic state (valence-hole or A^+B^-). We believe that the valence-hole state is an important but hitherto neglected feature in the electronic structure model. The C_2 molecule offers a perfect platform to study the role of valence-hole states in causing fundamental changes of the global electronic structure landscape. The valence-hole-induced curve crossings in C_2 occur at much lower excitation energy than the analogous ones in N_2, CO, NO, and O_2. The effects from these curve crossings are gloriously and uniquely sampled in the molecular constants of low-lying states of C_2.

RL09 **10:32 – 10:33**

EXAMINING HYPERMETALLIC OXIDE MgOMg WITH LASER INDUCED FLUORESCENCE AND PHOTOIONIZATION SPECTROSCOPY

THOMAS D. PERSINGER, MICHAEL HEAVEN, *Department of Chemistry, Emory University, Atlanta, GA, USA.*

Despite the fact that diatomic alkaline earth monoxides are deeply bound, closed shell molecules, hypermetallic species of the form MOM are also found to be stable. Formally these molecules have ionic bonds of the form $M^+O^{2-}M^+$. Each M^+ ion hosts an unpaired electron, and the interactions between these well separated electrons are weak. As a consequence the singlet-triplet energy interval is small, and the lowest energy singlet state is strongly multi-reference in character. In the present study we have characterized MgOMg by means of laser induced fluorescence and resonance enhanced multi-photon ionization (REMPI) spectroscopy. Rotationally resolved electronic spectra have been recorded for multiple bands of the $A^1A_1 - X^1\Sigma_g^+$ transition in the range of 21500 – 23000 cm^{-1}. The spectra were consistent with bent and linear equilibrium structures for the excited and ground states. Fluorescence decay lifetimes were found to be 39±1 ns. The attribution of the observed excitation bands to MgOMg was confirmed by recording REMPI spectra with mass-resolved ion detection. Two-color ionization measurements defined an ionization energy of 53071(20) cm^{-1}, close to a computational prediction of 53330 cm^{-1}.

RL10 **10:36 – 10:37**

STUDY OF LiMg AND $LiMg^+$ USING LASER INDUCED FLUORESCENCE AND TWO-PHOTON IONIZATION

THOMAS D. PERSINGER, JIANDE HAN, MICHAEL HEAVEN, *Department of Chemistry, Emory University, Atlanta, GA, USA.*

Heterodimers consisting of an alkaline and alkaline-earth metal, such as LiMg have the potential for being laser cooled to ultra-cold temperatures. The $X1^2\Sigma^+$ ground state of LiMg allows manipulation by both magnetic and electric fields, and its non-zero dipole moment offers the possibility that it could be used in quantum computing devices. Current experimental data on LiMg and $LiMg^+$ are sparse[1,2]. In the present study we used resonance enhanced two-photon ionization spectroscopy (RE2PI) and laser induced fluorescence (LIF) to record rotationally resolved spectra of the $X1^2\Sigma^+$, $2^2\Pi$ and $3^2\Sigma^+$ states. Near-UV spectra previously assigned as E-X and F-X transitions were also reevaluated. Vibrationally resolved spectra of the $X1^2\Sigma^+$ and $1^2\Pi$ state were observed using dispersed LIF. Pulsed-field ionization - zero kinetic energy photoelectron spectroscopy (PFI-ZEKE) was used to determine the ionization energy (IE) and the low-energy states of $LiMg^+$. An IE of 4.7695(4) eV for LiMg was found, and vibrationally resolved spectra yielded molecular constants for $LiMg^+$ that were consistent with a substantial strengthening of the bond upon ionization.

1. Berry, K.R. and Duncan, M.A., (1997) Photoionization spectroscopy of LiMg. Chem. Phys. Lett., 279, 44-49

2. Pichler, G., Lyyra, A.M., Kleiber, P.D., Stwalley, W.C., Hammer, R., Sando, K.M., and Michels, H.H., (1989) Laser-induced chemiluminescence of the lithium-magnesium (LiMg) excimer. Chem. Phys. Lett., 156, 467-71

RL11 **10:40 – 10:41**

INTERPRETING THE ELECTRONIC STRUCTURE OF SUPERATOMIC $AU_8(PPH_3)_7^{2+}$

JONATHAN WOOD FAGAN, CHRISTOPHER J. JOHNSON, *Chemistry, Stony Brook University, Stony Brook, NY, USA.*

Atomically-precise gold nanoclusters (AuNCs) in the tens to hundreds of Au atoms size range can exhibit superatomic characteristics where the geometric and electronic stability of the cluster is driven by "shell-closing" electronic configurations. The superatomic model predicts that Jahn-Teller-like distortions stabilize clusters near the closing of a shell by rearranging the molecular orbitals. We have collected a highly-resolved electronic absorption spectrum of an ellipsoidal phosphine-protected AuNC that supports the qualitative model for non-spherical superatomic clusters. The lower energy transitions reasonably match the metal-metal transitions predicted by density functional theory (DFT) calculations. In addition, we confirm these results by a qualitative "particle-in-a-box" numerical calculation that treats the core electrons as particles in an ellipsoidal potential. The results of this qualitative model are consistent with both the results of the DFT calculation as well as the electronic structure predicted for superatomic clusters with non-spherical cores.

RL12 **10:44 – 10:45**

SPECTROSCOPIC STUDIES OF SMALL POLYATOMIC MOLECULES NEAR ION-PAIR DISSOCIATION THRESHOLDS

CARLA KREIS, URS HOLLENSTEIN, FRÉDÉRIC MERKT, *Laboratorium für Physikalische Chemie, ETH Zurich, Zurich, Switzerland.*

At high vibrational quantum numbers, ion-pair states (A^+–B^-) behave like high Rydberg states. Their level structure can be approximately described by Rydberg's formula after replacing the Rydberg constant R_∞ by the appropriate mass-scaled value $R_{IP} = R_\infty \frac{\mu_{A^+-B^-}}{m_e}$.[a]

We present the results of spectroscopic investigations of high-lying excited ion-pair states of small polyatomic molecules in the vicinity of ion-pair dissociation thresholds. Such states have been extensively characterized in diatomic molecules (see ref. [a,b] and references therein) and are at the heart of the technique of threshold ion-pair production spectroscopy.[c] Only few studies have been carried out on polyatomic molecules.[d,e] Polyatomic molecules exhibit denser series of ion-pair dissociation thresholds corresponding to the different rovibrational levels of the positively and negatively charged fragments. We will present the results of our investigations of OCS and H_2S in the vicinity of their lowest ion-pair dissociation thresholds. The experiments are carried out using cold samples in skimmed supersonic expansions. The region of the lowest ion-pair dissociation threshold is reached by single-photon excitation from the neutral ground state using narrow-band VUV radiation. The experiments provide access to the ion-pair dissociation energies from which the level structure of the ionic fragments can be determined as well as other thermochemical data such as electron affinities, ionization and dissociation energies.

[a] E. Reinhold and W. Ubachs, Mol. Phys., 103:10, 1329-1352, (2005)
[b] S. Mollet, F. Merkt, Phys. Rev. A., 82, 032510, (2010)
[c] J.D.D. Martin, J.W. Hepburn. Phys. Rev. Lett., 79, 3154, (1997)
[d] R. C. Shiell, X. K. Hu, Q. J. Hu, J. W. Hepburn, J. Phys. Chem., 104, 19 (2000)
[e] Q. J. Hu, Q. Zhang, J.W. Hepburn. J. Chem. Phys., 123, 074310, (2006)

RL14 **10:52 – 10:53**

DETAILED VIEW INTO THE Au_2^+ POTENTIAL ENERGY SURFACES

MARKO FÖRSTEL, KAI POLLOW, TAARNA STUDEMUND, ROBERT G. RADLOFF, *Institut für Optik und Atomare Physik, Technische Universität Berlin, Berlin, Germany*; ROLAND MITRIC, *Institut für Theoretische Chemie, Ludwig-Maximilians Universität Würzburg, Würzburg, Germany*; OTTO DOPFER, *Institut für Optik und Atomare Physik, Technische Universität Berlin, Berlin, Germany.*

Gold is a versatile material with unique properties that underpin its importance in medicine, catalysis, electronics and basic research. The theoretical description of even very small Au clusters remains challenging due to relativistic effects, d electrons participating in the bonding, spin-orbit coupling and charge-transfer effects. Using photodissociation spectroscopy, we have obtained the first optical spectrum of Au_2^+. The quality of the spectrum is high enough to allow a detailed analysis of the ground and excited state surfaces of this important model system.[1,2] The results presented show that standard TD-DFT methods completely fail to describe this seemingly simple, H_2^+ like system. Only with a relativistic multireference treatment including spin-orbit coupling were we able to obtain a qualitative agreement between experimental results and theory.

[1] M. Förstel et al., Angew. Chem. Int. Ed., 2020, 123, 21587-21592.
[2] M. Förstel et al., Rev. Sci. Instrum., 2017, 88, 123110.

RM. Action spectroscopy (incl. PE, PD, PI, LIR)

Thursday, June 24, 2021 – 10:0 AM

Room: 2021 Online Everywhere

Chair: Michael D. Morse, University of Utah, Salt Lake City, UT, USA

RM01 **10:00 – 10:01**

OBSERVATION OF A DIPOLE-BOUND STATE IN THRESHOLD PHOTODETACHMENT SPECTROSCOPY OF THE INTERSTELLAR ANION C_3N^-

MALCOLM JAMES SIMPSON, MARKUS NÖTZOLD, TIM MICHAELSEN, ROBERT WILD, FRANCO A. GIANTURCO, ROLAND WESTER, *Institute for Ion Physics and Applied Physics, University of Innsbruck, Innsbruck, Austria.*

The existence of negative molecular ions in space has been known for over a decade. Despite the determinations of anion abundances within various regions of the interstellar medium, questions remain as to how these weakly bound systems are formed within such harsh environments. The proposed formation mechanism, radiative electron attachment (REA), in which the negative ion is formed through a collision between the neutral parent molecule and a free electron with the emission of a photon is considered too slow to explain observed abundances. REA rates may be augmented however by the electron first transitioning through a dipole-bound state (DBS) close to the threshold for attachment. The C_3N molecule possesses a permanent dipole of magnitude supercritical for the formation of DBS. In this talk, we present the results of threshold photodetachment spectroscopy of C_3N^-. Observed excitation in the detachment cross section below threshold at room temperature is attributed to activation of the two lowest energy bending modes in the trapped ion. This excitation disappears at cryogenic temperatures leading to a very sharp threshold. High resolution scans of the threshold region resolve two features which we assign to the P and R rotational branches of a two-photon detachment process via a DBS with $^1\Sigma^+$ symmetry. Our group recently presented results from threshold photodetachment spectroscopy of CN^- in which the energy dependence of the cross section was explained in terms of a model function [Simpson et al, J. Chem. Phys. **153**, 184309 (2020)]. By adapting this model to C_3N^- and including the resonant interaction, we are able to determine both the rotational origin of the DBS and an improved value for the electron affinity of the C_3N molecule thereby confirming the bound nature of the observed state.

RM02 ***Post-Deadline Abstract*** **10:04 – 10:05**

A GENERAL PATH TO INFRARED SPECTROSCOPY OF SINGLE MOLECULAR IONS

DAVID PATTERSON, *Physics, University of California, Santa Barbara, CA, USA.*

Definitive identification of single molecules is a natural limit of analytic chemistry. While single molecule spectroscopy is routinely performed on select classes of molecules, a general method for identifying individual molecules - including molecules without optical transitions - is beyond the current state of the art. I will present progress from my group towards a general method for realizing infrared spectroscopy, and thus identification, on molecular ions with masses between 20 and 200 amu. While the technique presented today will have modest spectral resolution, I will also present straightforward extensions that will allow for high-resolution spectroscopy of single molecules, and chiral recognition of single molecules.

RM03 10:08 – 10:09

THE ZEEMAN EFFECT IN CO^+ OBSERVED WITH ROTATIONAL ACTION SPECTROSCOPY

ARAVINDH NIVAS MARIMUTHU, KIM STEENBAKKERS, BRITTA REDLICH, SANDRA BRÜNKEN, *FELIX Laboratory, Radboud University, Nijmegen, The Netherlands.*

The fine-structure components of the $N = 0 \rightarrow 1$ and $N = 1 \rightarrow 2$ transitions of CO^+ ($^2\Sigma^+$) have been measured using the action spectroscopic technique ROSAA (Rotational State-dependent Attachment of rare gas Atoms) [1,2] in a cryogenic 22-pole ion trap. The recorded high-resolution spectra show resolved Zeeman splittings caused by the Earth's magnetic field, which are analyzed with an effective Hamiltonian approach. The ROSAA signal intensity of rotational transitions depends intrinsically on a difference in the ternary attachment rate of helium atoms to the molecular ion for the participating rotational fine-structure levels, as well as on experimental parameters such as temperature, excitation power, and helium gas pressure. Numerical simulation results of the underlying kinetics are compared to the observed CO^+ spectra.

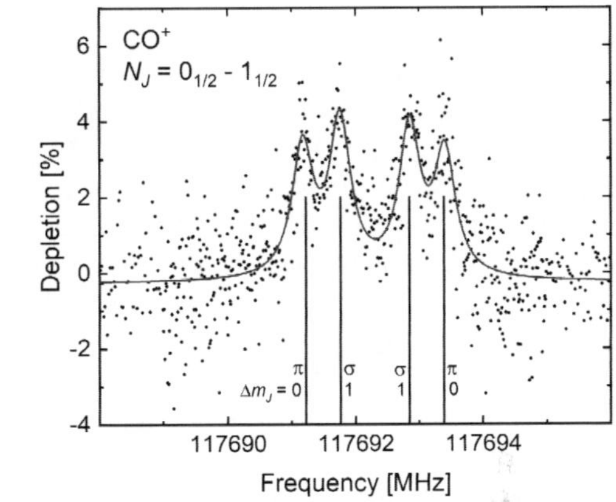

[1] S. Brünken, L. Kluge, A. Stoffels, O. Asvany , S. Schlemmer, Astrophys. J. 783 (2014) L4.
[2] S. Brünken, L. Kluge, A. Stoffels, J. Pérez-ríos, S. Schlemmer, JMS, 332 (2017) 67-78.

RM04 10:12 – 10:13

STRUCTURE AND OPTICAL PROPERTIES OF THE $Si_4C_2^+$ CATION

ROBERT G. RADLOFF, MARKO FÖRSTEL, KAI POLLOW, TAARNA STUDEMUND, OTTO DOPFER, *Institut für Optik und Atomare Physik, Technische Universität Berlin, Berlin, Germany.*

The chemistry of matter surrounding stars depends strongly on the elements that the center star produces during its lifetime but also on the transport of these elements to the outer layers of the star. Stars like IRC+ 10216 transport large amounts of carbon into their outer layers creating a carbon/oxygen ratio >1. Thus not all C is bound into carbon monoxide and a variety of carbonaceous molecules like silicon carbides can form. Small molecules like SiC, SiC_2, SiC_3, SiC_4, Si_2C but also μm-sized silicon carbide dust grains have been observed around these stars, but intermediates remain unknown. In this contribution, we concentrate on $Si_4C_2^+$ as an example for a possible grain seed. We present the first gas phase UV/VIS spectrum of the $Si_4C_2^+$ cation obtained by photodissociation spectroscopy in the range 208–330 nm and compare the experimental results with possible ground state structures and vertical absorption spectra obtained via DFT and TD-DTF calculations.[1]

[1]M. Förstel et al., J. Mol. Spectrosc., 2021, 377, 111427

RM05 **10:16 – 10:17**

PHOTODEPLETION SPECTROSCOPY OF IO^- WITHIN THE ACTINIC RANGE

BENJAMIN McKINNON, SAMUEL MARLTON, BORIS UCUR, *School of Chemistry, University of Wollongong, Wollongong, New South Wales, Australia*; BERWYCK POAD, STEPHEN J. BLANKSBY, *Central Analytical Research Facility, Queensland University of Technology, Brisbane, Queensland, Australia*; EVAN BIESKE, *School of Chemistry, The University of Melbourne, Melbourne, Victoria, Australia*; ADAM J. TREVITT, *School of Chemistry, University of Wollongong, Wollongong, New South Wales, Australia.*

Iodine oxides (I_xO_y) are atmospherically important due to their high reactivity with ozone. The I^- anion has been detected in the atmosphere, along with $IO_2{}^-$ and $IO_3{}^-$ however, IO^- is yet to be directly detected despite being a key intermediate to their formation.[a] A recent gas phase study[b] confirms I^- will react with ozone to form IO^- with subsequent step-wise ozone reactions to form $IO_2{}^-$ then $IO_3{}^-$. The aim of the present study is to investigate the photodepletion of IO^- within the visible range of 650 - 450 nm (15385 - 22222 cm^{-1}) *via* photodetachment and photodissociation spectroscopy. Gas phase spectra are obtained at room temperature by coupling a tuneable OPO laser with a linear ion-trap mass spectrometer. A bound excited state is present in this visible range, which will either undergo autodetachment *via* electron loss ($IO^\bullet$ + e^-) or undergo photodissociation (I^- + $O(^3P)$). Depending on the vibrational energy level of the excited state, either photodissociation or photodetachment is favoured. Investigation of the potential energy surface using the multireference configuration interaction (MRCI) method shows that within the investigated energy range IO^- will excite from the $X^1\Sigma^+$ ground state and populate the $1^1\Pi$ excited state and, in the Franck-Condon region, this is close to the curve crossing that mediates the photodissociation and close to the electron affinity for electron detachment. From this study IO^- has been shown to photodeplete at visible wavelengths and, with previous studies showing that IO^- will react with ozone to form higher order iodine oxides, may together contribute to the low abundance of IO^- in the atmosphere and therefore why it has eluded detection.

[a]Frege C. et al., Atmospheric Chemistry and Physics, 2017 / Koenig T. K. et al., Proceedings of the National Academy of Sciences, 2020 / He X.-C. et al., Science, 2021
[b]Bhujel M. et al., Physical Chemistry and Chemical Physics, 2020

RM06 **10:20 – 10:21**

HIGH-RESOLUTION PHOTODISSOCIATION SPECTROSCOPY OF N_2O^+

ANTHONY ROUCOU, XAVIER URBAIN, CLÉMENT LAUZIN, *Institue of Condensed Matter and Nanosciences (IMCN), Université catholique de Louvain, Louvain-la-Neuve, Belgium.*

The nitrous oxide cation (N_2O^+) is an important intermediate in the upper atmosphere[a]. The photodissociation spectra of N_2O^+ have been measured in the UV range using the new STARGATE instrument (Spectroscopy of Transient Anions and Radicals by Gated and Accelerated Time-of-flight Experiment) developped in UCLouvain.

This talk will present the rovibronic analysis of the $\tilde{A}^2\Sigma^+(002) \leftarrow \tilde{X}^2\Pi(000)$, $\tilde{A}^2\Sigma^+(101) \leftarrow \tilde{X}^2\Pi(000)$ and $\tilde{A}^2\Sigma^+(003) \leftarrow \tilde{X}^2\Pi(000)$ bands measured at 550 K in the 30500-32500 cm^{-1} range. A global vibronic fit has been performed including these bands, Q-branch head of overtones, combination bands and data from other studies[bc]. The Renner-Teller effect involving the $\tilde{X}^2\Pi$ and $\tilde{A}^2\Sigma^+$ states is taken into account in the global fit procedure. The improvement of the description of the vibronic energy level will be discussed.

[a]G. Chambaud, H. Gritli, P. Rosmus, H. J. Werner, and P. J. Knowles, Mol. Phys. 98, 1793 (2000)
[b]M. Gharaibeh and D. Clouthier, J. Chem. Phys. 136, 044318 (2012).
[c]C. E. Fellows and M. Vervloet, Chem. Phys. 264, 203 (2001).

RM07 **10:24 – 10:25**

ROVIBRATIONAL SPECTROSCOPY OF THE CH^+-He AND CH^+-He_4 COMPLEXES

THOMAS SALOMON, *I. Physikalisches Institut, Universität zu Köln, Köln, Germany*; JOSÉ LUIS DOMÉNECH, *Molecular Physics, Instituto de Estructura de la Materia (IEM-CSIC), Madrid, Spain*; PHILIPP C SCHMID, *I. Physikalisches Institut, Universität zu Köln, Köln, Germany*; ERNEST A MICHAEL, *Department of Electrical Engineering, University of Chile, Santiago, Chile*; STEPHAN SCHLEMMER, OSKAR ASVANY, *I. Physikalisches Institut, Universität zu Köln, Köln, Germany.*

A cryogenic 22-pole ion trap apparatus is used in combination with a table-top pulsed IR source to probe weakly bound CH^+-He and CH^+-He_4 complexes by predissociation spectroscopy at 4 K. The infrared photodissociation spectra of the C–H stretching vibrations are recorded in the range of 2720–2800 cm^{-1}. The spectrum of CH^+-He exhibits perpendicular transitions of a near prolate top with a band origin at 2745.9 cm^{-1}, and thus confirms it to have a T-shaped structure. For CH^+-He_4, the C-H stretch along the symmetry axis of this oblate top results in parallel transitions.

RM08 **10:28 – 10:29**

INFRARED SPECTROSCOPY OF THE $Co^+(H_2O)$ COMPLEX WITH He, Ne, AND Ar TAGGING.

JOSHUA H MARKS, *Department of Chemistry, University of Georgia, Athens, GA, USA*; EVANGELOS MIL-IORDOS, *Chemistry and Biochemistry, Auburn University, Auburn, AL, USA*; MICHAEL A DUNCAN, *Department of Chemistry, University of Georgia, Athens, GA, USA.*

Cobalt cation-water complexes are generated in a pulsed supersonic expansion by laser vaporization. Complexes are mass-selected in a time-of-flight mass spectrometer and their spectra are measured using infrared laser photodissociation of the rare gas tagged complexes. The spectrum of $Co^+(H_2O)$ was measured with He, Ne, and Ar_3 tags. These spectra reveal that the water remains intact in the metal cation-water complex. The Ar_3 tag is found to cause a small blue shift of the O-H stretches relative to that observed with helium tagging. Rotational structure observed for $Co^+(H_2O)$ and $Co^+(D_2O)$ with helium tagging reveal perturbations to the rotational constants introduced by the motion of the helium in the ground vibrational state. Nuclear spin statistics were found to maintain a room temperature population of states which indicates an antisymmetric ground electronic state. Spin-rotation coupling was observed to vary between isotopologues and differed from values obtained in untagged measurements.

RM09 **10:32 – 10:33**

AN ION MOBILITY MASS SPECTROMETRY CRYOGENIC ION TRAP INSTRUMENT COUPLED TO THE FRITZ HABER INSTITUTE INFRARED FREE ELECTRON LASER

MAIKE LETTOW, EIKE MUCHA, JAN HORLEBEIN, GERARD MEIJER, GERT VON HELDEN, *Department of Molecular Physics, Fritz-Haber-Institut der Max-Planck-Gesellschaft, Berlin, Germany.*

The coupling of ion mobility with mass spectrometry (IM-MS) allows for the selection of isolated, gas-phase molecular ions with defined mass/charge as well as geometrical size/charge ratios. When coupled to cryogenic ion traps, those molecular ions can be tagged with atoms or molecules to allow for action spectroscopy of very well defined cold species, and several instruments to do so have been developed in laboratories worldwide. We recently upgraded our drift tube IM-MS instrument that is coupled to the Fritz Haber Institute FEL to perform IR multiple photon dissociation spectroscopy with a cryogenic ion trap to allow for messenger atom/molecule action spectroscopy. The cryogenic ion trap itself implements a novel concept by having a segmented trap consisting of a high and a low pressure region. Ions can be injected cw or at a high repetition rate into the high pressure region, portions of the ions can then be transferred at a variable rate to the low pressure region from which they are ejected to the laser interaction region at a rate, matched to the laser repetition rate and independent from the injection rate into the trap. First results on the IR spectroscopy of biological molecules will be presented.

RM10 **10:36 – 10:37**

CIVP SPECTROSCOPY OF PYRIDINIUM IONS: SURPRISING PERTURBATION BY TAG MOLECULES

ALEXANDRA TSYBIZOVA, ENO PAENURK, VLADIMIR GORBACHEV, PETER CHEN, *Department of Chemistry and Applied Biosciences, ETH Zurich, Zurich, Switzerland.*

In cryogenic ion vibrational predissociation (CIVP) spectroscopy, the tag's influence on the spectrum is an important consideration. Whereas for small ions, several studies show that the tag effects can be significant, these effects are less understood for large ions, or for large numbers of tags. Nevertheless, common assumptions are that i) if the investigated molecular ion is large enough, the perturbations arising from the tag are small, and ii) the more weakly bound the tag is, the less it perturbs the CIVP spectrum. Under these assumptions, CIVP spectra effectively represent infrared (IR) absorption spectra of the free molecular ion.
In the Chen group, we have recently started studying IR spectra of large ions in the gas phase.[1] To understand the complicated IR fingerprints of those systems, we employ several theoretical methods. Density functional theory is a common tool for calculating IR spectra. An alternative approach is to calculate the IR spectrum by the Fourier transform of the dipole moment autocorrelation function from a classical trajectory,[2] e.g., from Born-Oppenheimer molecular dynamics (BOMD). In contrast to the harmonic approximation, BOMD includes vibrational couplings and conformational sampling at a given temperature. Having observed unexpected splittings in otherwise unproblematic CIVP spectra of some tagged ions, we calculated IR spectra by BOMD simulations with the semi-empirical GFN-xTB methods.[3,4] Our simulations indicate that mobility among the more weakly bound tags leads to the surprise splittings. We compared the behavior of two tags commonly used in CIVP spectroscopy (H_2 and N_2) with a large pyridinium cation. Our experimental results surprisingly show that the more weakly bound tag can, under the appropriate circumstances, perturb the CIVP spectra more than the more strongly bound tag, by not just shifting, but also splitting the observed bands.

References:

[1] A. Tsybizova, L. Fritsche, V. Gorbachev, L. Miloglyadova, and P. Chen, J. Chem. Phys. 151, 234304 (2019).
[2] D.W. Noid, M.L. Koszykowski, and R.A. Marcus, The Journal of Chemical Physics 67, 404 (1977).
[3] S. Grimme, C. Bannwarth, and P. Shushkov, J. Chem. Theory Comput. 13, 1989 (2017).
[4] C. Bannwarth, S. Ehlert, and S. Grimme, J. Chem. Theory Comput. 15, 1652 (2019).

RM11 **10:40 – 10:41**

OPTICAL SPECTRUM OF THE ADAMANTANE RADICAL CATION

PARKER B. CRANDALL, DAVID MÜLLER, MARKO FÖRSTEL, OTTO DOPFER, *Institut für Optik und Atomare Physik, Technische Universität Berlin, Berlin, Germany.*

Known for their stable structural and thermal properties, diamondoids and their radical cations are viable candidates as carriers for diffuse interstellar bands.[1] While previous diamondoid research has mainly focused on neutral molecules and their derivatives, little is known about their radical cations, which may form in interstellar environments by ionizing radiation.[2] We report the first experimental optical spectrum of the simplest diamondoid cation, the adamantane radical cation ($C_{10}H_{16}{}^{+}$), obtained via electronic photodissociation spectroscopy at 5 K between 310–1000 nm. The optical spectrum reveals a broad peak between 420–850 nm, assigned to the $D_2(^2E) \leftarrow D_0(^2A_1)$ transition. This feature exhibits no vibrational structure, despite an experimental temperature below 20 K, due to lifetime broadening and/or Franck-Condon congestion. A second band system originating at 345 nm does reveal a vibrational progression and is attributed to the overlapping $D_5(^2A_1)/D_6(^2E) \leftarrow D_0(^2A_1)$ transitions split by the Jahn-Teller effect. Comparison of the spectrum with known diffuse interstellar bands suggests that $C_{10}H_{16}{}^{+}$ is not likely to be a carrier. However, the strong absorption features in the UV to near IR show promise in the investigation of higher order diamondoid cations as potential candidates.[3]

[1] T. Henning and F. Salama 1998, Science, 282, 2204. [2] C. W. Bauschlicher Jr., Y. Liu, A. Ricca, A. L. Mattioda, L. J. Allamandola, 2007, ApJ, 671, 458. [3] P. B. Crandall, D. Müller, M. Förstel, J. Leroux, O. Dopfer, 2020, ApJL, 900, L20.

RM12 **10:44 – 10:45**

DETERMINATION OF SPECTROSCOPICALLY-STRUCTURAL CONNECTION IN THE PYRIDINIUM SERIES TO PROBE LONDON DISPERSION FORCES

VLADIMIR GORBACHEV, ALEXANDRA TSYBIZOVA, LARISA MILOGLYADOVA, PETER CHEN, *Department of Chemistry and Applied Biosciences, ETH Zurich, Zurich, Switzerland.*

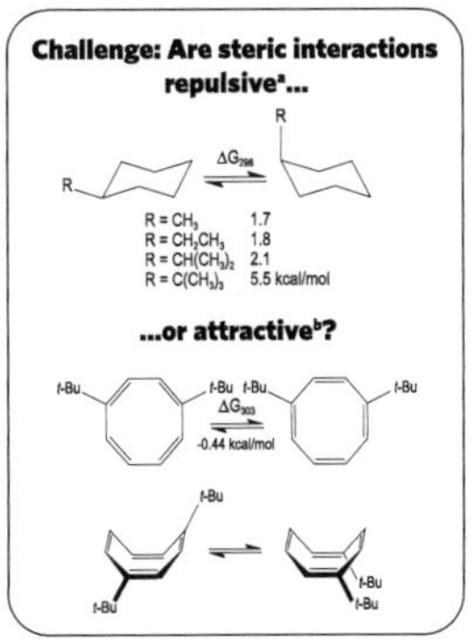

London dispersion, the attractive part of the van der Waals potential, is an omnipresent force in molecules. However, even a cursory glance at presumably driven by the London dispersion two systems from references[a,b] gives curiously conflicting answers, raising a legitimate question: are steric interactions repulsive or attractive?
To address this issue a new molecular torsion balance was proposed.[c] Obtained systematic CIVP-spectroscopic pattern – structural connection in the series of large molecules, *o,o*-disubstituted pyridiniums, could be used as an effective tool to explore London dispersion experimentally. Analysis of the conformer spaces: energies, frequencies, geometries as well as an extensive data set: X-ray and solid-state FT-IR data unambiguously link the gas-phase fingerprint with well-determined structures for all test-compounds in the series. Even among homologues, London dispersion significantly affects the resulting geometry starting from a change in the pendant substituents' relative position with respect to each other and ending with a total change of conformation. Remarkably, for the pyridinium featuring the highest DED-properties in the series, dispersion corrected methods appear to overestimate the magnitude of London dispersion forces, which leads to the principal improper assignment of the conformer in contradiction to the experimental data.

[a]Muller, P. *Pure and Applied Chemistry.* **1994**, *66*, 1077.
[b]Lyttle, M. H.; Streitweiser, A. Jr.; Kluttzt, R. Q. *J. Am. Chem. Soc.* **1981**, *103*, 3232.
[c]Tsybizova‡, A.; Fritsche‡, L.; Gorbachev‡, V.; Miloglyadova. L.; Chen, P. *J. Chem. Phys.* **2019**, *151*, 234304.

RM13 **10:48 – 10:49**

TEMPERATURE DEPENDENCE IN RELATIVE POPULATIONS BETWEEN ISOMERS HAVING DISTINCT HYDROGEN BOND STRUCTURES OF PHENOL-METHANOL CLUSTER CATIONS

MASATAKA ORITO, MASAYOSHI OZEKI, HARUKI ISHIKAWA, *Department of Chemistry, School of Science, Kitasato University, Sagamihara, Japan.*

Gas-phase hydrogen-bonded clusters are treated as microscopic models of hydrogen bond networks. We have been investigating the temperature effect on microscopic hydrogen bond structures. In our previous study, we measured ultraviolet photodissociation (UVPD) spectra of hydrated phenol cations $[PhOH(H_2O)_5]^+$ trapped in our temperature-variable ion trap. We revealed temperature dependence of relative populations between two isomers having distinct hydrogen bond structures.[a] It is known that water and methanol molecules construct different hydrogen bond networks. Thus, we measured UVPD spectra of phenol-methanol cluster cations $[PhOH(MeOH)_n]^+$ $(n = 3, 4)$ in the present study. As in the case of $[PhOH(H_2O)_5]^+$, isomers having ring type hydrogen bond structures are dominant in cold condition for both $n = 3$ and 4 cases. As the temperature elevates, populations of the chain type isomers become large in the case of the $n = 3$. Both bands for the ring and chain type isomers exhibit red shifts of the band positions and broadening of the band widths along the temperature elevation were observed. These changes were attributed mainly by hot bands of the intermolecular vibrational modes. In contrast, only the bands assigned as the ring isomers were observed with the temperature below 150 K. However, changes in the band profiles indicate structural changes within a ring type hydrogen bond motif.

[a]H. Ishikawa, I. Kurusu, R. Yagi, R. Kato, Y. Kasahara, *J. Phys. Chem. Lett.* **8**, 2641 (2017).

RM14 **10:52 – 10:53**

DIRECT OBSERVATION OF IR INDUCED ISOMERIZATIONS OF HYDROGEN-BONDED PHENOL CLUSTER CATIONS

MASAYOSHI OZEKI, MASATAKA ORITO, KENTA MIZUSE, HARUKI ISHIKAWA, *Department of Chemistry, School of Science, Kitasato University, Sagamihara, Japan.*

Since gas-phase hydrogen-bonded clusters are treated as microscopic models of hydrogen bond networks, numerous spectroscopic studies have been performed, so far. Structural fluctuations are one of features of hydrogen bond network. Such fluctuations correspond to isomerizations among isomers having distinct hydrogen bond structures in the cases of clusters. To investigate microscopic natures of structural fluctuations of hydrogen bond networks, we observed IR-induced isomerizations of hydrogen-bonded phenol cluster cations trapped in a cold ion trap. In a cold condition, all hydrogen-bonded phenol-methanol cluster cations $[PhOH(MeOH)_3]^+$ have a ring type hydrogen bond structures. In contrast, isomers having a chain type hydrogen bond structure are dominant in a hot condition. In the present experiment, we excited the ring isomers in a cold condition by IR laser pulses. Since the energy of IR laser photon exceeded the height of isomerization barriers, isomerizations from the ring to chain isomers occurred. We successfully detected the chain type isomers in ultraviolet photodissociation spectra. Additionally, we also observed reverse isomerizations from the chain back to the ring isomers by the collisional cooling with the buffer gas. Details of the observations are presented in the paper.

RM15 ***Post-Deadline Abstract*** **10:56 – 10:57**

HIGH RESOLUTION ANION PHOTOELECTRON SPECTRA OF NDO^-

MARK C BABIN, *Department of Chemistry, University of California - Berkeley, Berkeley, CA, USA*; MARTIN DeWITT, *Chemistry, University of California, Berkeley, Berkeley, CA, USA*; JESSALYN A. DeVINE, *Department of Chemistry, The University of California, Berkeley, CA, USA*; DAVID C McDONALD, *RVBXB/Plasma Chemistry Lab, Air Force Research Lab, Albuquerque, NM, USA*; NICHOLAS S. SHUMAN, ALBERT VIGGIANO, *Space Vehicles Directorate, Air Force Research Lab, Kirtland AFB, NM, USA*; LAN CHENG, *Department of Chemistry, Johns Hopkins University, Baltimore, MD, USA*; DANIEL NEUMARK, *Department of Chemistry, The University of California, Berkeley, CA, USA.*

High-resolution anion photoelectron spectra of cryogenically cooled NdO^- obtained using slow photoelectron velocity-map imaging (cryo-SEVI) are presented, providing insight into the vibronic structure of the corresponding neutral metal oxide.

FA. Mini-symposium: Spectroscopy with Undergraduates

Friday, June 25, 2021 – 8:0 AM

Room: 2021 Online Everywhere

Chair: AnGayle (AJ) Vasiliou, Middlebury College , Middlebury , VT, USA

FA01 *INVITED TALK* **8:00 – 8:02**

RESEARCH WITH UNDERGRADUATES: SPECTROSCOPY IS JUST THE BEGINNING

LAURA R. McCUNN, *Department of Chemistry, Marshall University, Huntington, WV, USA.*

Undergraduate research is considered the best pedagogical practice for engaging chemistry students in their curriculum and encouraging independent problem-solving. This presentation will explore many aspects of the undergraduate research experience in chemistry, beginning with the author's efforts in constructing instruments and conducting matrix-isolation FTIR experiments with undergraduate students. To expand the impact to more students and increase their exposure to modern physical chemistry research, journal club sessions have been brought to the classroom. Finally, a faculty-created, comprehensive summer research program and large group trips to national meetings have helped chemistry majors understand how their independent research advances not only the field of chemistry but also their professional development.

FA02 **8:08 – 8:09**

OBSERVATION OF THE C_6H_7 RADICAL IN AN ARGON MATRIX USING MATRIX ISOLATION INFRARED SPECTROSCOPY

JAY C. AMICANGELO, LIA TOTLEBEN, JACOB OSLOSKY, YEN JUI SU, NICOLE ORWAT, *School of Science (Chemistry), Penn State Erie, Erie, PA, USA.*

The cyclohexadienyl radical (C_6H_7) was observed in a low temperature argon matrix with matrix isolation infrared spectroscopy. The C_6H_7 radical was produced from the reaction of H atoms with benzene (C_6H_6) in the argon matrices. The H atoms were produced by either vacuum ultraviolet (VUV) photolysis or direct microwave discharge of H_2S in argon and co-deposited with C_6H_6 in the argon matrices. The most intense peak of the C_6H_7 radical was observed at 621.0 cm^{-1}, with several other weaker peaks observed at 512.0, 865.9, 910.9, 961.2, 973.7, 1290.3, 1390.2, 1394.9, 1425.9, 2758.7, and 2781.3 cm^{-1}. The yield of the C_6H_7 radical was found be approximately 40 percent larger for the direct microwave discharge experiments as compared to the VUV photolysis experiments. The identification and assignment of the C_6H_7 radical peaks was accomplished by comparisons to co-deposition spectra without VUV photolysis or direct discharge, the H_2S and C_6H_6 monomer spectra with and without VUV photolysis/direct discharge, filtered (400 - 900 nm) and unfiltered Hg-Xe lamp photolysis, and 35 K annealing. Experiments were also performed in which H atoms were reacted with C_6D_6 producing the C_6D_6H radical, with peaks observed at 460.0, 747.8, 830.0, 1237.5, 1245.5, 1246.7, and 2792.0/2796.8 cm^{-1}. Quantum chemistry calculations for the C_6H_7 radical were performed at the DFT and MP2 levels of theory with the aug-cc-PVTZ basis set to obtain the theoretical infrared spectrum to support the assignments. The peaks of the C_6H_7 radical observed in argon matrices are in good agreement with the values reported in xenon matrices[a] and *para*-hydrogen matrices[b].

[a] V. I. Feldman, F. F. Sukhov, E. A. Logacheva, A. Y. Orlov, I. V. Tyulpina, and D. A. Tyurin, Chem. Phys. Lett. 437, 207 (2007)

[b] M. Bahou, Y. J. Wu, and Y. P. Lee, J. Chem. Phys. 136, 154304 (2012)

FA03 **8:12 – 8:13**

HELIUM NANODROPLETS AND LIQUID HOT NAGMA: WHAT STUDENTS CAN LEARN ABOUT THERMODYNAMICS FROM INFRARED SPECTROSCOPY AND A MODEL DIPEPTIDE

ALAINA R. GUNN, *Natural Sciences and Engineering, University of South Carolina Upstate, Spartanburg, SC, USA.*

Students taking physical chemistry often find the thermodynamics section of the course confusing and even downright uninteresting. In part, this is due to the abstract nature of concepts, such as entropy and enthalpy, as well as the math skills that are required and/or the transference of skills that students already possess.

An activity was created and implemented for use in an undergraduate physical chemistry course to guide students through an application of thermodynamics through the lens of spectroscopy. The activity combines current spectroscopic research techniques[a] together with concepts covered in class to give students a complete picture of this topic. In this talk, the activity and its implementation will be discussed along with preliminary outcomes.

[a] Leavitt, C. M.; Moore, K. B.; Raston, P. L.; Agarwal, J.; Moody, G. H.; Shirley, C. C.; Schaefer, H. F.; Douberly, G. E. Liquid Hot NAGMA Cooled to 0.4 K: Benchmark Thermochemistry of a Gas-Phase Peptide. J. Phys. Chem. A 2014, 118 (41), 9692–9700.

FA04 **8:16 – 8:17**

WEAK HYDROGEN BONDING IN COMPLEXES OF SELENOPHENE AND WATER: A MATRIX ISOLATION FTIR AND COMPUTATIONAL STUDY

JOSH NEWBY, *Chemistry, Nazareth College, Rochester, NY, USA*; TIARA SIVELLS, *Department of Chemistry , Hobart and William Smith Colleges, Geneva, NY, USA.*

Weakly-bound complexes containing aromatic species have been the subject of study for many years. Here, a study of the weakly-bound complexes of selenophene (C_4H_4Se) with water will be presented. In this study, matrix isolation FTIR and computational methods were used to examine stable 1:1 complexes of selenophene : water (Sp:H_2O). Multiple density functional theories along with MP2 calculations were used to find a total of seven stable geometries which could be sorted into four categories defined by the intermolecular forces observed in the complex. The interactions include O−H···Se, O−H···π, and C−H···O. The Sp:H_2O geometries were found to be within 16 kJ/mol of each other across all computational methods. All calculated structures were similar to those found for complexes of furan : water and thiophene: water. Matrix isolation FTIR experiments identified several peaks that were not associated with isolated water or selenophene, implying the bands are due to weakly-bound complexes of the two monomers. In addition to normal water, D_2O and HDO complexes with selenophene were also observed. Possible interpretations of the experimental and computational results will be presented.

FA05 **8:20 – 8:21**

HELIUM NANODROPLET ISOLATION SPECTROSCOPY IN AN UNDERGRADUATE TEACHING LABORATORY

PAUL RASTON, *Department of Chemistry and Biochemistry, James Madison University, Harrisonburg, VA, USA.*

A home-built helium nanodroplet isolation spectrometer has been utilized by undergraduate students in course-based experiments to investigate the rovibrational dynamics of small molecules. Helium nanodroplets are well known to simplify the spectroscopy of embedded molecules owing to their low temperature (0.4 K) and weakly interacting nature. In the infrared spectral region, this results in a small number of rotationally resolved lines that can often be collected and analyzed in several lab periods. We demonstrate the advantages of using this technique in an upper-level undergraduate chemistry course for which the laser spectroscopy of helium solvated ^{13}C-labelled formic acid was investigated for the first time.

FA06 **8:24 – 8:25**

COMPOSITIONAL ANALYSIS OF TITAN'S ATMOSPHERE USING SPITZER INFRARED SPECTROGRAPH DATA

BRANDON PARK COY, CONOR A NIXON, *Planetary Systems Laboratory, NASA Goddard Space Flight Center, Baltimore, MD, USA*; NAOMI ROWE-GURNEY, *Department of Physics and Astronomy, University of Leicester, Leicester, United Kingdom.*

Saturn's moon Titan exhibits the most complex and diverse atmospheric chemistry of any body in the solar system other than the Earth. Photochemistry in the upper atmosphere starts with methane and nitrogen and produces a rich array of hydrocarbons and nitriles, and also some oxygen compounds due to an external oxygen source from Enceladus. Since the 1970s, infrared spectroscopy has been the primarily mechanism for probing the composition of the neutral atmosphere, using ground-based telescopes, visiting spacecraft such as Voyager and Cassini, and space-based observatories including the Infrared Space Observatory (ISO) and Herschel. We present for first time infrared spectra from the Spitzer space telescope (2004-2009) in both the short wavelength-low resolution channels (SL, $R \sim 60 - 127$, 5.13 to 14.29 microns) and short wavelength-high resolution channels (SH, $R \sim 600$, 9.89 to 19.51 microns) showing the emissions of CH4, C2H4, C2H2, C2H6, HCN, CO2, HC3N, C3H4 and C4H2. We compare the results obtained for Titan from Spitzer to those of ISO, Herschel and Cassini CIRS, and comment on the effect of spectral resolution on retrieved information content. We conclude by recommending gaps in current spectroscopic knowledge of molecular bands that could be addressed by theoretical and laboratory study to aid future astronomical studies of Titan.

FA07 **8:28 – 8:29**

A BROADBAND ROTATIONAL SPECTROSCOPIC STUDY OF DIETHYL PHTHALATE

RAIDEN SPEELMAN, ARSH SINGH HAZRAH, *Department of Chemistry, University of Alberta, Edmonton, AB, Canada*; NATHAN A. SEIFERT, *Chemical Sciences and Engineering Division, Argonne National Laboratory, Lemont, IL, USA*; WOLFGANG JÄGER, *Department of Chemistry, University of Alberta, Edmonton, AB, Canada.*

Diethyl phthalate (DEPh), a diethyl ester of phthalic acid, is commonly used as a plasticizer in products such as plastic packaging films, toiletries, and plastic bags.[1] The two ester groups can rotate about the respective single C – C bonds, making the conformational landscape of DEPh quite complex, and further investigation may improve our knowledge about the conformational landscape and dynamics of DEPh. Additionally, the close proximity of the two substituent groups and the resulting non-covalent interactions that will occur between them will ultimately dictate the monomeric structure. A thorough experimental investigation and assignment of the DEPh conformers may not only provide valuable insights into non-covalent intramolecular interactions, but also valuable conformational benchmark data for theory. We use rotational, microwave, spectroscopy to experimentally probe the conformational diversity of DEPh, as it has been shown before to be an excellent tool to investigate conformationally flexible molecules.[2] A broadband rotational spectrum was recorded in the 2-6 GHz region using a chirped pulse Fourier transform microwave spectrometer (CP-FTMW). With the help of the Conformer-Rotamer Ensemble Sampling Tool (CREST)[3] and DFT calculations, we identified 16 unique theoretical conformers. Using these results as an assignment aid, a total of 7 conformers were identified in our rotational spectrum. Non-covalent interactions (NCI)[4] analyses were carried out to examine the intermolecular interactions present within the DEPh conformers.

1. J. Sekizawa, S. Dobson, R. J. Touch III, DIETHYL PHTHALATE, CICAD. 2003;2. F. Xie, N. A. Seifert, M. Heger, J. Thomas, W. Jäger, Y. Xu, Phys. Chem. Chem. Phys. 2019. 21, 15408-16.; 3. P. Pracht, F. Bohle, S. Grimme, Phys. Chem. Chem. Phys. 2020., 22, 7169-7192; 4. E. Johnson, S. Keinan, P. Mori-Sánchez and J. Contreras-García, J. Am. Chem. Soc., 2010, 2010, 132.;

FA08 **8:32 – 8:33**

FABRICATION AND CHARACTERIZATION OF HIGHLY EFFICIENT DYE-SENSITIZED SOLAR CELL WITH COMPOSITED DYES

GARRIS H.C. RADLOFF, FEVEN M NABA, *Chemistry, Earlham College, Richmond, IN, USA*; DOROTHY B OCRAN-SARSAH, MAKENZIE E BENNETT, KATHRYN M STERZINGER, *Biochemistry, Earlham College, Richmond, IN, USA*; ABIGAIL T ARMSTRONG, *Chemistry, Earlham College, Richmond, IN, USA*; NAHOM ZEWDE, *Biochemistry, Earlham College, Richmond, IN, USA*; CAMERON GRAY, *Physics, Earlham College, Richmond, IN, USA*; MAHESH B. DAWADI, *Chemistry, Earlham College, Richmond, IN, USA.*

As a representative of the next-generation solar cells, dye-sensitized solar cells (DSSCs) offer the efficient and ease of implementation of new technology for future energy supply. Herein, four commercially available dyes including, curcumin, betanin, crystal violet, methylene blue, their compositions, and two naturally extracted dyes were used as sensitizers for fabrication of titanium oxide photo-anode based DSSCs. All dyes were fully characterized using absorption and emission spectroscopy. Both DFT and TDDFT studies were also carried out to probe the electronic structure of these dyes. The power conversion efficiencies of each DSSCs prepared using the individual and composited dyes were measured and compared. Particularly, this is the first study to combine four different dyes for DSSCs, leading to a remarkable increase of power conversion efficiency. The DSSCs with combined curcumin, betanin, crystal violet, and methylene blue (in 1:1:1:1 respectively) in ethanol exhibited the highest power conversion efficiency of 3.62%.

FA09 **8:36 – 8:37**

EFFICIENT COMPRESSION OF MOLECULAR LINE LISTS: APPLICATION OF 'SUPER-ENERGIES' TO THE EXOMOL DATABASE

XUDONG KE LIN, SAMUEL WRIGHT, ALEC OWENS, JONATHAN TENNYSON, SERGEI N. YURCHENKO, *Department of Physics and Astronomy, University College London, London, UK.*

A new compression algorithm for the efficient storage of molecular line lists has been recently presented[a]. The algorithm is based on the effective 'super-energies' developed to produce a compact HITEMP line list for methane. This method assumes a set of artificial lower state (super-)energies and corresponding reference intensities for an approximate description of the temperature dependent molecular absorption (absorption coefficient) on a grid of wavenumbers. The super-energies compression is applied only to the majority ($> 99\%$) of the lines representing the weaker, continuum part of the molecular absorption, while the strongest lines ($< 1\%$) are preserved in the original form to maintain the accuracy of the line list.

Here we adopt and develop the HITEMP compression algorithm to be applicable to the ExoMol data format and generate new compressed line lists for SiO_2,[b] H_2O,[c] KOH and NaOH.[d] We find that using artificial Einstein A coefficients instead of reference intensities provides a more accurate description of the temperature dependence. A typical compression of a line list consisting of, e.g., 40 billions SiO_2 lines is to about 40 million data points. Advantages and limitations of the 'super-energies' approach will be discussed. The compressed molecular line lists will be included in the ExoMol database (WWW.EXOMOL.COM) and their use should greatly facilitate atmospheric retrievals in exoplanets and other hot astronomical bodies.

[a] R. J. Hargreaves, I. E. Gordon, M. Rey, A. V. Nikitin, V. G. Tyuterev, R. V. Kochanov, L. S. Rothman, *Astrophys. J. Suppl.*, 2020, **247**, 55.
[b] A. Owens, E. K. Conway, J. Tennyson, S. N. Yurchenko, *Mon. Not. R. Astron. Soc.*, 2020, **495**, 1927–1933.
[c] O. L. Polyansky, A. A. Kyuberis, N. F. Zobov, J. Tennyson, S. N. Yurchenko, L. Lodi, *Mon. Not. R. Astron. Soc.*, 2018, **480**, 2597–2608.
[d] A. Owens, J. Tennyson, S. N. Yurchenko, *Mon. Not. R. Astron. Soc.*, 2021, **502**, 1128–1135.

FA10 **8:40 – 8:41**

INVOLVING HIGH-SCHOOL STUDENTS IN COMPUTATIONAL CHEMISTRY MOLECULAR DATA GENERATION FOR EXOPLANET SPECTROSCOPY

LAURA K McKEMMISH, ANNA-MAREE SYME, *School of Chemistry, University of New South Wales, Sydney, NSW, Australia*; CLARA SOUSA-SILVA, , *Harvard-Smithsonian Center for Astrophysics, Cambridge, MA, USA.*

"I get to help find aliens" - what better motivation for high school students getting into research for the first time! The identification of molecular biosignatures on exoplanets is a powerful example of the diverse role of spectroscopy in science that strongly motivates student interest and understanding of the fundamental principles of spectroscopy and its applications.

Though of course, the scientific journey to actually finding exoplanet molecules, particularly biosignatures, is long and far beyond the scope of current high school or undergraduate student projects, we can involve students in this journey. In my research, I focus on molecular spectroscopic data production computationally. In this presentation, I briefly describe how I involve students in this research project and identify good practice recommendations and common challenges. I focus on two programs involving high-school students in scientific research, the first as collaborators and publication co-authors (ORBYTS, UK, twinkle-spacemission.co.uk/orbyts/) and the second as independent researchers (SciX@UNSW, Australia, http://unsw.to/scix). I will also discuss how this research area can be used to motivate deep outreach engagement (Depth Studies, UNSW, Australia) and as the venue for small publishable undergraduate projects.

FA11 **8:44 – 8:45**

EPR SPECTROSCOPY OF RUBY IN THE UNDERGRADUATE PHYSICAL CHEMISTRY TEACHING LABORATORY

BRYAN LYNCH, *Department of Chemistry, University of Evansville, Evansville, IN, USA.*

We describe an exercise for the undergraduate teaching lab that uses EPR spectroscopy to determine the g and D values for the chromium(III) ion in a ruby ball lens. Students use a polarized light stereomicroscope to identify the ruby c-axis; once found, ruby orientation is locked in place with a teflon screw at the end of a teflon post. The post can then be rotated in the magnetic field of an X-band EPR spectrometer using an inexpensive rotation platform. Spectra are obtained from 0 to 90 degrees in 5 degree increments; the result is a huge amount of data, which is more easily handled using Igor Pro software.[1] Resonance field positions are found and plotted as a function of angle, and the values of g and D are determined from the 0° spectrum.[2] Using their experimental g and D values, students diagonalize the spin Hamiltonian using a procedure written in Igor Pro. Calculated resonance field positions at each angle can then be compared with experimental results.

1. WaveMetrics, Inc. 10200 SW Nimbus, G-7 Portland , OR 97223
2. L.A. Collins, M.A. Morrison, P.L. Donoho Am. J. Phys., 42 (1974) 560-571.

FA12 **8:48 – 8:49**

GUIDED-INQUIRY SPECTROSCOPIC PROJECTS IN THE PHYSICAL CHEMISTRY LAB

STEVEN SHIPMAN, *Department of Chemistry, New College of Florida, Sarasota, FL, USA.*

Based on discussions and suggestions received during the "Spectroscopy in the Classroom" 2015 ISMS mini-symposium, I have implemented guided-inquiry based spectroscopic projects in the upper-level undergraduate physical chemistry lab course. In this course, the first half of the semester is now primarily devoted to gaining familiarity with spectrometers and computational chemistry, and the second half is devoted towards students projects, with 3-4 weeks devoted to characterization of a student-chosen compound and 3-4 weeks to student-designed experiments on that compound. Time is built into the schedule for student experiments to fail, be revised, and be attempted again with the revised procedure. This talk will describe how this approach works in practice in our local context, where both chemistry and biochemistry majors take the course but biochemistry majors do not generally take quantum mechanics. Examples of student feedback will be provided as well as reflection about the strengths and weaknesses of this approach.

FA13 **8:52 – 8:53**

BUILDING A RESEARCH PROGRAM AT A PRIMARILY UNDERGRADUATE INSTITUTION

JACOB STEWART, *Department of Chemistry, Connecticut College, New London, CT, USA.*

Developing and building a research program in spectroscopy at a primarily undergraduate institution is a challenging and rewarding experience. In this talk, I will discuss my personal experience developing a research program in infrared spectroscopy applied to atmospheric chemistry at Connecticut College, a small liberal arts college located in the northeast of the United States. Working with undergraduate students in a research setting provides an excellent opportunity to mentor students one-on-one, but also comes with challenges related to student time and expertise. I will present strategies that I have found useful in addressing the unique needs of undergraduates performing research in molecular spectroscopy.

FB. Clusters/Complexes

Friday, June 25, 2021 – 8:0 AM

Room: 2021 Online Everywhere

Chair: Daniel A. Obenchain, Georg-August-Universität Göttingen, Göttingen, Germany

FB01 **8:00 – 8:01**

HOW SOLVENTS CHANGE THE CONFORMATIONAL LANDSCAPE IN MOLECULES WITH WEAK INTRAMOLECULAR INTERACTIONS: METHYL 2-METHOXYBENZOATE

ALBERTO MACARIO, JUAN CARLOS LOPEZ, SUSANA BLANCO, *Departamento de Química Física y Química Inorgánica, Universidad de Valladolid, Valladolid, Spain.*

The conformational behavior of methyl 2-methoxybenzoate has been explored using rotational spectroscopy. The two conformers identified show for each rotational transition a quadruplet attributable to two sets of splittings due to two tunneling motions, the internal rotation of the ester methyl group and the internal rotation of the entire ester group with respect to the benzene ring, which in addition interconverts both observed conformers. The analysis of such splittings allowed the determination of the potential energy barriers for the tunneling vibrations. The spectra of the complexes of methyl 2-methoxybenzoate with water and formic acid have also been analyzed. In both cases, only the global minimum structure could be identified in the spectra. In contrast with the observations in many other systems, the conformational landscape of the monomer is altered upon complexation. In the complexes the relative stability of the conformers observed in the monomer turn out to be inverted. Ester group torsion and methyl group internal rotation splittings were observed in the monohydrated complex, but not in the complex with formic acid.

FB02 **8:04 – 8:05**

PROBING AZULENE-WATER INTERACTIONS AND AZULENE AGGREGATION BY BROADBAND ROTATIONAL SPECTROSCOPY

SHEFALI SAXENA, ECATERINA BUREVSCHI, *Department of Chemistry, King's College London, London, United Kingdom*; YANG ZHENG, QIAN GOU, *School of Chemistry and Chemical Engineering, Chongqing University, Chongqing, China*; M. EUGENIA SANZ, *Department of Chemistry, King's College London, London, United Kingdom.*

Noncovalent interactions of aromatic complexes are highly significant in biological systems such as DNA, in materials science and in supramolecular chemistry. Gas phase studies of small aromatic complexes allow the determination of their preferred structural arrangements and of the relative contributions of various intermolecular forces to the interaction energies, laying the foundation for understanding the properties and interactions of larger systems. Azulene is one of the smallest aromatic hydrocarbons with a dipole moment. Here we present the investigation of azulene aggregation and its interactions with water using chirped-pulse Fourier transform microwave spectroscopy. Experimental observations are compared with predictions by various theoretical methods to evaluate their performance.

FB03 **8:08 – 8:09**

UNRAVELLING THE MICROSOLVATION FRAMEWORK AROUND PROTOTYPE POLYCYCLIC AROMATIC HYDROCARBON, NAPHTHALENE, BY HIGH-RESOLUTION INFRARED SPECTROSCOPY

KUNTAL CHATTERJEE, TARUN KUMAR ROY, JAI KHATRI, MARTINA HAVENITH, *Physikalische Chemie II, Ruhr University Bochum, Bochum, Germany.*

Solvation of aromatic molecules is a fundamental chemical process. Stability and function of almost all biomolecules are governed by the surface water molecules, typically known as biological water. Despite a plethora of reports available for the prototype aromatic molecule, benzene,[1] studies related to the solvation of larger aromatic moieties are rather scarce. Herein, we probe the microsolvated structures of the simplest polycyclic aromatic hydrocarbon, naphthalene (Np), by high-resolution infrared (IR) spectroscopy inside helium nanodroplets and quantum chemical calculations. Our results show that in the monohydrated Np-water dimer, solvent water preferentially binds to the π electron cloud of the two fused phenyl rings via OH-π hydrogen bonds (H-bond) and acts as a double H-bond donor. This binding motif is strikingly different from the corresponding cationic Np-water complex, in which water lies in the Np-ring plane and acts as a double H-bond acceptor by the simultaneous formation of two CH-O H-bonds.[2,3] Therefore, we see the presence or absence of charge causes a substantial modification of solvent binding motif. Further stepwise water-addition to neutral Np-water complex leads to evolution of H-bond network as reflected from the IR spectra. In larger Np-(water)$_{2,3}$ clusters, hydration motifs mimic the bare water network and thus leads to the formation of linear H-bonded water dimer and cyclic water trimer, which simultaneously interact with Np π electrons. Changing the solvent from water to methanol does not change the qualitative π bonding motif. However, in this case, the solvent only interacts with a single phenyl ring via a OH-π H-bond due to the presence of a single proton donor. The addition of the second solvent molecule leads to the formation of H-bonded methanol dimer that interacts with Np.

References:

1. R. N. Pribble and T. S. Zwier, Science, 1994, 265, 75 2. K. Chatterjee and O. Dopfer, Chem. Sci., 2018, 9, 2301. 3. K. Chatterjee and O. Dopfer, Phys. Chem. Chem. Phys., 2017, 19, 32262

FB04 **8:12 – 8:13**

MICROWAVE SPECTROSCOPY OF THE 2-METHYLAMINOETHANOL-WATER COMPLEX

DYLAN S VALENTE[a], *Department of Chemistry, University of Scranton, Scranton, PA, USA*; DINESH MARASINGHE, MICHAEL TUBERGEN, *Department of Chemistry and Biochemistry, Kent State University, Kent, OH, USA.*

The rotational spectrum of the 2-methylaminoethanol-water (2MAE-water) complex has been observed using a cavity based Fourier-transform microwave spectrometer in the range of 10-19 GHz. 2MAE exists in *trans* and *gauche* conformations[b,c,d]. We modeled 10 possible conformers of the 2MAE-water complex, five trans and five gauche conformers, using ab initio calculations (MP2/6-311++G(d,p)). 14 rotational transitions were fit to Watson's *A*-reduced Hamiltonian: A=3368.02 MHz, B=2282.60 MHz, and C=1538.00 MHz. ^{14}N nuclear quadrupole hyperfine splittings were resolved, and the 38 hyperfine components were fit to χ_{aa} = 1.543(7) MHz and χ_{bb} = -1.083(25) MHz. The measured spectrum is assigned to the lowest energy model structure of the complex, which has two intermolecular hydrogen bonds: from hydroxyl group to water and from water to the methylamino group. The structure of 2MAE-water is compared with 2-aminoethanol-water (2AE-water) and 2-methoxyethylamine-water (2MEA-water) complexes.

[a]Summer 2019 REU student at Kent State University.

[b]R. E. Penn and L. W. Buxton, *J. Mol. Spectrosc.* **56**, 229-238 (1975).

[c]C. Calabrese, A. Maris, L. Evangelisti, A. Piras, V. Parravicini and S. Melandri, *Front. Chem.* **6:25** (2018).

[d]Y. Liu, C.A. Rice and M.A. Suhm, *Can. J. Chem.* **82**, 1006-1012 (2004).

FB05 **8:16 – 8:17**

MICROWAVE SPECTRUM AND LARGE AMPLITUDE MOTION OF METHANESULFONIC ACID

ANNA HUFF, NATHAN LOVE, KENNETH R. LEOPOLD, *Chemistry Department, University of Minnesota, Minneapolis, MN, USA.*

Microwave spectra have been recorded for methanesulfonic acid (CH_3SO_3H) and its –OD isotopologue. No internal rotation of the methyl group was observed, consistent with the calculated high barrier of 2.7 kcal/mol. A pair of tunneling states has been observed for both species, however, and is attributed to large amplitude wagging of the hydroxyl hydrogen from one side of the molecule to the other. The predicted barrier to this motion, obtained from M06-2X/6-311++G(3df,3pd) calculations, is 0.7 kcal/mol. For CH_3SO_3D, the tunneling energy was directly determined to be ΔE = 6471.9269(17) MHz from the measurement of *c*-type spectra. In the case of the parent species, however, transitions displaced by the tunneling energy have not been located and are likely above the maximum frequency accessible by the spectrometer (20 GHz). Thus, the value of ΔE could not be experimentally determined. Nonetheless, a satisfactory fit was obtained for transitions involving J"= 0 and J" = 1 (nine frequencies for each state). Suggestions for further work at higher frequencies will be presented.

FB06 **8:20 – 8:21**

MICROWAVE SPECTRUM OF THE METHANESULFONIC ACID – WATER COMPLEX

ANNA HUFF, NATHAN LOVE, KENNETH R. LEOPOLD, *Chemistry Department, University of Minnesota, Minneapolis, MN, USA.*

The methanesulfonic acid water - complex (CH_3SO_3H-H_2O) has been observed using pulse-nozzle Fourier transform microwave spectroscopy. The rotational spectra for the CH_3SO_3H-D_2O and CH_3SO_3D-D_2O isotopologues have also been obtained and analyzed. DFT calculations predict the two lowest energy conformers of CH_3SO_3H-H_2O to form a strong hydrogen bond between the water molecule and the acidic proton and a second, longer hydrogen bond with one of the S=O oxygens to form the 6-membered ring-like structure that is typical of oxyacid monohydrates. The observed rotational constants and isotope shifts are in best agreement with those predicted for the global minimum structure of CH_3SO_3H-H_2O, where the unbound H_2O hydrogen atom is oriented away from the methyl group. In contrast to the triflic acid monohydrate (CF_3SO_3H-H_2O) spectrum, there was no evidence of a pair of tunneling states arising from internal motion of the water. A and E internal rotor states were not resolvable in the observed spectrum, consistent with the predicted high barrier for methyl group internal rotation (V_3=1000 cm^{-1}).

FB07 **8:24 – 8:25**

ATTENUATED STABILITY OF DEUTERIUM-BOUND COMPLEXES AT ROOM TEMPERATURE

ALEXANDER KJÆRSGAARD, EMIL VOGT, HENRIK G. KJAERGAARD, *Department of Chemistry, University of Copenhagen, Copenhagen, Denmark.*

We have recorded gas-phase Fourier transform Infrared spectra at room temperature of several hydrogen (H) and deuterium (D) bound bimolecular complexes. These complexes were formed using methanol and ethanol as OH donors, and methanol-d_1 and ethanol-d_1 as OD donors, to compare isotopic effects in H/D-bond stability. The stability of these complexes are governed by the Gibbs energy of complex formation. By combining experimental and calculated intensities, the pressure of the complex can be determined, and from that and monomer pressures the Gibbs energy of complex formation. At room temperature, we find similar Gibbs energies for corresponding H/D-bound complexes. For the pair of H/D-complexes, methanol·dimethylether (OH·O) and methanol-d_1·dimethylether (OD·O), Gibbs energies of 8.3 and 7.7 kJ/mol were determined, and for methanol·trimethylamine (OH·N) and methanol-d_1·trimethylamine (OD·N) were determined Gibbs energies of 3.2 and 2.7 kJ/mol. Our findings of similar Gibbs energies for H/D-bound complexes at room temperature, is in contrast to what has been observed in spectra recorded in cold conditions. The deuterium bound complex is heavily favored, at low temperatures due to a lower zero-point vibrational energy. From calculations, we find that the difference in stability of the H/D-bound complexes become smaller with increasing temperature. The change in stability with temperature, arise from changes in both the rotational and vibrational entropic contributions.[1]

[1] A. Kjaersgaard, E. Vogt, N. F. Christensen, H. G. Kjaergaard, *J. Phys. Chem. A.*, **2020**, DOI: 10.1021/acs.jpca.9b11762.

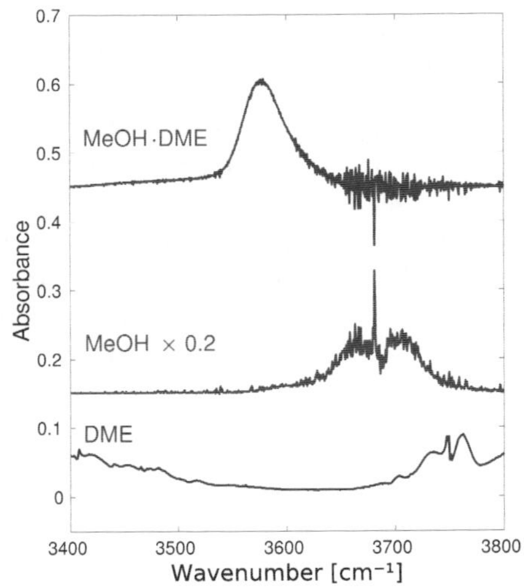

Figure 2: Spectrum of methanol (MeOH), dimethylether (DME) and the bimolecular complex (MeOH·DME).

FB08 **8:28 – 8:29**

ROTATIONAL SPECTRA OF THE CH_3CN-CO_2 COMPLEX: OBSERVING A CARBON 'TETREL BOND'

SHARON PRIYA GNANASEKAR, ELANGANNAN ARUNAN, *Department of Inorganic and Physical Chemistry, Indian Institute of Science, Bangalore, India.*

The CH_3CN-CO_2 complex was investigated using a pulsed nozzle Fourier transform microwave spectrometer. Nitrogen containing compounds generally form a T-shaped complex with CO_2 having a N-CO_2 'tetrel bond'. For example, microwave spectrum confirmed this structure for HCN-CO_2 back in 1984, though specific names of intermolecular bonds were not used those days[a]. We have observed two structures for the CH_3CN-CO_2 complex, the T-shaped and a π-stacked (the CO_2 is parallel to the CH_3CN). The ab initio calculations show that the two structures have similar binding energies. The T-shaped structure has a nearly prolate 'a'–type spectra with the K=1 lines missing, which is consistent with the C_{2v} symmetry of the T-shaped structure. All rotational transitions observed show hyperfine splitting due to nuclear quadrupole coupling of the nitrogen atom. Measurements with isotopic substitutions have been carried out to ascertain the assignment of the rotational transitions.

[a]Leopold, K. R.; Fraser, G. T.; Klemperer, W. J. Chem. Phys. 1984, 80, 1039–1046.

FB09 **8:32 – 8:33**

BOUND STATE CALCULATIONS OF THE VAN DER WAALS NH_3−Ne COMPLEX AND FIRST MICROWAVE DETECTION OF THE MISSING (*para*)-NH_3−Ne NUCLEAR SPIN ISOMER[a]

LEONID SURIN, IVAN TARABUKIN, *Institute of Spectroscopy, Russian Academy of Sciences, Troitsk, Moscow, Russia*; CRISTOBAL PEREZ, MELANIE SCHNELL, *FS-SMP, Deutsches Elektronen-Synchrotron (DESY), Hamburg, Germany*; JEROME LOREAU, *Chemistry, KU Leuven, Leuven, Belgium*; AD VAN DER AVOIRD, *Institute for Molecules and Materials (IMM), Radboud University Nijmegen, Nijmegen, Netherlands.*

The microwave spectrum of the NH_3−Ne van der Waals complex has been observed in a supersonic molecular jet expansion via broadband (2-8 GHz) chirped-pulse Fourier-transform microwave spectroscopy. Together with the well-known lines related to the (*ortho*)-NH_3−Ne spectrum[b], new transitions were detected and attributed to the missing (*para*)-NH_3−Ne nuclear spin isomer. The assignments were guided by the rovibrational bound state (J = 0 ... 10) calculations based on the recent *ab initio* NH_3−Ne intermolecular potential surface[c]. The hyperfine structure arising from quadrupole ^{14}N nucleus of NH_3−Ne was resolved, and the quadrupole coupling constant associated with the (*para*)-NH_3 subunit was precisely determined. This constant provided the dynamical information about the angular orientation of ammonia indicating that the average angle between the C_3 axis of NH_3 and intermolecular axis is about 68°.

[a]The authors acknowledge the Deutsche Forschungsgemeinschaft (SCHN 1280/5), Russian Science Foundation (17-02-01395) and Russian Foundation for Basic Research (19-03-00998).

[b]J. van Wijngaarden and W. Jäger, *J.Chem.Phys.* **115**, 6504 (2001).

[c]J. Loreau and A. van der Avoird, *J.Chem.Phys.* **143**, 184303 (2015).

FB10 **8:36 – 8:37**

ETHANOL TRIMER CONFIGURATIONS REVEALED BY CP-FTMW SPECTROSCOPY AND COMPUTATIONAL CALCULATIONS

S. INDIRA MURUGACHANDRAN, ISABEL PEÑA, *Department of Chemistry, King's College London, London, United Kingdom*; AL MOKHTAR LAMSABHI, MANUEL YÁÑEZ, *Departamento de Quimica, Universidad Autonoma de Madrid, Madrid, Spain*; M. EUGENIA SANZ, *Department of Chemistry, King's College London, London, United Kingdom.*

The study of hydrogen-bonded complexes in the gas phase aims to advance our knowledge of the intermolecular forces at play in these systems. To this end, ethanol clusters are of particular interest as archetypes of the interplay between hydrogen bonding and London dispersion forces. Here we present an investigation into the preferred isomers of ethanol trimer using computational methods in combination with broadband chirped-pulse Fourier transform microwave spectroscopy. The potential energy surface of ethanol trimer has been investigated through DFT and *ab initio* calculations, showing that the –OH groups forms a hydrogen bonded cyclic structure in the lower-energy isomers. From the analysis of the rotational spectrum, four distinct rotamers of ethanol trimer have been detected. All rotamers display O-H$\cdots$O hydrogen bonds between the three hydroxyl groups, where each hydroxyl group simultaneously acts as hydrogen bond donor and acceptor.

FB11 **8:40 – 8:41**

CONFORMATIONAL LANDSCAPES OF 2-FUROIC ACID MONOMERS AND DIMERS BY ROTATIONAL SPECTROSCOPY AND DFT CALCULATIONS

QIAN YANG, FAN XIE, WOLFGANG JÄGER, YUNJIE XU, *Department of Chemistry, University of Alberta, Edmonton, AB, Canada.*

2-furoic acid (FA), a heterocyclic carboxylic acid, is a significant precursor of esters, acrylic chloride, and acid anhydride, and is often used for medical purpose, for example in an orally active antidiabetic vanadyl complex.1 FA monomer may exist in a number of possible conformations based on the orientation of the COOH group with the ring O atom and on the relative orientation of the C=O and OH in the COOH group. Some of these possible conformations were investigated before.2 In this work, we studied conformational landscapes of the FA monomer and dimer by using a chirped pulse Fourier transform microwave (FTMW) spectrometer and DFT calculations. Conformational searches were performed to identify possible conformations using a conformer-rotamer ensemble sampling tool (CREST).3 The resulting candidates were further optimized at the B3LYP-D3(BJ)/def2-TZVP level of theory. Three FA conformers and four (FA)2 conformers 2-furoic acid dimers were predicted. Experimentally, rotational spectra of three monomeric conformers and two binary conformers were assigned. Two other FA dimers predicted have zero electric dipole moments. Detailed analyses of the double proton tunneling motion and conformational conversion barriers will also be presented.

1 M. Yin, X. Lei, M. Li, L. Yuan, J. Sun, J. Phys. Chem. Solids, 2006, 67, 1372-1378. 2 A. Halasa, L. Lapinski, I. Reva, H. Rostkowska, R. Fausto, M. J. Nowak, J. Phys. Chem. A, 2015, 119, 1037-1047; H. Ghalla, N. Issaoui, M. V. Castillo, S. A. Brandán, H. T. Flakus, Spectrochim. Acta A Mol. Biomol. Spectrosc, 2014, 121, 623-631. 3 S. Grimme, J. Chem. Theory Comput., 2019, 15, 2847-2862.

FB12 **8:44 – 8:45**

ROOM TEMPERATURE GAS-PHASE GIBBS ENERGIES OF WATER AMINE COMPLEXES

EMIL VOGT, ALEXANDER KJÆRSGAARD, HENRIK G. KJAERGAARD, *Department of Chemistry, University of Copenhagen, Copenhagen, Denmark.*

A hydrogen bound bimolecular complex consists of a hydrogen bond donor and acceptor unit. The OH-stretching fundamental transition of the hydrogen bond donor is typically redshifted and its infrared intensity enhanced upon complexation.[1] This facilitates detection of weak complexes even though the equilibrium is strongly shifted towards the monomers at room temperature. The ratio of a measured and calculated intensity of a vibrational band is proportional to the complex abundance, which with known monomer pressures gives the equilibrium constant.[2] We calculate absolute transition intensities with a reduced dimensionality variational local mode model that also includes low-frequency vibrations. Calculated and experimental intensities of multiple bands are combined to give the equilibrium constant of complex formation for the water·dimethylamine and water·trimethylamine complex.[3] The equilibrium constant obtained from different bands should be equivalent, and the detection of multiple bands therefore allows us to validate the accuracy of our combined experimental and theoretical approach.

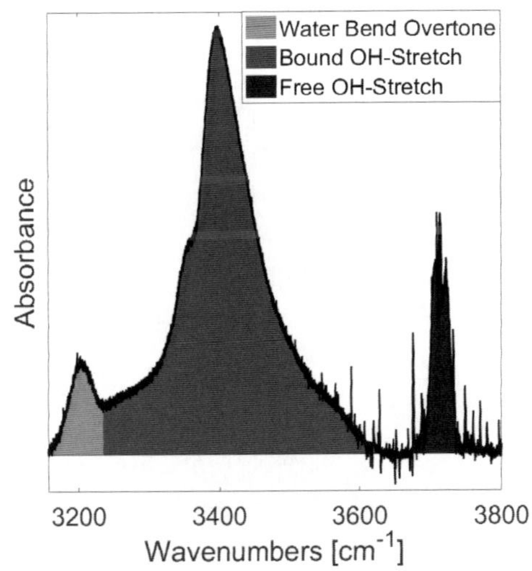

Figure 3: Room temperature gas-phase infrared spectrum of the water·dimethylamine complex.

[1] Arunan, Elangannan, et al. Pure Appl. Chem., 2011, **83.8**, 1619.
[2] A. S. Hansen, E. Vogt, and H. G. Kjaergaard, Int. Rev. Phys. Chem., 2019, **38.1**, 115.
[3] A. Kjaersgaard, E. Vogt, A. S. Hansen, and H. G. Kjaergaard, J. Phys. Chem. A., 2020, **124.35**, 7113.

FB13 **8:48 – 8:49**

MICROSOLVATION OF CARBENES IN SUPERFLUID HELIUM NANODROPLETS

JAI KHATRI, TARUN KUMAR ROY, STEFAN HENKEL, KUNTAL CHATTERJEE, GERHARD SCHWAAB, MARTINA HAVENITH, *Physikalische Chemie II, Ruhr University Bochum, Bochum, Germany.*

Carbenes are classified as an important reactive intermediate in chemical reactions owing to their multiple spin states. Recent studies in matrix isolation technique (3 K) demonstrated that a single water molecule is able to switch the spin state of diphenylcarbene[1] (triplet to singlet) and furthermore confirmed the formation of the carbenium ion in the LDA ice matrix[2]. In this line helium nanodroplet spectroscopy provides an ideal environment to study such solvation processes at ultracold temperature (0.37 K) by successive addition of water molecules. Here, we aim to determine the minimum number of water molecules required for the formation of the carbenium ion from its parent carbene molecule.

To understand the solvation process of diphenylcarbene, it is crucial to investigate the initial hydration framework of the precursor molecule, diazodiphenylmethane. Therefore, the present study elucidated the IR spectroscopic investigation of diazodiphenylmethane ($C_{13}H_8N_2$)-water (D_2O) complexes in helium nanodroplets. To assign the observed bands corresponding to $C_{13}H_8N_2$-D_2O complex, we also performed ab-initio calculation at B3LYP-D3/def2-TZVP level.

References: 1. Costa, P.; Sander, Angew. Chem. 2014, 126, 5222– 5225. 2. Costa, P.; Fernandez-Oliva, M; Sanchez-Gracia, E;Sander, W., J.Am. Chem. Soc. 2014, 136, 15625-30.

FC. Astronomy

Friday, June 25, 2021 – 8:0 AM

Room: 2021 Online Everywhere

Chair: SERGIO IOPPOLO, Queen Mary University of London (QMUL), London, United Kingdom

FC01 **8:00 – 8:01**

SUBLIMATION OF LABORATORY ICES MILLIMETER/SUBMILLIMETER EXPERIMENT (SubLIME): IDENTIFICATION AND QUANTIFICATION OF ORGANIC SPECIES FROM A UV PHOTOLYZED METHANOL ICE

KATARINA YOCUM, *Chemistry and Astronomy, University of Wisconsin-Madison, Madison, WI, USA*; STEFANIE N MILAM, PERRY A. GERAKINES, *Astrochemistry, NASA Goddard Space Flight Center, Greenbelt, MD, USA*; SUSANNA L. WIDICUS WEAVER, *Chemistry and Astronomy, University of Wisconsin-Madison, Madison, WI, USA.*

Millimeter/submillimeter spectroscopy is a powerful analytical technique for identifying the components of complex gas mixtures. In this work, millimeter/submillimeter spectroscopy has been utilized to detect and quantify organic species sublimated from a UV photolyzed methanol ice. Eleven species were uniquely identified by their structure-specific pure rotational transitions, and the integrated intensities of their rotational transitions were used to determine their rotational temperatures and gas densities by a rotation diagram analysis. This talk will outline the experimental design and the latest results with SubLIME. The abundance ratios of detected organic species will also be compared to those detected in star-forming regions and cometary comae.

FC02 **8:04 – 8:05**

REVEALING THE CHEMISTRY OF POLYCYCLIC AROMATIC HYDROCARBONS BY PLASMA SOURCES

DONATELLA LORU, *FS-SMP, Deutsches Elektronen-Synchrotron (DESY), Hamburg, Germany*; DANIEL RAP, *FELIX Laboratory, Radboud University, Nijmegen, The Netherlands*; SÉBASTIEN GRUET, AMANDA STEBER, MELANIE SCHNELL, *FS-SMP, Deutsches Elektronen-Synchrotron (DESY), Hamburg, Germany.*

Detected through the aromatic infrared bands (3-20 μm), polycyclic aromatic hydrocarbons (PAHs) are considered to lock up a large fraction of the carbon in the interstellar medium (ISM) and to significantly impact its physics and chemistry. Despite their importance, much is unknown about their formation and reactivity under the harsh conditions of the ISM.

We are looking at the reactivity of these molecules in the laboratory by means of an electrical discharge nozzle coupled with chirped-pulse Fourier transform microwave (CP-FTMW) spectroscopy in the 2-12 GHz frequency range. Under such energetic conditions, PAHs are expected to undergo fragmentation processes and/or a recombination chemistry. The formed species are then unambiguously identified via their unique microwave signature.

Herein, we present our results obtained from discharge experiments on the PAHs naphthalene ($C_{10}H_8$) and phenanthrene ($C_{14}H_{10}$), both pure and in mixture with acetonitrile (CH_3CN), a simple nitrogen-containing interstellar molecule. An interesting chemistry has been observed for the investigated PAHs, which will be compared and discussed.

FC03 **8:08 – 8:09**

IR ABSORPTION AND CALCULATED FREQUENCIES OF FORMALDEHYDE DISSOLVED IN LIQUID Kr

SURESH SUNUWAR, CARLOS MANZANARES, *Department of Chemistry and Biochemistry, Baylor University, Waco, TX, USA.*

Using a Fourier transform infrared spectrophotometer and a low temperature cryostat, we have obtained the IR spectra of formaldehyde dissolved in liquid krypton between 125 K and 137 K. Monomeric formaldehyde in gas phase was prepared by thermal decomposition of para-formaldehyde. Peak positions (ν), wavenumber shifts($\Delta\nu$), and full widths at half maximum ($\Delta\nu_{1/2}$) are reported. Influence of the solvent on fundamental vibrational frequencies are studied using the polarizable continuum model (PCM). When used in combination with calculated anharmonic frequencies, the PCM model shows qualitative agreement with frequency shifts in liquid Kr. The importance of formaldehyde IR characterization around 100 K will be discussed in reference to its detection in the interstellar medium [a], the IR detection of the ν_1 vibration in the protostar W33A[b], and although the Cassini infrared spectrometer (CIRS) was not able to detect methanol, formaldehyde, and acetonitrile in Titan's atmosphere, upper limits on their abundances and formation conditions have been proposed. [c,d]

---

[a] B. Zuckerman et al., Observations of Interstellar Formaldehyde, Astrophys. J., 1970, 160: 485–506.

[b] E. Roueff et al., Infrared Detection of Gas Phase Formaldehyde Towards the High Mass Protostar W33A, A&A, 2006, 447: 963–969

[c] C.A. Nixon et al., Upper Limits for Undetected Trace Species in the Stratosphere of Titan. Faraday Discuss. 2010, 147: 65–81.

[d] B.N. Tran et al., Titan's Atmospheric Chemistry: Photolysis of Gas Mixtures Containing Hydrogen Cyanide and Carbon Monoxide at 185 and 254 nm, Icarus, 2008, 193: 224–232

FC04 **8:12 – 8:13**

FORMATION OF PYRUVIC ACID AND 1,2-ETHENEDIOL IN INTERSTELLAR ANALOG ICES

N. FABIAN KLEIMEIER, *Department of Chemistry, University of Hawaii at Manoa, Honolulu, HI, USA*; ANDRÉ K. ECKHARDT, *Department of Chemistry, Massachusetts Institute of Technology, Cambridge, MA, USA*; PETER R. SCHREINER, *Institute for Organic Chemistry, Justus Liebig University of Giessen, Giessen, Germany*; RALF INGO KAISER, *Department of Chemistry, University of Hawaii at Manoa, Honolulu, HI, USA.*

More than 200 molecules have so far been detected in the interstellar medium (ISM), of which close to one third are complex organic molecules containing six or more atoms. Over the last decades, laboratory experiments simulating the conditions in cold molecular clouds have demonstrated that these COMs can form from interaction of ionizing radiation with simple ices deposited on interstellar dust particles. These experiments have unveiled multiple pathways towards the formation of acetaldehyde (CH_3CHO) in such ices, explaining its detection in many interstellar and circumstellar environments including tentative detections in interstellar ices. By condensing acetaldehyde and carbon monoxide at 5 K and irradiating the ice with 5 keV electrons, we simulate secondary electrons generated in the track of galactic cosmic rays interacting with ices around cosmic dust particles. Combined infrared and photoionization reflectron time-of-flight mass spectrometry studies were employed to unambiguously identify pyruvic acid ($CH_3COCOOH$) and its enol, 2-hydroxyacrylic acid ($CH_2(COH)COOH$), as reaction product from the irradiation by a barrierless radical-radical reaction of the acetyl (CH_3CO) and hydroxycarbonyl (HOCO) radicals. These results present an abiotic pathway towards the formation of this prebiotic molecule in the interstellar medium. Pyruvic acid constitutes a key starting material for the Krebs cycle, which supplies living organisms with energy. Furthermore, it is a precursor for more complex biomolecules such as lactic acid or alanine.

In a second experiment, condensing pure methanol and mixed methanol and carbon monoxide ices, 1,2-ethenediol (HOCH=CHOH) was detected after irradiation with 5 keV electrons at 5 K. Three distinct pathways to its formation could be inferred from isotopic substitutions. 1,2-ethenediol, the enol of glycolaldehyde, is the reactive key intermediate in the formose cycle to form complex sugars from formaldehyde but has hitherto not been isolated. The detection of 1,2-ethendiol in such simple ices therefore suggests a facile reaction network to enable complex sugar formation.

FC05 **8:16 – 8:17**

SPECTROSCOPIC STUDIES OF METHYL FORMATE AND ITS FORMATION PATHWAYS IN SPACE UPON ION IRRADIATION

ALEJANDRA TRASPAS MUIÑA , *Electronic Engineering and Computer Science Department, Queen Mary University of London , London, UK*; SERGIO IOPPOLO, *School of Electronic Engineering and Computer Science, Queen Mary University of London, London, GREATER LONDON, United Kingdom*; PETER HERCZKU, ZOLTAN JUHÁSZ, SÁNDOR T. S. KOVÁCS, *Atomki, Institute for Nuclear Research, Debrecen, Hungary*; DUNCAN MIFSUD, *Center for Astrophysics and Planetary Science, University of Kent, Canterbury, kent, United Kingdom*; ZUZANA KAŇUCHOVÁ, *INAF Osservatorio Astronomico di Roma, INAF Osservatorio Astronomico di Roma, Roma, Italy*; NIGEL MASON, *School of Physical Sciences, University of Kent, Canterbury, United Kingdom*; ROBERT W McCULLOUGH, *Department of Physics and Astronomy, Queen's University Belfast, Belfast, United Kingdom*; BÉLA SULIK, *Atomki, Institute for Nuclear Research, Debrecen, Hungary.*

All isomers of $C_2H_4O_2$, i.e. glycolaldehyde ($HCOCH_2OH$), acetic acid (CH_3COOH) and methyl formate ($HCOOCH_3$), have been observed abundantly around the Galactic center, in dark clouds, and hot cores of the interstellar medium (ISM), as well as in some comets of the Solar System. However, their exact gas-grain formation and destruction pathway is still unclear. According to El-Abd et al. (2019), the observed column densities of methyl formate and acetic acid are well-correlated, and are likely simply tracking the relative total gas mass in star forming regions. Methyl formate and glycolaldehyde, however, display a stark dichotomy in their relative column densities. The latter finding suggests that different formation/destruction routes are at play for the three isomers. To date, there is a strong laboratory evidence for an efficient production of glycolaldehyde, methyl formate, and acetic acid in the ISM (Gerakines et al. 1996; Bennett and Kaiser 2007; Modica et al. 2012). However, so far models and laboratory studies cannot fully reproduce the observed mutually exclusive presence of specific isomers in certain star formation regions. Understanding the formation of the $C_2H_4O_2$ isomers is an important step to verify the formation of yet more complex molecules that are necessary for life. In this talk, I will present our latest results obtained at the ion accelerator ATOMKI facility in Debrecen (Hungary) using the novel ultrahigh vacuum ICA end station. Results will be discussed in light of upcoming JWST mission.

FC06 **8:20 – 8:21**

DISCOVERING NOVEL GAS-PHASE NITROGEN-HETEROCYCLE FORMATION PATHWAYS WITH AN AB INITIO NANOREACTOR

SOMMER L. JOHANSEN, LISA OH, LEE-PING WANG, KYLE N. CRABTREE, *Department of Chemistry, University of California, Davis, Davis, CA, USA.*

Nitrogen-containing heterocycles pose an intriguing astrochemical mystery. 45 different varieties have been detected on meteorites with non-terrestrial isotopic abundances, but none have been detected in space, despite numerous search attempts. It is unclear if these species are more likely to form through low-temperature gas-phase chemistry, photoprocessing of icy grains, aqueous chemistry in a meteorite parent body, or a combination of processes. Further exploration of this question requires a broader catalog of potential N-heterocycle precursors, particularly for low temperature gas-phase chemistry. Here, results of *ab initio* molecular dynamics simulations of gas-phase N-heterocycle forming reactions will be discussed. These simulations were performed with an *ab initio* nanoreactor, a computational tool developed for chemical reaction discovery. Multiple novel gas-phase N-heterocycle formation pathways have been revealed, and many reactants are similar to known interstellar molecules. These simulations also reinforce previous experimental and theoretical studies which demonstrated that smaller N-heterocycles are potential precursors to larger ones. While these simulations cannot provide direct insight into interstellar chemistry, they have revealed nonintuitive N-heterocycle precursors that warrant further experimental and astronomical study.

FC07 **8:24 – 8:25**

MEASURING THE DIFFERENCE IN COLLISIONAL INTERACTION OF HCN/HNC WITH He AT LOW TEMPERATURES USING THE CPUF TECHNIQUE

BRIAN M HAYS, THEO GUILLAUME, DIVITA GUPTA, FRANCK THIBAULT, FRANÇOIS LIQUE, IAN R. SIMS, *CNRS, IPR (Institut de Physique de Rennes) - UMR 6251, Univ Rennes, F-35000 Rennes, France.*

The T_2 time of HCN and HNC in He was measured at low temperatures using chirped pulse Fourier transform millimeter wave spectroscopy, to compare to scattering calculations and to investigate the difference of interaction between the two structural isomers. These molecules are commonly observed in the interstellar medium (ISM), where their abundance ratio can be used to elucidate conditions within an interstellar environment. Within these environments, they are expected to collide with He and H_2, which could lead to non-thermal excitation. Previous ab initio calculations of the collisions with He and H2 with HCN and HNC have shown that the rates for HNC with these colliders are much greater, despite their similarities in structure. We have performed CPUF (Chirped pulse in Uniform Flow) experiments to measure the difference in T_2 of HCN and HNC at cold temperatures in He. The J=1-0 transitions of HCN and HNC were observed in under CRESU (Reaction Kinetics in Uniform Supersonic Flow) conditions using cold flows of He. Pulsed laser photolysis of vinyl cyanide was used to produce HCN and HNC under comparable conditions. The T_2 time was fit directly from the free induction decays of these experiments at different temperatures, which is directly comparable to the linewidth in the frequency domain. This was then compared to pressure broadening cross sections produced from close coupling scattering calculations performed on ab initio potential energy surfaces. We find that there is a difference in interaction of HCN and HNC with He at low temperatures and will discuss the impacts this may have for observing these species in the ISM.

FC08 **8:28 – 8:29**

LOW-TEMPERATURE KINETICS MEASUREMENTS OF THE GAS-PHASE REACTIONS BETWEEN AROMATIC SPECIES AND THE CN RADICAL

DIVITA GUPTA, ILSA ROSE COOKE, *CNRS, IPR (Institut de Physique de Rennes) - UMR 6251, Univ Rennes, F-35000 Rennes, France*; JOSEPH P. MESSINGER, *Chemistry, California Institute of Technology, Pasadena, CA, USA*; MITCHIO OKUMURA, *Division of Chemistry and Chemical Engineering, California Institute of Technology, Pasadena, CA, USA*; IAN R. SIMS, *CNRS, IPR (Institut de Physique de Rennes) - UMR 6251, Univ Rennes, F-35000 Rennes, France.*

It remains an open question as to whether polycyclic aromatic hydrocarbons (PAHs) can be efficiently formed in the ISM by bottom-up mechanisms involving growth from small aromatic precursors like benzene. However, the lack of dipole moment renders benzene invisible in the radio regime making estimation of the abundance of benzene in the ISM difficult. The recent detection of benzonitrile in the Taurus Molecular Cloud (TMC)-1 has caused excitement in the astrochemical community as it is the first aromatic molecule detected in the interstellar medium (ISM) using radio astronomy. Benzonitrile is thought to form via the neutral-neutral reaction between the CN radical and benzene, and therefore may serve as a chemical proxy to determine the abundance of benzene. The abundances of aromatic species in ISM environments are not well understood, in part due to a lack of experimental kinetics data. Both rate constants and product-branching ratios for the reactions of aromatic molecules must be measured at low temperature in order to input these reactions into astrochemical models and accurately predict abundances. Benzene and toluene are two of the aromatic species detected in the atmosphere of Titan and their reactions with the CN radical have been studied down to 105 K by Trevitt et al. Here, we have extended this study down to 15 K to approach dense cloud conditions and have measured the rate constants of the reactions of benzene and toluene with the CN radical using the well-established CRESU technique (Cinétique de Réaction en Ecoulement Supersonique Uniforme, or Reaction Kinetics in Uniform Supersonic Flow) combined with the Pulsed Laser Photolysis-Laser-Induced Fluorescence method. I will also discuss our recent progress in combining chirped-pulse micro/mm-wave spectroscopy with the CRESU method and how we plan to employ this technique to measure product branching ratios for reactions of the CN radical with aromatics at low temperatures.

FC09 **8:32 – 8:33**

REACTION RATE MODELING TO OPTIMIZE $O(^1D)$ INSERTION INTO METHYLAMINE FOR THE DETECTION OF AMINOMETHANOL

HAYLEY BUNN, CHASE P SCHULTZ, CHRISTOPHER M JERNIGAN, *Department of Chemistry, University of Wisconsin-Madison, Madison, WI, USA*; SUSANNA L. WIDICUS WEAVER, *Chemistry and Astronomy, University of Wisconsin-Madison, Madison, WI, USA.*

$O(^1D)$ insertion reactions with methylamine are a predicted pathway to form aminomethanol[a,b], a possible glycine precursor in the interstellar medium. In a preliminary study, $O(^1D)$ insertion into methane and ethylene have shown to successfully result in the formation and spectral detection of methanol and vinyl alcohol, respectively[c]. Despite the detection of these insertion products, the complex mixture resulting under these conditions has not been well characterized. Likewise, $O(^1D)$ insertion reactions with methylamine have proven more troublesome. We have examined the reaction pathways of the chemical mixtures resulting from the 248 nm laser photolysis of ozone + methane and ozone + methylamine. Millimeter/submillimeter spectra have been collected in both the frequency and time domain. The observed product pathways have been modeled using F0AM (Framework for 0-D Atmospheric Modelling) with the aim of determining the ideal experimental conditions to extend the lifetime of aminomethanol to enable its spectral detection. The results of both the laboratory studies and the modeling work will be presented.

[a] B. M. Hays, S. L. Widicus Weaver, J. Phys. Chem. A, 117, 32, 7142-7148 (2013)
[b] M. E. Wolf, P. R. Hoobler, J. M. Turney, H. F. Schaefer III, Phys. Chem. Chem. Phys., 2019,21, 24194-24205
[c] B. M. Hays, N. Wehres, B. Alligood DePrince, A. A.M. Roy, J. C. Laas, S. L. Widicus Weaver, Chem. Phys. Lett., 630, 18 (2015)

FC10 **8:36 – 8:37**

TESTING DUST-SURFACE FORMATION MODEL OF PREBIOTIC MOLECULE CH_3NCO IN STAR-FORMING CORE SAGITTARIUS B2(N1) BY ALMA

KYOICHI IZUOKA, *Faculty of Science Division I, Tokyo University of Science, Tokyo , Japan*; MITSUNORI ARAKI, *Research Institute for Science and Technology, Tokyo University of Science, Noda, Japan*; YUKI OHNO, *Faculty of Science Division I, Tokyo University of Science, Tokyo , Japan*; TAKAHIRO OYAMA, *Department of Materials and Life Sciences, Sophia University, Tokyo, Japan*; SHURO TAKANO, *College of Engineering, Nihon University, Fukushima, Japan*; NOBUHIKO KUZE, *Department of Materials and Life Sciences, Sophia University, Tokyo, Japan*; KOICHI TSUKIYAMA, *Faculty of Science Division I, Tokyo University of Science, Shinjuku-ku, Tokyo, Japan.*

Origin of organic molecules on Earth is discussed to be interstellar clouds, because comets carried molecules produced in clouds. Methyl isocyanate CH_3NCO is presumably one of the delivered organic molecules at the primitive earth. However, observed abundance ratios of $[CH_3NCO]/[HNCO]$ in molecular clouds [1] are clearly lower than that in the comet 67P [2]. Recently a theoretical study has suggested that this abundance anomaly can be explained by a model of dust-surface formation of CH_3NCO in molecular clouds [3]. If that is the case, high-temperature CH_3NCO desorbed from dust surface makes a compact distribution in a central region of a star-forming core. To examine this temperature and distribution condition, the spatial and spectral data of CH_3NCO toward the (N1) core of the star-forming region Sagittarius B2 observed by ALMA were investigated in the 94–113 GHz region for 24 rotational lines. Considering intensity maps and velocity structures, a compact distribution relating to a bipolar molecular flow and an accretion disk already suggested [4] was imaged by CH_3NCO. Rotational temperatures are 20–60 K and column densities are 10^{15} cm^{-2}. These results suggest hot and dense conditions of this molecule in the central region of the core. Hence, CH_3NCO detected in the present data is likely to be produced on dust surface. The model explaining the abundance anomaly is observationally supported. [1] Halfen et al., 2015, ApJL, 812, L5. [2] Goesmann et al., 2015, Sci., 349, 6247. [3] Majumdar et al., 2018, MNRAS, 473, L59. [4] Lis et al. 1993, ApJ, 402, 238.

FC11 **8:40 – 8:41**

REEVALUATION OF THE C_4H ABUNDANCE BASED ON THE REVISED DIPOLE MOMENT

TAKAHIRO OYAMA, *Department of Materials and Life Sciences, Sophia University, Tokyo, Japan*; YOSHIHIRO SUMIYOSHI, *Division of Pure and Applied Science, Faculty of Science and Technology, Gunma University, Maebashi, Japan*; MITSUNORI ARAKI, *Research Institute for Science and Technology, Tokyo University of Science, Noda, Japan*; SHURO TAKANO, *College of Engineering, Nihon University, Fukushima, Japan*; NOBUHIKO KUZE, *Department of Materials and Life Sciences, Sophia University, Tokyo, Japan*; KOICHI TSUKIYAMA, *Faculty of Science Division I, Tokyo University of Science, Shinjuku-ku, Tokyo, Japan.*

C_nH molecules are the simplest linear carbon chains in space. They are crucial for not only probes of young clouds but also benchmarks of calculations of chemical reaction network. However, their abundances occasionally show anomaly. For example, observed column densities of C_4H in various sources are one order of magnitude higher than theoretically estimated values. Herbst & Osamura suggested that these excesses of C_4H come from the theoretically determined dipole moment of C_4H.[a] The dipole moment in the electronic ground state of $^2\Sigma^+$ was calculated to be 0.87 D by the RCCSD(T)/aug-cc-pVDZ level of *ab initio* theory.[b] However, the mixing of wavefunctions between the ground state and the low-lying electronic excited state of $^2\Pi$ having the large dipole moment of 4.4 D occurs, giving a higher dipole moment to the ground state. By using a higher dipole moment, a smaller column density is derived via observed line intensities. In the present study, we re-calculated the dipole moment of C_4H by quantum chemical calculations including the mixing.[c] The calculations were carried out by the multi-reference configuration interaction level of *ab initio* theory using the cc-pVQZ basis set. The new dipole moment was derived to be 2.10 D, which is about 2.4 times larger than the value of 0.87 D used so far. Reported lines of C_4H were analyzed to revise column densities by using the new dipole moment. Revised values are about a factor of 6 smaller than those in the previous works. Using the revised column density of C_4H, abundances of the $C_{2n}H$ (n = 1–4) series show exponential smooth decreases with carbon-chain length in various sources.

[a]Herbst & Osamura, 2008, *ApJ*, **679**, 1670. [b]Woon, 1995, *Chem. Phys. Lett.* **244**, 45. [c]Oyama *et al.*, 2020, *ApJ*, **890**, 39.

FC12 **8:44 – 8:45**

ANALYSIS OF THE CH_2OH RADICAL SPECTRUM WITH AN IAM TUNNELING APPROACH

L. H. COUDERT, OLIVIA CHITARRA, JEAN-THIBAUT SPANIOL, MARIE-ALINE MARTIN-DRUMEL, OLIVIER PIRALI, *Institut des Sciences Moléculaires d'Orsay, Université Paris Saclay, CNRS, Orsay, France*; J.-C. LOISON, *Institut des Sciences Moléculaires, Université de Bordeaux, Talence, France.*

Early *ab initio* calculations[a] revealed that the hydroxymethyl radical (CH_2OH) is a non-rigid species exhibiting a complicated potential energy surface. It displays 4 C_1 non-superimposable, energetically equivalent, equilibrium configurations and 4 C_s maxima, approximately 300 and 1500 cm^{-1} above the equilibrium configurations. The large amplitude motion of the radical can be pictured as an internal rotation of the CH_2 group with respect to the OH group. The axis of internal rotation is the CO bond and the two-fold symmetry hindering potential is characterized by a barrier height of 1500 cm^{-1}. Aided by new *ab initio* results, the torsional levels associated with this torsional motion were computed. The energy levels display a tunneling splitting which, for the ground torsional level, was found to be smaller than 0.1 cm^{-1}.

As the large amplitude motion of the hydroxymethyl radical seems to be well described by the high barrier approximation, the tunneling IAM water dimer formalism[b] was used to derive a fitting approach aimed at accounting for its rotation-tunneling energy. The effects of the fine spin-rotation and hyperfine spin-spin couplings were also included since there is an unpaired electron.

In the paper, the analysis with the IAM approach[b] of already available[c,d] and newly measured sub-millimeter wave spectroscopic data will be reported. The fitted value of the tunneling splitting will be compared to that retrieved from the torsional energy level calculation. The rotational dependence of the tunneling splitting will be discussed.

[a]Saebø, Radom, and Schaefer, *J. Chem. Phys.* **78** (1983) 845; Marenich and Boggs, *J. Chem. Phys.* **119** (2003) 3098; and Ibid., *J. Chem. Phys.* **119** (2003) 10105
[b]Hougen, *J. Mol. Spectrosc.* **114** (1985) 395; and Coudert and Hougen, *J. Mol. Spectrosc.* **130** (1988) 86
[c]Bermudez, Bailleux, and Cernicharo, *A&A* **598** (2017) A9
[d]Chitarra, Martin-Drumel, Gans, Loison, Spezzano, Lattanzi, Müller, and Pirali, *A&A* **644** (2020) A123

FC13 **8:48 – 8:49**

HIGH-LEVEL ROVIBRATIONAL CALCULATIONS ON KETENIMINE

MARTIN TSCHÖPE, BENJAMIN SCHRÖDER, SEBASTIAN ERFORT, GUNTRAM RAUHUT, *Institute for Theoretical Chemistry, University of Stuttgart, Stuttgart, Baden-Württemberg, Germany.*

From an astrochemical point of view ketenimine (CH_2CNH) is a complex organic molecule (COM) and therefore likely to be a building block for biologically relevant molecules. Since it has been detected in the star-forming region Sagittarius B2(N), it is of high relevance in this field. Although experimental data are available for certain bands, for some energy ranges such as above $1200\,cm^{-1}$ reliable data virtually do not exist. In addition, high-level ab initio calculations are neither reported for ketenimine nor for one of its deuterated isotopologues. In this paper, we provide for the first time data from accurate quantum chemical calculations and a thorough analysis of the full rovibrational spectrum. Based on high-level potential energy surfaces obtained from explicitly correlated coupled-cluster calculations including up to 4-mode coupling terms, the (ro)vibrational spectrum of ketenimine has been studied in detail by variational calculations relying on rovibrational configuration interaction (RVCI) theory. Strong Fermi resonances were found for all isotopologues. Rovibrational infrared intensities have been obtained from dipole moment surfaces determined from the distinguishable cluster approximation. A comparison of the spectra of the CH_2CNH molecule with experimental data validates our results, but also reveals new insight about the system, which shows very strong Coriolis coupling effects.

FD. Small molecules

Friday, June 25, 2021 – 8:0 AM

Room: 2021 Online Everywhere

Chair: Qian Gou, Chongqing University, Chongqing , China

FD01 **8:00 – 8:01**

IN SEARCH OF PHOSPHORUS IN ASTRONOMICAL ENVIRONMENTS: THE REACTION BETWEEN THE CP RADICAL ($X^2\Sigma^+$) AND METHANIMINE

SILVIA ALESSANDRINI, FRANCESCA TONOLO, *Scuola Normale Superiore, Scuola Normale Superiore, Pisa, Italy*; CRISTINA PUZZARINI, *Chemistry G. Ciamician, University of Bologna, Bologna, Italy.*

Phosphorus belongs to the group of the so-called "main biogenic elements", which includes the most abundant elements in living systems. Accordingly, when seeking to better understand the evolution of the universe -with a keen eye on abiogenesis- phosphorus and its compounds cannot be overlooked. However, the chemical evolution of such element in the interstellar medium (ISM) is still far from an accurate characterization.
To provide a contribution in this direction, a recent work investigated the reactivity beetween the CP radical ($X^2\Sigma^+$) and methanimine (CH_2NH), both detected in the carbon-rich circumstellar shell IRC+10216. This type of reaction is particularly promising because it fits into a peculiar reactivity of methanimine with different radicals, among which we find the isoelectronic CCH and CN radicals, the reactions with these latter being very well characterized. This supports the idea of a general mechanism for the formation of complex imines in the interstellar clouds.
An accurate investigation of the reactive CH_2NH + CP potential energy surface (PES) revealed the presence of submerged formation pathways for three main reaction products, namely E- and Z-2-phosphanylidyneethan-1-imine (HNCHCP) and N-(phosphaneylidynemethyl)methanimine (CH_2NCP).
Despite the proof of concept of their feasible formation in gas phase from an energetic point of view, the laboratory synthesis of species like HNCHCP and CH_2NCP is particularly complex. This could hamper the identification of their rotational transitions required in view of predicting and confirming their presence in the ISM.
In order to provide a useful support to experimental measurements, computed spectra represent a mandatory starting point. This talk will delve into the accurate spectroscopic characterization of these latter species with a methodology at the state of the art, which is able to predict rotational transitions with accuracy better than 0.2%.

FD02 **8:04 – 8:05**

THE STRUCTURE OF ScC_2 ($\tilde{X}^2A_1$): A COMBINED FOURIER TRANSFORM MICROWAVE/MILLIMETER-WAVE SPECTROSCOPY AND COMPUTATIONAL STUDY

MARK BURTON, *Department of Chemistry and Biochemistry, University of Arizona, Tucson, AZ, USA*; QIANYI CHENG, *Chemistry, University of Memphis, Memphis, Tennessee, USA*; DeWAYNE T HALFEN, *Department of Chemistry and Biochemistry, Department of Astronomy, The University of Arizona, Tucson, AZ, USA*; J. HAYDEN LANE, *Department of Chemistry and Biochemistry, University of Arizona, Tucson, AZ, USA*; NATHAN DeYONKER, *Department of Chemistry, University of Memphis, Memphis, Tennessee, USA*; LUCY M. ZIURYS, *Dept. of Astronomy, Dept. of Chemistry, Arizona Radio Observatory, The University of Arizona, Tucson, AZ, US.*

Pure rotational spectra of $Sc^{13}C_2$ ($\tilde{X}^2A_1$) and $Sc^{12}C^{13}C$ ($\tilde{X}^2A'$) have been obtained using Fourier Transform microwave/millimeter-wave methods. These molecules were synthesized from the combination of scandium vapor, produce via laser ablation, with mixtures of $^{13}CH_4$ or $^{13}CH_4/^{12}CH_4$, diluted in argon. The four lowest a-type rotational transitions were observed for both species in the frequency range of 14 – 61 GHz. Each exhibit hyperfine splittings due to the nuclear spins of ^{13}C (I = 1/2) and/or Sc (I = 7/2). Rotational, spin-rotation, and hyperfine parameters have been determined for these isotopologues, and a refined structure for ScC_2 established. In addition, a quartic force field was calculated for ScC_2 and its isotopologues using a highly accurate coupled cluster-based composite method, incorporating complete basis set extrapolation, scalar relativistic corrections, outer core and inner core electron correlation, and higher-order valence correlation effects. The ratio of experimental to theoretical (B+C) values is 1.005 for all calculated isotopologues, yielding a promising route towards predictive gas phase rotational spectroscopy for new metal-carbon bearing radicals.

FD03 **8:08 – 8:09**

THE MILLIMETER WAVE SPECTRUM OF RARE IRON MONOXIDE ISOTOPOLOGUES: A MASS INDEPENDENT ANALYSIS

BJÖRN WAẞMUTH, ALEXANDER A. BREIER, GUIDO W FUCHS, THOMAS GIESEN, *Institute of Physics, University Kassel, Kassel, Germany.*

The role of iron containing molecular species in the interstellar medium is not fully understood. Iron monoxide was tentatively detected toward Sagittarius B2.[a] In the laboratory the isotopologues ^{56}FeO and ^{54}FeO were rotationally measured in all five spin states in their $X^5\Delta_i$ ground state by Allen et al.[b] We present laboratory measurements of rotational lines of the rare isotopologues ^{57}FeO, ^{58}FeO, and ^{56}Fe^{18}O, including the hyperfine structure splitting due to the nuclear spin $I = 1/2$ of ^{57}Fe.[c]

We performed a mass independent analysis[d] with the new isotopic data and data from the literature. This enables us to predict molecular parameters and line transitions of the radioactive isotopologue ^{60}FeO. Kamiński *et al.* detected the radioactive molecule ^{26}AlF in the merger CK Vulpeculae by means of rotational spectroscopy [e]. This is a powerful novel approach to use molecular transition to search for iron and its isotopes. Iron monoxide is a well suited candidate for a astronomical search for ^{60}Fe.

[a]C.M. Walmsley *et al., Astrophys. J.*, **566**:L109-L112, (2002).
[b]M.D. Allen *et al., Chem. Phys. Lett.*, **257**, 130-136, (1996).
[c]B. Waßmuth *et al., Mol. Phys.*, **118**, 19-20, (2020).
[d]A.A. Breier *et al., J. Mol. Spectrosc.*, **355**, 46-58, (2019).
[e]T. Kamiński *et al., Nature Astronomy*, **2**, 778-783, (2018).

FD04 **8:12 – 8:13**

HYPERFINE STRUCTURE OF NITROSYL IODIDE (INO)

AKIKO NISHITSUNOI, HIROYUKI OZEKI, *Department of Environmental Science, Toho University, Funabashi, Japan*; KAORI KOBAYASHI, *Department of Physics, University of Toyama, Toyama, Japan*; STEPHANE BAILLEUX, *Laboratoire PhLAM, Université de Lille - Sciences et Technologies, Villeneuve d'Ascq, France*.

INO or Nitrosyl iodide is the simplest form among the family of INOx (x=1 to 3), which may be viewed as important temporary reservoir species for iodine and nitrogen oxides. Since the corresponding chlorine and bromine species have already been well characterized by microwave and millimeter-wave spectroscopy, spectroscopic information of the iodine compounds is very limited. We have successfully measured submillimeter-wave spectrum of INO in 2016, without resolving any hyperfine splitting due to iodine and nitrogen nuclei.[a] Completion of this task is mandatory for full understanding of the molecule. We have observed millimeter-wave spectra of INO at millimeter-wave region. Hyperfine splitting were observed at the frequency of around 150 GHz. The electric quadrupole coupling constants for iodine nucleus was determined for the first time.

[a]S. Bailleux, D. Duflot, S. Aiba, S. Nakahama and H. Ozeki, hem. Phys. Lett. **650**, 73-75 (2016)

FD06 **8:20 – 8:21**

HIGH-RESOLUTION ANALYSIS OF THE 83.3 μm TORSIONAL BANDS OF THE $ClONO_2$ MOLECULE

F. KWABIA TCHANA, ANUSANTH ANANTHARAJAH, JEAN-MARIE FLAUD, *CNRS - Université de Paris - Université Paris Est Créteil , LISA, Créteil, France*; LAURENT MANCERON, *Synchrotron SOLEIL, CNRS-MONARIS UMR 8233 and Beamline AILES, Saint Aubin, France*; JOHANNES ORPHAL, *Karlsruhe Institute of Technology, IMK, Eggenstein-Leopoldshafen, Germany*.

Chlorine nitrate ($ClONO_2$) is a very important atmospheric "reservoir" of ClO and NO_2, destroying stratospheric ozone through catalytic cycles[a]. It was detected for the first time by infrared (IR) spectroscopy[b], a detection confirmed and extended by the MIPAS[c] and the ATMOS satellite experiments[d]. Many high-resolution microwave and mid-IR spectroscopy studies of $ClONO_2$ have been published[e]. However, $ClONO_2$ presents 4 fundamentals in the far-IR region below 600 cm^{-1}, with the lowest one corresponding to the torsional mode ν_9 around 83.3 μm. This band has been observed at low resolution[f] but without precise determination of the band center. More recently, the analysis of the mid-IR ν_8 and $\nu_8 + \nu_9$ band spectral regions of $^{35}ClONO_2$ allowed the indirect but accurate determination of the ν_9 band center[g].

In this work, the 83.3 μm region of $ClONO_2$ has been recorded at high resolution (0.001 cm^{-1}) using a Fourier transform spectrometer and the SOLEIL synchrotron light source. The spectrum corresponds to the absorption of the torsional mode, ν_9 around 123 $cm^{-1}$and a series of $n\nu_9$-(n-1)ν_9 hot bands. In this talk, the analysis of the ν_9 bands of $^{35}ClONO_2$ and $^{37}ClONO_2$ and $2\nu_9$-ν_9 band of $^{35}ClONO_2$ will be presented. In turn, this will enable an analysis of the hot bands involving low energy levels in the mid-IR region where $ClONO_2$ is detected and modelled.

[a]P. J. Crutzen, *Quart. J. Royal Met. Soc.* **96**, 320 (1970); M. J. Molina and F. S. Rowland, *Nature* **249**, 810 (1974).
[b]D. G. Murcray *et al.*, *Geophys. Res. Lett.* **6**, 857 (1979).
[c]H. Fischer *et al.*, *Atmos. Chem. Phys.* **8**, 2151 (2008).
[d]R. Zander *et al.*, *Geophys. Res. Lett.* **13**, 757 (1986).
[e]J. Orphal, M. Birk, G. Wagner, and J.-M. Flaud, *Chem. Phys. Lett.* **690**, 82 (2017).
[f]J. W. Fleming, *Infrared Phys.* **18**, 791 (1978); K. V. Chance and W. A. Traub, *J. Mol. Spectrosc.* **95**, 306 (1982).
[g]J.-M. Flaud, W. J. Lafferty, J. Orphal, M. Birk, and G. Wagner, *Mol. Phys.* **101**, 1527 (2003).

FD07 **8:24 – 8:25**

HIGH-RESOLUTION FAR INFRARED SPECTROSCOPY AND ANALYSES OF TRIOXANE

CYRIL RICHARD, VINCENT BOUDON, *Laboratoire ICB, CNRS/Université de Bourgogne, DIJON, France*; OLIVIER PIRALI, *Institut des Sciences Moléculaires d'Orsay, Université Paris-Sud, Orsay, France*; PIERRE ASSELIN, *CNRS, De la Molécule aux Nano-Objets: Réactivité, Interactions, Spectroscopies, MONARIS, Sorbonne Université , PARIS, France*.

Trioxane, $(H_2CO)_3$, is a symmetric top that belongs to the C_{3v} symmetry group. The molecule owns 20 fundamental modes that are dispatched as 7 symmetric vibrations of type A1, 3 vibrations of type A2 and 10 doubly degenerate vibrations of type E.

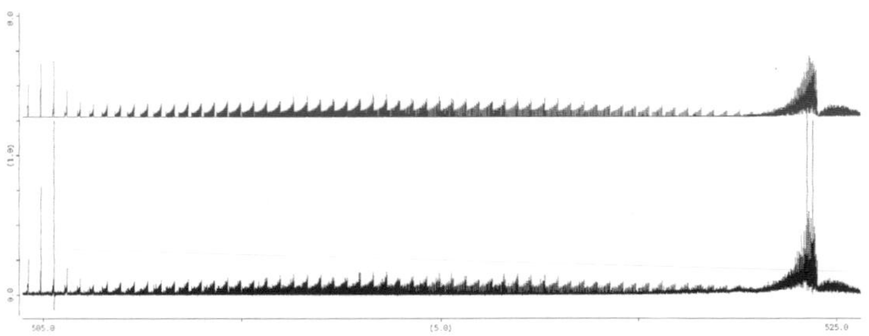

Infrared spectra of trioxane have been recorded in the 50–650 cm^{-1} range using a high resolution Bruker IFS 125 interferometer located at the AILES beamline of the SOLEIL synchrotron facility. Owing to its higher brilliance in the far-infrared region, the SOLEIL synchrotron radiation was used to improve the signal-to-noise ratio of the spectrum at the maximal resolution of 0.001 cm^{-1}.

We present here a detailed analysis and modeling of intense OCO deformation ν_7 and ν_{19} modes as well as weaker CH_2 torsion ν_{20} mode and its first overtone $2\nu_{20}$. Thanks to the formalism and programs developed in Dijon, we could determine accurately the effective Hamiltonian parameters for these 3 modes.

FD08 **8:28 – 8:29**

HIGH RESOLUTION INFRARED SPECTRA OF THE LINEAR DIALUMINUM MONOXIDE Al-O-Al

DANIEL WITSCH, EILEEN DÖRING, *Institute of Physics, University of Kassel, Kassel, Germany*; JÜRGEN GAUSS, *Institut für Physikalische Chemie, Universität Mainz, Mainz, Germany*; THOMAS GIESEN, GUIDO W FUCHS, *Institute of Physics, University Kassel, Kassel, Germany.*

In the vicinity of evolved stars cosmic dust forms via nucleation processes. Many of the initial steps of nucleation are not well understood but the investigation of small di- and triatomic molecules at radio or infrared wavelengths in these stellar environments can help elucidating the dust formation process. Especially molecules made of refractory material that condense already at temperatures above thousand Kelvin, like aluminum, are thought to act as seed molecules for dust grains. In this work the gas phase spectrum of the symmetric linear dialuminum monoxide Al-O-Al is investigated in our laboratory. Because Al_2O has no permanent electric dipole moment it can not be detected at radio wavelengths but it has a unique infrared ro-vibrational spectrum around 10 μm. We recorded the ro-vibrational absorption spectrum of Al_2O by using a frequency modulated quantum cascade laser in combination with Herriott-type multipass optics. The molecules were produced and rotationally cooled down to around 120 K by laser ablating an aluminum rod and purging the resulting ablation plume with a N_2O/He buffer gas mixture that subsequently underwent an adiabatic expansion into a vacuum chamber. The spectra reveal a line intensity alteration due to the spin-statistical weight induced by two identical spin 5/2 ^{27}Al atoms. The fundamental ν_3= 1-0 as well as five hot band transitions could be observed. Highly precise molecular constants could be determined and a l-type resonance was analyzed. The here presented transition frequencies will allow for astrophysical searches of this molecule in space.

FD09 **8:32 – 8:33**

SUB-DOPPLER DOUBLE-RESONANCE SPECTROSCOPY OF METHANE USING A FREQUENCY COMB PROBE

VINICIUS SILVA DE OLIVEIRA, ISAK SILANDER, ALEXANDRA C JOHANSSSON, OVE AXNER, ALEKSANDRA FOLTYNOWICZ, *Department of Physics, Umea University, Umea, Sweden*; LUCILE RUTKOWSKI, *IPR (Institut de Physique de Rennes)-UMR 6251, Univ Rennes, CNRS, Rennes, France*; GRZEGORZ SOBOŃ, *Faculty of Electronics, Wrocław University of Science and Technology, Wrocław, Poland*; KEVIN LEHMANN, *Departments of Chemistry and Physics, University of Virginia, Charlottesville, VA, USA.*

Methane is the first organic molecule detected in hot-Jupiter exoplanets [1] and the observed spectra carry information about the atmospheric conditions, the photochemistry, and planetary formation. To extract this information, we need accurate theoretical models of the spectra verified by high-precision laboratory measurements. However, the energy level structure of highly excited CH_4 is poorly understood; there exist limited line-by-line assignments of laboratory spectra above the Icosad polyad (6,000 cm^{-1}). We performed double-resonance spectroscopy using a 3.3 μm continuous wave pump and 1.67 μm frequency comb probe to measure sub-Doppler transitions in the $3\nu_3 \leftarrow \nu_3$ range (up to 9000 cm^{-1}) [2-3]. We detected 36 (J'=0-2) transitions with 1.7 MHz frequency accuracy, limited by the stability of the pump. We assigned the transitions using the intensity ratios measured with parallel and perpendicular pump-probe polarizations, and by comparison of transition frequencies and intensities to predictions from the TheoReTS database [4]. Recently, we implemented an enhancement cavity for the comb probe and improved the absorption sensitivity by two orders of magnitude, allowing detection of a wider range of transitions with better signal-to-noise ratio. Our work is the first measurement of sub-Doppler molecular response using a frequency comb and the first verification of the accuracy of the theoretical prediction that start from highly vibrationally excited methane states. [1] M. R. Swain, G. Vasisht, and G. Tinetti, Nature 452, 329 (2008). [2] A. Foltynowicz et al., Phys. Rev. Lett. 126, 063001 (2021). [3] A. Foltynowicz et al., Phys. Rev. A 103, 022810 (2021) [4] M. Rey, A. V. Nikitin, Y. L. Babikov, and V. G. Tyuterev, J. Mol. Spectrosc. 327, 138 (2016).

FD10 **8:36 – 8:37**

NEW LINE POSITIONS ANALYSIS OF THE ν_3 BANDS OF $^{35}ClNO_2$ AND $^{37}ClNO_2$ AROUND 370 cm^{-1}

ANUSANTH ANANTHARAJAH, F. KWABIA TCHANA, JEAN-MARIE FLAUD, *CNRS - Université de Paris - Université Paris Est Créteil , LISA, Créteil, France*; LAURENT MANCERON, *Synchrotron SOLEIL, CNRS-MONARIS UMR 8233 and Beamline AILES, Saint Aubin, France*; JOHANNES ORPHAL, *Karlsruhe Institute of Technology, IMK, Eggenstein-Leopoldshafen, Germany.*

Nitryl chloride ($ClNO_2$) is of atmospheric interest, since it is produced by heterogeneous reactions, in the marine troposphere, between NaCl sea-salt aerosols and gaseous N_2O_5[a], in the polluted continental air[b], and possibly also on polar stratospheric clouds, between N_2O_5 and solid HCl[c]. Many high-resolution spectroscopic studies of $ClNO_2$ in the microwave and mid-infrared regions are available[d]. However, $ClNO_2$ presents two fundamentals in the far-infrared region below 600 cm^{-1}, with the lowest one corresponding to the Cl-N stretching mode, ν_3 around 370 cm^{-1}.

A new investigation of the ν_3 bands of $^{35}ClNO_2$ and $^{37}ClNO_2$ has been performed using a high resolution (0.00102 cm^{-1}) Fourier transform spectrum recorded at SOLEIL with highly improved experimental conditions as compared to a previous study[e], leading to a *well resolved spectrum*. As a consequence, significantly better results than previously were obtained. The line assignments were pursued up to higher J and K_a quantum number values, J = 83 and K_a = 44. For both isotopomers, a total of 6331 transitions were reproduced with a root-mean-square deviation of 2×10^{-4} cm^{-1}using a Watson-type A-reduced Hamiltonian. Improved band centers, rotational and centrifugal distortion constants for the ν_3 fundamental bands of $^{35}ClNO_2$ and $^{37}ClNO_2$ have been determined. The synthetic line list obtained in this study will be interesting for future measurements of $ClNO_2$ in the atmosphere, e.g. using the new satellite mission FORUM (ESA) covering the 150-1400 cm^{-1}spectral region.

[a]B. J. Finlayson-Pitts *et al., Nature* **337**, 241 (1989); W. Behnke *et al., J. Aerosol Sci.* **24**, 115 (1993); H. D. Osthoff *et al., Nat. Geosci.* **1**, 324 (2008).
[b]L. H. Mielke *et al., Environ. Sci. Technol.* **45**, 8889 (2011); G. J. Phillips *et al., Geophys. Res. Lett.* **39**, L10811 (2012).
[c]M. A. Tolbert, M. J. Rossi, and D. M. Golden, *Science* **240**, 1018 (1988); M. T. Leu, *Geophys. Res. Lett.* **15**, 851 (1988).
[d]J.-M. Flaud, A. Anantharajah, F. Kwabia Tchana *et al., JQSRT* **224**, 217 (2019).
[e]J. Orphal, M. Morillon-Chapey, S. Klee, G. C. Mellau, and M. Winnewisser, *J. Mol. Spectrosc.* **109**, 101 (1998).

FD11 **8:40 – 8:41**

ISOTOPIC RELATIONS FOR TETRAHEDRAL AND OCTAHEDRAL MOLECULES

MICHEL LOETE, CYRIL RICHARD, VINCENT BOUDON, *Laboratoire ICB, CNRS/Université de Bourgogne, DIJON, France.*

The study and analysis of heavy spherical-top molecules is often not straightforward. The presence of hot bands and of many isotopologues can lead to a high line congestion very difficult for assignment.

In this work, using a low-order model we have derived very simple isotopic relations in order to determine initial parameters of the analysis.

We also show that an identical approach can be used for XY_4 and XY_6 molecules and all these results are illustrated by the comparison of numerical computations and experiments for different molecules: CH_4, GeH_4, RuO_4 (as shown in the figure on the right) and SF_6.

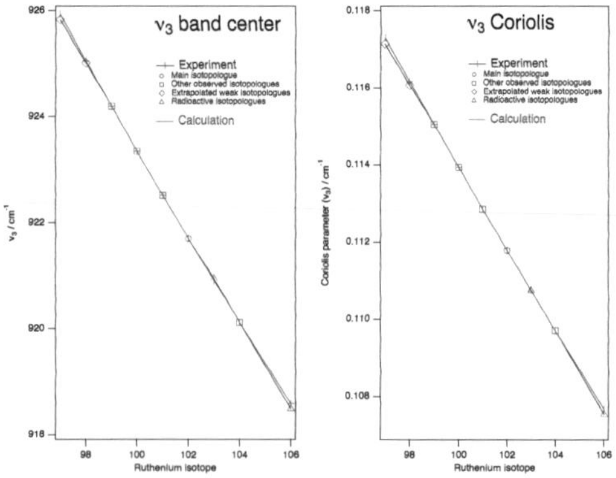

Reference: M. Loëte, C. Richard and V. Boudon, *J. Mol . Struct.* **1206**, 127729 (2020).

FD12 **8:44 – 8:45**

ROTATIONAL ANALYSIS OF A NEW [15.05] Ω=0^+ – $X\ ^3\Sigma(0^+)$ ELECTRONIC TRANSITION OF TUNGSTEN SULFIDE (WS) IN THE 14,900 - 16,100 cm^{-1} REGION OBSERVED USING ILS-FTS

KRISTIN N BALES, JACK C HARMS, JAMES J O'BRIEN, *Chemistry and Biochemistry, University of Missouri, St. Louis, MO, USA*; LEAH C O'BRIEN, *Department of Chemistry, Southern Illinois University, Edwardsville, IL, USA.*

Three bands of tungsten sulfide, WS, in the 14,900 - 16,100 cm^{-1} region have have been recorded in high resolution using Intracavity Laser Spectroscopy integrated with Fourier Transform detection (ILS-FTS). WS was formed in the plasma discharge resulting from a 0.05 A – 0.15 A DC current applied to a tungsten-lined copper hollow cathode within the resonator cavity of a dye laser using gas flows of Ar, CS_2, and H_2 at a pressure of approximately 1 torr. Based on isotopologue shifts, the observed WS bands are assigned as the (0,0), (1,0), and (2,0) bands of a new [15.05] Ω=0^+ – $X\ ^3\Sigma(0^+)$ electronic transition, with bandheads near 15,050, 15,575, and 16,094 cm^{-1}, respectively. The observed line positions were rotationally analyzed using PGOPHER, and spectroscopic constants are compared to a previous computational work [L.F. Tsang *et al.*, J. Mol. Spec. 2019 (359), 31-36]. The results of the analysis will be presented.

FD13 **8:48 – 8:49**

CHARACTERIZATION OF THE $A^2\Sigma^+$ STATE OF SH/SD RADICALS BY PHOTODISSOCIATION SPECTROSCOPY

YUAN QIN, XIANFENG ZHENG, YU SONG, GE SUN, *Department of Chemistry, University of California, Riverside, CA, USA*; JINGSONG ZHANG, *Department of Chemistry and Air Pollution Research Center, University of California, Riverside, CA, USA.*

Vibrational levels of the $A^2\Sigma^+$ state of SH (v' = 0-7) and SD (v' = 0-8) radical are investigated via photodissociation using high-n Rydberg atom time-of-flight technique. By measuring the H-atom product translational energy distributions, contributions from overlapping transitions can be separated, and the H/D-atom photofragment yield (PFY) spectra are obtained across various SH/SD $A^2\Sigma^+ \leftarrow X^2\Pi$ rovibrational bands. The upper $A^2\Sigma^+$ state vibrational levels v' = 5-7 of SH and v' = 3-8 of SD are observed for the first time. Analysis of the PFY spectra using the simulation program PGOPHER[a] gives vibrational origins along with rovibrational linewidths of the $A^2\Sigma^+$ state of SH/SD. The fitted linewidths in the PFY spectra for SH v' = 1-6 and SD v' = 2-6 states are broad ($\geq$ 1.5 cm^{-1}), demonstrating that those levels undergo rapid predissociation with lifetimes on the order of picosecond. While the lifetime of SD v' = 0, N'= 1 and 2 levels are determined to be 247 $\pm$ 30 ns and 168 $\pm$ 40 ns from pump-probe time delay measurements, respectively. The experimental lifetimes are in reasonable agreement with the theoretical predictions.

[a]Western, *J. Quant. Spectrosc. Radiat. Transfer*, 186, 221 (2016)

FE. Atmospheric science

Friday, June 25, 2021 – 8:0 AM

Room: 2021 Online Everywhere

Chair: Hamzeh Telfah, University of Louisville, LOUISVILLE, KY, USA

FE01 **8:00 – 8:01**

COMPUTATIONAL KINETICS STUDY OF ATMOSPHERIC RING-CLOSURE AND DEHYDRATION REACTIONS OF 1,4-HYDROXYCARBONYLS IN THE GAS PHASE[a]

PARANDAMAN ARATHALA, CHANIN B. TANGTARTHARAKUL, AMITABHA SINHA, *Department of Chemistry and Biochemistry, UC San Diego, San Diego, CA, USA.*

Several experimental studies have shown that 1,4-hydroxycarbonyls can undergo sequential reactions involving cyclization followed by dehydration to form dihydrofurans.[b] As dihydrofurans contain a double bond, they are highly reactive towards OH, O_3, and NO_3 in the atmosphere. In this work, we investigate the energetics and kinetics of the cyclization and dehydration reaction steps associated with 4-hydroxybutanal (4-OH-BL), a prototypical 1,4-hydroxycarbonyl molecule using ab initio calculations. The cyclization step transforms 4-OH-BL into 2-hydroxytetrahydrofuran (2-OH-THF), which can subsequently undergo dehydration to form 2,3-dihydrofuran. Since the barriers associated with the cyclization and dehydration steps for 4-OH-BL are respectively 34.8 and 63.0 kcal/mol in the absence of any catalyst, both reaction steps are not feasible under atmospheric conditions. However, the presence of a suitable catalyst can significantly reduce the reaction barriers. Therefore, we investigate the effect of a single molecule of H_2O, HO_2 radical, HC(O)OH, HNO_3, and H_2SO_4 as catalysts on the reaction. We find that H_2SO_4 lowers the reaction barriers the greatest, with the barrier for the cyclization step being reduced to -13.1 kcal/mol and that for the dehydration step going down to 9.2 kcal/mol, below their respective separated starting reactants. Interestingly, our rate calculations shows that HNO_3 provides the fastest rate due the combined effects of larger atmospheric concentration and reduced barrier. Thus, our study suggests that with acid catalysis the cyclization reaction step can readily occur for 1,4-hydroxycarbonyls in the gas phase. The 2-OH-THF products, once formed, likely undergo reaction with OH radicals in the atmosphere because the dehydration step involves a large barrier even with acid catalysis. The reaction pathways and rate constant for this reaction in the presence of molecular oxygen ($^3O_2$) were also investigated using computational chemistry over the 200-300K temperature range. The main products found from the 2-OH-THF + OH/$^3O_2$ reactions are succinaldehyde + HO_2 and 2,3-dihydro-2-furanol + HO_2.

[a]The authors are grateful to NSF for support of this work.

[b]Atkinson, R. et al. Atmos. Environ. 2008, 42, 5859; Ranney, A. P.; Ziemann, P. J. J. Phys. Chem. A 2016, 120, 2561.

FE03 **8:08 – 8:09**

TEMPERATURE-DEPENDENT WATER UPTAKE BEHAVIOR OF CLUSTERS RELEVANT TO NEW PARTICLE FORMATION

JOHN J. KREINBIHL, *Department of Chemistry, Stony Brook University, Stony Brook, NY, USA*; NICOLINE C. FREDERIKS, CHRISTOPHER J. JOHNSON, *Chemistry, Stony Brook University, Stony Brook, NY, USA.*

New particle formation is a process in which trace vapors in the atmosphere cluster and grow into larger particles. Recently, we have employed a multi-trap gas-phase ion preparation technique and cryogenic ion vibrational predissociation (CIVP) spectroscopy to identify common structural motifs for the uptake of water into cationic clusters relevant to NPF. Here we further extend this exploration using a multi-trap gas phase variable temperature mass spectrometry (VTMS) technique in which we probe the water uptake of clusters as a function of temperature to determine the associated thermodynamic parameters. We then seek to correlate these water uptake parameters to structural motifs present in the dry clusters.

FE04 **8:12 – 8:13**

A SPECTROSCOPIC AND COMPUTATIONAL PEEK INTO THE STRUCTURE OF ATMOSPHERICALLY RELEVANT DRY AND HYDRATED AMMONIUM BISULFATE CLUSTERS

NICOLINE C. FREDERIKS, *Chemistry, Stony Brook University, Stony Brook, NY, USA*; JOHN J. KREINBIHL, *Department of Chemistry, Stony Brook University, Stony Brook, NY, USA*; CHRISTOPHER J. JOHNSON, *Chemistry, Stony Brook University, Stony Brook, NY, USA*.

New particle formation (NPF) plays a crucial role in the formation of secondary aerosol particles, which in turn actively influence the climate radiative forcing balance. The magnitude of this impact is currently unclear, which limits the accuracy of climate models and their predictions. In order to minimize this radiative forcing uncertainty due to aerosol particles, information regarding surface structure and growth mechanisms of these precursor NPF clusters is necessary. Using a combination of mass spectrometry and infrared spectroscopy, these clusters containing sulfuric acid, ammonia, and water can be mass selected and irradiated with infrared light as a means to gain insight into bonding and structure of the smallest atmospherically relevant clusters. Quantum chemical calculations also provide important supplementary information regarding potential isomer stability at varying cluster sizes. However, even at the smallest cluster sizes there are several isomers that contribute to the experimental spectrum and there are even more potential isomer arrangements to explore computationally. As cluster size increases, computational expense increases exponentially, and water further complicates the computational process. Combining these experimental and computational efforts allows key structural features impacting cluster growth and stability to be identified for a subset of simple clusters. Cationic clusters containing two ammonium and one bisulfate as well as cationic clusters containing four ammonium and three bisulfate molecules are the focus of the study, as well as their singly hydrated counterparts. By understanding these small cluster binding motifs, growth models can be developed and applied to larger atmospherically relevant clusters, and ultimately help improve the accuracy of climate models.

FE05 **8:16 – 8:17**

LOW-PRESSURE YIELDS OF STABILIZED CRIEGEE INTERMEDIATES PRODUCED FROM OZONOLYSIS OF A SERIES OF ALKENES

LEI YANG, MIXTLI CAMPOS-PINEDA, *Department of Chemistry, University of California, Riverside, CA, USA*; JINGSONG ZHANG, *Department of Chemistry and Air Pollution Research Center, University of California, Riverside, CA, USA*.

Ozonolysis of alkenes is an important oxidation pathway of alkenes in the troposphere because it is involved in the production of organic aerosol and OH radicals. The mechanism of ozonolysis of alkenes involves the formation of a primary ozonide (POZ), which then decomposes into a carbonyl and a high-energy carbonyl oxide (Criegee intermediate). Criegee intermediates are produced with a broad internal energy distribution. High energy Criegee intermediates decompose into atmospherically important compounds (e.g. vinoxy, OH radical). Stabilized Criegee intermediates (sCIs) undergo reactions to produce secondary ozonides and organic aerosols.

Cavity ring-down spectroscopy (CRDS) was utilized in combination with chemical titration with sulfur dioxide (SO_2) to quantify sCIs. The reaction is carried out under various flow and low-pressure conditions. Reference cross-sections of products and reactants are fitted with spectral features to obtain product number densities.

The yields of sCIs were measured at different low pressures and the nascent yields were determined by extrapolation to zero pressure. Endocyclic alkenes show no sCI production at the pressures studied. However, acyclic alkenes show pressure-dependent sCI yields. Formaldehyde oxide (CH_2OO) from the alkenes studied has a high nascent yield due to its relatively high energy barrier for dissociation. Cis-2-butene produces higher nascent sCI than trans-2-butene, possibly due to different syn- and anti-CI branching ratios, or different POZ conformations. There is an indication that alkenes larger than 2,3-dimethyl-2-butene would have higher nascent sCI yields. The information on low-pressure yields from the current studies can be used as a benchmark for theoretical calculations.

FE06 **8:20 – 8:21**

LONG-OPEN-PATH MONITORING OF GREENHOUSE GASES BY NEAR-IR SPECTROSCOPY

HANS A SCHUESSLER, *Department of Physics and Astronomy, Texas A&M University, College Station, TX, USA*; JINBAO XIA, *State Key Laboratory of Crystal Materials, Shandong University, Jinan, China*; CARLOS RODRIGUEZ, *Department of Physics and Astronomy, Texas A & M University, college station, TX, USA*; ALEXANDRE KOLOMENSKII, *Department of Physics and Astronomy, Texas A&M University, College Station, TX, USA.*

Greenhouse gases were monitored on an open-path over kilometer length with calibrated wavelength modulation spectroscopy (WMS). A movable platform was developed capable of detecting atmospheric variations of the concentrations of methane and carbon dioxide. Two single-mode continuous commercial Distributed Feedback Diode Lasers (DFB-DL) with a fiber tail were employed as the laser sources with the wavelengths 1654 nm and 1602 nm (corresponding to the absorption features of methane and carbon dioxide, respectively) and the output powers of 10 mW each. These near-IR wavelengths give advantages of weaker interference of water absorption and readily available emitting and receiving equipment developed for applications at telecommunication wavelengths. The intensity modulation caused by turbulence was also observed. We realized an automated continuous monitoring of methane for more than 30 hours [1]. Similar measurements of carbon dioxide were performed for about 10 hours. The results show that the detection limits of methane and carbon dioxide are 2 ppb and 20 ppm with integration times of 60 seconds and 20 seconds, respectively. The developed sensor is a promising tool for monitoring of greenhouse gases. This work was supported by the Robert A Welch Foundation (grant No A1546) and a T3 grant from Texas A and M University and Open Fund of State Key Laboratory of Applied Optics (SKLA02020001A12).

[1] J. Xia, Feng Zhu, Sasa Zhang, Alexandre Kolomenskii, Jian Dong, Kunihiro Okada, James Strohaber, Hans. A. Schuessler, Probing greenhouse gases in turbulent atmosphere by long-range open-path wavelength modulation spectroscopy, Optics and Lasers in Engineering, 117, 21-28 (2019). [2] Jinbao Xia: State Key Laboratory of Applied Optics, Changchun Institute of Optics, Fine Mechanics and Physics, Chinese Academy of Sciences Changchun, 130033, China

FE07 **8:24 – 8:25**

MULTICHARME : A NEW CHERNIN TYPE MULTIPASS CELL FOR LONG PATHLENGTH TERAHERTZ SPECTROSCOPY EXPERIMENTS IN AN ATMOSPHERIC SIMULATION CHAMBER.

JEAN DECKER, JONAS BRUCKHUISEN, EIRC FERTEIN, NICOLAS HOUZEL, PIERRE KULINSKI, ROBIN BOCQUET, FRANCIS HINDLE, GUILLAUME DHONT, GAËL MOURET, CÉCILE COEUR, ARNAUD CUISSET, *Laboratoire de Physico-Chimie de l'Atmosphère, Université du Littoral Côte d'Opale, Dunkerque, France.*

For the first time, THz spectroscopy was used for a direct monitoring of molecular species in the Dunkirk atmospheric simulation chamber called CHARME for Chamber for the Atmospheric Reactivity and the Metrology of the Environment[a]. Within this chamber, we have developed a specially designed Chernin multi-pass cell "MULTICHARME" allowing to adjust a pathlength from 120 m. (24 paths) to 280 m. (56 paths) coupled to a submillimeter wavelength radiation. We demonstrate the capability to detect and quantify greenhouse gases at trace levels by probing their rotational transitions close to the Doppler broadening limit. Significant absorbances of 400 ppm residual N_2O traces at 577.58 GHz and 200 ppm O_3 traces have been measured with a path-length adjusted to 200 meters.[b] Right now, the accessible detection levels for both compounds are limited to tens of ppm. We are presently developing a model of the baseline in order to correct the strong variations caused by multiple interfering stationary waves in the Chernin cell. The first results obtained in CHARME coupling a THz source to the MultiCHARME Chernin cell opens new possibilities especially for the monitoring of stratospheric reaction processes at low-pressure. In particular, the versatility of the submillimeter electronic sources will allow to perform time-resolved quantitative spectroscopies of reactants, oxidants and products involved in targeted reactions occurring in the high altitude atmospheric layers.

[a]Meng, L.; Coeur, C.; Fayad, L.; Houzel, N.; Genevray, P.; Bouzidi, H.; Tomas, A.; Chen, W., *J. Atmos. Environ.*, **240, 1117740, 2020.**

[b]Cuisset, A.; Hindle, F.; Mouret, G.; Bocquet, R.; Bruckhuisen, J.; Decker, J.; Pienkina, A.; Bray, C.; Fertein, É.; Boudon, V., *Appl. Sci.*, **11, 1229, 2021.**

FE08 **8:28 – 8:29**

MOLECULAR TRANSITION FREQUENCES OF CO_2 NEAR 1.6 μ WITH KHZ-LEVEL UNCERTAINTIES

ZACHARY REED, *Material Measurement Laboratory, National Institute of Standards and Technology, Gaithersburg, MD, USA*; BRIAN DROUIN, *Jet Propulsion Laboratory, California Institute of Technology, Pasadena, CA, USA*; DAVID A. LONG, JOSEPH T. HODGES, *Material Measurement Laboratory, National Institute of Standards and Technology, Gaithersburg, MD, USA.*

We present measurements of molecular transition frequencies based on the comb-locked cavity ring-down spectroscopy technique [1], reporting vacuum transition frequencies of Doppler-broadened $^{12}C^{16}O_2$ in the 1.6 μm region for the (30012) $\leftarrow$ (00001) and (30013) $\leftarrow$ (00001) bands with an average combined standard uncertainty of 1 kHz. A global multi-state model was fit to these data and literature values to provide spectroscopic parameters and a best-case fit precision of 4 kHz. We identified and assigned an interaction between the (30012) and (33301) states which was manifest as an observed Fermi resonance in the (30012) $\leftarrow$ (00001) band. This interaction was accounted for in the global fit, significantly reducing uncertainties in the spectroscopic parameters of the (30012) state. We find excellent agreement with literature values, including better than 1 kHz RMS deviation with a recent saturation cavity ring-down study of the (30013) $\leftarrow$ (00001) band [2]. Agreement is excellent with CDSD 2019 [3] and HITRAN 2016 [4] for the (30013) $\leftarrow$ (00001) band, but much poorer for the (30012) $\leftarrow$ (00001) band.

[1] Z. D. Reed, D. A. Long, H. Fleurbaey, and J. T. Hodges, Optica 7, 1209-1220 (2020).
[2] H. Wu, et al., Phys. Chem. Chem. Phys. 22, 2841-2848 (2020).
[3] S. A. Tashkun, et al., J. Quant. Spectros. Rad. Trans. 228, 124-131 (2019).
[4] I. E. Gordon, et al. J. Quant. Spectros. Rad. Trans. 203, 3-69 (2017).

FE09 **8:32 – 8:33**

HIGH ACCURACY NEAR-INFRARED CARBON DIOXIDE INTENSITY MEASUREMENTS TO SUPPORT REMOTE SENSING

DAVID A. LONG, ZACHARY REED, ADAM J. FLEISHER, *Material Measurement Laboratory, National Institute of Standards and Technology, Gaithersburg, MD, USA*; JOSEPH MENDONCA, SEBASTIEN ROCHE, *Environment and Climate Change Canada, Toronto, Canada*; JOSEPH T. HODGES, *Material Measurement Laboratory, National Institute of Standards and Technology, Gaithersburg, MD, USA.*

We used two previously described [1,2] cavity ring-down spectroscopy systems to accurately measure line intensities in the following three $^{12}C^{16}O_2$ rovibrational bands near 1.6 μm: (30012) $\leftarrow$ (00001), (30013) $\leftarrow$ (00001), and (30014) $\leftarrow$ (00001). These bands are commonly used in remote sensing applications, including the Total Carbon Column Observing Network (TCCON) [3]. We estimate relative combined standard uncertainties for these band intensities of less than 0.1% and obtain percent-level deviations in the measured intensities relative to those in the literature and several spectroscopic databases. However, we find 0.1% level agreement with the (30013) and (30014) band intensities given in the HITRAN 2016 [4] database, which were calculated using ab initio dipole moment surfaces. Incorporation of the resulting line intensities into TCCON retrievals leads to significantly reduced biases in the (30012) and (30013) bands. These results indicate that refinements of spectroscopic databases are required to meet increasingly stringent remote sensing uncertainty targets.

[1] Lin, H. et. al. J. Quant. Spectrosc. Radiat. Transfer, 161, 11-20.
[2] Truong, G. W. et. al. (2013) Nat. Photonics, 7(7), 532-534.
[3] Wunch, D. et. al. Philos. Trans. Royal Soc. A, 369(1943), 2087-211
[4] Gordon, I. E., et al. (2017), J. Quant. Spectrosc. Radiat. Transfer, 203, 3-69.

FE10 **8:36 – 8:37**

DOPPLER-FREE SATURATED ABSORPTION SPECTROSCOPY OF CH_4 IN THE MID-INFRARED REGION USING A CONTINUOUS-WAVE OPTICAL PARAMETRIC OSCILLATOR

S M SHAH RIYADH, *Department of physics and astronomy, University Of Louisville, Louisville, KY, USA*; HAMZEH TELFAH, MEAGAN NICOLE HAASE, BRIANNA PAIGE HAASE, JINJUN LIU, *Department of Chemistry, University of Louisville, Louisville, KY, USA*; CUNFENG CHENG, *Hefei National Laboratory for Physical Science at Microscale, University of Science and Technology of China, Hefei, China.*

The fundamentals of XH stretching modes typically lie in the 2,500 – 3,700 cm^{-1} (2.7 - 4.0 μm) range. Continuous-wave optical parametric oscillators (CW OPOs) enable high-resolution spectroscopy in this region. A Doppler-free saturated absorption spectroscopy apparatus with a high-power, widely tunable CW OPO as the light source has been built in our lab for high-resolution, high-precision spectroscopy of gas-phase molecules. We have obtained the Doppler-free spectrum of the Q branch of the ν_3 band of CH_4 in a proof-of-principle experiment. Preliminary results from the experiment will be reported in this talk. A cavity-enhanced two-photon spectroscopy setup using the same CW OPO is under construction.

FF. Spectroscopy as an analytical tool

Friday, June 25, 2021 – 8:0 AM

Room: 2021 Online Everywhere

Chair: Carlos Manzanares, Baylor University, Waco, TX, USA

FF01 **8:00 – 8:01**

GENERATIVE ADVERSARIAL LINEAR DISCRIMINANT ANALYSIS FOR DISTINGUISHING API POLYMORPHS BY RAMAN SPECTROSCOPY

ZIYI CAO, CASEY J SMITH, YOULIN LIU, ALEX M SHERMAN, GARTH SIMPSON, *Department of Chemistry, Purdue University, West Lafayette, IN, USA.*

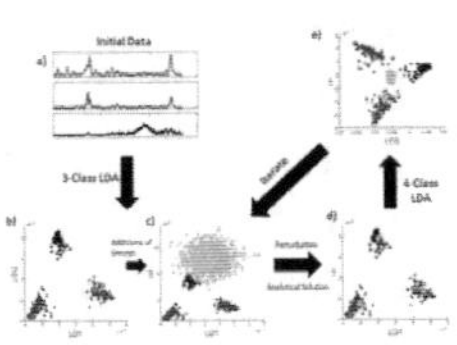

Raman Spectroscopy is a great way to distinguish different kinds of API polymorphs.[a]However,adversarial attacks on spectral classifiers were shown to enable identification of potential vulnerabilities in common dimension reduction analyses of Raman spectra. We tackled this susceptibility with the Generative Adversarial Linear Discriminant Analysis (GALDA) approach. GALDA is analogous to Generative Adversarial Nets (GAN) in the machine learning context. Conceptually in a typical GAN, two models were simultaneously trained, a generative model G that attempts to estimate the sample distribution and a discriminative model D that classifies the output of G.These two models seek to achieve Nash equilibrium during the iterative adversarial training process.[b] We herein incorporated this concept into spectral classification. Spectral classification in the spectroscopic context seems to lag albeit the mass development in the computer science area. As such, the analyzation methods' robustness and susceptibility to malicious attack is considered even less. Therefore, GALDA aims to test against the robustness of LDA classifiers and provide a new framework for considerations for classification strategies less susceptible to spurious misclassification.

[a]Shijie Zhang, et al. Dynamic Sparse Sampling for Confocal Raman Microscopy, Analytical Chemistry 2018
[b]Goodfellow, Ian, et al. Generative adversarial nets, Advances in neural information processing systems. 2014

FF02 **8:04 – 8:05**

IDENTIFYING UNKNOWN MOLECULES WITH PROBABILISTIC DEEP LEARNING AND ROTATIONAL SPECTROSCOPY

KELVIN LEE, *Radio and Geoastronomy Division, Harvard-Smithsonian Center for Astrophysics, Cambridge, MA, USA*; MICHAEL C McCARTHY, *Atomic and Molecular Physics, Harvard-Smithsonian Center for Astrophysics, Cambridge, MA, USA.*

A major bottleneck in the analysis of broadband chirped-pulse microwave spectra is the identification of unknown molecules. Often, a set of molecular frequencies are fit to an effective Hamiltonian, whereby a set of spectroscopic parameters are used to infer the molecular carrier. These constants are reproduced with electronic structure calculations through a trial and error process, accompanied by chemical intuition involving the precursors used, and the reaction conditions (e.g. electrical discharges). As the size of the molecules increase, the combinatorics of many hundreds to thousands of possible isomers becomes an intractable problem for chemical intuition alone.

Since spectroscopic parameters are only weakly informative, we turn to statistical inference to complement conventional spectroscopic analysis. In this talk, I will discuss a new framework for identifying unknown molecules by performing inference on spectroscopic parameters with probabilistic deep learning. Using a series of decoder architectures, we are able to infer the approximate molecular composition/formula and what functional groups are present using only the rotational constants and derived quantities κ (the asymmetry parameter) and Δ (the inertial defect), and approximate magnitudes and projections of the dipole moments.

FF03 ***Post-Deadline Abstract*** **8:08 – 8:09**

EXHAUSTIVE PRODUCT ANALYSIS OF THREE BENZENE DISCHARGES BY MICROWAVE SPECTROSCOPY

MICHAEL C McCARTHY, *Atomic and Molecular Physics, Harvard-Smithsonian Center for Astrophysics, Cambridge, MA, USA*; KELVIN LEE, *Radio and Geoastronomy Division, Harvard-Smithsonian Center for Astrophysics, Cambridge, MA, USA*; BRANDON CARROLL, *Atomic and Molecular Physics, Harvard-Smithsonian Center for Astrophysics, Cambridge, MA, USA*; JESSIE P PORTERFIELD, *Radio and Geoastronomy Division, Harvard-Smithsonian Center for Astrophysics, Cambridge, MA, USA*; BRYAN CHANGALA, *JILA, National Institute of Standards and Technology and Univ. of Colorado Department of Physics, University of Colorado, Boulder, CO, USA*; JAMES H. THORPE, JOHN F. STANTON, *Quantum Theory Project, University of Florida, Gainesville, FL, USA.*

By means of chirped and cavity microwave spectroscopies, automated double resonance, new high-speed fitting and deep learning algorithms, and large databases of computed structures, the discharge products of three benzene mixtures – alone or with oxygen and nitrogen – have been exhaustively characterized between 6.5 and 26 GHz. In total, more than 3300 spectral features were observed; 88% of these, accounting for roughly 97% of the total intensity, have now been assigned to 160 distinct chemical species and 60 of their variants (i.e. isotopic species and vibrationally excited states). Roughly 50 of the products are entirely new or poorly characterized at high resolution, including many heavier than the precursor benzene. These findings provide evidence for a rich architecture of two- and three-dimensional carbon, and indicate that benzene growth, particularly formation of ring-chain molecules, occurs facilely under our experimental conditions. The present analysis vividly demonstrates the utility of microwave spectroscopy as a precision tool for complex mixture analysis, irrespective of whether the rotational spectrum of a product species is known a priori or not. From this large quantity of data, for example, it is possible to derive a mass spectrum for each discharge that is analogous to a traditional mass spectrum, but with exquisite isomeric resolution.

FF04 **8:12 – 8:13**

IS IT CHIRAL?TOWARDS IDENTIFYING CHIRALITY IN UNKNOWN SAMPLES WITHOUT PRIOR SPECTRAL ASSIGNMENT.

GRETA KOUMARIANOU, LINCOLN SATTERTHWAITE, *Chemistry and Biochemistry, UCSB, Santa Barbara, CA, USA*; IRENE WANG, DAVID PATTERSON, *Physics, University of California, Santa Barbara, CA, USA.*

Current spectroscopic methods [a,b]can only detect and quantify chirality if the molecular composition of the sample has been determined. Therefore, before extracting enantiomeric information from a spectrum of an unknown sample, one needs to compare it to previously measured spectra, or to simulated spectra generated with previously determined rotational constants.

We describe new developments towards an updated version of the microwave three-wave mixing technique (M3WM)[c] in a buffer gas cell, that can unambiguously identify the presence of chiral species in an unknown sample with no need for prior spectral assignment or knowledge of the sample composition. This work combines the established sensitivity of 3WM in a buffer gas cell in determining enantiomeric information with broadband microwave fields, and an optimized sample input, and it opens up new directions in chirality detection towards real-life molecular samples and complicated mixtures.

[a]Sérgio R. Domingos et al. ,Sensing Chirality with Rotational Spectroscopy Annual Review of Physical Chemistry 69:1, 499-519 (2018).

[b]Nafie, L. A.; Dukor, R. K.; Freedman, T. B. Handbook of Vibrational Spectroscopy: Vibrational Circular Dichroism; Wiley Online Library, 2006.

[c]Patterson, D. Et al , Enantiomer-specific detection of chiral molecules via microwave spectroscopy. Nature 497, 475–477 (2013).

FF05 **8:16 – 8:17**

TIME-RESOLVED ROTATIONAL SPECTROSCOPY OF CARBOXYLIC ACIDS. IDENTIFICATION AND QUANTIFICATION OF THE COMPONENTS FROM HEATING ADIPIC ACID.

PABLO PINACHO, WENHAO SUN, *FS-SMP, Deutsches Elektronen-Synchrotron (DESY), Hamburg, Germany*; DANIEL A. OBENCHAIN, *Institute of Physical Chemistry, Georg-August-Universität Göttingen, Göttingen, Germany*; MELANIE SCHNELL, *FS-SMP, Deutsches Elektronen-Synchrotron (DESY), Hamburg, Germany.*

Adipic acid ($C_6H_{10}O_4$), a linear dicarboxylic acid, is of great importance in industry as a precursor for the production of nylon and as food additive (E355) to regulate the acidity of the product. Adipic acid is a stable compound at standard conditions; under heating it decarboxylates giving cyclopentanone as the main product and adipic anhydride as a by-product. This behavior is contrary to other aliphatic dicarboxylics acids, which tend to produce the anhydride analogue rather than the ketone.[a] We investigated the self-reaction of adipic acid under heating employing high-resolution rotational spectroscopy, which allows identifying each component in the gas phase, together with structure elucidation and quantification of molecules. The microwave spectrum was measured using a segmented chirped-pulse Fourier transform microwave (FTMW) spectrometer working in the 18-26 frequency range. The most intense lines were assigned to cyclopentanone, but we were able to identify also two conformations of the adipic anhydride, one conformation of adipic acid, and even a complex between cyclopentanone and one water molecule. We have analyzed the spectrum in time segments of one hour each to investigate the reaction pathways of adipic acid and the temporal evolution of the components of the spectrum.

[a] J. W. Hill, *J. Am. Chem. Soc.* **1930**, 52, 4110–4114.

FF06 **8:20 – 8:21**

CHIRPED PULSE MILLIMETER WAVE SPECTROSCOPY OF COMPLEX MOLECULES

MARIUS HERMANNS, NADINE WEHRES, BETTINA HEYNE, FRANK LEWEN, STEPHAN SCHLEMMER, *I. Physikalisches Institut, Universität zu Köln, Köln, Germany.*

Our chirped pulse millimeter wave spectrometer for complex molecules of astrophysical interest is operational between 75 and 110 GHz, which is coincident with the Atacama Large Millimeter/Submillimeter Array (ALMA) Band 3. High sensitivity and stability is a focus of our research to be able to measure isotopic species of molecules in natural abundance on the one hand and to observe fragments of molecules, which are produced with a high voltage DC discharge in combination with a supersonic jet on the other hand. For the latter application, first tests were performed with methyl cyanide (CH_3CN). We observed HCN as well as HNC discharge products. As the detector side of our instrument coincides in many aspects with our emission spectrometers [1,2] a comparison of chirped pulse measurements and emission spectroscopy will be discussed briefly. Additionally, we show and discuss current improvements and developments of our chirped pulse instrument. Other candidate molecules are ions or radicals created by the discharge and other means with the aim to record their fingerprint-like rotational spectra.

References:

[1] N. Wehres, B. Heyne, F. Lewen, M. Hermanns, B. Schmidt, C. Endres, U. U. Graf, D. R. Higgins, and S. Schlemmer, Proceedings of the International Astronomical Union, 13(S332), 332-345. DOI:10.1017/S1743921317007803

[2] N. Wehres, J. Maßen, K. Borisov, B. Schmidt, F. Lewen, U. U. Graf, C. E. Honingh, D. R. Higgins, and S. Schlemmer, Phys. Chem. Chem. Phys. 20, 5530–5544 (2018), DOI:10.1039/C7CP06394F

FF08 **8:28 – 8:29**

LASER SYNTHESIS AND SPECTROSCOPY OF PYRENE DIMERS

IAN WEBSTER, MICHAEL A DUNCAN, *Department of Chemistry, University of Georgia, Athens, GA, USA.*

Laser desorption time-of-flight mass spectrometry (LD-ToF-MS) experiments on pressed-pellet samples of polycyclic aromatic hydrocarbons (PAHs) exhibit the formation of covalently-bonded dimers at masses (m/z) of 2M-2 and 2M-4 (where M is the parent mass). Through replication of these LD-ToF-MS conditions at higher throughput, PAH dimers have been produced and collected in milligram quantities. The formation of the covalently-bonded dimers was confirmed under similar LD-ToF-MS conditions and through HPLC separation with a UV-Vis detector. For collected samples of pyrene, differential sublimation has removed the residual monomer to leave a mixture of dimerized pyrene. Decrease of the monomer mass peak was confirmed using LD-ToF-MS, and the samples are analyzed using several spectroscopic methods, including UV-Vis, IR, and Raman spectroscopy. Theoretical studies of possible dimer structures have been calculated using density functional theory with the CAM-B3LYP method at the def2TZV level of theory using the Gaussian 09 program. Theory calculations were calibrated and checked by comparison with the monomer samples, and used to determine the lowest energy dimer structures. The simulated spectra were compared with collected spectra of isolated dimers to determine the contributing structures of the dimerized PAHs.

FF09 **8:32 – 8:33**

DEEP REPRESENTATION LEARNING OF SPECTROSCOPIC GRAPHS

KELVIN LEE, *Department of Chemistry, MIT, Cambridge, MA, USA*; CHRISTINE LI, *Department of Chemistry, University of California, Davis, Davis, CA, USA*; BRETT A. McGUIRE, *Department of Chemistry, Massachusetts Institute of Technology, Cambridge, MA, USA*; KYLE N. CRABTREE, *Department of Chemistry, University of California, Davis, Davis, CA, USA.*

Graph representations of spectroscopic information have been increasing in popularity due to their efficiency and scalability in encoding large volumes of data; simply, energy levels are represented as nodes, and transitions as edges between each level. Thus, all quantum mechanical information pertaining to a molecule can be readily manipulated and transformed using a single data format, allowing computations and visualizations to be performed with ease.

One application of spectroscopic graphs is to assist in the analysis of high resolution spectra of complex mixtures, comprising many observed transitions from an unknown number of molecules. Analysis of such mixtures comprises two coupled tasks: assignment of features to their respective signal carriers, and to decompose the full spectrum into known molecules. Viewing this problem from the perspective of spectroscopic graphs, our task is to fully reconstruct the subgraphs (i.e. molecules) from sparse information obtained with techniques such as AMDOR and MST.

Here, we apply the use of deep graph learning techniques for spectroscopic graph reconstruction. Using convolutional autoencoder architectures, we experiment with the possibility of parameterizing graph neural networks to reproduce complex graphs when given only a limited number of "observed" energy levels and/or transitions. As part of this work, we perform a comprehensive investigation into the successes and challenges of our approach, including the interpretability of learned representations, how they can be manipulated and analyzed, and its applicability in complex mixture analysis.

FF10 **8:36 – 8:37**

COMBINED ROTATIONAL AND VIBRATIONAL CARS SPECTRA OF O_2 FOR SIMULTAENOUS TEMPERATURE AND PRESSURE MEASUREMENTS

AMAN SATIJA, ROBERT P. LUCHT, *Mechanical Engineering, Purdue University, West Lafayette, IN, USA.*

Coherent anti-Stokes Raman scattering (CARS), a four-wave mixing parametric process, is used for flow diagnostics due to its excellent spatial and temporal resolution. In this work we present a dual-pump combined CARS (DPCC) system for simultaneously obtaining the pure-rotational and vibrational spectra of O_2. O_2 is a an important molecule in combustion as well as in many high-speed non-reacting aerodynamic flows. Excellent temperature accuracy, in DPCC, is obtained via sensitivity in Boltzmann distribution of the pure-rotational CARS spectra. Pressure information, in DPCC, is obtained via relative sensitivity of the rotational and vibrational CARS spectrum to collision dynamics. As pressure increases, at a fixed temperature, the frequency of molecular collisions also increases. Only the vibrational spectra of O_2 undergoes collisional narrowing due to mixing between the closely-spaced Q-branch transitions. We employed the DPCC system in an underexpanded jet outside the exit of a converging nozzle. Figure shows a single spectrum, obtained 250 μm downstream of the nozzle exit, along the jet centerline. We compared different Raman lineshape models for extracting temperature and pressure from the DPCC spectra. The rotational diffusion model for collisional narrowing predicts a higher pressure compared to the Voigt model.

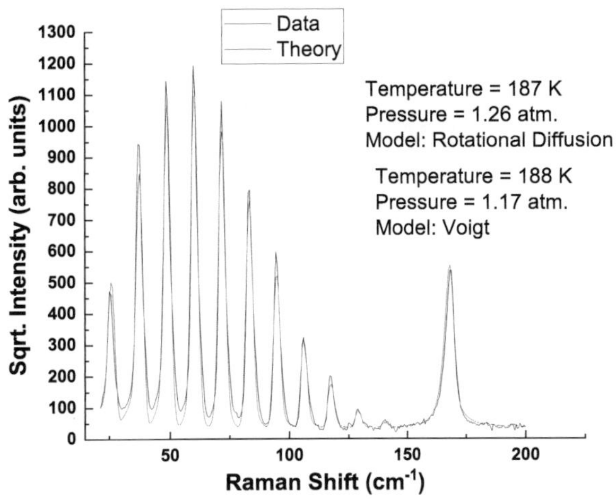

FF11 **8:40 – 8:41**

USING ULTRAVIOLET LASER ABSORPTION SPECTROSCOPY TO MEASURE VIBRATIONAL TEMPERATURE TIME HISTORIES OF SHOCK-HEATED OXYGEN

AJAY KRISH, JESSE WILLIAM STREICHER, RON K HANSON, *Mechanical Engineering, Stanford University, Stanford, CA, USA.*

Here, a two-color O_2 vibrational temperature diagnostic was developed by utilizing spectroscopic models to inform optimal wavelength candidates for both a continuous-wave (CW), ultraviolet (UV) laser and a picosecond pulsed, UV laser. Cross-sections of shock-heated O_2 were measured using a CW UV laser, and results over a range of wavelengths and temperatures are compared against a Stanford model, developed to simulate oxygen absorption cross-sections in the Schumann-Runge system under vibrational non-equilibrium conditions, and Specair, a spectroscopic model for high-temperature air species developed by Laux et al. All measurements were completed behind reflected shocks in 2% and 5% O_2 in argon (Ar) mixtures.

Vibrational temperatures for cross-section measurements were calculated for plateaus and peaks in experimental absorbances using a Bethe-Teller relaxation model up to 6,000 K and a steady-state approach above 6,000 K. Temperature sweep measurements were fixed around 223.237 nm, while wavelength sweep measurements were taken around 4550 K and ranged between 223.23 nm to 223.27 nm. Temperature sweep cross-sections agree to within 15% of Specair modeled cross-sections, with most measurements falling within 10% of Specair predictions. Wavelength sweep cross-sections agree at shorter wavelengths with Specair cross-sections, but longer wavelength features are offset from both the Stanford model and Specair predictions.

Using the spectroscopic model developed here to inform appropriate wavelength selection, the UV laser systems in this work become tools for directly tracking both vibrational temperature and populations in specific vibrational states of O_2 as it undergoes vibrational relaxation and dissociation behind strong shock waves. These temperature and population time histories provide important experimental data needed to evaluate current computational models that seek to capture the molecular energy transfer present in high-enthalpy airflows.

FF12 **8:44 – 8:45**

BROADBAND FREQUENCY COMB VERNIER SPECTROSCOPY IN THE MID-IR WITH VIDEO-RECORDING RETRIEVAL OF ABSORPTION SPECTRUM

HANS A SCHUESSLER, JAMES R BOUNDS, ALEXANDRE KOLOMENSKII, *Department of Physics and Astronomy, Texas A&M University, College Station, TX, USA.*

A spectroscopic technique based on the principle of Vernier frequency comb spectroscopy is developed, which combines the broadband spectral coverage and high spectral resolution with the signal enhancement due to a resonant optical cavity. The resonant cavity serves the dual role of optical path enhancement along with Vernier filtering of the comb modes, allowing individual comb modes to be resolved with a grating. The method uses only one frequency comb laser and by using multiple exposures and taking a sequence of images of enhanced comb modes (i.e. taking video-recording) a constraint imposed on the bandwidth can removed. The bandwidth can be expanded even more by simultaneously recording with the IR camera frequency comb modes from different spectral intervals. The methane absorption spectrum in ambient air in the mid-IR with a frequency comb obtained as a difference frequency generation was measured. Processing the sequence of images recorded with the mid-IR camera as the resonant cavity length is scanned allows the retrieval of the absorption spectrum. The experimental results and the discussion of the advantages and limitations of this techniques are presented. This work was supported by Robert A. Welch Foundation(grant No A1546) and a T3 grant from Texas A and M University.

FG. Plenary

Friday, June 25, 2021 – 9:0 AM

Room: 2021 Online Everywhere

Chair: Anthony Remijan, NRAO, Charlottesville, VA, USA

FG02 **9:03 – 9:43**

CHIRALITY RECOGNITION/TRANSFER/AMPLIFICATION: ROTATIONAL SPECTROSCOPIC AND CHIROPTICAL SPECTROSCOPIC STUDIES

YUNJIE XU, *Department of Chemistry, University of Alberta, Edmonton, AB, Canada.*

A molecule is chiral if its mirror image cannot be superimposed onto itself. Chirality serves an essential function in life. Our research program centres on understanding mechanisms of chirality recognition/transfer/amplification at the molecular level. To achieve this goal, we apply and develop new spectroscopic tools to characterize structural and dynamical properties of chiral molecules and non-covalent interactions among them in the gas phase, solution, cold rare gas matrices and at liquid-liquid interfaces.

We emphasize the connection between the gas phase and condense phase results obtained using high resolution spectroscopy and several chiroptical spectroscopies, respectively. For example, we examined the conformational landscape and chirality recognition in the binary adducts of tetrahydro-2-furoic acid using chirped pulse Fourier transform microwave spectroscopy. The unusual conformational distributions and chirality controlled conformational preferences will be discussed. Using vibrational circular dichroism, we followed the first few steps of self-aggregation of this acid in cold rare gas matrices and compared the results to those obtained in the gas phase and in solution previously. In the second example, I will discuss the unusually strong solvent 'Raman optical activity' features observed in a solution of a chiral nickel complex even though the solvent is achiral and the search for its origin. The interplay between experiment and theory is essential for all the work described.

FH. Mini-symposium: Spectroscopy with Undergraduates

Friday, June 25, 2021 – 10:0 AM

Room: 2021 Online Everywhere

Chair: Jacob Stewart, Connecticut College, New London, CT, USA

FH01 *INVITED TALK* **10:00 – 10:02**

UNDERGRADUATE MOLECULAR SPECTROSCOPY APPROACHES IN RESEARCH AND TEACHING AS AN EXPERIENTIAL LEARNING ENTERPRISE AT MISSOURI S&T

G. S. GRUBBS II, *Department of Chemistry, Missouri University of Science and Technology, Rolla, MO, USA.*

As most every person at this conference can appreciate, spectroscopy, especially at the undergraduate level, is often considered one of the most difficult subjects to undertake and, due to this mentality, is often avoided at all costs. To overcome this stigma and make the material resonate with undergraduates, it is important to give them avenues by which to actually get involved in the processes of spectroscopy. In this way, the students become invested in some aspect of the subject which is applicable to their own personal interests. At Missouri S&T, this is achieved in multiple ways. In the research lab, students are given tasks that align with their interest, but also achieve a common goal of a spectrometer enhancement or molecular target of interest in microwave spectroscopy. They are given the tools and instruction to succeed as well as the leeway to fail in a project as this is the cornerstone of discovery. When given this freedom, they become leads in a project, guided and mentored by both the graduate students and myself. If a student is interested in teaching, we have had undergraduates create physical chemistry labs and instruct them in order to guide other students through the process of learning, thereby augmenting their own knowledge. For expanded or more general undergraduate spectroscopy outreach, I serve as the physical chemistry lab instructor and the Associate Advisor of our university's Mars Rover Design Team, which always builds and implements an onboard spectrometer for field analyses. The overarching theme of the talk is to get students interested early and keep them involved. The university helps with this by having programs that will get the students involved as young as the high school level. How we have utilized these programs, reached, and kept student interest while also mitigating the costs of such endeavors at Missouri S&T will be discussed.

FH02 **10:08 – 10:09**

OODLES OF UNDERGRADS UNDERGROUND: CLASSROOM UNDERGRADUATE RESEARCH AT WIND CAVE NATIONAL PARK

JOSHUA A SEBREE, *Department of Chemistry and Biochemistry, University of Northern Iowa, Cedar Falls, IA, USA.*

For the past three years, the Department of Chemistry and Biochemistry at the University of Northern Iowa has been leading undergraduate students on spectroscopic expeditions into the depths of Wind Cave National Park in South Dakota. Using some of the newest miniaturized spectrometers, portable XRFs, and Lego Mindstorms Kits, the team has been working with NPS park rangers to look at the cave in a new light while providing unique experiences for the students involved.

FH03 **10:12 – 10:13**

USING COMPUTATIONAL TOOLS TO ENHANCE LEARNING IN AN UNDERGRADUATE MOLECULAR SPECTROSCOPY COURSE

M. REZA POOPARI, SHYAM PARSHOTAM, YUNJIE XU, *Department of Chemistry, University of Alberta, Edmonton, AB, Canada.*

In molecular spectroscopy, our models of the molecular world are built on rigorous spectroscopic experimentation and rich interplay between theory and experiment. To instill such appreciation to undergraduate students, who have little experience in either spectroscopic experiments and theory, is challenging. We have developed a new computational laboratory component to complement the material covered in a senior undergraduate course on molecular spectroscopy. Specifically, we focus on illustrating molecular spectroscopic concepts (some of which can be quite abstract and complicated) taught in class with electronic structure calculations. This talk will describe our implementation and the learning outcome. Two particular examples will be discussed. One is related to the misconception that electron density is the main factor responsible for NMR chemical shifts and how we utilize both experimental data and calculations to help students overcome this common misconception. The other deals with differences in geometries, for example, those obtained using rotational constants directly, isotopic substitution procedures, and electronic structure calculations. This talk will also discuss how the above activities worked in practice and the improvements we plan to implement next time.

FH04 **10:16 – 10:17**

BIOMOLECULAR STRUCTURE OF TROPINE DETERMINED FROM QUANTUM CHEMISTRY SIMULATIONS OF VIBRATIONAL SPECTROSCOPY

EMILY LYN YANG, *Henry Eyring Center for Theoretical Chemistry, University of Utah, Salt Lake City, UT, USA*; RYAN P STEELE, *Department of Chemistry, University of Utah, Salt Lake City, UT, USA.*

For biologically relevant molecules, determining the structure of the compound– and the manner in which it changes upon interaction with other molecules– is a central scientific challenge. However, many biomolecules exhibit multiple low-energy conformers at biologically relevant temperatures. In this work, the vibrational responses of tropine and its protonated analogue are used to explore the structural diversity of these pharmaceutical mimics. Quantum chemistry-based calculations were employed to identify the low-energy conformers and their vibrational signatures, in order to predict and explain these molecules' response to infrared light in experiments. These calculations also allowed for an assessment of the energetic and spectral consequences of protonation on tropine.

During initial attempts to simulate anharmonic behavior, strongly coupled low and high-frequency modes (which are commonly excluded in such calculations) yielded unphysical transition frequencies. A portion of this presentation will be devoted to techniques that allowed for the inclusion of these anharmonic effects without some of the pitfalls that befall traditional anharmonic approaches.

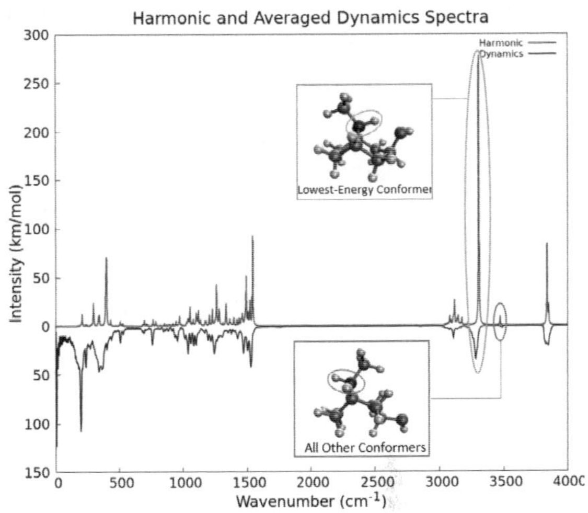

FH05 **10:20 – 10:21**

AN EXOMOL LINE LIST FOR SO: ROVIBRONIC SPECTRUM OF SULFUR MONOXIDE

RYAN BRADY, *Department of Physics and Astronomy, University College London, London, UK*; GAP-SUE KIM, *Dharma College, Dongguk University, Seoul, Korea*; WILFRID SOMOGYI, JONATHAN TENNYSON, SERGEI N. YURCHENKO, *Department of Physics and Astronomy, University College London, London, UK.*

The work we present here is a diatomic molecule line list study on the molecule sulfur monoxide (SO), suitable for characterising exoplanetary atmospheres up to temperatures of 4000 K. The motivation of this project is to provide comprehensive line list data applicable to modelling high temperature spectra in environments such as e.g. exoplanetary atmospheres, where current spectroscopic databases provide only limited coverage. The new SO line list will be included into the ExoMol database.[a] A production of such a line list first includes the creation of a MARVEL[b] set of rovibroic energies, calculation of high-level *ab initio* potential energy curves (PECs), spin-orbit curves (SOCs), electronic-angular momentum curves (EAMCs) and transition moment dipole curves (TDMCs) using MOLPRO at MRCI level of theory and a solution of coupled ro-vibronic Schrödinger equations using the variational code DUO[c]. The PECs, SOCs and EAMCs are represented by analytical parametrised functional forms and refined by fitting to the MARVEL energies. A rovibronic line list for SO consists of energies, frequencies, Einstein coefficients and a partition function covering all electronic states up to 50 000 cm^{-1}, including $X\,^3\Sigma^-$, $A\,^3\Pi$, $A'\,^3\Delta$, $A''\,^3\Sigma^+$, $B\,^3\Sigma^-$, $C\,^3\Pi$, $a\,^1\Delta$, $b\,^1\Sigma^+$ and $c\,^1\Sigma^-$. IR/Vis/UV absorption and emission spectra of SO for a set of temperatures are generated using the program ExoCross.[d]

[a] J. Tennyson et al. *J. Quant. Spectrosc. Radiat. Transf.*, 2020, **255**, 107228; *www.exomol.com*.

[b] T. Furtenbacher, A. G. Császár, J. Tennyson, MARVEL: measured active rotational-vibrational energy levels, J. Mol. Spectrosc. 245 (2007) 115–125.

[c] S. N. Yurchenko, L. Lodi, J. Tennyson, A. V. Stolyarov, *Comput. Phys. Commun.*, 2016, **202**, 262 – 275; publicly available at *https://github.com/Trovemaster/Duo*.

[d] S. N. Yurchenko, A. F. Al-Refaie, J. Tennyson, *Astron. Astrophys*;, 2018, **614**, A131; publicly available at *https://github.com/Trovemaster/ExoCross*.

FH07 **10:28 – 10:29**

COMPUTATIONAL SPECTROSCOPIC SIGNATURES OF PROTEINOGENIC GLUTAMIC ACID AND ITS ISOMERIC SPECIES OF ASTROPHYSICAL IMPORTANCE [a]

NAMRATA RANI, VIKAS, *Department of Chemistry and Centre of Advanced studies in Chemistry, Panjab University, Chandigarh, Chandigarh, India.*

The interstellar medium (ISM) is abundant in diverse network of molecules from simple diatomic to interstellar complex organic molecules (COMs). There have been continuous growing attempts to search the molecules of biotic potential such as proteinogenic amino acids. Notably, the amino acids are confirmed in meteoritic composition with considerable enantiomeric excess. Such large sized molecular species in ISM are investigated via their rotational and vibrational spectroscopic traits. Towards this our group performed the computational quantum-mechanical calculations of rotational and vibrational parameters of Glutamic acid and its isomeric species proposed along its stereoinversion pathways in gas phase under conditions akin to the ISM. DFT and MP2 methods are employed in anharmonic calculations utilizing vibrational second order perturbation theory to predict the rotational and vibrational transitions, particularly in millimetre (mm), sub-mm, mid- and far-infrared regions. The varied isomeric species studied, including zwitterionic ammonium ylide, di-carboxylic acid, gem-diol, vicinal-diol and imine can act as a significant aid for the search of Glutamic acid and its isomers in the ISM.[b]

[a]The authors acknowledges a grant from Science and Engineering Research Board (SERB), India, under as research project (sanction order No. EMR/2016/002074), Namrata Rani thanks UGC for SRF.

[b]Reference: Rani, N.;, Vikas. J. Mol. Spectrosc. 2020, 369, 111271(1-9).

FH08 **10:32 – 10:33**

NARROWING DOWN THE POSSIBLE GEOMETRIES OF A MOLECULE FROM ISOTOPOLOGUE ROTATIONAL CONSTANTS WITH STRUCTURAL FILTERS

JIEYU YAN, DAVID PATTERSON, *Physics, University of California, Santa Barbara, CA, USA.*

A computer algorithm is developed to narrow down the list of possible structural geometries of a molecule from the analysis of its isotopologue rotational constants. Based on Kraitchman's equation, the absolute values of the position coordinates of the atoms in a molecule may be obtained from the corresponding isotopologue rotational constants. The algorithm, in attempt to take a step further, narrows down the list of possible combinations of atom positions and bond connections within the molecule. Compared to a previous work by Mayer et al.[a] which focused on carbon atoms, the algorithm extends the application to more atoms including oxygen, nitrogen, etc. More molecular geometry filters are integrated in the algorithm as well. Five filters involving interatomic distance, bond type, valence, bond angles, and coplanarity based on VSEPR theory are developed. As a result, the algorithm was able to narrow down the number of possible structures for Aspirin, a molecule with 13 non-hydrogen atoms, from 10^{10} to 110. However, the exact geometry of molecules could not be determined by the algorithm directly, especially when the molecule is large (usually more than five non-hydrogen atoms). In addition, large errors from Kraitchman's equation near the principle axes of the molecule leads to ambiguous results on those atoms. It leads to the belief that our current understanding may be insufficient to resolve the molecular geometry directly from the isotopologue rotational constants.

[a]Mayer, Kevin J., et al. "The Feasibility of Determining the Carbon Framework Geometry of a Molecule from Analysis of the CARBON-13 Isotopologue Rotational Spectra in Natural Abundance." *74th International Symposium on Molecular Spectroscopy.* 2019.

FH09 **10:36 – 10:37**

USE OF STUDENT-SPECIFIC MOLECULES AND THEIR SPECTROSCOPIC PROPERTIES IN PHYSICAL CHEMISTRY COURSES

DAVID E. WOON, *Department of Chemistry, University of Illinois at Urbana-Champaign, Urbana, IL, USA.*

Spectroscopy is a fundamental component of physical chemistry courses. To encourage students to take more interest in the critical contributions of spectroscopic properties to the subject, I assign different molecules to the students. In the second semester of a two-semester course that covers statistical and classical thermodynamics, the students draw molecules from a hat on the first day of class. They look up spectroscopic properties for their molecules on the web and use the values in various homework, quiz, and exam problems. In a one semester "principles" course, they build a closed-shell molecule from a limited set of atoms. I then provide the students with calculated values of spectroscopic properties, which they use in a term project about their molecules that covers structure, spectra, partition functions, and properties derived from partition functions.

FH10 *Post-Deadline Abstract* **10:40 – 10:41**

THE CHIRPED-PULSE CLUB: MICROWAVE SPECTROSCOPY RESEARCH IN HIGH SCHOOL

JOSUE CERVANTES, EMILY GERAGHTY, ANISH KANTHAMNENI, ZIWEI LIU, SHAMITHA NANDI, ELIC WEEKS, GARRETT YOUNGBLOOD, GORDON G BROWN, *Chemistry, SC Governor's School for Science & Mathematics, Hartsville, SC, USA.*

A new course offering a research experience in microwave spectroscopy to high school students has been developed at the South Carolina Governor's School for Science and Mathematics. Seven students working in small groups completed research projects in microwave spectroscopy during the fall semester of 2020. The students measured the spectra of previously unstudied chemicals, performed relevant *ab initio* calculations, analyzed the spectra to find the rotational and distortion constants, and prepared presentations for the school's Annual Research Colloquium. Chemicals studied include 2-fluorobenzotrifluoride, trans-2-pentenal, and 2,6-difluorophenol. The spectra were measured on a 8 - 18 GHz chirped-pulse Fourier transform microwave (CP-FTMW) spectrometer. The spectrometer employs an Analog Devices AD-9914 direct digital synthesizer to generate a chirped pulse with a bandwidth of 1 GHz. The chirped pulse is mixed with a tunable carrier frequency and the spectrum is measured in 2 GHz (the output of the mixer includes the lower and upper sidebands) sections. Chemical samples are introduced through a small hole in a spherical mirror in order for the pulsed molecular beam to be coaxial with the microwave pulse. Experimental rotational parameters of the three chemical species will be presented along with a description of the spectrometer.

FH11 **10:44 – 10:45**

EXPLAINER: EFFECTS OF NUCLEAR QUADRUPOLE COUPLING TENSOR MAGNITUDE, ASYMMETRY, AND ORIENTATION ON THE APPEARANCE OF ROTATIONAL HYPERFINE STRUCTURE

S. A. COOKE, *Natural and Social Science, Purchase College SUNY, Purchase, NY, USA.*

Towards easier high resolution spectral assignment for asymmetric molecules bearing nuclei with spins greater than $\frac{1}{2}$ a systematic study has been performed examining how different nuclear quadrupole coupling (NQC) tensors cause different hyperfine patterns. The asymmetry of the NQC tensors principal components, the overall magnitudes of the components, and the orientation of the NQC tensor principal axes with respect to the molecular principal axes are considered from the perspective of directly *observable* rotational transition splittings. Effects of different molecular asymmetry are also considered. Also, while $I = \frac{3}{2}$ is the nuclear spin most thoroughly investigated, different nuclear spins are also examined. The SPCAT/SPFIT software has been used to simulate many thousands of spectra with the goal of identifying recognizable patterns which will be presented.

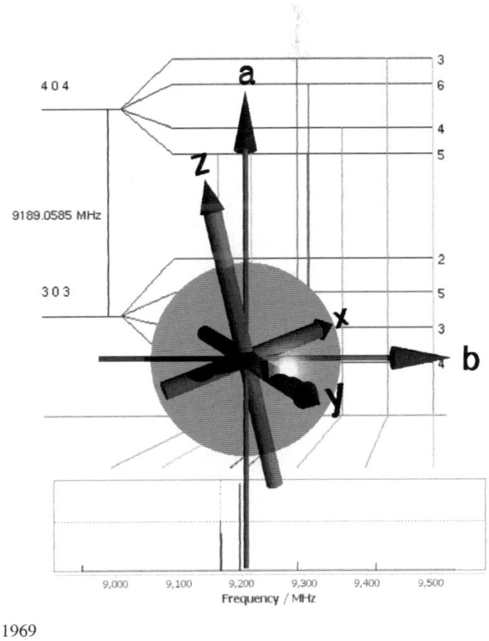

Thoughts concerning the incorporation of this material into the undergraduate curriculum will be presented together with a reflection on the statement "*An electrostatic field gradient is a classical quantity and presents no conceptual problem to the undergraduate student in their first year; nuclear quadrupole coupling constants can thus be introduced quite early...*"[a].

[a] *Nuclear Quadrupole Coupling Constants*, E. A. C. Lucken, Academic Press Inc. New York, New York, 1969

FH12 **10:48 – 10:49**

IMPLEMENTING EXTENDED CROSS CORRELATION AS A TOOL FOR SEMI-AUTOMATED MICROWAVE SPECTROSCOPIC ANALYSIS OF WEAKLY BOUND CLUSTER SPECTRA

HANNAH FINO, REBECCA A. PEEBLES, SEAN A. PEEBLES, *Department of Chemistry, Eastern Illinois University, Charleston, IL, USA*; CHANNING WEST, BROOKS PATE, *Department of Chemistry, The University of Virginia, Charlottesville, VA, USA.*

Rapid recording of molecular spectra of complex mixtures has facilitated acquisition of high sensitivity data sets. In studies of weakly bound clusters, these spectra may contain a wide range of cluster sizes and abundances, leading to intensities spanning many orders of magnitude between the strongest and weakest spectra present. The line densities and wide dynamic ranges of these high sensitivity spectra often lead to bottlenecks at the spectroscopic assignment and analysis stages of an experiment. Recent developments in artificial intelligence and machine learning have the potential to lead to fast, automated approaches to the spectroscopic assignment process. Here, we present an implementation of Jacobson, *et al*'s extended cross correlation (XCC) approach[a] to separating transitions arising from different species. While not leading to fully automated spectroscopic assignment on its own, XCC provides simplified data sets that can be more easily analyzed by visual pattern recognition or combined with other automated approaches. Initial XCC results will be compared with our previous implementation of principal component analysis-based examination of microwave spectra of complex mixtures of fluorinated ethylene/CO_2 clusters. In addition to simplifying raw datasets, these semi-automated analyses may provide insights that help identify the species present in the mixture, as well as helping guide searches for spectra of new species.

[a]M.P. Jacobson, S.M. Coy, R.W. Field, Extended Cross Correlation: A Technique for Spectroscopic Pattern Recognition, *J. Chem. Phys.* 107 (1997) 8349–8356.

FH13 **10:52 – 10:53**

ENGAGING UNDERGRADUATE STUDENTS IN SPECTROSCOPY RESEARCH VIA DEVELOPMENT AND INCORPORATION OF ADVANCED DATA ANALYSIS TECHNIQUES

REBECCA A. PEEBLES, SEAN A. PEEBLES, PRASHANSA KANNANGARA, HANNAH FINO, *Department of Chemistry, Eastern Illinois University, Charleston, IL, USA.*

The rapidity with which large amounts of spectroscopic data can now be collected is presently driving interest in developing techniques to improve the speed with which spectra can be analyzed. While desirable in a research setting to avoid bottlenecks in the lab, these techniques will also be essential to the commercialization of high resolution spectroscopic methods for analysis of complex mixtures. At the same time, many undergraduate students are intrigued by the concept of data analytics and attracted by the growing job market related to this field. We will present our incorporation of analysis techniques appropriate for large data sets into undergraduate spectroscopy research experiences. Through analysis of high sensitivity microwave spectra of complex mixtures of weakly bound complexes, undergraduate students from a wide range of majors gain skill sets that put them ahead of their peers in areas such as problem solving, basic coding, and computer skills (Excel, DOS, Linux, Python, Mathcad). The majority of spectroscopy undergraduate research students at Eastern Illinois University do not go on to chemistry careers, and these additional skills that they learn provide excellent preparation for a wide range of career choices.

FI. Clusters/Complexes

Friday, June 25, 2021 – 10:0 AM

Room: 2021 Online Everywhere

Chair: Wenhao Sun, DESY, Hamburg, Germany

FI01 **10:00 – 10:01**

INFRARED SPECTRA OF $(CO_2)_n$ - (RARE GAS)$_m$ TRIMERS AND TETRAMER, (n, m) = (1,2), (1,3), (2,1)

A. J. BARCLAY, *Department of Physics and Astronomy, University of Calgary, Calgary, AB, Canada*; A.R.W. McKELLAR, *Steacie Laboratory, National Research Council of Canada, Ottawa, ON, Canada*; ANDREA PIETROPOLLI CHARMET, *Dipartimento di Scienze Molecolari e Nanosistemi, Università Ca' Foscari, Venezia, Italy*; NASSER MOAZZEN-AHMADI, *Physics and Astronomy/Institute for Quantum Science and Technology, University of Calgary, Calgary, AB, Canada.*

***(n,m)* = (1,2).** CO_2-Ar_2 has previously been studied in the microwave[a] and infrared.[b] Its structure has two Ar atoms occupying equivalent positions around the 'equator' of the CO_2, giving C_{2v} symmetry. Here we report observation of analogous infrared spectra of CO_2-Ne_2 and CO_2-Xe_2. Meanwhile, for CO_2-Ar_2 we observe a new a-type combination band giving an intermolecular bending frequency of 32.2 cm^{-1}. Unlike the fundamental band, the combination band is free of interference from stronger CO_2-Ar transitions. Also, we observe CO_2-Ar_2 in the CO_2 (01^11) - (01^10) hot band region, as well as weak fundamental band spectra of the mixed trimers CO_2-Rg-He, with Rg = Ne, Ar, Xe.

***(n,m)* = (1,3).** An interesting band near 2345.2 cm^{-1} is assigned to CO_2-Xe_3, whose structure appears to have C_s symmetry containing a xenon trimer (near equilateral triangle) and a CO_2 positioned so that two of the Xe atoms are in equivalent near equatorial positions.

***(n,m)* = (2,1).** We have assigned spectra of new trimers, $(CO_2)_2$-Rg. The Xe-containing species was noticed first, and this led us to identify weaker spectra with Ar and (even weaker) Ne. Their structures resemble having a CO_2 dimer (planar slipped parallel) with the Rg atom located 'above' the dimer plane on (or close to) the dimer symmetry axis, analogous to $(CO_2)_2$-CO.[c] In the future, it should be possible to assign the various Kr clusters and to optimize each cluster by varying the expansion gas mixtures.

[a] Y. Xu, W. Jäger, and M.C.L. Gerry, *J. Mol. Spectrosc.* **157**, 132 (1993).
[b] J.M. Sperhac, M.J. Weida, and D.J. Nesbitt, *J. Chem. Phys.* **104** 2202 (1996).
[c] A.J. Barclay, A.R.W. McKellar, and N. Moazzen-Ahmadi, *Chem. Phys. Lett.* **677**, 127 (2017).

FI02 **10:04 – 10:05**

INFRARED SPECTROSCOPY OF $[H_2O\text{-}(Kr)_n]^+$ (n=1-3): HEMIBOND FORMATION WITH WATER

TOMOKI NISHIGORI, TOSHIHIKO MAEYAMA, MARUSU KATADA, ASUKA FUJII, *Department of Chemistry, Tohoku University, Sendai, Japan*; JING-MIN LIU, JER-LAI KUO, *Institute of Atomic and Molecular Sciences, Academia Sinica, Taipei, Taiwan.*

Spatial overlap of two non-bonding orbitals of ionized and neutral molecules can result in formation of a hemibond (two-center three-electron (2c3e) bond). Though hemibond formation between water and rare gas atom has been theoretically predicted, no definite experimental evidence has been reported. In the present study, we perform infrared spectroscopy of $[H_2O\text{-}(Kr)_n]^+$ (n=1-3) clusters in the gas phase. Comparison of the observed spectral features in the OH stretch region with the ab initio anharmonic vibrational simulations demonstrates the hemibond formation between water and Kr in all the observed cluster sizes.

FI03 *Post-Deadline Abstract* **10:08 – 10:09**

NEUTRAL IRON (III) SPECIES OBSERVED BY SECOND HARMONIC GENERATION SPECTROSCOPY AT THE AQUEOUS INTERFACE

KA CHON NG, *Chemistry and Biochemistry, The Ohio State University, Columbus, OH, USA*; HEATHER C. ALLEN, *Department of Chemistry and Biochemistry, The Ohio State University, Columbus, OH, USA*.

Iron is the most abundant metal on Earth and is involved in many critically important processes. Iron is commonly found in nature in its mineral forms, and in aqueous solutions as a complex with other soluble salts where hydration also plays a key role in its subsequent speciation. Aqueous interfaces are the gateway to many natural and biological reactions, including those that involve soluble Fe(III). Yet, interfacial iron complexation and surface prevalence are not well understood, especially under the inherently acidic conditions of $FeCl_3$ solutions. In this study, we investigate interfacial Fe(III) species using second harmonic generation (SHG) combined with surface tension and UV/visible absorption. Surface selective techniques such as SHG have been widely applied to unveil the unique properties of substances within the air-aqueous interface. Here, we observe two different interfacial regions with increasing concentration marked by two distinctly different SHG electric-field (E-field) trends. Below 2.0 mol/kg water aqueous $FeCl_3$, nonresonant SHG behavior is observed, similar to the E-field generated from the aqueous sodium iodide surface, but much larger in magnitude than aqueous NaCl and NaBr solution surfaces. Above 2.0 mol/kg water, a significant increase in the SHG slope is observed, much larger than that of the aqueous sodium halide electrolyte surfaces. Through further evaluation of symmetry and resonant behavior, we determine the existence of the neutral $[FeCl_3](H_2O)_3]$ complex.

FI04 **10:12 – 10:13**

A CLOSE COMPETITION BETWEEN OH-O AND OH-π HYDROGEN BONDING: IR SPECTROSCOPY OF ANISOLE-METHANOL COMPLEX IN HELIUM NANODROPLETS

TARUN KUMAR ROY, DEVENDRA MANI, GERHARD SCHWAAB, MARTINA HAVENITH, *Physikalische Chemie II, Ruhr University Bochum, Bochum, Germany*.

Anisole has two prominent hydrogen bonding sites, namely oxygen and the π-electrons of the phenyl ring. Earlier studies on anisole-water[1,2] and anisole-methanol[3] complexes show that in both cases the interaction with the oxygen atom is preferred and complex formation takes place via OH-O hydrogen bonding, where water/methanol acts as hydrogen bond donor.

We have studied anisole-methanol complexes in superfluid helium droplets, using high-resolution infrared spectroscopy.[4] Several bands corresponding to $(\text{anisole})_m$-$(\text{methanol})_n$ complexes (where m=1,2 and n=1) were observed. The size of the clusters corresponding to the observed bands was determined by recording the band intensity as a function of the partial pressures of the constituent molecules, resulting in so-called pickup curves.[5] A comparison of the observed spectra with the calculated spectra, at MP2/6-311++G (d,p) level of theory, suggests the formation of four different conformers of the anisole-methanol dimer in helium droplets. Among them, the two structures with the largest binding energies are predominantly stabilized via OH-O hydrogen bonds and the other two via OH-π hydrogen bonds.

References:

1. B. Reimann, K. Buchhold, H.-D. Barth, B. Brutschy, P. T arakeshwar, and Kwang S. Kim, J. Chem. Phys., 2002, 117, 8805.

2. M. Becucci, G. Pietraperzia, M. Pasquini, G. Piani, A. Zoppi, R. Chelli, E. Castellucci and W. Demtroeder, J. Chem. Phys., 2004, 120, 5601.

3. M. Heger, J. Altno, A. Poblotzki and M. A. Suhm, Phys. Chem. Chem. Phys., 2015, 17, 13045.

4. Tarun Kumar Roy, Devendra Mani, Gerhard Schwaab, Martina Havenith, Phys. Chem. Chem. Phys., 2020, 22, 22408.

5. M. Lewerenz, B. Schilling and J. P. Toennies, J. Chem. Phys., 1995, 102, 8191.

FI05 **10:16 – 10:17**

HIGH-RESOLUTION INFRARED STUDY OF THE C_3Te AND TeC_3Te CLUSTERS

SVEN THORWIRTH, THOMAS SALOMON, *I. Physikalisches Institut, Universität zu Köln, Köln, Germany*; SOPHIA BURGER, JÜRGEN GAUSS, *Institut für Physikalische Chemie, Universität Mainz, Mainz, Germany*; STEPHAN SCHLEMMER, *I. Physikalisches Institut, Universität zu Köln, Köln, Germany*; JOHN B DUDEK, *Department of Chemistry, Hartwick College, Oneonta, NY, USA.*

To date, carbon-rich clusters harboring heavy elements have received little attention from both experiment and quantum chemistry. Recent high-resolution infrared survey scans of laser ablation products from carbon-tellurium targets in the 5μm wavelength regime show two vibration-rotation bands not observed previously. On the basis of comparison with results from density-functional theory and high-level quantum-chemical calculations performed at the CCSD(T) level of theory these bands are attributed to two new linear chains, C_3Te and TeC_3Te.

FI06 **10:20 – 10:21**

STRUCTURE AND INFRARED SPECTRA OF NEW AEROSOL PARTICLE FORMATION SEED CLUSTERS

DANIEL P. TABOR, JEZRIELLE R. ANNIS, *Department of Chemistry, Texas A & M University, College Station, TX, USA*; NATHANAEL M. KIDWELL, *Department of Chemistry, College of William & Mary, Williamsburg, VA, USA.*

One of the largest unknowns in the understanding of aerosol particles is the structure and growth process that drives new particle formation, particularly from a *molecular* point of view. These processes are dictated by the underlying interplay of hydrogen-bonding interactions of the organic molecules with water and water with itself. The presence of amine groups may further accelerate new particle formation; thus we model the vibrational spectra of clusters of several heterocyclic molecules complexed with water and ammonia. We model the OH and NH stretching regions of the clusters' IR spectra through a suite of approaches that have favorable computational scaling and cost compared to standard anharmonic approaches. This acceleration allows us to consider the numerous cluster candidates and provide assignments. Finally, the wealth of spectral data (both theoretical and experimental) allows us to test the performance of data-driven spectroscopic models.

FI07 **10:24 – 10:25**

AB INITIO STUDY ON THE VIBRATIONAL SIGNATURES OF Ar_nH^+ (n=2–3)

JAKE A. TAN, JER-LAI KUO, *Institute of Atomic and Molecular Sciences, Academia Sinica, Taipei, Taiwan.*

A progression of strong bands in the 900–2200 cm^{-1} region are observed in the infrared laser photodissociation spectrum of Ar_3H^+.[a] In this talk, computational studies were conducted to examine the structures, binding energies, and infrared spectra for Ar_nH^+ (n=2–3). We found that the minimum structure for Ar_2H^+ is linear and centrosymmetric, while Ar_3H^+ can be either T-shaped or linear.[b] A series of potential energy surfaces at the CCSD(T)/aug-cc-pVTZ level of theory and basis set was constructed and used for the calculation of anharmonic spectrum using discrete variable representation (DVR).[c] Anharmonic theory can reproduce the observed strong bands, which were associated with the core Ar_2H^+ ion. These bands are assigned as combination bands of the asymmetric Ar-H$^+$ stretch with multiple quanta of the symmetric Ar-H$^+$ stretch.

[a]D.C. McDonald II, D.T. Mauney, D. Leicht, J.H. Marks, J.A. Tan, J.-L. Kuo, and M.A. Duncan, J. Chem. Phys. 145, 231101 (2016).

[b]J.A. Tan and J.-L. Kuo, J. Phys. Chem. A 124, 7726–7734 (2020).

[c]J.C. Light, I.P. Hamilton, and J. V. Lill, J. Chem. Phys. 82, 1400 (1985).

FI09 **10:32 – 10:33**

NEW INFRARED SPECTRA OF CO_2-Xe: MODELING Xe ISOTOPE EFFECTS, INTERMOLECULAR BEND AND STRETCH, AND SYMMETRY BREAKING OF THE CO_2 BEnd

A. J. BARCLAY, *Department of Physics and Astronomy, University of Calgary, Calgary, AB, Canada*; A.R.W. McKELLAR, *Steacie Laboratory, National Research Council of Canada, Ottawa, ON, Canada*; COLIN WESTERN, *School of Chemistry, University of Bristol, Bristol, United Kingdom*; NASSER MOAZZEN-AHMADI, *Physics and Astronomy/Institute for Quantum Science and Technology, University of Calgary, Calgary, AB, Canada.*

The infrared spectrum of CO_2-Xe is studied in the region of the carbon dioxide ν_3 fundamental vibration (near 2350 cm^{-1}), using a tunable OPO laser source to probe a pulsed supersonic slit jet expansion. We generally think of Xe or Kr isotope effects to be mostly unresolved for infrared spectra of weakly-bound van der Waals complexes. But here we model the Xe isotope dependence of the spectrum by scaling the vibrational and rotational parameters with the help of previous microwave data,[a] using features built into PGOPHER.[b] This model provides a very good simulation of the observed broadening and (partial) splitting of transitions in the fundamental band. More importantly, it is essential for understanding the intermolecular bending combination band, where many transitions are completely split by isotope effects. The combination band is influenced by a significant bend-stretch Coriolis interaction and by the relatively large Xe isotope dependence of the intermolecular stretch frequency. It turns out that K_a = 1 levels of the stretch lie above K_a = 2 levels of the bend for CO_2-^{129}Xe, but below them for CO_2-^{136}Xe. This greatly enhances the Xe isotope dependence of the Coriolis interaction.

The weak CO_2-Xe spectrum corresponding to the (01^11) - (01^10) hot band of CO_2 is also detected and analyzed, providing a measurement of the symmetry breaking of the CO_2 ν_2 bending mode induced by the nearby Xe atom. This in-plane / out-of-plane splitting is determined to be 2.14 cm^{-1}, with the out-of-plane mode lying higher in energy.

[a] M. Iida, Y. Ohshima, and Y. Endo, *J. Phys. Chem.* **97**, 357 (1993).

[b] PGOPHER, A Program for Simulating Rotational, Vibrational and Electronic Spectra, C.M. Western, University of Bristol, http://pgopher.chm.bris.ac.uk

FI10 **10:36 – 10:37**

$\mathrm{Si_nO_m^+}$ – OPTICAL ABSORPTION AND PHOTODISSOCIATION PROPERTIES

TAARNA STUDEMUND, MARKO FÖRSTEL, LARS DAHLLÖF, KAI POLLOW, ROBERT G. RADLOFF, OTTO DOPFER, *Institut für Optik und Atomare Physik, Technische Universität Berlin, Berlin, Germany.*

Interstellar dust contains to a large extent μm-sized silicate particles. The origin and evolutionary processes of these are still poorly understood. Only one possible precursor, molecular SiO in a circumstellar disk, has been observed so far.[1] We present experimental data and quantum chemical calculations on the absorption and dissociation properties of small $\mathrm{Si_nO_m^+}$ clusters ($n = 10 - 12$, $m = 1 - 2$) that are potential intermediates between the circumstellar SiO diatomic molecule and silicate grains observed in the interstellar medium. The spectra are the first optical absorption spectra of $\mathrm{Si_nO_m^+}$ cations and obtained by photodissociation of mass-selected ions generated in a laser desorption source.[2] We compare our experimental results to TD-DFT calculations and discuss them in an astrophysical context.

Literature:

[1] R. Wilson et al., Astrophys. J., 1971, 167, L97.
[2] M. Förstel et al., Rev. Sci. Instrum., 2017, 88, 123110.

FI11 **10:40 – 10:41**

INFRARED SPECTRA OF $(CO_2)_2$-X, CO_2-X_2, AND CO_2-X_3, X = CO OR N_2

A. J. BARCLAY, *Department of Physics and Astronomy, University of Calgary, Calgary, AB, Canada*; A.R.W. McKELLAR, *Steacie Laboratory, National Research Council of Canada, Ottawa, ON, Canada*; ANDREA PIETROPOLLI CHARMET, *Dipartimento di Scienze Molecolari e Nanosistemi, Università Ca' Foscari, Venezia, Italy*; NASSER MOAZZEN-AHMADI, *Physics and Astronomy/Institute for Quantum Science and Technology, University of Calgary, Calgary, AB, Canada.*

We previously observed the spectrum of $(CO_2)_2$-CO in the region of the CO fundamental band (2150 cm^{-1}).[a] Its structure resembles that of a CO_2 dimer (planar slipped-parallel) with a CO monomer aligned along the dimer C_2 symmetry axis in a C-bonded configuration, giving a trimer with C_2 symmetry. We have now observed three bands of the same species in the CO_2 ν_3 region. Two of these bands are fundamentals, one a/c-type and the other b-type. The presence of this b-type band establishes that the CO_2 dimer subunit within the trimer is actually not planar. The third band is a b-type combination band near 2376 cm^{-1}.

A new c-type fundamental near 2349.5 $\mathrm{cm}^{-1}$and an a-type combination band near 2365.2 $\mathrm{cm}^{-1}$are assigned to CO_2-$(CO)_2$. The structure has two C-bonded CO monomers in equivalent positions around the CO_2 'equator', giving a C_{2v} geometry analogous to that of CO_2-Ar_2. A similar fundamental is observed for CO_2-$(N_2)_2$ near 2350.0 cm^{-1}.

The weak parallel band of a symmetric or near-symmetric rotor near 2349.2 $\mathrm{cm}^{-1}$is assigned to CO_2-$(CO)_3$, together with an analogous band of CO_2-$(N_2)_3$ near 2349.8 cm^{-1}. We think that these tetramers are accidental symmetric rotors having C_s symmetry. They are obtained by taking the C_{2v} trimers from the previous paragraph and adding a third CO or N_2 to the 'side' of the first two, in the plane bisecting them.

[a] A.J. Barclay, A.R.W. McKellar, and N. Moazzen-Ahmadi, *Chemical Physics Letters* **677**, 127 (2017).

FI12 **10:44 – 10:45**

THE INFRARED SPECTRUM OF CO_2-Kr, INCLUDING THE INTERMOLECULAR BENDING MODE AND SYMMETRY BREAKING OF THE CO_2 BEND

SYE GHEBRETNSAE, *Physics and Astronomy, University of Calgary, Calgary, AB, Canada*; A. J. BARCLAY, *Department of Physics and Astronomy, University of Calgary, Calgary, AB, Canada*; NASSER MOAZZEN-AHMADI, *Physics and Astronomy/Institute for Quantum Science and Technology, University of Calgary, Calgary, AB, Canada.*

The infrared spectrum of CO_2-Kr in the region of the carbon dioxide ν_3 fundamental vibration (near 2350 cm^{-1}) was first studied by Randall *et al.*[a] Here we reexamine this spectrum, using a tunable OPO laser source to probe a pulsed supersonic slit jet expansion of a dilute mixture of CO_2 and Kr in helium. The bending combination band, which is observed near 2378 cm^{-1}, yields an intermolecular bending frequency of 29.43 cm^{-1}, in fairly good agreement with a theoretical prediction of 30.02 cm^{-1} by Chen *et al.*[b]

The spectrum of CO_2-Kr in the region of the CO_2 (01^11) - (01^10) hot band is also observed, following on our recent study of this transition in CO_2-Ar.[c] This gives a measurement of the symmetry breaking of the CO_2 ν_2 bending mode caused by the Kr atom. The out-of-plane mode turns out to be about 1.42 cm^{-1} higher than the in-plane mode for CO_2-Kr, as compared to splittings of 0.06 cm^{-1} for CO_2-Ne, 0.88 cm^{-1} for CO_2-Ar, and 2.14 cm^{-1} for CO_2-Xe.

[a] R.W. Randall. M.A. Walsh, and B.J. Howard, *Faraday Discuss. Chem. Soc.* **85**, 13 (1988).
[b] R. Chen, H. Zhu, and D. Xie, *Chem. Phys. Lett.* **511**, 229 (2011).
[c] T.A. Gartner, A.J. Barclay, A.R.W. McKellar, and N. Moazzen-Ahmadi, *Phys. Chem. Chem. Phys.* **22**, 21488 (2020).

FI13 **10:48 – 10:49**

TUNNELING DYNAMICS IN $N_2 - D_2O$ OBSERVED IN THE OD STRETCHING REGION

R. GLORIEUX, CLÉMENT LAUZIN, *Institue of Condensed Matter and Nanosciences (IMCN), Université catholique de Louvain, Louvain-la-Neuve, Belgium*; A. J. BARCLAY, *Physics and Astronomy/Institute for Quantum Science and Technology, University of Calgary, Calgary, AB, Canada*; MICHEL HERMAN, *SQUARES, Université Libre de Bruxelles, Brussels, Belgium*; NASSER MOAZZEN-AHMADI, *Physics and Astronomy/Institute for Quantum Science and Technology, University of Calgary, Calgary, AB, Canada.*

The rovibrational spectra of $N_2 - D_2O$ and $N_2 - DOH$ were measured around the OD stretching region. A combination band involving the in-plane N_2 bend intermolecular vibration was also observed in the same frequency range. These bands were measured at the University of Calgary using a pulsed-slit supersonic jet expansion and a mid-infrared tunable optical parametric oscillator. The spectra were analyzed by considering the feasible tunneling motions and fit to a series of independent asymmetric rotors. The rotational constants of the four tunneling components of $N_2 - D_2O$ were retrieved for the excited vibrational states. Small vibrational blue shifts of $0.6\ cm^{-1}$ and $1.8\ cm^{-1}$ compared to the D_2O monomer band origins were determined for the symmetric and asymmetric stretches, respectively. A two order of magnitude larger tunneling splittings is observed for the asymmetric OD stretching excitation compared to the symmetric one. This last finding indicate a significant change of the intermolecular dynamics due to the intramolecular asymmetric OD vibration.

FJ. Photodissociation and photochemistry

Friday, June 25, 2021 – 10:0 AM

Room: 2021 Online Everywhere

Chair: Katharine Moore Tibbetts, Virginia Commonwealth University, Richmond, VA, USA

FJ01 **10:00 – 10:01**

DYNAMICAL SIGNATURES FROM COMPETING, NONADIABATIC FRAGMENTATION PATHWAYS OF S-NITROSOTHIOPHENOL

K. JACOB BLACKSHAW, *Department of Chemistry, College of William & Mary, Williamsburg, VA, USA*; MARCUS MARRACCI, ANDREW S. PETIT, *Department of Chemistry, California State University, Fullerton, Fullerton, CA, USA*; NATHANAEL M. KIDWELL, *Department of Chemistry, College of William & Mary, Williamsburg, VA, USA*.

S-Nitrosothiols (RSNOs) are derived from the combination of sulfur and nitric oxide (NO) radicals in the Earth's atmosphere and fragment to products following photolysis. Extensive theoretical studies have focused on the thermodynamic and, to a lesser extent, photochemical properties of RSNOs. However, experimental studies of these compounds have been limited due to the inherent instability of RSNOs at room temperature. Using velocity map imaging (VMI), we explore the photodissociation dynamics of jet-cooled S-nitrosothiophenol (PhSNO) from 355 nm photolysis. We report the translational and internal energy distributions of the NO and thiophenoxy (PhS) co-fragments, which are determined by spatial detection of the ionized NO photofragments using 1+1 resonance-enhanced multiphoton ionization (REMPI). The velocity distributions indicate competing PhSNO nonadiabatic dissociation pathways, in which PhS is formed in the ground and first excited electronic states when probing high- and low-energy NO ($X^2\Pi_{1/2}$,v",J") rovibrational states, respectively. The results of multireference electronic structure calculations suggest that direct dissociation on the bright S_2 state results in PhS formed in its excited electronic state, whereas intersystem crossing into the triplet manifold leads to population of PhS in its electronic ground state. The dynamical signatures from the dissociation processes are imprinted on the fragments' quantum states and relative translation, which we explore in rigorous detail using state-resolved imaging and high-level theoretical calculations.

FJ02 ***Post-Deadline Abstract*** **10:04 – 10:05**

THE PHOTOCHEMICAL PATHWAYS FOR THE NONREACTIVE ELECTRONIC QUENCHING OF NO ($A^2\Sigma^+$) BY CO AND H_2O

JOSE GUARDADO SANDOVAL, *Department of Chemistry, California State University, Fullerton, Fullerton, CA, USA*; NATHANAEL M. KIDWELL, *Department of Chemistry, College of William & Mary, Williamsburg, VA, USA*; ANDREW S. PETIT, *Department of Chemistry, California State University, Fullerton, Fullerton, CA, USA*.

Nitric oxide (NO) is an important pollutant produced in combustion. Laser-induced fluorescence (LIF) on the $A^2\Sigma^+ \rightarrow X^2\Pi$ band is a common approach for quantifying the amount of NO and determining the physical conditions inside operating combustion engines. However, NO ($A^2\Sigma^+$) is known to undergo reactive and nonreactive electronic quenching with molecular species, providing alternative photochemical pathways that compete with fluorescence. For example, the nonreactive electronic quenching cross sections of NO ($A^2\Sigma^+$) with CO and H_2O at 300 K are 6 Å^2 and 120 Å^2, respectively. The underlying photochemical mechanisms responsible for this electronic quenching are not well-understood.

In this talk we describe our efforts to develop high-quality potential energy surfaces (PESs) that provide insights into the long-range interactions and conical intersections that facilitate nonreactive electronic quenching of NO ($A^2\Sigma^+$) by CO and H_2O. In order to ensure a balanced treatment of the valence and Rydberg electronic states as well as an accurate description of the open-shell character of NO we use the electron-attachment equation of motion coupled cluster with singles and doubles method (EOM-EA-CCSD). Our results demonstrate significant differences between the NO ($A^2\Sigma^+$)+CO and NO ($A^2\Sigma^+$)+H_2O systems in terms of the strength of the long-range attractive interactions, the impact of neighboring Rydberg states, and the shape of the PESs in the vicinity of the conical intersections responsible for the electronic quenching. In particular, we rationalize the large electronic quenching cross section of NO ($A^2\Sigma^+$) with H_2O by the presence of relatively strong long-range attractions that steer the NO ($A^2\Sigma^+$)+H_2O system into an excited-state collision complex that is bound by over 4500 cm^{-1}. Overall, this work sheds new light on the mechanisms for nonreactive electronic quenching of NO ($A\ ^2\Sigma^+$) with molecular partners.

FJ03 **10:08 – 10:09**

UNIMOLECULAR DISSOCIATION OF PEROXYFORMIC ACID INITIATED BY VIBRATIONAL OVERTONE EXCITATION TO THE 6νOH STATE[a]

JOSUE EMMANUEL PEREZ, MADHUSUDAN ROY, AMITABHA SINHA, *Department of Chemistry and Biochemistry, UC San Diego, San Diego, CA, USA.*

Photodissociation is an important loss mechanism for atmospheric hydroperoxides (R-O-OH) leading to the production of OH radicals via the rupture of the weak O-O bond. Photodissociation can either occur through electronic excitation to a repulsive excited electronic state or, alternatively, through unimolecular dissociation on the ground electronic surface. Here we present results from the unimolecular dissociation of peroxyformic acid (PFA) initiated by exciting the molecule in the vicinity of its fifth OH stretching overtone state (6νOH) at both 615 and 626nm. Based on the estimated heat of formation of PFA and its fragments, the O-O bond dissociation energy (D_0) in PFA is estimated to be 45.1 kcal/mol. Thus, exciting room temperature PFA molecules at 615 nm and 626 nm is expected to leave the OH + HCO_2 fragments with roughly 3.3 kcal/mol and 2.5 kcal/mol of available energy, respectively. Using laser induced fluorescence (LIF), we have probed the OH fragments from the near threshold unimolecular dissociation and have determined the partitioning of the available energy in to its internal and translational degrees of freedom. These results, along with the insight they provide regarding the unimolecular dissociation dynamics of HC(O)OOH, will be presented.

[a]The authors are grateful to NSF for support of this work.

FJ04 **10:12 – 10:13**

ROTATIONAL COOLING DYNAMICS OF HOT TRAPPED OH^- IONS PROBED BY VMI PHOTOELECTRON SPECTROSCOPY

ABHISHEK SHAHI, SAURABH MISHRA, DHANOJ GUPTA, ODED HEBER, DANIEL ZAJFMAN, *Department of Particle Physics and Astrophysics, Weizmann Institute of Science, Rehovot, Rehovot, Israel.*

A VMI photoelectron spectroscopy inside an electrostatic ion beam trap (EIBT) is used to probe the time dependent dynamics of rotational states population. The photodetachement of OH^- ion results neutral OH in its $\Pi_{3/2}$ and $\Pi_{1/2}$ states and corresponding VMI photoelectron spectra of unresolved P-branch transitions are shown in figure for different times in the EIBT. As storage time increases, the peak radius of P-transitions decreases indicate that population of high rotational levels shift to the low rotational levels. Intersting findinds on internal dynamics of OH^- as a function of storage time, change in individual rotational states population as a function of storage time, rate coefficients of such cooling process will be discussed in details during presentation.

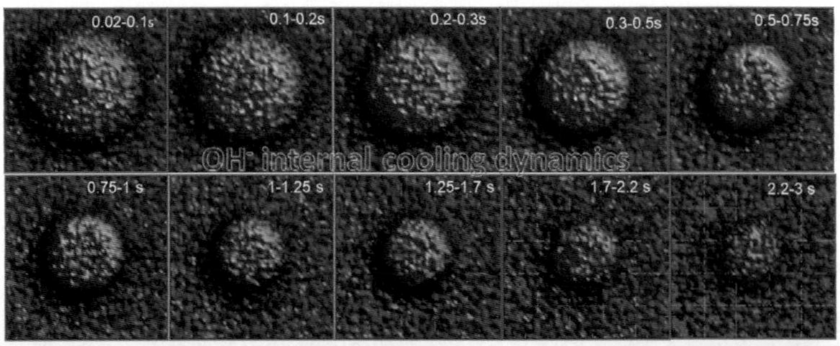

FJ05 **10:16 – 10:17**

BOND DISSOCIATION DYNAMICS AND THERMODYNAMICS OF NiO^+ AND NiS^+

SCHUYLER P LOCKWOOD, RICARDO B. METZ, *Department of Chemistry, University of Massachusetts, Amherst, MA, USA.*

Transition metal oxide and sulfide cations activate C-H bonds in the gas phase; several oxide cations activate methane and convert it to methanol at room temperature. However, a lack of experimental data on the energetics and dynamics of these species makes it difficult to model their reactions with hydrocarbons. We perform photofragment ion imaging experiments and ab initio calculations to determine the bond strength and photodissociation dynamics of the nickel oxide (NiO^+) and nickel sulfide (NiS^+) cations.

NiO^+ photodissociates broadly from 25000 to 32000 cm^{-1}via an excited $^4\Sigma^-$ state, exclusively forming Ni^+ (^4F) + O (^3P) products at photolysis energies above 29000 cm^{-1}. Photofragment images of NiO^+ show resolved Ni^+ ($^4F_{9/2}$) + O (^3P) and Ni^+ ($^4F_{7/2}$) + O (^3P) product spin-orbit channels; the lower energy (J = 9/2) channel dominates at photolysis energies of 29000 to 32000 cm^{-1}. The photofragment spectrum of NiS^+ from 19800 to 23200 $cm^{-1}$is highly structured, with 12 distinct vibronic peaks each containing underlying spin-orbit structure. Photofragment images of NiS^+ collected over this region show slight parallel anisotropy, suggesting the highly structured photodissociation spectrum of NiS^+ in this region predominantly arises from a $\Delta\Lambda = 0$ transition. Above 21600 cm^{-1}, the Ni^+ ($^2D_{5/2}$) + S (^3P) and Ni^+ ($^2D_{3/2}$) + S (^3P) product spin-orbit channels compete, with a branching ratio of 0.5. Temperature-dependent spectra suggest peaks below 20150 cm^{-1}result from hot bands. Images taken slightly above the dissociation threshold (20600 cm^{-1}) show resolved S ($^3P_2$) and S ($^3P_1$) spin-orbit channels. Our D_0 measurements for NiO^+ (D_0 = 244.6 +/- 2.4 kJ/mol) and NiS^+ (D_0 = 240.3 +/- 1.4 kJ/mol) are more precise and closer to each other than previously reported values.

FJ06 **10:20 – 10:21**

SPECTROSCOPIC STUDIES OF TRANSITION METAL AND LANTHANIDE BORIDES WITH RESONANT TWO-PHOTON IONIZATION SPECTROSCOPY

DAKOTA M. MERRILES, KIMBERLY H. TOMCHAK, CHRISTOPHER NIELSON, ERICK TIEU, MICHAEL D. MORSE, *Department of Chemistry, University of Utah, Salt Lake City, UT, USA.*

Metal boride compounds have unique properties that make them as chemically interesting as they are relevant in a multitude of disciplines. As more applications are discovered for metal borides, improved chemical models are needed to accurately predict the behavior of these species.

To assist in this effort, we have developed a method for the precise and accurate measurement of bond dissociation energies (BDEs) and have applied it to the diatomic transition metal borides (MB), triatomic transition metal diborides (MB2), and triatomic lanthanide metal borides (LnB2). The method relies on the fact that in the open d-subshell and open f-subshell metal boride molecules, there is a large density of electronic states present at energies about the molecule's dissociation limit. Spin-orbit and adiabatic couplings among the large number of potential energy curves in this region enable the molecules to hop from curve to curve, finding their way to dissociation as soon as sufficient energy is available for this process. In our resonant two-photon ionization experiments, the high density of states in this region leads to a quasi-continuous spectrum below the dissociation energy, followed by a sharp drop to baseline when the molecules are excited above the dissociation limit. The sharp drop in signal occurs at a wavelength that corresponds to the BDE of the molecule.

Using this method, the BDEs of 18 diatomic borides and 10 triatomic boride molecules have been measured to high accuracy with the majority of these species having no previous experimental data or observations recorded. These data provide important benchmarks for the development and testing of improved computational methods for these species which will be helpful for modeling larger metal boride clusters and nanoscopic materials. Of equal importance, a comprehensive set of bond dissociation energies for these species allows for a quantitative and qualitative landscape of the transition metal-boron bond to be elucidated.

FJ07 **10:24 – 10:25**

BOND DISSOCIATION ENERGIES OF DIATOMIC LANTHANIDE SULFIDES AND SELENIDES

JASON J SORENSEN, *Department of Chemistry and Biochemistry, Old Dominion University, Norfolk, VA, USA*; ERICK TIEU, MICHAEL D. MORSE, *Department of Chemistry, University of Utah, Salt Lake City, UT, USA.*

Bond dissociation energies pose a major challenge for modern computational methods. This is largely due to the need to treat electron correlation to the same level of accuracy in the molecule as in the separated atoms. This becomes especially difficult in transition metal and lanthanide containing species, as the electronic state densities are particularly high. As important as this issue is, the problem has been largely unassailable due to a long-standing dearth of highly accurate experimental data that is suitable for use as computational benchmarks. In this study, we use the sharp onset of predissociation in a highly congested, quasicontinuous optical spectrum to precisely measure the bond dissociation energies of 10 diatomic lanthanide sulfides, LnS, along with the corresponding lanthanide selenides, LnSe. These studies provide lanthanide thermochemistry of unparalleled accuracy, while also providing an opportunity to analyze the bonding in terms of the separated atom states to which the ground states diabatically correlate. From this analysis, it is proposed that most of the LnS and LnSe molecules diabatically correlate to the Ln^+ ($4f^N$ $5d^1$) + S^-($3s^2$ $3p^5$)/ Se^-($4s^2$ $4p^5$) separated ion limit. Our previous observation that the bond dissociation energies of the diatomic transition metal sulfides are universally about 15% stronger than their selenide analogs is extended to these 10 LnS/LnSe molecules, and the trend is observed to hold.

FJ08 **10:28 – 10:29**

EXOMOLHD: PHOTODISSOCIATION OF DIATOMIC MOLECULES

MARCO PEZZELLA, SERGEI N. YURCHENKO, JONATHAN TENNYSON, *Department of Physics and Astronomy, University College London, London, UK.*

The destruction of molecules by photodissociation influences the composition and dynamics of exoplanets, particularly in the presence of a UV-rich stellar environments, where molecules are hot. Current photodissociation calculations generally assume $T = 0$ K, appropriate for the cold interstellar medium but inadequate for hot (exo)planets and stars. We compute temperature-dependent photodissociation cross sections for molecules found in these atmospheres. The cross sections are calculated by solving the nuclear-motion Schrödinger equation as part of the ExoMol project using codes Duo and Exocross[a], and averaging results obtained as discrete spectra. We benchmark our results for three systems. The general validity of the methodology is tested considering the $A^1\Pi \leftarrow X^1\Sigma^+$ transition of HCl at low T. Our cross sections and rates agree with published results[b] ($2.31*10^{-10}$ s^{-1} versus $2.10*10^{-10}$ s^{-1} respectively). We also reproduce calculated photodissociation cross section of BeH^+ at T=1800 K.[c]

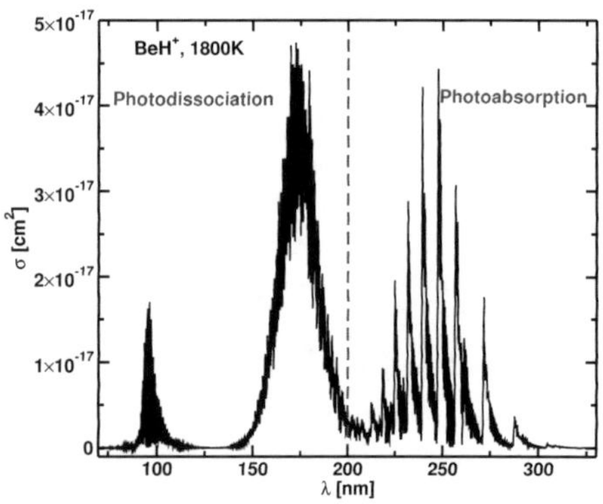

We performed the simulations considering the three excited states, $A^1\Sigma^+$, $B^1\Pi$ and $C^1\Sigma^+$, see figure. The photodissociation spectrum of NaCl varies consistently with T: at $T = 100$ K, there two peaks at 240 nm and 260 nm; while at $T = 1500$ K the peaks merge.

[a] Yurchenko *et al* Comput Phys Commun 2016 **202** 262–275;Yurchenko *et al* A&A 2018 **614** A131
[b] Dishoeck *et al* J. Chem. Phys. 1982 **77** 3693
[c] Yang *et al* J Quant Spectrosc Radiat Transf 2020 **254** 107203

FJ09 **10:32 – 10:33**

AB INITIO STUDY OF THE HIGHLY EXCITED ELECTRONIC STATES OF C_2 AND ITS PHOTODISSOCIATION

ZHONGXING XU, LEE-PING WANG, *Department of Chemistry, University of California, Davis, Davis, CA, USA*; STEVEN FEDERMAN, *Physics and Astronomy, University of Toledo, Toledo, OH, USA*; WILLIAM M. JACKSON, CHEUK-YIU NG, KYLE N. CRABTREE, *Department of Chemistry, University of California, Davis, Davis, CA, USA*.

Dicarbon (C_2) is one of the most abundant molecules in space and has been detected in different astronomical environments, including the interstellar medium, comets, and stars. In diffuse clouds, the dominant destruction pathway for C_2 is photodissociation by UV photons through the $F\,^1\Pi_u$ state and other higher $^1\Pi_u$ and $^1\Sigma_u^+$ states excited from the ground $X\,^1\Sigma_g^+$ state. However, the only laboratory study of the $F\,^1\Pi_u$ state was more than half a century ago and did not provide detailed information about its photodissociation, while no MRCI+Q level calculation has been done on the F state to date. Thus, considerable uncertainty exists about the photodissociation rate of C_2 in space and its atomic branching ratios, limiting the accuracy of simulations given by astrochemical models. Here we present a high-level *ab initio* study of C_2 photodissociation, focusing on the $F\,^1\Pi_u - X\,^1\Sigma_g^+$ transition. Potential energy curves of C_2 electronic states were calculated at the SA-CASSCF/MRCI+Q level using the aug-cc-pV5Z basis set with additional diffuse functions. To represent the Rydberg state nature of F state, the active space consisted of the valence orbitals and several additional σ_g orbitals. A total of 57 potential energy curves for singlet, triplet and quintet states were calculated, as well as transition dipole moments, nonadiabatic coupling matrix elements, and spin-orbit couplings. The F state lies near three $^3\Pi_u$ states that are likely responsible for its predissociation via spin-orbit coupling.

FJ10 **10:36 – 10:37**

PHOTOINDUCED CHARGE TRANSFER PROCESSES

ETHAN M CUNNINGHAM, CHRISTIAN VAN DER LINDE, MILAN ONCAK, MARTIN K BEYER, *Institute for Ion Physics and Applied Physics, University of Innsbruck, Innsbruck, Austria.*

Charge-transfer processes, particularly in hydrated iodide and salt clusters, depend sensitively on the chemical environment and number of water molecules solvated around the iodide ion. Studying such charge-transfer behaviour is ideally suited to gas-phase clusters, whereby the size and chemical composition, along with number of water molecules, can be controlled. For example, when hydrated iodide interacts with ultraviolet light, the electron fully separates from the iodine ion, forming a solvated electron. Charge-transfer transitions are also observed in ionic systems such as metal-halide clusters. To understand these charge-transfer processes at a molecular level, laser spectroscopic measurements in the ultraviolet and visible region are utilised and, initially, focussed on the ionic salt systems. Electrospray ionization is employed producing salt clusters, which can then be stored in the cell of a Fourier transform ion cyclotron resonance mass spectrometer. Laser systems using optical parametric oscillators are implemented, providing intense tuneable laser light in the 225 – 2600 nm region. For each size-selected salt cluster, evaporation of stoichiometric and non-stoichiometric fragments are recorded, elucidating photochemical pathways connected to charge-transfer transitions. These evaporation channels are revealed by mass spectrometry, whereby an electronic absorption spectrum can be generated in each case, in addition to wavelength-specific photochemistry. These experiments are complemented with simulated spectra generated using quantum chemical calculations. Unanswered questions such as where the charge is located, and where it moves to within the cluster, along with whether the charge is localised to one atom, are yet to be fully understood. Isolating size-selected hydrated iodide alongside a systematic series of salt clusters and exploring their photochemistry offers a targeted approach to tackle such questions. Studying these systems not only provides fundamental insight into charge-transfer mechanisms in cluster physics, but also offers a laboratory model system for a molecular level understanding of reactions occurring during marine aerosol ageing or radiation-induced cell damage.

FJ11 **10:40 – 10:41**

PROTOMERS OF FLAVIN RADICAL ANIONS PROBED WITH PD ACTION SPECTROSCOPY

SAMUEL MARLTON, BENJAMIN McKINNON, BORIS UCUR, JAMES P BEZZINA, *School of Chemistry, University of Wollongong, Wollongong, New South Wales, Australia*; STEPHEN J. BLANKSBY, *Central Analytical Research Facility, Queensland University of Technology, Brisbane, Queensland, Australia*; ADAM J. TREVITT, *School of Chemistry, University of Wollongong, Wollongong, New South Wales, Australia.*

Protonation or deprotonation sites mediate many cases of biological photochemistry. For example, flavin ions have several photobiological functions such as initiating DNA repair (occurring in some bacteria and frogs for example) and are central to quantum mechanical compass used by birds for navigation. These pathways involve various stages of flavin protonation and deprotonation, isomers and redox states. Furthermore, intermediate flavin radicals (which are formed in the biological photoredox pathways) have several possible protonation isomers (protomers) that are challenging to characterize due to their reactive nature and the additional challenge of separating isomeric species. Using photodissociation (PD) action spectroscopy coupled with mass spectrometry, reactive species (such as flavin radical ions) can be isolated in a vacuum and characterized based on their spectroscopic properties without reacting away. By photodissociating flavin adenine dinucleotide dianion (FAD) in an ion trap, multiple flavin radical anion fragments are formed. Photoproduct flavin ions in three redox states can each be separately re-isolated in the ion trap, in turn, and assigned by photodissociation action spectroscopy. Franck Condon simulations confirm that noncanonical protomers of these flavin radical ion are formed by direct photodissociation of larger flavins. These results reveal the structure of radical-anion products and provide assigned gas-phase spectra for reference and with these in hand, can provide new insights into the complex redox chemistry of FAD in biochemical systems.

FJ12 **10:44 – 10:45**

DELIBERATE FUNCTIONALIZATION AND THE CONSEQUENTIAL ELECTRONIC RELAXATION PATHWAYS OF THE PYRIMIDINE CHROMOPHORE

SEAN J. HOEHN, SARAH E. KRUL, CARLOS E. CRESPO-HERNÁNDEZ, *Chemistry, Case Western Reserve, Cleveland, OH, USA.*

The nucleic acid bases that we know today are thought to have originated from simple precursors also referred to as proto-biotic RNA. These molecular ancestors of RNA and DNA may have formed from a vast number of organic compounds found on early Earth and/or delivered by meteorite infall. Understanding the evolution of chemical synthesis ranging from those precursors to today's canonical nucleobases is essential in answering questions to the chemical origins of life. Among other factors, ultraviolet radiation (UVR) from the sun should have played a key role in shaping and selecting the building blocks of life. Whether the carbonyl and/or amino group substituents played any role in regulating the photostability of the canonical pyrimidine nucleobases is currently unknown. The biological relevance of the pyrimidine chromophore and its carbonyl- and amino-substituted derivatives make these molecules excellent candidates for investigating how their interaction with UVR may have enabled the selection of the RNA and DNA pyrimidine nucleobases on early Earth. Time-resolved spectroscopic results, complemented with quantum-chemical calculations, will be presented, which lend support to the idea that functionalization at the C2 and C4 positions of the pyrimidine chromophore has a preponderant role in controlling the inherent electronic relaxation mechanisms and photostability of the DNA and RNA pyrimidine nucleobases and their derivatives.

The authors acknowledge the National Science Foundation (Grant No. CHE-1800052) for financial support.

FJ13 **10:48 – 10:49**

ELECTRONIC RELAXATION MECHANISM OF GUANINE DERIVATIVES IN SOLUTION

SARAH E. KRUL, SEAN J. HOEHN, CARLOS E. CRESPO-HERNÁNDEZ, *Chemistry, Case Western Reserve, Cleveland, OH, USA.*

The natural RNA and DNA nucleobases absorb harmful ultraviolet radiation but the ability to dissipate this excess electronic energy efficiently to the ground state makes them highly photostable. Understanding how minor structural modifications affect their photochemical properties is important for advancement in biological applications. For example, 7-deazaguanosine (7dza) has been used for decades to probe the charge transfer dynamics in DNA, due to its lowered oxidation potential relative to guanosine. However, the electronic relaxation mechanism of 7dza has not been investigated until recently.

Using steady-state and time-resolved electronic spectroscopic techniques, combined with quantum-chemical calculations, we have investigated the excited-state dynamics of guanosine 5'-monophosphate (GMP) and 7dza in in aqueous solution and in a mixture of methanol and water following excitation at 267 nm. The following relaxation mechanism has been proposed for both molecules: $L_b \Rightarrow L_a \Rightarrow {}^1\pi\sigma^*(ICT) \Rightarrow S_0$, where the ${}^1\pi\sigma^*(ICT)$ stands for an intramolecular charge transfer excited singlet state with significant $\pi\sigma^*$ character. In 7dza, however, the relaxation dynamics is slightly slowed compared to GMP, which adjudicate to stabilization of the two lowest-energy singlet states and to the alteration of the topology of the excited state potential energy surfaces.

The authors acknowledge the National Science Foundation (Grant No. CHE-1800052) for financial support and the High-Performance Computing Resource in the Core Facility for Advanced Research Computing at Case Western Reserve University.

FJ14 **10:52 – 10:53**

POTENTIAL DEPENDENT PLASMONIC CATALYZED CLEAVAGE OF C-BR BOND OF 8-BROMOADENINE ON SILVER ELECTRODES OF NANOSTRUCTURE

DE-YIN WU, ZHONG-QUN TIAN, *College of Chemistry and Chemical Engineering, Xiamen University, Xiamen, China.*

Localized surface plasmon resonance (LSPR) has offered a unique way to trigger photocatalyzed chemical reactions on nanoscale. 8-Bromoadenine was one of the halogenated nucleobases could be applied in the tumor tissue upon irradiation as a potential DNA radio-sensitizer. To utilize the high spatial resolution properties of noble metal nanostructure and improve the selectivity of plasmon catalytic reaction, we investigated the cleavage of C-Br bond in 8-bromoadenine in electrochemical interface. Surface-enhanced Raman spectroscopy (SERS) provides an excellent opportunity to probe and monitor plasmonic photochemical reactions in situ and in real-time. The EC-SERS spectra contour map can explain the potential effect in the reaction, the plasmon catalyzed reaction rate constant in different potentials. Analyzing the intensity change of the characteristic peak of adenine in electrochemical SERS (EC-SERS) spectra was used to investigate the reaction kinetics of the cleavage of C-Br bond could be estimated by intensity integration of the SERS peak.

FK. Structure determination

Friday, June 25, 2021 – 10:0 AM

Room: 2021 Online Everywhere

Chair: Helen O. Leung, Amherst College, Amherst, MA, USA

FK01 **10:00 – 10:01**

SEMI-EXPERIMENTAL EQUILIBRIUM STRUCTURE (r_e^{SE}) OF METHACRYLONITRILE(C_4H_5N)

HOUSTON H. SMITH, SAMUEL M. KOUGIAS, DANNY J LEE, BRIAN J. ESSELMAN, R. CLAUDE WOODS, ROBERT J. McMAHON, *Department of Chemistry, University of Wisconsin-Madison, Madison, WI, USA*.

Methacrylonitrile is believed to be an astrochemically relevant molecule due to the detection of acrylonitrile (C_3H_3N) in Saturn's moon, Titan, and in the interstellar medium. We synthesized methacrylonitrile via the hydrocyanation and subsequent dehydration of acetone and obtained its rotational spectrum in the 130 – 360 GHz frequency region. The main isotopologue ground state has been least-squares fit to a sextic Hamiltonian accounting for internal rotation splitting from the 3-fold symmetric methyl rotor, and resulting spectroscopic constants compare well with those previously reported. The improved determination of centrifugal distortion constants improve the spectral prediction over a broad frequency range and thus the radioastronomical search for this molecule. Additionally, a study of pyrimidine, using 16 isotopologues, demonstrated that it is possible to determine very accurate semi-experimental equilibrium structures (r_e^{SE}) using multiple isotopic substitution combined with coupled-cluster calculations treating the vibration-rotation interaction and the electron mass correction. With the goal of such a structure determination for methacrylonitrile, we have analyzed the spectra of all singly-substituted heavy-atom isotopologues (^{13}C and ^{15}N), which were detectable at natural abundance, and least-squares fit them to sextic Hamiltonians. To obtain deuterated isotopologues, the synthesis of methacrylonitrile was modified by using partially deuterated or fully deuterated acetone to yield samples of varying deuterium incorporation. We have currently assigned the rotational spectra of 22 isotopologues, with additional isotopologues yet to be analyzed. The current r_e^{SE} will be presented and compared to theoretical r_e structures.

FK02 **10:04 – 10:05**

SEMI-EXPERIMENTAL EQUILIBRIUM STRUCTURE OF 1H- AND 2H-1,2,3-TRIAZOLES ($C_2H_3N_3$)

MARIA ZDANOVSKAIA, BRIAN J. ESSELMAN, SAMUEL M. KOUGIAS, *Department of Chemistry, University of Wisconsin-Madison, Madison, WI, USA*; JOHN F. STANTON, *Quantum Theory Project, University of Florida, Gainesville, FL, USA*; R. CLAUDE WOODS, ROBERT J. McMAHON, *Department of Chemistry, University of Wisconsin-Madison, Madison, WI, USA*.

1H-1,2,3-triazole (C_s; $\kappa = 0.94$; $\mu_a = 4.1$ D, $\mu_b = 1.6$ D) and 2H-1,2,3-triazole (C_{2v}; $\kappa = 0.82$; $\mu_b = 0.52$ D) are tautomers ($C_2H_3N_3$), the former of which is formally the product of a 1,3-dipolar cycloaddition of two explosive compounds, hydrazoic acid and acetylene. We have analyzed the rotational spectra of these tautomers in the 130 – 360 GHz frequency range and least-squares fit the observed transitions to sextic Hamiltonians with low error ($\sigma < 50$ kHz). While ^{13}C and ^{15}N isotopologues have been observed at natural abundance and similarly analyzed, several synthetic techniques had to be employed to access deuterium-substituted isotopologues. The rotational constants of the numerous isotopologues, along with vibration-rotation interaction and electron mass corrections predicted using coupled-cluster and density functional theories, have been used to determine highly precise semi-experimental equilibrium structures (r_e^{SE}) of the 1,2,3-triazoles. Equilibrium structures calculated at the above-mentioned levels of theory, as well as a computational prediction using basis set extrapolation and additional corrections for the 2H structure, are compared to the semi-experimental structures.

FK03 **10:08 – 10:09**

DETERMINATION OF SUBSTITUTION EFFECTS ON THE STRUCTURES OF 2-, 3-, AND 4-PICOLYLAMINE USING FOURIER TRANSFORM MICROWAVE SPECTROSCOPY

RYAN G BIRD, CALEB B SHIERY, KAYLEE X SHOOK, *Chemistry, University of Pittsburgh Johnstown, Johnstown, PA, USA.*

This is a continued discussion regarding the substitution effectcts on the three-dimensional shape and electron distribution of three methylamine substituted pyridines, 2-, 3-, and 4-picolylamine. The microwave spectra of all three molecules were collected over the frequency range of 4-18 GHz. In addition, the ^{13}C and ^{15}N isotopologues, along with the deuterated amine groups, were collected for each molecule in natural abundance. From these spectra, exact structures were determined which allowed for accurate rotation of the quadruple constants from the molecular frame into an internal axis. Next, an extended Townes and Dailey analysis was used to determine the lone pair density around each nitrogen and then compared to those of benzylamine and pyridine. Results of this analysis and how it explains the configuration of the methylamine group in each of the picolylamines will be discussed.

FK04 **10:12 – 10:13**

OXAZOLE: PRECISE SEMI-EXPERIMENTAL EQUILIBRIUM STRUCTURE DETERMINATION BY ROTATIONAL SPECTROSCOPY

TAYLOR K. ADKINS, MARIA ZDANOVSKAIA, *Department of Chemistry, University of Wisconsin-Madison, Madison, WI, USA*; KAORI KOBAYASHI, SHOZO TSUNEKAWA, *Department of Physics, University of Toyama, Toyama, Japan*; BRIAN J. ESSELMAN, R. CLAUDE WOODS, ROBERT J. McMAHON, *Department of Chemistry, University of Wisconsin-Madison, Madison, WI, USA.*

The rotational spectrum of oxazole (c-C_3H_3NO, C_s), an astrochemically relevant aromatic heterocycle, has been studied from 40 GHz to 360 GHz. Transitions of the ground vibrational state of the main isotopologue, as well as those of the five heavy-atom isotopologues (^{15}N, ^{18}O, and three ^{13}C), were detectable at natural abundance and have been fit to sextic centrifugally distorted Hamiltonians. All species are well fit with statistical uncertainties less than 40 kHz. Precise rotational and centrifugal distortion constants obtained for these species are compared to those obtained via B3LYP and CCSD(T) calculations. The experimental rotational constants have been corrected for vibration-rotation interactions and electron mass distributions. Preparation of deuterated isotopologues is underway and these data should yield a highly precise, semi-experimental equilibrium (r_e^{SE}) structure of oxazole, on par with the most precisely determined molecular structures.

FK05 **10:16 – 10:17**

PRECISE SEMI-EXPERIMENTAL EQUILIBRIUM STRUCTURE OF THIAZOLE (C_3H_3NS)

BRIAN J. ESSELMAN, MARIA ZDANOVSKAIA, *Department of Chemistry, University of Wisconsin-Madison, Madison, WI, USA*; JOHN F. STANTON, *Quantum Theory Project, University of Florida, Gainesville, FL, USA*; R. CLAUDE WOODS, ROBERT J. McMAHON, *Department of Chemistry, University of Wisconsin-Madison, Madison, WI, USA.*

Thiazole (C_3H_3NS, C_s, μ_a = 1.286 D, μ_b = 0.966 D) is a five-membered aromatic heterocycle containing a 1,3-substituted sulfur and nitrogen. We analyzed the rotational spectra of thiazole and twenty-one of its isotopologues from 130 – 360 GHz. Heavy atom ^{13}C, ^{34}S, ^{33}S, and ^{15}N isotopologues were observable in the rotational spectrum of the normal isotopologue at their natural abundance. Two syntheses were performed to generate a variety of deuterium-substituted isotopologues, resulting in multiple isotopic substitutions of each atom in the molecule. The resultant determinable rotational constants were computationally corrected for vibration-rotation interactions and electron mass with CCSD(T) calculations and 22 total isotopologues were least-squares fit to afford the semi-experimental equilibrium structure (r_e^{SE}). Theoretical structures were computed at several levels of theory up to CCSD(T)/cc-pCV5Z. The quintuple zeta structure was further refined to account for extrapolation to the complete basis set limit, residual electron correlation beyond CCSD(T), relativistic effects, and the diagonal Born-Oppenheimer correction. The resultant r_e^{SE} structure and best theoretical structure are compared.

FK06 **10:20 – 10:21**

PROPANE ISOTOPOLOGUES: HIGH RESOLUTION SYNCHROTRON FAR-IR SPECTRA OF THE SYMMETRICALLY DEUTERATED SPECIES $CH_3CH_2CD_3$, $CD_3CH_2CD_3$ AND C_3D_8. FIRST EXPERIMENTALLY DETERMINED GROUND STATE CONSTANTS FOR THESE SPECIES

STEPHEN J. DAUNT, ROBERT GRZYWACZ, *Department of Physics & Astronomy, The University of Tennessee-Knoxville, Knoxville, TN, USA*; COLIN WESTERN, *School of Chemistry, University of Bristol, Bristol, United Kingdom*; BRANT E. BILLINGHURST, JIANBAO ZHAO, *EFD, Canadian Light Source Inc., Saskatoon, Saskatchewan, Canada.*

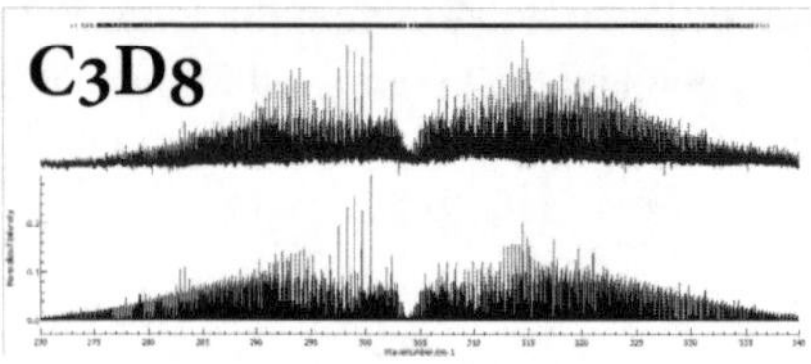

We are continuing our project of obtaining high resolution vibration-rotation spectra of propane isotopologues using the Far-IR beamline at the Canadian National Synchrotron (CLS). We have already reported on all the singly ^{13}C and singly D substituted varieties as well as the 2,2-D_2 species at previous ISMS meetings (2017-19) and in a recent paper on 2-^{13}C-Propane [a]. These studies have allowed us to determine ground state inertial and centrifugal distortion rotational constants for these molecules that have no pure rotational spectra in the literature except for the 6 lines reported by Lide[b] in 1960 of normal propane and two ^{13}C and D versions. In this talk we will present the high resolution spectra (0.00096 cm^{-1}) for the CCC skeletal bendings of $CH_3CH_2CD_3$, $CD_3CH_2CD_3$ and C_3D_8. These studies have yielded corrected observed band origins[c] and rotational constants for the three species. Preliminary values for each species are listed here in wavenumbers. $CH_3CH_2CD_3$: ν_9 = 335.664740(40), A_0 = 0.8185513(12), B_0 = 0.24400666(39), C_0 = 0.21852642(41); $CD_3CH_2CD_3$: ν_{16} = 306.4, A_0 = 0.711202, B_0 = 0.213021, C_0 = 0.193244; C_3D_8: ν_9 = 303.936065(23), A_0 = 0.58742224(42), B_0 = 0.20872437(23), C_0 = 0.18588200(18).

[a] Daunt, Grzywacz, Western, Lafferty, Flaud, Billinghurst, and Hutchings, J. Mol. Structure, in press (doi:10.1016/j.molstruc.2020.127851).
[b] D. R. Lide, J. Chem. Physics 33, 1514-1518 (1960).
[c] Gayles and King, Spectrochim. Acta 21, 543-557 (1965); K. M. Gough, W. F. Murphy and K. Raghavachari, J. Chem. Phys. 87, 3332-3340 (1987).

FK07 **10:24 – 10:25**

SEMI-EXPERIMENTAL EQUILIBRIUM STRUCTURE DETERMINATION OF THIOPHENE (C_4H_4S)

VANESSA L. ORR, *Department of Chemistry, University of Wisconsin-Madison, Madison, WI, USA*; YOTARO ICHIKAWA, *Department of Physics, University of Toyama, Toyama, Japan*; BRIAN J. ESSELMAN, AATMIK R. PATEL, SAMUEL M. KOUGIAS, ANDREW N. OWEN, *Department of Chemistry, University of Wisconsin-Madison, Madison, WI, USA*; KAORI KOBAYASHI, *Department of Physics, University of Toyama, Toyama, Japan*; JOHN F. STANTON, *Quantum Theory Project, University of Florida, Gainesville, FL, USA*; R. CLAUDE WOODS, ROBERT J. McMAHON, *Department of Chemistry, University of Wisconsin-Madison, Madison, WI, USA.*

Thiophene (C_4H_4S, C_{2v} symmetry, μ_a = 0.55 D) is the sulfur analog of furan. With the intent of improving its gas-phase structure determination, its rotational spectrum was collected from 8 – 360 GHz, and 21 deuterium containing isotopologues were synthesized and their rotational spectra were collected from 130 – 360 GHz. The heavy atom ^{13}C, ^{34}S, and ^{33}S isotopologues were observable in the rotational spectra of the normal isotopologue and several deuterium containing forms at natural abundance. The resultant determinable rotational constants (A'', B'', C'') were computationally corrected for vibration-rotation interactions and electron mass with CCSD(T) calculations and 24 total isotopologues were least-squares fit to afford the semi-experimental equilibrium structure (r_e^{SE}). For comparison, theoretical structures were determined at several levels of theory up to CCSD(T)/cc-pCV5Z. The quintuple zeta structure was further refined to account for extrapolation to the complete basis set limit, residual electron correlation beyond CCSD(T), relativistic effects, and the diagonal Born-Oppenheimer correction. The resultant r_e^{SE} structure and "best" theoretical structure are compared.

FK08 **10:28 – 10:29**

IMPROVED SEMI-EXPERIMENTAL EQUILIBRIUM STRUCTURE DETERMINATION AND THEORETICAL PREDICTION OF PYRIDAZINE (o-$C_4H_4N_2$), AND THE IMPACT OF THE ISOTOPOLOGUE DATA SET

ANDREW N. OWEN, MARIA ZDANOVSKAIA, BRIAN J. ESSELMAN, *Department of Chemistry, University of Wisconsin-Madison, Madison, WI, USA*; JOHN F. STANTON, *Quantum Theory Project, University of Florida, Gainesville, FL, USA*; R. CLAUDE WOODS, ROBERT J. McMAHON, *Department of Chemistry, University of Wisconsin-Madison, Madison, WI, USA.*

We obtained an improved semi-experimental equilibrium structure (${r_e}^{SE}$) of pyridazine (o-$C_4H_4N_2$) by improving the distorted-rotor least-squares fits of previously reported experimental data by incorporating fits of four previously unobserved isotopologues and by using higher level, isotopologue-dependent *ab initio* corrections from CCSD(T)/cc-pCVTZ in the ${r_e}^{SE}$ determination. As a result, we improved the determination of the parameters of pyridazine by a factor of two, obtaining 2σ uncertainties of less than 0.001 Å and $0.04°$ in the bond distances and angles, respectively. Additionally, we have obtained an improved theoretical prediction of the structure by using a CCSD(T)/cc-pCV5Z optimization and applying corrections to account for extrapolation to the complete basis set limit, for effects of electron correlation, for relativistic effects, and for the Born-Oppenheimer approximation. The resulting theoretical structural parameters are almost all within the corresponding uncertainties of the improved ${r_e}^{SE}$ parameters. Finally, we analyzed the effect of including additional isotopologues on the ${r_e}^{SE}$ structure and extended the analysis for comparison to the minimal set of isotopologues as used in substitution structure determinations.

FK09 **10:32 – 10:33**

MICROWAVE SPECTRUM AND IODINE NUCLEAR QUADRUPOLE COUPLING CONSTANTS OF 1,1-DIIODOETHANE

MICHAEL J. CARRILLO, WEI LIN, *Department of Chemistry, University of Texas Rio Grande Valley, Brownsville, TX, USA*; YASUKI ENDO, *Department of Applied Chemistry, National Yang Ming Chiao Tung University, Hsinchu, Taiwan.*

Only a few molecules with two iodine atoms have been studied using rotational spectroscopy probably due to the complex hyperfine splitting structure arising from the presence of two iodine nuclei. The high resolution rotational spectroscopic observation of 1,1-diiodoethane is investigated using a pulsed jet, cavity Fourier transform microwave (FTMW) spectrometer over the frequency range 11.5–18 GHz for the first time. The rotational constants, the centrifugal distortion constants, the nuclear spin-rotation coupling constants, and the complete tensor components of the nuclear quadrupole coupling for both iodine nuclei have been determined and reported. The fitted rotational constants are A = 4548.320446(47), B = 625.629141(55), C = 558.798939(43) MHz and the nuclear quadrupole coupling constants are χ_{aa} = -1089.8125(7), $\chi_{bb} - \chi_{cc}$ = -542.3162(13), $|\chi_{ab}|$ = 1215.7505(10), χ_{bc} = 340.8983(14), and $|\chi_{ac}|$ = 562.4206(19) MHz. No A-E splittings due to the methyl group internal rotation were observed. Many dipole-forbidden/electric quadrupole coupling allowed transitions were observed in the spectrum due to the large iodine quadrupole coupling effect. Quantum chemical calculations were performed at the CCSD(T)/aug-cc-pVTZ-pp level of theory. The calculated rotational constants, centrifugal distortion constants, and hyperfine constants were used to guide the data analysis.

FK10 **10:36 – 10:37**

A MICROWAVE STUDY OF THREE BROMINE-CONTAINING MOLECULES: CBr_2F_2, AgBr, and H_2-AgBr

JOSHUA A. SIGNORE, CHRISTOPHER FALLS, *Department of Chemistry, Wesleyan University, Middletown, CT, USA*; COREY J EVANS, *Department of Chemistry, University of Leicester, Leicester, United Kingdom*; WALLACE C. PRINGLE, *Department of Chemistry, Wesleyan University, Middletown, CT, USA*; S. A. COOKE, *Natural and Social Science, Purchase College SUNY, Purchase, NY, USA*; STEWART E. NOVICK, *Department of Chemistry, Wesleyan University, Middletown, CT, USA*; DANIEL A. OBENCHAIN, *Institute of Physical Chemistry, Georg-August-Universität Göttingen, Göttingen, Germany.*

In preparation for our FTMW study of the complex between hydrogen and silver bromide, H_2-AgBr, we have investigated the microwave spectra of our source of bromine, dibromodifluoromethane, CBr_2F_2. Previous sources of bromine to produce AgBr proved either too damaging to the instrumentation in the long term (Br_2), or did not produce enough AgBr to be useful ($CHBr_3$). In addition, silver bromide, originally studied by Hoeft, Lovas, Tiemann, and Torring in 1971,[a] and remeasured by Evans and Gerry in 2000,[b] was remeasured once more. We plan to produce H_2-AgBr, using laser ablation of a silver rod within a supersonic expansion of an argon carrier gas containing H_2 and CBr_2F_2. This is part of our ongoing study of hydrogen complexed with metal halides which include H_2-CuF,[c] H_2-AgCl,[d] and H_2-AuCl.[e] These molecules are "models" of the molecular hydrogen storage in the cavities of metal organic frameworks (MOFs).

[a]J. Hoeft, F. J. Lovas, E. Tiemann, T. Torring, Z. Naturforsch. 25a, 35 (1970).
[b]C. J. Evans, M. C. L. Gerry, J. Chem. Phys. 112, 1321 (2000).
[c]D. J. Frohman, G. S. Grubbs II, Z. Yu, S. E. Novick, Inorg. Chem. 52, 816 (2013).
[d]G. S. Grubbs II, D. A. Obenchain, H. M. Pickett, S. E. Novick, J. Chem. Phys. 141, 114306 (2014).
[e]D. A. Obenchain, G. S. Grubbs II, H. M. Pickett, S. E. Novick, J. Chem. Phys. 146, 204302 (2017).

FK11 **10:40 – 10:41**

STRUCTURE OF THE MODEL GRIGNARD-TYPE REAGENT $ClZnCH_3$ ($\tilde{X}^1A_1$) BY MILLIMETER-WAVE SPECTROSCOPY

MARK BURTON, *Department of Chemistry and Biochemistry, University of Arizona, Tucson, AZ, USA*; NAZIFA TABASSUM, *Department of Molecular and Cellular Biology, University of Arizona, Tucson, AZ, USA*; LUCY M. ZIURYS, *Department of Chemistry and Biochemistry; Department of Astronomy, Arizona Radio Observatory, University of Arizona, Tuscon, AZ, USA.*

Pure rotational spectra of the $^{37}ClZnCH_3$, $ClZnCD_3$, and $ClZn^{13}CH_3$ isotopologues of monomeric $ClZnCH_3$ ($\tilde{X}^1A_1$) have been recorded using millimeter-wave direct absorption techniques in the frequency range 263 – 303 GHz. These species were synthesized in the gas phase in a DC discharge by the reaction of zinc vapor, produced in a Broida-type oven, with $^{37}ClCH_3$ (in natural chlorine abundance), $ClCD_3$, or $Cl^{13}CH_3$. The data for each isotopologue were analyzed with a symmetric top Hamiltonian and rotational and centrifugal constants determined. In combination with previous measurements of $Cl^{64}ZnCH_3$, $Cl^{66}ZnCH_3$, and $Cl^{68}ZnCH_3$, an $r_m^{(2)}$ structure was determined for this organozinc compound. The bond lengths were calculated to be r_{Cl-Zn} = 2.0831(1) Å, r_{Zn-C} = 1.9085(1) Å, and r_{C-H} = 1.1806(5) Å. The H-C-H bond angle was found to be 110.5° – slightly larger than that in methane. These data serve to benchmark future structure calculations of organozinc compounds, which are widely used in organic synthesis.

FK12 **10:44 – 10:45**

RO-VIBRATIONALLY AVERAGED MOLECULAR STRUCTURE OF BENZENE I. ALMOST THE SAME BOND LENGTHS FOR THE C–H AND C–D BONDS.

MASAAKI BABA, *Division of Chemistry, Graduate School of Science, Kyoto University, Kyoto, Japan*; UMPEI NAGASHIMA, *Foundation for Computational Science, Kobe, Japan*; TSUNEO HIRANO, *Department of Chemistry, Ochanomizu University, Tokyo, Japan.*

Contrary to the common sense that the C–H bond-length is longer than that of the C–D bond due to the anharmonicity of the potential, Baba group found, from high-resolution laser spectroscopy, that ro-vibrationally averaged bond lengths of C–H and C–D are observed as being almost identical ($r_{0,\text{eff}}$(C–H) $\cong$ $r_{0,\text{eff}}$(C–D)) for planar aromatic hydrocarbons, such as benzene[a], naphthalene[b], and anthracene[c]. The vibrationally averaged bond lengths of benzene deduced from experimental rotational constants and *ab initio* geometry[b] are r_0(C–H) = r_0(C–D) = 1.0831 Å.[a]

In this study, the vibrationally averaged structures of benzene are derived from the DVR (Discrete Variable Representation) wavefunction based on the 3D potential energy surface at the level of valence-CCSD(T)/[aVQZ(H,C)] theory. The zero-point C–H(D) bond-length, $r_{0,\text{eff}}$(C–H(D)), determined from the experimental effective rotational constants, is, in definition, the r_0 bond-length projected onto the *a-b* principal axis plane, $r_{0,\text{proj}}$(C–H(D)). The DVR wavefunction gives $r_{0,\text{proj}}$(C–H) = 1.0815 Å and $r_{0,\text{proj}}$(C–D) = 1.0819 Å, so that the difference is of a negligibly small value -0.0004 Å. Thus, the seemingly strange experimental finding ($r_{0,\text{eff}}$(C–H) $\cong$ $r_{0,\text{eff}}$(C–D)), which is controversial to the common sense, is resolved. The details will be given in the next presentation (part II.)

[a] S. Kunishige, M. Baba, et al., J. Chem. Phys. **143**, 244302 (2015).
[b] M. Baba, U. Nagashima, et al., J. Chem. Phys. **135**, 054305 (2011).
[c] M. Baba, U. Nagashima, et al., J. Chem. Phys. **130**, 134315 (2009).

FK13 **10:48 – 10:49**

RO-VIBRATIONALLY AVERAGED MOLECULAR STRUCTURE OF BENZENE II. COMPUTATIONAL MOLECULAR SPECTROSCOPY STUDY.

TSUNEO HIRANO, *Department of Chemistry, Ochanomizu University, Tokyo, Japan*; UMPEI NAGASHIMA, *Foundation for Computational Science, Kobe, Japan*; MASAAKI BABA, *Division of Chemistry, Graduate School of Science, Kyoto University, Kyoto, Japan.*

Since the 30 dimensional potential energy surface is beyond our reach, we tried to disclose why the C–H and C–D bond-lengths are observed as being almost identical[a] in terms of C–H stretching ($\mathbf{L}_{\text{str}}$), out-of-plane ($\mathbf{L}_\perp$), and in-plane ($\mathbf{L}_\parallel$) local modes with respect to the C_α–H(D)$_\alpha$ bond in the virtual triatomic molecules [C_5H(D)$_5$]–[C_α]–H(D)$_\alpha$. The potential energy surface was determined at the valence-CCSD(T)/[aVQZ (H,C)] level of theory, and r_0-structure was determined from the DVR3D wavefuctions in Discrete Variable Representation. The virtual [C_5H(D)$_5$]–[C_α]–H(D)$_\alpha$ molecule has its energy minimum at the linear configuration, so that our theory for linear triatomics[b] can be applied.

The C_α–H(D)$_\alpha$ stretching local mode ($\mathbf{L}_{\text{str}}$) gives, as usual, longer C_α–H_α than C_α–D_α bond-lengths due to its anharmonicity. However, in both $\mathbf{L}_\perp$ and $\mathbf{L}_\parallel$ modes, the vibrationally averaged bond-length projected onto the principal axis is shorter for C_α–H_α than for C_α–D_α due to the larger averaged bending angle for the former bond. When we consider bond-lengths projected onto the *a-b* principal axis plane, $r_{0,\text{proj}}$, these antithetical factors, i.e., one in the $\mathbf{L}_{\text{str}}$ mode against the others in $\mathbf{L}_\perp$ and $\mathbf{L}_\parallel$ modes, nearly cancel ($\Delta = r$(C–H) $-$ r(C–D) $= -0.0004$ Å), resulting in almost the same C–H and C–D bond lengths as is experimentally reported. The vibrationally averaged structure of benzene in the zero-point vibration state is predicted to be planar, but non-flat in the peripheral C–H bonds moiety, which is confirmed from the theoretical and experimental values of the inertial defect.

[a] S. Kunishige, M. Baba, et al., J. Chem. Phys. **143**, 244302 (2015).
[b] T. Hirano, U. Nagashima, P. Jensen, J. Mol. Spectrosc. **343**, 54 (2018); T. Hirano, U. Nagashima, M. Baba, J. Mol. Spectrosc. **369**, 111252 (2020); and references therein.

FK14 **10:52 – 10:53**

THE EQUILIBRIUM STRUCTURE OF SMALL RADICALS: THE SEMI-EXPERIMENTAL APPROACH AT WORK

SILVIA ALESSANDRINI, *Scuola Normale Superiore, Scuola Normale Superiore, Pisa, Italy*; MATTIA MELOSSO, *Dept. Chemistry "Giacomo Ciamician", University of Bologna, Bologna, ITALY*; CRISTINA PUZZARINI, *Dep. Chemistry 'Giacomo Ciamician', University of Bologna, Bologna, Italy.*

A new data set of accurate semi-experimental equilibrium strctures (r_{SE}) for small open-shell species will be presented. In the semi-experimental approach, equilibrim rotational constants (B_e) of different isotopologues are used in a least-square-fit to retrieve the equilibirum parameters, thus implying the validity of the Born-Oppenhaimer approximation. The required B_e are obtained by correcting experimental rotational constants of the vibrational ground state (B_0) for the computed vibrational (ΔB_0) and electronic (ΔB_g) contributions. The latter have to be computed using *ab initio* methods and this imposes several constrains on the theoretical methodologies that can be employed. The ΔB_g's have been retrived from HF/aug-cc-pVTZ computations of the ***g***-tensor and the ΔB_0's have been obtained at the either UCCSD(T)/cc-pVTZ or the UB2PLYP-D3/cc-pVTZ level of theory, according to the level of spin-contamination.

The new data set includes several radicals for which experimental rotational constants of different isotopologues have already been reported in the literature, such as CCS, C_nH with n = 1-7, NH_2, CCP, CH_2, PH_2, H_2CCN, CP, CN and more. This collection of equilibrium structures has three ultimate purposes: (i) to serve as benchmark-reference for electronic structure methods, (ii) give new insights, based on experimental data, on the molecular structure of unstable species and on how these structures changes across a group of the periodic table and (iii) to predict the rotational spectrum of less abundant isotopologues. The semi-experimental approach leads to r_{SE} that can have an accuracy below 0.1 mÅ for bond lenghts and 0.01° for angles. For example, in the case of CCS radical, the C-S bond is predicted to be 1.31349(2) Å while the C-C bond lenght is found to be 1.56379(1) Å. For angles, the NH_2 molecule can be used as reference, with N-H bond distance of 1.023618(2) Å and an HNH angle of 103.1488(3)°.

FL. Small molecules

Friday, June 25, 2021 – 10:0 AM

Room: 2021 Online Everywhere

Chair: Kyle N. Crabtree, University of California, Davis, CA, USA

FL01 **10:00 – 10:01**

THE (1,0) BAND OF THE [13.10] Ω=1 – X $^3\Sigma^-(0^+)$ TRANSITION OF TUNGSTEN SULFIDE, WS, OBSERVED BY ILS-FTS

JACK C HARMS, *Chemistry and Biochemistry, University of Missouri, St. Louis, MO, USA*; BRENDAN M. RATAY, *Chemistry and Biochemistry, University of Missouri - St. Louis, St. Louis, MO, USA*; KRISTIN N BALES, JAMES J O'BRIEN, *Chemistry and Biochemistry, University of Missouri, St. Louis, MO, USA*; LEAH C O'BRIEN, *Department of Chemistry, Southern Illinois University, Edwardsville, IL, USA.*

The (1,0) vibrational band of the [13.10] Ω=1 – X $^3\Sigma^-(0^+)$ transition of tungsten sulfide (WS) has been measured in absorption using Intracavity Laser Spectroscopy with Fourier transform detection (ILS-FTS). WS was synthesized in a 0.05-0.15 A DC current plasma discharge within a tungsten lined hollow cathode at 625 mTorr with 65% Ar, 17.5% He, 17.5% H_2, and a trace amount of CS_2. The spectrum was calibrated using literature values for argon lines and PGOPHER's calibration feature [C.M. Western, J. Quant. Spectrosc. Radiat. Transfer 2016 (186), 221-242]. Three rotational branches (P , Q-, and R-branch) with four WS isotopologues (^{182}WS, ^{183}WS, ^{184}WS, and ^{186}WS) were observed in the spectrum. Molecular constants for these isotopologues were determined for both electronic states. The line positions of the (0,0) band of this transition [L.F. Tsang et al., J. Mol. Spectrosc. 2019 (359), 31-36] were included in the fit. The results of the analysis will be presented, and compared with calculations [L.F. Tsang et al., 2019].

FL02 **10:04 – 10:05**

DETECTION AND IDENTIFICATION OF PLATINUM FLUORIDE, PTF: ANALYSIS OF THE (0,0) BAND OF THE [15.3]Ω=3/2 – X $^2\Pi_{3/2}$ TRANSITION USING INTRACAVITY LASER SPECTROSCOPY

CAROLINE A WELCH, JACK C HARMS, JAMES J O'BRIEN, *Chemistry and Biochemistry, University of Missouri, St. Louis, MO, USA*; LEAH C O'BRIEN, *Department of Chemistry, Southern Illinois University, Edwardsville, IL, USA.*

A new electronic transition of PtF has been recorded at high resolution using Intracavity Laser Spectroscopy (ILS). The PtF molecules were produced in a current regulated RF discharge operating with 0.20-0.80 A applied to a Pt-lined Cu hollow cathode in 0.50-1.25 Torr total pressure comprised of 1-5% SF_6 in an Ar/He sputter gas mixture. This hollow cathode was located within the resonator cavity of a tunable DCM dye laser operating over the 14,500-16,500 cm^{-1} range, and effective pathlengths of 0.4-2.0 km were utilized with the ILS method. The band system observed corresponds to the (0,0) band of the [15.3]Ω=3/2 – X $^2\Pi_{3/2}$ transition. Rotational assignments for the transitions have been confirmed through combination difference analysis using known ground state constants. The data were fit using PGOPHER with a standard Hund's case (c) energy level expression. Spectra and results of the analysis will be presented.

FL03 **10:08 – 10:09**

OBSERVATION AND SPECTRAL ANALYSIS OF THE $A\ \Omega$=1 – $X\ \Omega$=0^+ ELECTRONIC TRANSITION OF DIATOMIC PLATINUM SULFIDE, PtS, BY INTRACAVITY LASER ABSORPTION SPECTROSCOPY WITH FOURIER TRANSFORM DETECTION (ILS-FTS)

LEAH C O'BRIEN, *Department of Chemistry, Southern Illinois University, Edwardsville, IL, USA*; JACK C HARMS, JAMES J O'BRIEN, *Chemistry and Biochemistry, University of Missouri, St. Louis, MO, USA*; WENLI ZOU, *Institute of Modern Physics, Northwest University, Xi'an, China.*

Using ILS-FTS, we have recorded the $A\ \Omega$=1 – $X\ \Omega$=0^+ transition of diatomic PtS. Strong bands were observed at 15,520 and 15,910 cm^{-1}, which have been identified as the (0,0) and (1,0) vibrational bands. The P- and R-branches show a regular pattern for the ^{194}PtS, ^{195}PtS, ^{196}PtS and ^{198}PtS isotopologues, but quite interestingly the Q-branch shows significant hyperfine splitting for ^{195}PtS. Although P- and R-branches were easily assigned based on the known ground state constants, the Q-branch seems to be perturbed, requiring q, q_D, and q_H parameters to achieve only a sub-par fit. This indicates the presence of a nearby Ω=0^- state that is perturbing the f–levels in the $A\ \Omega$=1 state. A successful deperturbation analysis and fit were performed in PGOPHER, and molecular constants for the $A\ \Omega$=1 and perturbing Ω=0^- states were obtained. High-level *ab initio* calculations support this assignment and predict an Ω=0^- state in close proximity to the A state. Results and discussion of this analysis will be presented.

FL04 **10:12 – 10:13**

DISPERSED LASER INDUCED FLUORESCENCE STUDY OF $CaNH_2$ AND CaSH [a]

TIMOTHY STEIMLE, *School of Molecular Sciences, Arizona State University, Tempe, AZ, USA*; ANH T. LE, *School of Chemistry and Biochemistry , Georgia Institute of Technology , Atlanta , Ga, USA*; CHAOQUN ZHANG, LAN CHENG, *Department of Chemistry, Johns Hopkins University, Baltimore, MD, USA*; BENJAMIN AUGENBRAUN, JOHN M. DOYLE, *Department of Physics, Harvard University, Cambridge, MA, USA.*

The visible electronic transitions of the simple asymmetric top molecules CaSH and CaNH2 have been extensively studied both field-free [b], [c], [d] and in the presence of static electric field [e], [f]. The diagonal Franck Condon factors for these metal-centered transitions make these molecules appealing for optical cycling studies[f]. These molecules can be readily aligned in the laboratory frame with the application of relatively small static electric field because of their small asymmetry splitting, and relatively large permanent a- and b-components of the electric dipole moments making them attractive as venues for quantum simulation and for investigation of fundamental physics (e.g. parity non-conservation). Here we report on the analysis of the dispersed laser induced fluorescence spectrum induced by both high-resolution and medium resolution laser excitation of the A-X, B-X and C-X bands of $CaNH_2$ and the B-X and C-X transitions of CaSH. The experimentally determined branching ratios are compared to those predicted based on high-level electronic-structure calculations of potential energy surfaces. The molecules were generated via laser ablation/supersonic expansion and the 2D spectra (excitation *vs* DLIF) recorded. Implications for laser cooling of the species will be presented.

[a]Funded by the Heising-Simons foundation

[b]Z. Morbi, C. Zhao, J.W. Hepburn, and P.F. Bernath, J. Chem. Phys. 108, 8891 (1998).

[c]Z. Morbi, C. Zhao, and P.F. Bernath, J. Chem. Phys. 106, 4860 (1997).

[d]P.M. Sheridan, M.J. Dick, J.-G. Wang, and P.F. Bernath, Mol. Phys. 105, 569 (2007).

[e]C.T. Scurlock, T. Henderson, S. Bosely, K.Y. Jung, and T.C. Steimle, J. Chem. Phys. 100, (1994).

[f]A.J. Marr, M. Tanimoto, D. Goodridge, and T.C. Steimle, J. Chem. Phys. 103, (1995).

FL05 **10:16 – 10:17**

HIGH RESOLUTION LASER INDUCED FLUORESCENCE AND ZEEMAN EFFECT IN THE [18.6]1.5-$X^2\Sigma^+$ TRANSITION OF YbOH[a]

COLAN LINTON, *Department of Physics, University of New Brunswick, Fredericton, NB, Canada*; TIMOTHY STEIMLE, EPHRIEM TADESSE MENGESHA, *School of Molecular Sciences, Arizona State University, Tempe, AZ, USA*; ALLAN G. ADAM, *Department of Chemistry, University of New Brunswick, Fredericton, NB, Canada*; ANH T. LE, *School of Molecular Sciences, Arizona State University, Tempe, AZ, USA.*

We report here on the high resolution (~30 MHz FWHM) laser induced fluorescence spectrum of an electronic transition of YbOH observed in the 18500 - 18600 cm^{-1}region. The YbOH was produced in a supercooled molecular beam by the reaction of laser ablated Yb with methanol. Because of the large number of Yb isotopes, the rotational structure, though well resolved, was very dense. The rotational structure of three of the isotopologues, ^{172}YbOH, ^{174}YbOH and ^{176}YbOH was identified and assigned. The rotational analysis showed that the transition was from an excited Ω = 3/2 state, labelled [18.6]1.5, to the ground $X^2\Sigma^+$ state and having an origin of 18577.5 cm^{-1}. In order to try and determine the nature of the Ω = 3/2 state (possibly $A^2\Pi_{3/2}$?), external magnetic fields were applied and the resulting Zeeman spectra assigned and analyzed. The previous analysis[b] of a high temperature source assigned a state near 18677 cm^{-1}as $A^2\Pi_{3/2}$. The results of the analysis will be presented and their interpretation discussed.

[a]Funded by a grant from the Heising-Simons Foundation
[b]T.C. Melville and J.A. Coxon, J. Chem. Phys. 115, 6974 (2001)

FL06 **10:20 – 10:21**

A COUPLED-CHANNELS POTENTIAL FIT DESCRIBING THE LOW-LYING $X^2\Delta$, $^2\Pi$ AND $^2\Sigma^+$ STATES OF NiH TO EXPERIMENTAL ACCURACY

ILVIE HAVALYOVA, IVAYLA BOZHINOVA, ASEN PASHOV, *Faculty of Physics, Sofia University, Sofia, Bulgaria*; AMANDA J. ROSS, PATRICK CROZET, *Inst. Lumière Matière, Univ Lyon 1 & CNRS, Université de Lyon, Villeurbanne, France.*

A direct potential fit to Hund's case (a) potential curves for the low-lying 'supermultiplet' states ($X^2\Delta$, $^2\Pi$, $^2\Sigma^+$) of NiH and to R-dependent spin-orbit and rotational coupling functions has reproduced the experimental term values of ^{58}NiH, ^{60}NiH, ^{62}NiH up to 6500 cm^{-1}, with a root mean square deviation very close to the estimated uncertainty of 0.01 cm^{-1}. Second-order Born-Oppenheimer breakdown corrections to the rotational Hamiltonian had to be included to achieve this result. The spin-orbit interaction A_{so}(R) associated with Ni^+ is large compared to the energy separations between the three electronic states, so that most of the observed rovibrational states are strong mixtures of the Ω-components of the multiplet. This made the fitting procedure particularly difficult, because there were no perturbation-free data to determine the starting values for the model functions. Potential curves were optimized from RKR turning-points generated from earlier work using an effective Hamiltonian approach[a], and the spin-orbit and rotational coupling functions from theoretical predictions[b]. We believe that this model may be reliably extrapolated to higher rotational states, with potential applications in the simulation of high temperature spectra, for example in the context of stellar atmospheres.

[a]M. Abbasi *et al*, J. Mol. Spectrosc. 349 49-59 (2018)
[b]C. Marian, J. Chem. Phys., 93(2) 1176-1186 (1990)

FL07 **10:24 – 10:25**

PHOTOELECTRON VELOCITY MAP IMAGING SPECTROSCOPY OF THE BERYLLIUM TETRAMER ANION Be_4^-

NOAH B JAFFE, *Chemistry Department, Emory University, Atlanta, GA, USA*; MICHAEL HEAVEN, *Department of Chemistry, Emory University, Atlanta, GA, USA.*

Beryllium is known to be a challenging test for even high level *ab initio* methods due to high electron correlation contributions. There is fundamental interest in understanding how well computational methods can predict physical properties of beryllium containing molecules, but very little available experimental data on these molecules. We have continued in our exploration of beryllium molecules, and have acquired preliminary spectra for the beryllium tetramer, Be_4. In this talk we will present our work to date on Be_4^-, with comparisons to high level theory and the beryllium dimer.

FL08 **10:28 – 10:29**

HIGH-RESOLUTION LASER SPECTROSCOPY OF LEAD OXIDE (PbO) IN 400-450 NM

KATSUNARI ENOMOTO, TAKEHIRO SUZUKI, *Department of Physics, University of Toyama, Toyama, Japan*; MASAAKI BABA, *Division of Chemistry, Graduate School of Science, Kyoto University, Kyoto, Japan.*

We observed rotationally resolved excitation spectra of PbO for transitions from the X(0^+) $v'' = 0$ vibronic ground state in a wavelength range of 400−450 nm. PbO molecules were produced by laser ablation in a cold helium buffer gas. The cold environment was useful to resolve overlapping rotational bands of different vibronic states. Absolute transition frequencies were measured with the uncertainty of about 10 MHz by using an ultralow expansion etalon for the laser frequency calibration. Since the previous work [1], we have continued the measurement and have observed about 1000 lines so far. The transitions to the B(1) ($v' = 2 - 6$), A(0^+) ($v' = 6 - 8$), and C(0^+) ($v' = 0$) states were clearly assigned, and spectroscopic constants were determined precisely for three isotopic molecules ^{206}PbO, ^{207}PbO, and ^{208}PbO. We analyzed perturbation of the B(1) levels due to the spin-orbit interaction with other $\Omega = 1$ levels. In this talk, we will present these results and analyses, including the latest data.

[1] K. Enomoto, A. Fuwa, N. Hizawa, Y. Moriwaki, and K. Kobayashi, *J. Mol. Spectrosc.*, **339**, 12 (2017).

FL09 **10:32 – 10:33**

EVOLUTION OF IRON AND CALCIUM MONOOXIDES' BANDS IN LASER PLASMA UNDEL LOW PRESSURE

ALEKSANDR ZAKUSKIN, BABKEN BEGLARYAN, TIMUR A. LABUTIN, *Department of Chemistry, Lomonosov Moscow State University, Moscow, Russia.*

Laser-induced plasma is widely used as an emission source for laboratory simulations of different objects. The properties of laser plasma vary significantly depending on the pressure and composition of the environment, as well as during the evolution of the plasma plume. This property combined with the typical range of electron temperature (from 0.2 to 4 eV) and electron number density (10^{15} - 10^{19} cm^{-1}) make it a promising object for study of radiation from various plasma sources in atmosphere (combustion of meteors, airglow) and in outer space. The aim of the present work was to study structure and evolution of CaO and FeO bands in laser plasma under low pressure (0.16 to 32 Torr) that corresponds to the known spectra of Benešov bolide.

We obtained emission spectra of laser plasma under different pressures and observation times while ablating samples of Fe_3O_4, $CaCO_3$ and chondrite. In each case plasma temperature was calculated by Boltzmann plot method using 20 to 30 atomic lines. We also estimated electron number density by Saha-Boltzmann equation where possible. Study of spatial distribution of emitting atoms and molecules in plasma with precise plasma diagnostics allows to make conclusions about existence or absence of the local thermodynamic equilibrium. The obtained data show that the formation of FeO in plasma occurs with involvement of oxygen from the ablated material, but not from the surrounding atmosphere. On the contrary, CaO if formed primarily using oxygen from atmosphere. Therefore, abundance and of FeO and intensity of its emission in space objects may not depend on the pressure of the surrounding media, while CaO should have a strong dependency.

FL10 **10:36 – 10:37**

FREQUENCY COMB REFERENCED SPECTRA OF $A-X$ TRANSITIONS IN SH

ARTHUR FAST, SAMUEL MEEK, *Precision Infrared Spectroscopy on Small Molecules, Max Planck Institute for Biophysical Chemistry, Göttingen, Germany.*

Recent observations of a possible SH absorption feature in the atmosphere of a hot Jupiter exoplanet have sparked a renewed interest in the molecule's electronic spectroscopy, motivating the creation of a new line list.[a] This list currently relies on absolute transition frequencies measured nearly 70 years ago with a grating spectrograph.[b] While the $0.03\ \mathrm{cm}^{-1}$ accuracy achieved in these experiments was impressive for the time, measurements using modern laser spectroscopy techniques can do much better. In this talk, I will present our measurements of the $A\,^2\Sigma^+, v'=0 \leftarrow X\,^2\Pi_{3/2}, v''=0, J''=3/2$ transitions in SH using a continuous-wave ultraviolet laser stabilized to an optical frequency comb. The same apparatus was previously used to measure $A-X$ transitions in OH[c]. Due to the broader linewidths and lower fluorescence detection efficiency caused by a short A state predissociation lifetime, the SH transition frequencies could not be determined as precisely as those in OH. We were nevertheless able to determine the frequencies of 12 transitions from the rotational ground state with an absolute uncertainty of less than 1.2 MHz ($4\times10^{-5}\ \mathrm{cm}^{-1}$).

[a]Gorman et al., *Mon. Not. R. Astron. Soc.* 490, 1652 (2019)
[b]Ramsay, *J. Chem. Phys.* 20, 1920 (1952)
[c]Fast et al. *Phys. Rev. A* 98, 052511 (2018)

FL11 **10:40 – 10:41**

REVIEW OF DIATOMIC SPECTROSCOPIC DATA

LAURA K McKEMMISH, *School of Chemistry, University of New South Wales, Sydney, NSW, Australia.*

Accurate and comprehensive diatomic molecular spectroscopic data have long been crucial for measuring and monitoring gaseous environments, e.g. astrophysically, as well as for benchmarking theoretical approaches and, increasingly in ultracold physics. Theory and experiment can be used independently or together to produce useful data that can be highly detailed (e.g. line lists) or summative (e.g. molecular constants).

Accessing these data can be challenging; when data is compiled, knowing the right database can be sufficient, but in many cases data is not compiled or is severely out of data and manual literature searching and data extraction is thus required.

Here, I will summarise my recent review of diatomic spectroscopic data (WIREs Comput Mol Sci. 2021;E1520). I will summarise the key diatomic data types and their interconnectivity. I will also provide strategies to strengthen the connection between data producers (e.g. ab-initio electronic structure theorists and experimental spectroscopists), data modellers (e.g. line list creators) and data users (astronomers, chemical physicists, etc). A particular focus is ensuring that new data is optimally utilised with appropriate attribution.

FL12 **10:44 – 10:45**

IR, VISIBLE, AND UV LINE LIST OF SILICON MONOXIDE (SiO) – A HACKATHON PROJECT

AHMAD Y. ADAM, *Faculty of Mathematics and Natural Sciences, University of Wuppertal, Wuppertal, Germany*; VICTORIA H.J. CLARK, *Department of Physics and Astronomy, University College London, London, UK*; BRIDGETTE COOPER, *Physics and Astronomy , University College London, London, United Kingdom*; PRIA DOBNEY, *Department of Physics and Astronomy, University College London, London, UK*; SHAUN T. E. DONNELLY, MAIRE N. GORMAN, *Department of Physics, Aberystwyth University, Aberystwyth, UK*; ANTHONY E. LYNAS-GRAY, *Physics, University of Oxford, Oxford, United Kingdom*; THOMAS MELTZER, ALEC OWENS, QIANWEI QU, MIKHAIL SEMENOV, WILFRID SOMOGYI, *Department of Physics and Astronomy, University College London, London, UK*; ANNA-MAREE SYME, *School of Chemistry, University of New South Wales, Sydney, NSW, Australia*; JONATHAN TENNYSON, APOORVA UPADHYAY, SAMUEL WRIGHT, SERGEI N. YURCHENKO, *Department of Physics and Astronomy, University College London, London, UK*; JUAN C. ZAPATA TRUJILLO, *School of Chemistry, University of New South Wales, Sydney, NSW, Australia.*

We have produced a new line list for SiO covering IR, visible and UV regions by extending the ExoMol EBJT line list for SiO to include the $A\,^1\Pi$ and $E\,^1\Sigma^+$ electronic states. The line list was computed using empirical potential energy curves of the states A and E refined by fitting to 2168 experimentally derived energy levels of SiO determined from 38 vibronic bands from the X–X, E–X and A–X systems states through the MARVEL procedure. The transitions dipole moments for E–X and A–X were computed with ab initio methods at the MRCI level. The line list is suitable for temperatures up to 10000 K and for wavelengths up to 150 nm. We have run the SiO line list as a Hackthon project. It was carried out internationally across different time zones. The team was composed of subgroups responsible for different tasks: the MARVEL procedure, literature review, ab initio calculations, rovibrational calculations, spectrum simulations, etc. We believe it was a successful networking event during the COVID-19 pandemic time which facilitate a collaboration in the absence of travel.

FL13 **10:48 – 10:49**

HIGH RESOLUTION LASER SPECTROSCOPY OF RUTHENIUM MONOXIDE

ALLAN G. ADAM, GEOFFREY M. CHENARD, *Department of Chemistry, University of New Brunswick, Fredericton, NB, Canada*; COLAN LINTON, DENNIS W. TOKARYK, *Department of Physics, University of New Brunswick, Fredericton, NB, Canada.*

Ruthenium monoxide (RuO) molecules have been studied by laser-induced fluorescence in the UNB laser-ablation molecular-jet apparatus. Spectra with line widths of $\sim$115MHz have been obtained allowing the seven different isotopologues of ^{n}RuO (n=104, 102, 101, 100, 99, 98, and 96) to be observed. In addition, hyperfine structure due to the nuclear spin I=5/2 for the odd isotopes of ruthenium has been resolved. The 2-0, 1-0, and 0-0 bands of the [18.1]4 - $X^5\Delta_4$ have been analyzed and the results will be compared to the earlier work of Cheung et al.[a] Studies of the red [16.0]5 - $X^5\Delta_4$ transition are continuing and will also be presented.

[a]N. Wang, Y.W. Ng, and A.S.-C. Cheung, J. Phys. Chem. A 2013, 117, 13279-13283.

FL14 **10:52 – 10:53**

EXPERIMENTAL AND THEORETICAL ANALYSIS OF THE INTER- AND INTRA-MOLECULAR DYNAMICS OF FORMYL RADICAL TRAPPED IN SOLID CO

YURIJ DMITRIEV, *Division of Plasma Physics, Atomic Physics and Astrophysics, Ioffe Institute, St. Petersburg, Russia*; AATTO LAAKSONEN, *Department of Materials and Environmental Chemistry, Arrhenius Laboratory, Stockholm University , Stockholm, Sweden*; NIKOLAS PLOUTARCH BENETIS, *Department of Chemical Engineering, University of Western Macedonia, Kozani, Greece.*

A comparative experimental and theoretical EPR study of HCO and DCO radicals, stabilized in solid CO at the liquid helium temperatures, revealed the crucial role the radical inter- and intra-molecular motions play in the spin-Hamiltonian parameters and spectral line-shapes. The HCO and, especially, DCO spectra of the highest resolution made possible thorough comparison between the experimental results and theoretical EPR spectra obtained using a variety theoretical methods.

The effect from vibrational, rotational, and librational motion observed in the molecular states of formyl as a probe under low-temperature CO matrix isolation condition was obtained by motional averaging and revealed the clear proton isotope effect in the spectrum shape anisotropy using both classical and quantum approaches.

As the rovibrational/librational averaging of the EPR magnetic parameters of formyl is not incorporated in standard quantum chemistry calculations, a significantly smaller Fermi contact interaction is obtained for the lighter hydrogen nucleus in the HCO isotopomer compared to experimental values in solid CO matrix at cryogenic temperatures. However, no measurable effect of this kind was detected for the deuterated DCO formyl under identical considerations. This isotope effect is discernible by the disagreement of the theoretical gyromagnetic ratios of the H/D nuclei in the quantum mechanical computations of the Fermi contact interaction.

FM. Chirality and stereochemistry

Friday, June 25, 2021 – 10:0 AM

Room: 2021 Online Everywhere

Chair: Guojie Li, University of Alberta, Edmonton, Canada

FM01 **10:00 – 10:01**

ASSESSING THE PERFORMANCE OF ROTATIONAL SPECTROSCOPY IN CHIRAL ANALYSIS

SERGIO R. DOMINGOS, *CFisUC, Department of Physics, University of Coimbra, Coimbra, Portugal*; CRISTOBAL PEREZ, *FS-SMP, Deutsches Elektronen-Synchrotron (DESY), Hamburg, Germany*; MARK D. MARSHALL, HELEN O. LEUNG, *Chemistry Department, Amherst College, Amherst, MA, USA*; MELANIE SCHNELL, *FS-SMP, Deutsches Elektronen-Synchrotron (DESY), Hamburg, Germany*.

The application of rotational spectroscopy-based methods as tools to deliver accurate and precise chirality-sensitive information are still breaking ground, but their applicability in the challenging field of analytical chemistry is already clear. In a recent study, we explored the current capabilities and challenges of microwave 3-wave mixing (M3WM) and chiral tag rotational spectroscopy - two emerging techniques for chiral analysis based on rotational spectroscopy. In this presentation, we compare the performance of these two techniques with respect to solving the absolute configuration and the enantiomeric excess (ee) of a sample prepared by others and containing a mixture of enantiomers of styrene oxide with a composition unknown to us.

FM02 **10:04 – 10:05**

CHIRALITY RECOGNITION IN THE TERNARY AGGREGATES OF PROPYLENE OXIDE: EXPERIMENTALLY GUIDED THEORETICAL CONFORMATIONAL SEARCHES

FAN XIE, *Department of Chemistry, University of Alberta, Edmonton, AB, Canada*; MARCO FUSÈ, *Scuola Normale Superiore, Scuola Normale Superiore, Pisa, Italy*; ARSH SINGH HAZRAH, WOLFGANG JÄGER, *Department of Chemistry, University of Alberta, Edmonton, AB, Canada*; VINCENZO BARONE, *Scuola Normale Superiore, Scuola Normale Superiore, Pisa, Italy*; YUNJIE XU, *Department of Chemistry, University of Alberta, Edmonton, AB, Canada*.

Propylene oxide (PO), a simple chiral cyclic ether, has served as a valuable prototype molecule for the theoretical development of chiroptical activities[1] and for rotational spectroscopic studies of chirality recognition. Although a study of the PO dimer was completed more than ten years ago where six homo- and heterochiral structures were identified experimentally[2], no similar studies of larger chiral aggregates such as a PO trimer have been reported so far. Aided with the recent development in chirped pulse Fourier transform microwave techniques[3] and in meta-dynamics conformational search algorithms[4], we have explored the conformational space of the PO trimer. Several hundred possible PO trimer structures were predicted the first two most stable homochiral trimers were assigned. The number of possible conformers of the heterochiral PO trimer predicted is about three times of the homochiral trimer. Even so, no match could be made for the heterochiral trimer conformers detected, despite additional exhausted conformational searches. By studying all monosubstituted 13C isotopologues of the most stable homochiral and heterochiral PO trimer in natural abundance, we experimentally determined their C atom backbone structures. Guided with this information, additional PO trimer structures were calculated which match the observed rotational constants and dipole moments. The study showcases the power of rotational spectroscopic experiments and highlights the necessity of intensive interplay between experiment and theory in dealing with large aggregates.

1.R. W. Kawiecki, F. J. Devlin, P. J. Stephens, R. D. Amos, J. Phys. Chem. 1991, 95, 9817. 2.Z. Su, N. Borho, Y. Xu. J. Am. Chem. Soc. 2006, 128, 51. 3.G. Barratt Park, and Robert W. Field, J. Chem. Phys. 2016, 144, 20090. 4.P. Pracht, F. Bohle and S. Grimme, Phys. Chem. Chem. Phys., 2020.

FM03 **10:08 – 10:09**

CHIRAL TAG ROTATIONAL SPECTROSCOPY FOR CHIRAL ANALYSIS OF CARBOXYLIC ACIDS

HALEY N. SCOLATI, *Department of Chemistry, University of Virginia, Charlottesville, VA, USA*; KEVIN J MAYER, BROOKS PATE, *Department of Chemistry, The University of Virginia, Charlottesville, VA, USA.*

Chiral analysis, the determination of the absolute configuration of a chiral molecule and its enantiomeric excess, is a challenging analytical chemistry problem. Rotational spectroscopy can perform chiral analysis through either three-wave mixing spectroscopy, as introduced into the field by Patterson, Doyle, and Schnell, or through the chiral tag method. In chiral tagging, a small, chiral molecule serves as the chiral resolving agent and is attached to the analyte through noncovalent interactions. This work considers suitable tags to perform chiral analysis on carboxylic acids. 2-phenylpropionic acid was used to illustrate the proof-of-principle for chiral analysis of carboxylic acids using propylene oxide and butynol as the chiral resolving agent. Propylene oxide is found to have a functional group specific binding motif. Candidate chiral tag complex structures were evaluated using DFT calculations (B3LYP GD3BJ def2TZVP). The presence of these complexes in the pulsed jet sample were verified by comparison between experimental and theoretical rotational constants. Chiral tag measurements with propylene oxide pose a challenge because there are geometries for homochiral and heterochiral complexes with nearly identical rotational constants and dipole moment components. The close similarity makes it difficult to determine the absolute configuration to high confidence. However, the tag complexes of similar geometry have different relative energies for homochiral and heterochiral interactions. The lower energy conformers were more likely to be observed, indicating efficient cooling in the jet pulse. In this case, it appears that energetic considerations can be used to establish the absolute configuration. Methodology and analysis, as well as C^{13} structure fits and EE determination, will be further discussed.

FM04 **10:12 – 10:13**

REACTION CHEMISTRY OF EPOXIDES WITH FLUORINATED CARBOXYLIC ACIDS

KEVIN J MAYER, BROOKS PATE, *Department of Chemistry, The University of Virginia, Charlottesville, VA, USA*; HALEY N. SCOLATI, *Department of Chemistry, University of Virginia, Charlottesville, VA, USA*; MARTIN S. HOLDREN, REILLY E. SONSTROM, CHANNING WEST, *Department of Chemistry, The University of Virginia, Charlottesville, VA, USA.*

During measurements designed to develop a chiral tag rotational spectroscopy methodology for establishing the absolute configuration of a known persistent fluorinated carboxylic acid pollutant (FRD-903), an interesting reaction chemistry was observed. In several cases, highly fluorinated carboxylic acids participate in ring opening of epoxides under ambient conditions. Reactions of three fluorinated carboxylic acids, difluoroacetic acid, trifluoroacetic acid, and pentafluoropropionic acid, with propylene oxide (PO) were explored. The reactions were performed externally to the spectrometer and internally in the gas phase by flowing PO over the fluorinated acid samples. Reactions were performed by adding 4:1 molar equivalents of PO to carboxylic acid, and each reaction was highly exothermic. The reaction mixtures were analyzed by rotational spectroscopy using a chirped-pulsed Fourier transform rotational spectrometer. These measurements showed that the reaction products are created through epoxide ring-opening at both epoxide ring carbons. This reaction chemistry, in principle, offers a way to perform chiral analysis through covalent tagging, but this application would require retention of configuration in the reaction. The reaction products were subsequently chiral tagged to determine the extent of configuration retention. These experiments show that the products, both the ring-opening at the least- and most-substituted carbon on the epoxide ring, are racemized. While these results are not useful for obtaining the absolute configuration, these results further our understanding of the chemistry involved in these reactions. Covalently modifying fluorinated carboxylic acids can be achieved, and establishing absolute configuration could be possible with a more controlled reaction to prevent racemization of the chiral center on the epoxide.

FM05 **10:16 – 10:17**

A BROADBAND ROTATIONAL SPECTROSCOPIC AND THEORETICAL STUDY OF CIS AND TRANS (-)-CARVEOL

ARSH SINGH HAZRAH, MOHAMAD AL-JABIRI, RAIDEN SPEELMAN, WOLFGANG JÄGER, *Department of Chemistry, University of Alberta, Edmonton, AB, Canada.*

Carveol, a primary constituent in spearmint and peppermint oil, is a monocyclic monoterpenoid alcohol that is produced in nature by the photooxidation of limonene.[1] Structurally, carveol contains two chiral centers with three substituents (methyl group, hydroxyl group, and propylene group) attached to it's cyclohexane ring. The combination of the three flexible substituents, ring puckering, and two chiral centers introduce a complex conformational topography that is non-trivial to elucidate. However, a thorough study of the topology of chiral carveol may provide valuable insights into complex conformational dynamics, as well as chirality recognitions studies. We believe chirped-pulse Fourier transform microwave spectroscopy (CP-FTMW) is an excellent tool for this investigation as it is able to unambiguously distinguish structural conformers within a complex mixture.[2] The broadband rotational spectrum of cis and trans (-)-carveol was recorded using a chirped pulse Fourier Transform microwave spectrometer in the 2-6 GHz region.[3] To aid in experimental assignment, a theoretical conformational search was carried out using a combination of a two dimensional potential energy scan, which scans over the propylene group and hydroxyl group, and the Conformer–Rotamer Ensemble Sampling Tool (CREST).[4] The theoretical results yielded a total of 23 conformers for the trans and 19 for the cis. Utilizing these results, a total of five experimental conformers were then assigned: two for the trans conformer and three for the cis conformer. For trans, it was determined both experimental conformers occupy the equatorial position. For the cis conformer, two equatorial and one axial conformer was experimentally assigned. The conformational cooling pathways and intermolecular interactions within each conformer were also analyzed to further understand the conformational landscape of cis and trans (-)-carveol.

1. J. Laothawornkitkul, J. E. Taylor, N. D. Paul and C. N. Hewitt, New Phytol., 2009, 183, 27–51.; 2. G. Barratt Park, and Robert W. Field, J. Chem. Phys., 2016, 144, 20090.; 3. N. A. Seifert, J. Thomas, W. Jäger and Y. Xu, Phys. Chem. Chem. Phys., 2018, 20, 27630–27637.; 4. P. Pracht, F. Bohle, S. Grimme, Phys. Chem. Chem. Phys. 2020., 22(14), 7169-7192

FM06 **10:20 – 10:21**

CHIRAL MOLECULAR RECOGNITION TRENDS IN AROMATIC AND HELICAL SYSTEMS REVEALED WITH ROTATIONAL SPECTROSCOPY

SERGIO R. DOMINGOS, *CFisUC, Department of Physics, University of Coimbra, Coimbra, Portugal*; CRISTOBAL PEREZ, *FS-SMP, Deutsches Elektronen-Synchrotron (DESY), Hamburg, Germany*; NARCIS AVARVARI, *MOLTECH-Anjou, University of Angers, Angers, France*; MELANIE SCHNELL, *FS-SMP, Deutsches Elektronen-Synchrotron (DESY), Hamburg, Germany.*

The rules of engagement for chiral molecules have evolved beyond the static "three-point" interaction picture. Models where weak intermolecular interactions compete and have a decisive act in establishing the molecular fit are the new travel guides to molecular recognition.[a] Moreover, molecules with dominant aromatic substructure foresee more unconventional intermolecular contact schemes given their delocalized electron distribution. This notion is valid for planar and helical motifs, as is the case of the smallest polycyclic aromatic hydrocarbon with a screw sense, tetrahelicene.[b] Given their compatibility with theoretical calculations, studies of cluster formation in the gas phase are pertinent approaches to disclose the ruling intermolecular forces at play and their role mediating molecular recognition.[c] In this scope, broadband rotational spectroscopy experiments are ongoing, and we will discuss our latest insights from studies on planar and helical aromatic systems.

[a] A. Zehnacker, M. Suhm. *Angew. Chem. Int. Ed.* 47, 6970–6992 (2008).

[b] S.R. Domingos, K. Martin, N. Avarvari, M. Schnell. *Angew. Chem. Int. Ed.* 58, 11257–11261 (2019).

[c] S.R. Domingos, C. Pérez, N.M. Kreienborg, C. Merten, M. Schnell. *Commun. Chem.* accepted (2021).

FM07 **10:24 – 10:25**

CHIRAL TAG ROTATIONAL SPECTROSCOPY FOR STRUCUTRE ANALYSIS OF CHIRAL METHYLPHENYL OXIRANE

HALEY N. SCOLATI, KEVIN J MAYER, MARTIN S. HOLDREN, BROOKS PATE, *Department of Chemistry, The University of Virginia, Charlottesville, VA, USA.*

In chiral tagging, a smaller chiral molecule of known stereochemistry is non-covalently bonded, or "tagged" to the analyte of interest. This enantiomeric conversion results in a diastereomeric mixture of complexes whose stereochemistry can be spectroscopically resolved. In this work, rotational spectroscopy coupled with the chiral tag methodology was used to elucidate the multiple isomers produced by the analyte and tag motif of methylphenyl oxirane (MPO). The chosen tagging agent, 1,1,1-trifluoro-2-propanol (TFIP), has an energy difference of about 2 kJ/mol between its two possible monomer conformations. In this study, the 10 kcal/mol (42 kJ/mol) of internal energy available during the tag complex formation stabilizes the MPO/TFIP tag through non-covalent interactions, making it possible to observe the low energy isomers of the chiral complexes of both TFIP monomer conformations. The cooling of the TFIP monomer in the pulsed jet allows the population of the lowest energy conformer to be larger by at least a 10:1 ratio. As a result, the complexation energy can be viable tool in the exploration of the system's potential energy surface and conformational preference of the tag. Experimental data was collected on a 2-8 GHz CP-FTMW spectrometer, with additional 6-18 GHz measurements for the analysis of less abundant conformers. Additional tagging agents, such as propylene oxide (PO), were also screened. Candidate chiral tag complex structures were evaluated using DFT calculations (B3LYP GD3BJ / def2TZVP). From quantum chemical calculations, optimized geometry structures of the tag complexes can be assigned to the observed spectra. By combining these optimized geometries with known energy and dipole information, a high confident determination of the absolute configuration of MPO can be made. A survey of candidate structures as well as the experimental assessment of observed conformers will be discussed.

FM08 **10:28 – 10:29**

MANIPULATION OF COLD CHIRAL MOLECULES USING ELECTRONIC AND ROTATIONAL SPECTROSCOPY

A. O. HERNANDEZ-CASTILLO, JOHANNES BISCHOFF, JU HYEON LEE, GERARD MEIJER, SANDRA EIBENBERGER-ARIAS, *Department of Molecular Physics, Fritz-Haber-Institut der Max-Planck-Gesellschaft, Berlin, Germany.*

The two non-superimposable mirror images of a chiral molecule are referred to as enantiomers. Their structures cannot be transformed into each other by pure translation or rotation. Even though most physical properties of enantiomers are identical – which makes them intrinsically difficult to separate – their handedness often determines their functionality. Chiral analysis, particularly for complex samples, is still challenging, thus there is a need for fast and reliable methods that can differentiate and/or separate enantiomers. Recently, the enantiomer-specific state transfer method[1] was developed. This method provides the means to populate or depopulate a rotational state of a chosen enantiomer. We have designed, built, and characterized a compact spectrometer capable of performing chirped-pulse Fourier transform microwave spectroscopy, including chiral analysis, and electronic spectroscopy. By combining optical methods with microwave spectroscopy, we seek to maximize the state-specific enantiomeric enrichment. Our recent studies mainly focus on the chiral alcohol 1-indanol. We have acquired and understood its rotationally resolved electronic spectra,[2] as well as performed microwave-UV double resonance measurements. The gained structural insight serves as a foundation for future, more sensitive enantiomer-specific measurements. I will discuss recent experimental results as well as details of our new experimental setup.

[1]Eibenberger, S. et al., Phys Rev Lett 118, 123002 (2017). [2]Hernandez-Castillo, A. O. et al., Phys Chem Chem Phys, (2021).

FM09 **10:32 – 10:33**

EXPLORING CONFORMATIONAL SPACES AND AGGREGATION PREFERENCES OF SERINE-ASPARAGINE AND VALINE-ASPARAGINE DIMERS BY IRMPD SPECTROSCOPY AND QUANTUM CHEMISTRY

MATTHIAS HEGER, HAOLU WANG, MOHAMAD AL-JABIRI, YUNJIE XU, *Department of Chemistry, University of Alberta, Edmonton, AB, Canada.*

Amino acids, often refered as the building blocks of proteins, are not only crutial in our body for all sorts of biological functions they support, but also are significantly important to chemistry and life sciences for their chirality properties. The mirror-imaged pair of a chiral amino acid share the same chemical formula but may respond very differently when interacting with a chiral acceptor site. In this presented work, the protonated dimers of asparagine with either serine or valine in their homochiral and heterochiral forms were investigated using an Infrared Multiple-Photon Dissociation (IRMPD) spectrometer. A three-tiered approach was developd to identify possible homochiral and heterochiral dimers. Harmonic frequency calculations were further carried out to interpret the observed IRMPD spectra. Analyses of these ensembles reveal a strong preference for the migration of the excess proton during the photodissociation process from serine and valine to asparagine. The structural and energetic relationships in the protonated homochiral and heterochiral serine-asparagine and valine-asparagine dimers will also be discussed in this talk.

1. M. Heger, J. Cheramy, F. Xie, Z. Chen and Y. Xu, J. Mol. Spectrosc., 2018, 352, 36–44.

FM10 **10:36 – 10:37**

CAN PHOTOELECTRON CIRCULAR DICHROISM WORK FOR CHIRAL ANIONS?

MALLORY GREEN, JENNY TRIPTOW, GERARD MEIJER, *Department of Molecular Physics, Fritz-Haber-Institut der Max-Planck-Gesellschaft, Berlin, Germany.*

Photoelectron Circular Dichroism (PECD) is a method of chiral discrimination, which can aid in our fundamental understanding of electron dynamics and holds promise for future analytical techniques of chiral compounds. In PECD, ionization of a non-racemic sample by circularly polarized light results in a forward-backward asymmetry of the photoelectron angular distribution. This technique has significant advantages over other optical CD methods, such as absorption circular dichroism, as sensitivity to the molecular chirality can manifest within the electron-dipole approximation, bypassing the need for observation of weak interactions with a molecule's magnetic moment. PECD as it pertains to neutral chiral species has flourished, evident by the many theoretical and experimental works now available. However, PECD of anions has yet to come to fruition. The use of anions for this technique would provide benefits such as mass-selectivity and eliminating the need for X-ray based ionization sources. Also, it is expected that anion PECD would provide insights into the specific role of long-range and short-range forces in the PECD effect. As such, this talk will detail the progress made towards achieving PECD for anions. An overview of the different experimental approaches attempted and considerations of the inherent differences between PECD of neutrals and anions will be included. This discussion will provide the necessary context to answer the question: Can anion PECD work?

FM11 **10:40 – 10:41**

MATRIX ISOLATION-VIBRATIONAL CIRCULAR DICHROISM SPECTROSCOPIC STUDY OF TETRAHYDRO-2-FUROIC ACID AND ITS AGGREGATES

YANQING YANG, JOSEPH CHERAMY, YUNJIE XU, *Department of Chemistry, University of Alberta, Edmonton, AB, Canada.*

Vibrational circular dichroism (VCD) spectroscopy is a powerful spectroscopic tool for determination of structural properties of chiral molecules directly in solution, including their absolute configurations and conformations. More recently, the matrix-isolation (MI) technique which allows substantial control over the sample(s)/carrier gas ratio(s) and deposition conditions has been combined with VCD. It can avoid the solute-solvent interactions and have the molecular target largely in its isolated monomeric form. The MI technique generally yields much narrower IR and VCD bandwidths than those obtained in solution, providing the opportunity to investigate possible conformations of the target molecules in considerable details.

In the current study, the conformational landscapes of tetrahydro-2-fuoric acid (THFA) and its binary aggregates in a cold argon matrix have been investigated. MI-IR and MI-VCD spectra have been obtained at three different deposition temperatures of 10, 24, and 30 K. In addition, extensive searches have been carried out to find stable conformers of the THFA monomer and dimer in an argon matrix. The well-resolved experimental MI-IR and MI-VCD features at 10 K allows one to identify the dominating monomeric conformations. Interestingly, the inclusion of argon using the polarizable continuum model improves the agreement between the theoretical and experimental IR and VCD spectra. At the 24 and 30 K deposition temperatures, the experimental IR and VCD spectral features reveal appearance new species, most likely binary aggregates of THFA, although the IR and VCD features differ greatly from those observed in the previous solution study. Further analyses indicate that these new species are due to the much less stable conformers of the THFA dimer, not observed experimentally before. The structures and the formation mechanism of these unusual species will also be discussed.

1. C. Merten, Y. Xu, Angew. Chem. Int. Ed., 2013, 52, 2073-2076. 2. T. Kuppens, W. Herrebout, B. Veken, P. Bultinck, J. Phys. Chem. A, 2006, 110, 10191-10200.

FM12 **10:44 – 10:45**

COMPUTATIONAL INSIGHTS INTO THE CHIRAL SUM FREQUENCY GENERATION RESPONSE OF WATER SUPERSTRUCTURES SURROUNDING AN ANTIPARALLEL β-SHEET

DANIEL KONSTANTINOVSKY, ETHAN ALEXANDER PERETS, SHARON HAMMES-SCHIFFER, *Department of Chemistry, Yale University, New Haven, CT, USA*; ELSA YAN, *Chemistry, Yale University, New Haven, CT, USA.*

Hydration modulates the structure and function of biomacromolecules. However, probing water structures in hydration shells remains difficult due to a large background signal from bulk water and the dynamic nature of the solvation layer. Chiral vibrational sum frequency generation (SFG) spectroscopy can probe the solvation shell around a chiral solute without interference from the bulk. Computational modeling can guide the interpretation of chiral SFG spectra of water structures in hydration shells. We develop and apply computational methods to predict chiral SFG responses of water around a model protein system, the antiparallel β-sheet $LK_7\beta$, at the air-water interface. The SFG response of chiral water superstructures around the protein is modeled with molecular dynamics simulations and an electric field mapping strategy. Our computed spectra agree qualitatively with experimental results and flip when the amino acids are replaced with their (D-) enantiomeric equivalents. We show that the spectroscopic response of the chiral water assemblies arises from both strong and weak hydrogen bonds between water and protein. Intra- and intermolecular vibrational couplings of water molecules are shown to be necessary for generating the chiral SFG response. These results will improve our understanding of macromolecular solvation, a key factor in protein folding, denaturation, and ligand recognition. This study establishes a computational framework to support further development of chiral SFG in revealing the structure of biomacromolecular solvation shells, complementing current structural biology methods.

FM13 **10:48 – 10:49**

CHIRAL SUM FREQUENCY GENERATION SPECTROSCOPY REVEALS HOW MIRROR-IMAGE β-SHEETS ORGANIZE WATER SUPERSTRUCTURES WITH OPPOSITE CHIRALITY

ETHAN ALEXANDER PERETS, DANIEL KONSTANTINOVSKY, *Department of Chemistry, Yale University, New Haven, CT, USA*; TY SANTIAGO, LUIS VELARDE, *Department of Chemistry, University at Buffalo, Buffalo, NY, USA*; SHARON HAMMES-SCHIFFER, ELSA YAN, *Department of Chemistry, Yale University, New Haven, CT, USA.*

The structure and function of biomacromolecules depend on water structures in the hydration shell. However, elucidating the architectures of hydration shells around biomacromolecules has proven challenging. We used heterodyne chiral vibrational sum frequency generation (SFG) spectroscopy to study the structure of the solvation shell around an antiparallel β-sheet protein.

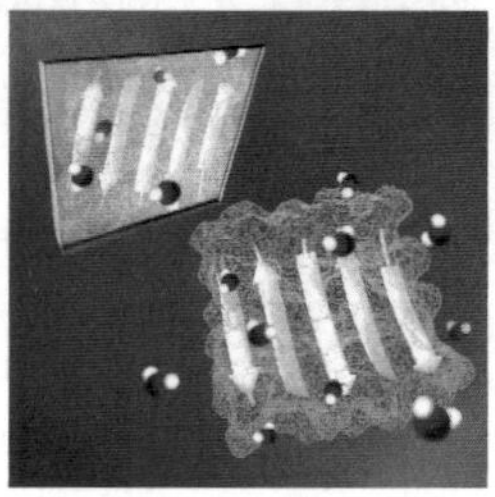

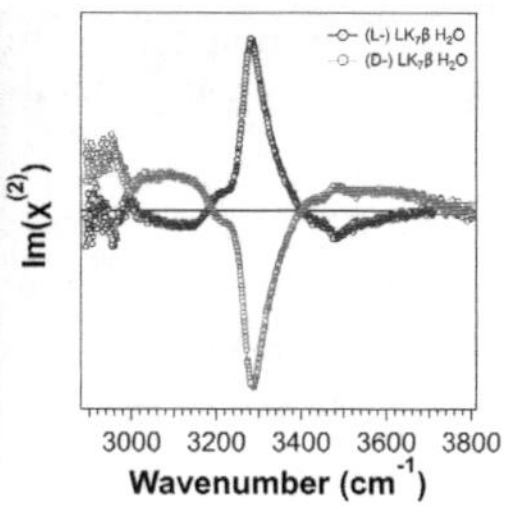

Heterodyne chiral SFG spectroscopy reveals that water molecules form chiral superstructures around the protein, and that these water superstructures are induced by the chirality of the protein. Enantiomeric (L-) or (D-) proteins give rise to enantiomeric water superstructures. Molecular dynamics simulations expose the chiral architecture of the water superstructures around the protein. Modeling the chiral SFG response of the hydration shell suggests that hydrogen bonding between water and protein is a driving force behind the formation of the chiral water superstructures.

Our work demonstrates the promise of chiral SFG spectroscopy to reveal structures and dynamics of hydration shells around biomacromolecules. We speculate on the involvement of chiral water superstructures in biomolecular recognition, and the role of chiral water superstructures in the origins of biological homochirality.

AUTHOR INDEX

C

D

E

F

G

H

I

J

K

L

M

R

S

T

International Symposium on Molecular Sprectroscopy-University of Illinois
170 Roger Adams Laboratory
600 South Mathews Avenue
Urbana, IL 61801

ISBN 978-1-7138-3523-3

CURRAN ASSOCIATES INC.
proceedings
.com

23rd Deloitte-University of Kansas Auditing Symposium 2016

Increasing Audit Quality

Lawrence, Kansas, USA
19 - 21 May 2016

KU SCHOOL OF BUSINESS
The University of Kansas